W9-BXA-688

"GRIPPING AND ILLUMINATING...

One of the most engaging biographies I have read in years."
The Nation

"One of the finest treatments of an American 20th century performer ever written...Not merely a biography...It is social history... written knowledgeably, in a brilliant style."
San Francisco Examiner

"Exemplary."
The Washington Post

"What a life! What a book!"
Detroit Free Press

Also by Joe Klein
Published by Ballantine Books:

PAYBACK

WOODY GUTHRIE

A·L·I·F·E

JOE KLEIN

BALLANTINE BOOKS • NEW YORK

Sale of this book without a front cover may be unauthorized. If this book is coverless, it may have been reported to the publisher as "unsold or destroyed" and neither the author nor the publisher may have received payment for it.

Copyright © 1980 by Joe Klein

All rights reserved under International and Pan-American Copyright Conventions. Published in the United States by Ballantine Books, a division of Random House, Inc., New York, and simultaneously in Canada by Random House of Canada Limited, Toronto.

Library of Congress Catalog Card Number: 80-7634

ISBN 0-345-33519-8

This edition published by arrangement with Alfred A. Knopf, Inc.

Printed in Canada

First Ballantine Books Edition: April 1982
First Mass Market Edition: August 1986
Fourth Printing: July 1992

For my children,
Christopher and Terry,
and for Woody's grandchildren

I'm going down that long, lonesome road
And I ain't gonna be treated this a-way . . .

— *"Lonesome Road Blues"*

CONTENTS

ILLUSTRATIONS

BOUND FOR GLORY *publicity shots, 1943 (Eric Schaal, LIFE, © Time, Inc.)*

With Cisco Houston, at Communist Political Association Rally, 1944

With Joe Louis and Earl Robinson

The Roosevelt Bandwagon, 1944

Portrait photograph of Woody

Pages from the Railroad Pete notebook

Woody and Marjorie

In the army, 1945

Marjorie and Cathy at Coney Island, 1946

Nora, Joady, Woody, and Arlo, 1951

On horseback, 1949

Woody and Marjorie, a publicity shot for their children's hootenannies

With Jean Ritchie, Fred Hellerman, and Pete Seeger at WNYC, 1949

With Anneke, around 1953

With Ramblin' Jack Elliot at Washington Square Park, 1954 (Arthur Dubinsky)

Bob Dylan (Barry Feinstein, Columbia Records)

Standing for the ovation after the 1956 benefit

With Nora, Marjorie, and Joady at Howard Beach

With Joady, Marjorie, Nora, and Arlo at Café Society, 1960 (Dave Gahr)

Woody's writing in 1955

Receiving the Conservation Service Award in 1966, with Harold Leventhal, Arlo, and Marjorie (John Cohn)

With Arlo (John Cohn)

following last page of text

Facsimile of "This Land Was Made For You & Me"

(All pictures not otherwise credited are from the Marjorie Guthrie Collection.)

PREFACE

This book is the result of a process, and an obsession, that began with a story about Arlo Guthrie that I wrote for *Rolling Stone* magazine early in 1977. I was a political reporter then and hadn't written much about music, but Arlo represented a tradition I considered important, and which seemed to be dying.

It was a primitive tradition, carried through the ages by common people who wished to express their joy and anger and frustrations through music. It had been passed on to Arlo from his father, the legendary Woody Guthrie, via Pete Seeger—and it extended back to socialist balladeers like Joe Hill . . . and further, to the unnamed, unknown slaves and farmers and cowboys and sailors who'd written and sung about the drudgery and occasional triumphs of their lives. In mid-twentieth-century America, it was given a name—*folk* music—and had enjoyed a brief vogue, but now it was quite out of fashion.

When I began work on the story about Arlo, I didn't know all that much about Woody Guthrie. I knew that he had written some famous songs, like "This Land Is Your Land," and that he'd died from a rare disease, and that he was supposed to have been a major influence on Bob Dylan and other folk singers of the 1960's. There also was a distinct image in my mind: a little man who wandered the country as a hobo, riding the boxcars, occasionally stopping in a town to take an odd job and write a ballad of social significance, before drifting off into the sunset. There was, in addition, a cloying, cutesy, unduly optimistic and child-like sensibility that I associated with Woody Guthrie—and there was little that I subsequently read in his modestly titled autobiography, *Bound for Glory*, or saw in the film version of that book, or read in the other published volumes of Woody's writing (with titles like *Born to Win* and *Woody Sez*) that did much to alter or deepen my impression of the man.

And yet, there were passages in *Bound for Glory*—especially the sections in which Woody described his childhood—that were beautifully written and belied the simplistic mythology that he obviously was trying to create around himself. Even more impressive was his music—so basic and powerful and true that it dwarfed all else in the movie version of *Bound for Glory*, which portrayed Woody in somewhat more depth than the book but covered only a few years of his travels in the 1930's (inaccurately, I later learned).

As I proceeded with my research about Arlo, the sense that Woody's story had never been adequately told became the common thread in all my interviews. Pete Seeger said, rather matter-of-factly, "You know, Woody was a Communist." And Arlo himself expressed dismay about his father's simplistic public image. He thought Woody's final years, his battle against Huntington's disease, were every bit as dramatic and important as his more publicized earlier travels. "You know what I remember?" he said. "I remember him coming home from the hospital and taking me out to the backyard, just him and me, and teaching me the last three verses to 'This Land Is Your Land' because he thinks that if I don't learn them, no one will remember. He can barely strum the guitar at this point, and—can you imagine—his friends think he's a drunk, crazy, and they stick him in a puke green room in a mental hospital with all these crazy people. . . .

"And then—and this is so weird you really can't even begin to figure it—when he can't write or talk or do anything at all anymore, he hits it big. All of a sudden everyone is singing his songs. Kids are singing 'This Land Is Your Land' in school and people are talking about making it the national anthem. Bob Dylan and all the others are copying him. And he can't react to it. Here's this guy who always had all these words and now that he's making it really big, he can't say anything. But his mind is still there. The disease doesn't affect his mind. He's sitting there in a mental hospital, *and he knows what's going on,* and he can't say anything or tell anyone how he feels. It's Shakespearean. Only Shakespeare could write something like that. . . ."

* * *

Well, I wasn't Shakespeare . . . and there was a new administration in Washington to write about, so I finished the story about Arlo and moved on to other things.

Several months later, though, I bumped into Harold Leventhal—the man who'd been Woody's agent and was now Arlo's. He said that no one had ever written a full-scale biography of Woody (a children's biography called *A Mighty Hard Road* had been published by McGraw-Hill in 1970), and asked if I'd like to try it. "It couldn't really be done before," he added, "because many of Woody's friends would have found it difficult to speak candidly about their past associations, but I think the political climate has changed enough so that they can now."

Then I spoke with Marjorie Guthrie, Woody's second wife, who said that many people had wanted to write books about Woody over the years, but she'd always refused: "I didn't think any of them were mature enough to write about my personal life." But she, too, thought the time was right and was willing to cooperate fully and give me access to all of Woody's private papers. She asked nothing in return—no editorial control, no financial consideration. "It's your book," she said. "Just try to be fair." Indeed, her only request was that I put in a plug for her Committee to Combat Huntington's Disease. (Here it is: the committee's address is 250 West 57th Street, New York, N.Y. 10019.)

At the time, I wasn't aware of the full significance of Marjorie's comment about her personal life, but I soon found out. She led me to a room filled with file cabinets—Woody's unpublished writings. I spent much of the next year in that room, reading stacks of letters and diaries that described, in astonishing detail, the most intimate aspects of their life together. Marjorie also subjected herself to dozens of hours of interviews, patiently answering questions that often were so personal as to embarrass the interviewer. She is a courageous and remarkable woman and, needless to say, this book could not have been written without her support and cooperation.

There were others whose help was crucial to my work: Woody's first wife, Mary Boyle, cooperated fully, as did his third wife, Anneke Van Kirk, and all his children, relatives, friends, and a few enemies. Their respective roles will be documented in the notes that follow the text.

Early on, Alan Lomax told me that I'd never really know Woody until I understood where he came from. In November of

1977, a friend—Tom Lunde—and I toured Oklahoma and Texas in a red pickup truck (I returned alone for a second look in July and August of 1978), interviewing not only Woody's relatives and childhood friends but also several old-timers who'd known his parents. I came to love and appreciate that bleak, open stretch of country, especially the desert near the Chisos Mountains, where one afternoon Lunde and I stumbled across the wagon road that led to the ruins of an old adobe house where Woody had lived briefly with his father, brother, and Uncle Jeff, and which was, in many ways, a symbol of the peace of mind he never found in his life.

My research also led me to such diverse spots as Beluthahatchee Swamp in Florida, Los Angeles, Denver, London, Coney Island, Brooklyn State Hospital, the Library of Congress, the National Institutes of Health, and the abandoned gold-mining town of Columbia, California. Although I resisted the temptation to travel by boxcar, it was a grueling journey nonetheless . . . and friends like Victoria Kaunitz, Paul Solman, Susan Bolotin, Paul Cowan, Janet Klein, my agent Elizabeth McKee, my parents, and my children helped ease me through the rough spots along the way.

Woody Guthrie was a man who was born on the frontier and died in the city. At times, I've been tempted to view his progress from Okemah, Oklahoma, to the Creedmoor State Hospital in Queens, New York, as a perverse metaphor for America's progress through the twentieth century—but it really isn't. It is only one life, sad and triumphant and utterly unique, and I have tried to present it as accurately as possible.

New York
January 1980

CHAPTER 1

Life's Other Side

Woody Guthrie's maternal grandfather was a Kansas dirt farmer named George B. Sherman. He married Mary Maloney, a schoolteacher from Tennessee, and they had four daughters. Sometime in the early 1890's, with the Oklahoma Territory opening to white settlement, the Shermans packed their belongings into a covered wagon and moved south. They found a piece of land near Welty in the Creek Indian Territory.

One day while crossing the Little Deep Fork River, George Sherman fell off his horse and drowned. He was a young, strong man at the time; the river was narrow and shallow. In later years his death would be dismissed as another of the strange tragedies that seemed to haunt the Shermans, but it was never really explained.

At about the same time and not very far away, a family of Texas cowboys, the Guthries, settled into a farm on the banks of the Big Deep Fork. They were a rowdy bunch, the sort of people who actually did all the things that cowboys are supposed to do: they herded cattle, shot bandits, played the fiddle and guitar around the campfire, and didn't talk much. The patriarch was a taut raisin of a man named Jeremiah Pearsall Guthrie—Jerry P. to all who knew him—who rose to middle management in the cowboy business. He'd borrow enough money from some city-

1

slick cattle agent in Tulsa or Kansas City to buy a small herd, then he'd raise them, sell them, and halve the profits with his backer.

His brother Gid owned a ranch down around the Big Bend of the Rio Grande, and sometimes Jerry P. would help out there—chasing cows, guarding against the Mexicans who'd come across the river hoping to make off with the Guthrie stock (several wild gun battles were fought, it is said)—but never for very long. He wasn't the sort to be tied down. No raggedy patch of prairie was interesting enough to contain his ambitions or curiosity. He was a first-class carpenter and mechanic with visions of becoming an inventor, always toying with various contraptions when he wasn't out with the cows. He also was a wild hoedown fiddler, as was Gid (and their father before them), until someone shot him through the right arm and cut a tendon. He was Scottish and Irish, with intense brown eyes and a wild handlebar mustache, a mixture of pragmatism and romance. He was always on the lookout for gimmicks, for deals, for new *possibilities*. And so, when he heard they were giving away land in Oklahoma to anyone who could prove he was an Indian, Jerry P. Guthrie packed up his family and went. His second wife—the first had died in childbirth—was one-eighth Creek, and Jerry P. figured it was worth a shot.

Oklahoma, known officially as Indian Territory in those days, was the scene of a great American madness. It was the one area east of the Rockies that hadn't yet become a state; it was a gaping hole in the commercial map of the country, a vacuum the railroad magnates and land speculators desperately wanted to fill. But the land was held by the "Five Civilized Tribes"—the Choctaws, Cherokees, Chickasaws, Creeks, and Seminoles. The tribes were called civilized because they had tried to impress the white man by imitating his culture, hoping for civilized treatment in return. They established legislatures, developed written languages, and owned slaves—all of which did them very little good, as they were routed from their homelands in the Southeast in the 1830's and sent off on a humiliating march along "the Trail of Tears" to Indian Territory west of the Mississippi, which, they were assured, would be theirs "as long as the grass shall grow and the waters run. . . ."

Actually, given the brutal range of possibilities, it wasn't such a bad deal. The Indians settled and re-established their various nations in a beautiful land of graceful, rolling hills that gradually flattened and dried out into the Great Plains to the west; it was good cotton land, and fine for grazing cattle. But the five tribes soon made a rather serious mistake: because they held black slaves (and perhaps out of sheer orneriness, to get back at the United States government for their humiliation), they sided with the South in the Civil War. When the war ended, the government promptly announced that the Indians had forfeited their right to the lands.

The confiscation did not occur all at once, though. First the western half of the area—the plains, mostly—was lopped off and called Oklahoma Territory; the eastern half remained the province of the five tribes, each ruled by its own government. There followed a bewildering series of land rushes, special sales, and assorted power grabs as the western territory was opened, piece by piece, to white settlement. Whites began pouring into the Indian Territory as well: some leased land from Indians, others simply claimed a plot and established residence. The question of who owned what was becoming very confused.

The confusion was compounded by the utter lawlessness of the area. White criminals were able to escape prosecution by fleeing to the Indian Territory, where they were exempt from both tribal law and extradition. The James brothers, the Dalton gang, the Doolins, Belle Starr, and Cherokee Bill (who claimed to be half black, half white, and half Indian), among others, sought refuge in the eastern hill country from time to time, often surprising their neighbors with their peaceful demeanor (there was more mileage in robbing banks than dirt farmers) and starting a tradition in Oklahoma of regarding outlaws as populist heroes. In fact, the Daltons had a hideout on Big Deep Fork, not far from where the Guthries settled.

In 1893, the United States government decided it was time for a final solution of the Oklahoma situation. Congress established the Dawes Commission to negotiate the dissolution of the tribes and to divide the land equally among their members. Needless to say, there was a wild rush of white people trying to pass themselves off as Indians, but the land was divided strictly among those whose names already were on the tribal rolls. Jerry P. Guthrie and his wife, Martha, obviously didn't have much of a case.

Having moved all the way to Oklahoma, though, Jerry P. decided to stay for a while. He bought some cattle, puttered around with his inventions, and sired more children. Eventually there would be eight, four by each of his wives. One child, a boy by his first wife, proved especially helpful in running the business: Charley Edward Guthrie, born in 1879, was a fine ranch hand but, more than that, he had brains. After chasing cows and doing chores all day, Charley would sit in a corner and read books all night. He sent away to Chicago for correspondence courses, which he completed religiously. He learned bookkeeping and developed a beautiful handwriting. Soon Jerry P. found himself actually going to the boy for advice—basic advice like when to buy and when to sell—and was sorely disappointed when Charley decided, at the age of eighteen, to go off and seek his fortune. Not long after that, Jerry P. packed up the remaining family members and went back to the Rio Grande Valley to help his brother Gid.

Charley started his career by hiring on as a cowboy at H. B. Spaulding's huge ranch near Clear Creek, hoping eventually to work his way into the business end of the operation. Not having much luck there, he found a job as a clerk, bookkeeper, and assistant postmaster for J. B. Wilson, who ran the general stores in the tiny hamlets of Welty and Castle. Before long, Charley had opened a small school as well—teaching handwriting to local children three nights a week. "Let your hand run free," he would tell them as they drew page after page of equally spaced circles. "Always let your hand run free."

Inevitably, Charley Guthrie found his way to the Tanner farm outside of Welty. Mary Tanner, a teacher at the local Indian school, was one of the few people around as interested in books as he. She was the widow of George Sherman, the man who'd drowned crossing Little Deep Fork, and was now married to a farmer named Lee Tanner. They loved having Charley out to their place—he'd already developed a reputation as the best storyteller and quickest wit in Okfuskee County. People would go down to Wilson's store just to hear him talk, and then invite him home to dinner to hear him talk some more. But it wasn't just the intellectual stimulation that made his visits to the Tanners more interesting (and frequent) than to the others: Mary had four attractive daughters by her first marriage.

Nora Belle was not the prettiest of them, but she seemed more *alive* than the others. She was nine years younger than Charley, having been born in Kansas in 1888, and was about fifteen years old when he first met her. She was the type of girl people described as "clever" in those days—sharp eyes, sharp tongue, a bit of a tomboy. She could ride a horse as well as a man, and she did it sidesaddle. She'd gallop across the rolling hills and slash through the tangled stands of blackjack and post oak on a blind horse named Frank, guiding him with her hands. Charley's younger brother Claude, when he first met Nora, described her as a "cowpuncher." She loved to sing the maudlin, old-time hill country ballads her mother had taught her—she sang in a high-pitched nasal twang as she rode along on her horse, with Charley at her side entranced. Unlike most of the other young women he met, she wasn't twittery or fawning. After courting for about a year, they were married on St. Valentine's Day: February 14, 1904.

Charley bought a small house in Castle, and they settled into their new life with a great deal of optimism. He was, quite obviously, a man with a future. He was reading law now, and dreamed of a political career when Oklahoma achieved statehood. He'd even attracted the passing attention of the local newspaper. In September of 1904, the editor of the Okemah *Independent*, a tiny paper that had started publishing in the next town over, came through Castle and visited with Postmaster Guthrie. "I found Mr. Guthrie to be a pleasant and courteous individual," he reported, "and prevailed on him to furnish *Independent* readers with news of that neighborhood from time to time."

The editor was traveling from the all-white town of Okemah to find out what life was like in the all-black town of Boley, ten miles to the west. Though residents of neither place were likely to admit it, the two towns mirrored each other. Each had about a thousand people, both were founded with the strong encouragement of the Fort Smith and Western Railroad, which was hoping for commercial development along its route, and both towns had pipe dreams. There was talk that Okemah was about to be graced by a second railroad and transformed into a major commercial center; but the second railroad never arrived, and Okemah languished. Boley hoped to become the spiritual center of a national black separatist movement, perhaps the seat of an all-black county, and, for a time, it seemed *that* dream might actually come true.

Blacks were more independent in turn-of-the-century Oklahoma than in most other places. The Indian slaveholders hadn't been as oppressive as whites, and sometimes gave their chattels major responsibilities. Black slaves often acted as intermediaries, conducting business with the white world for their tribal masters, who usually were too proud to learn English. After emancipation, the area also attracted a small but steady trickle of former slaves from the Deep South—"Exodusters"—looking for real freedom and a chance for prosperity in the West. They tended to be more ornery and independent than those who remained as sharecroppers on the old plantations, and soon a defiant black separatist movement was flowering.

The dream of political power flourished in Boley until the first statewide election in 1907, when the local whites discovered that the blacks—who tended to vote as a bloc for the former liberators, the Republicans—held the balance of power in Okfuskee County. Faced with the vexing question of black power, the county commissioners—Democrats appointed by the territorial government— came up with a novel answer: they simply decided not to put any voting boxes in Boley. When asked by the Republicans where the residents of Boley were to vote, the commissioners said they might vote over in Van Zandt, a backcountry town the size of a mailbox.

All these machinations were watched closely by Charley Guthrie. He was the Democratic candidate for District Court Clerk, having won the June primary by a three-to-two margin. With his handwriting and his law books, the clerkship seemed just the right spot to begin his political career, and Charley threw himself into the race. He campaigned vigorously for the Democratic ticket and its platform, which the Okemah *Independent*, a Republican newspaper, succinctly described as "the old familiar howl: Nigger! Nigger!"

On September 18, 1907, Oklahoma went to the polls to elect its first government. In Okfuskee County, the Republicans romped by 350 votes across the board, their totals immeasurably helped by the 395 Republican votes that came in from the tiny precinct of Van Zandt. The election commissioners once again faced a serious problem. There were several ways of dealing with the Van Zandt situation, but they chose the most direct: they simply threw out the 395 votes, citing "force and fraud practiced by the Negroes at Van Zandt." The Republicans sued, but the Democrats were sworn into office on statehood day and Charley Guthrie was now District Court Clerk, the winner by 319 votes.

Charley celebrated by asking his father, recently returned from Texas, to build him the sort of home in Okemah that might befit a rising young politician. Then he took Nora and their two children—Clara had been born in November of 1904 and Lee Roy in December of 1906—over to George Farnum, the Okemah photographer, for their first official photographs. Charley looked directly into the camera, a serenely confident and handsome man who seemed younger than his twenty-eight years. Nora was dressed in dark velvet with a white lace collar. She looked quite well, but there was a slight, almost imperceptible unease about her. She did not give herself to the camera as readily as Charley; there was a hint of fear in her eyes.

In 1907, Okemah was a dour little village, alternately sun-baked and windswept, that was located pleasantly, if somewhat improbably, atop a rocky hill. In the early days the combination of rocks and mud often made it difficult for wagons to get into town—another indication, along with the railroad that never arrived, that Okemah had its limitations as a commercial mecca. The rocks were gradually removed to construct stolid homes and buildings (with few of the Victorian Gothic indulgences that graced other small towns of the period), but the mud remained a seasonal bother until the streets were paved in the 1920's. It was a town that was working hard to achieve a veneer of respectability, the sort of place where propriety was mistaken for civilization. Okemah was born into middle age—its adolescence would come later—in a country that was still wild and young.

Charley Guthrie, every bit as wild and young as the country, caused an instant sensation. At ten o'clock each morning, a crowd would gather at Parsons' drugstore to listen to him talk as he drank his coffee. He was a man of vast enthusiasms, always looking to improve himself, always reading—his goal was to read *all* the classics, whatever that meant—always on top of the latest news, always the first in town to try the newest inventions. As early as 1909, the local newspaper reported that he and Nora had taken a trip to Kansas (probably to visit her relatives) by *automobile*. He had an unbridled, ingenuous optimism. He didn't stash money away to cushion future setbacks; the possibility of failure simply didn't cross his mind. He spent lavishly. He bought Nora a hundred-dollar sidesaddle so they could prance through town on Sunday afternoons, a bit too well dressed, he on his white stallion and she on a black mare.

Somewhere along the line, he had become a physical-fitness nut. He had learned to box—perhaps through another correspondence course—and could often be found working out over at the gymnasium in the National Guard armory. Of course, simple workouts weren't enough for Charley, and he soon had a punching bag installed in his office. He taught his younger brothers, Claude and Jeff, how to box. He taught his children: at the ages of six and four, Clara and Roy would put on gloves almost as large as they were, and stage exhibitions in the front yard for the neighbors. He was called "One-Punch" Charley Guthrie, the man who always grinned when he fought, even when he was taking a punch. He would paw-paw-paw at his opponent's face with his left hand, then stuff a powerful right in the fellow's ear. He was of average size—taller than his father—but was able to demolish men much larger because he was fast and in great shape.

The upper crust in town thought this was all a bit too flashy and never invited the Guthries into the supper club that passed for high society in Okemah. The club members included the local doctors and lawyers, and the more substantial merchants. The Guthries were considered too rough, too *pushy* for such refined company; they weren't even regular churchgoers, several of the wives pointed out. But the men enjoyed Charley's company when they could pry themselves loose from the pretension of "society." He was an inveterate poker player and always seemed to know where to get the best rotgut whiskey, the sort of man who'd invariably be the life of a stag party.

Charley also was known as the town's most creative practical joker, a reputation he earned one afternoon in June of 1911 when court was out of session and the building vacant. He persuaded the sheriff to "arrest" an innocent farm boy named Martin Bennett, who was in town running errands for his mother, on a charge of "unbecoming conduct," and to bring him to the courthouse, where Charley had assembled a judge, a jury, a prosecuting attorney, a number of witnesses, and a packed audience. Guthrie himself assumed the boy's defense. In a memorable summation, he attacked the credibility of his own witnesses, the intelligence of the jury, and the personal morality of the judge. At one point, the defendant tried to bolt but was forcibly restrained. The highlight of the trial, though, was something that not even Charley

Guthrie could have anticipated. Sam Gray, a local farmer, had come to town to buy some heavy rope at the general store. Noticing the relative calm, he asked where everyone was and the clerk told him they were all down at the courthouse. Sam decided to find out what was up and banged into the courtroom, heavy rope in hand, just as the judge was delivering his verdict. When the laughter subsided, the boy was acquitted. The local press reported the trial as front-page news and said that "everyone had bushels of fun except the defendant."

For a while, Okemah had to contend with the entire Guthrie clan. Jerry P. moved to town with his wife and kids soon after Charley was elected clerk. He rented a farm on Cemetery Hill just north of town, received backing from a Colonel Woodley in Tulsa to buy some cattle, and set about building his son a house. They chose a lot on the south side, next to the home of a prosperous merchant, W. H. Field, and built a large six-room house, ringed by a porch on three sides. Everyone helped out—Jerry P. even sent the kids up to the roof to nail on shingles—and the result was splendid. It was painted yellow, and had built-in bookcases, an exercise room for all of Charley's muscle-building contraptions, and an organ for Nora to play when she sang her old sad tunes. Work was completed in the early autumn of 1909.

And then, about a month later, it burned down.

The fire started next door, in Field's kitchen, and quickly spread to the Guthrie house. School was let out so the children could help with the bucket brigade, and neighbors pitched in and managed to pull out many of Charley and Nora's possessions, but much was lost. Field had been fully insured, but, the local newspaper reported, "Mr. Guthrie carried $300 insurance on his house though the building was worth $800, leaving him a pretty heavy loser. . . . Mr. Guthrie moved at once to the Dr. Bewley property."

Nora, who'd been there to watch her dream house go up in flames, was terribly depressed. She seemed haunted by the fire, and would talk endlessly about the house for years after. Charley took it in stride. The loss of the respectability that came from owning such a house seemed as serious to him as the financial loss. He was wiped out for the time being, but his political future looked brighter than ever, no one had been hurt, and fortunes could be made and new houses built anytime. Jerry P. Guthrie, no doubt dismayed to see his handiwork gutted, moved his family out of town a few months later, driving his cows to market at Sand Springs.

Early in 1910, Charley Guthrie announced he would run for re-election as District Court Clerk and was immediately endorsed by the Okemah *Ledger*, which said he'd been "one of the most satisfactory and popular of our county officers." He would have an easier time this year than in 1907. For one thing, the county Democratic organization was behind him now. For another, the black vote would no longer pose a problem. In August, blacks had been neatly severed from the body politic in a statewide referendum which added an incredible amendment—called the "Grandfather Clause"—to the Oklahoma constitution: any prospective voter would have to pass a literacy test unless he could prove he was a lineal descendant of someone who could vote prior to 1865 or resided then in a foreign nation (as had the Indians).

Boley's dream of political power was over, and the town seethed. A sign went up on Main Street: "White Man, Don't Let the Sun Set on Your Back in This Town." And the following spring a race war nearly erupted when a white deputy sheriff from Okemah named George Loney went to a poor black farm near Paden to arrest a man named Nelson for stealing sheep. Nelson's thirteen-year-old son, Lawrence, thinking that he saw the deputy go for his gun, pulled out a rifle and shot Loney in the leg. The deputy bled to death in the yard, and whites were especially outraged because Loney died begging for water, which the blacks refused him. A posse was organized, with Charley Guthrie a member, and the entire Nelson family was arrested. They were brought to Okemah, where the husband was placed in one cell and the wife, the son, and a nursing infant in another. The Okemah *Ledger*, not exactly a voice of reason in all this, described Lawrence Nelson as "rather yellow, ignorant and ragged."

A week passed, presumably time enough for everyone to calm down. But then a mob burst into the jail one night—a mob composed of many of Okemah's finest citizens, including Charley Guthrie—and dragged Laura Nelson, her son, and her baby to the bridge over the Canadian River about six miles west of town, where she and Lawrence were lynched and the baby left crying helplessly by the side of the road. The Okemah *Ledger* reported the news rather huffily: "It is generally thought the negroes got what would have been due them under due process of law.'' The *Ledger* also published a grisly photo of the lynched bodies, which later was reprinted as a postcard and became a popular novelty item in local stores.

Boley was so outraged by the news that there was talk of organizing a black posse and marching on Okemah. Rumors of the impending battle sent the whites into a panic. Women and children were evacuated to a field outside town, and the men stood watch with rifles on Main Street all night. But the blacks—who realized, no doubt, that such an attack would be suicidal—never marched, and militant separatism faded into second-class citizenship in Boley.

With blacks no longer an electoral problem, Charley Guthrie turned his attention to the other major threat facing the Democrats in Okfuskee County—the Socialist Party. In 1910, Charley noticed, as he was handily beating the Republican by 994–665, that the Socialist candidate had pulled 345 votes . . . and the party's strength seemed to be growing. Oddly enough, there were more dues-paying Socialists in Oklahoma in 1910 than in any other state in the Union. There was a strong heritage of agrarian radicalism in the area, dating back to the populists of the late nineteenth century, and the Socialists found eager supporters among the proud dirt farmers who'd been forced into renting from absentee landlords, especially from bankers and land speculators. It was a constituency that included more than half the farmers in Oklahoma, according to the 1910 census. The party sponsored huge summer encampments with rousing speeches by Eugene V. Debs and the legendary Mother Jones, among others, and the dirt farmers attended by the thousands, their wagons festooned with red flags. More than 40,000 Oklahomans subscribed to the *Appeal to Reason*, the Socialist newspaper, which was the largest-selling weekly in America, with more than 750,000 subscribers. Debs, probably the most popular left-wing orator in American history, was getting ready to run for President again in 1912, and the Socialist threat seemed very real.

It certainly was upsetting to Charley Guthrie. He had become a land speculator by then—the very sort of man the Socialists were campaigning against. He had started dabbling in real estate even before he was elected clerk; but hanging around the courthouse, where deals were made and deeds filed, whetted his appetite for more. Because he was able to speak both Creek and

Cherokee, Charley became known as especially adept at relieving Indians of their property. It was more fun than work—he enjoyed the game of deal-making more than the money that came of it. He wasn't interested in empire-building; he couldn't hold on to his money long enough to become a real land baron, but he had his farms and, no doubt, his tenants. The Socialists, with their insistence that tenants should control the land they worked, obviously had to be dealt with.

On October 4, 1911, the Okemah *Ledger* published a short essay entitled "Free Love the Fixed Aim of Socialism," by C. E. Guthrie. In a decidedly sarcastic tone, the author quoted a variety of "kumrids" from Friedrich Engels on down. He quoted Engels, for example, as saying that prostitution and monogamy were two poles of the same condition, and that one couldn't disappear without the other. It was the sort of approach guaranteed to hit home with Oklahoma dirt farmers. It was masterful.

The next week, Charley was back with "Socialism the Enemy of Christian Religion" and then "Socialism Guards Secret Philosophy" and then "Socialism Seeks to Destroy Christianity." By the third installment, the Okemah *Ledger* was featuring him on the front page. Charley, soaring, renamed the *Appeal to Reason* the "Squeal of Treason" and Debs, "Almighty-High-Gene."

The Socialists, caught off balance by a man who attacked them by accurately quoting their own philosophers, responded with J. Fleming Jones, the leading Socialist writer in Okfuskee County. The best Jones could do was to say that Thomas Jefferson, the founder of the Democratic Party, was himself "an infidel and free lover. Can Mr. Guthrie swallow Tom Jefferson, infidelity, free love, nigger children and all, and gag at socialism, because out of thousands of socialist writers he finds five or six whose views on marriage appear to be quite unorthodox?"

Charley's polemics also brought a response from the Executive Committee of the Socialist Party of Oklahoma City, which said: "Sincere thanks to C. E. Guthrie for the valuable aid and assistance he is giving the cause of socialism. Mr. Guthrie is doing what we socialists have all tried to do—namely, getting the people to study socialism."

It was a rather lame response, and Charley kept plugging. There was "More Evidence of Socialist Free Love" and "Is It True Socialists Never Do Graft?" and "Socialism Urges Negro Equality," in which he explained that under socialism "the race problem would be solved by intermarriage.'' In late December, he began a series of debates with a Socialist named Thurman, who, he later reported in the *Ledger*, hurled "vile epithets at the stars and stripes. . . . He was wishy-washy, slippery, slimey and dangerous.'' For his part, Charley defended Jefferson and said, "No body of men can establish pure government unless that body of men are pure in themselves.''

The debates quickly went out of control. In February, Thurman made a personal attack: "While charging free love on the socialists, do you deny you are a practical free lover?'' Charley, outraged, knocked Thurman through a bank window on Main Street—at least that's what his younger brother Jeff later swore.

In March, all of Charley's articles were collected into a pamphlet called *Kumrids*, whose publication was bannered in the *Ledger* with a large picture of the author (looking more severe and angular than in his earlier photo). In his introduction, Charley admitted he once had been tempted by socialism. "For more than seven years, I have been an earnest, patient and faithful student of socialism, the first three of which I was uninterrupted by any opposing politics. . . . I hasten to confess that the contents of this little book will not be looked on as one of the literary classics of this enlightened age. . . . The purpose is to give the reader an idea of the poisonous and dangerous fangs of the tempting serpent which is lurking behind the advance claims of socialism.''

At about the same time, he announced the establishment of a semi-monthly newspaper called *The Kumrid*, and promised that each issue would contain "actual proof of the charge that socialism is morally wrong, economically unsafe, politically unsound and socially it is rotten.''

Obviously all this ranting, raving, and fistfighting was not going to improve the Guthries' standing among the better elements in town, but Charley was hoping the Democratic Party would be grateful for his efforts and allow him to run for a more important office. He was wrong. He began 1912 by announcing that he would not run again for court clerk, but was considering a campaign for state representative. The friendly *Ledger* endorsed him at once, saying: "He wants the rate of taxation as low as possible.'' Unfortunately, the incumbent, J. J. Roland, decided to run for re-election, and when the Democratic organization endorsed him, Charley backed out. Next he announced for County Assessor, but the party had another man in mind there as well. Too proud, perhaps, to be pushed around like this, Charley decided to run for Assessor anyway and take on the machine in what was sure to be a losing fight.

Meanwhile, Nora was pregnant again. Charley hadn't had much time to think about the prospect of another child, preoccupied as he was by politics. But on Sunday, July 14, 1912, with the temperature standing at 99 degrees and not a cloud in the sky, Nora gave birth to a boy. Charley named him Woodrow Wilson Guthrie, in honor of the man the Democrats had nominated for President just the week before.

The birth was announced with appropriate fanfare in the *Ledger*. An article by C. E. Guthrie entitled "A Baby Defined" appeared on page two. In his inimitable fashion, Charley announced he had been searching for the best definition of a baby in "many volumes of the latest and most up to date works which deal with the theories of Creation, Evolution, and the origin of the family; brushing away the cobwebs to gain entrance into the antiquated libraries of our ancestors, I have finally succeeded in finding a definition. I have selected . . . one given in England in the hope of receiving a prize which had been offered by a London newspaper. 'A baby—a tiny feather from the wing of love dropped into the sacred lap of motherhood; an inhabitant of lapland; a padlock on the chains of life . . . the morning caller, noonday crawler, midnight bawler; the latest edition of humanity of which every couple think they possess the finest copy.' I concur in the definition as given and trust it will meet with the approbation of our splendid populace which is composed of real home-builders. To say the least, I am as happy as a lobster."

Nora called him Woodrow, not Woody as everyone else did, and sang him the songs her mother had brought from Tennessee, songs that had come over on the boats from England and Ireland and had been passed from mother to daughter (men, by and large, thought them too sappy) ever since. She sang of murders and jealous lovers and natural disasters. She sang about the woman who left her family to run off with the dashing outlaw, about the town that had been crushed by a cyclone, about families wrecked by bad luck. She sang lullabies to put the children to sleep and nonsense songs to cheer them up. She was alone with her children much of the time, and seemed even more alone when she was singing.

After the first house burned down, the family moved from place to place. Woody's earliest memories were of the London house, which had a dank, stone first floor and a wooden second floor with a back porch that overlooked the rolling countryside at the edge of town. But the family didn't live there long; Nora hated it. She felt most comfortable in her mother's new home, on a beautiful farm that Lee Tanner had bought five miles northwest of Okemah. He built an impressive Victorian house there, six rooms filled with interesting nooks and crannies, cedar paneling, window seats, and porches on all sides. It was located at the crest of a grassy hill, surrounded by cedar, pecan, and blackjack trees. There was a warmth to the house, a feeling of security and privacy . . . and calm. In addition to the regular Sunday visits with Charley and the children, Nora would bring Woody there during the week after his sister and brother went to school. She would sit at the Price and Deeple upright piano and sing ''A Picture from Life's Other Side,'' an utterly gruesome song, filled with images of good families gone bad, brothers turned violently against each other, and mothers left to commit suicide by drowning. The chorus was burned into Woody's brain:

> A picture from life's other side
> Somebody has fell by the way
> And a life has gone out with the tide
> That might have been happy some day.
> Some poor mother at home
> Is watching and waiting alone.
> Longing to hear from her loved one so dear,
> That's a picture from life's other side.

It was a song that exaggerated Nora's high-pitched nasal wail, and the Tanner boys—her mother's sons by the second marriage—would hide out in the bushes and tease her by holding their noses and screeching along.

Charley devoted himself to the real estate business after losing his race for County Assessor to the Democratic organization's candidate in 1912. He installed his punching bag in a small office above the Citizen's National Bank on Main Street, and took an ad in the paper saying he was interested in buying and selling farmland. He remained a frequent visitor to the courthouse, often serving as a handwriting expert who claimed to be able to distin-

guish between one Indian's "X" and another's. Sometimes he
would help lawyers to develop strategy in the more interesting
criminal trials, and he was said to be especially adept at figuring
out good alibis. There were those in town who thought he actually was a lawyer, but even though he probably had the knowledge to pass whatever examinations there were, he never became
one. No doubt he considered the courthouse a hobby; his real
future was in land speculation and, as World War I caused the
farm economy to boom, he became quite successful. At times he
owned as many as thirty farms. In 1918, he was involved in
twenty-eight different land transactions filed at the county offices.
He was able now to buy a fine home on North Ninth Street, and
also to keep a little forty-acre farm on a hill southwest of town
where he bred prizewinning Hereford cattle, as well as hogs and
pedigreed hunting dogs.

The house on Ninth Street seemed more Charley's than Nora's.
He filled it with his exercise paraphernalia and his books, and
cluttered the walls with ribbons his cattle and hogs had won,
pedigrees for his hounds, and even framed doggerel like:

> Smile and the world smiles with you.
> Kick and you kick alone.
> For a cheerful grin
> Will let you in
> Where a kicker is never known.

Charley doted on his children. When he completed a big land
deal, he'd invariably arrive home with his arms full of toys.
Neighbors remember the yard as filled with wagons and bikes
and other wheeled contraptions he'd bought. Each of the children
was taught to ride horseback. Woody—who never did become
much of a cowboy—fell off an Indian pony at an early age and
broke his elbow in three places. Charley took him to a doctor
who gave him chloroform and reset the arm. But Woody promptly
went and fell out of a tree. "I felt my arm burn and sting," he
later wrote. "I knew it was broke in the plaster cast. . . . I didn't
want to go under chloroform again so the bone grew back
crooked." More likely, it wasn't set properly the first time. In
any case, he spent the rest of his life with a right forearm that
looked as if it had been hooked onto his elbow the wrong way.

Woody was small for his age, a rag doll with curly hair. He

would sit on the front porch in the evenings, waiting for the sound of his father's horse on the hard clay street; then he'd run to meet him and jump up, and Charley would sweep him into his lap, and they'd play one of the silly word games they both loved. Woody was always hopping around the house, making up snatches of rhyme and trying to sing them like his mother. He loved the way she sang and would get angry at the Tanner boys when they mocked her. He commanded more attention within the family than his serious and reserved brother Roy, but the star of the show unquestionably was his sister Clara, a beautiful child with golden-brown hair and very much her father's daughter. She was quite intelligent—all her teachers agreed to that—but head-strong and, perhaps, a bit spoiled. Once when she was made to stay after school and told to write "naughty girl" fifty times, she drew a picture of herself with fifty curls, each of which said "naughty girl." Clara was difficult for Nora to handle, but Charley loved her free spirit . . . and Woody idolized her.

With his business doing well, Charley decided to run for political office again. The Socialists had lost much of their popular support when they opposed World War I and no longer consti-tuted a threat, but Charley had more serious enemies now. His opposition was the local Democratic organization, run de facto by W. N. Barry, the incumbent state representative. In 1918 he decided to run directly against Nick Barry for the legislature, to settle a grudge and clear his name.

Despite his electoral defeat in 1912, Charley had remained a political force. His appearances at the courthouse and his morn-ing coffee at Parsons' drugstore kept him in circulation. He was a popular figure—now also known as the man who wrote the names on Okemah's diplomas—and a worrisome presence to the Democratic organization, becoming more formidable as his fi-nancial position improved. In 1915, he had begun his political comeback by being elected justice of the peace, a minor position but a necessary first step. It was probably no coincidence that a state auditor arrived soon afterwards from Oklahoma City and began an investigation of Charley's record as District Court Clerk. The auditor "found" that Charley had received $834.25 in illegal fees and also discovered a $585 discrepancy in the money he turned over to his successor. The case went to court in 1916, but never was resolved. In a full-page ad that he bought at the be-ginning of the 1918 campaign, Charley said the charges had been conveniently left hanging after the judge asked the state for more "definitive proof." He said the $834.25 came from fees granted to him under a rate structure approved by the local judge and by Nick Barry himself, then one of the county commissioners. He went on to attack Barry for playing fast and loose with bridge construction bonds.

It was a wild campaign. Barry was rather nonchalant, saying, "Charley Guthrie only *thinks* he's running for the legislature," but Charley kept pushing. Woody later remembered traveling around the county with his father as he made speeches from the back of hay wagons to crowds of grimy farmers. As an extra campaign service, Charley—still a sucker for the latest inventions—bought a soil-testing device and offered a free soil analysis to anyone who wanted one. When Okfuskee County held its primary in early August, Guthrie was a decisive winner: 529 votes to 461 for Barry and 164 for Bartow, a third candidate.

It was a sweet victory until the recount. Nick Barry had been right all along: Charley Guthrie never had a chance. Nearly half the ballot boxes were tampered with after the initial count. In one case, the Okfuskee County *News* reported: "Some party or parties gained access to the [voting] box, selected six ballots voted for Guthrie and stamped a cross in front of the name of A. C. Bartow," thereby invalidating Charley's votes. What's more, eighteen ballots that originally had been voted blank now were stamped "with a cross in front of Mr. Barry's name." The new totals read: 499 for Barry, 477 for Guthrie, and 121 for Bartow. Even the relentlessly Democratic *Ledger* was forced to concede that this was the "first indication of a crooked election since the organization of the county."

Charley appealed to the state election board, but also took matters into his own hands. Apparently he never caught up with Barry himself, but he did locate several of his henchman and left at least one of them spraddled across a pool table. He didn't expect much relief from the election board and, indeed, in mid-October it awarded the nomination to Barry. The *Ledger* said on October 25, in an election preview: "W. N. Barry . . . one of the recognized leaders of [Oklahoma's legislature] will be able to again wield influence that will place our community in a commanding position." It was as though the fraud had never occurred.

Meanwhile, the strain of the election was causing real tension in the Guthrie family. Nora would sit anxiously waiting for her husband to come home each evening. She knew the threat of violence was more serious this time—the Socialists at least had some principles, but these guys were crooks. Sometimes Charley came home spattered with blood, his hands all busted up from fighting. He wasn't a young man anymore; he was almost forty now and, she thought, much too old for that sort of thing.

A fourth child, George, had been born in February of 1918 and Nora was finding it increasingly difficult to care for all her family. She was becoming forgetful: there were days when Roy would come home from school and find that she'd gone off and left the wash sitting in a tub of cold water, and he'd finish the job himself. The neighbors noticed that she wasn't mending the children's clothes anymore, and they were beginning to look raggedy at school. Sometimes she would wander, aimlessly it seemed, around town. She would dawdle over a piece of fabric in the dry-goods store and not even notice when someone said "Good day, Mrs. Guthrie . . ."

At about the same time, she broke her arm—probably in a fall from her horse—and it had healed poorly (the local doctor apparently didn't specialize in broken bones). When her stepbrother Lawrence Tanner and his new bride stopped by, they found Nora in pain, with her left arm fixed in a curious half salute. She was temporarily cut off from her one source of relaxation: with her arm in a sling, it wasn't possible to play the piano while she sang her songs.

Saddest and most frightening of all, though, was her temper. She was having trouble controlling herself at times—especially when it came to Clara. There had always been a subtle tension between them, but now the rivalry became more pronounced as Clara reached a difficult age: she was fourteen, and beginning to bloom. She was almost the same age Nora had been when she first met Charley. Nora was only thirty-one herself, but she felt much older. She'd had four children and thought of herself as ugly and disheveled. As Nora increasingly withdrew from the world, Clara hungered more and more to become part of it. They fought continually.

One day in late May of 1919, Nora kept Clara home from school to help with the housework. Clara protested: she *had* to go to school, there was a final exam that day; if she didn't take it, she wouldn't graduate. Nora said she didn't care. They argued back and forth—the neighbors later said they knew something horrible was happening inside the house that morning—and finally Clara, half crazy with anger, doused her dress with coal oil and touched a match to it. She later explained she'd only intended to scare Nora, who'd been unnaturally afraid of fire since the first house burned down, but the dress exploded in flames. Clara ran out of the house, screaming and crying, tumbling over and over in the grass. Nora was frozen in the doorway, shocked beyond any ability to respond. The woman next door had to rush out with a blanket and smother the flames.

Charley Guthrie was sitting in his real estate office when he heard the fire whistle blow. He saw people heading up Ninth Street and broke into a run. When he got there, he found Clara partially wrapped in a blanket. She was seared from her neck to her knees; the skin seemed to be hanging in sheets off her arms and legs. She'd been burned so badly that her nerve endings were destroyed and she couldn't feel the pain. Charley sank down in front of her, sobbing uncontrollably. "Why are you crying, Daddy?" she asked. "I'm all right."

They brought her inside and swathed her in bandages. That afternoon a steady stream of friends and relatives came to visit. It was a macabre scene: a crowd had gathered outside the house, and Clara, much the most cheerful person there, would ask from time to time if one or another of her friends were outside, and summon them in for a chat. Woody later wrote that Clara asked him not to cry like everyone else. "I'm gonna jump out of bed and start singing and dancing in about two minutes and a half," she said. "You go in there and tell Papa, and make Mama and Roy quit their carrying on." Indeed, Clara even granted the Okemah *Ledger* a brief interview. "I put coal oil on my clothes," she was quoted, "and was going to burn them a little to scare my mother."

Through the afternoon she lay there, "displaying the most superb fortitude and courage," the Okfuskee County *News* said. But with much of her skin gone, there was no way to prevent the loss of body heat. She gradually froze to death. At the end, her teacher, Mrs. Johnston, was there and Clara asked if she would graduate despite her absence that day. "Of course you will," the teacher said, and Clara closed her eyes and died.

For the rest of his life, Charley carried a small envelope in his coat pocket. On the outside he had written: "My Little Angel."

Inside there was a picture of Clara and the death notice. He held it in his hand the day he died.

The town blamed Nora. As if Clara's deathbed interviews hadn't been damning enough, there were those who now said the girl was covering up for her mother—that Nora had actually set her on fire. Others remembered the first Guthrie house had burned ten years before and said Nora probably was mixed up in that one too. Rumors about Nora's odd behavior had been circulating even before Clara's death, and now the simplest domestic problems were blown up and twisted ominously: Nora had chased Clara around with a broom; she had refused to wash or mend Clara's clothes, and when the girl complained, Nora told her to go hide in the closet. But there were other stories, far more chilling: Clara came home from school one day and heard a strange, muffled cry from the baby. "Where's George?" she asked. "He's gone away," Nora replied. But Clara heard the crying and searched the house, eventually finding the baby wrapped in newspapers in the oven.

Talk of the tragedy was so widespread that even the *Ledger* noted that it was "the chief topic of conversation" in town. School was let out for the funeral, and all of Okemah was there. Charley, in his starched white shirt and best dark suit, was no longer the dashing young man; he was stooped, and beginning to look old. Nora seemed more distant than ever. No doubt she felt the weight of every eye in town upon her. She knew what they were saying . . . and she agreed.

Clara was all she talked about now. If only she had let Clara go to school that day, the girl would still be alive. If only she hadn't been so harsh . . . all Clara wanted was to graduate and go on to the eighth grade. Nora twisted the events over and over in her mind, and nothing could wrench her free of them. Charley tried to get her interested in other things, offered to take her riding again. But when Nora pranced through the streets of Okemah now, all the looks were stares and everyone who talked was whispering.

Charley decided to get her out of town, at least until the talk died down and her nerves were calmer. He moved the family to one of his farms, about two miles north of town. It had a quiet little house next to a small pond, surrounded by fields of oats and cotton. But Nora seemed no more capable of caring for the family in the country than she had in town. Charley asked his sister Ethel, a relentless housekeeper, to come and help out for a week or so.

One day during Ethel's visit, Charley said he wanted to invite some business associates home for noon dinner. Nora fretted: "What shall we make for them?" Ethel reassured her: "We'll figure out something." But the next thing she knew, Nora had yanked out a slab of bacon and was down on the floor stabbing it with a knife, ripping it to pieces.

The rest of the family noticed Nora's odd behavior the following spring when Jerry P. Guthrie decided to hold a big family reunion at his farm in Drumright. Guthries from as far away as Texas came, and there was fiddle music and plenty of food. At one point, though, Woody and Roy were talking about Clara's fire. They talked on and on, describing every detail to their breathless cousins . . . and Nora exploded. She started screaming, and Charley had to restrain her.

Her depressions were becoming deeper. At times she would sit for hours, crying. She would go around the house muttering about killing herself, about getting a knife and cutting her throat from ear to ear. "She would be all right for a while," Woody later wrote, "and treat us kids as good as any mother, and all at once it would start in—something bad and awful—something would start coming over her, and it come by slow degrees. Her face would twitch and her lips would snarl and her teeth would show. Spit would run out of her mouth and she would start out in a low grumbling voice and gradually get to talking as loud as her throat could stand it; and her arms would draw up at her sides, then behind her back and swing in all kinds of curves. Her stomach would draw up into a hard ball, and she would double over into a terrible-looking hunch—and turn into another person, it looked like, standing right there before Roy and me." One day she dashed out of the house, got on her horse, and careened into town. Bill Stanford happened to be looking out his barbershop window and saw her blur past, dark hair flying crazily and her clothes all askew. The strangest thing, though, was that Nora Guthrie wasn't riding sidesaddle as she usually did; she was riding astride, like a man. She didn't stop for anything, just buzzed through and returned home.

Charley wasn't doing too well either. It was a terrible irony: now that he was growing older, Okemah had turned wild and young. The Oklahoma oil boom had hit, fortunes were being made every day, and the town was jammed with boomers and roughnecks. In 1920, oil was discovered at Spring Hill, nine miles east of Okemah. "Although the townsite is but a few days old," the Okfuskee County *News* reported, "it is estimated that it is now the home of 800 people." From there, the boom moved on to Garrison City, just south of Okemah, and then southwest to Cromwell, which became known as the "Meanest City in the Nation," and west again to the sleepy little village of Seminole, which exploded from a population of 700 to 30,000 in a matter of weeks.

Not much oil was ever discovered in Okemah proper, but the town's railroad station made it a major supply center. Lumberyards (oil rigs were made of wood in those days) and drilling-supply companies popped up around town. Oil-equipment wagons, paced by teams of ten rushing horses, rattled through the streets. Within months, Okemah's hotels were filled to capacity and men were roaming the streets, knocking on doors and asking for lodging. One local widow rented her spare bed to six men, two at a time in eight-hour shifts. A shack town sprouted on Okemah's east side to accommodate the boomers, but hundreds more steamed into town each day on the Fort Smith and Western train. The streets, still unpaved and swampy, were clogged with cars and wagons, and all manner of men clomped along on the wooden sidewalks. The population of the town, which had just nudged past 2,000 in 1920, quintupled overnight.

The boomers tended to spend their money as quickly as they made it, and now there were gambling casinos and loose women in Okemah. Crime became a problem for the first time. The local police seemed entirely unable to stem the violence in the streets. There were several grisly murders, as well as assorted shootings and stabbings. Alarmed by the near anarchy, the local businessmen decided—as the "better sorts" were deciding in towns all over eastern Oklahoma—that vigilante action was needed, and they formed a chapter of the Ku Klux Klan. This particular incarnation of the Klan wasn't much concerned with blacks, Catholics, or Jews; it functioned more as the martial arm of the Chamber of Commerce, almost as a hooded collection agency. Charley Guthrie, still yearning to be considered a "better sort," was an enthusiastic member.

The sheer animal force of the boom left Charley at something

of a loss; a new generation of outrageous, flashy young men wa
elbowing its way to prominence. He remembered the days whe
he had been on the cutting edge, full of vinegar, a real force i
town . . . and he wondered where it had all gone. He soug
desperately to regain control of his life and business, whic
seemed to be slipping away from him. He tried to ape the oi
field jauntiness in his real estate ads: "Still for Sale," read one
"It may be that you already know the way to a still; however,
have reference to another kind of still. If you still want to se
your property, list it with me. . . . My facilities for handling th
sale of your property are unexcelled. . . . Remember—same ol
stand—Room 9—over F. B. Thurman's store." But the oil boor
had transformed land speculation into a different, more volatil
proposition than it had been when he was going around peddlin
80-acre tenant farms. The high-stakes action had brought som
real sharks into the game, the kind of operators who ate small
timers like Charley Guthrie for breakfast. His business fortune
were declining rapidly.

He became wantonly decisive. He decided that what Nor
really needed to bring her back was another baby to take Clara'
place, and Mary Josephine was born in February of 1922. The
he decided that what *he* really needed was to run for office again
perhaps he'd feel better if he were out there making speeches an
raising hell the way he did in the old days. He wasn't going to
run for any puny local office this time, either; he'd make a statewide race. He grandly announced his candidacy for the Oklahoma Corporation Commission, a populist remnant that wa
supposed to monitor the activities of corporations, but really didn'
do much of anything. "Politically I am a lifelong Democrat. My
pre-election promises are few, very simple and, therefore, quite
easily understood," he announced. "My platform is a perfec
marvel of brevity. Here it is: If nominated and elected, I shall do
my very best to see that my conduct in office brings no regrets."
He sent Woody and Roy around the countryside tacking up campaign posters, and spent entirely too much money. It was madness from the start. He didn't have a chance. He ran fifth in a
field of eight for the one opening on the commission. He pulled
10,614 votes, about 60,000 behind the man who won.

By the beginning of 1923, Charley was stone-cold broke.
What's more, he was in physical agony: his hands, which he had
broken and abused in many a fistfight, were now swollen and

crippled with arthritis, the fingers drawing down painfully into his palm. In the evenings, the children took turns massaging his fingers and knuckles. "I'm the only man who ever lost a farm a day for thirty days," he would moan. "Nobody ever lost fifty thousand dollars any quicker than me."

He struggled to keep his dignity. He still would go downtown each day, dressed in a dark suit, clean white shirt, and tie. At first he'd just sit in his empty office, waiting for business that never came; then, for a time, he went out into the booming streets trying to sell fire extinguishers, of all things, door to door. But he was going nowhere and he hated the smell of failure. He had the feeling that they were staring and talking about *him* now, as well as Nora, and he couldn't stand it. He decided it was time to get out of there, try someplace new. He packed the family into a Model T truck and moved to Oklahoma City in July of 1923. They rented a shotgun shack on Twenty-eighth Street there, and everyone went to work. Roy pumped gas, Woody delivered milk, and poor Charley was forced to deliver groceries in return for a dollar's worth of food a day.

Then, for a moment, it seemed that things might turn out all right. Nora's stepbrother, Leonard Tanner, was a motorcycle daredevil who was making quite a name for himself in stunt shows throughout the Southwest. The Ace Motorcycle Company offered him a dealership in Oklahoma City, and Leonard asked Charley to run the business end for him. But just as they were about to close the deal, Leonard piled his motorcycle into an automobile in Chickasha, fractured his skull, and died.

So they limped back to Okemah in the summer of 1924, and settled in a little boomer shack—living room, bedroom, and lean-to kitchen on the half-deserted east side of town. The boom was pretty much over by now. The wells had been drilled, the pipe-lines built, the leases bought and sold, and the boomers gone off to prairie oil fields further west.

But the town had survived in fine fashion, its streets finally paved. The oil-equipment wagons were gone, but farmers still came with the wagonloads of cotton and pecans. Many of the burghers, their mild boom-time speculations and expansions having paid off, walked about with the puffed assurance of one-shot gamblers who'd quit while they were ahead. They could point with some satisfaction, and not very much pity, to carnage like

the Guthrie family as proof that the waters had indeed been
treacherous. With the boom safely tucked away, Okemah's propriety turned into pretense. By 1925, the Okfuskee County *New*
was running an "In Society" column.

Charley managed to latch on as a bookkeeper for the Hudson
Essex automobile dealer downtown and, hoping that he'd have
better luck now that the boom had died down, he placed an ad
in the newspaper: "Let's Trade. For real and rare bargains in
real estate and slightly used automobiles, see me AT ONCE." But
the customers didn't come. His tenure as bookkeeper ended after
four months when he was given the job of issuing auto licenses
in Okfuskee County, most likely a small political handout from
a courthouse friend. He would be paid fifty cents for each license
issued. He was still in terrible pain, and apparently began to drink
more heavily. He kept a fruit jar filled with white lightning beneath the front seat of his car, and Woody would see him going
out there for a snort every so often.

Nora was worse. She hated the musty shotgun shack they were
forced to live in. She hated the tiny rooms and the old, battered
furniture. Sometimes she'd lose her temper and knock the furniture around; once she threw it all out into the yard. Sometimes
she'd empty the icebox and throw all the food out there, too.
Woody and Roy picked up after her, did most of the housework,
covered for her so Charley never really knew how bad things
were. Her nerves seemed to be deteriorating: often she was shaky
and uncertain, losing her balance, dropping cups, dishes, and
matches. There were several small fires that utterly terrified her.
She went to the doctors at the clinic down on Main Street, but
they didn't know what to tell her. She'd come out of the clinic
and walk the streets in a daze, crying. She didn't have a piano
anymore, and had stopped singing the old songs.

In fact, the only real enjoyment in Nora's life now was going
to the movies at the Jewel Theater, where it was dark and no one
could see her and she couldn't see herself. The Jewel had a policy
of showing two new films every day, and Nora would almost
always be there. Sometimes she brought the children with her in
the afternoon, and Woody sat at her side as they watched the
cowboys and the pirates and the sheiks. Their favorite, though,
was Charlie Chaplin. They loved watching the little tramp with
the ratty clothes and the wild mop of hair make fools of the
snooty rich, the bullies, and the police. The tramp was far more

clever than he appeared at first; he was shy and looked sort of clumsy, but actually moved with a delicate grace. His poverty beggared their vacant gentility—it almost seemed a matter of choice on his part. He played the fool, and stood apart, and saw clearly all that went on around him.

In the empty afternoon darkness of the Jewel Theater, Woody heard his mother laughing. He hadn't heard her laugh in years, but the little tramp had the ability to make Nora forget her troubles, at least for a while . . . and Woody, who was small and wore ratty clothes and had a wild mop of hair, obviously took note.

He became known around town as an "alley rat," a loner, a scavenger who went around collecting junk in a burlap sack. Perhaps his first harmonica was a random item picked out of a trash barrel and stuffed in his sack; perhaps it really happened as he later told it: the French harp was given to him by a "colored shoeshine boy" he met in a barbershop who was able to make it sound like a railroad train, so sad and lonesome and distant. He asked the man to play it over and over, and tried to learn how to play it the same way. In any case, Woody Guthrie was soon a fixture on the bench near the produce market, playing around with his French harp for hours each day.

He moved at the periphery of Okemah, and met the leftovers from a wilder time—the cowboys, the boom flotsam, the down-and-outers, fogies and misfits who dated back to frontier days. They told him all the old stories, and some new ones. He'd go down to the barbershop and hear how Pretty Boy Floyd had come by just the other day, got his hair cut, and left a five-dollar tip; and how that old man out there, the one with the long beard who always hung out on the street, claimed to be none other than Jesse James. It just may have been true, too, because when the police swept him in, they stripped him down and turned a fire hose on him to give him a bath, and damned if he didn't have the same identical bullet holes as Jesse was supposed to have. At least, that's what they said.

The Indians were as interesting as the outlaws. A few of them—at least, a few of those who hadn't been tricked out of their land—struck it rich in the boom and went busting through town in new Lincolns. Most still came to town in wagons on Saturday afternoons, though. The men would do the shopping while the women remained, sitting straight up and stock-still, wrapped in blankets,

with solemn children on their laps. Woody tried to entertain them:
he'd go up close to the wagons, start playing his harmonica and
dancing a little jig, hoping to get the Indian kids to crack a smile.

There were all sorts of interesting people, too, over in the
shacktown on the east side and back of the hill. Some of them
were hanging on to the few remaining oil-field jobs, others were
trying to figure out where to go next or wondering where they'd
already been. Woody's closest friend among them was a tall, slim
oil-field worker named Gantz, who'd come home late in the afternoon, wash up, then sit out in the doorway of his shack singing
and playing a guitar. He sang the same sort of songs as Nora
Guthrie, only his seemed a little happier, and Woody especially
liked the one about Stewball the racehorse.

Nearby was the tumbledown tin shack where old lady Atkins
lived with her two grown sons. She kept a shelf of the finest
clothes there, colorful silks and satins that she'd worn in the days
when she'd been a fancy lady in Kansas City. She would tell
Woody stories about life in the big city and sometimes take a
notion to put on all her finery once again, and go promenading
through the streets of town with a gaggle of children trailing after
her, laughing. Mrs. Atkins didn't give two hoots if they laughed
or not, and Woody was impressed by her defiant pride: why *not*
parade around town in her musty satins? She wasn't hurting anyone. One day, though, she left town without telling anyone and
the tin shack was empty. When no one moved in after her, Woody
decided to use it as a hideout.

There was much to hide out from. There was, for example,
school. Compared to all the people he met and the things he
learned in the back alleys of Okemah, school was pretty boring.
It also was filled with kids who made fun of him because he was
runty, and had an Adam's apple that bobbled up and down, and
hair that was nappy like a black man's; and because he sometimes
came to class wearing shirts that were missing a button or weren't
ironed; and because his father had lost all his money; and because—but they'd never say this to his face—his mother was nuts.
He wouldn't give them any satisfaction, though. He would *never*
let on that he cared when they didn't invite him to their parties,
or when they whispered behind his back. In fact, his only reaction
to the pettiness of his classmates was to entertain them—after all,
it wasn't easy to laugh and whisper at the same time. He would
play his harmonica and dance jigs out in the schoolyard, and in

class he'd draw wonderfully funny cartoons. He was the sort of clever, inattentive student that teachers hate: the class clown.

It wasn't so much what he said. He never did *say* very much (although when he did mumble out a few words, they usually were choice). It was more the way that he used his face and his body—his expressions, his gestures. Like the time in seventh grade when he and Blanche Giles were supposed to be tightrope walkers in the class revue. Mrs. Price wrote the script a certain way, but Woody changed it to take advantage of his agility. The audience roared, but Mrs. Price kept him after school for six weeks for disobeying her.

Blanche was one of the few people—and the only girl—in class who'd talk to Woody. She sat next to him, and would give him her books to draw cartoons in. He was fine at caricatures, but best of all were his stick figures: the little men with the pointy knees and elbows who always seemed to be racing off somewhere . . . and always looked more than a bit like Woody himself. He would draw little lined faces on them, and top hats that he could shade just right to make them look shiny, and he did it all with astonishing speed.

"You're gonna be a great cartoonist someday," Blanche would whisper.

"Naw, they'll never let me," he'd reply.

"Yes, you will. You'll be famous someday, and have lots of money. Whatcha gonna do with your money, Woody?"

"I'll get my mother the best doctor I can to make her feel better again," and then he'd quickly turn away.

Blanche had a birthday coming in December—her thirteenth—and she decided to invite Woody to the party. It was a daring move and several of her girlfriends immediately announced they wouldn't come if Woody Guthrie was going to be there. "He's just trash," they said. Blanche held out, though, and the girls relented. She told Woody, "Now, you get all fixed up, and show them you can do it." So he cleaned himself up, ironed out a shirt, and tried (unsuccessfully) to plaster down his wild curls. He bought a bottle of dime-store perfume for Blanche's present, wrapped it in paper, and did just fine at the party.

After that, he'd sometimes walk Blanche home from school, and carry her books. It was all very innocent. But one day Grace Giles got a phone call from Mrs. Price at school: "You'd better look after your daughter more carefully. She's keeping the wrong sort of company at school." When Mrs. Giles realized the teacher was referring to Woody Guthrie, she couldn't believe it. She felt sorry for the poor kid. She'd see his mother wandering through the streets and sometimes hear her calling out the door, "Woodrow!" as though she were crying. But more than feeling sorry for Woody, Blanche's mother was amazed that Mrs. Price didn't see the same thing in the boy that she did: all you had to do was look into his eyes and it was quite apparent that a brain was cranking away behind there. He had the most beautiful, intelligent brown eyes Mrs. Giles had ever seen.

There were a few others, but not many, in town who noticed. Mrs. Chowning, the banker's wife, had a habit of picking out the "queer" children, the creative ones who were considered impossible to handle. She had a way, the way that Sunday-school teachers occasionally have, of caring without exactly understanding. She treated Woody as though the things he thought and said actually *mattered*, and before long she was hearing the back screen door creak open several days a week and he'd be sitting at the kitchen table, spinning out the wildest yarns about things he saw in town, telling epic tales about a family of squirrels—inventing personalities for each of them—or drawing pictures for her. Then there'd be an abrupt "S'long," and he'd be gone. She never knew when he'd come, how long he'd stay, or when he'd be back. And since he never offered, she never asked.

Occasionally, he'd tell her about his family. Once in a while, he'd even tell the truth. "I'm not going home for dinner tonight. They'll be fussing around, and I just ain't going."

"Don't talk nonsense. You surely are going," Mrs. Chowning would say. "Of course you are . . ."

"No, I ain't. . . . There probably won't be no dinner anyhow."

"Well, I'll give you a sandwich and a glass of milk, but you're still going home right after you finish."

Then: "I'm gonna have to do something about this. It just can't go on this way."

"What are you going to do, Woody?"

"Uh . . . what would *you* do?"

"I'd get an education if I had to steal for it," Mrs. Chowning would say.

". . . Yup."

"Really, Woody, it *is* the most important thing."

"Well, s'long . . ."

Indeed, the situation at home was much worse. One day when Nora set out an icy tub for little George to bathe in, he refused and she chased him around the house with a knife until he jumped out a window. Another time, they were sitting in the movies and three-year-old Mary Jo wandered down the aisle and out into the street. Luckily, a man rushed into Charley Guthrie's office and said, "Ain't that your little girl out there on the street in the middle of traffic?" Charley decided it was time to pack up Mary Jo and take her to his sister Maude's farm in the Texas panhandle, at least until things got better.

When school ended in 1926, Charley sent George out there too. Just before he left, though, there was a last family photograph, taken on the front step of their house. Woody, in a straw hat and bib overalls and looking very much like Huckleberry Finn, sat on the step next to his father, who was wearing his usual white shirt and tie but looked much older. George sat just in front of them in the yard, and Nora stood behind, staring straight into the camera this time, but with her arms pinned behind her back so no one could see their unsteadiness.

With the younger children gone, the last vestiges of family life disintegrated. Woody would be up like a shot in the morning and out of the house before breakfast. Invariably, he was the first one in the schoolyard. At night, he'd often get his dinner from friends he'd made among the cooks at the downtown cafés, knocking on the kitchen doors in back and playing his French harp for them. Then he'd fall asleep on a bench somewhere, rather than go home and face that day's particular horror. Sometimes Charley would go out looking for him and fetch him back. But more often, now, Charley himself wasn't going home. It was just too painful. For a long time—for the seven years since Clara had died, to be exact—Charley had tried to put the best face on the situation and held out hope that Nora would eventually put it behind her, that she'd regain control of her wits and nerves, but it only had become worse. Recently she had taken to attacking Charley with her fists or anything else that was handy, accusing him of being out with other women all the time . . . then she'd abruptly fall quiet. He knew there were times when he wasn't around that she'd affect a bizarre coquettish pose and go walking through the

streets wearing nothing but a slip. It was even rumored down at
the American Legion hall that she had become a loose woman.
She had no friends. Her mother, who desperately wanted to help,
couldn't come because her husband, Lee Tanner, wouldn't allow
it. He said Nora was a lost cause, an embarrassment, and it was
best to forget about her.

For his part, Charley was nearing the age of fifty and beginning
to shrivel up like a piece of bacon in a skillet. His shoulders were
stooped, his face was heavily wrinkled, and his hands were painful
knots of gristle. He was drinking heavily and pretty much confined
himself to a small circle of cronies, mostly boom people, with
whom he'd play cards and occasionally hunt. By force of will, he
kept his dignity. He insisted on dressing up in a suit for work every
day, and would never take a drink when women or children were
present. He still read all he could, although his hunger for new
ideas and his sense of boundless possibility that seemed to epitomize
the frontier spirit were gone forever. He didn't talk about his troubles, and when close friends would suggest, "Maybe you should
put her in some hospital," he'd switch the conversation off to something else. At the end of April 1927, he lost his job as auto license
clerk for the county and was unemployed.

Two months later, on a Saturday evening in late June, Charley
was taking a nap on the sofa in the front room, the newspaper
spread out on his chest. Woody had gone off to the Tanner place,
and Roy was working as usual; and Nora was alone there, watching her husband. At some point, she stood up and walked across
the room with the kerosene lamp . . . and then the lamp was
gone and there was an explosion and Charley was a bonfire. He
opened his eyes and, in an instant of recognition, saw Nora standing above him with a horror in her eyes beyond anything he could
have ever imagined, then he was out the door and rolling in the
grass until a neighbor came out with a blanket to smother the
flames.

At about 3 a.m., they called Charley's brother Claude, who
was living with a new wife over in Henryetta. He arrived at
Okemah's makeshift little clinic just before dawn and found
Charley all wrapped up in bandages. "What happened?" he
asked.

"No one will ever know," Charley said.

"But . . ."

"No one will ever know and that's all."

"Well, is there anything I can do for you, Charley?"

"I could use some cigarettes, Claude."

When he returned with the cigarettes, Claude said, "I guess I'll go down to the house and see about Nora . . ."

Charley closed his eyes and shook his head. "She won't even know you."

But when Claude pulled up to the house, Nora came right out with her hands clasped behind her back and said, "Morning Claude, you want some breakfast?" Claude wasn't so sure that he wanted Nora to fix breakfast for him, but decided that it might not be a bad idea to go inside and see about the kids, so he agreed.

Roy was there, but Woody still wasn't home from the Tanners'. Nora went back to the little kitchen and began making eggs. Claude noticed that she was cracking eggs and then throwing them into the skillet, shells and all. "Listen, Nora, don't worry about making me breakfast," he said. "I've got to be getting home."

Roy followed Claude out to the car and said, "Mama's just plumb gone, Uncle Claude . . ." That afternoon, the doctors came and took her to the state mental hospital at Norman. She was gone by the time Woody arrived home.

He went over to the Okemah hospital to see his father. Charley was in bad pain now; the burns covered his chest from his neck to his waist. It was one of the few times that Woody had ever seen him out of control. "It's all over for me now," he moaned. "I just want to die. I want to die and go the same way Clara went." But within a few days it became clear that he was going to live, and arrangements would have to be made. He called his sister Maude, who already had Mary Jo and George out at her farm in the Texas panhandle, and she said there would be plenty of room for him to recuperate there too.

The Okfuskee County *News* reported the fire in a small article at the bottom of the front page. The headline, "Pioneer Real Estate Man Painfully Burned," was accompanied by a brief but gaudy description of the tragedy: "At about 8:30 Saturday evening Mr. Guthrie was seen to run from the door of his home in east Okemah, seemingly ablaze from head to foot. His cries brought the assistance of a neighbor, who succeeded in getting the clothing off of the tortured man. . . . It is reported as an evident fact that kerosene had been poured over Mr. Guthrie, and rumors are many. However, he is now on the road to recovery and in a cheerful frame of mind.'' Charley's recent obscurity occasioned a biographical sentence describing him as a ''pioneer real estate man in this section,'' an image that conjured up visions of Daniel Boone, but it had been only twenty years since young Charley Guthrie arrived in town to assume his duties as District Court Clerk.

He remained at the hospital in Okemah for several weeks, then was taken to the Fort Smith and Western depot in a stretcher and lifted through a window onto the train. Woody stood on the platform and watched as the train pulled out, heading west toward the open prairie, and he was alone.

Of course, Roy had been left behind too, but he was twenty-one years old and expected to fend for himself. His reaction to the family tragedy had been the exact opposite of Woody's: he worked harder, dressed neater, and tried to be the most respectable young man in town. He never did approve of the way his little brother cavorted about, looking like a tramp and making a spectacle of himself—almost as if Woody wanted to *remind* people of all the Guthries had been through. Roy was tall and lanky, and looked a lot like his father; Woody, with his long nose, high forehead, and dark features, looked more like his mother. The two boys kept a polite distance.

Roy continued to work as a grocery clerk after his father left, and found room and board with a good family. The Masonic Lodge—Charley had been a 33rd degree Mason—tried to find a nice home for Woody too, but he was singularly unreceptive to the idea. He tried several different families—rich ones, poor ones, a farmer north of town—but never felt comfortable enough to stay for more than a couple of weeks. He worked as a bellhop, busboy, and night clerk at the Broadway Hotel for a while, but was fired for drawing cartoons all over the menus and the room-key tabs.

He felt best in the tin shack he'd taken over from old lady Atkins and, by mid-autumn, took up permanent residence there. By that time, he had developed a small group of friends—the children of boomers, mostly—who hung out in the shack with him. They called themselves a gang, and Woody was the leader. His closest friend probably was Colonel Martin, whom he called Abe because he was tall and awkward like Abraham Lincoln.

Nobody could recall Colonel ever getting angry. He had the low-key, accepting, and unbiased dispostion that Woody would demand of close friends all his life. There was also Casper Moore, a younger boy who was completely devoted to Woody and whom he nicknamed Tubba because he was chubby. The three of them were the core of the gang and would spend their afternoons rummaging through the back alleys with their burlap sacks, trying to find scraps of metal and other valuable items to take down to Mark's Junk Yard for appraisal. Then they would go back to the gang house—Woody named it the Eeny House because it was so small—where they'd stoke a fire in the large can they dragged in to serve as a stove. Woody ran a very moral gang: the Ten Commandments were tacked on the wall, and he promulgated a series of rules and regulations that, among other things, outlawed cursing—violators would be slugged on the arm by other gang members—but were enforced rather selectively. The gang members would go swimming and fishing together in the Canadian River. Sometimes they'd do crazy things like swim across the river with rocks tied around their necks, or go over to where the oil pipeline crossed the river, climb up, and play with the lineman's chair, suspended dangerously from a cable.

Ever since Clara died, Woody had been at the mercy of awesome and terrible forces he couldn't understand. But now, for the first time in years, he didn't have to worry about coffee cups flying or fires starting mysteriously. He didn't have to live in mortal fear that something he'd do or say would touch off another of his mother's screaming, crying fits. He didn't have to *behave* himself for her benefit anymore (it never had made much difference, in any case). He was his own man now. He took care of himself. He didn't have to worry about anyone else, and he liked it that way. In fact, it was easier to get by than he'd expected.

Once the question of lodging was settled, he found that food was no problem. He'd been cadging food successfully for years. Sometimes he and Casper Moore and his brother Red would follow the milk wagon from door to door, stealing quarts off the front stoops; then they'd go to the bakery and get some hot, fresh bread free from the baker. They'd buy a little butter and have a feast in the haunted house across from where the Moores lived. But Woody soon made another important discovery: he didn't have to steal to eat. All he had to do was go downtown, set his cap out in the street, and start playing his harmonica and dancing a jig. Not only did he make good money, but there also was the pleasure of seeing the crowd gather, and the feet tapping, and the applause. At times, he felt that he'd been sprung from a prison, and wonderfully free.

Of course, there were also times when he was desolate. He envied his pals going home each evening to supper and the security of their families. It had been a long time since anyone had fussed over him, and he missed that. He found himself going over to Mrs. Chowning's more often. She would set out tea, and they would chitchat politely and then she'd give her usual lecture about the importance of an education. He didn't put much stock in what she said, but he enjoyed her nagging and caring.

As winter approached and nights in the gang house grew damp and cold, it became obvious that he was going to have to make some accommodation with the civilized world. One day he showed up at Roy's house shivering and half delirious with fever. Roy's "family" took care of him for several days and Roy gave him money for medicine, but then he was gone again. Roy joked about Woody taking the money and buying cakes and moonshine for his gang, but he was concerned . . . as were several of Woody's close friends. Colonel Martin hung back, probably figuring that Woody was smart enough to find a solution for himself, but Casper Moore assumed Woody was too proud to ask any favors and took matters into his own hands. He pestered his parents, begged them to take Woody in.

His father, Tom Moore, had been part of the circle that played cards and drank with Charley Guthrie. He was a barber who'd followed the boom to Okemah and lost most of his business when the boomers went away. He had dark hair, bright blue eyes, and played at being a tough guy, but his heart went out to Charley Guthrie's ratty little kid. After the requisite pushing from his wife, Nonie, and prodding from the kids, Tom welcomed Woody into the family.

They got along famously. Tom played the fiddle and knew a raft of old Tennessee church songs, which he sang in a sweet tenor voice while Woody harmonized, or backed him on the French harp. He was amazed by Woody's remarkable ability to make up new, funny verses to old songs right while they were singing them. They would sit and play for hours most evenings, with the whole family (which also included two daughters and a grandmother) joining in on the choruses. Then Woody, Tubba, and Red would be sent off to bed—the *same* bed, which they slept in head to foot, so someone's feet were always sticking in someone else's face. The confusion was compounded by Woody's insistence that none of them sleep on their left sides because their hearts were located there, and it wasn't good for your heart to be slept on. Sometimes he'd poke Red and say, "You're sleeping on the wrong side," which would touch off a wild pillow fight and a booming response from Tom Moore.

Woody sensed the affection that lay behind Tom's gruffness, and saw that he wasn't being treated any differently from the other kids, and behaved himself accordingly. He'd obey Nonie's orders to clean himself up and actually tried to comb his hair, but it was so woolly that he'd often break the teeth of the big wooden combs the rest of the family used.

He even agreed to go to school, sometimes. During his gang-house period, he'd had a rare, and brief, burst of academic vigor, drawing huge murals filled with caricatures of students and teachers on the blackboards before anyone arrived at school in the morning. The administration put a stop to that quickly enough—it was "unsupervised activity"—even though it was bringing the kids to school more enthusiastically than anyone could remember. Aside from such occasional bursts of creativity, he received average grades with little effort. The exceptions were very interesting, though: he received A's in typing and geography, the two preoccupations of his adult life, and he flunked psychology. His favorite subject was typing because the teacher would allow him to use his imagination and write about anything he wanted if he finished his drills before the rest of the class.

He was a member of the school newspaper staff and joke editor of the yearbook, but he was best known as an entertainer. When the junior class wanted to raise money for its prom, Woody was placed atop a flatbed truck on Main Street and told to strut his stuff while a hat was passed. He had added a Jew's harp and bones to his repertoire, and seemed able to make music out of anything—pencils, combs, glasses filled with varying amounts of water, empty bottles. One night the Rotary Club hired him—perhaps out of charitable impulse more than appreciation of his talents—and the businessmen threw money as he danced and mugged. He came home that night with his cap stuffed with about sixty dollars in coin and Tom Moore said, "Well, Woody, don't you think it's time you bought yourself some new clothes?"

The next day Woody came back with two new shirts. "How about getting yourself some underwear?" Tom said. "You don't have any."

"Don't need it," Woody said.

"Then what are you going to do with all the rest of that money?" Woody stammered and mumbled and finally let on that he'd already given most of it away. Tom knew the boy was like that, and didn't go too hard on him. Money *bothered* Woody: getting it turned people into animals and losing it drove them crazy. He refused to acknowledge its existence in quantities beyond what he needed for immediate use, and squandered his windfalls.

Woody spent nearly a year with the Moores. It was a good, safe time for him, and he almost became part of the family. Almost . . . but he never surrendered himself completely. There was a whole range of emotions, of worries and fears, of questions about his past and future that he'd never discuss with them. He'd either be *on*—singing and dancing and cracking wise—or off into long, deep silences. Part of it, no doubt, was that men in the Southwest just didn't go around talking about those kinds of things. It would seem weak. But there was more: he sensed that if he stood apart, like the little tramp in the movies, he'd feel safer and be able to see more clearly. He sought *aloneness*, rather than privacy. It was an uneasy compromise, but the best he could do: he lived in the family, but wasn't part of it. Sometimes he would go to the kitchen and talk to Nonie about his mother. He wanted to visit her in the hospital. He wanted to see if there was anything he could do for her, and Nonie promised they would go to see her someday.

Gradually, during that year, he made the transition from the security of the gang house to the less certain precincts of Moomaw's drugstore, where all the kids—including girls—hung out. There were new ceremonies to learn, like rolling cigarettes from Bull Durham tobacco, which he'd buy in a pouch. How you *carried* the pouch was as important as rolling the cigarette tight and neat: it was stuffed in the breast pocket, with the little tag hanging out. When Woody and the Moore boys bought a pouch together, they would take turns carrying it that way. There were other, not so faint stirrings. He developed an unnatural interest in Sears catalogues, especially the women's lingerie section. He found himself slipping off with the catalogue to some secret place, and slowly turning the pages with one hand while he groped around under his bib overalls with the other. The idea of making actual physical contact with a girl was still beyond rational contemplation, but it was beginning to insinuate itself into his universe of possibilities.

Late in 1928, Tom Moore began to get itchy. Okemah was dead and gone as a boom town, but there were all sorts of interesting things going on out West. He had a friend who wrote him about the wonders of Arizona, and he was beginning to think about going there. As talk of leaving increased, so did Woody's requests to visit his mother, and finally, one day, they took him. Tubba and Red didn't go, but the younger daughter, Gladys, did. They drove west about sixty miles, into the prairie.

The hospital sat starkly in the middle of nowhere. It was prairie Gothic: a dark red brick building, with screened-in porches, that seemed much larger than it actually was. Woody went inside and the doctors took him through corridors of ravers and screamers, a great wash of crumpled and smelly humanity, through locked doors and into the room where his mother was sitting in a formless hospital smock, shaking and fidgeting. She didn't recognize him. The doctors said she was suffering from something called Huntington's chorea, a nervous disease that couldn't be cured and only got worse, and they told him other things too, but he wasn't listening very carefully: his own mother could not tell who he was. *She didn't even recognize him.*

He stumbled back out to the car in a haze, his lip trembling and him biting it, trying to be strong, but it was no use. He collapsed on the front bumper, sobbing deep and hard. Nonie wrapped him in her arms, and cradled him all the way back to Okemah. But before long, the Moores were gone to Arizona and he was alone again.

CHAPTER 2

Wheat Fields Waving,
Dust Clouds Rolling

An odd slant of light through the window, dust misting down, breaking the darkness of the dingy room. The old man sat in the shadows, tentative, trying to start a conversation after two years . . . but finding it difficult to pick up again as if nothing had happened. Woody held back too, and they circled each other cautiously like fighters at the beginning of a bout, looking for an opening. Luckily there was a knock at the door—a customer— and Woody was alone for a moment, free to look around and get his bearings.

There were two small rooms. The front one, where they'd been standing, was an "office" with two battered desks and not much else. Then a soiled, greasy curtain leading to the back room, where the old man lived. There was a double bed and a dresser in the back room, and his clothes hung from hooks along the thin pine walls. Woody went slowly to the dresser—it was covered with little notes and scraps of paper—and opened the top drawer: there was a .25-caliber automatic pistol and bullets resting on a sheaf of correspondence school courses. Woody felt a warm rush of recognition, and picked out one of the Jimmy DeForrest boxing lessons.

"Did you ever finish that boxing course I sent you?" Charley asked, returning to the room and sitting on the bed.

40

"No," Woody answered, embarrassed. "Just never did get the hang of it, I guess."

"Well, that's all right," Charley said, lighting a cigarette. "It doesn't matter one bit. You can learn something else. Whatever you pick out to do, I'll read a book on it and be your trainer."

Charley asked about Okemah, about politics and his old friends there. Woody mentioned the Moores and some of the others, but didn't say much about himself and said nothing at all about his mother. After the Moores had left for Arizona, Woody stayed around town for a while and then decided to get out and see the world. He headed south toward the Gulf of Mexico, playing his French harp and hitching rides, hoping to find the Mosiers, friends from his gang-house days, who'd moved to a farm down around there. He'd considered hopping a freight at first, but shelved that idea after an Okemah friend, Miles Reynolds, lost a leg when he fell between two boxcars (for the rest of his life, Woody only used the trains as a last resort: they were too dangerous and uncomfortable). Still, he did spend a lot of time in the hobo camps at the edge of railroad yards on his way south. Invariably, they'd have a fire going and a stew bubbling, and wouldn't be averse to sharing it. More often than not, the hoboes were simply migratory farm workers moving on to the next job. An estimated 200,000 of them followed the wheat harvest north across the plains each summer, and thousands of others were fruit pickers, cowboys, and boomers. It was a pretty dreary life, but they developed an elaborate mythology and customs to make it more palatable. They took names like Denver Fly and Mobile Mac, Poison Face Tim and Dick the Stabber. They told long, improbable tales around the campfire—"ghost stories," they were called—about legendary hoboes, good towns and bad, and railroad bulls like East Texas Red who took a special delight in making their lives miserable. They made up songs about life on the bum: some dripping with overripe romanticism, but others with a rough honesty that cut through the myths . . . and Woody soaked it all in.

He spent the early part of the summer of 1929 on the road, nibbling at the edge of hobo culture, but never really becoming part of it. He passed through Houston, reached the Gulf, and eventually found the Mosiers, who were happy to see him: they needed all the help they could get on the farm. But hoeing figs wasn't exactly Woody's style—manual labor never was—and he

soon headed back north to Okemah. When he arrived home, there
was a letter from his father waiting. Charley wanted him to come
to Texas and help run a rooming house in the oil-boom town o
Pampa.

Actually, Charley had been rather charitable in calling it a
rooming house. It was a long, rickety two-story building made
of cheap pine and corrugated tin slapped together—part of a tumbledown, sleazy block of fleabag hotels, ptomaine cafés, and
speakeasies. On the first floor, there was a long room with rows
of cots stretching out behind the office where Charley lived. The
beds were occupied in eight-hour shifts by oil-field workers who
paid a quarter for the privilege. They called it a "cot house,"
but with the young women who lived and worked in private rooms
upstairs, that wasn't an entirely accurate description either. On
warm nights the women would sit out on second-floor porches
all along the street soliciting customers, and the respectable people in town called the area "Little Juarez." Charley's job was to
collect the quarters from the oil-field boys, the weekly rent from
the women (who handled their other finances independently), and
make sure the place didn't become so disgusting as to force the
patrons elsewhere. It wasn't exactly dignified labor, but the family was happy to see Charley taking a step back into the world
again.

For a long time after they lowered him from the train, Charley
had seemed more dead than alive. He'd lie in bed all day, flat
on his back and quiet, smoking cigarettes. Occasionally he'd turn
on his side with a great deal of pain and effort, and read a book.
Mary Jo and George regularly harvested sheep pills from the
pasture to be made into poultices for his open wound. Sometimes
they would sit by his bed and ask questions. "How'd you get
burned, Papa?" Mary Jo would ask, and Charley would say that
some oil had spilled on him when he'd been working on a car
and it exploded when he lit a cigarette. "What happened to
Mama?" George would ask, and Charley would explain that she'd
been bitten by a mad dog and had to be taken to the hospital. He
rarely talked about what really had happened, not even with his
sister Maude, but often they'd hear him sobbing alone in his
room.

Maude refused to indulge his sadness. She was a tiny, eternally
cheerful woman with a scratchy voice who insisted on being called

"Skinny Granny" by all the children. She was married to a gaunt
farmer named Robert Boydstun, who was as quiet as she was
gregarious, and completely tolerant of her penchant for orchestrating family mob scenes. Maude and Robert had two daughters,
Allene and Geneva, but there always seemed to be a half dozen
other children running around the house, to say nothing of the
assorted aunts, uncles, and cousins. By some curious telepathy,
the entire Guthrie clan had decided to converge on the panhandle
simultaneously, and half of them usually could be found at the
Boydstun farm. Even Jerry P. himself had left Oklahoma to spend
his last few years with several of his children in Amarillo.

The Boydstun farmhouse was a speck of life in the vast emptiness of blue sky, quivering wheat, and rolling grassland that
stretched for hundreds and hundreds of miles in all directions. It
was a small house with large rooms, especially the kitchen, which
had broad plank floors that Maude scrubbed with lye water each
day. The furniture was threadbare and ordinary except for an old
pump organ, but there was an incredible abundance of food—a
vegetable garden, a meat locker, a basement filled with preserves
in glass fruit jars, a barn full of milk cows, and a wood-burning
stove that always seemed to be a confusion of steaming pots and
kettles. Maude was known to cook corn bread and beans for
entire threshing crews during harvest season . . . and even on a
slow day, there were nearly a dozen Guthries of all ages, sizes,
and dispositions ready to hunker down at the long kitchen table
when Maude dished out her specialties in a constant stream of
jabber.

By the time Charley arrived at the Boydstuns, one of the regulars at Maude's table was his youngest brother (half brother,
actually, since they had different mothers), Jeff Davis Guthrie.
Jeff was a large, windy man with pale red hair and blue eyes; a
garage mechanic in the town of Panhandle, but bubbling over
with extravagant plans for the future. He combined Jerry P. Guthrie's passion for get-rich-quick schemes with Charley's devotion
to self-improvement and, as a result, enrolled in some pretty exotic correspondence courses. He learned fingerprinting by mail,
and also was a graduate of Dr. Tarbell's Chicago school of magic.
The fingerprint diploma was immediately parlayed into a job on
the Pampa police force, but Jeff had no real ambitions in law
enforcement. His dream was to get into show business, mixing
magic with music. His father had taught him the Guthrie family

art of fiddle playing and it was generally acknowledged that Jeff was, hands down, the finest country fiddler in the panhandle. In fact, he'd won several contests to prove it. And after years of practice, he wasn't half bad at magic either.

It usually didn't take much prodding to get Jeff up and fiddling after dinner. Often he'd be accompanied on the accordion by Maude's oldest daughter, Allene, who had dreams of show business herself. She was an attractive girl who enjoyed dressing up and acting older than she was, which was fourteen. Soon Jeff was teaching her how to assist with his magic tricks, and then they were taking long evening walks together in the soft rustle and shimmer of the wheat fields. Although their marriage didn't come as much of a surprise to anyone who'd seen them together, it was still rather shocking. No one in the family was quite sure if it was legal: Allene was now Jeff's wife and niece. Maude was his half sister and mother-in-law. And Jerry P., who was now Jeff's father and grandfather-in-law, was totally outraged until Charley assured him that this sort of thing happened all the time in the royal families of Europe. Jerry P., who died soon after, never quite resigned himself to the situation, though.

Jeff moved Allene into an apartment in Pampa, which was busily transforming itself from a placid farming and ranching community into a boom town. It had been founded as a cattle depot in 1902 by the White Deer Land Company, an English firm that owned a massive chunk of rangeland in the panhandle. Two very proper Englishmen, C. P. Buckler and M. K. Brown, were dispatched to oversee the operation and, for approximately the next fifty years, Mr. Brown and Mr. Buckler, who quietly detested each other, were the two most powerful men in the area. Brown, a flamboyant Englishman who seemed to flaunt his accent, handled the management side. He wore expensive suits from London and often served high tea. Buckler, the financial officer, was less colorful but equally romantic. He had decided to come to Texas because it seemed a more adventurous option than India or Egypt. They ran a decent, civilized town of 7,500 until the oil boom broke in 1926—and even then, the boom was confined to an area south of the Santa Fe tracks, and didn't much disturb the more respectable north side.

Woody was seventeen years old when he arrived in Pampa, but seemed much younger. The upstairs girls at the cot house treated

him like a boy, not a man, and let him hang around. He drew
their pictures and made them laugh. They were, for the most part,
dull farm girls who'd come to town looking for adventure; they
painted their faces and tried to look fancy, but were more pathetic
than alluring. When Woody watched them at work through the
cracks in the pine and tin, their bodies moved with a sophistication that seemed beyond the comprehension of their blank, childlike faces. For some, it was a numbness that came naturally;
others, more sensitive, needed morphine to get them there.

Woody also drew pictures of the oil-field boys downstairs and
listened to their rough-and-tumble talk. His cartoons were plas-
tered all over the cot house and a new one appeared in the front
window each day, creating a happily implausible island of innocence in the dinge and muck of Little Juarez. Charley was thrilled
by his son's facility and ordered him a correspondence course in
cartooning. Shorty Harris, who owned the drugstore across the
street, wanted a little sunshine in his joint too and offered Woody
a job.

Actually, Shorty Harris's drugstore was about as much a drugstore as Charley's rooming house was a rooming house. To keep
up appearances, Shorty—who wasn't at all short, either—had several shelves of faded patent medicines and an ice-cream soda
fountain, but he was really in the liquor business. Woody's job
was to tend the fountain, fixing banana splits and milk shakes up
top and selling two-ounce bottles of bootleg Jamaica Ginger under the table, while Shorty took care of the more serious customers—like Charley and Jeff—in the back room. In addition,
Woody decorated the place with cartoons and clever signs in the
windows and on the mirror behind the fountain. His greatest
triumph, though, was the large "Harris Drug" which he painted
outside on the brick façade above the front window and signed
"Woody." It lasted through wind, snow, dust, and attempts to
paint it over for nearly fifty years, until it was sandblasted off in
1977.

Shorty was a garrulous man, always chewing on a cigar and
looking for a fight. He was known to mix it up with his customers
when they got too rowdy or didn't pay their bills, and once bit a
man's ear half off in a scuffle. But he was easy with Woody, and
didn't set down any specific rules or hours. If the boy came in,
that was fine. If he didn't, that was okay too. He paid Woody
out of his pocket each day, the amount depending on how much

Woody worked, or how entertaining he'd been, or how flush Shorty was, or how drunk. In truth, Shorty just liked having the kid around . . . and Woody didn't mind it much, either.

He found a beat-up old guitar in the back of the store and asked Uncle Jeff—with whom he'd established an immediate rapport— to teach him some chords. There was no formal instruction, just Jeff playing and Woody doing his best to keep up. Then he'd sit and practice in Shorty's, trying to figure out how to play the songs his mother used to sing. He still remembered the words and melodies all too clearly. Sometimes the black guy who shined shoes next door would come in and play some blues on the guitar for Woody, in return for a couple of shots of jake. Woody called him "Spider Fingers" because "his fingers walked up and down that old guitar neck just like a big, hairy tarantula."

In September of 1929, Woody made one more attempt to finish high school—with some prodding from his father—but the results were even less happy than they'd been in Okemah. He flunked algebra, English, and Latin, and barely passed history in the first semester. The second time around, he passed English and algebra, but once again flunked Latin. He started two more semesters after that, but finished neither. He wasn't involved in extracurricular activities as he'd been in Okemah. He wasn't well liked or remembered. The football players and other big shots tended to make fun of him for all the old reasons. In fact, high school probably would have been a complete waste of time if he hadn't met Matt Jennings.

Matt was an outsider too, a poor Irish Catholic from the south side. He was about six feet tall, had red hair, freckles, and a quiet intelligence that was successfully hidden from the teachers at Pampa High School. He was both curious and shy, an odd combination, with the same even-tempered kindness as Colonel Martin and yet more aggressively open to new ideas and possibilities. From the start, he was amazed and delighted by Woody Guthrie.

They met each other in study hall, but really didn't become friendly until Matt decided to buy a pawnshop fiddle and Woody offered to tune it for him, having seen his uncle do it dozens of times. After several hours of struggle, Woody suggested they visit Jeff and have *him* do it—a notion that frightened Matt, who only knew Jeff's reputation as one of the more violent members of the police force. Jeff, of course, relished any audience no matter how small and was more than happy to tune the fiddle, then play several rapid-fire hoedowns on it that left Matt gasping. After that, he and Woody were regulars at Jeff and Allene's apartment, always managing to show up just as Jeff got off work, hammering and sawing at their instruments like a pair of carpenters while Jeff fluttered and breezed off into the clouds on his. The two boys kept at it through hours of stumbling, gradually gaining speed and confidence together, testing new riffs and refining old ones, never talking but always in close communication, developing a musical knowledge of each other that was more intimate than anything that would ever be *spoken* between them.

When they did sit down and talk, Woody sometimes astounded Matt with his broad range of knowledge. He wouldn't show off, but things would just slip out—incredible things for a boy who didn't read books, like quotes from Chinese philosophers and amazing facts about ancient Egypt. What Matt didn't know was that Woody was cheating: he was sneaking off to the Pampa library, which was then stashed in the basement of City Hall. He'd become friendly with Mrs. Evelyn Todd, the librarian, who was married to a minister and fit rather neatly into the role Mrs. Chowning had played in Okemah. While still not very receptive to the idea of formal education, Woody had become addicted to reading. His tastes ran to psychology, religion, and Eastern philosophy—Mrs. Todd would later say that his name was written in every psychology book in the library. He seemed a very serious boy to her, never joking or cutting up, a loner . . . but continually surprising.

One day he shocked her by coming in with a psychology text that he had written, by hand, in a thick, bound notebook. It was an assimilation of all that he'd read about the search for self-knowledge through the ages, and owed more to Eastern spiritualism than to Viennese technicalities. It wasn't exactly erudite but it showed a good deal of thought, and certainly wasn't the illiterate ramblings of a shallow teen-ager. Mrs. Todd decided to put in on the shelf with the other psychology books . . . which is where it remained until she left Pampa and a new librarian took over and threw it away. Woody never told anyone, not even Matt Jennings, that he'd written it.

Charley Guthrie thought the time his son was spending in the library was impressive, but not very practical. There was nothing wrong with reading books—Charley would be the last person to discourage anyone from doing *that*—but Woody was showing precious little interest in doing anything else with his life, except maybe sitting around Shorty's and strumming the guitar. He had a distressing lack of ambition; he hadn't even finished the cartooning course that Charley had bought for him. And the worst part, the really frustrating part, was that Charley was finding it impossible to talk to him about these things. There was something about Woody, some way he had of putting you on the defensive without ever really *saying* anything. He tilted his head back, stared down his nose, and got that faraway, cloudy look in his eyes. It was like talking to someone through a window. When Charley pushed him too hard or lost his temper, Woody simply disappeared for a few days. Soon he was spending most nights at Uncle Jeff's or using the salary from Shorty's to buy a cheap hotel room.

As time went by, Matt Jennings began to notice that the way he looked at things, the very shape of the world, seemed to change when he was around Woody. It wasn't anything he could put his finger on; in fact, it barely dented his consciousness at first, but the little guy was downright . . . disorienting. He had no sense of perspective, or at least a different sense than normal people—especially when it came to things that Matt considered the basics of life, like time and money and planning for the future. Nor did Woody seem to care very much what people thought of his eccentricity, although—Matt soon realized—he *saw* everything, every nuance of each reaction was filed and catalogued.

But the oddest thing about Woody was that he could become, quite literally, childlike: when he was interested in something or someone—and, sooner or later, he was interested in virtually everything in town—he would dive in like a child, entirely preoccupied, losing all sense of time and place, and his wonderment was so infectious that sometimes Matt would be swept right along with him. More often, though, Matt was content to sit back and watch Woody watching the world. Once, for example, they visited the home of a rich banker in the little town of Canadian because Woody had heard that the banker's wife painted interesting pictures of horses. The paintings turned out to be massive and haunting and, staring at them, Woody seemed to drift off into a trance. It was as if he were doing more than just *looking* at the paintings, as if he were trying to physically incorporate them, and Matt was left shuffling and not quite knowing what to do, not wanting to break the purity of Woody's concentration.

At other times, they would just be boys. They went swimming at the ten-mile hole south of town, shot rats with .22-caliber rifles at the Pampa dump, drank Virginia Dare tonic—or V.D. tonic, as Woody called it—that he snaked from Shorty's and which packed a terrific wallop for a drink that was legal. They went to the Playmore auditorium for the wrestling matches and one night saw Dutch Mantell, who billed himself as the "Ugliest Man in West Texas," fight a bear. The bear mauled Dutch, then went berserk and terrorized half the audience.

On Saturday nights, the Playmore would become a ballroom, with the wrestling ring shoved into a corner to serve as a bandstand for the fox-trot and waltz orchestras who played the latest in popular music. Matt and Woody didn't go to many of those, preferring the old-timey country string bands at a place called the Red Barn. They'd sneak in sometimes: Woody carrying a mandolin and claiming to be one of the musicians, then handing it out the window to Matt.

One Saturday, after a dance, they went back to Woody's room at the Great Pampa Hotel and were drinking pretty heavily from a fruit jar filled with corn whiskey. Matt hadn't seen Woody all week, and he'd seemed quieter than usual throughout the evening. Matt knew better than to ask if anything was wrong—Woody had a tendency to flee when confronted with a direct question or request—but finally Woody volunteered, "We got word from Oklahoma this week. My mother died."

Slowly, quietly, he told Matt the family history: the fires, the death of his sister, the insane asylum. "When I went to visit my mother, she didn't even recognize me," he said. Then he talked about the disease: it ran in the family, crossing from father to daughter and mother to son.

"Does that mean you could get it?" Matt asked.

"No. There's no way I'm gonna get that disease," he said, and, in the whiskey haze, Matt believed him.

It was the only time they ever talked about it.

Charley had found it convenient to think of Nora as dead ever since she poured the kerosene on him, and the news from Oklahoma came as something of a relief. With the long ordeal finally over, he felt free to begin his life again. He was embarrassed by all the years he'd depended on the family; Maude was *still* caring for George and Mary Jo. It was time for the children to have a decent home of their own, and a real mother to care for them. He would remarry for their benefit, and also, perhaps, because he was lonely and getting old, and wanted someone to care for him too.

He went about the task of finding a wife in typical Charley Guthrie fashion: he sent away for one, much as he might send for a new correspondence course. He wrote to a Lonelyhearts Club and the name of Bettie Jean McPherson—a pleasant, solid enough name—came back in the mail. Gathering his dignity and courage, Charley wrote her a letter that was, no doubt, a masterpiece. She wrote back: she was a trained nurse, and had seen hard times too. So much the better, Charley thought: a trained nurse. He had been working as a bookkeeper for the police department—a patronage job, courtesy of Uncle Jeff—but had lost it when the sheriff was voted out in 1930, and needed a means of support. He wrote to her again.

All of the correspondence was quite secret. No one knew what Charley had up his sleeve. One imagines him ironing his dark suit on that fateful day in September of 1931, and putting on his best white starched shirt, then nervously walking—perhaps with a spring in his step for the first time in years—over to the Santa Fe station; and then his barely concealed disappointment when the woman who stepped off the train turned out to be positively Wagnerian, much larger than he, with severely cropped brown hair and a pinched face. But she had a surprisingly pleasant way about her and Charley *was* an honorable man, so he took her right over to City Hall, as promised, and they were married.

It was, no doubt, a bit later in the day that Charley got around to asking Bettie Jean about her nursing and learned that she was a trained nurse of a rather curious sort, a kind of mystic masseuse. She claimed expertise in chiropractic, phrenology, palmistry, Gypsy Dream Book, tarot cards, coffee grounds, tea leaves, Ouija board, and crystal ball. She had studied the occult with four different spiritualist mediums and two yogis, knew the nineteen points of Rosicrucianism, and could quote more than three hundred healing and gifted scriptures from the Old and New Testaments of the Bible. Her pride and joy, though, was the practice of "Electro-Magnetic Healing," which she had invented and named because it sounded modern, and you had to keep up with the times.

"Electro-Magnetic Healing" involved the laying on of hands and a lot of fast talk, which varied according to the patient's malady and gullibility. Aside from easing routine aches and pains, Bettie Jean often claimed to be able to remove tonsils and gallstones simply by placing her hands on the appropriate spot and could produce, on request, a jar full of stones she had removed from the rich and famous in California and elsewhere. She was a great believer in the restorative powers of eucalyptus oil, which she slapped on customers with great abandon, and the house reeked of the stuff, as did she.

Upon arriving in Pampa, she placed ads in the local newspapers and soon there was a trickle of customers visiting the little tourist court cottage Charley had rented for them on the southern edge of town. Many of her early customers were oil-field workers who'd somehow gotten the idea that she believed alcohol was a sure cure for cancer. The customers would wait in the parlor, then she would attend to them privately in the bedroom, wearing a very professional white outfit. Charley never did figure out what went on in that bedroom, and didn't much care. He was irked that Bettie Jean had immediately taken over the whole house—with the customers in the parlor and Bettie Jean in the bedroom, there wasn't much space left for him—but she *was* doing well by his children (Woody, especially, was enthusiastic about her and was visiting more often), and so he kept his peace. For her part, Bettie Jean quickly saw that Charley was more of an encumbrance than anything else—he wasn't bringing in any money and at least the kids did chores—and when Uncle Jeff started talking one night about taking a trip down to South Texas to look for Jerry P. Guthrie's lost silver mine, and Charley mentioned he might like to go along, Bettie Jean said yes, by all means, go.

The idea that Jerry P. Guthrie had discovered a rich vein of silver in the mountains near Uncle Gid's ranch was one of the least likely and most persistent of family legends. Jerry P. said he'd discovered it accidentally one day while stopping to take a drink from a mineral spring; the ore had glittered like pure diamonds in the sun, and he sent it to El Paso to be assayed. The report came back: $100 of silver per ton, and $10 of gold, plus copper, zinc, mercury, and other valuable minerals. But rather than cash in right then and lead a life of luxury, Jerry P. had decided to go to Oklahoma and try for the long-shot land he hoped would be coming to his one-eighth Creek wife. He left his name, though, on a piece of paper wired to a pile of flat rocks to mark his claim and fully intended to return someday.

It was a great story for sleepy children and drunken adults, and Jerry P. could even produce crude maps with colorful place names like Slick Rock Gap and Rough Run Canyon and a big "X" marking the spot. Jeff had heard the story all his life, and believed every word of it. Once he'd even made definite plans to take Jerry P. down there looking for the vein, but the old man had died just in the nick of time. After that, it became a subject that would arise at family get-togethers from time to time, late in the evening when the merriment had subsided. Jeff would say, "Someday we've gotta go down and find ol' Jerry P. Guthrie's silver mine." Everyone would promptly agree, and then forget about it.

Now, though, a curious logic was building in favor of the trip. It was probably nothing more than everyone just wanting to get out of town for a while: Jeff had lost his police job in the same election as Charley and now worked part-time shaking doors for the downtown merchants at night, and playing an occasional barn dance with Allene. Charley was married to a charlatan and, after three months of wedlock, looking for a quick out. Woody was always ready for an adventure, and even Roy, who'd just arrived in town looking for a clerk job, was game. There weren't any excuses left. It had reached the point where they'd either have to go or stop talking about it.

They went, and it was a strange, joyous, memorable debacle. They traveled in an old Model T truck that Jeff had bought from a farmer, with a box on the back for hauling wheat. Inside the box, which they covered over with canvas, they stuffed musical instruments, picks and shovels, provisions—mostly beans—and two big drums of gasoline they'd dripped, semi-legally, off the pipeline. Jeff and Roy did most of the driving and Charley sat up front with them, while Woody rode by himself in the back, playing his guitar all the way. They rolled from the top of Texas to the bottom in two days, from cold weather to warm, from wheat country down through cotton country, to scruffy grazing land and then the desert.

They went all the way to the Mexico border, where the road

naked along the thin ribbon of the Rio Grande, through rocky hills that looked like cement drippings. They passed the dun-colored town of Terlingua, with the silver-mine owner's mansion up on the hill and adobe shacks down below. Most of the miners were Mexicans, exotic-looking people who seemed to be baked the same color as their houses. From there, it was on across the dry expanse to the Chisos Mountains, which were a dramatic splash of watercolors in the middle of the desert: soft rose and purple, copper and ocher and, Woody later remembered, "eight different kinds of green." There were massive stone canyons, sheer cliffs, a jumble of crags; formations that seemed to shift and change every time he looked at them. The Chisos were the first real mountains Woody had ever seen, and they were awesome.

The Guthrie Expedition managed to find its way to Sam Nail's ranch, which once had been Uncle Gid's. Sam was happy to see them—visitors were rare in that part of the country, except for wetbacks trying to cross the river and border guards trying to catch them, and would-be prospectors were especially welcome: if they did manage to strike it rich on his land, Sam would get a percentage of the take. He didn't think there was much chance of that, though, especially after he saw the old maps they were carrying. They asked if he knew where the mineral spring was that Jerry P. had been drinking from the day he spotted the lode, and Sam told them there were literally thousands of little springs popping up and disappearing all the time. Then he pointed them toward an old adobe house a few miles up the dry creek from his ranch, and said it would be a decent place for them to stay. Jerry P. himself had used it when he worked for Gid around the turn of the century.

As soon as they dumped their equipment and set up camp, Woody, Charley, and Jeff hustled off in the general direction of Rough Run Canyon, about five miles to the northwest. Roy, though, had already decided the mission was hopeless. "This is crazy," he said. "Like trying to find a needle in a haystack, only a needle is bigger. You boys can go out and look all you want. I'm gonna stay here and cook."

They spent the first day stumbling eagerly through the desert, getting their hands, legs, and faces stabbed by cactus and ripped by stickers, and not finding anything except some pretty colored stones Woody insisted on bringing back. "Tomorrow we'll split up and look in different areas," Jeff said, a bit more subdued than he'd been. "Boy, we could use some horses out here."

And so, the next day: Woody making his way alone through the mesmerizing, dreamlike quiet of the desert, the bare sun and dry wind, the gray, hard ground like cement, the rough, tangled bushes struggling for life, and an occasional odd daub of color—a cactus turned purple and dying, a bright stone. He saw mule deer and wild pigs congregating around tiny springs in the dry gulches. The sharp, clean air tingled his face. He found nothing, but didn't care. At night they would all be together, eating Roy's beans and drinking corn whiskey from a seemingly endless supply of fruit jars. He and Jeff would get out their instruments and play square-dance tunes like Charley's favorite, "Old Judge Parker, Take Your Shackles Offa Me," the music swelling in the desert void: *"Turn me loose and set me free . . ."*

One morning Sam Nail came by with a gift—a goat he'd slaughtered for them. Roy cut off some steaks, and they hung the carcass high in the scraggly tree next to the adobe house as Sam had instructed. "You'll see why, tonight," he said, and sure enough, a carnival of animals—mountain lions, panthers, coyotes—approached the house that night, screeching and howling, fighting each other over a slab of meat that none of them could reach. Jeff barred the door and held their only weapon—a .22-caliber rifle, a peashooter really—just in case. The four of them huddled together in the musty adobe darkness, and it seemed to Woody that they were a family for the first time in years. They stayed for several days after that, then the food ran out and they went home . . . but the trip would haunt Woody for the rest of his life.

Matt and Woody gradually achieved a level of musical competence that was tolerable, with occasional intimations of becoming better than that. They joined a third boy, Cluster Baker, who actually was quite good on the guitar, called themselves the Corncob Trio, and set out to find some work. Their first job came from a friend's father, who owned a skating rink south of town and hired them for five dollars to play a Saturday-night dance. Woody picked up several hundred shirt cardboards from a tailor shop and painted clever signs which he tacked on telephone poles all over the county. They did well enough that first night, but didn't exactly touch off a land rush for their services. For the most part, they played house parties . . . which meant, in effect, they played for each other.

They'd usually start out a Saturday night at the Jennings house, where Matt's father always had cold cuts and home brew spread out for anyone who'd stop by. Sometimes they'd all go over to the Thomas Market on South Cuyler Street, where the owner loved country music and would welcome the musicians with sandwiches, drinks, and a warm fire. Pauline Thomas, the owner's daughter, was rather bored by it all: she thought the music was corny and old-fashioned—a feeling fairly widespread among young people in town, who preferred the jazz and pop they heard on the radio. The up-and-comers in Pampa wanted to seem sophisticated, *modern*, not hopelessly rural like their grandparents. The best jobs in town for musicians—Saturday night at the Playmore or the more exclusive Southern Club—went to orchestras with a smooth sound, the bands that could play the same sort of music as they played in the big cities. It was a strange time: fiddle and guitar music, the old folk culture, was both dying and about to be reborn with a vengeance.

The revival had begun several years earlier, in the early 1920's, when radio began to spread to the rural areas. Several of the more powerful stations in the South and West discovered they could attract astonishingly large audiences with old-fashioned barndance programs. By 1923, stations in Fort Worth and Atlanta had regular country music shows, and in 1925, WSM in Nashville started what would become the most popular barn dance of them all, "The Grand Ole Opry" (throughout much of the 1920's and 1930's, though, the "Opry" took a distinct back seat to Chicago's WLS "Barn Dance" as the best-known country music program). As successful as the various barn dances were, most southern stations still were dominated by popular, semi-classical, and, of course, religious music well into the 1930's. Local celebrities—like Fiddlin' John Carson in Atlanta and Jeff and Allene Guthrie in Pampa—might squeeze their way onto the air, but only occasionally, and at the least popular times of day.

Country music was roundly ignored by the record business until the mid-1920's, and even then it was considered outside the commercial mainstream, as was "race" or black music. Recording executives figured, not without reason, that neither blacks nor hillbillies were likely to buy large quantities of records, and few urban whites were interested in listening to anything so alien.

But radio almost killed off the record business in the mid-1920's: it usually sounded better (records were scratchy, fragile, and sounded as if the music were coming out of a tunnel), lasted longer (every few minutes you'd have to get up and change a record), and was free. Suddenly, the record companies had to become creative to survive, and they stumbled onto the idea of producing records in small quantities for limited audiences—like blacks and hillbillies—who weren't able to hear much of their favorite music on the radio. One of the earliest to realize this was Ralph Peer, of Okeh and then Victor Records, who at first didn't care for the music as much as for the market potential. In 1923, he recorded Fiddlin' John Carson and others in Atlanta—but mostly because a local phonograph dealer, who thought a few country records might boost his sales, had pestered him.

It all changed, though, during the first four days of August 1927, when Peer scored one of the most impressive coups in music history. On one of his periodic talent hunts, he held auditions in the sleepy town of Bristol on the Virginia-Tennessee border and discovered both the Carter Family and Jimmie Rodgers, who, between them, would transform country music during the next decade from something Grandpa did on the back porch into a huge business. The Carter Family was composed of A. P. Carter, his wife Sara, and his sister-in-law Maybelle. They sang old-time mountain standards and gospel hymns with a tight, pungent harmony and were virtuoso musicians. Maybelle's guitar style would be copied by a whole generation of players, including Woody Guthrie, who aped it assiduously (and also, later, lifted several dozen Carter Family melodies for his own purposes).

The Carters were, perhaps, the most respected of the early country music groups, but their commercial success was dwarfed by that of Jimmie Rodgers, a tubercular railroad brakeman from Meridian, Mississippi, who became the first hillbilly superstar. His style was a bit less traditional and more accessible than the Carters'. He borrowed from the blues (which he'd learned from black railroad workers) and popular music, and used such eclectic backup groups as Hawaiian and Dixieland bands. In addition, and most improbably, he yodeled. His first "blue" yodel, "T for Texas," became a smash hit and was followed by dozens more until his death in 1933.

By then, the record business had improved its sound quality and also gotten a boost from its old enemy, radio, as many local stations discovered that using recorded music was a lot cheaper than hiring live musicians. Rodgers' records were played throughout the South—he was virtually unknown in the North—but he was especially popular in Texas. In 1929, he'd moved to Kerrville, in the Texas hill country, because of the dry climate and built a mansion called the "Blue Yodeler's Paradise." He spent the next several years making appearances all over the state, and recorded several cowboy-style ballads. Soon he was a Texas institution of sorts—playing benefits for the Red River flood victims with Will Rogers and being made an honorary Texas Ranger—and his music became a matter of pride in the state, even among those who earlier had looked down their noses at country music. In Pampa, lines would form at the record stores every time a new Jimmie Rodgers single was released. Woody remembered crowds gathering around phonographs, listening to Jimmie sing about going to California, where "the water tastes like wine."

The Jenningses owned an old phonograph and a stack of 78's, much abused by Woody and Matt. The family lived in two small adjacent cottages; the one which housed the phonograph became a kind of clubhouse for the Corncob Trio. Even though the band wasn't very successful yet, it was much admired by a small group of friends who gathered for parties each weekend. Woody's personality seemed to change dramatically when the gang got together: he'd be more outgoing, always the center of attention, always performing in some way or other. Sometimes he'd even put out a little newspaper filled with all the latest gossip about the group and assorted jokes and tall tales. He staged boxing exhibitions (obviously he'd learned something from Jimmy DeForrest), told jokes, danced, and mugged. He did one dance that Cluster Baker, the guitar player, absolutely loved: he'd start out doing a very fast jig, then stop abruptly, frozen in a weird, funny position, then start up again. It was all in the gestures: the raised eyebrow, the exaggerated sweep of an arm as he brought it around to scratch his head or chin. When Woody was *on*, every move he made seemed distinctive.

His humor often was like that too. all in the timing and inflection. Woody told Cluster he could go onstage and crack up an audience without doing anything . . . and sometimes it did seem that the less Woody said, the funnier he was. It was impossible to describe just exactly how he did it, the humor was so dry that it virtually evaporated with the retelling. Once Cluster was watching Woody paint a sign that said "Sugar" in the window of a local market (after his success with "Harris Drug," several merchants had started hiring Woody to advertise the weekly specials in their windows). He'd been working on a rather stylized, almost abstract "Sugar" for about forty-five minutes when a man on the street stopped and said, "Woody, that don't look anything like an 'S.' Can't you paint no better than that?" Woody, up on a ladder, took a long, slow look at the sign, scratched his head, and said, "How'd you know it was an 'S'?" For the rest of his life, Cluster would be tickled every time he thought of the way Woody looked at the man, and the way he said it.

There was another, more bubbly and cornball side of Woody's humor that Cluster didn't like quite so much. Sometimes he seemed drunk with words, playing with them, rhyming them, reversing them, turning them every which way: "vice versa" might become "verse visa" or "Visalia Vesuvius," or a dozen other things. There were times when you just couldn't turn him off, especially when the Corncob Trio made one of its rare appearances on radio in Pampa, usually to plug its next dance. They'd work out a vague script with the announcer, a few brief words from each like "We'll be down at Oddfellows Hall this Saturday, hope y'all come . . ." then they'd play a tune and that would be it. Except Woody would change it all when they got on the air. He'd start talking about this or that—nothing in particular—and lose track of what was planned, and be off on some free association with the words rolling and flowing so easily that sometimes you just had to sit back and find out where he was headed. Matt was too easygoing ever to be seriously offended by something like that, but Cluster sometimes thought that Woody was just a little too smart for his own good, and not serious enough about life—if he ever pulled himself together, he could make a lot of money writing jokes for someone like Jack Benny.

Of course, Woody was dead serious about certain things, like his secret life in the library, but he wasn't about to share them with just anyone. He'd also become friendly with Reverend Eulys McKenzie of the Church of Christ, one of the more severe fundamentalist sects in town, and was quietly beginning to study—to devour—the Bible. McKenzie was a bear of a man, a friend of Uncle Jeff's, with a mad passion for country music. It was a passion that didn't sit too well with the more proper members of his flock who thought musical instruments were the devil's handiwork, to say nothing of the rumors that Brother McKenzie was attending parties where liquor was served. But he didn't care: he loved to sing bass, and when Jeff and Allene landed a spot on the Amarillo radio station, McKenzie came along as their announcer. He was a gentle man with a kind heart—even though he had a reputation for giving wild fire-and-brimstone sermons every Sunday—and he convinced Woody that it was important to make a spiritual commitment and be baptized by total immersion.

But Woody's eventual baptism into the Church of Christ didn't exactly signal the beginning of a new life. He attended church sporadically with Jeff and Allene for a while, then lost interest. He still loved the Bible, though, and would discuss passages with Matt, who was a devout Roman Catholic; and he'd amaze Cluster with his ability to come up with an appropriate quote from scripture to fit virtually any situation.

He was dreadfully alone. He was nearing the age of twenty-one, and it had been years since he'd had a home. He wandered from his father's house to his uncle's to a variety of cheap hotel rooms, never spending more than a few days in any one place. He felt best with Uncle Jeff, but Allene—who called him Woodrow—could be a pain at times, pushing him to take a bath or buy some underwear. Once she actually kicked him out of the house because he smelled so bad. After the Guthrie Expedition returned from the Chisos Mountains, though, she noticed that Woody was becoming marginally more respectable. He was neatly rolling up his shirt sleeves and getting his hair trimmed (there was only one barber in town, Jess Turner, who had the patience to snip through all those curls), and he didn't smell as bad.

Matt Jennings had two brothers, Fred and Blue, and a sister, Mary. Mary was about five years younger than he, a very quiet and sweet and innocent girl with long blond hair. She was part of the group that formed around the Corncob Trio, but not a very active part. No one could remember her ever expressing a strong opinion about anything, or showing any musical ability or being clever. She watched Woody Guthrie closely from the start, though, curious because Matt—whom she adored—was so impressed by him, but quickly realizing for herself that he was special. He wasn't at all like the other boys, who worked in markets and hardware stores and had definite if rather limited ambitions. He had no ambitions, and therefore wanted much more than any of them: he didn't want to be ordinary. Mary was fifteen years old and didn't want to be ordinary, either. She was dating Dink Altman, one of the boys who worked at the Thomas Market. He was very nice and would take her to baseball games, but she knew that Woody was interested (even though she'd see him occasionally with other girls) . . . and maybe even jealous. Once, when he was on the radio with Jeff and Allene, he dedicated a song to her: "Take Me Out to the Ball Game."

It all appeared quite normal, even cute, to their friends. They started going to movies together on two-for-one admission nights, and held hands at the Saturday-night parties. He played the guitar for her. She helped him put together his funny little newspapers. He bought her dime-store jewelry cases and bracelets. He made her laugh. But very soon after they started dating, Woody suddenly turned serious and asked her to marry him. It was completely unexpected—none of their friends were talking about marriage—and it seemed quite out of character. Later Mary realized that he was probably as much in love with the idea of becoming part of her family—he would be Matt's brother—as he was with her. At the time, his proposal seemed clumsy and laughably intense, but quietly so . . . and with his usual innocent charm. He wasn't at all demonstrative about it, just very insistent, and she said yes . . . almost in self-defense. The more she thought about it, though, the more she *liked* the idea of getting married to Woody Guthrie. It certainly would be interesting. Life would never be dull.

They went to her parents. Harry Jennings, a failed farmer and former saloonkeeper, was now scraping along as a salesman in a secondhand furniture store. He'd always been amused by Woody, liked having him around the house, and loved the way he sang "When You Wore a Tulip," but the idea that this boy was going to marry his one and only daughter was simply preposterous. Not only was Woody not a Catholic, not only was he unemployed (and without the prospect of, or even the desire for, gainful employment), but the girl was still a child. Harry said absolutely not, and Woody retreated for a time.

He went with Jeff and Allene to roam the countryside looking for work as a trio and also to visit Aunt Laura Moore, Jeff and Charley's sister, who lived in a fine brick house in Plainview. Her husband had died years before; her son Jess had been seriously injured in World War I and was receiving a pension; his brother Eddie had mental problems. Clearly she was a woman with more than enough troubles of her own, but she welcomed her relatives warmly and they immediately set up shop in her parlor, playing the piano, fiddle, and guitar all day and all night, often attracting wild hordes of local musicians, drinking and carousing until they fell over from exhaustion. When they weren't playing, Woody tended to become morose and lay on the couch, staring at the ceiling. Sometimes he wrote Mary long, passionate letters.

Aunt Laura, who obviously hadn't expected much more than a brief visit, grew somewhat less hospitable as the weeks dragged on. She finally exploded one night when the house was stuffed with people, screaming at Jeff, "I've heard too darn much of that violin and the piano's bang bang bang. I want you to go home and stay home. I'm so sick of that music, I could die."

She was sad to see Woody go, though: he was a good boy, who seemed to need a lot of mothering.

Back in Pampa, he renewed his quiet campaign for Mary Jennings. It continued through the summer of 1933, with everyone opposed to the marriage except Charley's new wife, Bettie Jean, who probably favored it simply because her husband hated the idea. Charley couldn't stand the thought of his son marrying a Catholic, and he went over to see Harry Jennings about it. The two men discovered they had much in common: both had been having hard times of late, both were unalterably opposed to the marriage, and strongly in favor of Harry's home brew. After sampling several quarts of the stuff, they became friends.

Woody and Mary had an oddly formal relationship for two people who wanted to be married. They rarely talked about deep, personal things. They would argue occasionally, usually about nothing very serious—although Woody did lose his temper once and yelled at her, "You don't want to marry me because my mother died in an insane asylum." Mary remembered that incident very clearly because it was one of the few times he ever said anything to her about his past, and she rarely asked questions. There was, from the very start, a gulf between them. She was sixteen years old and shy, and he seemed intent on achieving a bluff, southwestern manliness in his personal affairs, if not in any other part of his life. He remained stoic, too proud to plead his case again to Harry Jennings, while Mary quietly worked on her mother—who, like most motherly women, had a soft spot for Woody—and eventually convinced her to sign the consent form so they could be married.

The ceremony took place at the Holy Souls' Catholic Church in Pampa, on October 28, 1933. No members of the family were present, not even Matt. The service was performed by Father Joseph Wonderly, who made Mary promise that she would keep her religion and raise her children as Catholics, and it was witnessed by Claude and Catherine Sullins, acquaintances of Mary's who happened to be hanging around the church that afternoon.

They spent the first few months of married life in a small apartment above Jeff and Allene's. The four of them played poker for matchsticks through the early winter, watched Jeff rehearse his magic tricks, played music, and spent many hours speculating about how to become famous in show business. One day Jeff found, and answered, an advertisement in the Pampa *Times*: entertainers were needed for a traveling show.

The ad had been placed by a rancher named Claude Taylor from Hereford, Texas. He was a wealthy man, about forty-five years old, married to a young woman who found ranch life boring. She'd once been a Kansas City chorus girl—her stage name was Carlotta—and wanted to get back into the business. After watching Jeff perform several magic tricks and play the fiddle, Taylor invited the Guthries to spend the winter at his ranch and put together a show that would, of course, feature his wife.

The months at the ranch were comfortable and easy, a wonderful honeymoon for Mary and Woody, who got a kick out of watching Taylor and Carlotta trying to perfect their Spanish dance—she would fall back and he would try to catch her in his arms while Jeff played a tango on the fiddle, but it never worked out quite right. When spring came, they went to Fort Worth to buy a tent and equipment. Taylor, who had an uncanny ability to skimp on all the wrong things, insisted they buy a shabby old stockman's tent which reeked of cattle and had no sides. They bought canvas, rented sewing machines, and attached sidewalls, then headed south and west across central Texas.

Their first—and last, as it happened—stop was the town of Brownwood, where they pitched the tent in a field riddled with puddles and too far from the main road for many of the locals to see and get excited. Taylor, skimping again, printed up only 250 handbills to advertise the show and sometimes there were more people onstage than in the audience, but the Guthries played it as if it were the Palace. Jeff wore a tuxedo and Allene a jet-black gown that matched her hair and dramatized her pale white skin and red mouth. Woody was done up as an old farmer, with a gray wig and beard, and his face freckled with grease pencil. He'd wander onstage and peer at the audience, surprised and barely able to keep his balance. Then Mary would sashay across the stage very sexily, and he'd just about fall over watching her go by. With a wink and a shrug, he'd puff out his chest and try to impress her with a very shaky clog dance that gradually picked up steam as Jeff joined in with his fiddle and Allene with her accordion and the audience—what there was of it—whooped and stomped along in the dust and the cattle smell and steamy dampness of the tent.

Jeff had perfected some rather astonishing tricks during the winter at the farm. He'd had the Cabot Company in Pampa build him a special tank, which he'd climb into, chained. The tank would be filled with water, and several men (recruited from town) would come onstage with blowtorches and *weld* the thing shut. The tank would then be covered over with a wooden cabinet and, after a few minutes, Allene would instruct the men to break the welds, open the tank, and, of course, Jeff would have made his escape. He and Allene also performed the dollhouse illusion: she would climb into an oversized dollhouse, then he'd swing the house around and she'd disappear; then he'd shoot a pistol, swing the house around again, and she'd be back. It was all very professional.

Woody sometimes helped behind the scenes with the magic, but wasn't very trustworthy. There was one trick where Jeff waved his wand over a flower pot and a beanstalk was supposed to slowly sprout and rise. Woody's job was to control the beanstalk by pulling a thread backstage, but one night Jeff waved his wand and nothing happened. He waved his wand again . . . and again, smiling sheepishly at the audience. Then he started cursing and slammed the wand down, and Woody yanked on the thread, sending the beanstalk up like a rocket. The audience roared, but Jeff took his act seriously and never let Woody help with the magic again.

Woody worked best by himself, entertaining the crowd in front of the curtain while Jeff and Allene prepared the next series of tricks behind. He might play his guitar, French harp, or spoons, or just tell corny jokes lifted from Thomas W. Jackson's "On a Slow Train Through Arkansaw." He had a chalk-talk routine where he'd draw a picture of one thing, and then turn it over and it'd be something else. It was classic vaudeville humor, done in a laconic, Will Rogers style. The rest of the show consisted of some musical numbers he performed with Jeff and Allene, and Carlotta's dancing—with and without Taylor—which was so provocative as to lead some of the patrons backstage after each performance, asking if the "merchandise" was for sale.

The tour ended unceremoniously when Carlotta took up with the stage manager of a show passing through town called "The One and Only Original Life Story of the Famous Outlaw Jesse James." She was gone the next morning. Taylor closed the show, but gave Woody the battered old typewriter he'd been using to write copy for the handbills.

The marriage was turning out to be every bit as romantic and exciting as Mary had hoped. Even after they came back to Pampa and moved into a little shotgun shack on Russell Street around the corner from her parents, Woody managed to keep things hopping. He was interested in so many different things—he seemed to inhale whole areas of knowledge—that it was difficult to keep up with him from day to day. Their house was scattered with piles of library books on the most obscure subjects. For a time, he wanted to be a writer and would pound out steamy love stories, very loosely based on his own experiences, on the old typewriter and send them to true confession magazines in New York. He wrote an autobiography and sent that to a publisher too, but everything he wrote was rejected. It didn't matter; he'd already moved on to the law, reading all of Charley's dusty old books and taking Mary over to the courthouse every day to watch the trials. Then, flipping through a catalogue of government publications in the library one day, he found that the Department of Agriculture published a booklet on how to build adobe houses. He'd been fascinated by adobe ever since the trip to the Chisos Mountains, and he wrote away for a booklet. It seemed so logical, living *in* the earth on the earth, and practical: adobe wouldn't rot like wood, or burn. For the next few weeks, while waiting for the mail, he talked of nothing else. He'd lie back on the couch—his favorite position for speculation—rolling cigarettes and dreaming aloud with Matt of building whole cities of adobe. When the booklet finally arrived, he rushed out back and, following the instructions carefully, tried to make a brick—but the soil was the wrong consistency and, try as he did, he never succeeded.

Money wasn't a problem. He could always make money. His sign-painting business was flourishing, and he could now draw letters that looked icy, wooden, leathery, dusty, or sweaty and hot. What's more, he had begun to paint vast murals that often covered entire storefronts during the holiday season—steaming turkeys, chubby pink cupids, Santa Claus in his sleigh—and he'd attract large crowds as he worked on them. He did a sign for Cudahy bacon—showing an anguished husband with the caption "He brought home the bacon, but the wrong kind"—which attracted the attention of a Cudahy executive who happened to be passing through town; he offered Woody a job in advertising. There were other job offers, none of which he took seriously. Sometimes, just for the fun of it, he'd draw cartoons promoting some product or other, send them off to the company, and get money, job offers, or, at the very least, free product samples in return (Mary remembered a whole case of Listerine on one occasion). He'd take his sketch pad into the bars and do caricatures of the patrons—never asking for any money, but accepting a drink or a quarter or whatever else the subject wanted to throw his way in payment. He'd become interested in oil painting after visiting the banker's wife who painted horses, and now there was a stack of canvases in the living room next to an easel. His subjects depended on his interests of the moment. When he was studying the Bible with McKenzie, he'd taken to painting portraits of Jesus; when he was waiting for the government booklet, he painted adobes; he painted a portrait of Lincoln for Mrs. Todd at the library (who was ordering books with Woody in mind by now, but finding that she couldn't keep up with his shifting interests), and a portrait of Mary for her family. He did a rather sentimental picture for Uncle Jeff of a young boy with round red cheeks being slobbered over by his devoted dog. He did copies of "The Blue Boy" and other classics, and peddled them around the local bars—it was basic dime-store art and not very inspired, but eminently marketable.

He slept late in the mornings, and often sat outside in the afternoons, painting. He had become well known in Pampa as a harmless eccentric, and few expected him to behave the way

normal people did. He seemed to collect outcasts—like Heavy
Chandler, who weighed 290 pounds and was brain-damaged, a
combination that frightened almost everyone else in town. But
Woody had infinite patience with, and curiosity about, people
who were different, people who refused or were unable to conform—and even those, like Matt, who simply were open to the
idea of nonconformity. Heavy Chandler would come over afternoons and watch Woody paint. Sometimes they would have long
conversations, with Woody probing Heavy's mind and listening
carefully to what he had to say, *caring* about what he had to say.
One day Heavy brought over a model airplane he'd built and gave
it to Woody as a gift. And it was Woody's friendship that probably saved Heavy's life one afternoon when some joker bought
him some drinks to see what effect alcohol would have on someone who was brain-damaged. Heavy went berserk, tearing apart
a Little Juarez whorehouse and threatening several of the girls.
None of the police could handle him and they were beginning to
consider drastic action when Uncle Jeff came by and said,
"Howdy, Heavy. You remember me. I'm Woody Guthrie's uncle." Heavy calmed right down and said, "That's right. You
are, and Woody's my friend," and Jeff was able to bring him
peacefully to the police station.

The Corncob Trio was going strong now, playing weekends at
the Tokyo Bar, a rowdy joint on the south side, and occasionally
at barn dances and on the radio. But Woody also played with Jeff
and Allene and other combinations of country musicians. He was
part of a cowboy band that the Chamber of Commerce put together, complete with uniforms, for the Texas Centennial celebration. Most importantly, though, he had started toying with the
idea of writing his own songs . . . or rather, his own *words*,
usually to the old tunes his mother had sung. He always had been
quick at making up verses for hoedown songs like "Ida Red,"
which pretty much demanded that the singer improvise; sometimes he made up songs about members of the Corncob Trio and
their friends, but they were written spur of the moment and forgotten just as quickly. Now, though, he was writing down the
words (but not the music; he couldn't read music), and he was
saving them. As early as 1934, he saved a fairly traditional
ballad called "Old Gray Team of Horses," in which he is
riding along in a wagon with his girlfriend, Melinda Lou, when
a car chugs past and scares the horses. After a mad dash, he

brings the team back under control and Melinda Lou hugs and kisses him for the first time:

> And I married sweet Melindy
> So I'm happy in my soul
> That the old gray team of hosses run away.

In 1935, he put together a small typewritten songbook called *Alonzo M. Zilch's Own Collection of Original Songs and Ballads*, with an introduction that owed much to his recent fling with Charley's law books: "Every song in this book is an original wording of above stated author and all persons are warned not to throw nor shoot at said author under any circumstances during hours and periods of performance. . . . All songs having non-beneficial bearings, injurious exposings, etc., on any person or group of persons will be omitted from the book immediately. To which this day I have set my foot with all my might and main." None of the fourteen songs was exactly deathless, some were traditional ballads—all of which seemed to be about unfaithful women—and others were rewordings of popular songs like "The Isle of Capri." It's possible that the songs were intended for use on his local radio shows, for one of them is a distinctly unmemorable "Theme Song" ("Smile awhile, old pal/As round the dial you go/ And we hope you stop/ When you turn to us today"). There aren't many indications of the cleverness and inspired simplicity that were to come later, although one verse of a song called "Cowboy's Philosophy" has some bite to it:

> There ain't no fancy doctors
> Here to bind the cowboy's hurt;
> We jest warsh it at th' waterhole
> Then we dry it on his shirt.

Woody didn't consider the songs anything special; they were just something else he was doing, along with the signs and the cartoons, the painting and performing. He certainly didn't think of himself as a *songwriter* at this point. But he did save them.

One day in the library, he discovered the long narrative poem *The Prophet*, by Kahlil Gibran, and it was a revelation. He was amazed to find in it a philosophy that mirrored his own exactly;

it was as though Gibran had tapped his soul. He felt the same way reading it—tingly and alive—as he had in the desert. He loved the sonorous verities, the heavy mists and rhythms of it, the idea of the unity of all things, the idea that every living thing had value. Sometimes it seemed the Prophet said things that Woody *knew* but hadn't yet formulated in his mind: "The lust for comfort murders the passion of the soul, and then walks grinning in the funeral."

And: " . . . what is evil but good tortured by its own hunger and thirst? . . . You are good when you are one with yourself."

And: "Beauty is eternity gazing at itself in a mirror. But you are eternity and you are the mirror."

In the flat, dense heat and gathering dust of Pampa, Woody was transported to high mountains and lush green valleys, to murmuring fountains and pillared temples. He fell in love with the idea of mystery, with the Great Void and the Greater Unknown, with psychic phenomena and the occult, and all this eventually led him over to Bettie Jean's house.

She and Charley weren't getting along very well. Her business was steady enough so that she could rent a nice house over on the north side, but he was still unemployed and depressed. He was drinking heavily, remembering the past too much and talking about it very rarely. Once, when Mary Jo had her hair curled, he asked her not to wear it that way because it reminded him of Clara.

He and Bettie Jean would fight, sometimes violently, but he was no match for her. She became so angry with him once that she ripped the shirt off his back in front of the children. Another time, he ran screaming into the yard with a gun and said he was going to kill himself, but she wrestled it away from him. He was too embarrassed to stay around that house, useless, and began to spend more time on the road. At first he tried to sell sharpening stones to barbers, then he scouted around for a town where he could start his real estate business again. Soon he wasn't around very much at all.

Bettie Jean would be very harsh with the children, especially Mary Jo, when Charley wasn't there. She beat the girl, kept her a virtual slave in the house, and never allowed her out to see Aunt Maude, Woody, or the other relatives she loved; but Mary Jo never told anyone about it (Guthries, she had learned, didn't talk about such things), and no one knew except her brother

George. Nor did many people know that Bettie Jean was practicing voodoo on the side: there were nights when she'd place hundreds of candles in all the rooms and send the children out at 4 a.m. to plant beans around the house to ward off evil spirits; once she took special herbs and put them in one of Charley's shoes, then tossed it off a bridge to make him go away.

Woody, perhaps blinded by his new spirituality, didn't seem to notice how Mary Jo was being treated, nor did his father's problems trouble him very much. In fact, he was the only one in the family able to get along with Bettie Jean. She was one of the few people around who *understood*. She knew what he was talking about. She knew about the power of the Unknown, and was even able to harness it in small ways. She knew what those people who lined up in her parlor needed—perhaps it was just great sensitivity on her part, perhaps it was something more—and who could say that her gift wasn't spiritual, or divinely inspired? Even the doctors in town were threatened by her success, and looked for ways to close her down.

Mrs. Todd noticed Woody's new direction, not only in the books he was choosing—*The Secret of the Ages* was a favorite—but also in his conversation, and even his manner. One day he told her that Mary Jo was about to take a difficult math test and he was going to transmit all the answers to her by holding her hand that night while she was asleep. Several days later, he happily reported that Mary Jo had passed her test.

Now when he lay on the couch at home, he was meditating. He tried yoga and various other ways of putting himself into a trance, and claimed to have succeeded. Incense burned in the shotgun shack on Russell Street. He courted all the local cultists. A representative of the Rosicrucian Society came regularly to instruct Woody in the teachings of that medieval sect (which was then staging something of a comeback in Europe and America).

Matt, taking a classic Roman Catholic position, thought Woody was doing Satan's work and dabbling in witchcraft, although he nonetheless was lured into several of Woody's mental telepathy experiments. Mary was mildly alarmed; she liked the incense and didn't mind the trances, but was rather taken aback when he started putting ads in the paper and having business cards printed up: "Divine Healing and Consultation."

He was especially big on the consultation part. When the customers came—and they did come—to the house on Russell Street,

Woody would receive them in the parlor while Mary hid in the
bedroom. He would probe subtly and find out what was really
bothering them, then come up with an answer that was three
quarters common sense wrapped in a beautiful velvet cloak of
Gibran and other assorted gibberish from the Inscrutable East.
Unlike Bettie Jean, he never charged for his services but did
accept donations. He did this, off and on, for about a year.

Woody skipped blithely through his spiritual phase while the rest
of the country was suffering the Great Depression. He didn't
seem to notice. Nor did many other people in town, at first. The
oil boom and the basic prosperity of the area delayed the arrival
of hard times in Pampa, but the boom began to fizzle in the early
1930's, about the same time that a deep, hard drought began to
drive the local farmers to the wall. By 1935, after four summers
of drought, a patina of light brown dust seemed to hang in the
air all the time. The north winds blew the dust across a thousand
miles of open prairie into Mary Guthrie's kitchen, forcing her to
keep the pots covered while she was cooking, and preventing her
from setting the table. The dust was always there; she could
sweep out the house and it would still be there, on the floor and
covering the ratty old furniture that would have seemed dusty
enough in any case. It was in her hair and in her clothes and in
her lungs. Dust pneumonia became a local health hazard (Mary
Jo had a mild case of it), and people were beginning to pack up
and leave town, joining the great migration of Okies and Arkies
in secondhand trucks piled high with possessions and heading
west. Highway 66, which ran south of town, was the main road
out; it was swarming with migrants, some of whom found their
way to Pampa, begging meals at back doors and seeking sanc-
tuary in the churches.

On April 14, 1935, a great wall of blackness appeared to the
north of town, late on an unseasonably hot Sunday afternoon. It
extended as far as the eye could see to the east and west. There
were red flecks at the upper edges of the blackness which led
some of the faithful in town to believe that it was fire ("the fire
next time") and this was Judgment Day, but it was dust. It was
thousands of tons of dust from as far away as the Dakotas and
Nebraska, dark topsoil and red clay, carried on winds of 45 to
70 miles per hour, and it was chewing up the countryside. Flocks
of birds flew ahead of the storm; smaller animals caught in it

choked to death. The sky blackened and, for about forty-five minutes, Woody and Mary could barely see their house. The bare light bulb in the parlor glowed like a cigarette in the dark; they covered their faces with wet washcloths and hoped for the best. In three hours, the temperature dropped 50 degrees and the humidity plummeted to below 10 percent. After the first hour, the sky lightened somewhat but the winds kept blowing until after nightfall. The next morning, even the rich people who lived in brick houses needed shovels to clean out. That afternoon it began to blow again, but not as badly as the day before.

People called it "the Great Dust Storm" and for the next few days there was almost a holiday atmosphere in town as everyone shoveled out and listened to stories of how their friends had made it through (Violet Pipes, a neighbor of Woody and Mary's, had been trapped downtown in a car, wearing her brand-new white Sunday dress, and now the dress was black, with the dust so deeply embedded that she'd never be able to get it clean again), but the giddiness faded quickly and was replaced by fear. It had not rained in four years, and the wind was still blowing. A visiting journalist from Washington took a look around the Oklahoma and Texas panhandles and called the area "the Dust Bowl," and the name stuck. People were desperate. They were losing their jobs and homes; they were scrounging for food and shelter. Everyone seemed to be suffering in some way.

Except Woody. And, as the times got tougher, even his friends began to lose their patience with him. Here was a guy who had the talent to do virtually anything, who never had any trouble getting a job or making money, but ignored—*scorned*—all his opportunities. Most of his friends were locked into markets and hardware stores or brutal factory work, jobs with no future. He was still hanging out at Shorty's several afternoons a week, a twenty-three-year-old soda jerk, and it just wasn't funny anymore. Not only that, but he didn't seem to care much about money when he had it.

There was an outrageous old man in town named Joe Bowers who'd made a fortune in oil and liked to spread the wealth around. He'd show up at the police station at night, have Jeff take out a patrol car and pick up Woody, and then the two would serenade him. At the end of an evening, he'd give them each fifty dollars—an incredible sum in those days. One night he had Woody and Cluster Baker play "I Ride an Old Paint" over and over until

dawn. He did that sort of thing often enough to throw some big
money in Woody's direction, but Mary never saw much of it.
Woody was as likely to leave it on the table in the Tokyo Bar,
or give it to some old guy lying in the gutter, as bring it home
. . . and people began to talk about that. It simply wasn't right,
they said, especially now that his wife was expecting a baby.

Woody was tremendously excited by the idea of having a baby;
he just didn't give much thought to how he was going to support
it. He dragged Mary off to the library to read everything they
could find on the subject of parenthood, and then broadened his
interest to the whole field of biology, borrowing an old micro-
scope from Mary's doctor and spending hours hunched over it,
giddy with microbes. He recruited Bettie Jean to help with the
delivery—a dismal and not very magnetic attempt at anesthesia,
Mary remembered—and to make an initial analysis of the child's
personality using the "science" of phrenology. "This child was
born with a veil over her face," Bettie Jean announced when the
baby arrived in November of 1935. "She is going to be a very
mysterious person."

They named her Gwendolyn Gail and called her Teeny. She
was a beautiful, placid child with Mary's blond hair, the first
grandchild born to either side of the family and doted on shamelessly by her grandparents. All the affection that they had withheld from Woody and Mary, and from each other, in recent years,
seemed concentrated on the baby's crib, where Charley and Bettie Jean and the Jenningses congregated endlessly, gurgling and
cooing. Woody's major contribution was a traditional song,
"Curly-Headed Baby," that he had reworked to fit the occasion.
It sounded something like "Careless Love" and he sang it softly,
smoothly like a lullaby. There were times when he would be
enthralled by Teeny, amazed by her gradual discovery of the
world around her. Usually, though, he was indifferent, not much
help to Mary in taking care of the baby (he'd sleep right through
her crying at night), and perhaps even a bit unnerved by it all.
The house felt different now, smaller, with the force of another
life pressing against the bare pine walls. He was beginning to
feel trapped there.

He saw the migrants passing through town, telling tales about
the green valleys and thousands of jobs awaiting them in the
West, and many of them had "Help Wanted" handbills to prove
it. Aunt Laura already had left Plainview and gone to California.

Uncle John and Aunt Ethel had left Amarillo and were living in a place called Glendale. Woody wanted to head out too, but not just to California. He wanted to see it all. Sometimes he'd come across a matchbook cover with the name of a café in some town that struck his fancy—Grand Island, Nebraska; Bend, Oregon— and he'd stuff it in his guitar hole as a reminder that he was going to have to visit there someday. He'd had enough of Pampa. He had read all the books in the library, painted all the windows, played all the barn dances and radio stations, and heard everyone's life story half a dozen times. The town was played out, like an old mine. And he was bursting with energy. A simple letter introducing himself to Roy's new wife could, in April of 1936, become a giggly, half-crazed, near-hysterical eruption of cornball humor: "As far as drinking is concerned, Roy never touches a drop unless he is by himself or with somebody, and he never uses anything stronger than water—for a chaser. . . . About ten years ago I tried to offer him a drink and he threw it in my face. Last year I offered him another one and he threw it in his own."

And: "Since he was twenty, he has been more or less a long wolf. I mean, a *lone wolf*. He generally runs around by himself with four other guys. He goes to bed when there ain't noplace else to go and comes to work when it's time to get off and go home. If you ever want him and can't find him, just locate him and you'll know where he is. I used to lose track of him when he was giving me nickels and this was a distressing period in my life. So in my childish way I'd just start a conversation with some good-looking girl and Roy would show up pretty soon."

It went on like that, breathlessly, for three typed pages, single-spaced, pausing only briefly at the end for a serious note: "Your husband isn't impulsive or high strung like his brother, me. He takes everything . . . decently, and in polished order. He is making his life, and I am letting my life make me. He reminds me of a sailing vessel that is always under control no matter the storm at sea. He plies sensibly and safely, though sometimes slowly, into and out of the various high waters that foam all over we who attempt to ride this tight-rigged ship of life." He signed it "Your brother and a half, in law and a half," and added appropriate verses from Gibran on marriage and children.

An explosion was coming in Woody's life. It almost seemed a matter of natural law. For five years he had been sucking in knowledge like a vacuum cleaner, and now he had to let it out in some way or go crazy. He knew all about the growing antipathy toward him in town, and reacted to it by becoming more outrageous than ever. He let his hair grow out into a wild, curly bush that seemed to stand up straight in all directions, and he pretty much stopped taking baths. When he was home (and those appearances were increasingly rare), he was moody and irritable, either flat out on the couch and not talking or up and fidgety, rattling and tapping, down to the corner for some tobacco. He'd get angry with Mary for not being able to go out to barn dances with him as she had in the past, then would ignore her when she hired a baby-sitter and came. She was still little more than a child herself, and had no idea how to react to him. They didn't talk much. He'd stay in the saloons until closing time most nights and then come home (if he came home) with his shoes slung over one shoulder, playing his guitar and singing at the top of his lungs as he came down the street, waking all the neighbors. The song he invariably sang was one of several he'd written about the Great Dust Storm. He called it "Dusty Old Dust," and it proceeded in fairly traditional ballad style; the melody for the verses was borrowed from Carson Robison's "Ballad of Billy the Kid," but Woody composed the chorus himself. What was most striking, though, was the subtlety and bitterness of the words. He wrote verses mocking the people he knew—the ones who ran to the churches because they thought the world was ending, the merchants who'd probably raise their prices for Armageddon—and sometimes named them specifically. He even savaged old friends like Preacher McKenzie, whose reaction to the catastrophe was to "fold his specs, put down his text and take up collection." In the chorus, which eventually would become an American standard, he served notice that he'd had enough of Pampa:

> So long, it's been good to know you
> So long, it's been good to know you
> So long, it's been good to know you
> This dusty old dust is a-gettin' my home
> And I've got to be drifting along . . .

CHAPTER 3

Here Come Woody
and Lefty Lou

Woody didn't leave Pampa all at once. He drifted away, gradually. He started with short trips, visiting friends and relatives in the Southwest . . . and if Mary didn't exactly encourage these excursions, she certainly didn't mind them very much. Lots of men were out on the road, looking for work, looking for new opportunities and places to live. In fact, with Pampa curling up and dying in the dust, getting out of town seemed one of Woody's more *rational* impulses in recent years. There was always the possibility that he'd actually find something he wanted to do out there, some work that suited him.

So Mary wasn't terribly upset when, early in 1936, Woody decided to go to East Texas and visit Tom and Nonie Moore, his old favorites from Okemah. Tom was a barber in the town of Kilgore and Woody stayed with them for about a month, testing the waters. East Texas wasn't nearly as dusty as the panhandle, but it wasn't all that different, either. He found a job painting signs and soda jerking for the local druggist . . . and gave his first week's pay envelope to a crippled black man sitting in the street outside the store. "You haven't changed a lick," Tom Moore said, shaking his head. "How you gonna earn a living if you give it all away?" Woody shrugged, cracked a couple of jokes, and left town.

After a brief stay in Pampa, he was off again, this time to

Oklahoma to visit his brother Roy and his new wife, Ann, in the town of Konawa. Roy was working at yet another market, Streetman's, and he managed to get Woody a job painting the store's truck. He put "Here Comes Streetman's" on the front and "There Goes Streetman's" on the back, which was a big hit with everyone in town except the man who owned the truck; and then he moved on to Fort Smith, Arkansas, where his father was making one last attempt to start a real estate business.

Charley Guthrie was nearly sixty years old, but looked much older. His face was heavily lined, his shoulders stooped, and his hands were more crippled than ever by arthritis. He was a sad, feeble man sitting at an empty desk in a sorry little office (he'd borrowed the rent money from his brothers), without even the punching bag that had been his signature for so many years. His marriage to Bettie Jean was over, except for one nagging problem: he'd left his daughter, Mary Jo, at the mercy of that horrible woman and seemed incapable of figuring out a way to get her back. Bettie Jean had fled Pampa when a woman she was "treating" for breast cancer died and the bereaved husband threatened a lawsuit. Eventually she settled in Borger, with Mary Jo still in tow, and Roy finally decided to ease his father's mind and resolve the problem. He simply picked up Mary Jo one afternoon in Borger and took her to live with him in Konawa.

With that settled, Charley closed his real estate office and quietly slipped onto skid row in Oklahoma City a few months after Woody's visit. He would spend the rest of his life there, taking occasional odd jobs and receiving handouts from the family. To the end, he wore a frayed white collar and an old, soiled tie each day, offered free legal advice to anyone who needed it, and kept a notary seal pasted in the window of his fleabag hotel room.

For Woody, the pain of his father's tragedy blended with the agony of hundreds of broken, tormented men he was finding on the road in 1936. It was a strange moment in the Great Depression. The worst was supposed to be over, the economy was supposed to be improving . . . and life probably *was* better for some people. But for the rest—for those left hungry and jobless in a time of mild optimism—it seemed worse than ever. That certainly was true in the Southwest, where the dust and drought were only the most obvious signs of a general collapse. Even in fertile areas, small farmers were being driven out to make room for massive corporate entities that farmed with machines and could actually wring a profit from the land. The family farm simply wasn't economical anymore. A human convulsion of epic proportions was in progress. The whole countryside seemed to heave and groan as the farms emptied and the highways filled.

With all the homeless men cluttering the roadsides, Woody was finding it difficult to hitch rides, and often had no choice but to travel by freight train. It still wasn't the most pleasant way for him to go, but, with his guitar slung over his shoulder, he was a popular figure in the boxcars and hobo jungles. Inevitably, someone would ask him to play "Jesse James" or "Columbus Stockade" or "The Boll Weevil Song" or some other tune that a grandmother or uncle had sung back in the days when the family still had the farm; if he didn't know the words, they'd be more than happy to teach him. He was developing a repertoire of songs from all over the country—ballads from the Appalachians and Ozarks, cowboy songs, hoedowns and breakdowns, hymns and country blues from the black belt. Often, when he'd forget a verse, he'd make up another on the spot to replace it. The songs were always changing, reinventing themselves. With some, like "Lonesome Valley," it was hard to say where the traditional version left off and Woody's began.

He played a variety of four- and six-stringed instruments, but none of them well. His guitar picking would never be much more than adequate. His singing voice was dry, flat, and hard like the country. It wasn't a very good voice, but it commanded attention: listening to him sing was bitter but exhilarating, like biting into a lemon. In any case, his level of musical virtuosity never mattered very much to his audiences on the road.

They always wanted to hear the old tunes—there weren't many requests for fox trots in the boxcars—and Woody was amazed by the impact the songs had. Sometimes grown men would get all misty-eyed when he sang them, and their voices would catch when they tried to sing along. The whiny old ballads his mother had taught him were a bond that all country people shared; and now, for the migrants, the songs were all that was left of the land. Singing for these people was a totally different experience from playing a barn dance with the Corncob Trio. It wasn't just entertainment; he was performing their past. They listened closely, almost reverently, to the words. In turn, he listened to their life stories, and felt their pain and anger. An odd thought began to percolate. *He* was one of *them*. The collapse of his family wasn't all that unique; these people had seen hard times too. Almost every one of them had a story that was, if not as gruesome as his, bad enough. Despite all the lip service he'd paid to Eastern religion and the "unity of all things," Woody had never considered himself part of any group before. But here he was, an Okie, and these were his people.

He began to move in wider circles away from Pampa and during the next year was spotted everywhere from Ohio to California. He spent nights in jail on vagrancy charges when he was happy for the roof over his head; he spent nights in skid row flophouses that reeked of vomit and crawled with bedbugs; he spent nights out in the desert, freezing; he spent nights in the boxcars dodging randy old hoboes looking for boys to sleep with ("The Big Rock Candy Mountain," he learned, was a song about a homosexual tramp who seduces a young boy away from home); he learned to sleep on floors, in corners, on sidewalks, in alleys, anywhere. He was still learning, and quiet, and not yet ready to show very much of himself to the world . . . although he could, when necessary, stroll into a diner and start up a conversation with the orneriest waitress, spinning out tall tales about life on the road and serenading the customers with old favorites, and inevitably get someone—often the waitress herself—to pay for his bowl of chili.

A hobo named Curly the Kid (real name: James Isenberg) bumped into Woody several times during those years, and remembered him as distant, unpredictable, and charming. Once they were riding through Nebraska in a boxcar and spotted a circus tent sitting at the edge of a small town at dusk. They hopped off the train to investigate, and found it was a revival meeting—but the visiting evangelist hadn't arrived yet and the local church officials were in a quandary. Noticing Woody's guitar, they asked if he'd keep the congregation occupied with some hymns while they were waiting. The evangelist never did appear and Curly (who'd had some seminary training) eventually delivered a raucous sermon. When it was over, the elders of the church offered them the collection—mostly pennies, nickels, and dimes—but Woody refused to accept it, saying they needed it more than he did, which irked Curly a little.

Another time they hit skid row in Denver. Woody began to work the dive bars in his usual fashion, setting a cigar box or a cap between his feet and playing the Okie anthem, "Lonesome Road Blues." There were many different versions of the song, which Woody later claimed was a southern slave tune, but the one he usually sang was:

> I'm goin' down the road feelin' bad
> Yes, I'm goin' down the road feelin' bad
> I'm goin' down the road feelin' bad, Lord God
> And I ain't gonna be treated this a-way.

It was the sort of song that begged for improvisation, and sometimes Woody might sing it, "I'm blowin' down this old dusty road," and invent new verses like "Your two-dollar shoes hurt my feet," and "Takes a ten-dollar shoe to fit my feet," and "I'm goin' where the water tastes like wine," and probably about a thousand others.

Curly suggested that Woody's act was good enough to test in some of the ritzier bars in town, the ones where they served a free lunch. Woody agreed to try it, and while some bartenders ushered them out immediately, others were charmed by the graceful, dusty little tramp. Curly, meanwhile, was hitting the lunch bars, building huge sandwiches and stuffing them into paper sacks he carried with him for just such emergencies. After hitting five bars in two hours, they had enough food to feed an army and money enough to buy a bottle. Curly suggested a feast was in order, but Woody stopped abruptly and announced, "Nope. Gotta go home. S'long," and left Curly standing there in the middle of Laramie Street.

He always returned home to Mary sooner or later, usually bedraggled and without any explanations. Not knowing what else to do—his behavior was so far beyond her control that she was rendered nearly catatonic—she'd take him back in. He'd be fine for a while, wowing her and Teeny with songs and cartoons, playing out in the street with the neighborhood kids, and just being himself. Then he'd grow restless again, grumbling a little, going down to the corner for tobacco when he didn't need any, going down to the Tokyo Bar for a couple of snorts, over to Shorty's, over to Jeff's . . . and out. Sometimes he'd tell her where he'd be going and when he'd be back, other times he'd leave a note on the refrigerator door, but often he'd just be gone.

He went to California, but the water didn't taste at all like wine. It was an awful trip. The Los Angeles police, alarmed by the influx of migrants from the Southwest, had set up highly illegal roadblocks on the major highways at the California border, turning back people who looked like they might be "unemployables." Security on the railroads also was tightened—they called it the "Bum Blockade"—and Woody had to be careful not to get caught in the Glendale switching yards as he waited for a freight train heading north through the San Joaquin Valley toward his Aunt Laura's house in Turlock. But it was difficult to concentrate on anything but the scenery . . . California was the lushest, most beautiful place he'd ever been. It was raining, and the hillsides were an impossible kelly green; bright orange oranges dangled from thick, dark citrus trees; there were flowers everywhere, so unrealistically perfect they seemed artificial.

Woody simply could not believe the splendor of it all and, when his train stopped for a moment in the mountains north of Los Angeles, he hopped off to get a better look. He was so enthralled that he didn't notice the train had started up again until it was rolling downhill so fast that he just barely managed to grab a ladder and had to hang there, his arms and fingers aching, until it slowed down in Bakersfield and he stumbled off.

The trip north became a nightmare. He continued up the big valley in a driving rain, hopping the next train through, then off at the dismal valley town of Tracy, where he had to trade his sweater to get a plate of beans. The railroad stored sand in a dry, warm hut near the tracks and Woody decided to spend the night there—but he was quickly rousted by the railroad bulls and marched to the edge of town in the rain, and told never to come back to Tracy again. Down the road, he found a group of cold, shivering men under a highway bridge and spent the rest of the night snuggled together with a lumberjack, trying to keep warm.

He spent several weeks with Aunt Laura in Turlock, marveling at the size of the valley and its abundant harvest, the orchards stretching out forever in perfect lines of trees heavy with fruit. Laura's daughter, Amalee, took a special interest in him: she was newly married and entirely convinced that her house was haunted. Woody was supposed to be an expert in such things, and she wanted him to spend a night in the house to see what he could find. He did, and was mumbling something to Amalee in the morning about how she should search her past and meditate hard on the spirits that might want to torment her when a neighbor's shotgun went off accidentally and nearly killed the two of them standing there in the doorway. "You see?" Amalee said, and Woody decided it was about time to head home.

The trip obviously was jinxed, but it wasn't merely superstition that sent Woody packing. There was an anger in California, a bitterness toward his people—toward *him*—that Woody had never experienced before. It was frightening; he was stunned by the bigotry everywhere he went. In Los Angeles—a city where only 20 percent of the residents were natives—it was the nervous, priggish anger that recent immigrants often summon up to solidify their social standing in a new town. In the valley, it was the vicious, institutionalized violence of the vigilantes and hired goons who kept the migrants moving, meek and terrified.

The word "Okie" had become a slur, a word the goons spat out to describe *all* the migrants, all poor white people. About 500,000 "Okies" had entered the state since the beginning of the Depression, and there was widespread fear that California was being overrun. During Upton Sinclair's progressive campaign for governor in 1934, the conservative forces had played on the public's fear of "Okies." The movie studios released phony newsreels showing the seediest imaginable hoboes streaming off freight trains, anxious to take advantage of the radical reforms that Sinclair was promising. The propaganda worked: Sinclair, favored early in the campaign, lost decisively.

And now Woody began to listen more closely to the old radicals—all of whom seemed to be named Mac—who sat whispering around the campfires in the hobo jungles. They'd seen it all before. They had explanations. There were two sides, the rich and the poor, and you had to make your choice. They talked quickly, softly, insistently, hand on your elbow, about the workers organizing, facing down the bosses: it was possible; they had seen it. Some of them had been beaten and manhandled so many times their brains were soggy. They muttered half coherently about the capitalists, the rich bastards . . . and then, at the slightest encouragement, would reach into their pockets and pull out a battered old red card that proved they had been members of the wildest, woolliest, most violent, joyous, and completely disorganized gang of Reds ever to strike fear in the hearts of the American bourgeoisie: the International Workers of the World, or I.W.W., or more familiarly, the Wobblies. For a brief time before World War I, they had terrorized half the country and tried to organize the other half into One Big Union. They stood as a militant reproach to the moderate, cautious American Federation of Labor and the increasingly tame Socialist Party. They led violent, futile strikes and advocated sabotage as a weapon in the class struggle a little too openly to be serious about it. If Samuel Gompers of the A.F. of L. said that his goal for the workers was, simply, "More," the Wobblies wanted more than that: "Bread and Roses Too" was the slogan of their 1912 textile strike in Lawrence, Massachusetts. Their brazen, arms-and-elbows style of radicalism was especially popular with the lumberjacks, the miners, and the migrant workers out West. It fit perfectly into the self-conscious romanticism of the hobo culture. The blunt, overstated Wobbly style was summed up beautifully in the I.W.W. *Preamble*, a simple one-page document which began: "The working class and the employing class have nothing in common. There can be no peace as long as hunger and want are found among millions of working people and the few, who make up the employing class, have all the good things in life."

In 1906, the Wobblies in Spokane had realized their street speakers were being drowned out by the noisy Salvation Army brass band. Ever resourceful, they decided to form their own band to mock the Salvation Army. Mac McLintock (who later said he wrote "Hallelujah I'm a Bum") and Jack Walsh wrote several parodies of Salvation Army hymns that were so successful the Wobblies put them out in a *Little Red Songbook*. A few years later, an itinerant worker dropped into the headquarters with a parody of the Salvation Army hymn "In the Sweet By-and-By" which became one of the most famous Wobbly songs. The man's name was Joseph Hillstrom (*né* Joel Haaglund) and the chorus went:

> *You will eat, by and by*
> *In that glorious land above the sky (way up high)*
> *Work and pray, live on hay*
> *You'll get pie in the sky when you die (that's no lie).*

Joe Hill was probably more rogue than radical, and the songs he wrote were often little more than doggerel . . . but he came to symbolize the spirit of the Wobblies in the public mind, mostly because of the phenomenal success he achieved in orchestrating his own martyrdom. After arriving from Sweden in 1902, he

wandered through the West for the next thirteen years. Not much
was known about him, except that he often hung around the San
Pedro I.W.W. hall. Some of the old-timers suspected he made
his living as a robber, and only used the Wobblies as a social
club. Then, in 1914, he was arrested in Utah for the murder of
a market owner, a murder he probably didn't commit. But he
refused to say where he'd been at the time of the shooting (to
protect the honor of a lady, it was said), and was convicted. In
the years that followed, Joe Hill became a cause célèbre among
radicals and liberals all over the world. He did some of his most
inspired work while awaiting his death, including the famous line
he sent to Big Bill Haywood, the Wobbly leader, in a telegram
just before his execution: "Don't waste any time in mourning.
Organize."

Joe Hill's songs were given a prominent place in later editions
of the *Little Red Songbook*, along with the I.W.W. *Preamble*,
some serious songs like "The Internationale," and lots of lighter
parodies of popular tunes like "Barney Googles" ("Join the
Wobblies, join the Wob, Wob, Wobbly band . . ."). The book
was widely circulated in the boxcars and the migrant camps and,
somewhere along the way, Woody Guthrie got hold of a copy,
which he stuffed in his shirt and carried with him.

Woody discovered the Wobblies just as he was getting angry
about the horrors and deprivations all around him on the road.
The *Red Songbook* parodies, with their inspired use of humor and
music to convey anger, obviously had an impact. He began to
write some parodies of his own, songs about things he'd seen
like the Los Angeles police barricade at the California line—only
he put his words to the old country tunes the Okies loved, instead
of the popular melodies the Wobblies had used. His new songs
were more serious and direct than the "Alonzo Zilch" experiments but, at the same time, they were simpler and funnier.
Woody was beginning to discover his remarkable ability to transform his anger into humor. One way he did it was by using an
obscure Negro blues form, the talking blues, which was perfectly
suited to his sense of humor; he didn't have to sing at all, just
talk rhythmically while backing himself with a simple, bouncy
three-chord progression on the guitar. At the end of each four-
line verse, there was a spoken tag that Woody drawled out, often
to great ironic effect.

In "Talking Dust Bowl," which he wrote and rewrote end-

lessly while riding the freights in 1936 and 1937, he re-created
the migrant experience in six bitter, exquisitely simple verses,
The song begins in 1927, a small but happy farmer hauling his
crops into town, but then:

> Rain quit and the wind got high
> And a black old dust storm filled the sky
> And I swapped my farm for a Ford machine
> And I poured it full of this gasoline
> And I started. Rockin and a-rollin. Over the mountains,
>   out toward the old peach bowl.

The car has all sorts of trouble in the mountains, breaking down
and falling apart. He has to push it uphill and tries to coast it
downhill, but there's a hairpin turn and "I . . . didn't make it."

> Man alive, I'm a-telling you
> The fiddles and the guitars really flew
> That Ford took off like a flying squirrel
> And it flew halfway around the world.
> Scattered wives and childrens all over the side
>   of the mountain.

Finally, in the last verse, the family reaches the promised land:

> We got out to the west coast broke
> So dad gum hungry I thought I'd croak
> And I bummed up a spud or two
> And my wife fixed up a tater stew.
> We poured the kids full of it. Mighty thin stew, though;
>   you could read a magazine right through it.

Then, a *second* tag line:

> Always have figured that if it had been just a little bit
>   thinner,
>   some of these here politicians could have seen through
>   it.

When Woody said that word, "politicians," he rolled it over
in his mouth, luxuriated in it, pulled and tugged at it in such a

way—*pollli-TISH-uns*—that he was able to convey more rage and frustration than a dozen radical pamphlets.

Woody's growing political sense still wasn't very well defined, but it was beginning to intrude on the rest of his life. On the way home from California, he decided to stop in Santa Fe—a favorite town, a place that came very close to being the àdobe city he had dreamed about—and paint some pictures. To raise a little money, he took a job painting a huge sign for a curio trader. It would be a three-day job, and he asked fifty dollars for it. Soon, though, he began to notice how the trader treated the Indians who brought pottery and turquoise to be sold. One Indian came in with six gorgeous clay pieces, and the trader brusquely offered him $1.65, then threw the money on the floor so the Indian had to get on his knees to pick it up. Woody also learned that people in town had offered to paint the trader's sign for sixty dollars several years earlier, but he'd waited all that time just to find a sucker who'd do it for less. Woody was so angry that he quit the job, then climbed his painting ladder in front of the store and began making a speech to the Indians in the street, telling them they didn't have to take that kind of guff. It may have been just a coincidence, but that night three guys trailed him down a dark street near the Santa Fe cathedral and pounded on him until he wriggled free and ran away.

Then he was back in Pampa, and Mary was telling him she was pregnant again. He was numb to the idea, and to her, and didn't quite know how to react. The pain and anger of California had worn off, and all he could think about was the incredible green. Pampa seemed even less habitable than before, drab gray and brown in the bleak dust bowl winter. He tried splashing silver mica paint on the front of his little shack on Russell Street so the place would light up at night when a car's headlights shined on it . . . but the north wind still cut right through the flimsy pine walls. With Teeny getting older, there wasn't much peace and quiet in the house; and now, with another baby coming, there would be even less.

Jeff was still in town, working on the police force. Shorty Harris had converted his drugstore into a liquor store after prohibition went out. Matt Jennings continued plugging away at the market, but Cluster Baker had hopped a freight and gone off to Chicago to seek his fortune. When Cluster came home for Christmas that year and the Corncob Trio was reunited, Woody was so

happy that he gave him a painting of an old adobe house in Santa
Fe. On the back of the canvas he wrote: "This is adobe, a painted
clay, open air and sky. I was painting in front of the Santa Fe
art museum when an old lady told me, 'The world is made of
adobe,' and I said, 'So is man.' "

Spring came, still dusty. Mary was getting larger—the baby was
due in July—and Woody was growing quieter, even more remote
than usual. One afternoon in late spring, when Jeff and Allene
were visiting and they were all playing music together, Woody
popped up off the couch after a few songs and said, "Well, I'm
going," and started toward the door.

"Where you going?" Jeff asked.

"California."

There was a chorus of groans and various people—Mary, Allene, Mrs. Jennings—took turns trying to talk him out of it as he
gathered his things in a little bundle. Mary was stunned, heart-
broken. She was beginning to realize that all this traveling might
not be just a *stage* in Woody's life. She saw the future stretch
out before her—alone, with two children, in that rotten shack.
And then, before they could even talk about it, he was slinging
his guitar over his shoulder, kissing her on the cheek, and telling
her that he'd be in touch.

He hitched rides this trip, and slept in empty gas stations at
night, or by the side of the road. It was going to be better in
California this time, he knew it. He *felt* it. One night in the desert
outside of Wickenburg, Arizona, with a full moon and the coyotes howling, he could see the mountains all around him very
clearly, and the cactus, and the mineral crystals glistening in the
moonlight; and the worrisome fog that had settled on him in
Pampa—all those responsibilities—began to lift now, and his head
cleared in the sharp desert air. Several days later, when he reached
the California line, he found the Los Angeles police had taken
down their barricades. And when he arrived in Los Angeles a
few days after that, without a penny to his name, a dollar bill
floated down from one of the office buildings and landed at his
feet just as he was turning a corner. It was going to be *much*
better this time, no doubt about it.

In 1937, Los Angeles was more a concept than a city. It was a
network of independent little communities, each of them a replica

of a moderate to large midwestern town. It was known to the rest of the country for the glamour of Hollywood and as a haven for charlatans of every description—Westbrook Pegler once suggested that the whole area be "declared incompetent and put in the charge of a guardian," and it did seem to be the final roosting place for half the quacks in the country—but beneath the glitter, there was a solid base of prairie austerity. It was a clannish town. A newly arrived family from, say, Bosque County, Texas, might settle near some old friends from home who lived in Culver City and soon a dozen families from that same county would be living within a mile of each other. It was a standing joke in Long Beach that you had to come from Iowa to live there.

An amazing number of Guthries and assorted relatives congregated in the demure San Fernando Valley town of Glendale, just as they had converged on the Texas panhandle ten years earlier. Woody moved in with his Aunt Laura, who had tired of living up in Turlock, and he began hanging around with a cousin, Jack Guthrie, who was Uncle John and Aunt Ethel's son.

Jack was about Woody's age. He was tall, handsome in a boyish, western sort of way, and very talented. He had a beautiful, smooth tenor voice, played the guitar much better than Woody, and snapped a bullwhip with such accuracy that he could flick a cigarette out of a friend's mouth with little effort . . . and sometimes did, to the dismay of his friends. He was a reckless, sweet-talking, self-promoting sort with show business on his mind. He occasionally took his bullwhip and guitar on the local two-bit rodeo and vaudeville circuit, but supported his family—like Woody, he was vaguely married—by doing construction work.

It was the heyday of the singing cowboy in Los Angeles, a strange and rather wacky era that was mostly the result of Hollywood's desire to combine two of its most popular forms, the Western and the musical. It began with Gene Autry, who'd been a fairly big country music star on Chicago's WLS "Barn Dance," known for his cowboy posturing and his ability to yodel like Jimmie Rodgers. He was an immediate hit when he arrived in Los Angeles in 1934 and began making movies. Soon all the studios were looking for their own versions of Autry and the town was crawling with would-be cowpokes strutting around in boots, ten-gallon hats, silk kerchiefs, and shirts with all manner of spangles, baubles, buckles, and fringes. The music itself didn't bear the vaguest resemblance to the real cowboy ballads that Woody

knew, like "Sam Bass" or "Buffalo Skinners." With all the
yodeling and barbershop quartet harmony, it sounded more like
Switzerland than Texas. But it was one of the biggest things in
Los Angeles, and you couldn't turn on a radio without hearing
the Sons of the Pioneers (whose lead singer, Leonard Slye, would
become Roy Rogers) or some other group crooning a love song
to their cattle.

Jack Guthrie, whose nickname was "Oklahoma" or "Oke,"
was intent on becoming a singing cowboy star and invited Woody
along as his sidekick. Woody was doubtful about the project, but
it was a lot more interesting than washing dishes in Strangler
Lewis's restaurant in Glendale, which is what he'd been doing
until he tried to clean an aluminum pot with lye water and smoked
out the place.

A major roadblock to Woody's success as a singing cowboy,
though, was that he was going to have to ride a horse. There
were all sorts of horseback parades, singing contests, and rodeos
attended by large crowds, often including Hollywood talent
scouts. Jack was a daring rider, but Woody had been unlucky
with horses ever since he'd broken his elbow as a kid and he
soon found that his luck hadn't improved with age. When Jack
took him to a stable to pick a horse for his first cowboy parade,
Woody almost immediately fell off his mount and skinned an
elbow. Nonetheless, he and Jack trooped proudly into Gilmore
Stadium several days later, along with hundreds of other cowboy
acts. Jack was wearing a flashy cowboy outfit with a white silk
kerchief; Woody was done up as a raggedy hillbilly sidekick,
which is to say he came as he was. And it was going along just
fine until Woody lost control of his horse again and charged into
a group of Hollywood Indians marching in front of them, scat-
tering bows, arrows, and feathers in all directions. The crowd
loved it, whooping and hollering as several cowboys chased after
Woody and eventually brought the horse under control. "I was
picking feathers out of my hide for several days after that," he'd
later say.

Then Jack found work for them in a cowboy vaudeville show
that performed for several days between screenings of "Waikiki
Wedding" at the Strand Theater in Long Beach. Also on the bill
were the famous country music group the Beverly Hillbillies, as
well as Woody's distant cousins Possum Trot Bruce and the Poe
Boys. Jack stole the show with his beautiful rendition of "Empty

Bunk in the Cothouse Tonight,'' but Woody was far less prominent, coming on with the rodeo clowns and rattling his spoons. They were paid a couple of dollars apiece for the performances, plus five dollars for driving around a truck outfitted with promotional signs and cowboy regalia.

Buoyed by that success, Jack talked his way into a radio audition at KFVD, a station known more for its political commentary than its music. It was owned by a crusty old populist named J. Frank Burke, a small, florid man with white hair, whose major interest was his own ''Editor of the Air'' program each day at noon. Jack managed to convince Burke that the station needed a cowboy show to liven its programming and, on July 19, 1937, ''The Oklahoma and Woody Show'' made its debut at 8 a.m. on KFVD. They weren't paid anything for the privilege of appearing on the radio each day, but Jack didn't care: he saw the show as a promotional tool, a way to publicize personal appearances at rodeos, saloons, and other staples of the local cowboy circuit.

The show itself was mostly Jack, with only a smattering of Woody. They would sing their theme song, ''Lonesome Road Blues,'' and harmonize a few other songs together. Then Jack would take over, singing and yodeling in the Jimmie Rodgers fashion, with Woody backing him on the guitar and harmonica. Very rarely did Woody solo, usually a harmonica tune or some other novelty number. He didn't exactly enjoy this arrangement— cowboy music wasn't at all his style—but he *was* on the radio in Los Angeles and, what's more, the show was a success. They received more than three hundred fan letters in August and, by September, Burke had decided to put them on twice a day, adding another half hour at 11 p.m.

Early on, Jack had introduced Woody to his closest friends in California, the Crissman family. Jack had worked several construction jobs with Roy Crissman, an easygoing, eminently comfortable man who enjoyed having gangs of young people over to his house in Glendale. Roy and his wife, Georgia, had moved to California from Missouri in 1932. They had two daughters, both of whom avidly followed Jack and Woody's careers as singing cowboys. Even though he was married, Jack had his eye on the younger daughter, Mary Ruth, who was still in high school. The older daughter, Maxine, was a slim, elegant-looking woman with a husky voice who liked dressing up in high-fashion style. She worked in a dress factory for fourteen dollars per week, and hated it.

Maxine wasn't particularly impressed by Woody Guthrie the first few times Jack brought him by the house. He seemed quiet, and shy, and not very much fun. One night, though, they happened to sing together and a strange thing happened: Maxine started off in her usual deep alto, and Woody responded by going up high and harmonizing in a mountain tenor. Their voices meshed perfectly—it was almost eerie—in a natural two-part harmony. They were stunned by the sound they had created and began trying it out on some of the old country ballads, which, much to Woody's delight, were Maxine's favorite kind of music too.

In late August, Woody (who was obviously getting impatient with the same old cowboy stuff) asked Jack if he could invite Maxine on the show to sing a duet with him. Jack, always amenable, didn't mind at all. They sang "Curly-Headed Baby," and it went quite well, even though Maxine had a horrible case of stage fright and suffered a brief, but severe, attack of laryngitis just before the show. Afterwards, Woody drew a cartoon of the two of them singing at the KFVD mike, and Maxine shaking all over.

During the next few weeks, they made several public appearances and sounded great each time. Woody was very casual about it all: there were no rehearsals, no instructions, no planning, no worrying. He'd just step up to the microphone, say "Howdy" to the folks, start singing . . . and expect that she'd do the same. After appearing on the "Cowtown" radio program and at "Frontier Day" at Hermosa Beach, they returned to "The Oklahoma and Woody Show" on September 3; and Woody wrote a little introduction for Maxine. He called her "Lefty Lou from Ole Mizzoo . . . She's long-winded and left-handed, and she can jump a six-rail fence with a bucket of milk in each hand and never cause a ripple on the surface . . ."

Without any maneuvering or arranging on Woody's part, without any apparent effort at all—it was so maddeningly nonchalant—the breaks began to fall just right for them. In early September, Jack Guthrie realized he wasn't making enough money in show business to support his family, and decided to go back to construction work for a while. He hesitated, went on and

off the air several times, but was gone for good on September
14, and Woody asked Maxine to join him on both the morning
and evening shows. She happily quit her job in the dress factory,
and Woody wrote a new theme song to the tune of "Curly-Headed
Baby":

> *Drop whatever you are doing*
> *Stop your work and worry too;*
> *Sit right down and take it easy*
> *Here come Woody and Lefty Lou*

It was Woody's show now. He did the talking and he chose
the music, and Maxine didn't mind at all. The cowboy songs
were most definitely out; no more "Back in the Saddle Again."
They were replaced by old mountain ballads, hymns, and hillbilly
tunes. Now it was "What Would You Give in Exchange for Your
Soul?" and "Maple on the Hill" and "Bury Me Beneath the
Willow" and "I'm Thinking of My Blue Eyes."

There still wasn't very much planning or order. Woody and
Maxine would drive Roy Crissman's car to the station, which
was located in downtown Los Angeles. After Woody nearly totaled the car in the rain one night—"Hold the phone," he said
in mid-skid, a favorite expression—Maxine did the driving. They
often sang in the car on the way to work, but that was all the
rehearsing they ever did. Usually, they'd just walk into the studio, flip open Woody's loose-leaf songbook, and start singing.
There were no scripts, no song lists; in between numbers they'd
chat amiably about what to sing next, or read a letter from a
listener requesting a certain song. At least once a show, Woody
would spin off a tall tale, or a thought for the day. He called it
his "Cornpone Philosophy," and played at sounding like an utter
yokel, a device that enabled him to get off some good licks not
only at the city slickers but also at the narrow-mindedness and
insularity of country folk.

The warm, homespun style of the show found a natural audience in Los Angeles. The city was filled with people who missed
their old lives on the farm, who found urban life just a bit too
fast, who busily organized themselves into home-state societies—
clubs for natives of Iowa, Oklahoma, and so forth—that held
regular meetings in the downtown cafeterias and massive annual
picnics. They were an older, emotional, and unpretentious audi-

ence, who quickly adopted Woody and Lefty Lou as members of the family. And it wasn't just in Los Angeles: the 11 p.m. show skipped out across the country (often, on a good night, it could be heard clearly in Pampa), and there seemed to be people all over who were nostalgic for the sweet, simple country life. The mail poured in, 474 letters in September alone:

When you sing, it seems as though you are singing to each of your listeners individually . . .

I'm going to talk to you just like I do my own kids. You kids are real and natural. You sing the songs I use to sing 40 yrs ago.

Play "Ripsaw Blues"—it takes me back to milepost 1892 . . . I am 70, homesick, perhaps growing childish.

Oh boy what harmony!

Would love to have both of you out to a chicken dinner. We are just plain Texas people—your talk gives us a thrill, and those beautiful songs . . .

It floats me away from these hectic days of rush and heart-ache and jazz into a green valley of rest and peace. I have never heard any program like it—two perfectly blended voices, quiet, restful, unpretentious, singing sweet old melodies of the past, to me, alone.

We sure love to hear Lefty Lou laugh—it sounds just like I think people laugh in heaven.

Take this dollar bill and buy yourself and the lady a drink.

Please don't go modern.

The early days of the show were not without problems. There was a certain amount of jealousy and anger within the Guthrie family because Woody had asked an "outsider" to join him on the show, especially when there was so much talent in the family itself. There was Aunt Ethel, who screeched when she sang, and Uncle John, who mumbled, and Jack's sister Wava waiting in the wings. To say nothing of Possum Trot Bruce and the Poe Boys. At about the same time, too, Uncle Jeff and Allene arrived in California, figuring that if Woody could make it in big-time radio, they could too. Woody tried to resolve the problem by having them *all* on the show from time to time, which was pretty confusing and provoked some angry mail. For example: "Your charm lies in your individuality. When you have other than you two, it's just a hillbilly act. This is meant as constructive criticism, it's just so refreshing to have originality these days. Let's have more of [just] Woody and Lefty Lou." Apparently KFVD agreed, because they were taken off the evening program for several weeks in early October until the situation could be resolved. Maxine agreed with the station and the listeners, but Woody was stubborn. "You're just selfish," he said. It was the angriest he'd ever become with her. Finally, though, he relented, promised fewer guests, and the 11 p.m. program was restored.

In November, KFVD added yet *another* show for them, at noon each day. Instead of going back to Glendale after the morning show, they'd go exploring around Los Angeles and then return to the studio for the noon program. They went to used-book stores and Woody would have long conversations with the owners; once he read aloud to her from Kahlil Gibran, another time from the *Rubáiyát* of Omar Khayyám. He took her to the Los Angeles art museum, and showed her how the paintings worked. There was one, a jumble of dots by some Frenchman, that she couldn't understand at all until he pulled her back a few steps and she saw that it was a beautiful Impressionist landscape. It seemed Woody was having that same effect on the rest of her life, too. She was changing. She was becoming more open, less formal. She no longer dressed to the teeth or wore makeup; she'd go to the station wearing just slacks and a sweater. "Forget yourself and go, Lou," he'd say, and she would.

Even though Woody had become the most important man in Maxine's life, there was never any question in her mind of a physical relationship between them. She simply couldn't imagine going to bed with him. It wasn't that he was unattractive: Woody had beautiful, delicate features. But there was a pristine quality about the way he looked; it reminded her of pictures she'd seen of Jesus Christ. He was . . . sexless. He was an adult child. He saw life with a child's clarity and innocence, but there was more to it than that: sometimes he behaved like a child. One of his favorite pastimes was to race around the waiting room at KFVD, a room ringed with couches, with one foot up on the couches and the other on the floor, his arms outstretched, and making a "brrrrrrr" sound, pretending he was an airplane. In Griffith Park one day, he saw some kids rolling down an incline on their sides, and joined them.

He was like a little brother. He was playful, mischievous, small enough to wear her gray jacket with the blue window checks and look good in it. He stole cigarettes from her purse until she bought a new one made of suede—he hated the feel of suede, called it peach fuzz—and he stopped. A grown man didn't act like that. In fact, it didn't even occur to her that Woody might *have* a sex drive (although she knew he was married and had children) until she overheard him talking to her father one night about a girl he'd made love to in Santa Fe. "I turned her every way but loose," he said, and Maxine was shocked.

Often the Guthrie and Crissman families would spend weekends together, going for long drives and having picnics at the beach. Woody invariably was the life of the party at such times, mugging and joking, very much *on*, jabbering away at Roy and Georgia and Aunt Laura and the rest. One evening, a family picnic at Santa Monica beach was interrupted when forty blacks pulled up in a truck and raced onto the beach, intent on routing the white picnickers—or so it seemed to Woody and the Crissmans. Roy called the police, who eventually came and chased the blacks away.

Woody, whose social conscience had been rather dormant since he'd made it in radio, celebrated the event with a little newspaper of the sort that he'd always produced for the friends of the Corncob Trio. It was a blatantly racist document called the "Santa Monica Examine 'Er." The cover page was filled with cartoons of clichéd jungle blacks, and it was followed by two pages of gossip columns with jokes like: "What makes a nigger's feet fly the fastes'? Answer: A unifom." And a report of the event by "Rastus Brown" which begins: "After Joe Louise done won de crown fo bein the wuhlds mos bestas boxuh, all de Niggahs evah-wha automatickly got de idee dey wuz tuff too, so dey went out to celibrate how tough dey wuz. Santa Monica beach wuz de place an de white folks say dem coons got plum wile . . ."

The bulk of Woody's newspaper, though, was a long narrative poem, "Clippings from the Personal Diary of a Full-Fledged Son of the Beach," a parody of "Hiawatha" describing the events at

Santa Monica that night. Considering that the poem was merely a five-finger exercise, something he tossed off between radio shows the day after the incident, it was a surprising—and disturbingly clever—piece of work. It begins:

> *As in leisure there reclining*
> *In the firelight brightly shining*
> *On a coney hot dog dining*
> *On the ancient sands of time.*
> *I was with fond friends and neighbors*
> *There relaxing from their labors*
> *(And the trip was quite a favor*
> *'Cause I didn't have a dime.)*

The saga continues through sixteen more eight-line stanzas. Forsaking his hot dog ("Man cannot live on buns alone"), he decides to go swimming and, while in the water, hears someone yell: "What is that Ethiopian smell/Upon the zephyrs, what a fright!"

> *We could dimly hear their chants*
> *And we thought the blacks by chance,*
> *Were doing a cannibal dance*
> *This we could but dimly see.*
> *Guess the sea's eternal pounding*
> *Like a giant drum a-sounding*
> *Set their jungle blood to bounding;*
> *Set their native instincts free.*

Apparently, the "Santa Monica Examine 'Er" wasn't an isolated incident, either. On October 20, 1937, Woody received a letter from a listener that read in part: "You were getting along quite well in your program this evening until you announced your 'Nigger Blues.' I am a Negro, a young Negro in college, and I certainly resented your remark. No person . . . of any intelligence uses that word over the radio today." Woody was mortified. It was a word he'd used casually all his life. It was a word he'd used lightly, jokingly, without ever quite realizing its full implications. He took to the air immediately with an apology. He read the letter aloud, promised not to use the word again, and ripped all the "nigger" songs out of his book.

Woody's political naïveté did, at times, seem boundless. After Japan invaded China, he wrote a know-nothing parody of "The Martins and the Coys," called "The Chinese and the Japs," the point of which was summarized neatly in the last verse:

> *We don't know who will ever win the battle*
> *And as far as we're concerned we do not care*
> *If they bombard good ole Tokio*
> *Well, I guess that's okie dokio*
> *But let's pray they don't go droppin' 'em over here.*

Although he'd later be quite embarrassed by it (in a later notation in the songbook he writes: "When I made this one up, the war between China and Japan had just got started a few days and I didn't have sense enough to know that I was on China's side 10,000 percent—WG"), the song was a big hit with his listeners, and requests began to pour in for copies of the words. So Woody mimeographed the song and sent it—for a dime—to anyone who wanted it.

The audience was beginning to request the words to other songs as well and, as a promotional gimmick, Woody and Lefty Lou decided to publish a songbook. Frank Burke, the station manager, liked the idea and allowed them to use his office for the enterprise. Woody dived into the work, and spent his afternoons hammering away at the typewriter, working on the twenty-four songs to be included and jokes to fill the white space at the bottom of each page, such as: "Lefty Lou typed off a lot of theese songs and I tyyped off a bunCh. YoU WOnt HavE any Troubbel tellxng whech ones I rote." They printed about four hundred copies of the first booklet, a sheaf of pages stapled together and called:

OLD TIME HILL BILLY SONGS
Been Sung for Ages, Still Goin' Strong

Actually, with all the time they were spending on the air—almost two hours each day—they were running out of material, and getting bored with singing the same songs over and over. When "The Chinese and the Japs" was so well received, Woody decided to try out a few more of his own songs on the air. He tried "Talking Dust Bowl," which became an immediate favorite, and his song about the Los Angeles police barricades, "Do Re Mi." Then he began writing songs specifically for use on the show. When a listener sent a press clipping about a cowboy who killed a lawyer in a fight over a woman in Reno, Woody turned it into a ballad. The victim was a "Philadelphia lawyer" who was in love with a "Hollywood maid," and wooed her rather greasily:

> *Come, love, and we will wander*
> *Down where the lights are so bright*
> *I'll win you a divorce from your husband*
> *And we can get married tonight.*

Woody and Lefty Lou's audience was, of course, in sympathy with the cowboy husband, and quite happy when he killed the city slicker and there was "one less Philadelphia lawyer/in old Philadelphia tonight."

Maxine simply couldn't believe how quickly Woody was able to write songs. Usually he'd start off with a general idea—the newspaper clipping—and then a key phrase would come to him—"Philadelphia lawyer"—and he'd find a snatch of an old tune to fit the phrase, and then set the rest of the words to that tune. It wasn't a very conscious process, of course; in later years, he'd use Leadbelly's "Irene" as the tune for about a half dozen different songs, and always be amazed when someone would point out that he'd done it again. Sometimes he'd change the notes of an old tune here and there to make the melody fit his words better, thereby creating a new one—but the music usually was an afterthought. The words were most important. He wrote his songs at the typewriter; it was the instrument he played best.

One day he was sitting on the Crissmans' back step, strumming his guitar, when the boy next door came over and asked, "Hey, mister, where you from?"

"I was born in the Oklahoma Hills," he said. It was a pleasant-sounding phrase, "Oklahoma Hills," and he began to toy with it. In the next few minutes, just fooling around, he came up with a chorus:

> *Way down yonder in the Indian Nation*
> *Ride my pony round the reservation*

> *In them Oklahoma Hills where I was born*
> *Way down yonder in the Indian Nation*
> *Cowboy's life is my occupation*
> *In them Oklahoma Hills where I was born.*

Then he dashed inside, went to the typewriter, and had all the verses done in time for the 11 p.m. program that night. "Oklahoma Hills" would become a country music standard after World War II, made popular by none other than Jack Guthrie . . . and it would also be the source of some controversy within the family.

As Woody gained more confidence in his songwriting, he also grew more creative during the "Cornpone Philosophy" segment of the show. In addition to his own tall tales and homilies, he began holding contests. He asked listeners to send in their favorite tornado stories, the biggest lies they ever heard, the best miracles. One night he read off a list of thirty-five different types of miracle stories they might consider sending in, including: "1. A message that came to me . . . 9. How faith got me a job . . . 10. How faith got me out of trouble . . . 16. A warning that came to me . . . 20. How I found my lost relative . . . 30. God can cause strange things to happen . . ." Another night he suggested the possibility that there was a species of snakes that formed themselves into hoops and rolled across the desert like tumbleweed, and asked if anyone had ever seen or heard of one.

More often than not, though, he'd just talk for periods ranging up to fifteen minutes. He had a soft, lovely speaking voice with a graceful Oklahoma drawl that often seemed more melodious than his singing voice. Sometimes his "Cornpone" patter would be inspired, often it was just overdone hillbilly blab: "Of course, even when I'm gossippin about gossippers I realize that I'm a-gossippin myself, but I sorta figure that the only real gossippin that needs to be done is about gossippers," began a typical session. The audience was divided on Woody's talks.

> I don't enjoy that faked hill billy language that you give us, Woodie. The reason I know its faked is because I know that if you were really that ignorant, horses couldn't drag you up before a "microbephone," I come from the hills

myself but I never heard any talking quite so bad as yours . . .

I heartily disagree with those who claim that you talk too much.

I love that southern talk you put out.

With all the hoop snake stories, miracle stories, requests for songbooks, and debate over Woody's philosophizing, the mail for November became an avalanche: 1,509 letters, more than the previous three months combined. Woody loved the letters. He'd rip open the envelopes and read them aloud to Maxine, chuckling, as they drove home from work every day. He loved the stories and suggestions and requests that came in. There were very few hate letters or crazies. The listeners seemed a wonderfully good-natured and solicitous bunch; they bolstered Woody's belief in the essential goodness of humanity, a faith he'd been cultivating since his experiences on the road. His burgeoning love affair with "the people" was both a noble and an arrogant form of naïveté. He was charmed by their native wisdom, their kindness, their decency . . . and simply refused to acknowledge that they could also be selfish and petty and fearful. He willfully blinded himself to all but those who suffered the hard times with dignity. As long as the meetings were passing and by chance—as they were on the road—he was able to love them all without reservation. It was even easier to love them by mail.

Woody got along very well with Frank Burke, the man who owned the station. He respected the way Burke stood up for "the people" on his "Editor of the Air" program, and against the big shots and crooks running state and local politics at the time. Despite his seething oratory on the air, Burke was a rather formal man and Woody enjoyed teasing him. For his part, the station manager loved Woody's country humor and often invited him in to regale the business staff with bawdy stories.

One day Burke walked into his office and found Woody sitting with his feet propped up on the desk, working on the latest songbook, while Maxine had mimeographed sheets and envelopes spread out all over the floor. "I used to be top dog around here until you hillbillies came along," he said.

"Guess you'll just have to buy yourself another station," Woody replied. Burke smiled, and made a rash decision: he decided to give the hillbillies a contract. He offered to pay them twenty dollars per week base salary, plus fifteen dollars for each sponsor the ad salesmen could dig up.

It was an incredible windfall. Woody was so thrilled he wrote out several drafts of a "Corntract" for Burke to sign. In one draft, the hillbillies would be paid in corn bread; in another: "It is understood that the laundry of the party of the second part shall be done by the party of the first part, whether you bring all of it or part of it. This will save the party of the third part the job of doing part of the laundry of the party of the second part."

On November 12, 1937, Woody and Maxine signed a one-year contract with Standard Broadcasting Company. After receiving their first paycheck, Woody dragged her over to the bank at the Ambassador Hotel and had it cashed into silver dollars, big clunky pieces of metal they could stack and play with—ten for Maxine and ten for Woody.

The next thing he did was to send for Mary and the kids.

Mary had been waiting. At first, when he left in March, she hoped he'd be back in time for the baby. He'd never been gone for more than a month before. But her second daughter, Sue, was born in July, just about the time "The Oklahoma and Woody Show" was getting started in Los Angeles. As the months passed and another hot, dusty summer held Pampa in near-paralysis, and her parents railed against Woody's outrageous irresponsibility, and the people in town stared at her and took pity, Mary began to wonder if everyone was right and he really *was* gone this time.

Then, in September, there was new hope. The evening radio show began on KFVD. She and Matt would stay up late—11 p.m. in Los Angeles was 1 a.m. in Pampa—and listen to it each night. Her immediate reaction was tremendous pride. Woody had *shown* them; he had shown all the narrow-minded people in town who thought he'd never make anything of himself. And now, instead of hoping that he'd come back, she prayed that he would get her out of there. He wrote occasional letters describing the wonders of California, and dedicated songs to her on the air. He promised in the letters that he'd send for her when he got a little money, and so she wasn't at all surprised when he did.

But even then, her parents were skeptical. He'd drag her out to Los Angeles, they said, then get bored and go off somewhere else. With Woody, there was half a chance he'd be gone before the train arrived. And then she'd be all alone in a strange place. They protested all the way to the Santa Fe station, and put her and the two babies on board against their better judgment. She looked so young and helpless getting on that train. She was only twenty years old.

As if to confirm her parents' worst fears, Woody was nowhere to be found when she arrived in Los Angeles two days later. She and the children sat at the station for several frightening hours before he ambled in, kissed her, hugged the kids, said, "Sorry, got lost," and took them all to the beach, where Teeny played in the water even though it was December.

Woody, of course, hadn't given any thought to where they were going to live and so they moved in temporarily with Aunt Laura's daughter, Amalee, and her husband, Harlan "Chief" Harris, an Indian carpenter who was about as antsy as Woody. Amalee and Chief lived in a small bungalow in Glendale that was so close to the Griffith Park zoo they could hear the lions roaring at night. Woody often took Mary and the kids to the zoo in the afternoons that first month; in the evenings, they would play poker with Amalee and Chief. Woody drew up funny cartoon money for the games, and Amalee made huge pans of popcorn. But they spent much of those first few weeks looking for a place to live— never an easy proposition in Los Angeles, but especially difficult when there were children involved. As landlord after landlord refused them, Woody grew angry . . . and eventually started an anti-landlord campaign in his "Cornpone Philosophy" spot that was his first vaguely political effort on the air. It was quite popular with the audience:

This land lord business is the best yet.

Woody, my little girl had to hear those people say, "no children" and "sorry, we can't take children" until she [said to me], "Mother, if you didn't have me you could find a place," and at that point I just broke down and cried.

But the campaign didn't help Woody and Mary's chances of finding a place and, as the days passed, life at Amalee's became less tolerable. There wasn't much peace or quiet with all the

children running around, and the natural confusion among the
adults about who should buy the groceries, and the long bathroom
lines that formed at crucial moments during the day. Woody, who
needed a certain amount of privacy, had his three radio shows to
prepare for and began spending afternoons at the Crissman house,
which didn't sit at all well with Mary.

Through all those months of listening to the radio back in
Texas, she hadn't been very worried about Lefty Lou. The word
on the family grapevine was that there wasn't much to worry
about, that Lefty Lou went around dressed like a man. But the
first night Woody took Mary to meet the Crissmans, Maxine was
all decked out for a date and Mary was a bit surprised. Then she
began hearing a different set of rumors from the west coast Guthries, about how Woody and Maxine had been inseparable, about
how they'd been seen rolling around together in Griffith Park.
Woody hadn't done much to discourage the rumors—in fact, he
seemed to *want* everyone to think he and Maxine were having an
affair. As Mary grew more suspicious, Woody became more elusive. He began staying out late after the 11 p.m. show, and sometimes not coming home at all.

Maxine knew little of all this. She still idolized Woody, and
couldn't imagine him acting less than honorably. But years
later she realized he probably didn't always go straight into the
house when she dropped him off after the late show; sometimes
he'd go over to the saloons on San Fernando Road, where Jack
Guthrie also escaped his marriage. On occasion, "Oklahoma
and Woody" would crank up their old duo and make good
money in the bars, especially when they sang "Oklahoma
Hills." Maxine did notice that, instead of staying with Mary,
Woody was coming to her parents' house in the afternoon and
typing furiously in the living room, or painting pictures of California missions out in the garage . . . and sometimes falling
asleep on the floor.

She felt sorry for Mary, who seemed so confused and worn
out, with the haggard, too experienced look that often settles
in on women who have to raise families when they are still
children themselves. Once, when Maxine told her that Woody
had been quite worried in the days before Sue's birth, Mary
began to cry. It was the closest any of them ever came to a
personal conversation. Woody never said what was on his mind.
Mary, frightened again about the future, had retreated into her

Pampa stupor. Maxine, an outsider, didn't want to butt in, and was only dimly aware that she might be a source of the tension.

Just as the situation seemed ripe to explode, Matt Jennings arrived in town for a visit, calm and good-natured as always, and defused it. He and Maxine now were paired off at social occasions, which eased Mary's mind somewhat. Uncle Jeff and Allene also were back in town, after an unsuccessful attempt to make some money as musicians in the California gold country, and the family spent the holiday season together, going to the beach and the amusement parks, playing music at home just as they had back in Pampa, drinking wine out of a gallon jug, and watching Woody pace back and forth, giddily spinning out whoppers about the things he'd encountered on the road. On New Year's Eve, they all went over to KFVD—even the kids—and did the late show, then went to a restaurant owned by a listener who'd called in to invite them over to celebrate the New Year. Baby Sue sat on a counter as 1938 came in, munching on a doughnut, while the rest of them entertained the customers with their fiddles and guitars, and Mary figured that if her own life wasn't exactly terrific yet, it was a whole lot better than it had been the year before in dreary Pampa.

The radio show was reaching its peak of popularity. Woody and Lefty Lou had sponsors—the Victor Clothing Company, the Perfume Man, Sal-Ro-Cin Headache Pills were among them. There was also the gas station at the corner of San Fernando Road and Los Feliz which gave them free service in return for an occasional plug. They were splitting sixty-five dollars per week, and Woody was comfortably supporting his family for the first time.

There were all sorts of interesting offers coming in as well—personal appearances, guest spots on other radio shows, better deals elsewhere—most of which Woody shunned. He didn't care very much about fame or money, and was quite happy at KFVD, where Frank Burke gave him the freedom to do virtually anything he wanted on the air. One offer, though, was too good to pass up. In mid-January, a representative of the Consolidated Drug Company named Hal Horton called KFVD and asked Woody if he and Lefty Lou would like to sing on station XELO in Tijuana, Mexico, for seventy-five dollars per week. More important than the money to Woody, though, was that Horton wanted him to assemble a troupe of hillbilly performers to broadcast for three hours each night. It meant that Woody could hire the whole family, and still have room for more.

XELO was one of several stations located in border towns that the Mexican government let operate with two to three times the amount of wattage allowed to American stations. With their transmitters aimed north, the "X" stations, as they were called, could blanket a large part of the country—much to the dismay of American broadcasters, who couldn't do much about it. Since most of their audience was located in the South and West, the "X" stations tried to present, and became known for, the finest in country music. The Carter Family, for example, held forth on XERA from 1938 to 1941 (and communicated with Woody by mail several times during that period).

The "X" stations also were known, though, for a steady stream of awful commercials hawking products of a less than savory sort, especially quack cures too raunchy to make it past American censors and Better Business Bureaus. In fact, it was Dr. J. R. Brinkly, inventor of a goat-gland cure for sexual impotence, who started the "X" stations when he bought XERA in Villa Acuña, Mexico, in order to advertise his product after his Kansas broadcasting license was revoked in 1930. The Consolidated Drug Company, which Hal Horton represented, was a cut above the worst of the border advertising . . . but not much more. Woody, Lefty Lou, and the gang were hired to perform between loud, pushy, obnoxious ads for Peruna Tonic, which was Consolidated's cure-all, plus Colorback hair dye and other questionable items.

By January 25, 1938, Woody had assembled a strange assortment of performers in Tijuana, including Lefty Lou, Jack Guthrie, Jack's parents, Jeff and Allene, Matt Jennings, Possum Trot Bruce and the Poe Boys, a skid-row fiddler named Jimmy Busby, who always was afraid of the police for some reason, and a twelve-year-old boy wonder named Whitey McPherson. They performed three times a day on the station—a show in the morning, Woody and Lefty Lou at noon, and the main three-hour extravaganza at night, which also featured the station's resident cowboy band, Buck Evans and the Buckaroos. Woody was the central figure in all this, organizing the shows and acting as master of ceremonies, cracking jokes and introducing the various combinations—Jack Guthrie singing "Empty Cot" with the

Buckaroos in the background, Jeff Guthrie and Jimmy Busby doing a fiddle duet, and so on. He and Lefty Lou did a fifteen-minute segment in the middle of the show, and it was their theme song, "Here Come Woody and Lefty Lou," that opened the whole shebang each night.

During the day, the gang—which also included Mary and the kids, the Crissman family, and assorted stray relatives—lived in a tourist court in Chula Vista, just this side of the border. All the old scare stories about Okies taking over the state must have flashed through the minds of the motelkeepers as they watched the truckloads literally pour in, all of them with fiddles and guitars. Each day brought another member of the family, often carrying all of his or her possessions down from Los Angeles. The Crissmans, expecting a long, prosperous run in Tijuana, packed up their Glendale apartment and arrived in a truck the week after the show started, as did Whitey McPherson's parents. The shocked motel owners kept bumping the rent, but the hillbillies always found the money to pay it.

Woody, Matt, and Lefty Lou discovered the pleasures of the San Diego zoo and Balboa Park, and also enjoyed wandering through the streets in Tijuana. They weren't very sure of themselves in Mexico and one day when Woody disappeared after drinking several champagne cocktails with them, Matt and Maxine were alarmed . . . until they found him fast asleep on the back seat of the car.

The show went poorly from the beginning. Hal Horton was very much like the Consolidated Drug Company ads—noisy, pushy, and obnoxious. He kept flying down from Los Angeles and pestering them, demanding that they quit acting like hillbillies and organize their act a little better, be more professional. One day he began picking on Uncle Jeff for the casual way he played a tune, and Jeff got so angry he had to be forcibly restrained. Another time, Horton suggested a fake radio romance between Buck Evans and Lefty Lou, and Woody seethed, "Why in the hell don't you just stay up in Los Angeles and let *me* fly up and see *you* there when you have a problem?" Maxine was so disturbed by the smarmy advertising that she complained to Horton at lunch one day and he exploded, "You know, I can replace all of you with records."

Another problem was that Woody turned out to be a rather anarchic master of ceremonies, especially when he'd spent the afternoon rehearsing in Tijuana saloons. He developed a near-fatal penchant for Mexican ethnic slurs, like: "Here's another song for all you pepper-bellies out there." Or: "Well, the gang was out in Tijuana [he pronounced it "Tiawanny," which was bad enough] today, getting ourselves all chilied up," which offended one of the station's Mexican announcers. The most serious flap, though, came as a result of a relatively innocuous comment he made after receiving a postcard from some listeners in Canada. He said, "Here's a request we smuggled in over the border from Canada," and somehow the Mexican border guards misinterpreted this (apparently the word "smuggle" set them off) and hauled Woody in the next day when he was crossing the border. The Guthries went into a panic when they heard about the arrest—Mary was running around the tourist court screaming and crying, afraid they would take Woody to some awful jail in Mexico City—but he was released several hours later.

The Tijuana adventure ended soon after that, but it wasn't Woody's mouth that killed it. Hal Horton simply stopped paying them after the first few weeks, then strung them along for several weeks more before announcing that he couldn't get them work visas, and the show was over. It was the end of the line for Jeff and Allene on the west coast; they were broke and disgusted, and decided to head back to Pampa. Matt Jennings, who'd had no luck finding work as a butcher, decided to go home too. The rest of the group straggled back to Los Angeles. Later, Woody and Maxine learned that several other naïve country music groups had been similarly abused.

Within a month after they'd left, Woody and Lefty Lou were back on KFVD again. Frank Burke had allowed them to break their contract and go to Mexico with no fuss in the first place, and now he welcomed them home as though nothing had happened. Not only that, he advanced them money to rent tourist cottages in Burbank until they could find more permanent accommodations.

The only difference now was that Woody and Lefty Lou no longer had the 11 p.m. show—it had been filled successfully while they were gone—which meant less recognition, but also less worry for Mary. She was still wary of Maxine, although Woody's younger brother George soon arrived, as if on cue, to fill Matt's old role as Maxine's escort. George, who found work in a market, was a more persistent suitor than Matt had been, asking Maxine out on dates and wanting to buy her dresses with his paycheck. Maxine thought he was a nice kid. In any case, when Roy Crissman found a beautiful old Victorian bungalow on Chestnut Street in Glendale that was big enough for everyone— even George—to live in, Mary felt secure enough to make the move.

Woody began working on a third songbook as soon as he returned from Mexico, and Burke promised to have this one printed, instead of mimeographed like the others. The songs were mostly the same as before, but Woody's comments seemed less flip, more philosophical. At the end of "The Chinese and the Japs," he wrote: "They ain't but one thing in the world that can cause a war and that is somebody's greed. It's hard to track 'em down and find out whose it is, because it's a lot of fellers and they all try to lay it off onto somebody else. They even try to call it religion or something. If that's true, I rather not be quite as religious and stay alive, 'cause I got another song or two I want to write, and a lot of traveling to do."

After "Under the Weeping Willow Tree," he paid tribute to Omar Khayyám: "Omar Khayyám seems to have been sorta of a hillbilly hisself, because he took the words right out of my mouth. And he knew how to put down in a very few words just what it takes for a day's run."

And later, beneath "What Did the Deep Sea Say?" he apologized for the fact that the new songbooks were so fancy: "They is something about these here neatly printed books I don't like. It looks too neat to be anything that I done. Now them first books we mailed out was hand made, and very slouchy, but they had my brand on them, and there was something about them that I liked. They was a few mistakes in 'em, that's what made 'em so human . . ."

In the third songbook, too, he wrote brief biographies of Lefty Lou and himself. Lefty Lou's was warm and loving, and predictable enough; but there was something restless, almost uncomfortable, about the lines Woody wrote about himself. There were the old saws, and the refried Gibran, and the self-deprecation, but also a hard, troubled edge to it:

Well when I go to write about myself, I cain't say much, 'cause I ain't got no material to work on. I've been around the country a few years, a Hobo Hillbilly, eating twice a week whether I was hungry or not. I've worked a lot of places but never did have anybody write and tell me that my work was a bright spot in their day till I got on the airwaves in front of a microbephone. I never did drink anything stronger than water for a chaser, and never spend my money foolish unless I'm by myself or with somebody. I am a believer in everything and everybody, extry modern and extry old fashioned. My contract with KFVD don't give me enough money to get the bighead, but it gives me enough so that I don't care what other people think about me. I'm just a pore boy trying to get along. The dust run me out of Texas, and the Officers run me in at Lincoln Heights [jail]. But they was nice to me. They had bars fixed up over the windows so nobody could get in and steal my guitar. . . . I am never surprised or disappointed, for I have no regret or future ambitions. I am a lazy man, and cain't help it. Ugly and cain't fix it. The Universe is my home, and Los Angeles is just a vase in my parlor. I don't care if school keeps or not. I like pore people because they'll come out winner in the long run. And I like rich people because they need friendship.

The mail still poured in, about a thousand letters per month, and Woody still did surprising things on occasion—once he found a sound-effects machine in the studio and spent an entire half-hour broadcast creating strange noises and making up stories to fit them—but the show was less spirited than it once had been. Maxine couldn't put her finger on anything specific, although Woody did seem to be running off at the mouth more, and caring less. After Mexico, he became downright cynical about the job offers that came in, and ignored feelers from two of the more popular country music shows with national audiences—the "Hollywood Barn Dance" and Chicago's WLS "Barn Dance." Not only that, he delighted in offending prospective sponsors. He refused to suck up to them; indeed, it often seemed they were auditioning to meet *his* standards. In one instance, he drove a woman distraught by calling her Mrs. instead of Miss when he saw that it bothered her. Roy Crissman, who loved Woody like a son, was becoming impatient with him as he watched the good opportunities slip away.

Life at home wasn't much better. Woody was feeling trapped by his family responsibilities again, and restless, and a bit edgy. One day his cousin Amalee saw him go berserk when a dog bit a child in the Crissmans' front yard. He ran all around the house, screaming and cursing, trying to find a gun to shoot the dog—an understandable reaction, perhaps, but completely out of character for Woody. He treated Mary awfully. He pointedly ignored her. He'd come home from work and wouldn't even say hello. They rarely showed affection toward each other, or even touched. Mary seemed more faded and forlorn than ever. She just couldn't understand why Woody wasn't ambitious, especially with all the opportunities he had. She couldn't figure out what was going on inside his head. She wanted to talk to him about this, but didn't know how to begin—every time she tried, he'd slip away somehow. Her closest friend was Amalee and they'd sometimes sit around the house, cooking up a pot of beans and drinking, gossiping about show business and movie stars. She burned quietly most of the time, and suffered his public indignities, but occasionally lashed out at him. Once, when she lost her temper in front of the Crissmans, Woody shook his head with disgust and mumbled, "Aw, Mama, why don't you just go home?"

At the end of May, after several difficult and not very communal months, the Guthries—including George—moved into a small apartment down the block from the Crissmans. If Mary had the idea that a home of their own would improve things, she was wrong. He became more remote, and she knew he was going to leave again.

The radio show continued to fade. Maxine wasn't feeling well. She was exhausted after all the months of singing and excitement, and a doctor said she was anemic. Sometimes she didn't even have the strength to finish songs on the air, and she decided to ask Woody about taking a break from the show for a while. He said he was thinking of doing some traveling himself. "Hey, Roy," he asked her father one day, "how'd you like to hop a freight train and go on up the big valley?"

"Sure," Roy said, to Woody's surprise, and they began making plans for the trip.

Frank Burke was amenable to the idea of a sabbatical, and on Saturday, June 18, Woody and Lefty Lou performed for the last time on KFVD. George, who was very sad about the show ending, carved their initials on the station's back staircase. "At least this much will stay here," he said.

Several days later, a letter came from one of their most devoted listeners, Mrs. Martha Hammer, a woman who'd sent clothes to Woody and quilt pieces to Maxine: "I cried all during your last program. . . . I feel so sorry for Woody all alone on that freight train. But if it don't stop until he gets to where he is going maybe he will be all right. But so many get knocked in the head that [riding] makes me uneasy. But we will trust in God that he gets there all right . . ."

CHAPTER 4

I Ain't a Communist Necessarily, But I Been in the Red All My Life

During the year that she'd known Woody, Maxine Crissman had heard him talk about everything from the philosophy of Laotzu, the founder of Taoism, to French Impressionist painting; she'd heard him sound off, at length, on just about every conceivable subject . . . except politics. He would, of course, routinely defend "the people" against the evil *"pollli-TISH-uns,"* but he never went beyond those vague, easy generalities. He simply didn't concern himself with specific issues or political figures; he seemed to have a philosophy, but no opinions.

Woody's political education, begun on the road, had lapsed in Los Angeles as he turned his attention to other, more immediate matters. Singing with Lefty Lou, he'd come to realize that writing and performing songs was going to be more than just another of his casual pursuits, like sign painting or fortune telling. He'd become so wrapped up in music there hadn't been room for much else in his life. Although he scorned the concept of professionalism, that first year at KFVD had been an apprenticeship. He'd learned how radio worked, gained confidence in his ability to write songs, refined his craft. And now, as "Woody and Lefty Lou" began to wane, he was ready to move out into the world again.

The catalyst was Frank Burke, whose thunderous radio editorials had made him prominent in liberal circles (which, in Los

Angeles at the time, were little more than dots). Burke was one of a handful of reform types who occasionally met with Clifford Clinton in his famous downtown cafeteria and commiserated about California politics. The state government had been run by the same bunch of ultra-conservative Republicans for the past thirty years, and the city of Los Angeles was a swamp of land speculation and vice payoffs. The current mayor, Frank Shaw, was strip-mining the city with an ease and grace that shamed even his corrupt predecessors. There seemed little hope for reform, until Shaw ran into some bad luck involving a bomb.

The bomb was planted in a car owned by Harry Raymond, a police detective investigating vice squad corruption. It had been placed there by a fellow officer, Captain Earl Kynette, who happened to be the mayor's enforcer and collection agent in the department. In the spring of 1938, Kynette was tried, convicted, and sent to San Quentin. The Clinton's cafeteria reformers celebrated by launching a petition drive to recall Mayor Shaw—a drive that was a surprising success from the start and quickly gathered the signatures necessary for a new election to decide Shaw's future.

There were other optimistic signs. The prospects for toppling the Republican governor, Frank Merriam, seemed quite good. In 1934, Merriam had almost been beaten by the socialist upstart Upton Sinclair, who was considered a quack by many and certainly was not a political professional. This time, the Democrats were going to run a less exotic, but still progressive candidate: State Senator Culbert Olsen.

Frank Burke was bubbling with all these possibilities. He started a little newspaper called *The Light* to publicize the recall and Olsen campaigns. It appeared only occasionally and probably didn't have very much impact, but since most of the major newspapers in town were unremittingly right-wing and the one reformist daily, the Hollywood *Citizen News,* was in the midst of a long (and rather embarrassing) strike, Burke felt the need to do *something* to get the news out.

One of his first recruits to the paper was Woody Guthrie. He loved Woody's country humor and common sense, and had a vision of turning him into the "next" Will Rogers, whose daily political comment had been an institution in papers all over the country. Woody, who'd been creating his own little newspapers since the Corncob Trio, jumped at the chance to help out with a real one. He decided to follow current events more closely, and attempted some political cartoons for Burke. His early efforts were eclectic. One of them showed a rotting hulk of Shaw's "political machinery" with a captioned quote from the Buddha: "All things are transient, fleeting, destined to pass away."

Actually, Burke had bigger plans for Woody in the spring of 1938. He wanted to send him and Lefty Lou on a statewide tour for Culbert Olsen in a sleek, chrome bus along with a comedian who impersonated Franklin Roosevelt. That had to be shelved, though, when Maxine's health failed and the radio show fell apart. But Burke had another idea: as long as Woody seemed so intent on bumming around the state for a while, why not put his travels to good use? He asked Woody to investigate the living and working conditions of the migrant workers. He'd heard the valley jails were stuffed with Okies who'd been trying to organize a union. If that was true, it might be a good issue for Olsen. "You might even consider getting yourself arrested," he said. Woody didn't know about that, but he was happy to have a good excuse for Mary when he hopped the boxcar with Roy Crissman in mid-June. He was now "on assignment" for *The Light*, and had a letter to prove it.

Woody and Roy spent a week or so together, eventually landing in the pleasant town of Chico at the northern end of the Sacramento Valley. Roy, who'd been homesick for the country ever since he'd moved to Los Angeles, liked the area so much he decided to go right back to Glendale, pack up the family, and move them all to Chico. Woody said he was going to continue wandering around, perhaps do some investigating for Frank Burke, and promised to meet the Crissmans at noon in the town square of Chico a month later.

After a happy and secure year in Los Angeles, Woody was back on the road alone again, back among "his" people in the boxcars and the squalid migrant camps. But he was different now, and so were they. He was "Woody" from KFVD now. Not that he went around advertising that fact, nor did many people recognize him at first. But often, when he began to sing or play, someone would know his voice . . . and make a crack about hoop snakes or ask, "Where's Lefty Lou?" They treated him more like an old friend than a visiting celebrity, welcoming him into their orange-crate-and-cardboard hovels, offering him food and a place to sleep. Sometimes, when they asked him why a fellow with a radio job had to ride the boxcars and grub for food in Hoovervilles, he'd try to joke past it: "Just traveling around, looking for my family. Forgot which railroad bridge they're camped under."

But that sort of cornpone humor wasn't as funny in the real world as it had been on the radio. Eight families actually were found to be living under a highway bridge near Bakersfield, sick and hungry. Starving children with distended bellies were not an uncommon sight in dusty migrant camps located next to huge orchards spilling with fruit . . . and protected by armed guards. Other children had running sores, dysentery, lice, and worms; often their mothers had to draw water from infested streams. It didn't take Woody long to realize that the situation was not the same as the last time he'd passed through the valleys. The Okies were no longer quite so meek and yielding; there was a grim anger now, a barely controlled rage, a sense of pride trampled once too often. Some families had been there—living in the nooks and crannies of the big valleys, scratching for food, begging for jobs—for several years now.

The federal government had come in and opened a few model camps for the migrants: neat rows of khaki tents, running water, medical care, and sanitary facilities. The camps were supervised by the Farm Security Administration, and often were run by councils elected by the migrants themselves. Several of the camps even had newspapers and Saturday-night entertainment. But occupancy was limited and, for the rest of the migrants, the FSA camps were a reminder of how awful their own lives were. To make matters worse, the government sent around photographers to record the Okies in their misery. The migrants scavenged their last shreds of dignity for the cameras, straightened themselves up and stared proudly into the lenses; their gaunt Scots-Irish stoicism, in the face of having lost the farm and being tricked into the orchards by a handbill, was recorded for posterity. And there were others coming now to report their misery: newspaper reporters, usually from out of state. Book writers. An angry young lawyer named Carey McWilliams was putting the finishing touches on a history of the California agricultural system that he would call *Factories in the Fields*. Tom Collins, the supervisor of the FSA camp at Arvin, had brought in a young novelist named John Steinbeck to look around and talk with the people. Steinbeck, horrified, had written a stirring pamphlet called *Their Blood*

Is Strong, then organized a committee of Hollywood celebrities to give money and support to the migrants, and was starting work on a long novel that he hoped would record the entire dust bowl experience.

The migrants, imagining their awful reflections in the photographers' lenses and the reporters' questions, began to get angry. They were not worldly people. They had known only their farms and now this. From the photographers and the reporters and the FSA camps, they began to realize that an outrage was being perpetrated against them. It wasn't just their own stupidity that had gotten them into this fix. It wasn't all their fault: they were being victimized. A platoon of fiery, earnest young people—union organizers, predominantly Communists—had started coming around in 1937 and telling them, "No, it's not your fault. It's the system. It's the growers getting rich off your sweat," and a fledgling union was being formed.

But unions had been crushed before in California, most recently in 1934. The growers were immensely powerful. They controlled huge tracts of land, some of which dated all the way back to the Spanish land grants. In 1915, a legislative committee had found that a mere 310 proprietors owned more than four *million* acres in the state. They had been hiring armies of workers (and armies of thugs to control the workers) at starvation wages since the 1870's: first the Chinese, then the Japanese, then the Filipinos, and now the Okies (an estimated 50 percent of the farm labor force) and Mexicans (30 percent).

They had no qualms about using violence to keep their workers in line. In the early 1930's, some growers had formed a paramilitary group called the California Cavaliers whose stated purpose was to "stamp out all un-American activity among farm labor," and whose effect was to rout the attempt to organize the Cannery and Agricultural Workers Industrial Union. Usually, though, it wasn't as formal as that. A grower would simply hire and arm some local townspeople—who didn't like the Okies overrunning their communities in any case—to scatter a picket line or drive out a suspected union agitator or, in more drastic cases, bust up a whole migrant camp. They didn't have to worry about the law. The local police supported them, as did the conservative state government. They were favored, too, by economic realities. It was estimated that there were between four and ten workers competing for every available job in the fields. The growers could pay almost nothing and still have crowds of Okies lining up for work. In 1937, some families made as little as three dollars per week picking cotton in the San Joaquin Valley. An able-bodied man who made one dollar per day was doing very well indeed.

Woody mentioned none of this when he joined the Crissmans in Chico late in July. They set up camp in a beautiful state park on the banks of the Sacramento River and had a fine old time, fishing by day and singing at night. He seemed as happy-go-lucky as ever . . . but a little more antsy. He left them after only a week, doing a smooth soft-shoe on the side of the road to hitch a ride. Three weeks later he was back, with no explanation of where he'd been. Maxine, meanwhile, had rather abruptly fallen in love with a mechanic named Pat Dempsey, whom she'd met at the park, and was intending to settle down with him in Chico. Woody seemed happy for her, even though it meant the end of their singing team. They performed together one last time at a bar in Chico, singing for several hours and making a few dollars apiece . . . and then he ambled out of her life.

It was, perhaps, just as well. Woody was moving in a different direction. He was writing political songs again, and they were angrier and more direct than ever before. They were songs about the dust bowl and the people he was meeting in the camps. He wrote a song that summer called "Dust Bowl Refugees," which was a term he hated. He described them as homeless, moving from crop to crop like "whirlwinds in the desert." Often, he introduced the song by saying, "You know, there are different kinds of refugees. There are people who are forced to take refuge under a railroad bridge because they ain't got noplace else to go, and then there are those who take refuge in public office . . ." He had learned not to joke about the people who lived under railroad bridges, but he hadn't lost his sense of humor. He wrote a bitter parody of Jimmie Rodgers, who'd sent so many people yodeling out to California on the promise that the water there would taste like wine. Woody called the song the "Dust Pneumonia Blues," and announced right off that "there ought to be some yodeling in this song," but he couldn't do it because of the dust rattling in his lungs. He ended with an adaptation of a popular dust bowl joke:

> Down in Texas, my gal fainted in the rain.
> Down in Texas, my gal fainted in the rain.

> *Had to throw a bucket of sand in her face,*
> *Just to bring her back again.*

New song ideas were coming more frequently now. They could be triggered by a small change in the lyric of an old tune, or spring fullblown from his head. He always was refining the words, always juggling them around—playing with them seemed his greatest pleasure. He would forget old verses, and make up new ones as he sang. He would change lines to fit an audience or a situation. Everything seemed negotiable except the anger. And sometimes the anger became a near shriek, as in the opening verse of "Dust Can't Kill Me," a song that captured the defiant pride and anguish Woody had seen in the camps:

> *That old dust storm killed my baby,*
> *But it won't kill me, lord.*
> *No, it won't kill me.*

He returned to Los Angeles in early autumn, by way of Texas. Mary had stomped home angrily to the panhandle with the children, convinced that Woody was up to no good with Maxine Crissman in Chico. Before she would agree to return with him to California, Mary made Woody promise that he wouldn't sing with Maxine again, a promise he must have made with one of the half giggles that often insinuated themselves into the middle of his words, like "Wehell," as in "Wehell okay."

By the time Woody brought his family back from Texas, Mayor Frank Shaw had been voted out of office and replaced by a stolid judge named Fletcher Bowron. Culbert Olsen, the progressive Democrat, was on his way to a victory in the governor's race too, and Frank Burke was jubilant. Woody helped again with *The Light*, filling several notebooks with cartoons which showed, among other things, that his political views were still in flux. A two-paneled cartoon, for example, had a boss telling a worker (who looked suspiciously like Woody), "You can't do this job till you join a union . . ." And then a union guy telling the worker, "If you join this union, you can't take that job . . ."

But another cartoon—actually a neatly printed statement—was a scathing attack on both the government and the Consolidated Drug Company, his erstwhile sponsor in Tijuana. It also was an indication that Woody was developing an eye for the more subtle outrages in the news: "The big heads of the consolidated drugs trades company, Chicago, Illinois, who handle about 20% of the rottenest drugs, powders, chalks, salts, glues, oils, carbon black and quinine in the United States, and hoodoo every home in the country with a sly and witchy radio broadcast amounting to 60 hours a day, over which nothing as good, pure or honest as good witchcraft is used as sales talk—They've decided to get in good with the government by a makeshift adoption of the Poor Food and Drug Act—where the big business heads, between drinks of seltzer, will inspect their own lousy products and stick Uncle Sammy for the salaries of nine inspectors . . ."

Frank Burke liked the cartoons and still loved Woody, but didn't quite know what to do with him. Woody insisted on returning to the radio as a solo, but Burke didn't think it would work without Lefty Lou. Finally, they reached a compromise: Woody would have a half-hour program every day, but Burke wouldn't pay him (except for one dollar per day, for carfare) . . . which apparently satisfied all parties except Mary. Woody figured he could always make enough money to get by, singing in the skid-row bars at night and selling songbooks for a quarter on the air. Not getting paid also gave him the moral freedom not to show up when he had something better to do, like hitch up to the San Joaquin Valley and play for the cotton strikers in a big open field. Dorothy Healey, a young UCAPAWA (United Cannery, Agricultural, Packing and Allied Workers of America) organizer who spoke at that rally, was amazed by the easy rapport Woody had with the strikers, completely unlike any of the other celebrities who came up from Los Angeles.

On his visits to the migrant camps that autumn, Woody found that one of the more popular songs was a bouncy, jolly Baptist hymn called "This World Is Not My Home," which had been made popular by the Carter Family:

> This world is not my home
> I'm just a-passing through
> My treasures and my hopes are all beyond the blue
> Where many Christian children
> Have gone on before
> And I can't feel at home in this world anymore.

There was something about the song that bothered Woody. It was a mild annoyance at first, but it developed into a grating, pulsing anger as the weeks passed and he couldn't wipe either the tune or the idea from his mind. He was hearing the words in a different way than he'd ever heard them before. He was beginning to understand that the effect of this song was to tell the migrants to wait, and be meek, and be rewarded in the next life. It was telling them to accept the hovels and the hunger and the disease. It was telling them not to strike, and not to fight back. He was outraged by the idea that such an innocent-sounding song could be so insidious. An alternative set of words exploded out of him, and stood the song on its head:

> I ain't got no home
> I'm just a-roaming round
> I'm just a wandering worker, I go from town to town
> And the police make it hard
> Wherever I may go
> And I ain't got no home in this world anymore.

The rest of the song was unrelenting. In the second verse: "Rich man took my home and drove me from my door." In the third verse: "My wife took down and died, upon the cabin floor." And so on, unsparing, a statement of unrelieved anger.

Not only was "I Ain't Got No Home" a clever parody of the fundamentalist sensibility and a fine song in its own right, it also represented a clear turning point in Woody's life. It was a rejection of the passive Eastern spiritualism that had fascinated him since Pampa (and also a rebuke to his old idols, the Carter Family). It was, in a way, a call to arms—at the very least, an attack on inaction. Having spent most of the 1930's on the sidelines, Woody finally was spoiling for a fight. And, as he looked around, the people who seemed to be fighting hardest for the things he believed in were members of the Communist Party.

It was probably the only moment in American history when being a Communist seemed at all plausible to more than a tiny minority of the people. Woody had seen Communists working in the valleys, where virtually all the union organizers were party members. He had seen them involved in the Shaw recall and the Olsen campaign, always the hardest workers, often performing the most menial tasks with a breathless enthusiasm. They could stuff envelopes with the passion and intensity that most other people reserved only for sex and family arguments. Many of them were brilliant, most were good talkers, all seemed able to uncork a pretty fair speech at a moment's notice. They were impossible romantics, of course, who dreamed of a society based on complete equality—"from each according to his ability, to each according to his needs," a beautiful, hopeless ideal that most of them were willing to die for. But they masked their lavish humanism behind a tough veneer of logic and social science—a difficult pose for a humanist—and tended to strut about with the assurance of religious cultists, certain that poverty and injustice were easily cured by the simple application of Marxist principles, certain they represented the inevitable future.

For most of its history in America, the Communist Party had been a largely irrelevant and often laughable sect. It was founded after the Russian Revolution by a tiny sliver of native radicals, Wobblies and such, who admired the Russian achievement, and a larger group of socialist immigrants from Eastern Europe, who bubbled with nationalist pride. They were tremendously arrogant people. Not only did they believe that the overthrow of the capitalist system by the workers was inevitable, a scientifically proven *fact*, they also were convinced that the Bolsheviks had demonstrated the One True Way to bring it off, and thus looked to Russia for leadership in the coming struggle. Aside from that, they displayed a singular genius for splintering themselves into warring factions at the slightest provocation. They spent most of their time arguing over obscure points of rhetoric and the meaning of recent events in the Soviet Union . . . which was just as well, since few of them had any idea of how to reach the American working class they were supposed to be organizing. In fact, a sizable minority couldn't even speak English.

From the start, though, they attracted a degree of attention and repression from the government that was far out of proportion to their influence. The revolution in Russia had frightened the Western governments and many took harsh, immediate steps to prevent any chance of a workers' revolt in their countries. In the United States, there was a series of brutal, sweeping raids, organized in part by the Attorney General, A. Mitchell Palmer, in late 1919 and early 1920. Thousands of suspected radicals were rounded up, beaten, and deported. The various Communist factions were effectively crushed, their few remaining members forced underground.

All of which made for an organization that was as paranoid and myopic as it was passionate and idealistic. Throughout most of the 1920's, the party kept to itself. It lived a dream life dominated by the continual jockeying among the factions for a favorable nod from Moscow. Its presence in Russia, where it was an officially recognized member of the Communist International (the agency charged with furthering Marxist revolution around the world), often seemed more real than in the United States, where it was little more than a figment of its own imagination.

The stock market crash in 1929 changed all that, though. The predictions of capitalism's demise—which had sounded like utter insanity during the Roaring Twenties—seemed to be coming true. With unemployment soaring and the people desperate, the Communists were able to organize some fairly impressive demonstrations in 1930 and 1931. What's more, the Soviet Union seemed to be making real economic progress in the face of worldwide collapse. There was no unemployment in Russia. There was planning, and order. Joseph Stalin set a crisp, efficient style that permeated the American party. The Communists still were isolated in America, but now it was a smug isolation of their own choosing; they were sure history was on their side, and no compromises were necessary. Socialists were denounced as "social fascists." The Russian leadership was cemented in place.

Then, in 1934, there was another change. With the Nazi triumph in Germany and the growth of fascism elsewhere, history was beginning to seem slightly less inevitable. The Communist policy of ideological purity—indeed, of attacks on the socialists—had been a disaster in Germany; a united Left, much larger and stronger than the Nazis, might have prevented Hitler's takeover. And so, at the Seventh World Congress of the Communist International, the Bulgarian delegate George Dimitrov read a paper calling for a change in tactics around the world. He called for alliances with socialists and other progressives to fight the fascist threat.

The new policy was called the Popular Front and, in the United States, it led to the Communist Party's greatest period of growth and influence. For the first time there was a real effort to seem less alien and severe, to "Americanize," to join the mainstream. Earl Browder, who led the CP during this period, announced that

"Communism is twentieth century Americanism," and the party tried to align itself with the revolutionary past: Thomas Jefferson, Thomas Paine, and Abraham Lincoln joined the pantheon of heroes alongside Marx, Engels, and Lenin. The American flag began to appear at meetings, "The Star-Spangled Banner" replaced "The Internationale." Communist and socialist youth groups worked side by side in the American Youth Congress. With total economic collapse still a possibility and Hitler waiting in the wings, *everything* during the Popular Front period seemed crucial, dramatic, charged with meaning. American Communists were literally putting their lives on the line against the spread of fascism in Spain, where Francisco Franco was trying to overthrow the legitimate government with support from Hitler and Mussolini.

At the same time, Communists were playing a central role in the massive labor organizing that had been made possible by Franklin Roosevelt's legislative and moral support of the union movement . . . and by John L. Lewis's bravado. In 1935, Lewis had led his mine workers and eight other unions with a combined membership of 900,000 out of the tepid American Federation of Labor, and formed the Congress of Industrial Organizations. The idea was to begin organizing the workers in whole industries, instead of by individual skills—there would be one giant auto workers' union, for example, as opposed to a maze of smaller groups organized by craft. It was a near-impossible task, and Lewis realized he was going to need all the help he could get. He also realized that many of the toughest and most experienced union men around were Communists. They'd been trying to build their own industrywide unions for years (and, in eastern Kentucky, had even challenged Lewis's own mine workers), but now, because of the Popular Front, the Communists could shelve their rather ridiculous plans to build separate unions and could join the C.I.O. Ever the pragmatist, Lewis swallowed his personal disdain and welcomed them in. By 1937, C.I.O. membership was up to 3,718,000—larger than the A.F. of L.—and vast sections of it, whole unions in fact, were controlled either by Communists or by people closely associated with the party.

Between the Abraham Lincoln Brigade and the union organizers, the Communist Party presented a tough, muscular image in the late 1930's. It was a time within the party when, for once, action seemed more important than ideas, though the headlong rush to form coalitions with anyone who seemed even vaguely progressive often led to embarrassing excesses. A typical attempt by the Young Communist League to "sell" itself on a midwestern college campus read: "Some people have the idea that a YCLer is politically minded, that nothing outside politics means anything. Gosh no . . . There is the problem of getting good men on the baseball team this spring, of opposition from ping-pong teams, of dating girls, etc. We go to shows, parties, dances and all that. In short, the YCL and its members are no different from other people except that we believe in dialectical materialism as a solution to all problems."

Though they ran their traditional slate of candidates in the 1936 elections, the Communists worked hard for Franklin Roosevelt—the New Deal was seen as the ultimate Popular Front coalition—and the President responded with a degree of quiet tolerance. In local campaigns, their relationship with the candidate often was more direct. They were becoming a political force in some districts, a constituency to be courted, accumulating IOU's through their hard work. When Culbert Olsen was elected governor of California in 1938, he repaid his campaign debt to the Communists by freeing Tom Mooney, the well-known labor leader who'd been languishing in San Quentin for almost twenty years since he'd been convicted on evidence that was flimsy at best of planting a bomb that had killed a number of people during San Francisco's Preparedness Day parade in 1916. Mooney began a triumphant tour through the state, and one of his first stops was radio station KFVD in Los Angeles, where Frank Burke—always a stalwart defender of free speech—had actually allowed the local correspondent for the *People's World*, the west coast Communist newspaper, to have a radio show three times a week.

The *People's World* correspondent was an easygoing former gambler and social worker named Ed Robbin, and he was rather surprised when KFVD's resident hillbilly singer approached him the day after the Mooney interview and said, "I listen to your show all the time. Do you listen to mine?"

"Why, no . . . I'm sorry. I should," Robbin said.

"Well, why don't you stop in tomorrow?" Woody Guthrie said. "I think you'll like it."

The next day Robbin was shocked to hear Woody sing a song called "Mr. Tom Mooney Is Free" on KFVD, and then tell his listeners to check out Ed Robbin's *People's World* commentaries because "he tells the truth, and that's pretty rare in this town."

After the show, Robbin asked the hillbilly, "Do you have any other songs like that one?"

"Got a whole book of them," Woody said. "Had two books, but I lost one on the road."

Robbin invited Woody and his book home, and spent the rest of the day and night—Woody slept on the couch—looking through the songs. Ed had never met or heard of a progressive hillbilly before, and was amazed. "Woody," he said to the little man playing on the floor with his children and who seemed so much a child himself, "there's going to be a meeting for Tom Mooney tomorrow night at the Embassy Auditorium. If I can arrange it, I'd like you to sing your Mooney song there."

Woody said that would be fine with him, but Robbin—who still wasn't too sure about Woody's level of political sophistication—added, "You should know that this is going to be a left-wing political meeting. A lot of Communists will be there, in case you have any objections to that sort of thing."

"Left wing, chicken wing, it's all the same to me," Woody said.

Ed had to twist a few arms to get a singer on the program—there had never been any *entertainment* at party meetings in Los Angeles before, much less a hillbilly singer—but he prevailed, and the next night Woody Guthrie attended his first Communist Party rally. He took his place among the dignitaries on the stage, with his guitar resting between his legs, and sat quietly through long speeches by the youth representative, the black representative, the labor representative, the women's representative . . . along about the women's representative, Robbin noticed that Woody's eyes were closed and he was snoring gently. But when his turn came late in the evening, Ed nudged Woody awake and he brought the house down. The audience went wild over the last verse of the Tom Mooney song, where Woody suggested that the thing to do now was to free the *rest* of California. They wanted to hear more. So, while tuning his guitar between songs, Woody told a few stories about the goons and vigilantes he'd met on the road and then swung into one of his songs about the dust bowl refugees. He received another hooting, stomping ovation, and decided to sing another song. He'd never experienced anything like this before . . . and they, obviously, hadn't seen anything like him either. It was love at first sight.

After that, Ed Robbin became Woody's booking agent. There was a steady stream of requests to perform at fund-raising parties staged by the various Communist Party appendages and front groups, and Woody always was happy to drop by for a few songs. He'd play for a couple of dollars, or a couple of drinks, or a meal. It didn't make much difference to him, as long as they liked the music. Sometimes he'd play as many as three or four parties a night and then drag Ed down to skid row—where Woody appeared to be a rather well-known figure—and play some more.

Although he continued to write and sing the traditional country-style songs for his radio program (he called himself "Woody, the Lone Wolf" after Lefty Lou's departure), he began to devote more time to the serious, political songs his new audience—which was virtually his sole source of income—enjoyed. He wrote songs about the stuffed shirts and businessmen he'd hated since Okemah, including a clever waltz called "The Jolly Banker" (best line: "I take a great interest in all that I do"). He also wrote a series of ballads about outlaws, celebrating them as the populist heroes they'd been back in Oklahoma, as poor people who preyed on the rich. He wrote about the Dalton gang, who'd camped out near Jerry P. Guthrie's old farm on the Big Deep Fork, and about the brazen woman outlaw Belle Starr. But the most famous of his outlaw ballads, and one of his finest pieces of work, was "The Ballad of Pretty Boy Floyd," which he wrote in March of 1939.

It was a song that was calculated to outrage "proper" people and to entertain the Okies in the migrant camps: Woody's Pretty Boy was a heroic figure, a victim of circumstance who killed a deputy sheriff (in a fair fight) for insulting his wife, and then had to flee to the backwoods and live as an outcast as "Every crime in Oklahoma was added to his name." But if the police considered Pretty Boy a criminal, he was a hero to the poor farmers who gave him food and shelter and, in return for their hospitality, often found that their mortgage had been paid off or a thousand-dollar bill left at the dinner table. As the song progressed, Woody's claims for his hero became more extravagant: Pretty Boy even sent a truckload of groceries to provide Christmas dinner for all the families on relief in Oklahoma City. And if the point still wasn't quite clear, Woody hammered it home with two beautifully simple last verses:

Now as through this world I ramble
I've seen lots of funny men
Some will rob you with a six-gun
And some with a fountain pen.

But as through this life you travel
And as through this life you roam
You will never see an outlaw
Drive a family from its home.

Meanwhile, Woody had received his first notice in the *People's World*. It was a fleeting reference in an article about the growing success of Ed Robbin's Los Angeles radio show: "One of Ed's most ardent fans is an Oklahoma hill-billy whose program directly follows that of the *People's World*. One day the hill-billy, his name is Woody, came to Ed with a song he'd written about Tom Mooney's release from prison. It was real folk music, Ed says, ending on the militant note, 'and now lets free California too . . .' Woody, who has a native class consciousness, often picks up political angles from Ed's broadcasts and transforms them into song."

Actually, Woody was allowing his class consciousness to seem a bit more "native" than might normally have been the case. He sensed that the more proletarian he appeared, the more successful he'd be with his new fans. He had played the rube rather shamelessly on the radio with Lefty Lou, and now that tendency became more pronounced . . . especially after John Steinbeck's *The Grapes of Wrath* was published that April and the Okies achieved a new celebrity status in the party's martyrology of the oppressed. Woody, who was shabby and unshaven on a good day, could seem as oppressed as anybody. Even Robbin was convinced that he was almost totally uneducated and unread, that he came from a poor farm family, and had worked with the migrants picking fruit. Ed figured that Woody was too naïve politically to want to join the Communist Party, although he did bring him to group (in later, McCarthy, jargon: "cell") meetings, where Woody often performed to type by falling asleep during the heavy rhetorical discussions. One day when Ed asked him whom he admired most in the world, Woody said Jesus Christ and Will Rogers.

So it was pretty embarrassing, and Ed didn't quite know what to do, when Woody asked if he could write a column for "that there *People's World* newspaper you got there."

"Well . . ." Ed stumbled, trying to imagine Woody's cornball humor alongside the Olympian dispatches from Browder and the others, "why don't you write one or two sample columns and we'll see?"

The next day Woody appeared at KFVD with a sheaf of columns and cartoons—Ed hadn't known Woody was an accomplished cartoonist—and some of them were quite funny in a sly, political sort of way. Ed sent the material to Al Richmond, the newspaper's editor, at the main office in San Francisco.

Richmond was a talented journalist who had transformed a dour weekly called the *Western Worker* into the bright, daily *People's World*, which seemed to embody all the enthusiasm of the Popular Front. Despite the predictably turgid political analyses and "light" features about the Soviet Union with headlines like "Where There's More Freedom Than You Ever Dreamed Of," it was a surprisingly well-written newspaper, with lively sports and entertainment pages and columnists like Mike Quin, whose Irish saloon socialism usually took the form of finely crafted comic dialogues between members of the proletariat. It had a weekend magazine with comics, recipes, a teen-age page, and a women's column by Elizabeth Gurley Flynn (with much encouragement given to the ugly lisle stockings Communist women were supposed to wear while boycotting fascist Japan's silk). Still, it was considered a rather daring move when the editor agreed to publish Woody's country humor without, as Richmond later noted, "serious examination of his political credentials or antecedents, much less an ideological screening test." And also without pay.

On May 11, the column was announced on the front page and Woody was touted as "the dustbowl refugee, songster and homespun philosopher who has won thousands of friends through his program on KFVD." Thereafter, he appeared on the editorial page each day. The column rarely was longer than a paragraph, crushed at the bottom of the page under the weight of Harry Gannes's political philosophizings above. It was called "Woody Sez" and was often accompanied happily by one of his cartoons.

Cornball humor is a difficult trick under the best of circumstances, and Woody's task wasn't made any easier by the daily

format and the need for political relevance . . . nor did his taste-
less, condescending use of bad grammar and misspellings help
very much. Most of the early material he submitted was rejected,
and many of the early columns that appeared should have been,
but it was surprising how frequently Woody's blithe spirit burst
past the limitations:

> Here's a definition for Relief: Relief (noun): It is 2 people
> and one of them has accumulated the property of both; and
> then poses as some sort of a "giver." . . . They first re-
> lieve you of what you got, then "Relief" you for what you
> get. . . . An when the highups can invent a way to give
> you four bits and get back a dollar you will get some relief.

> The national debit is one thing I caint figger out. I heard a
> senator on a radeo a-saying that we owed somebody 15
> jillion dollars. I don't know their name but I remember the
> price. Called it the national debit. If the nation is the gov-
> ernment, and the government is the people, then I guess
> the people owes the people, that means I owe me and you
> owe you, and I forget the regular fee, but if I owe myself
> something, I would be willing to just call it off rather than
> have senaters argue about it, and I know you would do the
> same and then we wouldn't have no national debit.

> I never stopped to think of it before, but you know—a
> policeman will jest stand there an let a banker rob a farmer,
> or a finance man rob a workin man. But if a farmer robs a
> banker—you wood have a hole dern army of cops out a
> shooting at him. Robbery is a chapter in etiquette.

> You mite say that Wall St. is the St. that keeps you off
> Easy St.

> I ain't a communist necessarily, but I been in the red all
> my life.

One day in July, Ed Robbin introduced Woody to an old college
friend of his from Illinois, an actor named Will Geer, who'd just
arrived in town. Geer had a reputation as one of the more "political" people on the Broadway stage. He'd spent much of his
spare time back East doing agitprop theater work in factories and
coal mines for the radical New Theater League. He was closely

associated with the Communist Party—his wife, Herta Ware, was the granddaughter of a founder and still-active leader of the American party, "Mother" Ella Bloor—but, like Woody, Geer wasn't a member himself.

He was a happy, expansive blowhard of a man whose two great loves were gardening (he had a degree in botany) and performing. Although he was a well-respected Shakespearian and a celebrated character actor, Will Geer was at his very best on a makeshift stage in front of an audience of workers. He loved watching them grimace, cheer, hoot, and stomp as he played the villain—the evil landlord or factory owner—in the crudest of political skits. He didn't mind crudity. But he'd also recite passages from Walt Whitman, or Mark Twain, or Shakespeare, and encourage his audiences to fight fascism, organize a union, and read the *Daily Worker* or the *People's World* if they wanted to read the truth.

He'd fallen in love with country music back in 1927 when, as a young actor playing summer stock in West Virginia, he'd met a ballad singer named Jack Frost and invited him along on a tour of the coal mines. Not only did the miners love the music, but Will loved acting out the melodramatic ballad stories. After that, he tried to travel with a ballad singer whenever he did agitprop work. On his most recent trip, he'd taken a young, smooth-voiced Indiana college boy named Burl Ives. And now that he was in California, he wanted to bring theater to the migrant workers and was looking for a ballad singer to accompany him, which was one reason why Ed Robbin had brought Woody over to visit.

There was another reason: Mary Guthrie happened to be pregnant again, and Will was looking for pregnant women. He had come to Los Angeles to star in a movie about childbirth called *Fight for Life*, to be produced by the U.S. government and directed by the noted documentarist Pare Lorentz. He would play a doctor who runs a prenatal clinic and teaches poor women to give birth safely in their homes. Herta, who also was pregnant, would appear in the movie too.

Mary hadn't seen all that much of Woody in recent months, what with all the fund-raising parties and nights on skid row . . . but apparently just enough. She hadn't been very happy, at first, about being pregnant again, but now she was going to be in the movies (and so was Amalee, who *also* was pregnant), and Woody seemed genuinely happy that she was "fragrant" again, and went around saying clever things about trees and fruit. What's more, Will was starting to bring Woody to fancy Hollywood parties—they played for Eddie Albert, for the gang at the Hal Roach studios, for John Garfield and the Group Theater refugees from New York, and even for John Steinbeck himself one night. It looked to Mary as if Woody was finally hitting the big time, in spite of himself. A reporter for the Hollywood *Tribune* wrote a very favorable story about him: "There's never any bitterness in Woody, but his laughter just digs its hooks into the upper crust that has pushed his people around. . . . There are so many hillbillies who sing over the radio, so many voices that drum on through night and day, that this voice might be lost to some of us, which would be a shame, wouldn't it?"

Mary didn't even mind the left-wing business so much when it was glamorous (although it still tended to frighten her: these people were talking against America). She'd never met anyone like Will or Herta Geer before. They managed to drift through life with a distracted informality that made them seem completely accessible, just like normal people, and yet never quite there. They collected an odd, interesting group of friends and behaved in a way Mary often thought a bit risqué. Herta, especially, was a revelation: she'd traipse around wearing shorts even though she was quite pregnant.

Will and Woody made a marvelous team. Will was tall and substantial; Woody small and slight. Each was a compulsive trouper, happy to give a command performance in a telephone booth. Although there were some set pieces they developed, their performances together usually were haphazard affairs. Will loved acting out "The Philadelphia Lawyer," as Woody sang the song; Will, of course, played the lawyer, while Herta was the "Hollywood maid" and another friend, often Chuck Gordon, played the cowboy. Will also liked reciting Vachel Lindsay's poem "The Congo," with Woody pounding on the back of his guitar as though on an African drum. Within a week after Will arrived, the *People's World* was advertising "The Lustiest Party of the Year" for the benefit of Spanish war refugees, "MC'd by Broadway's Will Geer, and featuring Woody and his geetar." Several days later, the paper reported: "The Hollywood crowd that attended the affair for Spanish refugees a few days ago crackled with laughter when Woody took the mike, and then doubled up completely when Geer took over. . . . Looks like they're the new team.''

After several weeks of playing at Hollywood parties, they were ready to take the act out on the road. In midsummer, Will, Herta, Woody, and several other performers traveled north to a migrant camp near Bakersfield and performed in a big tent. Herta was amazed by the change in Woody when he stepped out in front of that audience. He was looser, more relaxed, more comfortable than she'd ever seen him in the city. And much funnier. The material was essentially the same stuff he used in his *People's World* column but, with his melodic Oklahoma accent and his impeccable sense of timing, it seemed completely different when it was spoken. He'd say something like: ''How many of you from Texas? . . . I spent some few years up in the panhandle town of Pampa, Texas, where the wheat grows and the oil flows, so they say . . . and the dust blows, and the farmer owes. Well, you know Texas is where you can see further and see less, walk further and travel less, see more cows and less milk, more trees and less shade, more rivers and less water . . . more fun . . . on less money . . . than anywhere else.''

And then, tucking his lit cigarette into the wild mess of wires at the neck of his guitar and tilting his chin up, he'd begin to sing. He seemed tiny and delicate onstage, an entirely unassuming presence and yet quite magical; an Okie, plainly enough, but with intimations of more than that: a visitor from Celtic mythology—a leprechaun, perhaps. ''True as the average,'' he often said of himself, and just as elusive. He was a haunting little man, Herta thought later, as they stopped the car and went skinny-dipping in the Kern River, still giddy from the performance, Woody flopping and splashing about like a puppy.

On August 23, 1939, the *People's World* reported, without comment, the incredible news that a delegation from Nazi Germany had arrived in the Soviet Union to discuss a non-aggression treaty between the two countries. By midafternoon that same day, the announcement of the Hitler-Stalin pact was all over the radio.

It sounded, at first, like capitalist propaganda of the basest sort. The Soviet Union, the bulwark of anti-fascism, had made common cause with Hitler. Even the staunchest of Communists were confused, sickened by the news. It was simply unbelievable. Ed Robbin, who had to go on the air that evening in Los Angeles and say something about the situation, struggled for some sort of explanation. He had no instructions from the party, just his instincts. So he blamed England. He said the Soviet Union had tried, all spring and summer, to negotiate a mutual defense treaty with the Western allies, but England and France had shown little interest—in fact, Neville Chamberlain had seemed interested in cutting a non-aggression deal with Hitler himself. So there was no choice. The Soviet Union had to protect itself *somehow* from the fascist threat. A non-aggression pact with Germany—it was not a mutual defense treaty—was the only way for the Soviet Union, for the future of socialism, to remain secure. It had to be done.

In the next several days, similar explanations began to splutter out of the party's New York headquarters. The Soviet Union wasn't pro-fascist, just pro-peace. It didn't want to get involved in a capitalist war (which, in fact, erupted a week later when Hitler used his pact with Stalin as a license to invade Poland). On August 26, the *People's World* ran Earl Browder's long, convoluted statement of the CPUSA's official position on the pact. Under his picture, there was the caption: "Wonders Why the Excitement: 'Pact Sets Peace Example for the World.' "

But there was plenty of "excitement," and dismay, throughout the party. It was as if some pagan test of faith had been sent down for the membership. Everything had flip-flopped overnight. The Popular Front came to a screeching halt, replaced by the old militant sectarianism of the early 1930's. Obviously, there was no longer a need to form alliances with moderates and liberals to meet the fascist threat; the fascist threat had been met with an alliance of an entirely different sort. Franklin Roosevelt, formerly a hero, was now a villain trying to drag America into a capitalist war on the side of the British imperialists. But worst of all, the party's attempt to build credibility as a plausible American radical alternative was shattered. If nothing else, the Hitler-Stalin pact made clear what had always been implicit—the American party was slavishly devoted to the interests of the Soviet Union. Even *that* hadn't seemed so bad during the 1930's: the Soviet Union was the home of socialism. Its occasional excesses were forgivable as the mistakes of a young, revolutionary society. But this was different . . . even if Lenin *had* said something about making deals with the devil to secure the revolution, this particular deal, with this particular devil, seemed the height of cynicism. For the first time, large numbers of Communists themselves began to wonder if the Soviet Union stood for anything more than its own preservation. The party hemorrhaged anti-fascists, especially Jews. The doubters fell away and, after the purification ritual, all that was left was a hard core of true believers able to construct brilliant, elaborate rationalizations in defense of the romantic vision they chose to believe was a "scientific" truth, but unwilling to ask themselves any of the basic questions that even a fledgling scientist must.

Woody remained true to the party, if still not a member. The pact with Germany didn't bother him very much. It was an abstraction, not nearly as important as the fact that Communists *still* were the only people organizing the migrants in the San Joaquin Valley to fight the cotton growers (who had proposed the ridiculous picking rate of sixty-five cents per hundred pounds—lower even than the year before—for the 1933 harvest). As long as the basic values stayed the same, the momentary posture of the Soviet Union wasn't important to him.

In fact, all the uproar seemed to make him *more* militant. He became outrageously outspoken in defense of the Communist Party now, in much the same way as he had responded to the attacks against his family and himself in Okemah and Pampa. He took a perverse pleasure in flaunting his radicalism, pushing it in people's faces, especially proper people, and putting them on the defensive. Sometimes he became downright silly about it, often taunting poor Mary mercilessly. When she asked him to start putting some money away for the birth of their child, he told her that in Russia the state would take care of all hospital costs. Another time, when Mary and Amalee wanted to go to the movies and asked Woody to baby-sit, he refused because "in Russia, the state does the baby-sitting."

Matt Jennings arrived in California the week after the Hitler-Stalin pact, and was distressed by the change in Woody. They went up to San Francisco to play a benefit for Harry Bridges, the Australian-born longshoremen's union leader whom the government was trying to deport because of his left-wing associations. On the way home, Woody and Matt fell into a bitter argument about religion. Woody said he simply didn't buy it anymore; he was an atheist. Religion was just hogwash intended to keep people quiet, to keep them from fighting back. Not only that, marriage was hogwash too. Free love, he said, was much more

honest. Matt, who remembered the long, sensitive talks they'd
had back in Pampa, was deeply hurt. He felt that Woody had
purposely steered the conversation in a direction guaranteed to
offend him. Matt had been endlessly patient, always defending his
brother-in-law's inexplicable behavior ("Aw, that's just Woody"
had become a stock phrase) to family and friends, but now he was
beginning to wonder if the guy wasn't just a total loss.

As the autumn progressed, Woody became more ornery. On September 18, the *People's World* reported that the peace-loving Red
Army had swept through eastern Poland, "liberating" land that had
"languished under a brutal Polish landlord and capitalist class . . ."
The Soviet invasion required a whole new level of rationalization
by the faithful. The Russians had crossed the Polish border, but
they hadn't "entered" the war. They simply had acted to "create
a buffer zone," and for the "salvation of the people of Poland
themselves . . ." Woody's response was to dig himself in deeper
with a talking blues called "More War News":

> I see where Hitler is a-talking peace
> Since Russia met him face to face—
> He just had got his war machine a-rollin',
> Coasting along, and taking Poland.
> Stalin stepped in, took a big strip of Poland and give
>   the farm lands back to the farmers.

> A lot of little countries to Russia ran
> To get away from this Hitler man—
> If I'd been living in Poland then
> I'd been glad Stalin stepped in—
> Swap my rifle for a farm . . . Trade my helmet for a sweet-
>   heart.

Meanwhile, Woody's newspaper column was beginning to reflect a countrified version of the Soviet Union's bellicose paci-
fism:

> Locate the man who profits by war and strip him of his
> profits—war will end. . . . [I'd] rather weed a few flesh
> eaters from the race than see ten nations of people hypno-
> tized to murder . . .

As long as the pore folks fights the rich folks war, you'll keep a-havin' pore folks, rich folks, and wars. . . . I wood have lots of fights if I had a nother feller to fight them for me. But since I got to do my own fightin', I try not to have no trouble. Same with everybody. Make 'em do there own fightin'—and you do away with fightin'.

Most weekends he still traveled with Will Geer and company to the migrant camps. They went to Marysville, Shafter, Indio, Brawley, and played for the construction workers on the big power dam at Redding. In early October, the cotton growers made a final offer of eighty cents per hundred pounds, but the union refused and went on strike. The situation quickly became violent. The *People's World* reported hundreds arrested, dozens beaten, and "armed bands of vigilantes" out looking for the strike leaders. A caravan of celebrities was organized to travel from Hollywood to the strike headquarters in Arvin in early October—just Mary's luck, it was the weekend she would give birth to her first son, Will Rogers Guthrie. Woody was well aware of her precarious state, but the cotton strike beckoned and he left the house on Friday without telling Mary where he was going or when he'd get back, and Amalee had to take her to the hospital.

The valley was as tense that night as Woody had ever seen it. A big warehouse had just burned, and the growers were blaming the strikers. He and Will Geer and Waldo Salt, who headed the Hollywood committee to aid the strikers, were sitting in a valley bar before the performance that evening, talking with Luke Hinman, one of the UCAPAWA organizers, when someone rushed in and said the sheriff was outside, looking for Luke . . . who calmly swallowed the last of his beer, said "G'night," and stepped out a window as the sheriff burst in the door. Inspired, Woody wrote a parody of "Greenback Dollar," which he performed an hour later in the big wooden union hall with people literally hanging from (well, sitting on) the rafters:

> I ain't gonna pick your 80¢ cotton,
> Ain't gonna starve myself that way.
> Gonna hold out for a dollar and a quarter.
> Will they take us back again?

Not exactly a memorable song, but a big hit among the strikers. It was the first of many picket-line songs he'd write. Almost all of them would be forgotten as soon as a settlement was reached, but Woody didn't mind. He loved watching the workers sing his words, loved seeing them used as *weapons* in a strike. It made him feel useful.

He was still the professional innocent, still the adult child—he reminded Ed Robbin of Mishkin in *The Idiot*—and, in the wonderful, dangerous way that children and naïfs have, could give himself completely to whatever he believed in. That autumn, he radiated a revolutionary fervor that seemed boundless and imposing to the Hollywood progressive types who accompanied him to Arvin. People like Waldo Salt, a talented screenwriter who would suffer later because of his left-wing views, were intimidated by Woody's effortless purity. They were merely weekend radicals, but he was the real thing—the ultimate proletarian, "the voice of his people," as they'd so often described him at fund-raising parties . . . and as he proved that night in Arvin. Woody—an innocent, but no fool—picked up on their deference and treated them with casual disdain, causing some to struggle all the harder for his approval . . . which, in his blunt, southwestern way, he never granted.

He was especially merciless toward Burl Ives, who was visiting California. Ives not only sang too sweetly (and pretentiously, Woody thought: "Burl sings like he was born in lace drawers," he later said) to be authentic, he tended to fudge his politics to fit his audience. He was a chubby, kindly sort who was defenseless against Woody's needling. "He had a chip on his shoulder," Ives would later say. "His mind worked so fast that you couldn't keep up with him, and sometimes I just felt like decking him, but Woody was so small and delicate that it just didn't seem fair." One day Ives visited the radio show and, after suffering a poisonous introduction, was asked to sing. When he finished, Burl suddenly realized that Woody had vanished . . . and wasn't about to come back and bail him out. He was left to fumble through the rest of the program on his own.

Actually, Woody's antics and his radicalism were beginning to cause him problems at the station. Not only had he lost much of his audience, but he was being red-baited for the first time—and by KFVD's cowboy singer, Stuart Hamblen, of all people.

Hamblen often made cutting remarks on the air about the two Commies, Woody and Ed Robbin. He was especially tough on Robbin, who unfortunately had just bought a *red* Chevrolet.

A far more serious problem, though, was Frank Burke. Like many other progressives, he'd felt personally betrayed by the Hitler-Stalin pact . . . and doubly betrayed because his protégé, Woody, had gone along with the Communists on it. He shuddered when he heard songs like "More War News" wafting out over his airwaves, and began to complain about them. Woody's response was to make fun of Burke's editorials on his show. When the Soviet Union, in another defensive aggression, invaded little Finland in November—and Woody once again stood firm— his relationship with Burke disintegrated beyond repair. He never told anyone the exact circumstances of the final break, but the radio show ended.

Then Will Geer returned to New York to play the lead in *Tobacco Road* on Broadway, and Woody was left to perform solo again at the fund-raising parties that were his livelihood. He didn't do very well at it. He'd played for each of the Communist groups in Los Angeles so frequently during the past year that they were tired of him—a hillbilly with politics was a novelty in the beginning, but there were only so many times you wanted to hear the joke about the dust being so thick the farmers ran their plows upside down. Even the Hollywood crowd, impressed but not very comfortable in his presence, steered clear of him. Ed Robbin still used him as the entertainment for a series of issues forums he held on Sundays, but he found that Woody was talking more and playing less, desperately searching for laughs, and the audiences were bored with him.

There wasn't much left to do in California. He decided that his best bet probably was to take Will Geer up on his (loose) invitation to join him in New York. First, though, he would go home to Pampa for the holidays and deposit Mary and the kids there while he went off to seek his fortune. He had sung and talked about the dust bowl so much that he was actually beginning to miss it a little. One of the last songs he wrote at KFVD was a wistful ballad called "I'm A-Goin' Back to th' Farm," in which he complained that he was tired of roaming around the country looking for work, that he was going back home to where there was "elbow room" and a man could settle down (although he added that it was kind of *hard* to settle down because "the rich folks own the land"). The same tone began to sneak into his newspaper column: "Wonder where we'll migrate to next? I hope folks choose a comfortable place to migrate to . . . but I reckon the world has always been short on comfortable places. Leastwise, I've never found 'em by huntin' for 'em."

By Thanksgiving, he had packed Mary and the kids into a not very impressive Plymouth he'd picked up eighth-hand, and they clattered back across the desert to Texas.

Pampa was agony. It was the same old dump, only worse. They moved back into the same little shack on Russell Street, which seemed shackier than ever. The same old furniture was there beneath a year's worth of dust. Within a few days—much too quickly—it felt as if they'd never left . . . except that news of Woody's political conversion had preceded him, and people tended to avoid him in town. The word was that he was peddling Commie pamphlets and talking against God. The neighbors were on the lookout for suspicious activities. Even Cluster Baker refused to invite him to his wedding, although he was more upset about the way Woody treated Mary than by any of the radical business.

Woody, hurt by the snub, wrote Cluster and his new bride a long, moody letter that seemed to reflect his old Pampa gushiness more than his new radical asperity. It was written in one endless paragraph on a sheet of white tissue wrapping paper and, even if the writing was so sticky sweet as to appear almost a conscious parody of Woody's former, spiritual self, there was a rolling power to it. He wrote that he'd been rousting about the Jennings house, looking for something to read, when he'd come across a book in which he had inscribed, years before, the names of the Corncob Trio: "It is a rather strange and heavenly accident that those three names are yet listed so closely together after so many separations and long journeys. For the winds of the years have blown between us and the clouds of many storms have danced around us and it was said many times that we were parted, but distance matters not to friendship and there is no such thing as time." He went on to reminisce about how they'd named the Corncob Trio at one of Cal Farley's "wrassling matches," and then:

"For me to bless your married life is like a cowboy trying to bless the sky. It is perfectly hung, perfectly balanced and perfectly blessed. Marriage is something bigger and greater than you or me, and it is as durable as the sky which always remains clear and endless in spite of the clouds or planets that whirl and spin there. And since love is as endless and empty as the clear blue eternal sky, all of my blessings whether written or spoken or prayed would fall short and not be complete. But I ask you to look many days and many nights into that empty blue above your head, and I wish that same peace and that same power and that same balance and that same freedom, that same wealth, that same health, that same harmony and that same quietness and that same love in life that is birthless and deathless; I wish you nothing else.

"On the day of your marriage, in the season of your awakening, in the year of your new birth, in the land of your people . . . Woody Guthrie, Mary, all the children and all your friends."

It was an odd, spontaneous outpouring and Cluster shook his head in amazement when he read the letter. It took a lot of sand for Woody to write about how marriage was all those wonderful things and "durable as the sky" after the way he treated Mary, and yet Cluster was moved by the words in spite of himself. He would keep the letter for the rest of his life.

Woody didn't hang around long after that. Just after New Year's Day of 1940, he drove the Plymouth to Konawa, where he sold it to his brother Roy for thirty-five dollars. He didn't want to be weighed down by any ramshackle crate when he rolled into the big city; he wanted to get there free and clear.

The trip north wasn't very pleasant, as Woody had to hitch rides in the wind and snow. Worse than the weather, though, was the fact that "God Bless America," Irving Berlin's patriotic pop tune, seemed to be everywhere that winter. He had heard it in Pampa, in Konawa, on car radios, in diners, and it seemed that every time he stopped in a roadhouse for a shot of warm-up whiskey some maudlin joker would plunk a nickel in a jukebox and play it just for spite. No piece of music had bothered him so much since "This World Is Not My Home," although Bing Crosby's narcotic, lay-down-and-die version of "Wrap Your Troubles in Dreams, and Dream Your Troubles Away" had come close. "God Bless America," indeed—it was just another of those songs that told people not to worry, that God was in the driver's

seat. Some sort of response obviously was called for and, as he
hitched north and east through Appalachia's foggy ghostlands, a
string of words began to take shape in Woody's mind.

CHAPTER 5

American Spirit

In 1940, New York was the greatest city in the world. It had a population of 7,454,995, one-third of whom were foreign-born. The mayor was Fiorello La Guardia. The Empire State Building was still a novelty. Rockefeller Center was brand-new. The subway system was modern, efficient, and cost only a nickel to ride. The port handled three times as many ships and twice as much cargo as London, its closest competitor. There were three professional baseball teams, more than six hundred theaters, and dozens of daily newspapers, written in a wide variety of languages. New York was the home of network radio, Tin Pan Alley, Wall Street, and the Communist Party. Although much of the city was still struggling out from under a decade of economic hardship, the feeling downtown was fast, brash, and confident: it was swing music, Tallulah Bankhead, Chinese food, the World's Fair, Henry Luce, and Joe Louis—a golden age.

Woody wandered the midtown streets, tickled by the size of the buildings and the bustle of the crowds. He went down to the Bowery, but found it less accommodating than skid row in Los Angeles—instead of unemployed Okies just passing through, there were hard-core alcoholics groveling for pennies. More to his taste, and far more profitable, were the Tenth Avenue bars where the merchant seamen hung out. Sometimes he'd pick up Will Geer after a *Tobacco Road* performance, stop for a bowl of chili (his

141

favorite meal), and then they'd hit the bars together and stumble home to Geer's West Fifty-sixth Street apartment, where Woody had pitched camp on the living-room couch.

He was not an especially easy house guest. For one thing, he'd come off the road smelling like a cattle car and didn't seem in much of a hurry to remedy that condition . . . which troubled Herta Geer, who had a newborn baby and wanted to keep the apartment as germ-free as possible. After several days of thudding hints, Will was forced to take direct action one morning when he found himself in the bath and a reeking Guthrie adjacent on the toilet, playing the guitar. He simply lifted Woody off the seat and deposited him in the tub, then poured in a bottle of pine oil and handed him a sloe gin fizz to mute any protests. The strategy worked so well that Woody's sloe gin fizz baths became a matter of course for the next few weeks.

Even when clean, though, he was something of a bother. Herta was on a strict timetable with the baby—it was the era when babies were kept antiseptic and scheduled—and Woody wasn't much for keeping time. She'd find him asleep on the couch in the middle of the day, forcing her into the kitchen or bedroom, cramping her life. He left her very little time alone with Will and, what's more, had somehow "borrowed" her new Martin guitar and was taking it out on the town with him each night. Still, Herta felt very close to Woody and protective of him. He was so innocent: when he asked what the rent was on the apartment and Will said a hundred fifty dollars, Woody thought it was for the entire year. He could be utterly charming at times, singing to the baby, lecturing Will on fatherly responsibilities, and leaving hastily written—but often clever—ballads in the refrigerator as payment when he helped himself to food. One was a version of "I Ain't Got No Home" called "I Don't Feel at Home on the Bowery No More," at the bottom of which he noted: "Written February 18, 1940, in the city of New York on West 56th Street in Will Geer's house, in the charge of his wine and the shadow of his kindness."

Herta couldn't imagine kicking him out. She confided her problem to a friend, who suggested that it might be best to write Woody a note, explaining her discomfort and leaving the solution up to him, which Herta did, depositing it on his chest one afternoon while he was taking a nap. Then she hid in the bedroom and waited until she heard him stirring. He was halfway out the door by the time she reached the living room. "Woody," she said, unable to look him in the eye, "you must come back and have dinner with us from time to time. Don't be a stranger now."

"Yeah, I'll do that. I'll do that," he said, and walked out the door with her Martin slung over his shoulder.

He bounced around the city for several days, spending a night with Burl Ives in his new, fancy apartment on Riverside Drive. They sang songs and caroused until very late, and Ives fixed the convertible sofa in the living room for Woody—his first guest—to sleep in, then passed out. He awoke to find Guthrie gone and the sofa a mess. Woody apparently had decided to sleep with his clothes on, including his heavy, dirty lace-up boots, which had soiled Ives's sheets beyond repair.

After that, he checked into Hanover House, a fleabag hotel on the corner of Sixth Avenue and Forty-third Street, near Times Square. Angry, frustrated, and feeling sorry for himself, he took it out on Irving Berlin, finally writing down the words that he'd been turning over in his mind for several weeks. At the top of a piece of loose-leaf paper, he wrote "God Blessed America," and began the first verse:

> This land is your land, this land is my land
> From California to Staten Island

He stopped, crossed out "Staten" and put in "New York."

> From the Redwood Forest, to the Gulf Stream waters
> God Blessed America for me.

He wrote five more verses in the dingy hotel room. The tune was taken from the Carter Family's "Little Darlin', Pal of Mine," which, in turn, had come from an old Baptist hymn, "Oh My Lovin' Brother."

> As I went walking that ribbon of highway
> And saw above me the endless skyway
> And saw below me that golden valley, I said
> God Blessed America for me.

> I roamed and rambled and followed my footsteps
> To the sparkling sands of her diamond deserts

And all around me, a voice was sounding:
God Blessed America for me.

Was a big high wall there that tried to stop me
A sign was painted said: Private Property.
But on the back side, it didn't say nothing—
God Blessed America for me.

When the sun come shining, then I was strolling
In the wheat fields waving, and dust clouds rolling
The voice was chanting as the fog was lifting:
God Blessed America for me.

One bright sunny morning in the shadow of the steeple
By the relief office I saw my people—
As they stood there hungry,
I stood there wondering if
God Blessed America for me.

He noted at the bottom of the page: "All you can write is what you see," and signed it—he was beginning to sign all his pages now—"Woody G."and marked the date, February 23, 1940, and the location. Then he completely forgot about the song, and didn't do anything with it for another five years.

While Herta Geer worried over the most gracious way to evict Woody, her husband had been busy lining up work for him. In addition to the usual assortment of fund-raising parties, Will had arranged several important concert appearances. The first, on February 25, was a huge benefit for Spanish refugees at Mecca Temple. Although Woody's dust bowl songs were well received that evening (the movie version of *The Grapes of Wrath* had just opened), he won the audience completely with a ballad describing the recent American Youth Congress convention in Washington, which he'd attended on his way north. The delegates, most of them leftists, had stood outside the White House in the rain, protesting war loans to Finland and demanding more public works jobs, and had received a scolding from the President. The song—called "Why Do You Stand There in the Rain?"—mocked Roosevelt as a myopic aristocrat unable to comprehend the "strange goings on, on the White House-Capitol lawn.'' The last verse brought the crowd to its feet:

> *Now the guns of Europe roar*
> *As they have so oft before*
> *And the warlords play their same old game again.*
> *While they butcher and they kill*
> *Uncle Sammy foots the bill,*
> *With his own dear children standing in the rain.*

Then, on March 3, Will Geer organized a ''Grapes of Wrath Evening'' to benefit the ''John Steinbeck Committee for Agricultural Workers,'' a show that changed the course of Woody's career and, perhaps, of American music as well. It was held at the Forrest Theater, home of *Tobacco Road*, and featured ''American Ballad Singers and Folk Dancers: Will Geer, Alan and Bess Lomax, Aunt Molly Jackson, Leadbelly, Woodie Guthrie, the Pennsylvania Miners and the Golden Gate Quartet.'' Most of the performers—notably Leadbelly and Aunt Molly Jackson—had appeared in New York before, but usually for small, often academic, gatherings. There had been other ''folk'' music recitals, but this would be remembered as the first really important one, the first before a large, mainstream audience.

Several days before the show, Woody was promoted in a *Daily Worker* blurb as ''a real dust bowl refugee and discovery of Geer's who was brought to New York recently, especially to appear on this evening's program. 'Woody' is a folk singer who chants not only the songs of his region, but composes unique and moving ballads of topical interest. His most recent effort, which will be heard Saturday evening, was dedicated to the American Youth Congress members who listened to President Roosevelt recently.'' Along with the story was a photo of a rather stern-looking Woody in the *Daily Worker* offices, strumming his (Herta's) guitar, a western hat pushed back on his head, and the caption: '''Woody'—that's the name, straight out of Steinbeck's 'The Grapes of Wrath'—sings People's Ballads.''

And so Woody wasn't entirely unheralded when he ambled out onto the stage of the Forrest Theater that evening, the second act on the program after Aunt Molly Jackson. He stood alone, fixed by a spotlight slanting down from the balcony, and seemed to fit in perfectly with Jeeter Lester's tarpaper shack on the *Tobacco*

Road set behind him. He scratched his head with a guitar pick and said, "Howdy," squinting up at the cheap seats in the same unassuming, slightly bemused way that he'd surveyed every house since the Taylor tent show: as if he'd wandered in by accident, but didn't mind hanging around and singing a few songs as long as he was there. Muttering something about how pleased he was to perform in a "Rapes of Graft" show, he tilted up his chin, leaned into his guitar, and began to sing. Off in the wings, Alan Lomax snapped to attention and felt a surge of adrenaline as he realized—quickly, viscerally, no question about it—that the little man onstage was someone he'd often thought about but feared he'd been born too late to meet: the great American frontier ballad writer.

Alan Lomax was twenty-three years old at the time, and did not suffer from a lack of enthusiasm. He was the assistant director of the Archive of Folk Song at the Library of Congress, and had already established his brilliance as a cultural historian and anthropological talent scout. He was the son of John Lomax, a college administrator and sometime banker who'd been, in his spare time, a legendary collector of cowboy songs (of which "Home on the Range" was his most famous find, though not his most interesting). In 1933, with his bank job gone in the crash and the family resources dwindling, John Lomax decided to see if he could earn a living doing what he loved. He managed to convince a New York publisher, Macmillan and Company, several charitable foundations, and the Library of Congress to support him. He also managed to persuade his seventeen-year-old son, Alan, to spend the summer helping him to haul a 350-pound Presto recording machine from prison to prison in the Deep South, in search of work songs sung by the black inmates. Alan was then a student at the University of Texas and, like many students of the period, something of a radical. He began the trip reluctantly, as a favor to his father, but soon realized that the songs they sought were not only beautiful and compelling but also *political.* Music was the way black prisoners, some of them wrongly convicted and all horribly mistreated victims of a racist system, communicated their anguish. By recording their songs, he could give them a voice. His father, a political conservative, loved the music because it was a distinctive, glorious American art form. It was privilege enough for him to collect it. Alan loved it for all the same reasons, and one other: it was, potentially, a weapon in the class struggle. Throughout his career, he'd see himself as a promoter as well as a collector, someone who found ways to bring the music and the message to the widest possible audience.

It was on this trip that the Lomaxes discovered, at the Angola State Prison Farm in Louisiana, Huddie Ledbetter, who was called Leadbelly by the other inmates. His ability on the twelve-string guitar, his range, creativity, and sheer magnetism, left the Lomaxes breathless. Ten years earlier, while serving a thirty-year sentence for murder in Texas, Leadbelly had sung and jived his way to a pardon by Governor Pat Neff. Now, serving ten years for assault with intent to murder, he made the same trick work again: John Lomax took his musical plea for clemency, on record, to Governor O. K. Allen, who set him free several months later. Hiring on as Lomax's chauffeur and traveling companion—Alan's former role—Leadbelly was brought to New York, where he charmed college audiences and caused a brief stir in the press. He left the elder Lomax after a year, chafing under his white paternalism, wanting to control his own money, and tired of having to wear his convict clothes each time he performed, ''for exhibition purposes,'' as John Lomax put it.

Leadbelly appeared almost exclusively before academic audiences up North because they were about the only white people who were interested. Folk music was a scholarly pursuit, the province of a small fraternity of professors who were mostly interested in finding out how Elizabethan ballads had crossed the Atlantic and changed over the years. The field was so far removed from reality that people like the Lomaxes and Carl Sandburg—who did it for fun—were considered vaguely disreputable. ''Presumably,'' the elder Lomax said after a snub from the American Folklore Society, ''the collector must go out among the people wearing a cap and gown.'' John Lomax's particular sin was that, when he published Cowboy Songs in 1910, he didn't simply reprint the best version he'd collected of, say, the classic Texas outlaw ballad ''Sam Bass,'' but mixed together his favorite verses from several versions—in other words, the folklorists felt he was tampering with the data. The very fact that he was interested in cowboy songs, which some early scholars considered peripheral, and Negro music, widely considered to be barbaric, made him suspect to begin with. And Alan Lomax, with his flagrant activism, was simply beyond salvage.

There were others, though, who understood that the Lomaxes

were onto something important. One was a gaunt, aristocratic musicologist named Charles Seeger. He had begun his career with classical training and hoped to pick up where Wagner left off, but he found himself intrigued by the early recordings of tribal music the anthropologists were bringing back from Africa and Asia in the late 1920's, and also was swept up by the radical politics of the times. He began to wonder about the socioeconomic differences between classical and folk music. By 1935, he was writing in a small Marxist journal called *Music Vanguard* that "fine art" music was the property of the dominant classes, for which it was made. Pop music was a bastardization of the "fine art" tradition; it was "crumbs from the table of the rich and powerful . . . combined with various story elements." But folk music was the music of the proletariat and, therefore, inherently progressive. Seeger and his second wife, Ruth Crawford, joined forces with the Lomaxes in the early 1930's, concentrating on the difficult question of how to write down the music—as opposed to the words—of the songs being collected.

Seeger was something of a renegade member of the Pierre Degeyter Club, a society of American Communist musicians, named after the co-author of "The Internationale." It was formed in the arrogant, separatist period of American Communism; the days of no alliances, no compromises, not even in the arts. Just as Communist labor organizers were attempting to form their own separate trade unions in the early 1930's, Communist musicians wanted to develop a new, distinct "proletarian" music—music the victorious workers would enjoy after the revolution. To the Degeyter group, this seemed to mean the ponderous, hortatory choral tradition of the German Communist Hanns Eisler. Their idea of proletarian music was a "workers' chorus" singing clangorous, oddly formal compositions like "The Scottsboro Boys Must Not Die" or "The Comintern." When Seeger brought Aunt Molly Jackson, fresh from the Harlan County coal wars, to the Degeyter Club and had her sing "I Am a Union Woman," the reaction was "That's very nice, but what does it have to do with proletarian music?"

One of the few others interested in the problem was the *Daily Worker* columnist Mike Gold, who was always searching for the proletarian writer-poet who'd become "Shakespeare in overalls." Gold would ruminate at length about the need for a "Communist Joe Hill," but didn't know where to look for him. He liked the

music coming out of the Harlan coal and Gastonia textile strikes—
the songs of Ella May Wiggin, who was murdered by company
thugs at Gastonia; of Aunt Molly Jackson and her brother Jim
Garland, and her stepsister, Sarah Ogan, who actually wrote a
song called "I Hate the Capitalist System"; of Florence Reece,
who tore an old calendar off the wall of her shack and wrote
"Which Side Are You On?"—but he regarded them more as
interesting oddities than proletarian artists: hillbillies with politics.

But then, in 1935, the Popular Front came in and Earl Browder's dictum that "Communism is twentieth century Americanism" sent many left-wing intellectuals scurrying off to find
out just what *Americanism* was. Now that the party policy was
to fight fascism by building alliances with liberals and "other
progressives," Communist artists looked for ways to bring their
work to the largest number of people, to simplify, to popularize,
to Americanize. They studied the country and its people and its
past, and came to be captivated by the color and diversity of it
all in the same intense way that they experienced everything else.
Although the process wasn't nearly as mechanical as it sounds in
retrospect, there was a burst of appreciation for America, of *pa-
triotism*, among left-wing artists starting in the mid-1930's that
swept across the political and cultural spectrum, and launched
one of the happiest, most accessible, demonstrative, and inspi-
rational periods in American cultural history.

This coincided with—and perhaps triggered—a widespread realization that the American people were surviving the Depression
without going completely haywire; that many had relied on re-
sourcefulness, wit, and sheer willpower to get by; and that only
an extraordinary people could suffer such hard times so extraor-
dinarily. There was a growing sense that the victims of the Depression, those who'd suffered and survived, were special . . .
perhaps even *superior* people; much could be learned from them.
Intellectuals who'd sneered at small-town America throughout the
cynical 1920's were awestruck by its resilience now.

There was a surge of journalists going out and talking to the
people, trying to *experience* the country. A raft of "I've Seen
America" books began to appear. Journalism—especially pho-
tojournalism—dominated the period. There was a "documentary" movement in all the arts, an attempt to accomplish in other
fields what the Lomaxes were doing in music, to rediscover "the

people" as a source of creativity. One way to do it was through oral history, the technique of simply recording for posterity what unsophisticated people—former slaves, folk singers, storytellers, anyone—had to say about their lives. But there were other ways: in painting, Thomas Hart Benton tried to splash all the folklore of the American West onto his canvases, cramming them with people and wheat fields and contraptions. In modern dance, the formerly harsh and remote Martha Graham moved into a warmer, more theatrical, "American" period. Her *American Document* (1938) was a minstrel show which surveyed the nation's history, using an "Interlocutor" who quoted from the Declaration of Independence and Emancipation Proclamation, and closed with a section called "Now," in which "the people" triumphed over economic adversity: "We are three women; we are three million women. We are the mothers of the hungry dead; we are the mothers of the hungry living," the Interlocutor announced as the women writhed onstage, followed by a strong, free-striding, confident man: "This is one man; this is one million men. This man has power. It is himself, and you," and, as the dancers moved into a series of triumphant leaps, the Interlocutor closed with a quote from Lincoln's Gettysburg Address: "that government of the people, by the people and for the people shall not perish from the earth."

The very notion of *culture* itself was overhauled and made more democratic. No longer did it merely refer to the European "fine arts" tradition: now it could include practically everything creative, the *style* of the country down to the simplest turns of phrase, which the noted folklorist B. A. Botkin called "folksay." It was an exhilarating, almost giddy discovery: America had a culture. It also had a new hero—the "common man" who suffered hard times and survived. Henry Wallace, who'd soon become Roosevelt's new Vice-President, called it the "Century of the Common Man."

In many ways, the Popular Front in culture was an attempt to create a mythology of "the people" using the guise of realism. It had its roots in "socialist realism," the Soviet poster art movement that really was nothing more than unabashed romanticism. "Before the Popular Front, you'd see a lot of paintings of bums lying in the gutter," said Joseph Solman, an activist painter of the period. "Afterwards, it was always murals of the workers marching off to glory." Among the 270,000 photographs taken of America during the Depression by such talented people as Dorothea Lange, Walker Evans, and Ben Shahn for the Farm Security Administration, very few showed people groveling, choking with hunger, or covered with filth. Roy Emerson Stryker, who headed the FSA unit, acknowledged this when he said of John Steinbeck: "He caught in words everything the photographers were trying to say in pictures: Dignity vs. despair. Maybe I'm a fool, but I believe dignity wins out. When it doesn't, then we as a people will become extinct."

But if the cultural style of the Popular Front was a bit more romantic than it acknowledged, the humanitarian spirit was very real and infectious. It was a burst of optimism and pride just when the country needed it—"the sweetest bandwagon in all history," a Communist intellectual said—and it virtually became the federal government's cultural policy in the late 1930's. Its cheerleaders were Archibald MacLeish (then Librarian of Congress), Eleanor Roosevelt, and Rexford Tugwell (who not only founded the FSA photography project but also employed Charles Seeger as a music consultant in the Resettlement Administration, which preceded FSA). Its home was, primarily, the various programs within the WPA to provide jobs for unemployed creative people: the Federal Writers Project collected folklore and other "American Stuff," and published an extensive set of guides to the states; there was a "living newspaper" produced by the Theater Project, and, of course, the Art Project's murals in libraries and post offices across the country.

In music, the Popular Front's American wave added to a growing movement among serious composers to incorporate folk themes, especially jazz, into their works. The movement's most famous proponent was George Gershwin, a popular songwriter whose early symphonic works like "Rhapsody in Blue" were sneered at by the classicists. By 1935, though, when Gershwin premiered his greatest work, *Porgy and Bess* (which he called a "folk" opera), the snobs were beginning to come around. Foremost among the "serious" composers seeking to Americanize their work was Aaron Copland. In 1938, he used snatches from several of John Lomax's cowboy songs—"I Ride an Old Paint," "The Old Chisholm Trail," and "The Dying Cowboy"—as themes in his ballet score *Billy the Kid*. But Copland apparently saw folk music merely as raw material waiting to be refined into a finished product. On one occasion, Alan Lomax brought him thirty-five variations on "John Henry" to consider for future use. Lomax played one version after another of the greatest American folk ballad, Copland dismissing each with a wave of the hand after a verse or two, as if it were an audition.

Even among those who were beginning to recognize the importance of American musical traditions, the folk performers themselves weren't very popular. The *idea* that Aunt Molly Jackson was singing the people's music was a lot more palatable than the harsh, nasal reality of her voice—she survived in New York, after being driven out of Kentucky, by running a restaurant. Even Leadbelly, easily the most impressive of the early folk singers in the city, was difficult to understand with his thick Louisiana accent and down-home ways. When Earl Robinson (whose "Ballad for Americans" had been performed by Paul Robeson in 1939) brought him to Camp Unity, the Communist Party's summer retreat, Leadbelly shocked and disheartened the audience with his songs about knife fights and "high yaller" women—those weren't the kinds of things they wanted to hear from a progressive Negro. After Robinson explained the problem, Leadbelly returned to win over the crowd with "Bourgeois Blues" and several of his other political songs.

Alan Lomax had taken over the day-to-day operation of the Library of Congress archives by then; his father, in semi-retirement, preferred to spend his time out on the road collecting. The younger Lomax was a precocious, arrogant, bearlike young man, of great appetites and greater enthusiasms. He was an idealist, inordinately protective of the music he loved, scornful of those who attempted to dilute or fancify it, and utterly contemptuous of the music executives who peddled garbage and refused to acknowledge the treasures in his storehouse. His great hope was to launch a folk music revival—a proletarian alternative to the corporate music—but that appeared to be a losing battle. The music, the *real* music, was a tradition whose time was passing with the spread of radio and mass culture. Instead of listening to Grandma sing "Barbara Allen" on the back porch, the kids—and often Grandma too—were listening to Bing Crosby on the radio. Just as New Orleans jazz had been bleached and diluted into swing music, the traditional mountain and cowboy songs were becoming "country and western." The most talented folk musicians were coming down from the mountains to follow Jimmie Rodgers' path, adapting their music to the popular styles, growing and changing with the times. Those few who remained true to their roots usually existed at the edges of society—among the oldest people, in the poorest and most remote towns, long-term convicts like Leadbelly or native radicals like Aunt Molly Jackson and her clan. They were museum pieces, priceless and rare, but not quite marketable in the mass culture. For the most part, folk music remained stranded in academia . . . although now it had at least moved into the educational mainstream and was taught to elementary school children as well as college students. In 1939, CBS radio gave Alan Lomax a weekly morning slot on its "Columbia School of the Air," so he could teach America's children their musical heritage.

And then Woody Guthrie wandered onto the stage of the Forrest Theater and breathed some life into a dying tradition. As he stood off in the wings and listened, Alan Lomax realized several things at once about the little man. Somehow, miraculously, Guthrie hadn't allowed himself to be touched by the popular styles—a little Jimmie Rodgers, maybe, and he'd certainly borrowed heavily from the Carter Family's more traditional material, but he was essentially an unwitting classicist, someone who understood the power and integrity of the traditional forms and sang the old songs in an old-fashioned way, his voice droning and nasal and high-pitched. At the same time, and even more miraculously, he was a political radical, a living affirmation of Charles Seeger's theories of the activist potential of the music— those were *political* songs he was singing in traditional fashion. Most important, though, Woody Guthrie was quite obviously a genius. His songs had the beautiful, easy-to-remember simplicity of the best of folk art. He was as good as the guy who wrote "Sam Bass" or "Jesse James" or any of the great frontier ballads—and probably better, Lomax would come to believe, because he was toting around at that moment at least a half dozen songs that were among the greatest ever written by an American. "Shakespeare in overalls," indeed.

He was also very funny. Having introduced himself with several of his dust bowl songs, Woody was now telling sly, clever stories about his first few days in New York, and the audience was roaring. "New York sure is a funny place. . . . The buildings are so high the sun don't come out until one-thirty in the afternoon, and then it's visible for seven minutes between the Empire State Building and the shoe sign over there." He started to play around with the guitar, strumming a talking-blues progression. "Actually, I believe there's more of New York underground than on top. . . . Seems like two or three times a day . . . I get lost down the old subway. . . . Electric train comes down the line . . . I catch out wrong most every time." He stopped playing, and leaned his arms on top of the guitar. "You know, they could have more people on these subway trains if they'd lay 'em down: when you got to your station, they could shoot you home like a torpedo. . . . Trains were so crowded today, you couldn't even fall down. I had to change stations twice, and both times I came out with a different pair of shoes on. . . . But you know, there *is* one thing about New York, and that is the way you can get tomorrow's paper last night, that is . . . *to*night. The capitalist papers are so far ahead of the news that they know tonight what happened tomorrow, but they never do go to the trouble of informing their readers what they really knew yesterday." And then he was off explaining what happened to the American Youth Congress in Washington, and moving toward his finale, "Why Do You Stand There in the Rain?"

Alan Lomax was tremendously excited by Woody, and invited him down to Washington. Alan loved everything about him, even the way he moved: the exaggerated way his arm swept around and his fingers came down to scratch the very top of his head like a steam shovel; the way he pooched his mouth and stroked his chin when he was thinking, the finger to the forehead when an idea came, and those eyes that seemed to take in everything and give out so very little. Woody had a repertoire far greater than that of any other folk artist Alan had ever encountered—not just the songs he'd written, but the songs he'd heard, and the places he'd been and the things he'd seen, and the things he *said*: "That feller's so rich he's got cattle in the bank and money out West," and "That boy don't care if school keeps or not," and "The barn crumpled like a calf hit with a sledge," and always, when leaving, "Take it easy, but take it."

Lomax and his wife shared a house in Arlington, Virginia, with a young director named Nicholas Ray, who'd been doing theater work for the government, and his wife. It wasn't a very formal house, but when Woody arrived about a week after the "Grapes of Wrath" concert, he made a point of flouting the few conventions there were. He refused to sit down at the table for dinner, preferring to eat standing over the sink: "I'm a road man," he said, "I don't want to get soft." Nor would he sleep in a bed, favoring a couch or the floor, his lumber jacket for a blanket: "I ain't used to them fancy feather mattresses." Nicholas Ray swears that Woody didn't remove his boots during the first two weeks he was in the house. He also drove everyone crazy by playing the same records over and over again, usually some Carter Family tune, more often than not their version of the outlaw ballad "John Hardy." One morning, as he headed off to work, Alan decided to give Woody something to keep him busy other than playing records all day. He asked him to write down a paragraph or two about his life, as background material for the recorded interviews they would be doing for the archives. When Lomax returned in the evening, Woody had finished twenty-five pages, single-spaced.

"When I began to read," Lomax later wrote, "I lost myself in the prose in the same way I was once absorbed by the first chapter of Joyce's *Ulysses*, except that what Woody had to say meant far more to me. The sentences were sometimes almost a page long, but . . . they had the looping grace and originality of the prose masters. He told of his childhood in Okemah, Oklahoma, the way he saw things when he was two and three years old. The boyhood gangs, the clubhouse, the fights in vacant lots, the drunken Indians, the half-corrupt cracker politicians and a score more original types were never so well described as here in front of my unbelieving eyes by Woody. Later I showed the manuscript to my father. As a Texan touched by the truth of his region, he agreed with me that it was one of the best American evocations of childhood."

When Lomax finished the manuscript he told Woody he was a great natural writer, and that he should never do anything else in his life. Surprised, Woody said, "About the only thing I ever learned in school was speed typing. All that stuff in books was second-hand, I thought. Writing's no profession for a man these days. With all these poor folks wandering around the country as homeless as little doggies, what I should do is strop on a couple of six-shooters and blow open the doors of the banks and feed people and give them houses. The only reason I don't do that is because I ain't got the guts."

Flattered by the tidal wave of superlatives, by the overwhelming interest Lomax took in all he did, Woody began to pull out everything he could remember (a noteworthy find was "So Long, It's Been Good to Know You," which he hadn't sung since Pampa), and Lomax was delighted by it all. After a week with Guthrie in Washington, Alan had the rapturous—and perhaps sinking—feeling that there was no need to go out *collecting* folklore any more; all he'd have to do was hang around Woody and half of America would spill out.

A constant presence during this period—he couldn't even be considered a visitor—was Charles Seeger's twenty-year-old son Peter, who was tall, thin, painfully shy, had a bad case of acne, and seemed much younger than his age. Peter was a Harvard dropout, a sometime artist and radical puppeteer who served as Alan's occasional (unpaid) helper at the Library. He had impressive native musical ability and sometimes would sit in Lomax's chinaberry tree playing the lute. He'd been in love with folk music ever since attending a North Carolina festival with his father in 1935, but hadn't decided yet where he fit in. Both his father and Alan were encouraging him to learn the five-string banjo, a folk instrument in danger of becoming extinct, and he was starting to fool around with that ("He just *looked* like a banjo," Alan would later say). On Will Geer's recommendation—they had done some radical theater work together—Peter attended the "Grapes of Wrath" benefit and immediately attached himself to Woody in Washington, watching and listening and learning all he could . . . and loving every minute of it.

In the evenings, there was a stream of visitors invited over by Alan to meet his new discovery. One of the first was his father: John Lomax was put off by Guthrie's politics and disgusted by his barnyard manners, as only a farm boy who'd raised himself by the bootstraps to gentility could be. Still, Lomax the elder had to admit he'd never heard anyone sing his beloved cowboy songs as well. Charles Seeger and his wife, Ruth, were captivated. Benjamin Botkin and other New Deal folklorists were similarly impressed. Sometimes there would be long, drunken singing contests. A topic would be chosen—dogs, faithless women, storms, eyes, *brown* eyes—and it would go around the room, each contestant offering a song until everyone was stumped. Usually it came down to Alan and Woody and, with the Library of Congress archives (Woody called them the "high dives") in his back pocket, Alan inevitably won. He rather hoped that these impressive displays of virtuosity would establish his credentials with

Woody (oddly, he felt it was *his* credentials that needed to be established), but he never really could be sure if they had their intended effect.

The ostensible purpose of Woody's visit to Washington was to record his songs for the Library of Congress archives, and that took place in three marathon sessions on March 21, 22, and 27 of 1940, at the Department of the Interior's studio. The interviews were planned in advance to sound free-form, impressionistic, and casual—more like a radio show than a collection of folklore. Indeed, Lomax had vague hopes of using the material as a radio pilot (with the two of them as a duet possibly, for at several points Alan commits his profession's ultimate sin by trying to *sing along* with his subject—although, in fairness, that may have been the result of his tendency to use liquor as an oral history lubricant). But despite the ulterior motives, the sessions went well from the start. Lomax, who'd done a wonderful series of interviews with Jelly Roll Morton the year before, knew what he was after and how to get it. He had a distinctive, reedlike *American* voice with a slight Texas lilt:

LOMAX (over instrumental): The song is "Lost Train Blues" played on harmonica and guitar by Woody Guthrie from Okemah, Oklahoma. Woody knows what that lost train means because he's ridden the "red ball" freights from one end of the country to another. In a few minutes we are going to begin a conversation with Woody Guthrie about life in the Southwest, about where he's from and where he went and what's happened.

Woody Guthrie is, I guess, about thirty years old from the looks of him [he was twenty-seven] but he's seen more in those thirty years than most men see before they're seventy. He hasn't sat in a warm house or a warm office. He's interested in looking out. He's gone into the world and he's looked at the faces of hungry men and women. He's been in hobo jungles. He's performed on picket lines. He's sung his way through every bar and saloon between Oklahoma and California. . . . And listen to that "red ball" roll. . . .

Even though he was being recorded seriously for the first time in his life, Woody didn't seem at all nervous. In fact, with his smooth, soft, mesmerizing voice and nimble mind, he dominated the proceedings, spinning yarns about Okemah, his childhood, his first square dances and early drinking experiences. Lomax, apparently trying to steer the conversation toward the nether reaches of folklore with a definite purpose in mind, asked if the boys back in Oklahoma ever made toasts when they were out drinking behind the barn:

GUTHRIE: Here's a pretty good one I used to hear down in that country: "Here's to her, and to her again. If you can't get to her, let me to her. I'm used to her."

LOMAX: Well, some of them were even worse off than that, weren't they, Woody? In the way of being a little off color, or something?

GUTHRIE: Yes, well they started there and went on down.

LOMAX: Where'd they go from there? What was the next stop?

GUTHRIE: Well, let's hear *you* say one, then I'll be remembering mine.

LOMAX: I wasn't brought up that way, Woody. You see, I didn't grow up in the country. I grew up inside a brick house. I didn't have that kind of experience. . . . I wish I had.

After Woody played a few square dance tunes, the interview glided into a surprisingly emotional moment, as Lomax asked if the Guthries had experienced hard times down in Oklahoma. Woody said yes, but "I don't know whether it's worth talking about or not. I never did talk it much," and then, as if propelled by a force he couldn't quite control, he began to describe his sister Clara's death: "Either [she] set herself afire or caught fire accidentally. There is two different stories got out about it. Anyway, she was having a little difficulty with her schoolwork, and she had to stay home and do some work"—his voice was getting tighter; he swallowed hard. "And she caught afire while she was doing some ironing that afternoon on the old kerosene stove. She run around the house twice before anyone could catch her, and the next day she died. . . .

"And my mother . . . that was a little bit too much for her nerves, her something . . ." He swallowed hard again, trying to hold his composure. Had he gone too far? "I don't know exactly how it was . . . but anyway, my mother died in the insane asylum at Norman, Oklahoma.'' And then Woody said the most extraordinary thing about his father: "My father, mysteriously for some reason, caught fire. There is some people say he set his self afire. Others say he caught fire accidentally. I always think he done it on purpose, 'cause he lost all his money. . . ." He moved on to telling funny stories about the various foster parents he'd had, careful not to mention any correct names (the Moores became the Whites). It never became personal again after that, although it was quite entertaining, with Woody singing and talking about his experiences as a hobo, in the dust bowl and California. When Alan's voice gave out during the March 27 session, his talented wife, Elizabeth Littleton, stepped in and asked the questions.

Although it would be twenty-five years before the Library of Congress recordings reached the public (in the form of a three-record set), Alan worked up a much-abbreviated version of the interview as the script for his "Columbia School of the Air" program of April 2. He arrived at the CBS studios in New York for dress rehearsal on the afternoon before the show only to find Guthrie (who was, perhaps, rather full of the fact that he was a newly discovered genius) in an inexplicably ornery mood. He just didn't like the director, George Zachary, who was among the network's top people and acted as though he expected to be treated accordingly. Alan tried to impress his protégé with the importance of the occasion—Woody's future in network radio and, perhaps, Alan's own were at stake—but Woody was having none of it. He sulked. Whenever Zachary gave him a speed-up signal, he slowed down. The half-hour script stretched into an hour and a half. Finally the director took the bait and blew his stack, and Woody stormed out.

Lomax, chasing right after him, took an intuitive gamble and decided to act as if nothing important had just happened. If Woody didn't want to mention it, he wouldn't either. They proceeded on down to Leadbelly's apartment on East Tenth Street and spent a raucous evening singing and drinking, tumbling into bed quite late and quite loaded. It was a double bed, and Alan made sure that Woody was securely sandwiched between himself and the wall, and couldn't get out.

They were up again at the crack of dawn, and Woody decided he wanted to go for a walk. They walked and walked, heading down toward Wall Street, and talked about all sorts of things . . . except the obvious one. They stopped in a cafeteria for breakfast, and several cups of coffee after breakfast.

Finally, Woody rather nonchalantly asked, "What's the time?"

"About seven-thirty."

"Well, shouldn't we go on up and do that show now?"

They brought it off without a hitch, of course, ending exactly at 29 minutes and 30 seconds, as planned, and Alan paid Woody the astronomical sum of two hundred dollars for his performance. Eventually the show won an award as the best educational program of the year.

Lomax had good connections at CBS, which tended to be a bit more progressive than the other networks, and he began to promote Woody. One executive who was immediately interested was Norman Corwin, a Popular Front-ish producer and writer of radio spectaculars in which "the people" always seemed to be on the march. The year before, he had produced the famous Paul Robeson broadcast of "Ballad for Americans." In addition to his extravaganzas, Corwin had a popular Sunday-afternoon variety show called "The Pursuit of Happiness," and Woody was invited to perform on the April 21, 1940, broadcast. He would be paid fifty dollars simply for singing one of his songs. He was introduced that afternoon by Burgess Meredith, the show's host: "Our next guest really has traveled. He is Woody Guthrie of Oklahoma, one of those Okies who, dispossessed from their farms, journeyed in jalopies to California. There, Woody, who always had been a great man at playing the guitar and making up songs of his own, managed to get some work performing at a small radio station. He got a lot of fan letters, one of which was from John Steinbeck, who wrote the saga of the Okies. Not long ago, he set out for New York and rode the freights to get here . . . and we've asked him to perform one of his own compositions. We present Woody Guthrie and 'If You Ain't Got the Do Re Mi.' "

Mike Quin, the *People's World* columnist, was so thrilled to hear his old colleague singing on network radio from New York that he wrote in the paper's April 25 edition: "Sing it, Woody, sing it! Karl Marx wrote it, and Lincoln said it, and Lenin did it. Sing it, Woody, and we'll all laugh together." Quin's column, reprinted in the *Daily Worker*, added to a small left-wing bandwagon that was beginning to roll—after all, it wasn't every day that a Communist newspaper columnist was a hit on network radio. Actually, Woody had been attracting attention since his "Grapes of Wrath" benefit appearance. On March 17, Art Shields wrote in the *Worker*: "Will Rogers had his points, but I don't mind telling you that I'd a heap rather have Woody . . . the most sparkling philosopher that ever hit the *Grapes of Wrath* trail." Several days later, the *Worker* began to run "Woody Sez" for the first time (the column had continued, sporadically, even after he left California), in a small box on the entertainment page. Woody was becoming a celebrity in New York Communism, which was a not inconsiderable achievement in those days.

"New York was then a very Russian city," another recent arrival from the hinterlands, Saul Bellow, would later write. "New York dreamed of leaving North America and merging with Russia." And, in a way, it was true: the city was the one place in America where Communism had virtually became a subculture—not just in the intellectual precincts of Manhattan, but also in many working-class sections of the Bronx and Brooklyn. The party ran schools, summer camps, a housing project in the Bronx, and controlled much of the local labor movement. The International Workers' Order (I.W.O.)—a predominantly Jewish fraternal order allied with the CP—provided low-cost doctors, health insurance, funeral arrangements, and, in some neighborhoods, even a social center.

But the party's influence went far beyond the hard-core members (never much more than 100,000 nationally). A large number of people in the creative professions in New York considered themselves "progressive"—a favorite euphemism—at the very least. Few were actually party members, since that involved a commitment something on the order of marriage, but most looked to the Communists for political (and often cultural) direction. In such an environment, Woody's clear-eyed "native class consciousness" more than made up for his frequent ideological flights of fancy (like his insistence that Jesus Christ was a socialist outlaw). His integrity seemed every bit as imposing as it had to the Hollywood radicals, especially his apparent willingness to take chances with his career by appearing in the *Daily Worker* each day. He even wrote in his column about "this false and silly thing called a reputation, which causes plumb good folks [to keep] from joining what they'd like to join and saying what they'd like to say. . . . This craving to get another step higher on the ladder of fame and fortune is a ball and chain on the good work of organizing . . . people into unions.''

All of which had some rather intriguing consequences for Woody, the most pleasurable being a sudden popularity with women. Out West, Maxine Crissman's reaction had been typical—he was a clever little guy, but she was looking for a man. In New York, though, he was the Noble Savage: exotic, intuitive, pure, proletarian, and especially alluring to young left-wing women curious to learn what ''twentieth century Americanism'' was *really* all about. Bedding down with him seemed the functional equivalent of a night out on the prairie.

For his part, Woody responded with the clumsy aggression of the formerly shy. He'd often embarrass Alan Lomax at parties by literally attacking—''haunching,'' as Lomax put it—young women. Amazingly, they seemed not to mind this very much: a certain amount of crudeness was expected from the Noble Savage and, in Woody's case, he was so innocent-looking and . . . *cute* that it was virtually impossible for him to appear very threatening. Often, he'd be adopted for several days of love and mothering, and then sent on his way. ''I think he worked his way through half the secretaries in the CBS building,'' Lomax estimated.

As a result, Woody didn't establish a permanent residence in the city—he received mail at the Forrest Theater—for nearly a year. He did spend a good many nights on the Murphy bed at Huddie and Martha Ledbetter's apartment, awed by the old man's ability and in love with his language. ''I heard Leadbelly say the other day, 'I woke up this morning and the blues was falling down like midnight rain,' '' he wrote in his column. It was difficult to tell what Leadbelly thought of Woody, although he appeared to enjoy his company. But then, it was difficult to tell what Leadbelly thought of any white man; he was unalterably servile in their presence, and addressed them formally as ''Mr. Alan,'' and even ''Mr. Woody.''

Lomax continued to work at promoting Woody's career. His most important breakthrough was to persuade Victor Records to produce a two-album, twelve-record set of Woody's dust bowl ballads. Victor agreed because it was curious about folk music's market potential, possibly as an educational item for use in the schools—its main rival, Columbia, was just then releasing an album by Burl Ives—but it also was hoping to capitalize on the popularity of the movie version of *The Grapes of Wrath*. In fact, Woody apparently was asked to write a song about the movie, and one night in New York, he asked Pete Seeger where he could get a typewriter. "The Victor people want me to write a song about *The Grapes of Wrath*," he said.

They went over to the Lower East Side, where Seeger had an artist friend named Jerry Oberwager, who owned a typewriter. Woody sat down to work with a half gallon of wine, getting up every so often to test a few lines on his guitar, and then back to the typewriter. Seeger watched for a while, but eventually dozed off. The next morning he found the bottle empty, Guthrie asleep on the floor, and a seventeen-verse ballad called "Tom Joad" sitting in the typewriter. In it, Woody had managed to summarize all the main action of the story, down to Tom's last words to his mother:

> "Ev'rybody might be just one big soul,
> Well it looks that-a way to me
> Everywhere that you look in the day or night
> That's where I'm gonna be, ma
> That's where I'm gonna be.

> "Wherever little children are hungry and cry
> Wherever people ain't free,
> Wherever men are fightin' for their rights,
> That's where I'm gonna be, ma,
> That's where I'm gonna be."

It was written to the tune of "John Hardy," the outlaw ballad Woody had been playing over and over at Lomax's house, and Victor was so impressed that it decided to use all seventeen verses even though it took both sides of a record to get it all down. Woody was tremendously—uncharacteristically—proud of the song, and when the *Daily Worker* gave much of its entertainment page one day to printing the words, he wrote, "I think the ballad of the Joads is the best thing I've done so far."

The songs were recorded, without much fanfare, on May 3, 1940, at Victor's Camden, New Jersey, studios. Woody simply stood in a studio and sang one after the other—"Dust Bowl Refugee," "Talking Dust Bowl," "I Ain't Got No Home," "Do

Re Mi,'' ''So Long, It's Been Good to Know You,'' ''Dust Can't Kill Me,'' and the others—and then took a train back to New York. He was paid three hundred dollars for the session, and was jubilant. He wrote his younger sister, Mary Jo, about his good fortune and exaggerated only a little: ''I made 14 Victor records and been in about 100 shows since I got to New York. I'm coming to Oklahoma as soon as I get a check from CBS—by the way, I was on a coast to coast broadcast last week with Burgess Meredith and Franchot Tone. Tone is a swell guy, and I got $50 for about six minutes work. Not bad if the six minutes was every day, or is that being a hog? Well, Columbia's got lots of money, I don't mind taking it from them. . . . I got $400 cash in advance and five percent royalties for the records. . . . I just bought a new Plymouth and it really splits the breeze.''

He also wrote about the recording session in the *Daily Worker*: ''The songs are liberal as the dickens and as progressive as the angels. . . . They came out of the hearts and mouths of the Okies. On no occasion have I referred to myself as either an entertainer or a singer, and I'd better not start now. . . . [If I'm] most proud of anything . . . [it's] the fact that I seem to have been born a shade pink, and didn't have to read too many books to become a proletariat, and you can guess that when you hear the records. . . . What I'm glad to see is working folks' songs getting so popular. I'm sure Victor never did a more radical album.''

R. C. Wetherald, the Victor executive in charge of the production, asked Woody to write a little booklet explaining the songs, which he did; he billed himself as ''The Dustiest of the Dust Bowlers,'' and told the tale once more: ''My relatives had wrote letters back from California a-telling how pretty the country was and about the big rains and the big ocean and the high mountains, and the valleys with green trees that was loaded down with most every kind of groceries, and they said the whole landscape out there just spelt the word 'Work' . . . and I got so interested in the art and science of Migratin' that I majored in it, in a school so big you can't get out of it.''

With the records finished and a few months to kill before they'd be released, Woody decided to visit Mary and the kids in Pampa. He still suffered from periodic spells of responsibility, writing to Mary and sending her money; he wanted to see the kids and break in his new Plymouth. Along the way, he stopped in Washington and was waylaid there for several days by another of Alan Lomax's projects: a book of protest songs. Lomax would provide the lyrics, Pete Seeger would transcribe the music (as his stepmother, Ruth Crawford, had done for Alan's collaboration with his father, *Our Singing Country*), and Woody would write introductions for each of the songs. Seeger provided a title for the book, *Hard-Hitting Songs for Hard Hit People*.

Lomax proceeded with the project with his usual enthusiasm, though none of the New York publishers seemed very interested (and the book wouldn't see print until 1962). He asked John Steinbeck to write a general introduction, and Steinbeck responded with several thousand rather predictable words about "the people" marching and triumphing. He did, however, include a memorable description of Woody:

"Woody is just Woody. Thousands of people do not know he has any other name. He is just a voice and a guitar. He sings the songs of a people and I suspect that he is, in a way, that people. Harsh voiced and nasal, his guitar hanging like a tire iron on a rusty rim, there is nothing sweet about Woody, and there is nothing sweet about the songs he sings. But there is something more important for those who will listen. There is the will of the people to endure and fight against oppression. I think we call this the American spirit."

While in Washington, Woody acquired Pete Seeger as a traveling companion for the trip to Oklahoma. They headed down through Appalachia in the fresh, clean spring air, stopping briefly to visit the Highlander Folk School, a training center for labor organizers in Tennessee where Myles and Zilphia Horton were experimenting with the use of music as an organizing tool. From there, they continued west in something of a haze, carrying on a running conversation about music and politics—after Highlander, Woody was preoccupied with the idea of writing union songs—but rarely talking about anything personal (Pete was making a major effort to become a "proletariat" and was especially reticent about his aristocratic past). Both were private, dreamy men who seemed to reinforce each other's unworldliness, and the simplest contacts with the realities of life often had dire consequences. A flat tire touched off a strange series of events that resulted in the loss of Pete's typewriter (he'd offered the machine as collateral for a cheap old recap and it disappeared when he and Woody went off to raise money for a new tire by singing in a couple of bars).

Lunch one day became a melodrama when they insisted on eating in a black café and the owner—who couldn't understand why white people would want to come in there, except to make trouble—refused to serve them.

They picked up hitchhikers along the way, including a man with no legs who said his name was Brooklyn Speedy and offered to share expenses. "Just set me down in front of Woolworth's for a few hours and I'll have plenty of gasoline money," and sure enough, he did. Before they left town, though, he asked Seeger to go to the drugstore and buy him several ounces of paregoric. "Tell them the baby has a stomachache and when they ask you to sign your name, don't sign your real one." Speedy downed the stuff in one gulp as Pete watched, amazed.

"What does it do for you?" Pete asked.

"I'm just sitting here," Speedy said, "and the world's moving past me, and going away . . ."

They traveled across Arkansas to Oklahoma, the country growing flatter and hotter, and stopped in Konawa to visit Woody's brother and sister, Roy and Mary Jo. Charley Guthrie was there too—a brief respite from skid row, another futile real estate attempt—but he didn't have very much to say to his son, at least not in front of strangers. Seeger sensed a real tension between them, and the visit lasted only a few hours.

Arriving in Oklahoma City, they contacted the local Communist Party organizers, Bob and Ina Wood, who put them to work singing for the poor, desperate people in the Hooverville on the banks of the Canadian River, and then for the striking oil workers and the Unemployed Workers' Alliance. Woody experimented that day with a variation on "You've Got to Walk That Lonesome Valley," which went: "You better go down and join the union," and noted in his songbook that night: "Sung on the banks of the Canadian River to a bunch of kids—best audience ever."

They spent the night with the Woods, who were the sort of unassuming, devoted, and quietly brave people that radical organizers often turn out to be in isolated outposts like Oklahoma City. Although Woody later wrote that his song "Union Maid" was inspired by the story of a southern Tenant Farmers' Union organizer who was "stripped naked and beat up, and then hung to the rafters of a house till she was unconscious," it's probable that Ina Wood was a more direct influence. A militant feminist, she criticized Pete and Woody for never singing any songs about the women in the labor movement, and Woody responded that night by writing a parody of "Redwing":

There once was a union maid who never was afraid
Of the goons and ginks and company finks,
And the deputy sheriffs who made the raids.
She went to the union hall when a meeting it was called
And when the company boys came 'round
She always stood her ground . . .

Oh you can't scare me I'm sticking to the union,
Sticking to the union, sticking to the union.
Oh you can't scare me I'm sticking to the union
Sticking to the union, till the day I die.

Pete's first reaction, when he saw the song the next morning, was that it was kind of dumb. But it began to grow on him. It was so artless and simple, and direct. "Stickin' to the union" had a nice, percussive feel when you sang it really fast . . . it was hard to get the chorus out of your head. Like almost everything else Woody wrote, including most of his prose, it was written for the ear more than the eye, it *sounded* better than it read. For the next decade, "Union Maid" would be Woody's most popular song, appearing in union songbooks and sung on picket lines all over the country.

Although Pete was prepared for something less than a mansion in Pampa, he was surprised by the dumpy little shack that Mary and the kids were living in. "It was like a shantytown," he remembered. "Just a tiny place, long and narrow like a trailer, maybe ten feet wide and thirty feet deep." It was an awkward situation, a side of Woody's life that Pete didn't want to intrude into . . . or even know about. And yet there they all were, trapped in that little house, the only relief coming when Uncle Jeff, Allene, and Matt Jennings came over and played music. Even then, Mary's mother grabbed Pete by the shoulders and shook him. "You've got to make that man treat my daughter right!"

Pete stayed a few days and then begged off, saying that he wanted to keep heading west and see more of the country. Woody didn't last much longer than that. He was moving too fast, too much was happening for him to be able to explain any of it to Mary. He breezed in and out so quickly that she was nearly breathless. He played with the kids, bounced them on his knee, and was gone. She wasn't even quite sure yet where the three hundred dollars he'd sent had come from. After little more than a week, he was on the road back north, stopping in Oklahoma City to pick up Bob Wood and several of his comrades and bring them to the big Communist Party convention about to be held in New York City.

He described the Oklahoma Communists' arrival in his *Daily Worker* column: "After we got out of the Holler Tunnel, I says, Well, Boys, what do you think of her? One old boy in the back said, I bet I sunburn the roof of my mouth—but it'll be worth it—he looked out the window as we drove down the street and he said, God a mighty, dadburn my hide, is ALL of them people here for the convention?—Another ol boy said, Well, yeah, but they just don't KNOW IT yet."

And then the convention itself: "All of you workers everywhere, you will see, you will know, who's on your side, who's working and fighting for you . . . and it won't be the rich guys, nor their hired guards . . . it'll be the 20,000 people who met last Sunday in Madison Square Garden."

Woody was so filled with the party spirit that he gave Bob Wood the Plymouth, so he'd have something to get back home with. It was the official car of the Oklahoma Communist Party for several years after that.

Woody bought a scrapbook that summer and began collecting the reviews of *Dust Bowl Ballads* when the albums were released in July. Most were pretty favorable. There was much talk of "Americana," and Steinbeck, though some treated Woody merely as a *Grapes of Wrath* spin-off. The Los Angeles *News*'s classical music critic suggested, in the best "fine art" tradition, that Woody's songs might prove helpful to serious composers. "They might make a tone-poem, symphony or suite by some American more American." Woody, perhaps beginning to realize that his radical politics might jeopardize his chances for commercial success, misunderstood the review and exploded in the margin of his scrapbook: "An American more American? What the hell do you mean? My dad and my dad's dad was born and raised in this country, and so was my ma and her ma. . . . I ain't out to spread no foreign ideas amongst the people over here, but I have been accused of being a Russian red . . ."

The most perceptive review came from Howard Taubman in *The New York Times*: "These albums are not a summer sedative. They make you think; they may even make you uncomfortable. . . . The albums show that the phonograph is broadening its perspective, and that life as some of our unfortunates know it can be mirrored on the glistening disks."

As it turned out, even Taubman was understating the case: *Dust Bowl Ballads* eventually would be recognized as a landmark, one of the most influential American recordings of the twentieth century. But aside from the handful of newspaper reviews, there wasn't much of a stir when the albums appeared in the summer of 1940. In fact, Victor released no more than 1,000—and perhaps as few as 500—copies. Woody waited for the big reaction, the acclaim, some notice. He wrote in his scrapbook: "Boy when I made them records and got that $300 I thought I was rolling rich. I thought all these here fellers that make records had money coming in all the time, but heck they're about as broke a bunch as you'll find. . . ."

The records weren't completely ignored, though. The few copies sold seemed to be played continually—especially in left-wing schools and summer camps, where the words and the simple, defiant optimism became a part of the curriculum . . . as did the image of a dusty little man wandering around the country with a guitar slung over his shoulder, making up songs that helped people to understand themselves and encouraged them to fight back. It was a powerful, romantic image, especially for kids growing up in the middle of New York City, and it would be central to the mythology of the generation of radicals coming of age.

Woody, meanwhile, was too busy to get very depressed about the albums' commercial failure. He wrote to Lomax: "Pete has been to Wisconsin with the Youths [American Youth Congress]. He's back now. We been singing around at the puppet workshop and other places. We're really getting set in the saddle. Going up to Camp Lakeland today and sing there tonight. Then 2 bookings here in New York tomorrow night. Then Sunday we're going out to Staten Island with the Spanish Relief Committee. Went to a party out at Bill Groppers house last week and got drunker'n old billy hell. I sung at the bar and everyone bought me drinks. The bar cleared 2 bushel baskets and one scoop shovel full of silver dollars, and they packed the small change off in a gunny sack. It was a howling success, with everybody howling about my singing."

He spent a good deal of time with Leadbelly that summer, and also with Aunt Molly Jackson and her clan, all of whom lived on the Lower East Side. He took great pleasure in their gruff integrity and wrote in his column: "[They] all come to Leadbelly's house almost every day. . . . Molly is the woman Leadbelly. She is in her cotton apron what Leadbelly is in his bathrobe. She talks to him exactly as to her reflection in the mirror. He speaks back to her like the swamplands to the uplands, the same as his river would talk to her highest cliffrim. She loves him in the same half jealous way that he loves her, because he sees and feels in Aunt Molly the woman who has found in her own voice the same power on earth that he has found."

From time to time, they would all sing on WNYC—New York's public radio station and one of the few places around where pure, undiluted folk music could be heard. Woody did a series of programs that summer with Sarah Ogan and Jim Garland, and mounted a successful campaign to get Leadbelly a weekly show of his own.

Woody probably could have had a regular show on WNYC too, but he already was moving in another, more lucrative direction. Throughout the summer, Alan Lomax had been working on yet another of his special projects—a regularly scheduled folk music program on prime time network radio. He'd write the shows from Washington, and Nicholas Ray would direct them in New York. Each would have a folksy theme—railroads, dogs, kids, getting married—like the drunken all-night singing contests. CBS was interested in the idea and a half-hour pilot version, called "Back Where I Come From," was aired on August 19, 1940, in the hope that a regular sponsor could be found. Woody was featured on that show (and paid eighty-three dollars), along with Burl Ives, the Golden Gate Quartet, a cornpone comedian named Len Doyle, and Clifton Fadiman as master of ceremonies. There also was an orchestra, a studio audience, and all the other accouterments of big-time network radio. The theme was "The Weather," a convenient showcase for Woody's dust bowl songs, especially "So Long, It's Been Good to Know You," which was the program's major production number. Fadiman introduced Woody, once again as a recent visitor to the city, and Woody once again told his joke about changing shoes on the subway trains. He sounded terrific: very southwestern, dusty, natural . . . and entirely professional. He began to sing "So Long," with dust storm sound effects in the background. An orchestra and chorus came in on the refrain, and between verses there were brief dramatizations of Pampa's reaction to the Great Dust Storm of 1935. After the verse about the sweethearts who "sat in the dark and sparked," for example, there was a scene between Woody and an actress, sparking. "Gonna kiss me, Cora?" Woody asked. The actress sighed rapturously, and he said, "Gonna kiss me again?" The song was used once more as the closing theme for the broadcast.

Even though "Back Where I Come From" was generally regarded as a success and greatly favored by the CBS hierarchy, no sponsor was willing to take it on. The music was too experimental and, with the casual mixing of blacks and whites in equal roles on the air, the politics were a bit suspicious. Still, CBS wasn't ready to give up the idea and decided to continue the program on a "sustaining" basis—without a sponsor—for a time, hoping it would catch on. Starting in late September, it would be aired for fifteen minutes at 10:30 p.m. on Monday, Wednesday, and Friday evenings. On August 27, Woody signed a contract for a hundred fifty dollars per week to be a regular on the show.

In the month before "Back Where I Come From" began, he played a few nightclub gigs and established a semi-permanent residence with Harold and Elizabeth Ambellan on East Twenty-first Street. Harold Ambellan was a sculptor and folk music fan with a large studio and plenty of extra space for Woody. Woody loved his weird, modern sculptures, which had all sorts of little holes in them, and wrote to Lomax after Ambellan had received an honorable mention in a sculpture competition: "One judge at the contest thought Harold was something his statues had carved. Honorable mentions ain't used among politicians, I don't think, but they're the best chiselers of the lot. . . ."

At about the same time, an old traveling companion from Will Geer's California troupe, a would-be actor named Gilbert "Cisco" Houston, arrived in town and Woody roped him into singing high-tenor harmony in his nightclub act, which Cisco did quite well. He was a tall, quiet man with dark, classic features and a degree of sensitivity that would have been rare in any case, but was particularly striking in someone so handsome. Not that Cisco wasn't vain about his looks—he had extremely poor vision, the result of a congenital eye condition, and yet refused to wear glasses (which would have helped only marginally)—but it wasn't an obtrusive vanity. He was the sort of man whom people would look at and assume that he lived a wild, colorful, outdoorsy life; it soon was rumored in New York that he'd been a cowboy out West. Actually, he'd spent nearly all his life with his stolid, working-class family near Pasadena. Woody found him to be a loyal friend, intelligent, kind, calm, and caring in all the ways Matt Jennings had been, but not so religious or straitlaced.

Will Geer landed Cisco his first job in the city—as a doorman, wearing a big fancy uniform with a cap and epaulets, at a burlesque house on Forty-second Street. He was still working there when Woody opened for a week in early September at Jimmy Dwyer's Sawdust Trail, a well-known midtown club, and asked him to come up for a few duets each set. It was the beginning of a long, if rather sporadic, collaboration, and probably the closest friendship of Woody's life. The act was well received in the local papers, especially in the *Sun*, where the nightclub columnist Malcolm Johnson swallowed everything Woody fed him, including the "fact" that "the Guthries worked their farm and worked hard."

Meanwhile, Woody was swamped with network radio offers after his performance on the "Back Where I Come From" pilot. He was invited to sing on Sanka's "We, the People," a new talent revue on CBS. Du Pont's "Cavalcade of America" on NBC offered him three hundred dollars to write and perform a ballad about Wild Bill Hickok that would serve as the backbone for a half-hour drama. And most important, the Model Tobacco Company wanted him to replace a cornball comedy team as the regular host of its weekly CBS show, "Pipe Smoking Time," starting in November, and to use a version of "So Long" as the theme song. They would pay Woody two hundred dollars each week for this, and he'd be able to continue with "Back Where I Come From," making his weekly salary a minimum of three hundred fifty dollars, plus any other radio shows, nightclub gigs, and record contracts he could fit in. It was a staggering turn of events. People seemed to be handing him wads of money each time he walked into the CBS offices. He wrote to Lomax, "They are giving me money so fast I'm using it to sleep under."

The sudden notoriety was exhilarating, confusing, and more than a little frightening. It also raised serious moral questions.

Clearly, hundreds of dollars weren't going to be dumped into his lap each week without some strings attached. He was going to have to modify his style. It just wasn't possible, for example, for a *Daily Worker* columnist to host a network radio show—and that would be only the first and most obvious hurdle. There would probably be a slew of compromises, little artistic and political concessions each week—songs he couldn't sing, cracks he couldn't make. Already he'd been red-baited in letters to the *Sun* responding to Malcolm Johnson's puffery, and Johnson had written a second column in Woody's defense: "One of our friends tells us that we have been accused of 'falling for fifth column stuff' in writing about Woody Guthrie, the singing Okie at Jimmy Dwyer's Sawdust Trail. The charge is that Guthrie is a communist. Well, we don't know whether he is or not, and we don't care. We didn't ask him, nor do we intend to do so, figuring that his politics, if any, comes under the head of his own business. We do know that we like Guthrie's songs. . . ." It was a brave response, but Woody couldn't expect the CBS or Model Tobacco moguls, who had so much more at stake, to act similarly when their turn came.

On September 19, he wrote a long, eloquent, nervous, unpunctuated, and defensive letter to Lomax. It took him several pages to warm up and get around to discussing what was really on his mind, and even then he came through the back door, talking about the way he wrote songs: "Usually I set down and knock off a song in about 30 minutes or an hour but in most of them I've been going around humming or whistling it and trying to get it all straight in my head what I want to say and why I want to say it and usually when I decide just exactly who the song is a going to help and if its the right bunch I can really beat or scribble her down in a hurry. The reason why you want to write songs is what keeps you going. If you got enough reason to write I say that you can knock off two or 3 pretty fair songs a week and a pretty darn good one over the weekend. . . . I get my words and tunes from the hungry folks and they get the credit for all I pause to scribble down. . . . Music is some kind of electricity that makes a radio out of a man and the dial is in his head and he just sings according to how he's a feeling. The best stuff you can sing about is what you saw and if you look hard enough you can see plenty to sing about. . . ."

From there, he went directly into the Malcolm Johnson episode. "Lots of people wrote in hollering that the reporter fell for a lot of fifth column stuff. They called me a communist and a wild man and everything you could think of but I don't care what they call me. I aint a member of any earthly organization my trouble is I really ought to go down in the morning and just join everything. . . . I always knowed that this was what I wanted to talk and sing about and I'm used to running into folks that complain but I don't ever intend to sell out or quit or talk or sing any different because when I do that drug store lemonade stuff I just open up my mouth and nothing comes out.

"And now I've got this CBS radio job and a salary that beats owning six farms in Oklahoma and I don't know just what or where or when somebody will raise up and try to put their foot in my good jungle stew because it is mighty apt to happen and it means so much not only to me but to my friends and relatives that I'll be able to help and my wife and three kids are feeling pretty good for the first time in a long time and a long time down there in the dust bowl where they've been cooped up is just naturally a mighty long time. If I thought for two minutes that anything I do or say would hurt America and the people in it I would keep my face shut and catch the first freight out of the country." At this point Woody pulled back a little, and cracked a few jokes. "The Library of Congress is good. It has helped me a lot by recording what I had to say and to copy all my songs and file them away so the senaters caint find them. Course they're always in there in case they ever get a few snorts under their vest and want to sing." Then, serious again, he wrote several lines that would become quite famous: "I think real folk stuff scares most of the boys around Washington. A folk song is what's wrong and how to fix it, or it could be whose hungry and where their mouth is, or whose out of work and where the job is or whose broke and where the money is or whose carrying a gun and where the peace is—that's folk lore and folks made it up because they seen that the politicians couldn't find nothing to fix or nobody to feed or give a job of work. We don't aim to hurt you or scare you when we get to feeling sorta folksy and make up some folk lore, we're a doing all we can to make it easy on you. I can sing all day and all night sixty days and sixty nights but of course I aint got enough wind to be in office. . . ."

* * *

As it happened, he stopped writing the column.

For the first time in his life, Woody appeared to back down, rein in, compromise his integrity. It must not have been easy, especially after having made such a big deal in the *Worker* of "this false and silly thing called a reputation which causes plumb good folks [to keep] from . . . saying what they'd like to say." It was not a decision that he discussed at the time, or wrote about or explained—the column simply ended in October. Years later, he'd tell friends that he was fired from the paper because he was too wild and undisciplined for the party, but that hardly seems likely since he'd been writing for more than a year with no such difficulties, and it was especially unlikely now that Woody was about to become a network radio star—unless, of course, he did something extraordinary to precipitate a firing. It certainly was a touchy time for the party; its neutrality on the war issue was beginning to seem more brutish and reprehensible than ever that September as Hitler pulverized England. It's probable, in any case, that Woody didn't have the same close ties to the Communists in New York as he'd had in California . . . and certainly not the direct contact with party people who were actually out there *doing* things, like the labor organizers in the San Joaquin Valley.

But he still felt an overwhelming guilt and anger about what he'd done, and tended to exorcise that guilt by redoubling his integrity in other areas. He became the avenging angel of "Back Where I Come From," challenging Nick Ray on every artistic compromise. He was especially vehement on the subject of Leadbelly, who was given only an occasional, subsidiary role on the program and, worse, often had to hear a smoother, more accessible black singer, Josh White, perform his songs so that white America could understand the words. Woody's incessant quibbling with Nick Ray led to a major blowout in late October, and he stormed off the show. Lomax, again moving deftly, wrote from Washington: "I am indeed sorry you are no longer on 'Back Where I Come From.' I wish there was some way you and Nick could get together again. The first program that you failed to appear on just about broke my heart. . . . I'd like to hear your side of the story and I'd like to try to do something about the situation."

Apparently Lomax was able to heal the breach, because Woody returned to the show and, gradually, assumed a larger, more important role. "He was about the smartest guy around that show,"

Burl Ives recalled. "We really needed him to help with the scripts, give us a quick line here or there—nobody could match him at that." Ray also eventually settled on Woody as the narrator for most of the broadcasts; he had the perfect casual tone for the program, which, despite the occasional bows to convention, was still the most daring thing on commercial radio. On the anniversary of the Thirteenth Amendment to the Constitution—the freeing of the slaves—Woody read the amendment aloud with the Golden Gate Quartet singing "Oh Freedom" in the background. It was a stirring, incendiary moment that Nick Ray would always remember as "Back Where I Come From" at its very best.

When the Model Tobacco program began in late November and the big money started rolling in, Woody no longer had any excuses and sent for Mary and the kids. She tacked a sign on the Russell Street house: "For Rent. Gone to New York. Yippee . . ." and hopped the next train north. Woody, as usual, was confused about when to pick them up and the family was left stranded at Grand Central Station for several hours—they'd never seen a place so crowded—before Mary took matters into her own hands, piled the kids into a taxi, and gave the driver the new address that Woody had sent her: 5 West 101st Street, just off Central Park uptown. The family was reunited, somehow, by the end of the day and Woody whisked them off to the Bronx Zoo in the new Pontiac he'd just made a first payment on. He seemed genuinely happy to see them, loving up the kids and writing a song called "The Rio Grande Valley" about his blond Texas woman.

The month of December 1940 was a wild, carefree blur for Mary. There was *so much* money: she kept three hundred-dollar bills in her wallet at all times, just for safekeeping, just to be able to remind herself that it was real. Not only was there enough money for baby-sitters whenever she wanted to go out with Woody at night, but also enough for a nanny to air out the kids in the park each day. They bought liquor by the half gallon, an absolute necessity given the crowds streaming through the apartment at all hours. Of all the remarkable things about New York, Mary was most amazed by the fact that it never seemed to stop: guitar players, writers, musicians, radio people, sailors, deadbeats would knock on their door at 3 a.m., expecting a party. A half dozen revelers might arrive at any hour, and then everyone would decide to go up to Harlem and hear some jazz, or down to the Village, or out to a movie, or to a burlesque show. One night the crowd drifted apart in an alcoholic haze and Mary found herself—*where* was Woody?—in a burlesque house trying to fend off some guy she barely knew.

Woody's success prompted another visit from the New York *Sun*, which found the Guthries ensconced in their "four room, furnished" apartment, certainly an improvement on their old Texas shack, as Woody took pains to point out: "I bought that little ole shack for $25 . . . I still owe $5 on it." And now he had a piano "which nobody plays," and a refrigerator, which the kids thought was quite a thrill. "They eat 'snow' all the time," he said. As for Mary, she wanted to see the sights of New York but still preferred California. "She doesn't want anything special now that Woody's making a decent living, except a home of her own," the *Sun* reported. There was a photograph of Woody, Mary, and the children sitting at the piano which no one played, and the headline: "Wrath's Grapes Turn to Wine?"

"Pipe Smoking Time," starring Woody Guthrie "and his guitar," began on November 25, 1940. The show opened that night with Ray Bloch's red-jacketed orchestra playing "So Long" and Woody singing:

> *Howdy friend, well it's sure good to know you*
> *Howdy friend, well it's sure good to know you*
> *Load up your pipe and take your life easy,*
> *With Model Tobacco to light up your way*
> *We're glad to be with you today.*

And it went on down from there. It was a tightly controlled, tightly scripted show, as most network programs were. There was no room for slyness or spontaneity, not to mention politics or "pollli-TISH-uns." Woody had been hired more for his on-the-air delivery than for his cleverness, or even his songs. It was his casual, natural country feel that was salable. But playing the rube wasn't much fun unless there was an element of surprise—the quick, caustic, understated, unexpected comeback that cut four or five different ways was the only thing that made the act morally defensible. Without the needle, he was just another singing hick who trafficked in a smarmy, vulgar sort of self-deprecation for the city folks, singing only the blandest songs and telling the limpest stories, introducing the comedy team of Fields and Hall that first night, and then the baritone Eddie Roeker, and closing with the bastardized "So Long" once more:

> *With Model and Tweed, Dill's Best and Old Briar*
> *It's good to be with you tonight.*

Woody did as he was told . . . for a couple of weeks. And quibbled for a couple more after that, burning all the while. "Wrath's Grapes Turn to Wine?" What an embarrassment! The headline was black-and-white proof of his worst fears, physical evidence of his betrayal. By midmonth he was boiling. Everything, everyone bothered him: the family, especially, in that bleak fourth-floor walk-up with somebody else's furniture. He wrote a parody called "It Takes a Married Man to Sing a Worried Song," and included the line: "The kids run out like cattle when you open up the door."

By late December, Mary was beginning to suspect that something was wrong. On Christmas Eve, Cisco came by and Woody choreographed the celebration over to the nearest bar—much to Cisco's embarrassment, Mary thought—and didn't return for several days. On New Year's Eve, some of the cast from "Back Where I Come From" piled into Woody's Pontiac and went up to Nyack to play a fund-raiser at Will Geer's new house (only Will Geer would have a fund-raiser on New Year's Eve). A good slice of Broadway was there that night, dressed to the nines in gowns and tuxedos, and Woody got ornery drunk. He sang three or four songs rather poorly, his eyes closed throughout.

"Why do you have your eyes closed?" Geer asked.

"All them white shirts and diamonds are blinding me."

The ride back to the city was accomplished at speeds ranging from 20 to 80 miles per hour, although the speed at any given moment had little to do with the difficulty of the road. When they reached Harlem, Woody insisted on screeching to a stop at each corner and asking pedestrians, "How do we get from here to the United States?" Leadbelly, in the back seat, scrunched down and mumbled, "Please, Mr. Woody, please . . ."

Several days later, Woody arrived home and announced to Mary, "Get packing. We're getting out of here."

Mary was numb. He'd blown New York too.

"C'mon. We're going to California."

Actually, he'd been planning the getaway for about a week—

a clean break, flushing all the garbage from his system. He'd given Nick Ray notice, gotten himself fired from "Pipe Smoking Time," and even had the presence of mind to get a letter of recommendation from CBS vice-president Davidson Taylor: "His work is practically unique. . . . His travel, his powers of observation and his creative ability have given him tremendous advantages in the field he's made his own."

They loaded as much as they could into the Pontiac (Sue Guthrie always would remember the tricycle—her father's Christmas present—that was left behind), trudging up and down the four flights of stairs, and headed for Washington. Mary was in a mild state of shock. There just wasn't any hope for the man. It was all over. When they arrived in Washington and Alan asked what on earth they were doing there, Woody said, "New car fever."

And it *was* a fever of some sort. It was an eerie, exhausting, panicky trip west, starting with the horrible wind and rain storm at the Lomaxes' that night which shattered several windows in the house as Mary was putting the children to bed, and then the strange, drunken party afterwards with the black woman who danced in circles around Mary, singing, "I'm gonna kill you, I'm gonna kill you . . ." A day or two later they were on the road again, swooping down through the South, Woody driving—silently, eyes dead ahead—until he collapsed; and Mary taking over somewhere in Mississippi and getting lost in the soft, wet night, and coming upon a group of men slaughtering a pig in a misty field. She asked them for directions, but they didn't speak English. They spoke French. They were Cajuns. This was Louisiana. "I got relatives in Louisiana," Woody said drowsily. "In Collinston."

They went to Collinston, looking for Lawrence Tanner—who was Woody's half uncle, his grandmother Mary Maloney's youngest child by Lee Tanner—and his wife, but found they had moved to Baton Rouge. The Tanners' daughter, Billie, happened to be in town visiting old friends, though, and offered to show the Guthries how to get to her parents' house. Along the way, they stopped in a gas station and Billie was amazed by the wad of bills Woody pulled from his pocket—she'd never seen so much money before.

Lawrence and Ora Tanner barely remembered Woody. They hadn't seen him since Okemah, and were a bit nonplussed by the visit, but hospitable nonetheless. Ora went off to the kitchen to cook up some dinner as Woody started talking about life in New York, and radio, and the trip south. Then she heard a commotion in the living room . . . somehow, the conversation had slipped into politics and Woody, feeling his freedom for the first time since Model Tobacco, said they hadn't eaten in anything but black restaurants since they'd left Washington.

Lawrence Tanner thought that was pretty disgusting, especially with Woody's wife and two little blond daughters along on the trip. "How'd you like one of them to marry a nigger?"

"Wouldn't mind it a bit."

This was too much for Tanner, who'd heard through the family grapevine that Woody had turned Communist and now believed it. "Get out! Get out! Get out of my house!" he screamed, and they were back on the road again, heading now toward Matt Jennings' new home in El Paso, Texas.

Matt was alarmed by the sudden arrival, but, as always, tried to make the best of it. He suggested that he round up the rest of the family (his brothers, Fred and Blue, also were in town), and they'd all cross the border to Juárez and celebrate. Woody, who was wearing a big, black, ridiculous cowboy hat that he'd bought somewhere along the way, had other ideas: El Paso was near the Big Bend country and the Chisos Mountains; he wanted to go down there for a few days and look for Jerry P. Guthrie's mine again. Matt had to work the next day and couldn't go along, but his brother Fred was game. So, promising to return in time for dinner in Juárez on Saturday, Woody and Fred headed out in the morning, bouncing the Pontiac over the rough desert trails, past the old silver-mining town of Terlingua again, along the Rio Grande again, and down to the adobe shack at the foot of Burro Mesa. It was beginning to wash away now, its roof gone, but there was still the same view of the lavender and brown Chisos range, craggy in just the same way it had been a decade before, the air still tingly-fresh, the desert expanse still dizzying. Woody proceeded to lose the keys to the Pontiac and a massive search was required before they were found. As a result, he and Fred were late getting back to El Paso . . . and Mary was steaming when they got there. It was the first time Matt ever heard Woody and his sister yell at each other; it was the first time he'd ever heard Woody raise his voice.

They did make it across to Juárez eventually that evening and stopped in a saloon that had a punch bowl full of eggnog sitting on the bar. Matt was busy socializing and didn't realize what was happening behind his back, when he saw the bartender's eyes bug out. He turned to find Woody, already pretty far gone after several drinks, dipping a hand into the eggnog and spreading the stuff on his face like shaving cream. Matt pulled him out of there and back across the Santa Fe bridge to the United States, where Woody picked up half a brick and hurled it through a store window. "Looks like a goddamn capitalist place to me," he said, and was about to toss another brick when Matt grabbed it away and hustled him into the car.

The mad dash west continued. Woody didn't want to go to Los Angeles. His Aunt Laura and cousin Amalee had moved from Glendale back upstate to the beautiful little town of Sonora in the California gold country, and he wanted to go there. Mary was pleased: she was looking forward to getting together again with her old confidante, Amalee. But rather than stay in Sonora itself, Woody decided to settle in Columbia, an empty, forgotten town nearby that once had been a center of the California gold rush. About 10,000 people had lived there, pulling approximately $87 million worth of gold out of the surrounding hills, but now it was decidedly ghosty . . . another strange way station in the flight from New York. They lived in an old hotel, in a single large room with high ceilings and windows with iron shutters that cranked open. They looked out across at the ancient scales in front of the Wells Fargo depot, where thousands of ounces of gold had been weighed.

Woody spent his days communing with the ghosts and pounding on the portable typewriter he'd bought from Matt Jennings for ten dollars. One of the first things he wrote was a long letter to Lomax, describing the town at length, and also the trip across country, but making only a few oblique references to the New York debacle that was still very much on his mind:

Howdy Alan. Well I guess the new car fever has wore down just a little bit but it aint run into the New York fever yet, and I feel pretty sure that it wont. . . . As far as music goes around here I am enjoying the shortage of it. I dont mean that like it sounds. I mean I am glad to be where you don't hear one of the jute boxes going full blast through every window. They got a little dance hall across the street. They got a band of some kind in there that ain't no good.

A tramp musician is almost a welcomed guest out here.
The saloons in some of the mining towns around here are
fixed up with nickel boxes but I've walked into them and
asked the boss man how about knocking off a few tunes to
pick a stake and seen him turn the nickel box face to the
wall and tell me to do the best I could. . . . We're all right
for the shape we're in. The wife feels better out here but
she likes New York City paychecks better than what I been
able to carve out of the mountains so far. She just wasn't
in New York long enough to get right good and sick of it.
She was never around there when she was flat broke and
she aint got no idea how far you can smell the garbage that
folks throw out of their windows over there in the low rent
district. I ruther to raise my kids like a herd of young
antelope out here in the fresh air. Maybe that's wrong, but
that's the way I feel about it. Everything around here is
good and clean and fresh and natural and if you aint got a
bag of money in the big city it's a lowdown rotten joint to
get caught in. We went up 7123 feet high coming over the
pass the other day after dark and it was snowed under and
the moon was hanging out and I just had to throw on the
brakes and stop the car and get out and just stand there
and look and think—man that was a pretty sight for sore
eyes . . .

He'd run away from the filth and capitalist temptations of the
big city all right, but he'd also left behind Leadbelly, Aunt Molly,
Pete Seeger, Cisco, Nick Ray, and Alan—the very people who'd
finally shown him what he was all about. Sitting in Columbia,
he wrote a meandering parable about Leadbelly (and himself) in
which the hero was a singing cricket with a hoarse and sour voice
who always hid out in the part of the house that most needed
repair: "Somehow or another, the best singing just naturally
comes from under the leakingest roof. You know why folks like
to hear a cricket sing? . . . Well, it's like this, when you hear a
cricket you can just look around a little and find a rotten board
or plank that needs to be jacked up and a new one run under it."
But since the cricket always was singing about the house falling
down, the other bugs (the ones who were actually eating away at
the place) began to blame him for *causing* the collapse: "Look
at that goddamn cricket, he was there all th' time!" And while

the hero was, in the end, crushed by a sullen and misinformed
shoe, his brothers and sisters and relatives carried on the singing
tradition.

A ghost town is a good place to recover from a fiasco, but only
for a little while. After two weeks of pounding the typewriter—
Woody also was starting to write an autobiography at Lomax's
behest—and no money coming in, he decided it was time to see
if there was some way to earn a living in Los Angeles. He told
Amalee he wasn't going to pay the grocery bill because the store-
keeper was a capitalist, and when she threatened to report him to
J. Edgar Hoover, he told her she was worse than Walter Winchell
and paid it.

They traveled down through the San Joaquin Valley on the way
to Los Angeles, but there was something strange here too—most
of the Okies were gone. The migrant camps had dried up, the
rattle-down cars and trucks brimming with furniture no longer
filled the roads, the union organizing had crumbled, the big growers were importing Mexicans to do the picking and then shipping
them back after the harvest. As for the Okies, many had found
work in the burgeoning war industries. There were plenty of jobs
available now. Los Angeles was booming. Tom Joad probably
was off building airplanes, and Woody was perplexed: this wasn't
the same town he'd left.

The housing shortage hadn't changed, though, especially for
families with children. In fact, with all the Okies coming in from
the valleys, it was worse . . . and the Guthries found themselves
stuck in a dingy tourist court while they looked for a place to
live. Woody was still thrashing New York over in his mind.
Model Tobacco wasn't worth thinking about, but he was beginning to wonder why he'd been so quick to quit "Back Where I
Come From" too. He wasn't ready yet to admit any second
thoughts, though, when he wrote to Lomax on February 15:

Give our regards to the cast in New York. Hope they are
all in good circumstances with a sponsor that likes them
good as we do and one that believes in freedom [of] speaking. . . . I couldn't see to save my neck any immediate
prospect of a commercial there. The fifteen minutes was a
little packed. The elevator run too straight up and straight
down and the studio had too many radioactivities in it, and

so I ducked off . . . and lit here in L.A. to get my old
program back where I know dam good and well that I ain't
gonna get no money and no sponsor and can rest with that
out of my head. . . . My program starts this coming Monday, three or four days. By the time you get this letter I'll
be a wheeling and a dealing . . .

But Woody was doing some wishful thinking about the radio
show. Apparently he assumed that he could just walk into KFVD
the following Monday and start work again as if the Hitler-Stalin
pact had never happened. He was wrong, though; for whatever
reason, Burke didn't want him back. By the time he wrote to
Lomax five days later, he'd already wired Nick Ray to ask for
his "Back Where I Come From" job again . . . and found *that*
was no longer a possibility either.

It is raining to beat the devil here and I'm sorry as hell to
hear that Back Where I Come From is kicked off the air. I
wired to Nick asking him if I could possibly go back to
work and he wired me that it was all off. Too honest again
I suppose? Maybe not purty enough. O well, this country's
a getting to where it cain't hear its own voice. Someday
the deal will change. I catch myself pretty often setting
around thinking just how hard a dam time you must have,
trying to get some of our upper crusts to listen to the real
thing. I suppose a feller gets to feeling like he'd like to
haul off and tell about 47 jillion of them to go to hell but
you are too smart to let yourself do it. I never was. . . . I
got awful downhearted about it up there in New York. But
it was about an even break. Some of the high collar joints
I went to had such a feeling about them that they just
drained my crank case. Then you'd go out and sing for a
bunch of working people—like the CIO, and they'd holler
and roar and yell and raise so much rukus that you just
know dam well the country was a gonna come out right in
the long run. The rich folks like to lull their selfs off to
sleep and sort of float 1/2 way between a drink of scot
liquor and a tile shit house—and listen to a raft of songs
that's about as close to the real as I am to foreclosing on
a farm. . . .

So he was stranded. There wasn't any work to be had on either coast. His family was still mired in a tourist court. It had been raining ever since they'd arrived in Los Angeles. The escape from New York had ended with a thud. . . . And then Ed Robbin came to the rescue.

Perhaps embarrassed by his New York sellout, Woody had delayed contacting his old friend, who was still the *People's World* Los Angeles correspondent. Ed was quite happy to see him, though. He offered the possibility of working some fundraisers together, and also an immediate solution to the Guthries' housing crisis—the cottage next to Ed's home in the Echo Park district was vacant. It was owned by an old woman anarchist poet who apparently believed that renting the place would be politically reprehensible. Woody had to serenade her for several hours (with Mary and the kids waiting in the car in the rain) before she agreed to let him have it for ten dollars per month. Ed rounded up some secondhand furniture from the neighbors and helped them move in.

Unpacking, Woody found his old "Alonzo Zilch" songbook from Pampa. It was six years old now. Pulling out his pen, he began signing his name to some of the songs—an odd impulse, since he found most of them embarrassing. He wrote comments on a few: "I figgered this was hot stuff when I wrote it. I don't know what it makes me feel now. I was trying to say something—didn't know what." And: "Here's one I used to sing over a little 2x4 bootleg radio station some boys made in 1935." And under his first theme song: "I guess this is one of the main reasons why never liked theme songs again—especially Tobacco ones—"

There were three blank pages in the book and, having nothing better to do, he filled them up. He hated the sight of an empty page. On the first, he wrote a clever rhyme about the people who used to come to his house in "superstitious shoes" thinking a "Psychic Reader can cure the worried blues." They wasted their time with "witchery" while their lives were being "lent and leased to wars across the ocean . . . to save—democracy (?)." He signed his name and the date, "2-27-41." On the next blank page, he wrote a paragraph about the weather which began: "Today is lonesome and sad as the devil and it makes me think of the sorry weather in an oil boom town," and ended: "Everything looks like it's all bogged down. But we'll pull through. Always do." On the last page, he delivered a brief sermon: "Every single human being is looking for a better way—and that way is coming to win. There is a lot better way on the way. Will it catch you out or in?'' He was playing with the words, rhyming "in" with "win," just passing the time, perhaps a little bored, without any real prospects for the first time since he'd met Jack Guthrie three years earlier. "When there shall be no want among you, because you'll own everything in Common. When the Rich will give their goods unto the poor. I believe in this way. I just can't believe in any other way. This is the Christian way and it is already on a big part of the earth and it will come. To own everything in Common. That's what the Bible says. Common means all of us. This is pure old commonism.'' Mary was calling. She wanted him to calm the girls down so she could put the baby to sleep. He wrote a last sentence: "Play a little game that's real quiet so the baby can sleep," and signed it: "Woody Guthrie.''

CHAPTER 6

Talking Union

Pete Seeger spent most of 1940 learning how to play the banjo. There were a handful of expert banjoists on record at the Library of Congress, and Pete set out to visit them all. He spent weeks sitting on front porches in obscure piney woods hamlets in Alabama, Florida, and Tennessee, trying to play along with the old masters, gradually learning their tricks. By the time he returned to New York that December, he wasn't half bad.

Nick Ray and Alan Lomax gave him some work on "Back Where I Come From" and, with his clean, boyish tenor style, Pete might have gone far in network radio . . . but he wasn't much interested in commercial success. Even though Woody Guthrie had weakened (temporarily, Pete was sure) and was playing for big money on the Model Tobacco show, Seeger had no intention of straying from the straight and narrow. Music and politics were inseparable in his mind. Music *was* politics. To sing was to organize. The struggle to popularize folk music, to make inroads against the domination of Tin Pan Alley, was a metaphor for the fight against capitalism itself. Pete was still quite young— just twenty-one—and uncompromisingly intense. He was determined to use folk music to organize workers and build the union movement, and soon after returning to New York, he learned there was at least one other young radical in town with exactly the same idea.

187

Lee Hays seemed as large and weather-beaten as an unpainted barn, and looked much older than his twenty-seven years. He had recently come north from Commonwealth Labor College in Arkansas, a small communal outfit which prided itself on being more radical than its rival, the Highlander Folk School. There, Hays had been a teacher, agitprop playwright, songwriter, song leader, and cook. He was a difficult sort who ate too much, drank too much, complained continually about his health, and combined a crabby, crotchety brilliance with an aura of defrocked southern religiosity. He was in perpetual rebellion against the values of his father, a strict Methodist preacher who died when Lee was a teen-ager; his hero was Claude Williams, a leftist Presbyterian minister and guiding spirit of Commonwealth College who'd become a near-legend in the South because of his organizing work with sharecroppers. Early on, Williams had discovered that gospel hymns and Negro spirituals could easily be transformed into rousing organizing songs—with some, all you had to do was substitute the word ''union'' for ''Jesus.'' Under Williams's tutelage, Lee Hays became a nimble lyricist with a knack for rewriting hymns, and the ability to make the songs spring to life with his glorious, rolling, church-house bass voice.

When Commonwealth folded in 1940, friends encouraged Hays to take the songs he and Williams had been collecting and developing—which included classics like ''We Shall Not Be Moved'' and ''Roll the Union On''—to New York, and see if they could be put to wider use by the labor movement. Hays had the vague hope of forming a group that would go around singing the songs in union halls and on picket lines. This was, of course, essentially the same thing Pete Seeger was intending to do, and it didn't take long for the two of them to find each other in New York's minuscule folk music community. They soon were singing together at small gatherings, Lee's bass mixing nicely with Seeger's tenor.

Hays had just started rooming with a young left-wing writer named Millard Lampell in a small, dark Chelsea apartment. Lampell was handsome, gregarious, and athletic, an all-American type, the son of a Jewish garment worker from Paterson, New Jersey. He'd attended the University of West Virginia on a football scholarship, but made his mark in school by infiltrating and exposing several local neo-fascist groups for his senior thesis . . . which then became the basis for an article in *The New Republic*.

Coincidentally, Lee Hays had written a brief, witty piece in the same issue and Lampell sent him a fan letter which burgeoned into a correspondence between them. As it happened, both men landed in New York at about the same time—Hays with his music and Lampell to work for *Friday*, a short-lived "progressive" version of *Life* magazine—and they decided to share an apartment.

They were an unlikely pair of roommates, to say the least. Lampell was aggressive, ebullient, a self-promoter, wise guy, and womanizer. Hays was slow-moving, painfully shy, with a subtle, rural style of humor, and admittedly terrified of big-city women. Lampell was too busy with his life to be much bothered by the living arrangements; Hays, more reflective, found his roommate rather grating . . . although he had to admit that when Pete Seeger came over and they all sat around trying to make up labor songs, Millard was the fastest and cleverest of the bunch. A little *too* fast, perhaps, but there was no denying his talent.

Within a matter of days, Seeger had established himself as a more or less permanent resident of the Chelsea flat. He and Hays worked together constantly, with Lampell an increasingly interested observer. One of their first visitors was Woody Guthrie—rather flush at that moment with his network radio success—who came by one afternoon with his wife and children. Hays had seen Woody perform with Will Geer once at a cocktail party; Lampell had never heard of him. Both were greatly impressed by his musical ability, and also by his *authenticity*: this guy was a real, down-home, proletarian Okie, with an egregiously Okie wife and blond Okie kids who spent most of the afternoon flushing the toilet, obviously a new and wondrous experience for them.

Later, Woody sent Mary and the kids home and dragged Seeger, Lampell, and Hays up to a burlesque house on Forty-second Street, where he introduced them to the doorman, who was standing outside the theater in a bizarre blue-and-gold uniform and, when Woody whipped out his guitar, began to sing along in a sweet country tenor. After that evening on the town, Guthrie whooshed out of their lives and wasn't heard from again until he started sending them letters from California.

His presence was felt, though. It was felt especially by Millard Lampell, who began to imitate Woody's songwriting style with startling ease. Mill had heard country music in college, had even played the harmonica some, but he hadn't been fully aware of the music's potential for political irreverence until he met Woody; he certainly felt more at home with Guthrie's playful, biting style than with Hays's more hortatory religious anthems. "The day after Woody left," Hays would later recall, "Millard began writing just like him. Millard always was a great assimilator."

One of Lampell's first efforts was called "The Ballad of October 16," written to the tune of "Jesse James," and it was a stunning success. It wasn't a labor song, but an attack on Franklin Roosevelt and Congress for passing the nation's first peacetime military draft bill. The chorus went:

> *Oh Franklin Roosevelt told the people how he felt,*
> *We damn near believed what he said.*
> *He said, "I hate war and so does Eleanor but*
> *We won't be safe till everybody's dead."*

The song was a turning point, of sorts. It opened a bold new direction for Seeger, Hays, and Lampell—*peace songs*—and their music began to take on a puerile, insolent tone that reflected the rather embarrassing political realities. The Communist Party, still asserting its neutrality in the war, was looking more and more ridiculous. As public sympathy shifted strongly toward England and against Germany (with an assist from Edward R. Murrow's rooftop journalism from London during the blitz), the Communists found themselves stranded in murky agreement with John L. Lewis, Henry Luce, a handful of aging isolationist politicians, and the right-wing's lunatic fringe. The party grew shrill attempting to explain this odd turn of events.

Throughout the winter of 1941, the three young men churned out their radical peace songs. They were assisted occasionally by Pete Hawes, a well-to-do Brahmin friend of Seeger's who took an interest in the radical arts, and also by Allen Sloane, a frighteningly intense college pal of Lampell's. Alan Lomax stopped by once or twice, and gave his blessings. "What you are doing is the most important thing in music today," he told them with characteristic understatement, and encouraged them to study Woody Guthrie's work. They hardly needed the encouragement. Much of their early material sounded distinctly like Guthrie, although it was burdened by a mocking, *collegiate* sort of humor that was more heavy-handed than anything Woody might have done.

In early February, Seeger was invited to perform for the American Youth Congress in Washington. He decided to bring Hays and Lampell along, and the three of them sang together publicly for the first time. The response was explosive. The delegates had never heard such songs before—songs which directly attacked the President—and more, *ridiculed* him. Seeger, intending to protect his father's job in the Roosevelt administration—and also to honor a Left tradition—chose a revolutionary pseudonym for the occasion: he was now Pete Bowers.

The trio performed regularly at Left functions in New York after that, and immediately were faced with the vexing question of what to call themselves. They spent several long evenings trying to find an appropriate name. Seeger flipped through the manuscript of protest songs he'd compiled with Lomax and Guthrie, shouting out words and phrases. Then they read several of Woody's letters aloud, hoping to find something clever and progressive. Finally, Hays remarked that most American families owned two books: the Bible and the *Farmer's Almanac*. The Bible was a guide to the next life, and the *Almanac* to this one; they hoped their music would prove as useful as the *Almanac* was. "How about the Almanac Singers?" someone said. It wasn't a name that touched off fireworks, but it would do.

The Almanac Singers turned out to be quite a novelty. Not only were they the first urban folk-singing group ever assembled, but they developed a life style that was fairly unique for New York in 1941. They moved into a huge loft on Fourth Avenue near Union Square just a block away from Communist Party headquarters—where they lived and worked communally, sharing all the money they received for performing and recording. The proximity to party headquarters was just a coincidence, but it was a rather appropriate symbol. The ties were certainly close, although less than formal. A number of people like Earl Robinson, the folk-oriented composer and member of the party's Cultural Section, served as unofficial political chaperones, giving advice but never orders. In the disciplined, puritanical world of the Communist leadership, the Almanacs were considered a bit rambunctious—the idea of living in a commune was considered rather racy—and unreliable. For the most part, the party left the group alone . . . although there were occasional brushes with lunkheaded functionaries. In one case, the Almanacs had to audition for a panel of American Youth Congress leaders before they'd

be hired to play at a convention; one of the panel suggested that
Lee Hays's song "Jim Crow" be changed to "Jim Crow Gotta
Go" in order to conform with an official AYC slogan. The song
remained as it was.

Despite their dangerously experimental and creative tenden-
cies, the Almanacs received a good deal of favorable publicity
from the *Daily Worker*, which had little else to cheer about that
awful winter. On March 24, the *Worker* ran its first long article
about them, an account of Bowers and Hays's appearance at the
League of American Writers conference. The story was titled
"America Is in Their Songs," and featured a picture of the two
of them—Lampell was elsewhere that evening—looking rather
rumpled in suits and ties. Bowers, it was reported, gave a talk
about ballads as a "people's form of expression" and then sang
a few with Hays. Afterwards, Theodore Dreiser was moved to
remark, "If there were six more teams like you, we could save
America."

Woody, meanwhile, was languishing in Los Angeles. He wrote
to Seeger: "Wife and kids are in pretty good shape. They like
settling down. I said they." With nothing much else to do, he
began hanging out at the library for the first time since Pampa.
Once again, his reading was eclectic: a book about soil erosion
touched off a flurry of letters to Seeger, Will Geer, and Lee Hays.
Woody seemed shocked to discover that certain crops depleted
the soil more than others—a surprising admission for the "Dustiest of the Dust Bowlers"—and that absentee landlords had helped
create the dust bowl by refusing to allow tenants to rotate their
crops. The letter to Hays was a lengthy, serious discussion of
strategies that "People's Organizations" might use in the South
to get through to the poor farmers. "If we approach farmers on
concrete things like soil reclamation, it'll be easier to approach
them on the poll tax." He also suggested that the Left form a
"National Committee on Soil Saving," and closed with a bene-
diction: "For Jesus said, 'The poor shall inherit the earth . . .'
and we don't want it to be all wore out and eroded down as slick
as an 8 ball when we get it."

Also at the library Woody found a fiction-writing textbook and
began working on practice assignments. Ed Robbin would come
over to visit and find him sitting at the typewriter, writing like
crazy and not at all distracted by the children crawling all over

his lap. He seemed to write the way other people doodled—mindlessly, easily, compulsively. When he wasn't typing, he'd spend long hours leafing through his old songbooks, filling each empty page with strings of words, aimless ramblings, really, that ranged from extravagant fears about the rich folks coming down on him for being too dangerously subversive to childlike dreams of the day when "the soldiers wake up and go over to the working folks side and then the rich crooks will be whipped and then the working folks will take over the country and they'll be the boss and run everything."

In the long, idle afternoons, Woody found himself growing closer to his children, *studying* them, discovering them for the first time: Gwen was quiet, reflective, and ladylike. Sue was bouncy and clever. Bill didn't talk much yet, but careened around the house precariously, always getting into trouble. One day Bill pulled down a vase of flowers and Woody wrote a verse about it:

> *Ubangi, Ubanger, Youbangie, You*
> *You bang Teeny and Billy bangs Sue*
> *Daddy and mommy are mad enough to kill,*
> *Picking up the flowers what Bill did spill . . .*

The kids loved it, went marching through the house reciting it, and Woody watched them, amazed. What an appreciative audience they were—like the Okies in the boxcars, hanging on his every word. He'd sit out on the porch with his guitar in the afternoons, entertaining them—soon Ed Robbin's children were coming over as well—with songs that were also games. He'd have them stick their fingers in the air, then on their noses, then on their chins . . . He could do this endlessly; as long as their attention held, his never wavered.

Mary watched these idyllic scenes happily, but without any illusions. She was almost beyond caring whether Woody was finally ready to settle down. Seven years of abandonments and disappointments had been more than enough. She was just treading water now, waiting for the right set of circumstances to make her move. She was twenty-three years old, and increasingly confident she could survive on her own. She'd find a job easily enough and, eventually, another man.

For now, though, life with Woody was relatively painless. Ed and Clara Robbin were ideal next-door neighbors. Ed was tall, calm, and soft-spoken; Clara was a tiny, twinkly Russian émigré who always was cooking more than the Robbins could eat, and inviting the Guthries over for dinner. Mary loved them for their warmth and hospitality, but was put off by their politics. Woody was in deep with the Communists again now too, and insisted on dragging her off to classes at the Workers' School, which she found utterly boring. Also, the Robbins would have fund-raising parties from time to time where she'd be expected to dance with Negro men and vodka was served. Mary was convinced that vodka was a dangerous Soviet hallucinogen of some sort: at one party, a man got drunk on the stuff and spent the whole night howling and crying like a dog in the backyard.

As the weeks passed and nothing changed, Woody grew restless again. There still wasn't much work to be had, just occasional left-wing meetings and house parties. A finance company was after him, threatening to repossess the Pontiac (which he'd managed to bang up pretty badly on the trip across country). He was drinking more heavily—though it never did take all that much to get him drunk—and went on a rampage one night, smashing beer bottles through the windows of the house. Mary, stronger now, was tolerating less; they argued fiercely over trifles. She was waiting for him to find an excuse and go.

He wrote to the Almanacs frequently, and longingly, giving encouragement and advice in a rather avuncular tone. In early April, he wrote to Lampell: "How's the loft? Lofty enough for you? Don't let Pete and Lee go highbrow on you. . . . Stick together you guys. . . . Sometimes I set around and picture you old boys up there hoeing your row and I never seen 3 fellers I'd of took more stock in. Always busy. You come and went and come and went, and after you come a time or two, you went. . . . [I] would shore like to get with you boys and steal some water mellons and splash some branch water." And it's likely that he would have slipped off to New York and joined the Almanacs right then if Gunther Von Fritsch hadn't entered his life.

Von Fritsch was a director of documentary films, working for the Bonneville Power Administration in Oregon. He'd already made one film, *Hydro,* about the building of the first of a series of dams across the Columbia River, and now he was planning to make another. He had a vague notion of centering the documentary on a homespun, folksy character who'd explain all the benefits the dams were bringing to the Pacific Northwest, and a friend of his in Los Angeles, a screenwriter named Eugene Solo, recommended Woody Guthrie.

In early April, Von Fritsch visited the Guthries and spent an afternoon listening to Woody sing and tell stories. "I could see he had the kind of talent I was looking for," the director would remember. "But I hadn't made up my mind—Guthrie was one of several possibilities I was playing with." Several weeks later, possibly in response to a letter from Woody, Von Fritsch wrote to say that he still wasn't sure about the job. The funding for the film wasn't set; there would be a delay before any decision was made.

But Woody had no other offers that were even tentative, and decided to force the issue. He loaded the family into the battered Pontiac and set out for Portland in early May. Mary was excited by the idea of Woody starring in a film—he'd neglected to tell her there wasn't any sure job—and decided to give him one last chance.

It was a difficult trip north. At one point, Woody was forced to hock the family radio for money to feed the kids. They arrived in Portland in awful shape, hungry and tired and dirty. Von Fritsch and his superior, Stephen Kahn, saw the car pull up—a new Pontiac, inexplicably battered, with a broken window, upholstery that was stained and ripped, possessions piled high inside, and blond children spilling out—and couldn't help taking pity. Even though it seemed increasingly unlikely that the movie would actually be made, Von Fritsch and Kahn asked Bonneville Power Administration director Dr. Paul J. Raver if there wasn't some way they could put Guthrie on the payroll for a while. Raver said he wanted to meet the man first, and Woody strolled into the office with his guitar. He emerged an hour later with a thirty-day contract as a temporary laborer, paid at the rate of $266.66 per month.

It would be the most productive month of his life.

In April, the Almanac Singers began using their loft for Sunday-afternoon concerts to help pay the rent. They were joyous, free-form affairs, attended by most of the folk musicians in the area: Leadbelly, always immaculate in his suit and tie; Aunt Molly Jackson and her clan; Burl Ives; Blind Sonny Terry, the harmonica player; Richard Dyer-Bennett, who sang the classic ballads in artsy, academic fashion; Josh White. Non-musicians were charged thirty-five cents admission, beer was sold for ten cents a cup, and sometimes as many as a hundred people crowded into the loft—which provided more than enough money to keep the Almanacs afloat.

But the mere experience of performing was more important than the money. The Almanacs were still experimenting, just beginning to discover their own possibilities, and the Sunday sessions were a laboratory of sorts. The afternoons glided easily from the exuberant amateurism of an audience sing-along to the scorching virtuosity of Sonny Terry's harmonica solos; there was room enough for everything from Burl Ives's commercial sweetness to Aunt Molly Jackson's rasp. One moment Richard Dyer-Bennett would be singing words that were hundreds of years old, and then the Almanacs would be using essentially the same music to improvise agitprop verses based on the week's headlines. It was as if a new source of energy had been discovered, a new power unleashed. Much to their amazement, Seeger and Hays and Lampell found they could get a hundred people—*city* people—singing and stomping, the walls of the old loft shaking with the music.

At the same time, the group was looking for someone willing to record their peace songs. They spent several months knocking on doors before Alan Lomax, Nick Ray, and Joe Thompson (of NBC radio) convinced Eric Bernay, who owned a small record store on Forty-fourth Street and a smaller distribution company called Keynote Records, to take the gamble. Bernay, formerly an editor of the Communist literary magazine *New Masses*, had a history of coming to the rescue of offbeat musical efforts. In 1938, he had persuaded the *New Masses* to sponsor John Hammond's landmark concert *From Spirituals to Swing*, a history of black music that was performed before Carnegie Hall's first integrated audience. But even Bernay was worried about the incendiary nature of the Almanacs' music: rather than risk his Keynote label, he released the six songs on "Almanac Records." The album was called *Songs for John Doe*.

The response to the album was much stronger than expected, although the Almanacs never learned exactly how strong, since Bernay never paid them royalties. Predictably, it sold best among New York leftists but the songs also reached a surprisingly wide audience. In fact, isolationist *Time* magazine felt the need to warn its readers: "Honest U.S. isolationists last week got some help from recorded music that they would rather have not received. . . . Professionally performed with new words to old folk tunes, *John Doe*'s singing scrupulously echoed the mendacious Moscow tune." *The Atlantic* magazine published an article by Carl J. Frederich, a Harvard professor of government, which described Communist infiltration in the arts—"Poison in Our System," it was called—and characterized the Almanac songs as "strictly subversive and illegal." The records even made it to the White House—probably via Nick Ray or Lomax—where Eleanor Roosevelt was said to think them clever, "but in poor taste." Her husband reportedly raged briefly and wondered if there was some way the singers could be arrested.

Soon the Almanacs were preparing a second album, labor songs this time, which Bernay apparently considered safe enough to release on Keynote itself. If the peace songs seemed primarily a reflection of Lampell's brashness, the labor songs owed more to Hays's southern religiosity. One of them even was called "Get Thee Behind Me Satan" and made joining a union seem as difficult as getting into heaven:

> *A redheaded woman took me out to dine,*
> *Says, "Love me baby, leave your union behind!"*

Lampell made his presence felt on the labor album too, though. He wrote a third verse to Woody's "Union Maid" and, sitting out on the fire escape with Seeger one warm spring afternoon, collaborated on "Talking Union," perhaps the Almanacs' most famous song. It was a classic, Woody-style talking blues, describing—in great detail—how to start a union. It moved from leaflets and meetings to the perils of stool pigeons and speed-ups, to the climax when the boss looks out the window and sees "a thousand pickets and they all agree . . . He's a *bastard*!"

The album of labor songs, called *Talking Union*, was recorded in late spring. As with *John Doe*, everything was credited collectively. No individual Almanac Singer was named as the writer or performer of any of the songs. It was a point of political principle: the Almanacs aspired to anonymity. They modeled themselves on the early Group Theater, which was established as a community of equals (but some of whose members, such as Clifford Odets and John Garfield, had too much talent to remain

equal for long). Another source of inspiration was the Anonymous movement, a group of poets in Paris in the early 1930's—
some well known, others not—who published collectively to
confound the critics and make sure all their work received equal
attention.

The strict anonymity didn't last for long with the Almanacs,
but it remained a strong influence—a shared ideal—within the
group. Actually, it would have been almost impossible to figure
out precisely who wrote what in any case. Sooner or later, each
of them contributed something, if only a line, to just about every
song. The process was rather casual, like a parlor game; whoever
happened to be around when songs were being written—even
guests—helped out. The Almanacs found they worked surprisingly well together, given their diverse personalities.

Seeger usually was the first one up in the morning, decidedly
un-hung over, tinkering with his banjo before any of the others
stirred. He was the musical heart of the group, the only accomplished musician of the three. But it was more than just his ability
to play the banjo: Pete had a *sense* of the music, he knew what
would work. He was always experimenting, trying old songs in
new styles and tempos. His discovery that when you slowed down
"Groundhog" it became a beautiful processional was the musical
foundation for Hays's words for "Jim Crow." He would drape
himself across a chair and start playing a bluegrass version of
"The Internationale" and sing, "Oh don't forsake me, little darlin' . . ." His musical inventiveness and political radicalism were
accompanied by a deep personal conservatism and orderliness.
He was the de facto manager of the group; he paid the bills, kept
a list of bookings, and probably did most of what little cleaning
was done.

Hays was the oldest, the theoretician, the most experienced
politically and in front of an audience . . . and the cook. He
would bake fifteen loaves of bread at a time, the aroma swelling
through the loft and out into the street; he would assemble great
foaming and mysterious soups and stews. He shuffled through the
loft sourly, though, often diverting pragmatic discussions about
this song or that performance into dark, theoretical alleys. He
was troublesome, bitter, and often sloppy drunk, but he came
from the same part of the country as the music did, which gave
him an authenticity—like Woody's, but watered down by his in-
tellectuality—that covered a multitude of sins.

Lampell seemed less involved than the others, possibly because he was the only one with an active sex life (though Seeger was beginning to take halting steps in that direction, courting an attractive young actress). He was a writer, not a musician or a performer. He saw the Almanacs as a lark, an adventure, something he happened to get involved in—temporarily, no doubt—that year. He was, when aroused, the group's promoter, always figuring out new angles, ways to get publicity, to gain a larger audience. It was probably Lampell's idea that the Almanacs should go on a cross-country labor-organizing tour that summer; it certainly was his plan to get the C.I.O. to sponsor them. Although the C.I.O. withheld a full endorsement, it agreed to help with an itinerary and Lampell began to make the arrangements. He was the easiest talker of the bunch, the best interview for the reporters who'd started coming around.

The three Almanacs soon were joined occasionally by two others. Pete Hawes, Seeger's Brahmin friend, had learned a few chords on the guitar and, as early as *John Doe*, could be heard singing along. Hawes wasn't much of a creative force, but he helped fill the stage (going by the name of Joe Bowers) and, perhaps more important, helped pay the rent. The other new member was Bess Lomax, Alan's younger sister, who joined the group after graduating from Bryn Mawr (and occasionally used the name Cora Jackson). Bess was, without doubt, the sanest person ever associated with the group. She was a sweet, plump woman, kindly and intelligent, a solid musician with a good voice and, like her brother, a vast repertoire of songs.

The pseudonyms and militant anonymity invested the Almanac Singers with a certain air of romance and drama. The members tended to mythologize themselves and each other shamelessly. They invented proletarian (especially rural) backgrounds for themselves, spoke with a southern lilt, and, as time went on, made quite a show of dressing like downtrodden workers. Few were aware that Pete Seeger had gone to Harvard; he seemed more a figment of Erskine Caldwell's imagination. Millard Lampell, formerly of Paterson, New Jersey, now claimed to come from Kentucky, except when he slipped and said West Virginia. Lee Hays's past was a mysterious raveling of dire illnesses and tragedies, which seemed to change slightly with each retelling. Most of it was harmless posturing, the sort of youthful playacting that would seem more embarrassing in retrospect than it was se-

rious at the time. Apparently, they brought off their respective
acts rather well though: Mike Gold, the *Daily Worker* columnist,
who became a regular at the loft on Sunday afternoons, certainly
was hornswoggled. "The boys are Southerners," he wrote, "born
with a sense for the right rhythm and drawl of these songs. When
they get going, they are irresistible. . . . Here, above the huffing
trucks and grimy factories of Fourth Avenue, an American folk
legend was being made right under one's nose. . . . Yet hasn't
the revolutionary workers' movement thus stimulated folk-art in
every land?"

Woody Guthrie hadn't written very many songs since leaving
New York, and certainly none that were memorable. But now he
burst out of his dry spell spectacularly. It wasn't simply that he
wrote twenty-six, or however many, songs in the thirty days he
was employed by the BPA (twenty-six would become the usual,
if unverifiable, figure). It was the maturity, grace, brilliance, and
diversity of the songs he wrote—anthems, work songs, ballads,
talking blues.

The anthems were particularly fine, filled with lush, dense po-
etic imagery. "Roll On, Columbia" was a stately and elegant
waltz (to the tune of Leadbelly's "Irene") that evoked the maj-
esty of the lower river as it flowed into the sea. By contrast,
"The Grand Coulee Dam" was wild and powerful like the river
upstream, where the dam—still under construction when Woody
visited it—was located. It was written to the "Wabash Cannon-
ball," and contained spectacular, detailed images and unsus-
pected rhymes:

> She heads down the granite canyon and she bends across
>   the lea
> Like a dancing, prancing stallion down her seaway to the
>   sea;
> Cast your eye upon the greatest thing yet built by human
>   hands,
> On the King Columbia river, it's the big Grand Coulee
>   dam.
>
> In the misty crystal glitter of that wild and windward spray,
> Men have fought the pounding waters and met a watery
>   grave.

*Well, she tore their boats to splinters, but she gave men
   dreams to dream
Of the day the Coulee dam would cross that wild and
   wasted stream.*

His songs were beginning to sound like Walt Whitman's poetry, drunk with details. In "Roll On, Columbia," he felt the
need to list all the river's tributaries. "The Grand Coulee Dam"
included one verse devoted to the different types of factories along
the river, and another stuffed with place names: Umatilla Rapids,
the Priest, Cascades, Shelillo Falls. He wrote the Almanacs ad-
vising them to include more details in their songs: if they ever
expected to reach the workers, they'd have to mention the
"wheels, whistles, steam, boilers, shafts, cranks, operators, tug-
gers, pulleys, engines and all of the well known gadgets that
make up a modern factory."

Each day he'd go out in a BPA car and inspect a different
portion of the river. The idea that the *government* was building
all these massive dams was especially thrilling. It was what socialism would be like when it came to the United States. He loved
to commune with the thousands of construction workers—sweaty,
muscular, pouring concrete, driving bulldozers, using machines
of all descriptions with consummate skill, doing *honest* work. He
celebrated their achievements in work songs like "Jackhammer
John" and "My Uniform's My Dirty Overalls . . ." and especially "Hard Traveling."

In his wanderings, he found that a number of Okies had come
up through California to the Pacific Northwest. Some were eking
it out as scrub farmers—Woody wrote a song suggesting that the
dams would finally bring electricity to their farms. Others still
lived in government camps. For them, he wrote the last and,
many would argue, the best of his dust bowl songs, "Pastures of
Plenty." It was one of his most solemn pieces, almost a dirge,
based on a version of the old folk tune "Pretty Polly." In it, he
once again traced the migrant experience, through the hard times
to the big, green valleys of the Pacific Northwest, and ended on
an unexpected patriotic note:

*It's a mighty hard row that my poor hands have hoed
My poor feet have traveled a hot dusty road,*

Out of your Dust Bowl and westward we roll,
And your desert was hot and mountain was cold.

I've worked in your orchards of peaches and prunes,
Slept on the ground in the light of the moon,
On the edge of your city you've seen us and then,
We come with the dust and we go with the wind.

California and Arizona, I make all your crops,
And it's north up to Oregon to gather your hops,
Dig the beets from your ground, cut the grapes from your
*   vines*
To set on your tables your light sparkling wine.

Green pastures of plenty from dry desert ground,
From the Grand Coulee Dam where the water runs down,
Every state in the union us migrants have been,
We work in your fight, and we fight till we win.

Well, it's always we ramble, that river and I,
All along your green valley I'll work till I die,
My land I'll defend with my life, if it be,
Cause my pastures of plenty must always be free.

He was greatly moved, once again, by his contacts with the
migrants and wrote to the Almanacs about going into the "tents
and shacks" and asking the people what songs they knew:

I made a little speech in each tent and I said you folks are
the best in the west, why don't you take time out and write
some songs about who you are, where all you come from,
where all you been, what you was a huntin for, what happened to you along the way, the work you done . . . the
things you want to do. Your songs are not your songs, but
songs somebody else has put in your head, and for that matter, why had you ought to sing like you're rich when you
ain't rich . . . why had you ought to sing like your satisfied
when you ain't satisfied, or junk like you hear over these
nickel machines, or over the radio? Every one of them would
lean and look toward me and keep so still and such a solemn
look on their faces, there in those little old greasy dirty hovels

that it would bring the rising sun to tears. In a few minutes
some young and dreaming member of the family would break
down and say, I been a thinkin' about that ever since I commenced to singin', and then the whole bunch would enter
into a deep religious conversation and decide that was right.
On more than one night, on more than one day, I've heard
my Oakie friends ask me, Say mister, you dont happen to be
Mister Jesus do you? Come back?

It was an extraordinary slip, the first real outburst of the mes-
sianism—combined with false humility, the idea that any old Okie
could write like him—that always had been a tacit part of his
work. It's probable that Woody simply was carried away by the
incredible flow of songs, the otherworldly surge of words that
month. Omniscient images had begun poking their way more
forcefully into many of his lyrics . . . as well as the unspoken
assumption that he could cram the whole country into his songs;
the belief—like Whitman's—that *he* could say what America was.
Usually he was more artful about it than in his letter to the Almanacs, but he was gradually being overwhelmed by a sense of his
own destiny. Sometimes, as in his famous bragging song, ''The
Great Historical Bum,'' he exorcised those feelings playfully:

I'm just a lonesome traveler, the great historical bum,
Highly educated from history I have come,
I built the Rock of Ages, it was in the year of one
And that's about the biggest thing that man has ever done.

I worked in the Garden of Eden, that was in the year of
two,
Joined the apple-pickers union and always paid my dues.
I'm the man who signed the contract to raise the rising sun
And that's about the biggest thing that man has ever done.

The song continued through ten more verses, on up to the Grand
Coulee Dam: Woody Guthrie's history of the world. And it *did*
sometimes seem that anything was possible that month. He wrote
one of his best talking blues, ''Talking Columbia,'' in which he
predicted that someday everything would be made out of plastic,
tossed in awful, wonderful lines about salmon having ''Senators,
politicians too . . . Just like a president, they run every four

years," and closed by saying that he didn't like "Dictatorship none, but I think the whole country ought to be run . . . by *Electtricity!*"

He would go out and scribble madly in notebooks each day, and then refine his ideas at home each night. He was lost in his work, numb to his family and the rest of the world. The finance company caught up with him and repossessed the Pontiac; he didn't care. Nor did he care very much when Mary, who'd found that moviemaking in Portland wasn't exactly Hollywood, began stepping out at night, bar-hopping with one of the other young women in their apartment building, leaving him to baby-sit and work on his songs. At times she'd even tempt fate by having men bring her home, at least to the trolley stop down the block, but Woody never seemed to be looking out the window, waiting for her to return.

By the time his thirty days on the BPA payroll ended, there was no longer much chance that Von Fritsch's film would be made: the government was diverting all nonessential funds into the war buildup. Several of the songs were recorded for possible future use, but Woody's job was done. He was stranded again, trying to figure out what to do next . . . and then the letter from New York arrived: the Almanac Singers were planning a summer tour. Was there any way he could join them?

Of course there was.

"Well," said Woody, arriving in New York smelly and bedraggled, having literally ridden across country in a cattle car, "I guess we won't be singing 'Why Do You Stand There in the Rain' anymore, will we?"

Indeed, the Almanacs were going to have to shelve much of their repertoire. The Germans had just slashed into Russia, shattering the non-aggression pact and ending the American Communists' clumsy neutrality. Socialism was now fighting for its life, and had to be defended. Peace songs were no longer appropriate.

In a way, the Almanacs' transition had begun well before the German attack. The group dived into union work that spring and became somewhat less interested in peace songs. Hitler was driving east across Europe and it hadn't required much insight, in any case, to realize that a change was coming. Even the *Daily Worker* would, on occasion, run stories about how "vigilant" Russia was, how well prepared defensively. When the attack came on June 22, the Almanacs didn't switch immediately to war songs—*that* would have been too obvious—but Woody, for one, began to squeeze savage verses about Hitler into his old songs. He seemed overjoyed to finally be able to hate the man without restraint. In fact, he became obsessed by Hitler, a villain who actually measured up to the level of evil required by Woody's comic-book fantasies of the struggle between the workers and the bosses.

Millard Lampell, meanwhile, was busy organizing the summer tour, working through a friend—Saul Mills—at the New York C.I.O. Council, figuring out a schedule and making all the necessary arrangements. The tour would begin at a July 4 rally in Philadelphia and end with a gala appearance before Harry Bridges' longshoremen in San Francisco. Between Philadelphia and San Francisco there was an entire country full of strikes and union organizing drives. More workers were on strike in 1941—an estimated 2,363,000—than in any previous year except 1919. Lampell took a map of the country and marked all the places where confrontations seemed likely; the *Daily Worker* listed all major union conventions and he marked those too. Then he set about finding a car for the trip. His brother-in-law was a lawyer in New Jersey with some less than savory clients. One of them, Willie Moretti, died rather instantly in June and left a massive 1929 Buick touring car, which could seat five in the back and got about seven miles to a quart of oil. It wasn't the most economical way to travel, but it had a certain flair.

The night before the trip began, the Almanac Singers—with Woody Guthrie for the first time (and without Pete Hawes, who had pneumonia, and Bess Lomax, who'd decided to summer in Europe with her family)—recorded two nonpolitical albums for General Records, a small jazz-oriented label that wanted to branch out. They received a two-hundred-fifty-dollar advance for recording *Sea Shanteys* and *Sodbuster Ballads* that night, enough to get them started on the road. The six songs on *Sea Shanteys* were mostly Seeger and chorus, although Woody was called on for a less than credible rendition of "Blow the Man Down." The *Sodbuster Ballads* were more his style. He sang lead on "Hard, Ain't It Hard," "The House of the Rising Sun," and "I Ride an Old Paint." Lee Hays had the lead on two others, including "The State of Arkansas," which he just barely got through because Woody—who loved word play, especially spoonerisms (as did

Hays)—persisted in reversing lines: "I dodged behind the depot, to dodge that prairie wind," became "I peed behind the dodge-pole," and the two phrases were so twisted in Hays's mind that he could never be sure which he'd sing . . . or whether he'd just burst out laughing.

As the Buick headed west, Woody at the wheel, he and Hays kept each other occupied with their word games. "Hoobert Heever . . ." Woody would shout out, giggling madly, slamming his fists down on the steering wheel, "Heebert Hoover . . . Hobert Heeper . . ." And Hays, from the back seat, in his best Arkansas-preacher fashion: "If any man deny the name of God, let him descend into the pittomless bot . . . the pottomless bit . . . the bottomless pot . . . let him go straight to hell!"

Woody's presence—and, perhaps, the freedom of the road—had a catalytic effect on the group: suddenly everyone was at the top of his game. The songs poured out. The ideas bubbled and ricocheted back and forth in the Buick. The four seemed to feed off each other, each new phrase was quickly met with a rhyme, and the rhyme, a verse. They kept a notebook handy in the car to record anything that might turn out to be deathless, but most of the songs were effervescent, immediate, and didn't survive the trip. There *was* one bizarre exception, however: sitting around a kitchen table in Pittsburgh, they collaborated on "Pittsburgh Is a Smokey Old Town," a song that would, through some mysterious folk process, be sung by generations of schoolchildren and eventually be used as the theme for Paul Hindemith's symphony celebrating the city's two-hundredth anniversary. The tune was based on "Crawdad," which Hays had brought with him from Arkansas, and Woody came up with the best line: "What did Jones and Laughlin steal in Pittsburgh?"

From there, they moved on to Cleveland for the National Maritime Union convention—a big deal, with delegates from all over the country. As a matter of youthful pride, the Almanacs wanted to be paid a set rate for their performance. They were, after all, workers just like anyone else and deserved to be paid accordingly, instead of having the hat passed for them like beggars. Blackie Meyers, the union's vice-president and leading "progressive" influence, took them aside and said, "Sailors are the most generous people in the world. You'll make more money passing the hat than you would any other way." The collection turned out to be a middling $45.84 according to Woody's tabulation, but they were lucky to be in the hall for a remarkable spectacle: the NMU president, Joe Curran, singled out two government spies who'd wormed their way into the union to hunt for Reds, and they were driven summarily from the hall—for a moment it seemed they might be stomped to death—in a hail of boos and hisses. The Almanacs, next on the program, were smart enough to open with "Which Side Are You On?" and quickly had the sailors up out of their seats, clapping and singing along. Woody sent a breathless dispatch to the *People's World* about the convention: "Made you feel good to see all of them guys, just hard working sailors . . . shooting the living hell out of Mister Hitler and anybody else of his particular way of thinking, the . . . hired thugs was called out, put on the spot, and exposed, and mailed back home. . . . Guys from the ships with their sleeves rolled up, voting the death of Rich Man's Fascism, whang, bang, right on down the line, point after point, driving the nails in clean up to the head. Must have been 400 or 500 of them, good guys, hard and tough, and not a single dam sissy nor a stuffed shirt in the whole shebang. . . ."

On to Chicago. They sang for the striking furriers in Cicero, spent the night in a horrible flophouse on North Clark Street (and wrote the "North Clark Street Blues"), and then played for an audience of three hundred—each of whom had contributed one dollar, the biggest payday of the trip—sponsored by a left-wing theater group. One of the actors, a recently married young man named Louis "Studs" Terkel, invited the Almanacs over to his house for the night. Terkel would later remember Woody going out to the neighborhood bar for several hours, then coming back and spending the rest of the night at the typewriter, clacking out descriptions of the things he'd seen and the conversations he'd heard . . . and then throwing all the pages in the wastebasket.

Woody had been feeling pretty good about himself ever since his songwriting binge in Portland, but he was goaded to new levels of arrogance now by a burgeoning competition with Lampell—they were the quickest members of the group, the cleverest, the most active sexually. The competition soon moved beyond songwriting into other, less creative, areas: Lampell, seeking to ingratiate himself with Guthrie, invited Woody along to visit a girl he knew in Winnetka, hoping she could round up a friend. She couldn't, and while Millard was off making time, Woody wandered through the girl's upper-class home, stealing things.

Lampell eventually caught him, and returned the stolen goods
. . . but war had been declared. In Milwaukee, several days later,
Woody got drunk at a C.I.O. picnic and began staggering about,
embarrassing everyone. Lampell pulled him aside several times,
trying to calm him down, but Woody only became more outrageous. Finally he tried to goose the C.I.O. district leader's wife
and Lampell grabbed him, slammed him up against the car, then
threw him inside and tied rope through all the doors so he couldn't
get out.

But the occasional conflicts and bickering usually were stowed
away, if not exactly forgotten. Too much else was happening.
Each new day seemed more thrilling than the last. In Minneapolis, they were marching and singing on the picket line at International Harvester when the National Guard was called out and
a tear-gas battle ensued. They were caught up in the excitement,
the *privilege*, of playing for huge crowds of men and women
who were sacrificing everything to build the C.I.O. And they
were entirely amazed by their own effectiveness: the four of
them—misfits, intellectual oddballs, amateurs really—had the
power to get thousands of workers—*workers*—up and singing,"Oh you can't scare me, I'm sticking to the union . . . sticking to the union, till the day I die . . ." They could charge up a
crowd, turn them around, weld them together, get them roaring.

It was a transcendent moment, a time that each of the four—
in one way or another—would always try to recapture. "It was
the first time I got a sense of the openness and solidarity of the
labor movement," Lampell would recall. "Wherever we went,
we'd check in at the union hall and they would have a family
ready, sometimes two or three, ready to take us into their homes.
They'd get a few people together that first night and serve beer,
and tell us what was going on in the strike, and then we'd write
a song about it. Somehow the music would open these people
up, and they'd talk with great dignity and simplicity about their
lives. We got to see how people worked, what they actually did
on the job. Very often they could get us into their plants, and
there was a kind of poetry that came of all that. It had a tremendous impact on all of us. Woody had a mystique about working,
but he'd never really seen *industrial* workers before. I think it
was the first time that Woody—or any of us—saw organized labor
with this kind of strength. There was such a sense of excitement

and dedication to everything they were doing . . . and the C.I.O. was almost like a religion.''

They glided west in their touring car, convinced they were an integral part of something very important: a major change was taking place in the lives of American workers—one by one the big companies were caving in, submitting to the C.I.O.—and it was being orchestrated in large part by radicals and, especially, by Communists . . . and the Almanacs were helping it along. Woody celebrated his twenty-ninth birthday on the road, happy as he'd ever been. He was the old master of the group, the most experienced road man, the most accomplished songwriter (even Lampell had to acknowledge *that*), the one the others deferred to. All the madness of the past year—quitting the tobacco show, busting out of New York—seemed justified now. This was the sort of thing he'd had in mind all along. This was honest work, his true audience. Somewhere along the way, he wrote in the Almanac notebook: "The worst thing that can happen to you is to cut yourself loose from people. And the best thing is to sort of vaccinate yourself right into the big streams and blood of the people. To feel like you know the best and the worst of folks that you see everywhere and never to feel weak, or lost, or even lonesome anywhere. There is just one thing that can cut you to drifting from the people, and that's any brand or style of greed.

"There is just one way to save yourself, and that's to get together and work and fight for everybody."

They arrived in San Francisco in early August and made, by most accounts, a triumphant appearance before Harry Bridges and his dock workers. At the end, they were given union cards and made honorary longshoremen. Then they went out to the docks and the dockside bars, and helped Blackie Meyers in his efforts to organize the National Maritime Union on the west coast. As often as not, the sailors would want to hear popular songs and had no idea what this hillbilly music was all about, but the Almanacs were still coasting on their recent triumphs and not about to be troubled by contradictions.

Having reached their destination, the Almanacs were enjoying themselves too much for the trip to end. Pete, Millard, and Woody decided to go on to Los Angeles, and began arranging a schedule there. Lee Hays, though, had had enough; in fact, his health had been in precipitous decline ever since they'd crossed the Mississippi. At times he was so badly off, suffering from dire, nebulous maladies, that he was unable to perform. One night he went into a wild, inexplicable sweat and the others had to help towel him off. Now he was complaining of a low fever, swelling in his arms and legs, and general exhaustion. He bought a bus ticket east, intent on recuperating at April Farms, the apple orchard owned by Mother Bloor (she'd been a frequent visitor to the loft that spring) in eastern Pennsylvania. The others pressed on.

They spent the rest of August in Los Angeles, playing for a variety of groups. Woody kept a record of their appearances:

August 15	American Peace Mobilization	$10
August 16	*People's World* party	$10
	Actor's Lab	$20
August 17	Gypsum Picket Line	Collection
August 18	*People's World* meeting	$20
August 19	Electrical Workers	Collection

And so on, a different group each day until Labor Day, when they marched proudly in the parade. One night there was a reception for them at the C.I.O. Council, and Woody described the scene in a letter to Lee Hays: "Mr. Theodore Dreiser was all 'thused up . . . and said he'd do his dadblamedest to rake us up some legal tender . . . The Soviet consul member was there, Nichi Somebody, and he listened to our songs and wanted to know where he could get all the records we ever made. He's gonna send a big batch of them over to the Soviet Union because, he said, this is the first time in America he's heard music that sounds like Soviet Workers' Music and Singing. If they take a sudden notion to reproduce these records over there, naturally, you know what that might lead to—hell, we might sell a whole flock of them. It's dam good to hear that the Almanacs and Union Folks over here in the USA guessed so close to the Real Truth in selecting and choosing to back this kind of music."

In the midst of all this, Mary and the children arrived in town from Portland. There was a final confrontation, and Woody asked her what she wanted to do. He made an offer: he was going to head back to New York eventually, and she was welcome to settle down there with him but, he warned her, he was expecting to be out on the road most of the time, organizing unions. "No, thanks," she said, and took a train back to El Paso and the security of her family.

Now it was September. They had been on the road for two months. Lampell was getting tired and said he missed his New York girlfriend. He decided to go home and begin work on a fall schedule for the group. Pete and Woody decided to start home too, but by the scenic route—up the coast to Seattle, then across the northern tier.

They headed north, just the two of them in the cavernous Buick. The first stop, Portland, was a disappointment. They visited Woody's old BPA friends, but couldn't find any unions to organize. They wrote a joint letter to Lampell, Pete starting off mournfully, in his thin, elegant handwriting: "Portland is a pretty poor union town, full of factional strife, but it is a lesson to us. We hear from Seattle that we are already booked up for a while there, so we are cheered up a bit. But right now we don't feel too good, what with being broke in a boss's town. . . ."

Then Woody jumped in, in his inimitable helter-skelter fashion, giving Lampell the needle for returning to New York to see his girl: "What's the matter back there we ain't heard no darn wedding bells yet? . . . I'm fairly well sure that if you was to test Pete's blood right about now, it would register ½ drinking water and the other ½ chili; and if you want to test his head about now, it wouldn't have but *one* big thought in it and that would have to do mainly with a purty little gal by the name of—well—her initials, at least, are—Ellen . . . Flash: Latest report from Europe says that everybody's surrounded everybody else."

Seattle was even better than Pete had hoped. The C.I.O. and the CP and even the Liberals threw all sorts of work their way. On September 20, a coalition of progressive groups sponsored a fund-raising party featuring "the famous Almanac Singers of New York" and they called this affair a "Hootenanny," which is what they often called their social get-togethers. Pete and Woody had never heard the word before, and had no idea what it meant—it was, apparently, the social equivalent of a thingamajig—but they loved it. Woody kept one of the advertisements for the party in his scrapbook and noted: "This was mortally a blowout and one of their most successful hoots. Pete and me aim to put the word Hootenanny on the market."

In addition to "Hootenanny," Woody brought several stories back from the Northwest which inexplicably tickled his fancy, and which he'd tell for the rest of his life. One was a joke he heard in Seattle: Mrs. Smith dies and goes to heaven, and asks St. Peter where she can find her husband, John. St. Peter says they've got lots of John Smiths in heaven. "Is there anything special you can tell me about your husband?" "Well," Mrs. Smith says, "before he died he said he'd love me forever and turn over in his grave if I ever made love to another man." "Oh," said St. Peter, "you mean *whirling* John Smith."

Then, driving through Montana, Woody and Pete stopped in a small town for gas and started a conversation with an old geezer sitting out on a porch, whittling. "Must get pretty cold out here in the winter," Woody said.

"Not so cold," the old man replied, ". . . but *pretty damn cold*."

And Woody kept repeating that line over and over again in the car, mimicking the old guy's inflections perfectly—"Not so cold . . . but *pretty damn cold*"—and he'd giggle and shake his head in amazement. The entire Almanac summer had been like that— the slightest incidents were memorable, the worst jokes funny, the merest insights earth-shattering. All of it had been special and dreamlike and would, in time, become part of the mythology of folk music, a feat to be endlessly attempted by groups of young singers, but never quite duplicated.

The mythologizing began even before the trip was over. In Minneapolis on the way home, Woody was interviewed for the local labor newspaper. He described singing for the longshoremen in San Francisco: "They patted us on the back so much, those big bruisers, [I] pert' near thought they'd tear us apart. One of the longshoremen says to me he says, 'Hell, I thought you was gonna sing us some a these sissified cowboy songs, but you boys talk our language. That's us.' That's why the workers like our songs. . . . This damn Hollywood stuff, the stuff about love and champagne and flowers, it don't talk a worker's language. It ain't his kind of stuff. [Our] songs are . . . right out of the workers' lives."

The Almanacs opened their fall campaign in new quarters: a classic New York town house, selected by Pete Hawes, near the corner of Tenth Street and Greenwich Avenue, in the heart of Greenwich Village. Almanac House, as it came to be known, offered more privacy than the old loft—the top two floors were bedrooms—but less space. The Sunday-afternoon concerts, now called hootenannies, were squeezed uncomfortably into the basement.

It was a busy autumn, filled with as many as six bookings per night, and a stream of distinguished visitors joining the group for dinner, crowding onto the picnic benches that lined the long kitchen table. Elizabeth Gurley Flynn, the Communist Party leader and former Wobbly who'd stolen Joe Hill's heart twenty-five years earlier (he'd written a song about her, "The Rebel Girl"), now brought many of Hill's private papers to the Almanacs—an official passing of the torch—hoping the group might find some inspiration in them. Mother Bloor came by with baskets of apples and vegetables from her farm. Walter Lowenfels, the poet, a friend of Lee Hays's, and founder of the Anonymous movement, considered himself a spiritual father of the group and was a frequent visitor. Nicholas Ray, in transit from network radio to Hollywood (where he would become famous as the director of *Rebel Without a Cause* and other psychological thrillers of the 1950's), weathered a bad period in his marriage on the Almanac couch. Sonny Terry, the harmonica player, and Brownie McGhee, a guitarist recently arrived from Tennessee who would become Sonny's longtime partner, moved in temporarily and made Almanac House an interracial commune for a time, before finding more private and comfortable digs uptown. And there were lots of others, musicians and intellectuals, philosophers and drunks, and a brigade of young women with a definite tendency toward long hair and peasant blouses who found the scene and the singers rather glamorous, and were more than happy to spend hours addressing postcards announcing the next hootenanny or doing other odd jobs.

There was trouble, too, right from the start. It began when Millard Lampell took Pete Seeger, just arrived from the West, out onto the front stoop and told him that the girl he'd been mooning over all summer had fallen in love with Pete Hawes and they were planning to be married. Seeger listened quietly, then—without saying a word—leaped up and took off down the street and wasn't seen for several days. He returned more intense and officious than ever, running the house, paying the bills, worrying about scheduling, even pressuring Woody to get back together again with Mary or, failing that, at least to send her some money (Camilla Siera, one of the young women helpers, was assigned the task of accompanying Woody to the post office, making sure he didn't spend the money in a bar along the way).

Seeger worked hard to keep the Almanacs going, but his efforts weren't much appreciated by the others, who seemed blissfully unaware of all the *details* that had to be handled each day. Pete hated their callousness and undependability; it burned him that the others didn't care as much about the Almanac Singers as he did. Usually, he'd submerge his anger beneath a veneer of relentless folksiness, but sometimes it just became too much. Once the Almanacs were traveling by car to a booking and became enmeshed in a long, rambling discussion—the *usual* long, rambling discussion, studded with picky complaints—about how to make the group operate more smoothly. Everyone always had ideas, but no one, except Pete, ever did anything. Finally, someone (possibly Hays, since he could be provocative almost without effort) said, "What the Almanacs really need is a manager," and Seeger smashed his foot through a mandolin.

For the most part, though, Pete kept it all inside. He was the most accommodating of the Almanacs, the perpetual yokel and student—a pose that was galling to friends who realized that Pete was much smarter than he let on and had much more musical talent than anyone else in the group, and yet he was always subservient to the others, especially Woody.

But then, everyone cowered before Woody. He was the group's inspiration, the moral leader, the old master . . . and he never let anyone forget it. He was forever intimidating the others with his political and musical rectitude, and his Oklahoma credentials—they were all dilettantes compared to him, even Hays, who was southern, yes, but middle class, a preacher's kid. Woody, the dust bowl refugee, was the group's repository of proletarian wisdom, the ultimate arbiter of taste. He was impossibly arrogant, affecting a general air of impatience with the other Almanacs' hopelessly urban, middle-class sensibilities, rarely raising his voice but maintaining his authority with grunts, shrugs, and paralytic stares. He had, Bess Lomax thought, the feeling of a loaded gun about him.

The rest of the group played to Woody shamelessly, even down to a less than conscious attempt to affect a southwestern accent when they were in his presence, hoping to win approval by seeming as tough and experienced and authentic as he. Of course, none of it ever worked. He remained aloof, and the others stumbled into an uncomfortable and debilitating parody of Okie-ism, which seemed to mean that you didn't admit to reading books, didn't talk philosophy in public, didn't wear bourgeois clothes like suits or ties, and, in extreme cases, didn't bathe.

Woody usually was at his worst at the songwriting meetings the group held several nights a week. It was *his* music, and he set the rules. Seeger, always experimenting, would on occasion come up with a calypso melody or an adaptation of a Jewish folk tune (to appeal to the garment workers, who weren't hillbillies), and he'd be slapped on the wrist by Woody for dealing in less than what *he* considered to be the genuine article. "Too Tin Pan Alley," he'd sniff, dismissing Pete's suggestion . . . and Seeger would get so angry that he'd literally be shaking as Woody went off on some extended, elliptical discourse about Okie farmers that had nothing to do with anything they'd been talking about.

It was Lampell, though, who usually bore the brunt of Woody's wrath. Woody despised Millard's facility, the ease with which he aped the southwestern mode, the awful attempts to put on a hill country accent and claim a Kentucky past—especially when his father frequently called Almanac House from Paterson and asked, "Is Miltie there?" When he was most frustrated by Lampell, Woody had a tendency to go overboard and claim that you actually had to *experience* something before you could write a song about it. He would, in passing, slash sweet, virginal Bess Lomax for trying to sing the whorehouse song, "The House of the Rising Sun."

Lampell would calmly respond, "Does that mean you have to get your legs cut off by a railroad train to write a ballad about some poor guy who gets mangled?"

Actually, Woody's feelings about songwriting were more valid than he made them sound. He took a classic high-culture position, arguing against agitprop exhortation. You didn't have to slam people over the head; it was more artful and effective to *show* than to *tell*. He argued that writing a ballad was the ultimate test of a songwriter. Taking the story of an individual and turning it into a metaphor, like "Tom Joad," was far more difficult than just telling people to go out and join the union. He would discuss these ideas frequently with Bess Lomax—whose musical knowledge he respected because of her family pedigree—and he'd even admit to her that "East Texas Red," a ballad he'd recently written about a railroad bull in Texas who bore a certain resemblance

to Adolf Hitler, was the best thing he'd ever done. It wasn't, but
he certainly was moving in an interesting theoretical direction.
Usually, though, he didn't have the patience or, perhaps, the
conversational tools (or, perhaps, the guts) to explain his ideas
about songwriting to the others; usually it just came out as "Too
Tin Pan Alley," or "You can only write what you see," or,
more frequently, "Aw, the hell with it," and he'd be up and off
to the nearest bar.

But there *were* other times when the Almanacs, with a minimum of thinking or arguing, were able to achieve a magical syn-
thesis of the Guthrie and Lampell styles. When the U.S.S. *Reuben
James* was torpedoed by the Nazis off the coast of Iceland in late
October, killing 86 and wounding 44, Woody was inspired to
write a ballad about the incident. He decided the best way to
humanize the tragedy would be to name all 86 victims, and he
set out to do just that (to the tune of the Carter Family's "Wild-
wood Flower"):

> *There's Harold Hammer Beasley, a first rate man at sea*
> *From Hinton, West Virginia, he had his first degree.*
> *There's Jim Franklin Benson, a good machinist's mate*
> *Came up from North Carolina, to sail the Reuben James.*
>
> *Dennis Howard Daniel, Glen Jones and Howard Vore*
> *Hartwell Byrd and Raymond Cook, Ed Musselwhite and*
> *   more*
> *Remember Leonard Keever, Gene Evans and Donald Kapp*
> *Who gave their all to fight about this famous fighting ship.*

Woody brought his completed work to a songwriting meeting in
early November and everyone agreed he'd come up with a sen-
sational idea for a song, but all those names were a bit . . .
boring. You didn't have to go through all that to personalize it,
Seeger argued. A rousing, agitprop chorus could get the same
message across. If you combined a chorus with ballad verses
describing the *event* in detail, it might make a better song. Woody
agreed to give it a try and reworked the verses, while Seeger and
Lampell developed the chorus that would make the song one of
the Almanacs' best-known:

Tell me, what were their names?
Tell me, what were their names?
Did you have a friend on the good Reuben James?

But in the highly charged atmosphere of Almanac House, even a successful collaboration could cause an argument—in this case, the revival of an old argument. Woody, who was a fitful communard at best, wanted credit for writing the song, and for "Union Maid" and the others he was primarily responsible for. Alan Lomax sided with Woody, arguing that giving individual credit was the only way to head off copyright battles in the future, but the others were strongly opposed and Woody invariably lost. "Reuben James" was officially written by "the Almanac Singers." In later years, though, Seeger would—typically—give Woody credit for writing not only the verses but also the chorus.

The kitchen, the warmest room in the house when the cold weather came, was a truce zone of sorts . . . especially late at night when Guthrie and Lampell would find themselves having to coexist in the general area of the stove, writing at the long table while the others were asleep. Woody turned out dozens of pages each night. He'd rework old songs or write aimless accounts of things he'd seen that day or continue with his vast, endless autobiography. He kept a large steamer trunk in his room into which he tossed many of his pages; many others were thrown in the trash—a random filing system that depended, apparently, on his mood. Occasionally, he'd turn out another of his little newspapers, "The Daily Almanac," with little gossipy items like: "Pete Bowers and Cora Jackson on the Columbia School of the Air—$33.16 for bank account," or "The Daily Almanac is really your own newspaper. Send in all of the thoughts that you think would help the Almanac House beat Hitler quicker."

While Woody diddled at the typewriter, Lampell—much more the professional writer—was at work polishing the libretto for a symphonic piece Earl Robinson was composing about Abraham Lincoln, to be called *The Lonesome Train*. Millard's text was inspired in large part by the Sandburg biography of Lincoln, and one line which became a recurring theme was: "You could hardly tell . . . Where Lincoln left off, and the people began . . . You could hardly tell . . ."

Woody took the line, rewrote it, and used it to batter Lampell every time he entered a room: "You could hardly tell . . . Where Sandburg left off, and began Lampell . . . You could hardly tell . . ." Millard, who did not suffer needling easily, was rapidly losing patience with the whole scene.

It grew worse. One weekend, needing a satchel to carry his things out to Paterson for a visit with his family, Lampell apparently absentmindedly lifted the attaché case with Joe Hill's papers in it that Elizabeth Gurley Flynn had left the group. By chance, Woody and the others decided to take a closer look at the papers that weekend, to see if they might develop some songs based on the material. They searched the house frantically before coming to the conclusion that Lampell had taken the briefcase with him to New Jersey. It was all Woody needed. He spent the rest of the weekend drawing cartoons ridiculing Lampell, and pasted them all over the walls of Almanac House, up the staircase, hung from the ceiling, and all over Lampell's room. The cartoons were filled with Woody's usual stick figures, and bitter, childish messages:

Where is he? Lead me to him. I'll picket him! You got to get me some protection though, if they see me picketing Lampell everybody will want to do it and I'm liable to get trompled in the crush . . .

Mermaid Union: Lampell is an awful fishy character . . .

Pete Bowers advocates: You know, I don't think Mill realized, you know, how important it is, you know what I mean. Well, as I was saying. I don't think he realizes, you know, well, golly . . .

It didn't take long after that for Millard to find himself an apartment nearby where he could write in peace and bring his girlfriends, and didn't have to hide his books under the bed for fear of seeming too intellectual. He remained an active member of the Almanac Singers, still eating dinner at the house, going out on bookings, and helping to write songs. He just didn't live there anymore.

While the hounding of Lampell kept everyone entertained that fall, the disintegration of Lee Hays was proceeding less noisily, but more conclusively. Hays had never really recovered from his arduous summer. He seemed to have no energy or enthusiasm

'or bookings, but discovered great reservoirs of strength when it
came to having meetings or arguments. Even before Pete and
Woody returned from the West, Lee had organized a seminar at
Pete Hawes's country estate in New Hampshire and invited various friends to discuss the future of the Almanacs. He prepared
a lengthy agenda, which was quickly disposed of by Mike Gold,
the columnist, who suggested that the future of the Almanacs
should be to keep on writing and singing political songs . . . and
that was pretty much that.

As the most openly cerebral of the Almanacs, Hays probably
would have been uncomfortable in any case. He was always trying
to impose formalities on an aggressively informal group of people. He enjoyed thinking and arguing for the sake of thinking and
arguing; any action—even getting up in the morning—seemed
drastic without several hours of discussion, pro and con. What's
more, Lee was drinking heavily, which made him even more
indolent and lethargic than usual. He seemed to take a perverse
joy in backbiting and encouraging tiffs among the others, especially after he couldn't find a suitable place for himself in the
post-tour dynamics of Almanac House: Woody had usurped his
role as the official Southerner, his friendship with Lampell was
long gone, and Seeger was angry with him for being so completely undependable. One night when Lee begged off an important booking at the last moment, Pete trooped upstairs and found
him slumped helplessly across the bed like a beached whale, and
played "Taps" on his recorder. A meeting was held after that.
The group decided that a more dependable and less divisive bass
was needed, and Hays was banished. Lee summoned what remained of his dignity and left Almanac House without too much
of a scene. He'd later claim that the doctors diagnosed a mild
case of tuberculosis as the root of all his problems, but no one
would believe him.

The group wasted no time in finding new members after Hays
was purged. There certainly were plenty of people to choose from.
There were all sorts of Sunday hootenanny regulars, some of
whom had even been brought along on bookings from time to
time. In fact, it was never quite clear who the "official" members
of the group were at any moment; organizations that hired the
Almanac Singers expecting the original quartet were often dismayed to find a formless mass of people enter their hall: the
Almanacs, plus girlfriends, plus hangers-on, all of whom would

get onstage and attempt to sing. Or, at other times, just Pete and some amateur, a last-minute recruit, might appear. On Thanksgiving night, for example, there were two jobs—an I.W.O. lodge in Manhattan and an old-age home in New Jersey—and Pete faced the prospect of playing them both solo. So he roped Arthur Stern, an art teacher by trade and one of the Sunday-afternoon regulars, into joining him for the night. Stern sang a passable bass, and Seeger asked him to replace Hays on a more or less regular basis.

Stern was the first member of the Almanac Singers who was unabashedly urban and Jewish. He loved the music and he loved the singing (although he wasn't nearly as good as Hays), but he refused to indulge in the rural proletarian façade. He joined the group on the Lampell plan—dinner and meetings, but no room in the house; he preferred his parents' home in Queens. He was intimidated by Guthrie, but refused to be cowed. In fact, he wrote a parody that mocked Woody as effectively as Woody had gotten Lampell:

> My name is Woody Guthrie, the great hysterical bum,
> Highly saturated in whiskey, rye and rum.
> I wrote a million pages, but never read a one
> And that's about the biggest thing that Guthrie's ever done.

Hays's old room was soon filled by Agnes "Sis" Cunningham and her husband, Gordon Friesen, a pair of hard-bitten Oklahoma Communists just arrived from the South. Sis Cunningham played the accordion and sang in a harsh, distinctly rural voice. She'd been a member of the Red Dust Players, an agitprop theater group in Oklahoma, and had met Pete and Woody when they'd come through the state in 1940. She did some songwriting, but was more valued for her performing ability. Gordon Friesen had no musical ability whatever; he was a writer, very witty in a countrified way, and an absolutely demonic cartoonist. His main function with the Almanacs, aside from carrying his wife's accordion case around, was keeping Woody in line. Gordon was uniquely qualified for the job, having grown up on a scraggly dirt farm in western Oklahoma, the heart of the dust bowl. Whenever Woody started flaunting his "authenticity" and going on about the migrants, Gordon would let him have it: "Woody, what on earth are you talking about? You never harvested a grape in your life. You're an intellectual, a poet—all this singin' about ackhammers, if you ever got within five feet of a jackhammer it'd knock you on your ass. You scrawny little bastard, you're shitting the public: you never did a day's work in your life.'' He'd say these things lightly, in jest—Gordon was one of Woody's staunchest fans, even to the point of having listened to him on the Model Tobacco show—and Woody usually took the gibes well enough, with a half smile and a shrug . . . but the message got through.

Throughout all the crises and the arguments, all the comings and goings that fall, the Almanacs continued singing. It didn't seem to matter that their quality varied greatly from one evening to the next, depending on who was singing and how sober they were; the bookings just kept rolling in. On a typical weekend night, they might start at about 7 p.m. by hitting a couple of union locals, then move on to larger affairs like banquets and dances, and keep going until 2 a.m. with smaller fund-raising parties, rarely singing anywhere for more than a half hour or forty-five minutes.

The various I.W.O. lodges and union locals and Russian War Relief benefits tended to blur together after a while, but there were some memorable performances . . . and others that were eminently forgettable. At times, the group's rampant yokelism clashed with the prevailing realities of the organizations they were performing for. Arthur Stern managed to land a booking—through his father—at the Meatcutters' Union's annual banquet, a fancy, catered affair at the Hotel New Yorker. The Almanacs showed up, as usual, in boots and work shirts, studiously sloppy. "We went on after some adagio dancers," Stern would recall. "The lights lowered and we started to sing our first number, and somewhere in that first number we heard this crash onstage. It was followed by another crash, and then hot and heavy. They were throwing china off the tables, actually skimming plates at us. They were literally doing this. It was because we looked like shit and all these people were in evening clothes. My mother had her hair blued and my father was dressed up, for once in his life, in good clothes. Working-class people dress up and they don't want their entertainers to look worse than they do during the work week, and we were putting on this big romantic, proletarian affectation. They finally told us to get the hell off and leave. They never even paid us.''

They certainly must have seemed an odd-looking group as they traveled from place to place in the city by subway, their guitars and banjos slung jauntily over their shoulders. In 1941, guitars weren't nearly so common in New York as they'd later become. In fact, a half dozen people carrying, sometimes even *playing*, guitars in the subway was about as likely a sight as a tuba sextet. The Almanacs created waves of curiosity wherever they went, and usually were more than happy to oblige their fellow passengers with a song or two about the world situation. Some of their best performances were in subway stations; the acoustics were wonderfully resonant. Pete Seeger would get so excited when the group was out and together and playing around like that, he'd dash up the down escalators in the subways and go clomping along the street, one foot on the curb and the other in the gutter, like a kid.

Woody in the subways, in bars, on picket lines, in spontaneous, informal groups of people was usually a much better performer than Woody in front of an audience. He still worked hard at the craft of performing, driving everyone in Almanac House crazy by playing the records he admired over and over, and singing along. Bess Lomax would never forget "The New Casey Jones," sung by an obscure black bluesman. There was one particular verse that ended with the words "on the same track," and Woody played that phrase on the phonograph—and only that phrase—until he could repeat it exactly. Sometimes, all his hard work was reflected on stage: he'd be as good as ever, a compelling performer, sharp and funny and seemingly able to hold a note forever, simply because he believed in what he was singing.

Increasingly, though, he was erratic in formal situations. Often he'd react sharply if he sensed a lack of interest in the audience, or insufficient respect for his work. He was particularly bad with the rich, pretentious, and intellectual crowds at fund-raising cocktail parties. On one occasion, he just stopped singing in mid-verse, picked up two full bottles of liquor, and walked out. At another party, hosted by a radio big shot in a snazzy penthouse, Woody started improvising verses that insulted many of the guests—who were too busy chatting and drinking to notice. He grew more and more abusive until he finally decided that the only way to get their attention was to pull down a drapery, wrap it around him like a toga, and stomp out.

Of course, drinking had a good deal to do with this sort of

behavior. Almanac House happened to be surrounded by some of the most eclectic saloons in New York City, places where longshoremen drank with poets, where eccentrics of every conceivable description hung out. Most days, Woody "negotiated" a dollar from Bess Lomax, the only Almanac with a steady job (she worked in the music division of the New York Public Library), and headed off to Julius's or the White Horse, and inevitably got himself involved in a flagrant, convoluted, marathon debate about the divinity of the proletariat, and he'd lose all track of time, space, and bookings. His drinking probably was as serious as Hays's, but less disturbing because he'd usually agree—after being fished from a neighborhood bar—to stumble along with the group wherever they were going, often falling asleep in the subway, on the sidewalk, or onstage . . . but, as often as not, pulling himself together and managing to fake his way through. Unlike Hays, he was a happy drunk. He'd make jokes about his drinking, about going down to the blood bank and donating a pint because they'd give you a shot of whiskey if you told them you felt faint afterwards. "I told them," he'd say, "that I was a Judeo-Christian and I believed in the laws of Moses: an eye for an eye, and a pint for a pint."

For a time, the Almanac Singers were doing so well they were able to hire a black woman to buy groceries and cook a big meal each night. But the bookings began to tail off as the cold weather set in. By January 1942, there wasn't enough money to buy coal . . . or pay *last* month's rent. The group was forced to move into less expensive quarters—back to a loft, in fact—around the corner at 430 Sixth Avenue. The move was accomplished furtively, in the middle of the night. A brigade of volunteers was organized to carry everything, by hand, from Tenth Street to Sixth Avenue. Rather than help out, Woody spent the night typing as all the furniture—kitchen table, benches, chairs—was moved out from under him. The next morning, he was the last item left in Almanac House, curled up asleep on the floor next to the stove.

In addition to the financial worries, there were serious creative frustrations. The group *still* felt a bit constrained by its peace-singing past. After all the publicity they'd received, especially in places like *Time*, a flip-flop on the war would seem rather fishy. So as Russia was clobbered by the Nazis that fall and America moved closer to the brink, the best the Almanacs could do was sidle up to the issue on occasion, as with "Reuben James," where they cleverly described an event, but never said it was time to go out and whip Hitler. This subtlety made for good art, but rather limp politics. They struggled to find other ways to get the point across. In a song called "Mister Lindbergh," they mocked Charles Lindbergh and the other "America First" isolationists without ever actually advocating intervention. The best line was: "They say America first, but they mean America next . . ."

"Mister Lindbergh" was one of six songs distributed to guests at the hootenanny on Sunday, December 7, 1941 (the others were: "Union Maid," "Reuben James," "The Ballad of Harry Bridges," "High Cost of Living," and "Jim Crow"). Early in the afternoon, there was a flurry in the back of the room and someone ran up front and whispered to the singers. Arthur Stern took the microphone and announced, "The Japanese have just attacked the American fleet at Pearl Harbor."

There were no more isolationists after that, and the Almanacs finally were free to vent their passions. Woody went just about berserk that week, converting all his old songs to a war footing. "So Long, It's Been Good to Know You" became a song for soldiers saying goodbye to their girls. And there was a new chore for the "Great Historical Bum":

> There's a man across the ocean, and I guess you know him well;
> His name is Adolph Hitler, god damn his soul to hell;
> We'll kick him in the panzers and we'll put him on the run
> And this will be the biggest thing that man has ever done.

Woody was so wound up that even as he sat—in a suit and tie—waiting to perform for the National Maritime Union's Women's Auxiliary five days after Pearl Harbor, he busily scribbled war verses to old songs on his program. To the tune of "Lonesome Valley":

> Uncle Sam, let me join your army
> Let me take my woman along
> I don't want to waste time traveling
> When I get a furlough home.

And "Curly-Headed Baby":

> *Guns are roaring all around me*
> *As my love to you I write.*
> *I'll be thinking of my darling*
> *As I crawl into the fight.*

By the week after Pearl Harbor, the Sunday hootenanny was being touted as "a preview of our new Anti-Axis Album of Songs . . . The Axis Buzzards have struck the first blow, but we will strike the last!" And for those with lingering questions about the Almanac Singers' ability to move so quickly from peace to war, Woody explained it obliquely, humorously, almost giddily, in a song called "Brand New Situation":

> *I fell in love with the prettiest gal*
> *In all this big wide nation.*
> *But her daddy won't let me go with her*
> *In view of the new situation.*

In subsequent verses, he courts the girl through the prewar buildup, through "war mechanization" and "unionization" and several other "ations," and eventually is allowed to marry her so they can have children and "outnumber the Axis gang, in view of the new situation."

Meanwhile, Seeger and Lampell and the others also were working on war songs. In fact, the Almanacs were so fertile and so clever, and their conversion so rapid, that they were now the first major group of entertainers turning out war propaganda in New York . . . and CBS radio, for one, was interested in using them as morale builders. There was even some talk of the Almanacs being hired by the network to write songs describing each new major event in the war. At which point, Alan Lomax—who saw the possibility of a huge political and commercial bonanza, but also the possibility that the group's past and left-wing ties might still ruin it all—intervened and began to plead with the Almanacs to take no chances. He wrote to Woody: "It's very important I think for [the group] to hurry up and change your name, and for heaven's sake make it a good old countrified name like the 'Oklahoma Rangers' or something of the sort. Your chief point of contact with America is that of the American soil and American folk songs. Don't become the 'Headline Singers' even though you may be singing the 'Headlines.' "

Lomax's suggestion touched off a heated debate within the group. Woody kind of liked the "Headline" idea, but Pete Seeger—perhaps the most radical, in his quiet way, of them all—was adamantly opposed. He was proud of the group's associations and, what's more, a name change at that point would seem rather sneaky. It would be found out eventually and the Almanacs would seem all the more subversive to their opponents, while alienating many of their old friends. When they appeared on their first network radio show, "We, the People," they were still the Almanac Singers.

That appearance brought all sorts of offers, including the possibility of a record contract with Decca. An agent from the William Morris theatrical agency came around and talked to the group about setting up a national tour, starting in a big Catskill Mountains resort and then moving across country—first-class clubs all the way—possibly in conjunction with the USO. It was probably the William Morris agent, too, who landed the group an audition at the Rainbow Room, the posh nightclub atop Rockfeller Center.

"As soon as we walked out the elevator door, I knew Woody was going to do something awful," Bess Lomax remembered. "It was like being in a Rosalind Russell musical. There were three tough Broadway producer types sitting there. We were sort of straggly, no class, nothing slick about us. Pete made a little speech about our first song—the sort of thing that always happens in folk music, but never in nightclubs . . ."

After the first, relatively innocuous war song, the group swung into "New York City," a song they used for improvisation, and Woody and Lampell began trading nasty verses about the Rockefellers and their Center:

> In the Rainbow Room, soup's on the boil
> They toss their salad with Standard oil
> In New York City,
> Hey, New York City
> Where you really gotta know your line . . .

And:

> This Rainbow Room, she's up so high
> You can see John D.'s spirit come driftin by . . .

And:

> *Well, this Rainbow Room's a funny place to play*
> *It's a long way from here to the U.S.A. . . .*

The tough producer types weren't at all offended; in fact, they were rather amused. They approached the group and began making suggestions about how the Almanacs could be developed into a *real* cabaret act: costumes, certainly; a Li'l Abner motif, perhaps gunnysacks . . . which sent the Almanacs scurrying toward the elevators.

The William Morris agent lost interest after that, but the group's commercial success grew. A music publisher put out an Almanac songbook, with a rather mythological introduction: "Not long ago, a long lean banjo player and a school teacher from Arkansas met in a sharecropper's cabin in Missouri. . . . They met by accident and started swapping the songs they had learned in all parts of the country . . ."

The Almanac Singers reached their commercial zenith on Saturday, February 14, 1942, when Norman Corwin used them on his ultimate Popular Front-style extravaganza, a program called "This Is War," broadcast simultaneously on all four networks as a national morale booster. The Almanacs sang a bouncy old square dance tune that Seeger had converted into a war song called "Round and Round Hitler's Grave." Oddly enough, the group was never formally introduced in the script. There was some gunfire and then the narrator, Lieutenant Robert Montgomery, read: "These are all battle noises. They're all related to the roaring cannon and the stuttering machine gun, notes and harmonies and music belonging to the United Peoples. Shells will whistle at their work and we at ours, each making their special music in a special way. . . . Songs will rise up from our singing people, some well worth the nation's ear. Songs to work to and to fight to and to set our quotas to . . ." and the Almanacs began singing to their largest audience.

Having reached the nation's ear, the Almanacs promptly lost it. Three days after the broadcast, the New York *World-Telegram* reported: "All that the sponsors were looking for were some hillbilly singers to help start off the 'This Is War' radio series last Saturday, the four-network nationwide morale broadcast. . . . The program's backers were much upset today to learn that the Almanac singers have long been the favorite balladeers of the Communists and their official publications, the *Daily Worker* and *New Masses*.'' Allen Meltzer, in charge of publicity for ''This Is War,'' was quoted as saying he was ''very upset,'' and promised that the Almanacs would not be included on any of the twelve remaining programs in the series.

The New York *Post* followed the next day with an article titled ''Peace Choir Changes Tune,'' which pretty much repeated the accusations from the old article in *The Atlantic*, adding that *Songs for John Doe* had been ''withdrawn from the market and is no longer purchaseable.''

Their commercial prospects were gone, but the Almanacs continued with their Sunday hoots, their bookings and songwriting, and even with plans for another national tour. They continued for nearly a year, until almost all the members had joined the armed forces and the group officially disbanded. Woody remained a part of the Almanacs throughout, but he wasn't as active or concerned as he'd once been. His mind and heart were elsewhere.

CHAPTER 7

Like a Wild Wolf in the Canyons of New York

A year earlier, in the spring of 1941, the Almanac Singers had flirted briefly with the idea of staging a revue. It was a time when anything seemed possible and, indeed, a troupe of left-wing theatrical people and dancers were recruited with very little effort. The Almanac Players performed twice that spring and received a favorable notice from the *Daily Worker* but little else, and it was quickly forgotten in the heat of preparations for the summer tour. Years later, all that would remain from the show was the vague memory of Pete Seeger singing a duet with a wide-eyed young actress named Carol Channing, and several charming dances, choreographed and performed by Sophie Maslow, to the music of Woody Guthrie's Dust Bowl Ballads.

Sophie Maslow was one of Martha Graham's most accomplished dancers. She'd been one of the three women writhing across the stage in *American Document* when the Interlocutor said, "We are three women; we are three million women . . ." and that was only one of many memorable performances. She had joined the Graham company in 1931, and was just now establishing herself as a choreographer. She was a cultural and political progressive, and had known about Woody Guthrie's work for several years. She followed his column in the *Daily Worker*, and was quite moved by the Dust Bowl Ballads when they were released by Victor. American folk music seemed a natural area for her to explore creatively—it reminded her of the rough simplicity of the Russian Jewish songs she'd loved as a child—and she developed a series of simple, yet deceptively difficult movements for "So Long, It's Been Good to Know You" and "Goin' Down the Road Feeling Bad," and danced them in a costume that included an apron and a western hat.

Shortly after she danced with the Almanac Players in June of 1941, Woody arrived in town and Sophie arranged to meet him at the loft. She explained what she'd been doing and suggested it might be fun to perform the songs together. Woody said he didn't see why not, and they spent a disastrous afternoon trying it out: Woody sang as he always did, with long, unexpected pauses which destroyed Sophie's timing and ruined the precise movements she'd developed from the records. After several false starts, she finally asked him, "Why do you have to stop all the time? Why can't you just sing it like you do on the record? Dancers can't work like that. They have to do it exactly the same way every time."

"Well," he said, "if I want to take a breath between verses, I play a few extra chords. And if I forget the lines and want to remember them, I play a few extra chords. And if I want to get up and leave town, I get up and leave town," and that was that.

But several months later, Sophie was desperately searching for a guitar player with a sense of humor and she turned to Woody again. She had choreographed a new, experimental dance called *Folksay* that used words from Carl Sandburg's poem "The People, Yes," as well as folk songs and country humor. It featured, in addition to the dancers, two narrators with guitars who'd sing songs and swap corny stories. Earl Robinson already had agreed to be one of the narrators, and he suggested Woody Guthrie would be perfect for the other. Against her better judgment, Sophie decided to give him another try.

She had recruited most of the dancers for the piece from the Martha Graham company, and one of them was a tiny, girlish, radiant young woman—she was twenty-five, but seemed much younger—named Marjorie Mazia, who was surprisingly interested when Sophie happened to mention one day that she was going downtown to ask Woody Guthrie to perform in *Folksay*.

"He's here in town?" Marjorie Mazia asked. She'd been moved to tears when she first heard "Tom Joad" at her sister's house (each of those five hundred albums seemed to have a special function), and just *had* to meet the man responsible for that song.

So Marjorie and Sophie went to Almanac House on an afternoon in late January of 1942, and brought some fruit along as a gift. They were met at the door by Arthur Stern, who did his best to discourage them from coming in. He said Woody was sleeping, or busy or something—women were always trying to find him—but Sophie and Marjorie wouldn't be deterred and pushed on into the large room where the hootenannies were held. They found Woody standing with his back to them, staring out the window onto Sixth Avenue, wearing a red-checked shirt that seemed—as always—three sizes too big. Sophie said hello, and when he turned around Marjorie was a bit shocked by her own reaction: she'd been expecting a tall, Lincolnesque figure, but this was a forlorn little man, wiry and tense, with delicate features . . . and eyes that seemed to make immediate, intelligent contact with hers. Her heart went out to him in that instant of recognition.

Both of them would later claim they fell in love right there.

Marjorie Greenblatt Mazia had been born on October 6, 1917, in Atlantic City, New Jersey. Her parents were Russian Jewish immigrants. Her mother, Aliza Waitzman Greenblatt, was a happy, creative woman who wrote poetry in Yiddish. Her father, Isidore Greenblatt, started off by selling bananas from a pushcart in New York, then ties, and then joined his father-in-law's garment firm in Philadelphia. He was a stern, intelligent, highly principled man, successful enough eventually to move his family to Atlantic City, where the air was better. But success in business was not the central fact of his life: the real passion was for Zionism and socialism and, more than anything else, the idea of *knowledge* itself. Business transactions weren't nearly as important to him as ideas. His home was often filled with visitors discussing—heatedly, invariably—the events of the day, especially the progress toward a Jewish state in Palestine. He loved scholarly argument. Everyone said he would have made a great rabbi. And it was dreams, ideals, abstractions, aesthetics that were at the center of his family's life: the children were taught to love books and fine music; they learned to play instruments and were encouraged in art.

The whole family seemed to exist in a higher, purer realm than the rest of the world.

The Depression, when it came, was a crushing and confusing experience for Isidore Greenblatt. He was forced to move the family back to Philadelphia. He was forced to rechannel his energies away from ideals, and back into the prosaic realities of bolts of cloth, and stitches, and sales. The family suffered, but refused to relinquish its dream life. Marjorie, who was well schooled in piano but increasingly interested in dance, managed an arrangement whereby she could take dance lessons in return for providing piano accompaniment for some classes. She was a bright girl, imaginative and orderly. Her model in elementary school had been Miss White, the music teacher, who could organize an entire auditorium into wonderful four-part harmony and do it effortlessly. Marjorie lived with a certain emotional economy; she was, without question, the most practical member of the family (though there wasn't much contest). When her father's business failed, Marjorie stepped in, reorganized the books, and worked part-time in the office. But she also continued with her music lessons and dancing.

Every so often, Marjorie and her older sister, Gertrude, would go to the Academy of Music and get the cheapest possible seats, in the highest balcony, for the symphony or the opera. One evening in 1932, they went to see Mary Wigman, the revolutionary German dancer, and were roused by the dark passion of her performance. Several months later, when Leopold Stokowski held tryouts for the Philadelphia Youth Symphony, the Greenblatt sisters auditioned with a rather startling modern dance to the music of "Ase's Death" by Grieg, wearing dark blue hooded costumes of their own design. When asked what else they could do, Marjorie sat down and played the piano while Gertrude improvised a dance, and then Marjorie danced while Gertrude played. They obviously were a talented pair.

From there, it was a natural progression for Marjorie to join a group of young modern dancers in Philadelphia (Gertrude began to concentrate more on painting) and then on to New York to see the already legendary Martha Graham perform . . . and then to audition for one of Graham's classes at the Neighborhood Playhouse in 1935.

Meanwhile, Marjorie spent the summers teaching dance at a leftwing Jewish camp. One of the other counselors there was a young accountant named Arnold Goodman*; he and his best friend, Frank Walz, constituted as formidable a pair as the Greenblatt girls. In fact, as in a Victorian romance, the Greenblatt girls often had stared across the Academy of Music audience at the two boys. With little prodding, both couples began courting and soon were engaged to be married. Arnold proposed to Marjorie one day as she was boarding the bus to go to New York for a dance class. She was eighteen years old, and accepted. Her parents were tremendously pleased; it was a good match. Arnold promptly bought a small, bandbox-style house—three stories, three rooms, one on top of the other—in Wilmington, Delaware, where he was now working, and prepared for a solid, durable marriage.

But there was a problem: Marjorie was terrified of sex. She'd spent most of her adolescence galloping from one cultural activity to the next, spending all of her emotional energy "creatively." She seemed forever organizing, discussing (she was a member of the high school debating team), and deflecting. She aggressively *befriended* boys, so as not to appear the least bit flirtatious, and steeled herself against the merest sexual advances. She was expert at transforming a vulnerable moment in the back seat of a car on a double date into a discussion of the student peace movement or some other such weighty matter.

The proposed union existed in her mind more as an attractive *concept*, a fortuitous piece of symmetry, than a physical reality. Her knowledge of the process itself was relatively virginal—a discussion of hydraulics would have been quite out of place in the ethereal Greenblatt home—and the prospect of marriage didn't improve the situation much. Before the wedding Marjorie went to a gynecologist to be fitted for a diaphragm, but when the details were explained, she panicked and refused. "I'll do without," she announced, and though she relented a bit subsequently, their sex life was marginal at best. Arnold, a gentleman throughout, accepted the situation as a temporary difficulty that would be overcome with time and trust.

But there never was much time. Marjorie spent more hours on the train back and forth to New York than she did at home. She was invited to join Martha Graham's company in 1936, and took

*Arnold Goodman is a pseudonym. I am not using his real name and have changed other facts concerning him out of respect for his privacy.

Mazia as her stage name. She quickly showed so much aptitude for teaching—as well as a light, delicate quality as a dancer—that Graham asked her to assist with the many classes she was forced to teach each week to keep the company afloat financially. In the mornings, Marjorie would teach movement to the actors at the Neighborhood Playhouse, then from one to three o'clock in the afternoon there would be rehearsal for the Graham company; and from four-thirty to six, the company class. Often she'd have to stay in the evening to assist with or demonstrate for other classes, and wouldn't arrive home in Wilmington until well after midnight, when Arnold would be (mercifully) asleep. Summers were spent at Graham's Bennington College encampment in Vermont . . . and then there were national tours each year, and occasional performances with experimental ensembles like Sophie Maslow's New Dance Group. With all of that, she pushed her husband off to the periphery of her life. Eventually she rented a room in a boardinghouse on Fourteenth Street in New York, and returned to Wilmington only on weekends to keep up appearances for the various parents.

She worshipped Martha. She was overwhelmed by the privilege of basking in the brilliance of the presiding genius of modern dance; she happily offered herself for any menial task that needed to be done and was, predictably, the most organized member of the company. On tour, Marjorie always took it upon herself to make sure the other dancers received their luggage and that all the arrangements were in order. What's more, she had the unique ability—and it was possible only because of her utter devotion—to criticize the tempestuous Graham when she treated the company or class poorly. "I remember one time," Marjorie recalled, "when I started the class and they were doing really well and I figured that if Martha walked in and saw them she'd be thrilled. And then she came in and started to yell. She actually slapped one girl. So later, at the right time—timing is everything in life—I said to her, 'You know, you yelled at the class and it had nothing to do with the class. What happened to you before the class is what you were yelling about, and that's really not fair.' I always said that sort of thing in a nice way at the right time . . . and if she couldn't handle it that day, I wouldn't say it."

It was a special, political sensibility that enabled Marjorie to remain completely subservient and yet exert a subtle control. She was quite aware of her own creative limitations—"Martha was far more important than me to the world," she would say—but she knew she could be a useful, perhaps even crucial accessory to genius. It was a role she had clearly staked out for herself before she met Woody Guthrie, and which she assumed naturally when the rehearsals for *Folksay* began in a drafty studio on Thirteenth Street.

Woody was having trouble with his pauses again. He was supposed to sing "The Dodger," a Lee Hays song that Sophie had lifted from the *Sodbuster Ballads* album, and he just couldn't get it right, even when he was *trying* to get it right. "I can't sing like Lee Hays," he'd complain. "I haven't got asthma." But he had trouble on other songs as well, even familiar ones like "I Ride an Old Paint." He simply wasn't used to singing with the precision required for modern dance, and despite his best efforts he'd often send the dancers bumping into each other. He was becoming frustrated with it all and Sophie was thinking about finding another guitar player, when Marjorie Mazia decided to take the situation, and Woody, in hand. She told him to get some shirt cardboards. Then she prepared an exact count for every word and every pause in each of the songs Woody had to sing, and marked them out on the cardboards. "Now, Woody," she said in her chirpy little voice, "if you can count, you can do this."

No one had dared speak to him like that in years: she was not awed by his authenticity; she cut right through the sullen stares and mysterious distance he had imposed upon himself. She told him what to do with respect, without guile, simply and directly. And he did it. He'd count and sing, "I'm goin' down the road feelin' bad two three four . . ."

With the counting problem solved, more or less, Woody began to have some creative influence on the development of *Folksay*. He was especially good at shaping the interludes in which he and Robinson would trade corny jokes, and he even managed to insert a few of his old favorites like:

ROBINSON: Rain much around here?
GUTHRIE: Naw . . . s'dry the grasshoppers gotta jump three times just to stay even.
ROBINSON: Must get cold in the winter.
GUTHRIE: Not so cold . . . but pretty damn cold.

It was a line that often reduced Sophie and the others to helpless giggling—no one was quite sure why—and soon they were all going around saying, "Not so cold . . . but *pretty damn cold*!"

Woody was fascinated by the dancers. They were beautiful women, even the ones who didn't have attractive features. They were poised and stately—he loved the way they walked about— and they worked so hard. The rehearsals for *Folksay* usually were held at night, after most of the dancers had spent all day preparing with the Graham company for an upcoming national tour. He was amazed by their dedication and stamina, by the difficulty of their art. And he was smitten by Marjorie Mazia, but didn't dare hope that she might feel the same way about him. Sometimes they'd sit on the floor of the bare studio during breaks, drinking sodas, talking—she did most of the talking—and she knew so much about cultural things, and came from such a different and mysterious and alluring background than he. Earl Robinson, who'd also half fallen in love with Marjorie, watched them sitting there and saw what was happening, and knew he didn't have a chance. For her part, Marjorie found herself desperately wanting to *take care* of the little man and, much to her surprise, wanting to sleep with him as well. She noticed that he was watching her too, and they both primly waited for their time.

The courtship began with little things. He saw her shivering in the cold studio one night and draped his cab-driver coat over her shoulders. "Got it for three bucks in Seattle," he said awkwardly, and that was the first move that was made. Another night, he offered to walk her home after a rehearsal. They went the long way through the Village, stopping in a restaurant in Sheridan Square for a cup of coffee and then continuing on, holding hands now, his finger touching hers through a hole in her glove.

Folksay debuted in early March as part of a program sponsored by *Dance Observer* magazine, and was very well received by the critics. At the cast party after the performance, Woody read everyone's palm—an old Pampa trick—and Marjorie asked him, in an uncharacteristically flirty way, "What can you tell me about my sex life?" He looked at her and smiled.

There was another party several nights later and Woody asked Marjorie if she'd like to go with him. It was their first real date and he surprised her by appearing at her door in a suit and tie which he said he'd borrowed from a friend. He looked ridiculous and lovable, and she *knew* she was going to spend the night with him—she'd be leaving on a tour with Martha the next day—and she was very, very nervous. The party passed in a fog, and then they were back in her little room on Fourteenth Street . . . and she was ready, but still very nervous, but ready nonetheless . . . and he didn't do anything. He just sat down on her bed and talked about his past, and asked questions about hers. They spent most of the night holding hands and talking quietly like that. Woody, always aware of the subtlest nuances in other people's behavior, had sensed her fear and wasn't about to take the chance of blowing it all on a lunge—for which she was eternally grateful, and impressed, and more in love with him than ever.

He told her that night about remarkable changes taking place in his life. People were beginning to pay him money to write stories. It had started with Charles Olson, an old professor of Seeger's from Harvard, who'd come to Almanac House for dinner one night. Pete had told him about Woody's writing ability, and Woody had shown him some things he'd written. Olsen was suitably impressed, and asked Woody if he'd like to write a story about how people out in the country learn to become musicians for *Common Ground*, a small scholarly magazine with which he was associated. Woody responded, within a matter of days, with a lovely story called "Ear Players," about his mother singing ballads, and the shoeshine boy in the barbershop in Okemah who played the long, lonesome railroad blues on his harmonica, and how he learned new songs on the road to the Gulf coast and California. The story was going to be published in the magazine's spring issue.

Then, soon after Olson's visit, some friends of Bess Lomax's came by: William Doerflinger had just arrived in town to become an editor at E. P. Dutton, the publishing house; his wife, Joy Homer Doerflinger, had recently completed a book about her experiences in China. Bess insisted that Woody let them read a piece of the autobiography he was always fiddling with, and he showed them a raw, colorful, exciting (and utterly preposterous) scene in which he fights the toughest kid in Okemah and whips him in front of half the town on Main Street. The Doerflingers were struck by the power and immediacy of the writing. It was, Bill Doerflinger thought (as Alan Lomax had before him), as fine an evocation of American childhood as he'd ever read. But it was wild and undisciplined, and would need a great deal of work before it could be published as a book. Woody then showed them an outline he'd done for the book in 1940, after Lomax had encouraged him to write, and several other sections he'd been toying with—mostly childhood scenes: the old gang house; his sister's death; his mother's strange illness. They were all as good as the first, and just as rough.

Doerflinger took a sample back to Dutton and was able to land Woody a contract—with the stipulation that his wife, Joy Doerflinger, would act as a free-lance editor for the book (it would be pretty much a full-time job) and double as Woody's agent, for which she would receive 20 percent of whatever profits accrued after publication. Woody was given a $500 advance: $250 upon signing the contract, with the other half to be sent to Mary in El Paso in ten monthly installments.

So it was official. He was being paid to write an autobiography, which he intended to call *Boomchasers*. All he had to do now was sit down . . . and do what? He didn't know where to begin. Writing had always been something he'd done without thinking, but now it was all so formal. Almanac House suddenly was full of distractions, people coming and going, always interrupting him, *dragging* him down to the corner for a drink. He couldn't concentrate, he told Marjorie that night as they lay on her bed. He needed some peace and quiet.

"Well," she said, "I'm leaving with Martha tomorrow for three weeks, and you can use this place until I get back."

He promptly accepted the offer, mostly because it was another tangible link they would have, a guarantee they would see each other again. He had no great hope that solitude would bring order and, indeed, he continued to flounder in his new quarters. The problem wasn't putting down the words themselves: he'd think of a scene or a feeling he'd want to describe, and it would just gush out. But he didn't know how to structure the various swatches of words, how long each should be, or how to link one to the next—it seemed a jigsaw puzzle for which he was continually inventing new pieces. He dawdled, stared out the window at crowded Fourteenth Street, thought about Marjorie . . . whoever she was. He wrote Sophie a long letter about performing in *Folksay* that eventually was turned into an article for *Dance Observer*. He filled his notebook with errant thoughts and verses:

Nora and Charley with Roy and Clara, 1907

Left: Charley in Okemah. *Right:* Nora (arms clasped behind her back, a sign of Huntington's chorea) and Charley with Woody (in hat) and George, around 1926. *Bottom:* Okemah High School, 1926-1927 (Woody is in the front row, sixth from the left)

Left: Woody and Matt Jennings, around 1935. Above: with Mary and the kids (Gwen, Sue, Bill) in Los Angeles, 1940. *Right:* Mary

Top: the Pampa Jr. Chamber of Commerce Band, 1936 (Woody is far left, with bass and moustache). *Right:* Lefty Lou

Top right: Jack and Woody, 1937. *Above:* the gang at XELO, 1938 (*left to right, seated*—Shorty, Buck Evans, Lefty Lou, Allene Guthrie, Whitey McPherson, Woody; *standing*—Smokey, Jack Guthrie, Rusty, Jeff Guthrie, Possum Trot Bruce, Slim, Jimmy Busby)

Top left: Will Geer. *Top right:* Woody with Lilly Mae Ledford and Alan Lomax during THE MARTINS AND THE COYS. *Bottom right:* Woody, Mary, and the kids in New York.

Top left: with Burl Ives in Central Park, a publicity shot for "Back Where I Come From," 1940. *Top right:* Pete Seeger and Woody at Highlander Folk School, 1940. *Bottom:* the Almanac Singers—Woody, Millard Lampell, Bess Lomax, Pete Seeger, Arthur Stern, Sis Cunningham

BOUND FOR GLORY publicity shots, 1943

Top: with Cisco Houston, at Communist Political Association Rally, 1944. *Left:* with Joe Louis and Earl Robinson. *Bottom:* the Roosevelt Bandwagon, 1944.

Pages from the Railroad Pete notebook. Woody and Marjorie (Woody's drawing, from back of photo)

In the army, 1945 (Woody is standing, disheveled, far left)

At Coney Island. Marjorie and Cathy, 1946. Nora, Joady, Woody, and Arlo, 1951.

Left: on horseback (untypical), 1949. *Top right:* Woody and Marjorie, a publicity shot for their children's hootenannies. *Bottom right:* with Jean Ritchie, Fred Hellerman, and Pete Seeger at WNYC, 1949

Top left: with Anneke, around 1953. *Bottom:* with Ramblin' Jack Elliot at Washington Square Park, 1954

Standing for the ovation after the 1956 benefit

Left: with Nora, Marjorie, and Joady at Howard Beach. *Right:* with Joady, Marjorie, Nora, and Arlo at Cafe Society, 1960. *Bottom:* Woody's writing in 1955

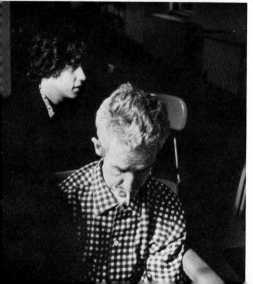

Receiving the
Conservation
Service Award
in 1966, with
Harold Leventhal,
Arlo, and Marjorie

I borrowed a room on 14th street
Just up above the hard concrete
And I can't sleep, I don't know why
But I'm gonna stay awake and try . . .

I believe that Pete Bowers with his banjo is saying just about as much as one man can.

Sometimes you get the feeling
Like you're on your last go-round
But there's always somebody else that comes along
It's for them that you start all over.
It's for them that you do your best.

I'm not a folklorist, I'm a poor folkist.

Come on train, split your guts.
You got someone on there that I want to be here.
Loving or being loved
Is a high class job of first class work.

Marjorie sent him postcards from the road: "I love you very much," and "You're the person that makes me love everyone more," and others like that. And Woody wrote letters to her that wouldn't be read until she returned to the little room that was rapidly becoming a mess of crumpled papers, tangled bedding, and empty bottles. He confessed to being "the world's most disorganized person" and "the biggest waster of time." And then, in a long, rambling, perhaps drunken letter, he invented a revealing alter ego: a little rat, who lived temporarily in the Fourteenth Street room, and read all of Marjorie's postcards and wanted to know: "Who the hell is this Woody bastard and who the hell is this Marjorie who always rides trains?" The rat, by contrast, rode through sewer pipes, tossed about by water and garbage, and eventually was drowned in some forgotten culvert . . . *but,* just before he died, he left a message to the pretty girl who lived in the apartment: "There are lots of little rats like me that live in the slums and die somewhere like this. Do all you can to help them. Maybe rats are good for something—goodbye."

It was obvious that they were going to sleep together when Marjorie returned . . . and there was, once again, more than a little tension when the time came. Marjorie had to clean up the apartment first, then take a bath and insist that Woody take one too, and then she slid into bed wearing a new pair of pink rosebud pajamas. Woody came in naked beside her and (in a moment he'd later write about with loving detail) began to tell her more about the little rat. It seemed the rat had really started out in life as a man, but had been turned into a rat by a mean man who had lots of money. Eventually, though, the rat was able to get his revenge. He stole a candle from the mean man, and ate the flame . . . so the man didn't have light anymore, and was forced to live in darkness. Which, of course, was painful for the rat (with all that fire in his belly) and aggravating to the man, who sent all sorts of dogs and cats to catch him. But the rat had a secret refuge. He could go to the pretty girl's apartment and hide out under the bedcovers. He had a key to the apartment, a key the pretty girl's husband had lost . . . and he wanted to tell the girl that if she took him in and treated him just like a man, he might *become* a man again, but he only talked rat language and she couldn't understand him. So he tried writing his feelings down on paper, which was better, and he finally was able to tell her just exactly how she could help him to become a man again: "She had to give the little rat the one thing in the world that she loved and valued most. And this just happened to be a pair of rosebud pajamas."

"Like these?"

"Just exactly."

And so she did, and the little rat became a man, and the pretty girl became a woman, and they might have lived happily ever after, if only they'd gotten a few breaks along the way.

She still commuted back to Wilmington from time to time, making an occasional cameo appearance in her marriage, but her emotional life was centered in the little room on Fourteenth Street where Woody was teaching her—with great, gentle patience—about physical love and she was getting him organized to write his book. "Even if you don't write, you should be sitting at that desk from nine to five each day," she'd tell him. "Something will happen. You have to be a daily worker, just like someone in a factory. Writing is your job now and you must take it seriously."

Although she didn't leave much room for the vagaries of creativity, he felt impelled to give her plan a try, and, in those first days after her tour, when she was on a light schedule and resting, she enforced it with vigor. When delegations arrived from Almanac House or elsewhere, hoping to steer Woody into a jam session or a tavern, Marjorie would answer the door and firmly tell them that Woody was working and wouldn't be available till five. He'd shake his head and laugh at this, and if the results of his enforced labor weren't the grand, free, swooping ungrammatical sentences that Alan Lomax had loved, if the prose was a bit more constrained and routine than before, it's also probable that this was the only way the book would ever have been written. He'd do a first draft in longhand, then he and Marjorie would take turns reading it aloud while the other typed. Often, she'd steer him gently by asking questions about what he'd written. Once, in the midst of a description of his mother's illness, Marjorie stopped and asked, "Woody, could you get sick like that?"

"No," he said. "Only women."

Completed sections were taken to Joy Doerflinger, who pared them down still further, eliminated repetitions, and shaped the words into a prose that was still rather wild and unfettered by conventional standards but tame by Woody's. At times she'd send him back to write connecting passages or elaborate on certain scenes, but mostly she cut and shaped. Woody accepted her guidance without much of a fuss and, once started, the work moved along quickly.

In May, the *Folksay* troupe reassembled for a series of performances before small audiences, mostly in high school auditoriums, many of them benefits for things like the Russian War Relief Committee of Passaic, New Jersey. Woody was singing again, too, with the Almanac Singers, who'd been on a tour of the Midwest (including a spectacular appearance before 100,000 auto workers in Detroit) while he pursued his literary career and Marjorie, and who were now resuming their Sunday hootenannies and some occasional bookings.

Marjorie had mixed feelings about the folk music scene. She loved the music itself, and the politics behind it, but the people were disturbingly raunchy—always drinking too much and smoking too much and having loose, smoky, sloppy parties. Marjorie didn't drink, smoke, or even use strong language . . . and though she tried to enjoy Woody's friends and their parties, she found them rather coarse for her taste and began to beg off, saying she was tired after a long day of dancing—which she was—and either leaving early or not going at all. Woody would taunt her then by very obviously lavishing his attentions on the nearest available woman, and sometimes would even stay out all night. But very early Marjorie accepted—though she didn't exactly relish—the fact that he needed those parties and that scene, and there would probably be late-night encounters with other women from time to time. She knew he'd always come back the next morning, guiltily. She knew he needed her (in fact, she was just beginning to sense how desperately he needed her). She would tolerate his misdemeanors and, perhaps, make some use of them. Intuitively, she understood that Woody wouldn't be Woody without an occasional insurrection, or the appearance of one.

Even so, the Almanac Singers were amazed by the change that had come over him. He'd been domesticated. Millard Lampell saw Marjorie as a visitor from the real world, the place where his parents lived, where people did their laundry and ate regular meals. "She seemed to take Woody in hand, like a little boy," Bess Lomax thought. "One night we were all walking along the street and Marjorie said, 'Okay, Woody, let's step out,' and I'll be darned if he didn't just step on out."

The Almanacs, like most American Communists, had lapsed into a fanatic, undifferentiated super-patriotism. Everything had to be sacrificed to the war effort, even another large chunk of the group's repertoire—union songs—since the party could no longer support labor organizing. Strikes would only cripple the war effort, so "Talking Union" was placed in mothballs for the duration. The important thing now was to support the American government, encourage the opening of a second front in Europe to ease the German pressure on Russia, and build a united front against fascism. The new spirit of alliance building was so strong among the Almanacs that they even reached out and made peace with Lee Hays. He and Lampell buried the hatchet in June and collaborated on the script for an extravaganza called *Folk Songs on the Firing Line*, which traced America's military history in song, and was hailed by the critics as an important morale booster.

Woody, of course, was the most frenzied anti-fascist of the bunch. He was bursting with new song ideas and lyrics—his "Talking Hitler's Head Off Blues" was printed in the *Daily Worker* in May—and he could often be spotted dashing through Union Square, almost in flight, on his way to some crucial appointment or engagement, with his guitar slung across his shoulder and a new slogan scrawled across the face of it in blue paint: "This Machine Kills Fascists."

He fired off letters to just about everyone—except the army—offering his services in the battle against the forces of darkness. He wrote to CBS radio suggesting that he'd be the perfect replacement for Burl Ives, who'd just been drafted, as the network's folk singer. He sent poems to the *New Masses*. He wrote to R. C. Wetherald at Victor Records asking to record some morale-building, beat-the-fascists songs: "I hear you are not able to put out as many records as before due to the shortage of materials, but if recording is cut down, I think it ought to be the cocktail numbers and not the songs about jackhammers and diesel engines and saws and axes. . . . There ain't no better way to get more work out of anybody than to tell them how proud you are of the work they already done, and the working folks I've met didn't build America in a sissy tone of voice such as the nickel machines are full of. . . ."

But that and all of Woody's other inquiries were rebuffed, and, frustrated, he was reduced to pestering innocent bystanders with his furious anti-fascism. A case in point was Marjorie's mother.

In June, Marjorie had decided to introduce them over lunch. It wasn't intended as any sort of announcement (though her mother quickly saw through *that*), merely the meeting of two kindred spirits—Yiddish poet and Okie balladeer—who might find each other interesting. And they did hit it off rather well: Aliza Greenblatt was so impressed by Woody's argument that artists should channel all their energies into the fight against fascism that she decided to help out by writing a rare poem in English. She then mailed a copy to Woody, who responded with a letter in which he lectured her—respectfully—about the best ways to fight fascism and proceeded to tear apart her poem line by line:

I gave my son to my
   country.   (This is a very good line)
My oldest I gave to my
   land.   (This line is very good)
A soldier so brave
My country to save   (Save? From what?)
He will fight for what's
   right

To the end.

(I suppose Hitler tells his
boys this. But give actual,
concrete proof that your
son's side is the right
side.)

*Cheer up! America
     mothers!*

(Very good line)

*Heads up! How proud we
     shall be!*

(Very good line)

Our Johnnies are young!

Our Johnnies are strong!

(The young will save the
world)

*All nations our Johnnies
     will free!*

(Free from what? Where is
the actual proof? The Nazis
also believe they are
freeing the world. Naziism
is doomed to lose. How do
we know?)

*I shall give my third to my
     country!*

*I shall give my babe to my
     land!*

(Two very good lines. But
for such a great gift of pa-
triotism, the next lines
should tell the best reason
on earth why you are giv-
ing, and why they are fighting and why we will win.)

Should the enemy dare

I am ready to share!

(The Axis powers are fa-
mous for daring. For striking deadly, murderously,
quickly and without warn-
ing. Millions of homes
wrecked. Families killed
and driven around over the
face of the earth like cattle!
Pearl Harbor. Over 300
American ships torpedoed.

> Europe and Asia blasted
> asunder! Are we still wait-
> ing for some undescribed
> enemy to dare?)
> (I am ready to share what?)

Nevertheless, Woody set the poem to music and sent it to Alan
Lomax, who had moved from the Library of Congress to the
Office of War Information, the government's official propaganda
arm, where "I Gave My Son" was promptly filed and forgotten
. . . by everyone but Mrs. Greenblatt, who was quite pleased to
be a small part in the struggle against fascism.

Of course, Marjorie had been interested in more than just the
potential for artistic camaraderie when she introduced Woody to
her mother. There were new, pressing considerations that made
her mother's reaction to him very important. On June 3, Marjorie
wrote to Woody from Wilmington and told him that she was
going to visit the doctor about her "side." She enclosed the
monthly rent for the Fourteenth Street apartment, and continued
on in her usual cheerful fashion: "You should be through another
50 pages by now! Assuming you're a decent 'Daily Worker'!"
She closed by reminding him to keep clean, "drink your milk,
orange juice etc . . . and let me find the little tater I'm dreaming
of."

The doctor did, in fact, discover that Marjorie was with tater,
which caused much jubilation on Fourteenth Street. Both Woody
and Marjorie were intrigued by the exotic possibilities—two distinctly talented people, coming from such different backgrounds,
couldn't help producing a spectacular child. For Woody, especially, there was a *mystique* about this child from the beginning
and he set about giving the fetus a personality. He drew cartoons
for Marjorie of "Railroad Pete," a tough little cuss who walked
around with his hands jammed into his pockets and a sock cap
over his eyes, the world's best union organizer and fascist fighter,
who could knock Nazi planes from the sky simply by spitting at
them and wipe out entire panzer divisions the same way.

They were so excited by the prospect of a baby that there
wasn't much talk, at first, about the severe logistical problems
they were facing. For starters, they both still happened to be
married to other people. Marjorie—who was, no doubt, far more

aware of the impending difficulties—quietly began to compute the
various options available to them as she spent July at Bennington
College with Martha Graham, teaching several dance classes each
day. They corresponded frequently through the month, Woody
sending Marjorie cartoons of Railroad Pete dispatching a variety
of enemies with gobs of spit; Marjorie sending Woody bits of
homey advice, "Put a wet towel around your neck (on a hot day)
and it'll work miracles. Eat lightly but well. . . . And please,
honey, take your *shower*!!!"

But there was a subtle tension in the letters back and forth, a
certain formality, an enforced gaiety. Marjorie to Woody: "Write
me again—how are you—the book—your drinking sprees—and
everything you know I love to hear about." Instead of writing
about his drinking sprees, though, Woody sensed there was
something amiss and wrote a warmly supportive (and also rather
strained) reply: "I can almost feel how glad you are, and Railroad Pete too. . . . So whatever makes both of you happy, makes
me the same way . . . . You feel more useful in Bennington now,
don't you? That's what you need. . . ."

In late July, Marjorie left Bennington, stopping in New York
on her way to Wilmington, and dropped something of a bomb.
She told Woody that she *had* to have the baby with the best
possible medical and hospital care; it was important, too, that the
child not be burdened with the stigma of illegitimacy. Therefore,
she'd decided to stay with Arnold, at least until the baby was
born, and then, afterwards, she'd leave her husband and come to
live with Woody in New York. The baby was due in February;
she promised she'd be in New York by April 15.

Woody was taken completely by surprise. He'd never considered the possibility that she might remain in Wilmington. It raised
all sorts of unsavory scenarios. Was she going to tell Arnold
whose baby it was? Did she *know* whose baby it was? Maybe it
was Arnold's baby after all, and this was just her way of letting
him down easy. But Marjorie reassured him and coddled him,
and encouraged him to tell her more stories about Railroad Pete,
and they fantasized together about living in a little white cottage
with honeysuckle vines and they would produce a songbook together (with Marjorie transcribing the music), and he grudgingly
accepted her plan.

But he was deeply wounded and needed an outlet for his pain.
So he began, in August, a diary addressed to Railroad Pete in

which he communicated, at some length, his hopes and fears and sense of the world. "You are the only person I can put my complete faith in," he began, "because you are not born yet." He wrote rather coldly of Marjorie, who "lives for work's sake and works to dig up more work." He told Pete about how she'd organized his book writing on Fourteenth Street and then launched into several long, terrible poems about the fascist menace and the role he intended for Pete in the future. He also filled the book with more cartoons, plus bits of random verse and wonderful aphorisms:

LENIN: Where three balalaika players meet, the fourth one
        ought to be a communist.
ME: Where three communists meet, the fourth one ought
        to be a guitar player.

"I read the Bible from Generous to Revolutions."—Leadbelly

> Gamblin' is my nature
> Ramblin' is my game
> Deal me out
> Your hardest card
> I'll win this goddamn game.

The diary stretched through August and into September. Woody began to confide in Railroad Pete as if he were a real person and, at one point, even alluded to his deepest fear of all: "I have dreams that tell me I'm not entirely as sane as is comfortable. . . . I don't know what kind of feelings are in me to cause me to write all the things I do. . . . One minute I'm nervous and afraid, and the next minute I'm as big and strong as anyone," and then he slid off in another direction: "You're gonna jump around and entertain all the docs and RN's and all the other little babies [in the hospital] and not only that—but convert them to socialism on the spot. . . . Don't let anything knock your props out from under you. . . . Why should I be fool enough to write all this down for you? You are young and new and ought to be giving me advice. . . . It ain't Pete that's the baby in this family. Not by a longshot—No, I really think I'm the baby in this family, don't you?"

* * *

With Marjorie living in Wilmington full-time now, there was no longer an excuse for her to keep the Fourteenth Street room and Woody had to leave. He moved into the latest incarnation of Almanac House, which was really just Gordon Friesen and Sis Cunningham's apartment on Hudson Street at the western edge of Greenwich Village. Woody had his own bedroom there, but he felt uncomfortable and confused—with Fourteenth Street gone, an important link with Marjorie had been broken. She visited him occasionally on Hudson Street—one night she helped him through a mysterious high fever and deep sweat that scared her half to death—but it just wasn't the same.

Much that had been implicit in their relationship now became quite obvious in their correspondence. He addressed her as "Mama," and she called him "Baby." In one letter, he pointedly noted that he'd been neglecting to brush his teeth, and she responded immediately: "I want to remind you to go into the bathroom and brush your teeth this very minute. No more of this foolishness!" He threw tantrums when he was with her—sputtering out thin-lipped lines of expletives—and then apologized profusely by mail. In a letter dated September 17, he regretted "all the things I said the other day. . . . There are red devils with pitch forks poking around in me somewhere and making me yell out some pretty bad things. It puzzles me to even try to think how a person with a mind like yours can even stand the presence of a mind like mine." He added that despite his protestations, he understood the virtues of family life in Wilmington: the quiet and health and eating the right things at the right time. "I don't guess I've developed much on that side," he concluded abjectly.

His rampaging self-pity began to have an impact on his professional life. In early September, he was recruited by Earl Robinson for a revue he was staging called *It's All Yours*. The American People's Chorus would sing Robinson and Lampell's Lincoln cantata, "The Lonesome Train," and then there would be a playlet starring Woody, among other folk singers, as a performer in a dingy basement nightclub where the real, pure folk music was played. After songs by Woody, Leadbelly, and others, establishing the utter purity of the atmosphere, an unscrupulous music publisher would barge in, attempt to buy off the performers, and water down their music. Woody, perfectly cast, would lead the counterattack. The script, written by Millard Lampell at the bottom of his form, called on Woody to say things like "You're wrong! You can't! You can't take our music from us!" Or some such approximation of proletarian outrage.

But Woody refused to put any emotion in his lines. "Yer wrong," he'd drawl. "Y'cain't . . ."

Earl Robinson tried his best to animate him, without much luck. "Woody, for Chrissake," he finally said. "Don't you ever get *angry* at people in Oklahoma? This guy is stealing our music!"

Woody leaned his head back and, slower than ever, said to Robinson, "Yup. We get angry. But when we get angry, we just give 'em a long, hard stare."

Still, despite problems with the script and cast, there were great hopes for *It's All Yours*, especially after the favorable reaction to *Folk Songs on the Firing Line*. The show would open at the Brooklyn Academy of Music and, if successful, move on to Broadway. Lampell apparently was in the midst of another promotional orgy, drumming up support from Broadway types.

One day Woody accompanied Millard on one of his forays and returned steaming to Gordon and Sis's apartment, slamming a new mandolin against the wall, shattering it and several of Sis's vases in the process. He asked them if they had seven dollars he could borrow to go to New Jersey and buy a gun so he could kill Lampell. They asked him why he wanted to kill Lampell, and he said that he'd been in some big producer's office with Millard, and he'd started fooling around on his harmonica while Lampell negotiated. Millard asked him to put it away and he did, but a few moments later he pulled it out again—absentmindedly, he said—and Millard had snatched it away from him.

He vowed that he wouldn't appear in *It's All Yours* as long as Lampell had anything to do with it and, the night of the dress rehearsal, he walked out as soon as he saw Millard walk in. Earl Robinson, who knew about none of this, was forced to take Woody's part at the last minute and sing "The Great Historical Bum," which nobody could do quite like Guthrie.

Interestingly enough, Woody went straight from the rehearsal to Penn Station, where he hopped a train to Wilmington, intent on finally confronting Arnold Goodman. By the time he arrived, though, his passion had cooled somewhat. He presented himself at the door as merely a friend of Marjorie's from New York, and had a spirited conversation with Goodman about the importance of opening a second front and other matters of political signifi-

cance. When he left finally, Marjorie accompanied him to the
train and he exploded along the way, demanding that she return
with him immediately . . . which she, of course, refused to do.

Arriving back home, he wrote her a massive letter, apologizing
for his behavior, agreeing at length that Wilmington was the best
place to be, promising to work hard to raise money for their
future:

> And, do you know that as you sit here and read this, these
> pages and pages and pages, that my whole life is taking on
> such a nice, pretty, hard working and useful shape, that it
> almost blows through me like a morning wind? And, do
> you know this is the first time in all my life that things
> have had this radiant glow and clear light around them?
> I'm, I guess, what you would call a happy man. And the
> old crazy tailspins I have gone into so regularly in the past
> few months, I see now, almost that they were absolutely
> necessary in order for me to get my head running right and
> my eyes to seeing. . . . And do you know that even that
> crappy, cheap and lousy speech I made . . . even that, I
> think, was my last gathering of all the planless and dream-
> less and thoughtless forces in my whole life, piling them
> on you, because *I really was thinking just the opposite of
> every word I said. . . .*
>
> How much I love you both spiritual and physical, every
> earthly way, is too much for me to try to tell. I feel like I
> was drowning in an ocean full of burning oil and you pulled
> me out. All I feel like I owe you is my work and myself;
> and you know how well I admire and love your dancing
> and even on this point, I think we can do lots of good and
> useful creating together; we'll have a billion ideas, and
> some of them's gotta be good. The very best. Pete will be
> our chief critic. He can rustle up the money and the audi-
> ences for both of us, and get me a printing press and you
> a nice slick-floored dance studio and all kinds of pupils
> staring with wide eyes at Pete wheeling in and out doing
> fifty or a hundred jobs at once.
>
> From Petie's standpoint, I still can't admit that you'd
> ought to make any changes now in your living quarters,
> doctors, nurses and whatnot. I really believe that since
> things are as they are, your little Band Box is best. Every-

thing will run smoother there, and I can come see you as often as the law allows. . . .

Marjorie responded, several days later, with an equally long and passionate effusion:

I know the first thing I want to tell you is what I've always wanted to tell you about you. . . . I know what I'm talking about when I say I love you. I've met lots of people I thought I loved, but never has there been anyone that I believed more in, trust in, confide in, work with, better than you. What more can there be? And when I go to sleep at night, I always think . . . are you sleeping . . . are you lonely and drinking out your blues . . . are you working . . . are you clean . . . is your bed clean . . . did you eat anything at all nourishing today . . . and a million other little things. . . . Imagine being worried because I know you don't scrub your teeth enough. But then I figure to myself . . . it's just those little things that make me realize how much you mean to me.

You know what your letter is to me?? It is a birth certificate of a new born baby named Woody. . . . I'm sorry Pete but you'll have to be my second born. I'm sorry I'm going to have to disappoint you . . . but I see now a new, beautiful, healthy baby . . . and I know he's mine and I've even got his name on a birth certificate. . . .

After that, Marjorie went on for several pages about the events of her life, comings and goings, her brother's recent arrival in town, cousins getting married, and then the big news:

And now I want to tell you what passed between Arnie and myself. He asked if you had wanted me to leave Wilm. I explained that you had. He wondered what my plans were. And after some meager explanations . . . I couldn't give the details . . . I will stay in Wilm. and have Pete, bring Pete into this world under decent living conditions and with proper care. It would be difficult to break up the home now and after Arnie has already volunteered for the army and will no doubt be with the armed forces quite soon. Then without any hub bub we can separate without disturbing our families and Pete will have a good start. . . . Now that your letter has arrived I don't feel too badly about staying here. I want you to know . . . I would leave if you rather . . . but it would be taking a chance with my life and Pete's. . . .

All of which cleared the air between them for about a week.

He was almost finished writing *Boomchasers*, but there were problems. The last several chapters, which were supposed to bring him up to the present, seemed flat. They lacked the insight and authenticity of his earlier work. Having started with a wonderfully complex and emotionally accurate—if not always truthful—description of his childhood, the book had deteriorated into a series of encounters with strangers along the road, each of which inevitably revealed a shallow and predictable political purpose. Woody's fudging of the facts and self-mythologizing became more obvious and, thus, less tolerable, as the book progressed. Mary and the children were never mentioned. The Almanac Singers were nowhere to be found, an absence that was particularly galling when he wrote about taking the stage at the Rainbow Room *solo*, in a much romanticized version of that audition. In fact, he had written more a novel than an autobiography—with few of the creative advantages of the former and all the self-indulgent disadvantages of the latter.

Joy Doerflinger, his editor-agent, was a stylish woman who'd sometimes appear for meetings with Woody at Sis and Gordon's dumpy apartment wearing high heels and dazzling clothes, with two large dogs on leashes that were twined around her legs and pulling in opposite directions. As the work neared completion, she began to make some important editorial decisions (and, perhaps, *not* make others). She cut the chapter describing the family's trip to find Jerry P. Guthrie's lost silver mine in the Chisos Mountains, and suggested it could be made into a separate book someday. She also decided to change the title from *Boomchasers* to *Bound for Glory*, a phrase she lifted from the song "This Train Is Bound for Glory," which Woody had described himself singing to a freight car full of homeless men in the book's opening and closing scenes.

He was worried about the latter change. He wrote to Marjorie: "[It] sounds like I personally am bound for glory, but . . . really

it is the common people who are.'' But Marjorie reassured him:
''I don't see why it should mean *you* are 'Bound for Glory,' ''
and as he began a series of ink drawings to illustrate the book,
he settled into the glum acceptance, punctuated by occasional
bursts of sheer terror, that is the common fate of incipient authors.

Meanwhile, a depleted version of the Almanac Singers struggled on. Pete Seeger was in the army, Millard Lampell was writing radio scripts, and several of the others had gone off to form
a Detroit branch after their spring success there (Arthur Stern,
Bess Lomax, and her husband-to-be, Butch Hawes—Pete Hawes's
younger brother—were the key figures in that group). Their places
were taken by a stream of young singers who drifted in and out,
plus old reliables like Sonny Terry, Brownie McGhee, and Leadbelly, who played occasional bookings. Cisco Houston, working
now as a merchant seaman, also sang with the group between
boats. But the only hard-core members were Sis Cunningham and
Gordon Friesen, Lee Hays (described in the *Daily Worker* as the
group's ''manager''), and, reluctantly, Woody, who found the
others to be much too strict ideologically.

''Political education, polish and smoothness'' were being over-
emphasized, he wrote to Marjorie in November. There were two
or three organizational meetings each week. ''Musical ability
should be the first requirement, not how good a Marxist or Len-
inist [you are].'' In fact, he argued, there had *always* been too
many hard-liners in the group. The only two real performers had
been Pete Seeger and himself: ''My singing and playing wasn't
quite as good as Pete's, but my composing of ballads and songs
was a little better. . . . I was voted down in meetings over and
over. . . . Most of them misunderstand me to say that music and
politics don't mix. I know it made several Almanacs pretty sore
to see me rehearsing with a dance group.''

Gordon Friesen would later claim that Guthrie was a member
of the Communist Party (as were they all) while living at Hudson
Street, and that Woody even was disciplined once for refusing to
sell copies of the *Daily Worker*. But his actual membership probably didn't last much longer than that first disciplinary warning
(or, perhaps, the second monthly dues payment) . . . and was a
moot point in any case, since he frequently bragged of his loyalty
to the party, and claimed to have been working with the Commu-

nists since 1936, which was three years before he'd ever attended a meeting.

Reduced to a dry, spiritless circle of ideologues, the Almanac Singers clearly had outlived their usefulness. When Nick Ray, working now with Alan Lomax in the government's Office of War Information, sought to hire the group to make some propaganda records, the daily press quickly jumped down his throat. In a front-page story, the *World-Telegram* reported: "The Office of War Information has engaged the favorite ballad singers of American communists to help present a picture of the American way of life to the world. . . . Previously, they have sung such morale builders as 'Plow Under Every Fourth American Boy.' " There didn't seem much point in continuing after that. Sis and Gordon were having trouble supporting themselves in New York and, hearing that there were plenty of factory jobs in Detroit, decided to go off and join the midwest contingent. By December, they had closed down the last Almanac House and moved west.

Woody, forced to fend for himself, found a small apartment—a fourth-floor walk-up—at 74 Charles Street in the Village, for which he paid twenty-seven dollars per month. It was so dusty and dingy that he called it El Rancho del Sol. With the Almanacs finished, he decided to start a new, more musically adept group—"Woody Guthrie's Headline Singers"—and sent out very official-sounding contracts to Sonny Terry, Brownie McGhee, and Leadbelly, stipulating that they would be paid at least $5.00 for a thirty-minute show when performing with him, and $7.50 when he was able to get them a separate booking (the rates were $7.50 and $10 for Leadbelly). All three returned signed contracts, which entitled them to sit around Woody's apartment drinking rye whiskey, cooking beans and ham hocks, neck bones and potatoes, and jamming through many long, cold nights.

Marjorie made an early appearance at Woody's new place, and brought with her yet another crisis: she was having second thoughts. Arnold had been such a prince through the whole affair that she wanted to give him one last chance, a limited period—perhaps a month or so—to see if she could really love him. She thought it was very important that families stay together, and suggested that Woody give Mary another try too—failing that, he was free to go out with other women. She didn't want to break off contact with him completely, though. She still loved him dearly and he was, after all, the father of her child—but, for the time being, she suggested they correspond in less steamy fashion, as friends rather than lovers, in order to give her the freedom to pursue her noble experiment.

Woody responded with, what was for him, remarkable calm. In his first letter after the new rules had been imposed, he described, at length, a visit to a Bronx high school: "I always get along best with young kids. They're more my age. I get a kick out of their natural looseness of tongue and lip, and the way they crack back at you." Then he showered her with praise: "Your decision to let these few months be a real chance to get to knowing your husband, I think is a fine and level-headed thing," and closed by asking, "Do you think the form and content of this letter are changed enough to make it come under the new rulin's? Or is it still too personal and small? Should I write about higher intellectual pursuits—or what?"

Marjorie's reaction to this display of high-mindedness was, surprisingly, a near-collapse: "Honey what can I do? I sit here and cry like an old woman. Will I ever stop? And every night since I've left New York, I hug my pillow like it's you. . . . Are you washing every day and scrubbing your teeth? God I wish I was there to do everything for you and kiss you."

But right after she mailed her "blue" letter, as it came to be known between them, she phoned to apologize and vowed to make a stronger effort to stick to the new rules.

Still, her outpouring had given him an excuse to blow off some steam and he bought a small school notebook and quickly filled it with his less high-minded thoughts, and mailed it off to her. He began rather bitterly, in capital letters: "HOW BAD DID *I* HAVE THE BLUES? PRETTY BAD, PRETTY BAD, BUT I'M SLOWLY DRINKING THEM AWAY. THE BLUES GOES SECOND, THE MONEY GOES FIRST." He wrote about getting drunk with Lomax and flirting with a cafeteria waitress, and other things calculated to get a rise out of her: but then admitted that he was confused by the latest turn of events and concluded with a long, acute, and often gorgeous account of why they'd fallen in love in the first place. He described himself as a scraggly, rebellious character, "living like a wild wolf in the canyons of New York" until he'd found her— a woman who could bring some order to his life.

He pours a dammed up love out on her—which she avows is the mental salvation of her own self because she has just

lived six years with a wrong husband—and had begun to
think her own self unnatural or abnormal. She welcomes
his wild love because she hated the thought of the human
soul getting too domesticated or tamed. He is a tonic for
her stiff and unsatisfied sex organs.

But there is more to it than sex. There is the attraction of oppo-
sites, a sense of completion. Each has qualities the other lacks,
and desires.

> She was so passionately aloof and cut apart from the crowds
> and crowds of men she'd met that she loved his careless
> way of cutting across all of the known social and moral
> barriers and shoving aside of conventions, good etiquette
> and customs, and taking her because she was a pretty,
> healthy, smart woman, sexually—heatedly—like an animal
> in one sense—hot—warm—naked for the one reason of sat-
> isfying his own human craving. This she wondered about
> and at the same time loved more than any earthly event
> that had taken place in her life, yet she hoped to awaken
> in him some of her own tastes. . . .
> He had a national reputation as a people's artist which
> he had built on pure blind instinct, passion, wild un-
> bounded, unhampered and unlimited imagination—that sort
> of inspiration that gets you just so far and no father—(far-
> ther!)—
> And he knew that he had come to the end of his animal
> inspirational rope and couldn't progress any farther unless
> he got the help of somebody—[he knew a woman] who had
> developed her mind along different lines and who was en-
> tirely different in outlook and approach than he was. He
> knew she possessed these qualities and he loved her for
> them. . . .

In the next few weeks, he unleashed a barrage of letters and
tried every trick in the book on her. At times he was cute—"Dear
Mama and Contents," one letter began—and at other times snotty:
"Have you fallen in love with your husband yet?" He was in-
spirational, he was clever, he wrote snatches of verse and songs.
He appealed to her better instincts, argued that their love was a
way of fighting fascism, tried to flutter her sex drive, shame her,

make her feel guilty. He groveled ("I've always looked at myself as a rat") and strutted and, when all hope seemed lost, appealed to Railroad Pete. It was a virtuoso performance, capped by another full notebook, this one utterly shameless, addressed to both Marjorie and Arnold, beginning very slowly and soberly, protesting his good intentions, claiming that he never wanted to disturb their happy home, and wishing them all the best: "If you two (three) decide to carry on together, I think Pete would like to see Arnold buy Marjorie a mandolin for a honeymoon present."

And he slid on down from there, gradually working his way to the topic of sex, which was "simply one way of people showing how glad and proud they are to be working together . . . sex shouldn't be a problem for two people who really love each other." Of course, there was always the question of frequency: certain "studious" people needed very little, others required it weekly, others daily, others still more frequently than that. "I don't quite agree with the ones who spread it out any fewer and farther between. . . ."

Eventually, though, he lost track of the fact that he was writing to both Arnold and Marjorie, and concentrated on her. He started edging in that direction by saying that sex only was good when two people were completely attuned to each other, in every way, and *they* certainly had been, and wasn't it a shame that all that attunement had to go to waste. Finally, he blurted: "I owe Arnold plenty. We all do. But we all owe each other the right to do our own thinking and to live and to love democratically. Intellectually. And right. I've put my nickel in."

Then he went on tour with Sonny Terry and Brownie McGhee for a week, and didn't write. He figured he'd get her response in person when he sang for a labor group in Wilmington, just before Christmas. He was feeling tense and frustrated, and not very confident of the outcome. In Baltimore, after they performed for a fraternal organization—Woody happily, provocatively, sandwiched between his two black partners onstage—Sonny and Brownie were led off to a special "Negroes Only" table and Woody was told he couldn't eat dinner with them. "I just *sang* with them," he protested.

"Well, it's different here than in New York," one of the hosts replied, huffily.

Woody quietly told Brownie to start leading Sonny out of the

hall and he'd meet them at the train station. Then he calmly
walked across to the long buffet table with all the food piled up
on it and tossed it over without a word, and was out of there
before anyone realized what had happened.

And then Wilmington. She was waiting for him at the station,
and threw her arms around him, and told him it hadn't been much
of a contest from the start: she loved him, and there was no
getting around it. She would have the baby in Wilmington, and
then come to New York as planned. It wouldn't be easy, what
with the families and all, but they'd figure it out. Or rather, she
would.

With *Bound for Glory* finished and his private life finally in order,
Woody wasn't quite sure what to do next. He began to read
heavily again, mostly books about the Communist Party and its
history. He loved Maxim Gorky's novel *Mother*, especially ad-
miring the way Gorky used a single family to illuminate an entire
movement. He wrote to Marjorie that Gorky had given him some
new ideas about how to tell a story. Other favorite books were
Mother Bloor's autobiography, *We Are Many*, from which he
took several ideas for ballads, and William Z. Foster's *Pages
from a Worker's Life*. He would, at times, go over to Lee Hays's
apartment on Jane Street to look at his books and abuse his typewriter, which had an extra-long carriage that allowed Woody to
stuff paper bags, wrapping paper, and long, multicolored sheets
of poster paper into the machine and type out long, long strings
of words. One day he discovered Hays's annotated, illustrated,
deluxe edition of Rabelais and went wild over it, pacing back
and forth across the floor, giggling madly and reading aloud—
shouting out—Gargantua's list of euphemisms for his penis: "My
little spout . . . my peg . . . my coral-branch . . . my stopper
. . . my plug . . . my centerbit . . . my ramrod . . . my gimlet
. . . my trinket . . . my rough-and-ready-stiff-and-steady . . . my
prop . . . my little red sausage . . . my booby-prize . . ."

He spent much of December and January writing lengthy,
beautiful letters and notebooks to Marjorie. He continually re-
played the early events of their courtship, as if he couldn't believe
it had actually happened, and finally decided to write a novel
about it. He dashed off several chapters—calling it *A Picture from
Life's Other Side*—and imagined himself as an actor named Tom
Harris, "an ugly young man, too little to suit his own self . . .

an easy-going guy, with a walk like a lonesome goat in hot weather.'' He wrote about the early rehearsals with the dance group, and then a rather interesting confrontation between Marjorie (''Ruthie'') and a drunk who suddenly appears in her room and tries to rape her. She cheerily talks him out of it and then convinces him to take a bath and vent his anger more creatively, on the fascists.

A Picture from Life's Other Side stopped there. Woody was filled with so many other ideas he couldn't seem to concentrate on any one of them for very long. He started another novel, called *I Want to Be Right*, about one of his Texas cousins whose wife died of cancer. ''I'm just a farmer when it comes to raising books,'' he wrote to Marjorie. ''I'm into the story so much that the actual writing is pouring out. Yesterday about 15 pages. The day before, 15 or 17 pages, and today although I've written three songs for the [National Maritime Union], I feel like going 20 pages this afternoon.'' But *I Want to Be Right* was dropped too, as he considered writing a folk opera with Marjorie . . . or, perhaps, a series of songs and dances for children (her idea). He began research for the latter by hanging around groups of kids in the street and taking notes on their conversations. He sent the notes to Marjorie in a letter, just as he kept her informed of all the other details of his life.

They gossiped easily back and forth now, with the emotional pressure finally off. They discussed possible names for the child. She suggested Conrad, ''because it sounds like Comrade,'' or Steven. He responded with Matthew, Frederick, Peter, Luther, and Mark: ''Conrad is fine. It ain't so worn out as lots of other names you hear. . . . I like Conrad Mark best I guess.'' Later, realizing an oversight, Marjorie suggested that if Pete turned out to be a girl, they should name her Cathy.

Much was made of New Year's resolutions. Marjorie sent Woody a very precise list of eight, which included ''Keep loving 'My baby,' '' and ''Get Arnold on a new road of life that will bring him happiness,'' and ''make my life even more organized.'' Woody responded, sitting at his table on New Year's Eve, with a hilarious list of thirty-three, each accompanied by an appropriate little cartoon: ''1. Work More and Better . . . 2. Work By A Schedule . . . 3. Wash Teeth If Any . . . 7. Drink Very Scant If Any . . . 8. Write A Song A Day . . . 13. Read Lots Good Books . . . 16. Keep Rancho Clean . . . 18. Stay

Glad . . . 23. Have Company But Don't Waste Time . . . 27. Help Win War—Beat Fascism . . . 32. Make Up Your Mind . . . 33. Wake Up and Fight . . .''

He titled one letter ''Views of News from Okies to Jews,'' and kept her abreast of all the latest professional developments. He was continuing to perform with the Headline Singers, but there were lots of other offers too. Although the Almanacs were too controversial to sing for the Office of War Information, Woody had no trouble recording for Lomax as a solo. Not only that, but Alan also managed to have four of Woody's songs placed in the U.S. Treasury Department songbook (although Woody wasn't quite sure why the Treasury Department needed a songbook). His songwriting had taken a prosaic, agitprop turn with Germany and Japan on the march throughout the world and the Allies still falling back, and not much that he'd written during the past year was up to his former standards. But he continued to churn them out, sometimes even writing songs to the specifications of groups like the National Maritime Union. He was paid two hundred fifty dollars by an outfit called the Am-Russ Music Company to adapt seven Soviet war songs to ''the American dialect,'' an assignment of which he was quite proud.

Cisco Houston was in town, and they were spending a good deal of time together—especially in the waterfront saloons, where Cisco's fellow merchant seamen hung out. On Christmas Eve, Woody invited Joy Doerflinger to join them for a night on the town to celebrate the end of work on *Bound for Glory*. Later, she would describe the evening (''It was far beyond any evening I could have conjured up in a fairy tale'') and Woody (''a pied piper . . . something of a legend in New York'') in a blurb she wrote for Dutton's in-house news bulletin, explaining what sort of man had written *Bound for Glory*. Her account was a frustrating mixture of upper-class condescension and true appreciation, the same qualities she had brought to the editing process: ''I have just spent five months cutting down his manuscript to a paltry hundred thousand words,'' she wrote, by way of introduction. ''Every time I would figure out a good chapter with Mr. Guthrie . . . the boy would go home and return gaily the next day with a hundred and seventy-five pages.''

She wrote of following Woody and Cisco as they wandered through the Village, looking for a suitably proletarian place to eat, singing and playing their guitars as they went, drawing a small crowd that followed them along the street and down into a subway to the Battery: "They began to sing a song Woody had made up: 'You're bound to LOSE, You Fascists, bound to LOSE!' There were many reasons given as to exactly why You Fascists are bound to lose, and each reason was better and funnier than the last. It was a good song. It went on for seven stations. In the last hop, between Rector Street and South Ferry, every single human being in that subway car was singing that song." They stopped then in a combination bar and cafeteria on the waterfront, and spent the next few hours alternating between Christmas carols and anti-fascist songs, and creating an international chorus of sailors (American, British, and a convenient Russian) in the process. "Woody Guthrie," she concluded, "who has spent a third of his life starving, a third working and a third creating, gave quite a lot of people that evening something you might call happiness or just plain faith. His book will do the same."

After that, Cisco began teasing Woody about his book-publishing friends and suggested that if Woody really were a man of the people, he'd sign up for the merchant marine. It was the sort of argument that held a little too much water with Woody, and he wrote to Marjorie: "I was pushed out of the main road pretty early and had to come up along the ditches and the mud and the weeds. . . . Now I'm picked up out of this kind of life and find myself camped along the trail of the intellectuals. . . . To put the matter mildly, I'm having a hard time. I hear their words that run like rainclouds and splatter a few drops across some hot pavement—and the sun and the wind turn the words to steam and they go up in the air like a fog."

His letters to her were filled with surprising admissions and lush descriptive passages like that (and without the disruptive misspellings and bad grammar of his public writing). He would chug along with a routine account of the latest gossip or what he'd had for breakfast or whom he'd bumped into and then, suddenly—*whoosh*—he'd explode off into a wild fantasy, the words spilling out effortlessly, on and on, for pages and pages, single-spaced, mad, brilliant, disorganized, uneven, impossible, unique.

Marjorie's letters back—how could she possibly respond to such outpourings?—were relentlessly chatty and earnest and loving: "All morning I've been imagining how nice it would be to hug you and run my hand through that crap you call hair." Occasionally, though, she would lapse into operatic depressions: "I went to bed and cried for a change! I'm lonely! I'm wretched! I'm blue! I just don't seem to live!'' She was worried about what effect her running away with this odd, *Christian* man would have on her family, especially on her militantly Jewish father. After seeing a movie about Paul Gauguin she wrote: "Can we really push aside all our backgrounds and morals, our so-called way of life and really do what we want, the way we choose, disregarding everything and everybody? I've been wondering . . . Why not!''

Usually, though, she was determinedly optimistic about the future. She seemed to take a special pleasure in fantasizing about spending their later years together, especially Woody's fiftieth birthday party, an event she'd write about again and again over the years: "No, I don't think you'll be tottering. I think you'll have a big bush of hair—a few wrinkles—about the same smallness and I hope a happy heart. I'll be about 45 and Pete just about 20! And we'll sing . . . and Pete might even read aloud this part of the letter and say—God what a sentimental mama. . . . And that night I'll tell you, 'See, I told you so!' And I guess I'll cry a bit and go to sleep laughing with a few salty tears on the pillow. . . .''

In return, he regaled her with more adventures of Railroad Pete, who had become a symbol of the remarkable intimacy they had developed in their correspondence over the months. The letters were a private world they shared and devoted much time to, quite apart from his New York drinking pals and her Wilmington family life . . . and sometimes it seemed as delicate a fantasy as Pete himself. It was a closeness that Woody had never experienced before and, at times, he was tempted to pull back and test its perimeters, to see just how much he could really trust her. In late January of 1943, he wrote to her: "I have been letting myself entertain little old hateful and doubtful thoughts about us . . . [and the] possibility that you'll make up your mind to stay in Wilmington.''

Cathy Ann Guthrie was born on February 6, 1943. She weighed a relatively meager five pounds fourteen ounces, which worried her natural father, restless in his New York rancho, struggling with the idea that Railroad Pete was no longer a viable concept. It was like losing a close friend.

"HOWDY LITTLE MISS CATHY ANN,'' he began his first letter afterwards, which became, in a way, his farewell to Railroad

Pete. In it, Cathy announces, "I was elected to be sent out into the world to fight fascism," and then reports that she *knew* Pete "in the land where babies come from." She had met him at a political rally where he "made a wonderful, brilliant, world-changing speech, his voice was like a symphony. . . . Pete spends most of his time now working or studying or listening to the radio." And, master strategist that he was, Pete had agreed that the times were more propitious for the arrival of Cathy Ann than himself because, as she declared in her opening remarks: "Men have enjoyed an artificial superiority over women for several centuries. I have got to work and fight and do all I can to break the old slavery idea of the woman being chained to her house which, in many cases, certainly isn't a home." Then she set out her political agenda: Neighborhood nurseries for all children. Equal pay for women. Complete equality for men and women—"They can't expect to know how to kiss or make love or have romance, love or marriage until they are equal in every way."

After such a powerhouse entrance, the tiny reality of Cathy Ann—who was, after all, just a baby among twenty-four others in the hospital nursery—might have proved unsettling to Woody when he finally visited her several days later. But no; he was transfixed. He stood at the window for about an hour, staring at her—the birth of this child, after all the crises and the fantasies, had become a much more significant event in his life than the arrival of any of his other children. Clearly, she was going to be wonderful. She had dancer's legs, Marjorie said . . . and also *his* dark curly hair.

Returning home, Woody unleashed a long (seventy-page), charming, free-verse poem describing what he'd seen in the hospital, how he felt as he stared through the window and tried to give her an appropriate nickname. The correct nickname was absolutely crucial, of course, and he considered hundreds before settling on . . . "Stackabones"—for no apparent reason other than its rhyming potential. His poem meandered sweetly through an explanation of germs—the reason why he couldn't come in and hold her—as Woody tried to communicate with her in baby talk and children's rhyme, a language she'd understand:

I FELT LIKE MOST OF ALL THINGS I WANTED
    WAS TO GET A HOLT OF YOU AND TO FEEL HOW
        GOOD AND HOW SMOOTH AND HOW

WARMSY WARMERY

YOUR SKIN IS RIGHT
                    HERE
                    AND RIGHT HERE
                        AND OVER YONDER
                    AND HERE
                    DOWN ALONG YOUR TOES AND
                    ALL DOWN ALONG
                            YOUR ARM
                                AND YOUR HAND
AND JUST ABOUT
            ALL OVER YOU
I WANTED TO LISTEN TO YOU GUGGLE AND GOOGLE
AND GURGLE AND GEEGLE AND SQUEAK AND SPEAK AND TALK
AND SAY ALL KINDS OF GROWED UP WORDS
            IN YOUR BABY LANGUAGE.

But Cathy's arrival also had some less pleasant side effects: it
put a new, strange distance between Woody and Marjorie, a distance exacerbated by the fact that, for whatever reason, she didn't
write or call him for several weeks after the birth. Later, she'd
say that she'd been cooped up in the house with no way to get
out and mail her letters, no way to reply to his withering fusillade
of postcards, which grew more acid—and pathetic—each day as
he waited for news from her:

Why ain't you wrote or nothing?

Have you decided to raise C in bandbox?
TOO DRUNK TO WRITE.
I'll pull out. Stay in your bandbox.
TOO DRUNK TO MAKE SENSE . . .
One bandbox is worth two hundred wild rancheros . . .

Early in March, Marjorie began sending letters again and
calmly tried to explain why she'd been unable to write. She reassured him that she still was going to leave Wilmington, as
planned, on April 15. She told him that, once in New York, she
intended to remain as independent as possible so that he'd never
have to worry about being chained down (if that was, as she
expected, part of what was troubling him now). But the postcard

offensive continued and, on March 8, she lost patience with him: "Just when everything good is about to happen you suddenly lose your hopes, your desires, your—love . . . I think you better take hold of yourself and think a little. . . ."

It was difficult, though. Not only was he finally on the brink of winning Marjorie for good and all, but *Bound for Glory* was done; he had held a copy of it in his hands, and was now waiting for the critical reaction. He kept himself busy by inscribing copies and sending them off to his Oklahoma relatives. To his father, he wrote: "To my papa, as good a dad as a kid ever had. I wrote this book wishing I had more of the stuff that made my dad the best fist fighter in Okfuskee County . . ."

There were all sorts of strange ceremonies and procedures cluttering his life now. He signed a contract with Publicity Associates to promote the book. "It's like a shirt," he wrote to Marjorie. "It takes more folks to sell it than it does to make it." A team of photographers followed him around one day taking publicity shots: Woody, dressed in pea coat and fisherman's cap, singing for a gang of kids; singing in McSorley's Old Ale House; in the subway; standing on the street, trying to look both tough and sensitive at the same time, with a cigarette dangling from his lower lip. Amy Vanderbilt, who was retained by Publicity Associates to help with the promotion, held a party in her fashionable apartment celebrating the book's publication. Other parties were planned by friends and professional acquaintances. And then, in early March, the first reviews began trickling in from the trade magazines:

Book Week: "A huge, rich, juicy chunk of life and it's bound for its share of glory too, I'll wager—I'm excited about it . . ."

Books: "The illustrations by the author are pretty bad and add nothing to the book's flavor. But it is a fine narrative job . . ."

Library Journal: "Too careful reproduction of illiterate speech makes for slow reading . . ."

Woody wasn't sure how to react to all this. The reviews seemed dull and strange and inconclusive. The fancy parties and publicity were frightening. He needed Marjorie to help steer him through.

Luckily, she came for a visit on a weekend in mid-March, but her mind was on other things. She was—understandably—more concerned with future living arrangements than with his inability to cope with success. She had to find an acceptable place to raise Cathy. The rancho, which Woody assumed would be their home, was definitely out. Marjorie wouldn't even sleep in the bed there until he sprayed it with roach killer. A four-flight walk-up would never do, in any case. She was thinking more in terms of a place by the ocean, near her parents' apartment in Sea Gate, way out in Brooklyn. Actually, she was thinking in terms of an interim arrangement: Woody would remain in the rancho, and *she* would live in Sea Gate with Cathy . . . and gradually prepare her parents for the shock of an Okie son-in-law. She was so taken up with (what seemed to him) pedestrian, domestic problems that there really wasn't much chance to talk. She just breezed in and out. It was beginning to seem that their letters were more intimate than their meetings, and he was left frustrated and angry. That night, after she'd gone, he wrote a vicious attack:

Dear Mrs. M. Mazia:

Tonight marks just about *365* days of this business of running back to the band box.

Week ends came and you ran back to your band box.

When the wind changed you ran back to your band box.

When you had a thought you phoned it back to your band box.

And when you found out you were going to have an idea you bought a $5 ticket back to your band box.

And when you took a deep breath of air you put in a call for your band box.

It's foolish for me to say it, but when you found out you were going to have a baby, in two minutes you called up your band box.

You went to your band box to find friendship, help, companionship and money, and love, neither of which you could find with me.

You valued the hairs on your leg more than all of the foolish and silly words we said in our sleep.

And this has gone on for more than 12 months.

When you had a dream worth dreaming you got in touch with your band box and the half-time kisses you dished out the honest ones at the band box. Those dry things called kisses that you gave to me were the old ones, the week old ones, the ones left over from your band box.

From the dates you told me, I judge that Cathy more

than likely came from your band box. You hate to admit this but never have you denied it. You say it "likely" came from either place. Well. For six whole years now there has been "something" fairly attractive keeping you in your band box. Just what that "something" is, I find it easy to imagine. . . .

You slept with your band box man every night. I haven't exactly been alone. But the deal is over. It's been carried on too far. If the least mental canyon ever existed between you and your band box man, ten hundred times more of a canyon is now between us. How could it be otherwise?

I'm sure and very sure that when me and you say the word "love" we mean entirely different things. In my mind you don't seem to even understand the first simple principles of "love" and I guess to you I appear the same. To me people that are in love wrap their little babies up in a rug or a blanket and cross deserts, wade swamps, cross icebergs, wade snow, do anything to be together, but it seems that you have always put a hamburger or an orange juice or your belly before any thoughts of love—and if I've not been raised to live in your way, I'm very sorry.

And now because you still, still make silly excuses to keep on staying in your band box, all I can say is to you "goodbye" and "good luck." Please let me know how much I owe you and I'll get the money.

I can't live insane any longer.

> Your friend,
> Me

You can lose a hundred dollars just trying to win a dime . . .

Marjorie, outraged by the letter and perhaps a bit frightened herself by the prospect of such a new, uncertain life, responded in kind:

Well I must say you must have enjoyed dragging me through the gutter. But I have plenty more to add and the words are coming so fast I can't even take the time to write them. . . . I've got all the strength and the courage in the world tied up like bundles in my muscles and you nor nobody can make

me feel like the rat you'd like me to feel like. I'm sorry if
this is not the letter you expected but you've done your share
of raving and I've got mine coming to me.

No thanks I don't need any of your money any more than
I need Arnold's. I am self sufficient and can stand on my
own two feet. I wasn't coming to New York only for you.
There is something else in my life and by God it's something
that won't call me names and it's something I can always
live for and with. I'm still coming to New York when and
how I choose. You were never much help in seeing to it that
I got there. You only cried that you were helpless . . . that
you were lost . . . that you were insane . . . that you were
lonely . . . always you and you and you. . . . Well Mr. YOU
I hope you find that there are some other things in this world
and they don't all begin with you. There is me and him and
her. And all of us . . . whether you like us or not and you
liking us or not doesn't make us die out or freeze up. I'm
going ahead with my plans just the way I want and when I
get to New York I'll be the happiest and the liveliest person
in that city and I'll do everything the way I know I can and
nothing will stop me. . . .

To which there was no possible response except utter, abject
retreat. "(Hello) (Can I sneak in for a moment)," he began his
next letter. "You have said more truth on a page and a half than
I could say in a whole book . . . I feel like an awful mean little
boy that's throwed a squalling walleyed fit and said every mean
old word he could think of to the little mama that he loved most
of all . . ."

And Marjorie's reply: "Yes, you really are my first and best
baby. You've got just as many troubles as Cathy."

The more prestigious reviews were beginning to come in now
and they, too, were largely favorable. Most reviewers were so
impressed by Woody's raw talent that they tended to forgive the
book's flaws. Though the politically convenient plot twists and
relentless self-deprecation seemed a bit obvious to New York
literary tastes, there was a crude vitality to the writing that could
not be ignored. With time and maturity and discipline and good
counsel, it was believed, Woody Guthrie had a chance to become

an important American writer. He already had a distinctive style and sense of the country.

Horace Reynolds, in *The New York Times Book Review*, compared him to the Irish playwright Sean O'Casey: "Woody is on fire inside, a natural born poet. . . . There's a glory hallelujah madness of imagery here which is exciting and compelling. . . . It's exciting and it's a little flat and empty. . . . There's a curious sense of withdrawal here which I believe is the result of omission and contrivance. . . ."

Orville Prescott, the *New York Times* daily reviewer: "Woody Guthrie might well be an American folk hero all by his own self. . . . Woody's travels, his brushes with the law, his succession of odd jobs and his guitar playing . . . all seem somewhat of an anticlimax after his stupendous childhood. . . . There certainly hasn't been anything like it before, an ecstatic, breathless, jutting geyser of scrambled words. . . ."

Clifton Fadiman, who had appeared with Woody on radio, writing in *The New Yorker*: "Some day people are going to wake up to the fact that Woody Guthrie and the ten thousand songs that leap and tumble off the strings of his music box are a national possession, like Yellowstone or Yosemite, and part of the best stuff this country has to show the world. . . ."

A dissenting view came from Oklahoma, where a majority of the Guthries were disappointed that Woody had chosen to air the family's dirty linen in public, especially in regard to his mother's illness. But most upset, by far, was Woody's cousin Warren Tanner, who was portrayed as a sadistic cat killer in a rather lurid scene. Warren decided to defend his good name by suing for libel, and Woody's father, who was still primly playing out his string in a dingy Oklahoma City hotel room, wrote: "I think the literary value of your book would have been enhanced if you had left Warren's name out altogether. . . ."

Woody wasn't much troubled by the Tanner lawsuit, though, or by the family's misgivings—all of that seemed far away, part of a different time and place; *Bound for Glory* had been so much a product of his imagination that it was hard to believe the people he'd brought to life on paper actually existed in the real world. Meanwhile, he was basking in the critical acclaim . . . while trying his best to hide his personal satisfaction and respond in a politically appropriate manner. He wrote to Marjorie: "Most of [the critics] come down too heavy on the rambling and gambling of a wild hobo with a guitar. . . . It was a lick at bad politics and racial barriers that I really wanted to hit.''

E. P. Dutton Company certainly was surprised and pleased by the book's critical success, and apparently looked forward to a long relationship with Woody. On April 7, 1943, Elliott Macrae, a Dutton executive, wrote to Mary Guthrie that he'd had a chat with Woody about his writing plans and was hopeful that several more books of ''literary merit and appeal to the reading public'' might be published in the years to come and, therefore, it had been agreed that Dutton would send Mary $25 per week out of Woody's royalty account for the next six months . . . and possibly thereafter. At the same time, Woody was negotiating a contract for a second book, *I Want to Be Right,* with Dutton. Once again, he would receive a $500 advance: $250 payable upon signing, $125 when half the manuscript was completed, and $125 when the whole thing was done—which was optimistically targeted for October 1, 1943.

Money seemed to be pouring in from all sides now. In May, Woody won a $1,700 Rosenwald Fellowship, having been nominated by Alan Lomax, to write ''books, ballads, songs and novels that will help people to know each other's work better.''

Suddenly, he was in great demand all over the city. The favorable reviews and parties and fellowship had given him a certain notoriety. Three *Life* magazine photographers followed him around town one day, taking pictures wherever he went. He appeared on network radio shows again: ''Report to the Nation,'' talking about folk songs and the war, and ''We, the People,'' singing war ballads and telling of ''his experiences while traveling through America.'' The *World-Telegram*, apparently unaware that it had exposed Woody as a Communist twice in the past two years, sent a respectful reporter for an interview and Woody told him, ''If I make some money [from the book], I'm gonna buy a war bond and see Maine and Florida, places I ain't seen.''

He was something of a New York celebrity again. His name appeared in the gossip columns (a result, no doubt, of the unseen hand of Publicity Associates). Walter Winchell noted: ''Woody Guthrie, the itinerant ballad singer whose new book *Bound for Glory* is getting rave reports, still earns his living by playing for nickels and dimes in waterfront saloons.''

Leonard Lyons ran two anecdotes Woody had told him. One concerned a decision Woody made to kill a man who'd been giving him trouble out West. He'd bought a gun and was heading off to the shootout when he met an attractive woman "who, for the first time, was responsive" (whatever that meant) and he told her to wait while he sold the gun, "and with the money, I took her to a show. That's how I lived to write a book instead of being hanged for murder."

The other anecdote was about a riot on a picket line: "This cop came up, hit me on the head with his club and said, get out of here, you radical you . . . And I bin lookin' for that cop ever since . . . 'cause he sure was psychic. . . ."

On April 15, as planned, Woody borrowed a car and, accompanied by Brownie McGhee, went to Wilmington and retrieved Marjorie and Cathy from their bandbox. After all the melodrama of the past year, the actual moment of victory was rather anticlimactic. Marjorie had organized everything, and the transfer was accomplished without a hitch.

As they drove back to New York along U.S. Highway 1, Woody may well have enjoyed a rare, peaceful, uncomplicated moment of triumph. He was thirty years old, just entering his prime, with all sorts of fascinating possibilities arrayed before him. His first book had gone into a second printing; his second book would soon be under contract. He was appearing on network radio shows again. He'd been compared in recent weeks to Sean O'Casey, Robert Burns, and Walt Whitman, among others, and called a "national possession" like Yosemite. It was springtime, the woman he loved was by his side, and they were, finally, heading home.

CHAPTER 8

Poems and Explosions

There was, of course, a war still going on.

Woody Guthrie figured that his job was to fight the war with his songs, his writing, and his guitar that "killed" fascists (even falling in love was a blow against Hitler, he told Marjorie, since fascism stood for hatred and love was the opposite of that).

The United States Army, however, was not at all convinced that maintaining high morale in the subways and waterfront saloons of New York was quite enough. And while Woody might have done wonders rousing the troops to battle, *that* wasn't exactly what the army had in mind either: to the military, he was no different than any of the other hillbillies who'd overrun virtually every barracks and foxhole with their sad songs and guitars. He was infantry.

At first, he was exempted from the service because he had a family to support. But as the supply of unmarried, eligible young men began to dwindle in the winter of 1943, the army was forced to become less choosy about its inductees. Even as Woody celebrated the publication of *Bound for Glory* that spring, his draft board was sniffing around. By May, he had received official notice—in June, he was to report for a physical.

At the same time, Cisco Houston continued his long-term campaign to recruit Woody into the merchant marine. His tactics were only marginally more subtle than the army's. He called

Woody a sissy for hanging around Amy Vanderbilt and all those other New York celebrities and phonies. He summoned up visions of the good old days when they'd traveled the California valleys with Will Geer, organizing the cotton strikers; Woody had been the old master then, teaching Cisco everything there was to know about organizing and hoboing and singing in bars . . . but now he'd grown soft, flabby, *bourgeois*. Cisco's position was unassailable: not only had he risked his life several times already at sea—despite the near-blindness that would have been an ironclad exemption from military service—but his younger brother, Slim, had drowned some months before when his ship was torpedoed by the Nazis. Slim, who suffered from the same congenital eye problem as Cisco, hadn't been able to see his way to the engine-room ladder in the rush of oil and water when the hull shattered.

Cisco's hectoring had an impact. Woody was edging off to sea even before the army sent its greetings, but the notice to appear for his physical iced it. He and Cisco headed off to the National Maritime Union hiring hall on Seventeenth Street, and signed on as mess boys on the *William B. Travis*, a Liberty ship carrying supplies by convoy across the Atlantic. Also along for the ride was Jimmy Longhi, a young, emotional, determinedly left-wing law student from the Bronx, whom Cisco had met the week before at Camp Unity, the Communist Party's summer retreat. Woody immediately handed Longhi a guitar and began teaching him to grunt some bass harmony for what he was sure would become a splendid shipboard trio.

Marjorie, convinced that Woody would be eaten alive in the army and that the merchant marine offered him a bit more leeway (and some protection, in the form of Cisco), gave her reluctant blessings. They hadn't had much time together. Marjorie had moved, at first, into a tiny room above her parents' apartment in Sea Gate, while Woody remained in his rancho. The strategy was to break the news to her parents gradually. First, the separation from Arnold. Then, the arrival of Woody. Then, the true story of Cathy's paternity. It was a plan that worked both better and worse than she expected. Her mother knew the whole story even before Marjorie told her; Aliza Greenblatt had sensed it from that first lunch with Woody, a year earlier. Marjorie's father, on the other hand, refused to acknowledge the facts even after he was told. He would not countenance his daughter taking up with a Gentile; he would never, he promised, set foot in their home.

Realizing the utter finality of her mother's acceptance and her father's rejection, Marjorie dropped all pretenses when it became apparent that Woody was going off to serve, and perhaps die, on the ships. They lived together briefly in her monastic Sea Gate cubicle, above her parents' apartment, still unmarried (though Woody was now officially divorced).

In the first days after he left, she would take Cathy in the carriage over to the beach and watch as the huge convoy—no fewer than a hundred ships—formed off the coast of Coney Island, getting ready to carry supplies for the Allied invasion of Italy, and she imagined that Woody was out there, somewhere, on one of those ships; as it happened, he was.

In a way, Cisco was quite right. Woody *had* been out of the mainstream for too long, cooped up in his rancho writing *Bound for Glory* and the long letters to Marjorie, completely distracted by the bizarre twists and turns of their courtship—all of his energy going to her, and to himself and his writing. But now, as he stood on the deck of the *William B. Travis* in Hoboken and watched the men busily loading the boat, he felt the same sort of excitement as when he'd watched them building the Grand Coulee Dam. It didn't even matter that it was a frightful cargo of two-ton bombs and gasoline they were dropping into the *Travis's* holds. He was so completely exhilarated by the prospect of being out in the world again, part of a great adventure, a man among men, that as the ship pulled out that first evening for a short cruise over to Red Hook in Brooklyn, its final mooring before sailing, Woody danced a little jig on the main deck (which had a nice hollow metal thonk to it) when no one was looking.

He luxuriated in the gruff, sweaty presence of the other men on the ship. He always carried a pencil behind his ear or in his shirt, a battered little notebook in his pants pocket; he was always scribbling down bits and snatches of their conversation ("So I showed her this chain around my neck here, and these medals, and I says, 'Yes honey, I know I could never be anything but a catholic, and I know you couldn't never change from a Baptist . . .' ") and observations ("Sailors talk to each other like most people think to themselves") and speculations ("How many scientific discoveries await the mind of man inside a can of garbage?

Acids. Plastics. Paints. Gasses. Drugs. Dyes. Moulds. Bacteria
. . .") and little poems:

> The sea
> Took off her clothes
> In the sun today
> And naked
> All night
> With the wild wind lay.

He had a wonderful, journalistic ear for the coarse rhythms
of the words all around him, could perfectly reproduce the
halting formality of the union meeting where Cisco was chosen
the ship's representative (despite a challenge from some red-
baiters), the back-and-forth bravado and swagger of a shipboard poker game. Theoretically, he wasn't supposed to be
taking down all those notes and observations; there were signs
posted all over the ship, warning against personal diaries because the enemy might seize them if the ship were captured or
torpedoed. There was also the constant fear of foreign agents
and sabotage. But Woody was so profoundly unthreatening that
no one seemed to mind. The men were, in fact, rather impressed. They would stare in amazement at Woody's bunk,
always covered with papers and books, a typewriter, a pile of
musical instruments . . . and they'd wonder not so much *what*
he was writing all the time, but why and how he did it. He'd
invite them in to read things he'd written—they watched him
compose a twelve-verse talking blues about the merchant marine in the first days he was on board—and he'd encourage
them to try it too. "Look at those sea gulls over there," he'd
say. "See how those two guys are fighting over that scrap of
garbage? You could write a story just describing that."

Jimmy Longhi remembers Woody coming aboard the first
day wearing a new, neatly pressed set of khakis (Marjorie's
doing, no doubt), with the pants three inches too long. "He
looked like a walking pawnshop with his guitar, his mandolin,
his violin, three or four different harmonicas, his Jew's harp,
his typewriter, his seabag, and some bottles of beer." He first
was assigned to washing dishes, but later was promoted to
messman, in charge of putting food on the table for the twenty-
man navy gun crew that was aboard, a job he performed with

great ardor but mixed success. He really tried hard to have everything just right for the men, but was easily distracted. Instead of setting the tables, he might lose himself in drawing a beautiful menu on the blackboard, garnished with ribbons and bows, twittering birds, children playing, a mermaid, and sumptuous, impossible descriptions of the meal. Beef stew became "Aunt Jenny's prize-winning Saturday night special made of choice chunks of prime Texas beef, braised in golden butter, cooked with 14-carat carrots, plump tomatoes, California celery and sweet Spanish onions seasoned and stirred every 10 minutes by a beautiful virgin, if available, or by the youngest member of the gun crew . . ."

"Sometimes Cisco and I had to bail him out," Jimmy recalled, "and help him set up at the last minute. But, all in all, people would rather eat in Woody's messroom than mine. They knew he was special. The attitude was: 'Lay a finger on him and I'll break your fucking legs.' "

There was, indeed, a tendency to protect him. Each of the men had a special task to perform in case of an emergency, each was given a little card telling him exactly where to go and what to do. Woody's card simply said, "Be there!" In the lonely and superstitious life at sea, he was a valuable commodity—a continual source of wonder, a good-luck charm, a mascot almost, but wilder and more unpredictable than the captain's cat; more like a dolphin skimming along portside, or a strange, exotic sea bird perched on the rail. His benign, near-mystical presence was practically enough, in itself, to guarantee special treatment. But there was also his music: he was uncanny about sensing the crew's mood with his songs, which ranged from morale-building rousers like "When the Yanks Go Marching In" to the sad, sweet cowboy ballads he'd harmonize with Cisco, to the juicy, unabashed bawdy verses he seemed able to spin out endlessly, sitting on the main deck as the sun set, surrounded by the incredible panorama of a hundred other ships in five long rows, the waves slapping gently against the welded metal sides of the *Willy B.*

They set out across the Atlantic in a rather precarious position—the next-to-last ship on an outside row of the convoy, one slot away from coffin corner, with only a thin line of destroyers to protect them from German submarines. It was a two-week journey across to Gibraltar, and the U-boats were out most nights, the destroyers trying to deflect them with a noisy curtain of depth

charges that boomed and splashed in the darkness . . . scant protection against the German torpedoes that shivered the waters all
around them, whanging into several ships, which expired in mad,
gasping balls of fire and black smoke. They saw one boat fold
precisely and slide under in a perfect Churchillian "V."

Returning to their cabin after the alert ended and the seas qui-
eted the first terrible night of the submarine attack, Jimmy and
Cisco fell into a surprisingly vehement discussion of immortality
and the eternal verities, fueled by a bottle of sweet rum. Jimmy,
normally a most rational person, suddenly found himself holding
out the possibility of a universal master plan, citing Einstein and
speculating about other levels of reality and time and space.
"Maybe," he said, "nothing ever ends."

"Bullshit," said Cisco, a no-nonsense atheist. And so it went,
Woody silent in his upper berth, chain-smoking Camels and sip-
ping Myers's rum, interrupting only once to tell Longhi he was
beginning to sound like a rabbi, which promptly became Jimmy's
nickname: "Rabbi," or "Reb" for short. When the nervous back-
and-forth subsided, Woody took over and began to tell them,
very calmly and in surprising detail, the story of his family and
the fires and his mother's illness. And then, in conclusion: "And
I'm pretty sure I've got the same thing my mother had . . ."

"That's a crock," Jimmy started, then: "How do you know?"

"Dunno, just feel *queer* sometimes."

The next day, Woody began an ingenious experiment that was
part object lesson, part inquiry in the nature of hope, but mostly
an attempt to divert everyone's attention from the German subs.
He appeared on the main deck with some empty fruit crates from
the galley, which he began whittling down into slats and shafts,
slowly attaching them together, building, refining. The crew
gathered around, intrigued, not asking at first—nor did he vol-
unteer—what it was all about. Finally, a young navy gunner
couldn't restrain himself: "Woody, what the hell is it?"

"A wind machine."

"A what?"

"It'll make the ship go faster."

"C'mon."

Gradually, attached to the rail, it grew into a Rube Goldberg
agglomeration of propellers and turrets and rubber bands and
shafts and pistons, becoming more complex and wonderfully ab-

surd each day until he finally announced, "It's done." And then
the bets—fives, tens, twenties, fifties—went down. Having divided itself rather clearly into opposing theological camps—believers and nonbelievers—the crew spent the next day watching
the machine churn and rotate. When it was over, faith was rewarded: the ship's log officially recorded that the *Travis* had done
thirteen miles better than the day before. The wind machine became an article of faith after that, helping the men through a
rough passage until it was swept away in a storm as the ship
neared Gibraltar.

The imminent possibility of death seemed a tonic to Woody.
Not only was he an inspiration to the other men, but he also
began to explore some interesting personal areas. Gradually, during the year he sailed with the merchant marine, he developed a
coherent philosophy that managed to encompass both his earlier
spirituality and his current Marxism. It began with Cisco and
Jimmy's running debate on hope and mortality, and burst into
full flower with a stray phrase from a shipboard chaplain one
Sunday morning: "As a rule, any activity of the mind which
tends to show us the real 'one-ness' of all things is great."

Woody took off from there, using the word "union" as a central proposition, tracing it from Buddha to the C.I.O. in a series
of letters to Marjorie. "The Chinese called it 'yogin' or 'union.'
The Indians called it 'prana' or 'energy,' " he wrote, adding that
every great religious leader had believed in the same unifying
concept . . . and Karl Marx too. When he reached Marx, Woody
tended to drift off into his standard good guys vs. bad guys scen-
ario, the forces of union against the fascists: "All I ever done
was to simply show here and there that the people in the fight all
around the world are lined up on one of two sides. Love. Greed.
There are no middle grounds—no halfway limbs. . . ." But the
fact that Woody could reduce his philosophy to comic-book di-
alectics wasn't what was important (he'd always been able to do
that). The important thing was that he'd found a spiritual ration-
ale for his politics that would serve him for the rest of his life.
He'd managed to reconcile Cisco and Jimmy's positions, as well
as his own past and present, at least in his own mind, and that
was cause for celebration. In fact, he wrote an anthem called
"Union's My Religion" announcing his insight:

I just now heard a salty seaman
On this deep and dangerous sea;
Talking to some Army chaplain
That had preached to set him free:
"When I seen my union vision
Then I made my quick decision;
Yes, that union's my religion;
That I know."

(And, that I know)

The *Travis* steamed into Gibraltar on July 10, and sat there for three weeks, awaiting orders. The men were denied shore leave and began to go a bit crazy, taking thirty-foot dives off the side of the ship just for the hell of it. Woody was quite content, though, writing in his notebook, losing at poker (two weeks' wages), losing at chess to Jimmy, but consistently winning the mental telepathy games that were organized to pass the time of day. He wrote to Marjorie: "Am really a deep chocolate brown. . . . You'd take me for a full-blooded cherokee. . . . I feel a whole lot better than I've felt in my life."

Finally, in midsummer, they moved out in a convoy to Palermo, Sicily. They remained there for about six weeks, unloading their cargo and waiting for new sailing orders. While the ship was moored, a reassuringly normal letter arrived from Marjorie, filled with routine, happy news. She was looking for a permanent home for them in Coney Island, and had cleaned all his belongings out of the rancho. "Some of the 'little strangers' that loved our mattress decided to come over here with some of your books." More important, she was dancing and teaching again. And as motherly as ever. In closing, she wrote: "Remember the ship is your home. Keep it tidy."

In mid-September, after rusting away in Palermo harbor for more than a month, the *Travis* received its next set of sailing orders. It was to proceed alone, without convoy, across the Mediterranean to Tunis with a cargo of thirty military police—an odd assignment that became odder still when, one night out from Tunis, a torpedo slammed into the side of the ship as most of the crew was sleeping. Woody, Jimmy, and Cisco scrambled to the deck, shocked but unhurt. One man was dead and another seriously wounded, but everyone else had survived. The ship was badly ripped apart, though, and it seemed likely that the *Trav* would sink right there. The men, terrified that the German su was still lurking about and waiting to finish the job, made read to abandon ship. Woody stood on the rail, shouting, "God ble the Red Army! They'll finish off the fascist bastards!" until I was silenced by a punch in the nose from a right-wing cool They waited there silently then, for hours it seemed, but neith the second torpedo nor the order to abandon ship ever came ar the captain managed to limp the *Travis* into Bizerte, where it san in the harbor, canceling all shipboard poker debts . . . much Woody's relief.

By the time he returned home in early November, Marjorie ha found a small, dark, one-bedroom apartment at 3520 Merma Avenue, in a drab street of three-story row houses, one bloc from the beach at Coney Island. Woody loved the place. H made sure to praise the little improvements Marjorie had made— the floor she had painted a bright electric blue; the wide she that would have to serve as a breakfast nook—and he didn't all mind the relentless gloom. At last, they had a home of the own.

He was tremendously happy those first few weeks back fro the war. Marjorie was off working and teaching most days, an so he'd roam the beach with Cathy in her stroller; then, whe Marjorie came home in the evening, he'd patiently massage h tired legs. He filled notebooks with poems about "Marjorina th Ballerina," including a very funny one in which he awakens find her already gone to work, but her spirit and "vapors" remai in the apartment: he wants sex with the spirit, but it insists tha he make the bed, fix the rug, and "brush your teeth good, honey you smell like vinegar."

Woody was so pleased with the new domestic arrangement that he sent out announcements, entitled "Sort of a Marriag License," to all their friends. He noted their new Coney Islan address and added: "We aim to live here awhile, and if this wa comes out okay and prices go down a little, we sorta might blov a buck or two for some real wedding papers and all. . . . If yo are our friend you won't give a dam, and if you aint our friend we dont give a dam."

There also was a private contract with Marjorie: "I solemnl promise to remain, books and all, as a resident at 3520 Merma

Avenue, first floor rear, for a period of six months. All words to the contrary, spoken in any state of mind, may only become effective after 5/21/44."

Once again, though, the army intruded. On November 14, Woody received another induction order. He wrote his draft board, protesting that he'd served in the merchant marine, had even been torpedoed, and now planned to honor his contract with E. P. Dutton and Company and finish the novel that he'd promised (which was already overdue): "I sincerely believe my writing is the best thing I have to offer the people who are winning this war. . . ." Obviously, the army didn't agree; he was told that he'd have to either report for induction or go back to the ships.

So, on December 7, he signed on the S.S. *Oliver Hazard Perry*. Three days later, he was transferred to the *Woodrow Wilson* and went on a brief East Coast jaunt. He managed to return home in time to celebrate the holidays with Marjorie. There also was a reunion with Jimmy, who'd been married in the interim, and Cisco, who'd been recuperating from the *Travis* at a left-wing Catskill Mountain resort and came back with a new, blond girl-friend named Bina Rosenbaum, who joined Marjorie at 3520 Mermaid Avenue when Woody, Cisco, and Jimmy decided to ship out together again in early January. Their new ship was the *William Floyd*, with a cargo of war supplies and two hundred Texas oil-field workers on their way to Oran in North Africa. It was a comparatively uneventful crossing this time.

Dissatisfied with the reading material on the first boat, Woody lugged a portable library onto the *Floyd*, along with his usual array of musical instruments, typewriter, and notebooks. Jimmy Longhi remembers Woody carrying volumes by Darwin, Gibbon, Rabelais, Emerson, and Engels. "We are at least reading some good books," he wrote to Marjorie. "I've got all wrapped up in politics and science and social doings which I like better [than fiction]. I had rather write stories than read them." In his present, scientific frame of mind, he grew scornful of the wild excesses of his old hero, Walt Whitman, and wrote a very funny parody called "I Go Singing of Bellies." He also turned out, from time to time, another of his little newspapers, making use of the ship's mimeograph machine; he called his publication "Union News" and laced it with N.M.U. propaganda directed mostly at the Texas oil workers.

But there wasn't the same magic as there'd been on the *Travis*
he was merely another messman and then, after a dispute with
the chief steward, demoted to washing dishes again. The contin
gent of brash, manly oil drillers seemed to bother him too. His
letters to Marjorie became nervous and uncertain: "I write like a
big man but I feel little and small," and later: "I would like to
be rough and tough as most of [the guys playing poker]. The
show business is full of sissy people." And to Cathy: "Your
mama is always right. The one time she really went wrong is
when she adopted me to raise. Personally, I think she is bound
to lose out because I will never grow up. . . ."

They arrived in Oran without serious incident, dropped off the
Texans and then moved on to Arzew, to unload their cargo. The
scene at the docks there was shocking: filthy, starving Algerian
longshoremen swarmed over the American crew, begging for
food, sticking their hands in the sailors' pockets, pushing, grab
bing, whimpering. Jimmy Longhi, much to his disgust, had to
punch one of them in the jaw. It was a level of poverty that
seemed beyond any sort of effective response; it was difficult
even to comprehend such desperation. The best the Americans
could do was to divide their garbage after each meal and hand it
out to the longshoremen in slop pails, which they took home to
their families. Woody, meanwhile, began a campaign to collect
soap from the crew and distribute it to the people—which wasn't
as condescending as it sounded—he knew the Moslems had strict
religious laws about cleanliness and, even in their current de
prived state, would welcome soap (of which there happened, also
to be a surplus on board) as gratefully as food. He proceeded to
collect pillowcases full of soap, and then took his guitar to the
center of town, where he performed a bit of magic, distributing
the soap to a crowd of grateful women while playing a wonderful
concert for their children, who learned his name before very long
and began chanting, "Woo-dee! Woo-dee! Woo-dee . . ."

He wrote in his notebook: "By far my best audience for folk
songs and ballads so far have been the kids. They look and they
listen and they don't make a single sound. The story you are
telling them in words goes through the minds like a news reel,
only plainer. . . ."

It was the music, more than anything else, that came to dominate the trip. He and Cisco practiced all the time, and were
getting to be quite good together. "I really think it would surprise

'ou to hear us play now," he wrote to Marjorie. "We have gotten so much practice you wouldn't recognize us."

When they arrived home in late March, Cisco joined Bina on the cot in Cathy's room at Mermaid Avenue, and he and Woody would be up and playing even before Marjorie left for work in the morning . . . and still going strong—sometimes, she'd later insist, on the same song—when she returned at night. Left to their own devices, it's possible that Woody and Cisco would have been content merely to sit around the house like that all day, making an occasional appearance on some Greenwich Village street corner or in a neighborhood tavern, but Marjorie and Bina began pressuring them to take their obvious talents and *do* something with them. The problem was, given the still obscure status of folk music in New York: do what?

As was so often the case in Woody's life, Alan Lomax had part of the solution. He was organizing another of his radio extravaganzas—a folk opera this time, written by Lomax and his wife, Elizabeth, about two feuding hill country families who decide to call a cease-fire and join forces to fight the fascists. Included in the cast for *The Martins and the Coys* were Will Geer, Burl Ives, Sonny Terry, and virtually every other folk musician who happened to be in town. Woody promptly was assigned one of the main roles, that of dashing young Alex Coy, who submits to his draft board and goes off to fight the war; Cisco was part of the chorus. Unfortunately, none of the American networks were very interested in the project, and the best Alan could manage was to have the whole thing recorded in the Decca studios in New York and shipped to London for use on the BBC, which financed the production.

It was probably in the course of rehearsals for *The Martins and the Coys* that Alan told Woody about Moses Asch, a man with a wisp of a record company and a tiny studio on West Forty-sixth Street, but with the solid intention of recording the real thing: American folk music without frills. Within days after that, Woody knocked on the door of the Asch Record Company, plopped himself on the floor, and announced, "I'm Woody Guthrie," as if that was supposed to have some tremendous effect on the dark, burly man sitting at the recording panel/desk of the miniature recording studio/office.

"So?" Moses Asch replied, in typical fashion. He was a grumbly, ursine man with an eclectic cultural background. His father was Sholem Asch, a prominent Yiddish writer, and he had spent much of his youth bouncing back and forth between Europe and America. He'd studied electronics in Germany, was a pioneer in the use of microphones and recording technology, and had fallen in love with American folk music one day in the early 1920's when he'd picked up a first-edition copy of John Lomax's *Cowboy Songs* on the Quay in Paris. "It was the words that were always most important," he'd recall. "More than the music, before I'd even heard the music, the words."

Moe Asch considered himself an intuitive judge of talent. He would later claim that he'd never heard of Woody Guthrie before, but sensed his genius from the moment the little man plopped himself down on the studio floor, dressed in what might charitably be called rags, with a berserk mop of hair and a full beard (which he'd cultivated at sea), and, after announcing his name, quickly added, "I'm a Communist, y'know."

"So?"

"I want to make some records."

"When do you want to start?"

During the course of the next week or so, Woody and Cisco—joined intermittently by Sonny Terry, Leadbelly, Bess Lomax, and others—committed hundreds of songs to acetate master discs. They included both traditional songs and Woody's own, and constituted, without doubt, one of the most memorable series of recording sessions in the history of American folk music.

The process itself was entirely informal. Asch would sit behind a glass partition with his recording equipment, in a room the size of a large closet; Woody and Cisco would stand before a microphone on the other side, in a room the size of a slightly larger closet. Asch would give them the signal to go ahead and they'd start plowing through their repertoire, song after song. Occasionally Woody might screw up the words or music irretrievably (sometimes he'd actually have trouble remembering which tune went with which set of words) and they'd have to start over again, but most of the songs were recorded in one take. The sessions usually took place in the evening. "He'd just come by and say, 'I've got some songs I want to do,' " Asch recalled. "And I'd say okay, and give him maybe twenty or twenty-five dollars, and afterwards we'd have dinner in a cafeteria. I never formally set up a recording session. If Sonny Terry happened to be around, he played. Same with Leadbelly. But nothing organized. It was their music, and I just let them go ahead.''

Several months later, *PM* described Woody's first sessions with Asch: "Recently Guthrie and Cisco Houston, Bess Lomax, Sonny Terry and Pete Seeger [not true; Seeger was in the South Pacific with the army] gathered in one of Asch's recording rooms and began singing to each other. Guthrie would do a ballad, and Bess Lomax would say, 'Oh yes, that reminds me of one,' and Cisco Houston would follow with one he remembered. This group recorded 132 master records.''

Asch's rather sketchy logbook shows that Woody Guthrie first recorded in his studio on April 16, 1944. It was a quick session, two songs: "Hard, Ain't It Hard" and "More Pretty Gals Than One." He returned three days later and staged a marathon with Cisco and the others—63 masters, including three different versions of his merchant marine ode "Talking Sailor." On April 20, they were back for 25 more. Then 20, 35, and 38 in subsequent sessions that month. One of the songs at the last, undated, session was Woody's old Irving Berlin parody, "God Blessed America," changed slightly, with a new tag line at the end of each verse ("This land was made for you and me . . .") and a new title, "This Land Is My Land." Woody didn't treat the song any differently than his others, but Moe Asch (later) claimed that *he* knew it was a very important composition from the start.

There wasn't much he could do about it, though. Asch didn't have the money to release any of the remarkable music he was recording. He did have a gut feeling, though, that what was happening in his studio was an important—historic—event, and the recording sessions might have continued indefinitely—just to get everything *down*—if the army hadn't decided to resume its rather dogged pursuit of Woody. Once again, he was forced to ship out with Cisco and Jimmy. The ship was called the *Sea Porpoise*, and the cargo was three thousand young soldiers, headed for what everyone assumed would be the invasion of Europe.

The *Sea Porpoise* was somewhere in mid-Atlantic when the first troops stormed ashore at Normandy on June 6, 1944. "We all heard the news about the invasion today," Woody wrote to Marjorie. "You should have heard the cheering and whistling from Cape Cod to Kingdom Come. We hope you are as glad as we are. . . .''

The invasion, which seemed to promise a quick end to the war, had Woody in high spirits throughout the crossing. He was deep into the ecstasy of his "Union's My Religon" period now, and wrote Marjorie long sermons interspersed with happy speculations about the beautiful cottage they would live in once the war was over, and the babies they would have. "Greetings and saturations," he began one letter. "How do you find yourselves? With your hands, I suppose. . . . I'm so lonesome I've already proposed wedlock and matrimony to three gulls." He had stumbled across a book of short stories by Guy de Maupassant and was quite impressed. He described several stories at length to Marjorie and added: "I can't help but feel that I can put together [my stories] the same as he." The reading made Woody anxious to settle down and finally do some serious work: "I am several months behind on the book for E. P. Dutton. I should also have prepared some kind of song book. I should also have knocked off several short stories . . . and here I am washing dishes and cleaning tables on a ship where anyone could take my place. . . . Nothing hurts me worse than to waste time, although I have poofed off a lot of it."

Woody neglected to mention that he was performing several other functions, aside from washing dishes and cleaning tables, that made the *Sea Porpoise* unique among the ships steaming toward France. It was, in fact, a terrifying passage: German submarines were prowling the North Atlantic even more determinedly than before, hoping to cut off the invasion at its source. Depth charges boomed about the convoy continuously. "We had three thousand soldiers on board," Jimmy Longhi remembered, "and lifeboat accommodations for no more than two hundred people. So if we got hit, it was going to be one big fucking mess. Naturally, I wanted to stay close to a lifeboat at all times. I wanted to *sleep* in one if I could, especially when we were under attack, and it seemed we were always under attack."

When the fireworks began the first night out, Woody grabbed his guitar and said to Jimmy and Cisco, "Let's go."

"Let's go where?"

"Down below."

"Down below?" Jimmy said. "You gotta be nuts."

"Okay," Woody said with a shrug, and took off without them, down to where the troops were quartered in the ship's five massive holds—frightening, cavernous rooms below sea level, where the depth charges boomed and echoed metallically; far too deep inside the ship for any of the men ever to reach the deck if there was a torpedo.

And there was Woody—utterly fearless, it seemed—heading down into the darkness to entertain the young soldiers. Jimmy and Cisco, shamed, scurried after him and found him already telling the boys to "Sing loud. It sends out shock waves that confuse the Nazi U-boats and makes 'em shoot crooked. . . ."

They played for hours down there, moving from hold to hold. They played mostly up-tempo tunes, trying to get the men to join in and forget the danger. Woody organized square dances, and played the rollicking hoedowns and breakdowns his Uncle Jeff had taught him. He'd hack away merrily at his fiddle, with Cisco backing him on guitar; then he'd drop the fiddle and improvise some square dance calls for the whooping, hollering men, who were dancing in the aisles:

> Grab your partner from his bunk
> Whirl him around and show some spunk.
> Don't listen to the depth charge, just be brave
> And we'll dance around old Hitler's grave . . .

By late June, the *Sea Porpoise* was moored off the coast of Ireland, the soldiers waiting nervously to join the invasion force. The men tried to busy themselves by playing poker—Woody lost a hundred dollars in an afternoon and attempted to rhyme his way out of it in a letter home: "The news will spread and go around by gossip everywhere/ That I tried to make an inside straight and lost to a little pair." There also was a great deal of fuss made over Erskine Caldwell's slightly blue novel, *God's Little Acre*: "What little of Caldwell's work I know is somewhat forced, but does a good job of tearing down old and useless conventions," he wrote to Marjorie. "Men yell and kick their feet in the air and laugh as they read the book. I sometimes wonder how many wars we'll have to fight before we get over our silly ignorance of the human body."

Finally, in early July, the *Sea Porpoise* moved toward Normandy in a turbulent gray sea filled with nervous, rocking ships surrounded by the floating effluvia of the initial assault force, bits of wooden crates and hints of unspeakable horrors, pieces

of cloth and, it seemed, rotting flesh and bones; a sky crazy
with planes from both sides executing brilliant dives and loops,
the air splotched with flak and, at night, festooned with the
gaudy red spurts of tracer bullets. Then, in the midst of all the
noise and heaving, the three thousand young soldiers shuffled
up to the deck and, with a grim flip, vaulted one by one over
the side and into the flimsy transport boats bobbing helplessly
in the chaotic sea.

And then the *Sea Porpoise* was empty, and riding strangely
high in the water. Woody, Cisco, and Jimmy sat dumbstruck in
their cabin, filled with the horrible reality that many of the men
they had worked so hard to entertain during the long passage
would soon be dead. As the *Sea Porpoise* silently extruded itself
from the incredible carnage, they lapsed into an idle conversation
about what they'd be willing to die for. Sex, Cisco said, the love
of a good woman. "Jane Dudley dancing the harmonica break-
down," Woody said, trying to break the solemnity.

"What?"

"Haven't you ever seen Jane Dudley dance the harmonica
breakdown?" he asked Jimmy, who allowed that he hadn't.
"Well, before you die, you simply must see Jane Dudley dance,"
and Woody began rising toward the ceiling at this point, floating
it seemed, his mouth still forming the words, "the har-mon-ica
break-down," which couldn't be heard because of the bursting
metal *brrannng* of the explosion. Jimmy blacked out, and the
next thing he remembered, really, was being on deck with Cisco
and Woody, waiting for the abandon-ship order. It hadn't been a
torpedo this time, but an acoustic mine that had exploded beneath
the ship, lifting it into the air briefly and ripping a gaping hole
below. The *Sea Porpoise* somehow managed to remain afloat,
though, and was towed into Southampton harbor, arriving just as
the Germans launched a rocket attack—thirteen separate V-2
rocket bombs, moaning and streaking across the sky, then ex-
ploding in the distance, a sight as strange and frightening as anything Woody had ever seen.

He, Cisco, and Jimmy were dispatched to London, where
they were to take a train to Glasgow for the passage home.
Woody had the presence of mind to drop by the BBC offices
in London, where he was welcomed as one of the stars of *The
Martins and the Coys* and asked to sing some of his railroad
songs on a program called "The Children's Hour" on July 7,

1944. There wasn't time for much else in London, but Woody and the others enjoyed the leisurely train ride through the countryside. They spent several days roaming the back streets of Glasgow and meeting the Scottish people, who "sound like they are singing even when they are talking," he wrote to Marjorie.

They had been promised first-class passage home, but were loaded aboard a troop carrier with cots stacked four and five tiers high. Woody later wrote about organizing a letter-writing contest among the bored, tired men, getting them to petition Congress for unemployment insurance for seamen, a G.I. Bill of Rights for seamen, and citizenship for alien seamen—all of which were current N.M.U. demands. More than a thousand letters allegedly were written, and he claimed to have polished off 112 himself, telling each congressman: "I'm a voter from your home town. Not only that, but from right in your own neighborhood. I'm facing buzz bombs, magneto mines, torpedos, stukas and hauling nitroglycerine to save your neck; surely you can pass three bills to save mine."

When not writing letters, Woody filled a notebook with the beginnings of a story about outgrowing the old gang house in Okemah and meeting his first girl; he also wrote a bawdy poem about the Virgin Mary, and some sea songs:

> I got a new way to roll
> I got a new way to roll
> I'm a torpedoed seaman,
> And I got a new way to roll.

Arriving home in early August, Woody made a decision: he was not going out in the boats again, no matter what. It was more a question of common sense than bravery; he'd already proven his bravery. He'd been blown out of the water twice and been lucky both times. Going back again would be asking for trouble, tempting the Fates. He figured his service on the three ships would be enough to satisfy even the most rapacious draft board. Barring that, he hoped the war would be over before the army could get him. It seemed unlikely that they'd want him at this late stage, in any case; he was thirty-two years old, with two women and four children to support. He decided to take his chances.

Anyway, there were more important matters to worry about. There was the re-election of Franklin D. Roosevelt for a fourth term, which had become something of a referendum on the pernicious influence of the Communist Party in American life—at least, in the eyes of the Communists, and perhaps among some of the Republicans, who were casting the aspersions. The Republican candidate, Thomas Dewey, ran a campaign that could well be considered the official beginning of the most vicious era of red-baiting in the nation's history. He called Roosevelt "indispensable to Earl Browder," and defined a Communist as anyone "who supports a fourth term, so our form of government may be more easily changed." And Dewey was moderate compared to many of the nation's newspapers.

For their part, the Communists happened to be floating through their meekest period since the Russian Revolution. The Communist Party didn't even *exist* anymore, officially. In the interests of the great Soviet-Anglo-American alliance, it had been dissolved by Earl Browder and replaced with the Communist Political Association, a rather Milquetoasty outfit that often seemed little more than a Roosevelt fan club. Browder, as might be expected, set the new tone with statements like: "If J. P. Morgan supports this coalition and goes down the line for it, I as a communist am prepared to clasp his hand. . . ." He predicted a great era of cooperation after the war and, at times, could barely be distinguished from idealistic, mainstream liberals like Wendell Willkie and Henry Wallace.

Sitting in Scotland and reading the early reports of the Dewey campaign strategy, Woody wrote to Marjorie that he was thinking of getting some of the old Almanacs group together and forming a group that would help not only Roosevelt but also people like New York's progressive congressman, Vito Marcantonio, and others whose campaigns might need a boost. "With the entire fascist rat nest on the Dewey bandwagon," he wrote, "we see our enemy now in one whole and solid camp."

As it happened, the Communist Political Association was having similar thoughts. It was hoping to put together an old-fashioned vaudeville show—a program with only folk music would have too limited an audience—and send it around the country for Roosevelt in October. Acting through producers and promoters with left-wing ties—the C.P.A.'s financial involvement was a rather poorly kept secret—a "Roosevelt Bandwagon" was organized: Will Geer would be the master of ceremonies, and Woody and Cisco were hired as a singing team. Other cast members included a pair of comedians, a jazz trio, a black woman jazz singer, and modern dancers Helen Tamiris and Daniel Nagrin. Jackie Gibson, Alan Lomax's old secretary and a sometime girlfriend of Woody's, became the tour's traveling secretary.

Woody had almost two months at home before the "Roosevelt Bandwagon" was scheduled to begin, though, and he was determined to finish his novel for Dutton. He had decided to write a book about his merchant marine experiences—the subject matter of "I Want to Be Right" had never been stipulated in the contract—but the work wasn't going very well. He just couldn't seem to get started, couldn't keep his concentration. Marjorie had built a small triangular piece of plywood into a corner of the living room to serve as a desk for Woody, but he was easily distracted by the phone, by Cathy, by visitors from the neighborhood, by Cisco, and especially by the local taverns. Nor was Joy Doerflinger around anymore to shepherd him through the morass of notes and random scenes and observations he'd jotted down during the past year. Both she and her husband, Bill, were overseas in the service. So Woody ranted and bleated around the house, stormed out and got drunk. He sulked, and Marjorie would get on him for sulking. There was a constant low level of tension in the house and it was becoming a rather serious crisis for them. By the time he left for the "Roosevelt Bandwagon" in late September, it wasn't entirely clear whether he was leaving of his own accord or being kicked out.

"Maybe we just can't live together," Marjorie said.

"Maybe we can't," he replied.

Neither of them meant it, of course, and he wrote her an apology the next day from his train en route to Chicago, where he and Cisco were to provide the entertainment at a huge rally for the Communist Political Association. "It may be good to get rid of me and my ashtrays for a spell once in a while," he wrote. "You can breathe a little and sleep a little and sort of stretch out and be comfortable. I so seldom show you any thanks when I'm there around you. A few days away and I see more and more of the reasons to want you. . . . I only hope and HOPE that we can work out some way to work together in the same unit or something. . . . Have a little patience and I'll try to live up to your way of life."

The next day, he sent her a giddy letter written on a paper bag: Chicago had been a triumph. He'd signed copies of *Bound for Glory* and then sung "All You Fascists Bound to Lose" with Cisco at the Chicago Stadium rally: "We sung better than we ever did, and got a nice hand." The program for the rally described Woody as "the Will Rogers of today, with his guitar and stirring ballads," which didn't please him very much (he never liked being compared to anyone, except Leadbelly). But the Chicago *Tribune*, then a virulently right-wing newspaper, was much worse—it reported that the "People's Rally for Victory and Unity" was attended by 10,000 people and entertained by Woody Guthrie, "an irresponsible hobo. . . . In recent years he has had a vogue, being talked up by young pinks and others who know nothing of the dust bowl."

The *Tribune* jab was the first of many he would receive when the "Roosevelt Bandwagon" began in earnest a week later in Boston. Throughout the tour, the Republican press made much of the fact that this was a barely concealed *Communist* effort to support the President. In Boston, on the very first night, the performance was routed by a barrage of stink bombs. The next evening, in Hartford, Woody began his set by saying: "Me and Cisco spent some time in the merchant marines this past year, hauling nitroglycerine and troops over to win the war. I was torpedoed twice and Cisco here was hit three times. Last night in Boston the fascist people threw a big string of firecrackers into Symphony Hall, but it didn't cause a runaway or a riot. The people in the crowd gave us a hundred dollars for every firecracker."

But the incident in Boston and the general right-wing assault had a telling effect on the tour—people stayed away in droves. Some of the concerts were successful, but those tended to be the ones packed by sympathetic labor unions and left-wing organizations. In fact, the Hartford audience was sufficiently—and obviously enough—progressive so that Woody felt free to crack: "I don't know how the minds of the people here in Hartford run, but all along the railroad tracks the trees are turning red."

From New England, the tour moved through the dour factory towns of the industrial crescent: Buffalo, Akron, Indianapolis, Cleveland, Minneapolis. It wasn't a very pleasant trip. Helen Tamiris was continually at Woody for the nonchalant way he sauntered through "Girl with the Roosevelt Button," which was supposed to be the climax of the show. "You are not a professional!" she would scream at him, which caused his performances to become progressively more unpredictable. For his part, Woody occupied himself on the endless train rides—it was, he claimed, the first time he'd traveled extensively *in* a train, instead of *on* one—by cataloguing every thing he saw out the window. He would actually list signs, scenes, details, interspersed with his own thoughts:

> *United Fence Erectors.*
> *Rusty barrels along wall of factory*
> *Fire is a good servant and a bad master*
> *National enameling and stamping company*
> *Budweiser Beer Brewery*
> *home home home home home home (new houses)*
> *Courtney Vs. Green for governor.*
> *No man in this world looks at you like a railroad conductor.*
> *Grab your baggage*
> *And hold your seat*
> *I'm selling sandwiches*
> *That Jesus couldn't eat.*
> *I believe that I could be a better poet than Walt Whitman if only I didn't have four children to support.*

Before long, Woody tired of the routine and was aching to get home. There were some great audiences and interesting nights out on the town with Cisco and Will, but for the most part, the "Roosevelt Bandwagon" was a succession of dreary towns, half-empty halls, and third-rate accommodations in second-rate hotels. Even the fling he'd hoped to have with Jackie Gibson (with whom he'd spent several nights in Washington) never materialized, as she usually traveled several days ahead of the tour.

In Cleveland, on October 20, he started writing Marjorie the umpteenth letter of apology since the tour began. "I'm coming home to you before long and I'm going to be a new person or a dead one. . . . It's not because I love you any less that I act so silly most times. It's because I'm sore at myself for not making you as happy as I could or should." But then, a rather odd thing happened: he drifted from how much he missed her, to how much he loved her, to how much he loved to make love with her, to a wildly passionate description of their lovemaking:

My mind only wants to draw you nearer and closer. And you make me the luckiest and the happiest man in the world when you move your body with mine, when you close your eyes and open your mouth and roll your belly and your hips, when you spread your legs apart slow and easy and let me put my mouth and tongue on the hairs of your womb. There is a smell that goes through me finer than the prettiest morning and the skin and the hair of your belly and womb are my whole life's desire. To touch your lips with my lips and lick my tongue in your hole of your vagina absolutely boils every drop of blood in my whole body.

I feel my penis fill up with its warm blood. I feel it stand up stiff and hard against your body. To press it tight and hard against you sends me to heaven and back nine times. Just to push my penis against you while I lick my tongue inside the hole of your womb.

Your juices taste to my mouth better than any meal or drink the world can brag about. Just to move my mouth against the lips between your legs. And when the juice from my mouth makes your little hole all warm and slick, then to move and kiss your face and eyes and to kiss your mouth and to suck the saliva from your tongue.

To slip the end of my penis up to your hairs while they are so wet and oily, and to feel the head of it enter into your little hole, mama, that warm feeling that is your very life bathes one all over, and your very electricity and magnetism runs all through me from end to end. Your breath from your nose and your mouth I want to suck into my lungs. I want to be closer yet and closer yet. I feel your pretty hips roll under my belly and I push my penis in a little bit deeper.

Your heat gets hotter as my penis goes farther and farther. Your organs inside your belly squeeze tight around my rod and I can feel your inner womb as it fits like a glove over the end of my penis. This is the most peaceful and beautiful feeling of life to me and I only want it to be as beautiful and as good to you.

You roll your belly and your hips and you squeeze my

hips between your legs, and mama, your legs, don't forget, are the world's prettiest. Your hips are as shapely as hips are made. Your stomach is as warm and as pretty inside as tummies come. You hold me with your arms around me and you pull me nearer and closer till we are as close and as warm as two people can get. My penis moves inside you and you move because you are glad and I want you to be glad. More than any other thing on earth I want you to be glad.

Roll your hips and your belly, mama, and hold me tight between your pretty legs. Squeeze my penis close as you can and whisper some nice things in my ear to make us one.

Don't you think we are one? Don't you? When I'm on top of you with my penis several inches inside your belly I know that we are one. One breath. One warmth. One saliva. One body. I feel your womb squeezing tight over the end of my penis and you hunch and move a tiny bit faster and faster and longer and longer till your entire being is moving and moving and rolling and hunching with mine.

I feel the hairs of your belly tangled with my own hairs and this is the most beautiful thought that I have yet thought in this particular trip through life. You are warmer. Oilier. You move with a perfect roll and rhythm and we move together and together because you want me to get the fullest joy out of it and I want you to do the same. Mama. God.

Roll your hips and your belly. Lift your hips up from the bed so I can push it in another half an inch. I'll put my hands here. I'll squeeze the muscles of your hips and I'll pull you another inch, another half an inch.

And I'll kiss you fifty hundred years.

And nine months later out will jump a little Petie.

Now boy, have you got nerve enough to mail this letter?

                                        Sh—
                                        Woody.

Bina Rosenbaum, who was still living with Marjorie when the letter arrived, remembers her blushing and giggling and trying to hide her obvious excitement and embarrassment as she read it. Marjorie was nonplussed. There was nothing she could say to such a letter. She didn't understand it, loved it, was flattered by it, aroused by it, and frightened a little.

Woody himself wasn't quite sure how to react. The following day he wrote to her from Akron:

> I suppose by now that you've got my real super-drooper sexy letter I drained out of my pen the other night. I have always craved more than anything else to write just such letters, but I didn't know who to write them to.
>
> Read it. Read it over to yourself. Read it in privacy and in silence. I meant it. I meant every word of it, and a bunch more I didn't put down. . . . It don't take no false stimulants to make me feel this way towards you. . . . Be sure of this, because you are going to find me hugging you and kissing you right here in this bed 50 years from now, and there aint no way out for you.

In early December, a month after Roosevelt's victory, Woody managed to land a weekly radio show on WNEW in New York. It wasn't much of a show—just fifteen minutes on Sunday afternoons at 4:45—and not much is remembered about it. Years later neither Marjorie nor the management of WNEW or anyone else would be able to recall how Woody had gotten himself hired, how much (if anything) he was paid, or why he lost the job twelve weeks later. Bess Lomax would remember going up to the studio with Woody once, as a guest, and being surprised by how absolutely happy he was, how comfortable he seemed behind the microphone as he swung into his theme song, "This Land," and then began chatting with his audience.

The WNEW program is probably best remembered for the script he wrote for his opening broadcast, December 3, 1944, which was later published in a book of Woody's writings. In it he begged the listeners to send in cards and letters asking the station to give him thirty minutes each week instead of fifteen; he described his background and set out, in concise and memorable fashion, his musical philosophy:

> I hate a song that makes you think you're not any good. I hate a song that makes you think you are just born to lose. Bound to lose. No good to nobody. No good for nothing. Because you are either too old or too young or too fat or

too slim or too ugly or too this or too that. . . . Songs that
run you down or songs that poke fun of you on account of
your bad luck or your hard traveling.

I am out to fight those kinds of songs to my very last
breath of air and my last drop of blood.

I am out to sing songs that will prove to you that this is
your world and that if it has hit you pretty hard and knocked
you for a dozen loops, no matter how hard it's run you
down nor rolled over you, no matter what color, what size
you are, how you are built, I am out to sing the songs that
make you take pride in yourself and your work. And the
songs that I sing are made up for the most part by all sorts
of folks just about like you.

Three days after Woody's first broadcast, *Variety* published a
snippet of a review: "The series promises to be a treat for the
growing number of enthusiasts of this fundamental American me-
lier. Guthrie, it must be admitted, sounded a little rusty in his
between song chatter—it might have been wiser had he included
more songs on his first program." As it was, the reviewer noted,
he sang only "Tokyo Talking Blues," "Hard Traveling," and
"Grand Coulee Dam." Still, *Variety* concluded: "Folk ballad
fans should go for this one. It's as authentic as a cook shack."

If Woody was going to have his own radio show again, he
would have to have a songbook to sell the folks—after all the
years at KFVD, it had become a necessary part of his act. He
recruited Marjorie to help with the project, transcribing music for
his songs, and a mimeographed booklet of "Ten Songs for Two
Bits" was ready for sale in early January.

It was about this time that Herbert Harris began to have some
peripheral influence on Woody's career. Harris was a devoted
Communist—he would commit suicide in 1956, after Khrushchev
"officially" revealed Stalin's atrocities—who parlayed the
concession to sell Soviet records at the 1939 World's Fair into a
small, progressive record store on Union Square. He continued
selling Russian records throughout the war, and eventually suggested to Moe Asch that his Stinson Trading Company might be
a good vehicle for the release and distribution of Asch's remarkable folk music recordings as well. Harris offered to put up the
money to release the records, and share equally whatever profits

accrued. Asch was amenable and plans were made to release modest series of albums, including one by Woody Guthrie.

When Woody's mimeographed songbook was finished in January, Harris offered to help pay for a more elaborate edition if Woody agreed to insert an ad for Asch Records and if he persuaded WNEW to pay the rest of the costs, so the books could be distributed free. Woody objected, though, "because the station is owned by Patterson McCormack and I wouldn't want for them to be censors as to what I put in the book. . . . Their system of censorship protects Franco, Churchill and Hitler, and puts the chains of slavery on the microphones and the legs of the people."

Obviously, Woody was beginning to have his usual problems at WNEW. Indeed, one song written specifically for the program called "When I Get Home," set out a radical political program for returning veterans to support—integration, full employment union organizing, and so forth—which surely couldn't have been very popular among the station's executives. In any case, the WNEW show was canceled in late February, and faded away as mysteriously as it had begun.

Woody, meanwhile, was performing *Folksay* with Sophie Maslow again, and making occasional appearances at Moe Asch' studios to record more songs. Cisco had returned to sea, and now that Woody was working as a solo again, he began to think seriously about writing the sort of ballads he'd started experimenting with in Almanac House. He suggested to Asch that he might even try a regular musical newspaper, with ballads describing the major events of the week or month. Asch was enthusiastic, and decided the series would be called "American Documentary." Woody tuned up for the project by writing several ballads about important events in American radical history, taken from Mother Bloor's autobiography. One ballad described the famous Ludlow Massacre of 1914, when National Guard troops fired on striking Colorado miners and their families. Another was about a more obscure incident: in 1913, during a copper strike in Calumet, Michigan, company thugs disrupted a Christmas party for the miners' children by shouting "Fire!" and then locked all the doors. According to Mother Bloor, seventy-three children were trampled and smothered in the crush. Woody's ballad, "1913 Massacre," was one of his most delicate, affecting, and personal works. In it, a first-person narrator introduces the listener to the miners in the midst of their happy, friendly Christmas party

"Before you know it, you're friends with us all") with images of a small girl playing the piano and children dancing around the tree. Then the "copper boss thugs" play their murderous joke, the crowd surges down a staircase toward the door, and:

> Such a terrible sight I never did see;
> We carried our children back up to their tree.
> The scabs outside still laughed at their spree,
> And the children that died there were seventy-three.
>
> The piano played a slow funeral tune
> And the town was lit up by a cold Christmas moon.
> The parents, they cried and the miners, they moaned,
> "See what your greed for money has done?"

In March of 1945, through the collaboration of Herbert Harris and Moe Asch, the first album of Woody Guthrie's songs since *Dust Bowl Ballads* was released. There were six songs, on three 78-r.p.m. records, a rather formless selection: there were two old ballads from the Southwest, "Ranger's Command" and "Gypsy Davy"; Woody's merchant marine song "Talking Sailor" and an improvising song based on an old blues by Blind Lemon Jefferson, "New York Town"; plus two of his standards, "Jesus Christ" and "Grand Coulee Dam."

Reviewing the album in early March, *Billboard* said: "Singing from the heart, rather than the throat, Woody Guthrie . . . is a folk singer of more than casual interest. They are all songs of social significance. Songs rich in democratic content, they appeal to the man in the back street."

And there was a second review, in *Pic* magazine: "Musically the performances are no great shakes and Woody's social comment doesn't cut deep, but the set is one that will recommend itself for use by unions and other groups."

Actually, both *Billboard* and *Pic* were wrong about the album's appeal. Neither "the man in the back street" nor "unions and other groups" seemed much interested. In fact, there was little interest in Woody's work at all, except among the small circle of New York leftists who'd been following his career since 1940. Still, he was quite pleased to have an album before the public again, even if it wasn't selling, and he sent Moe Asch plans for four more—pioneer songs, cowboy ballads, sea shanteys, and fiddle tunes—in addition to the "American Documentary" project.

But before he could proceed with any of those, there was, much to his surprise, the army to contend with again. Back in September he had written his draft board a charming letter, describing his adventures in the merchant marine and his domestic and professional responsibilities: "I'm not trying to make you think I'm a better writer than I am a dishwasher. I honestly believe I took great pride in my dishes until that torpedo busted them all. After a few more books hit the market, in all probability, I will be forced to re-enter the business of dishwashing. I might have to be a sudbuster all the days of my life." He didn't hear from the army for a while after that . . . and then he received another induction notice in late March of 1945. It seemed a bad joke. The Nazis were folding back toward Berlin. The war was nearly over. Japan was still hanging on, but that didn't seem likely to last much longer either. On April 9, Woody reported for his physical. He was in perfect health, except for his deformed right elbow, the one he had broken falling off the horse when he was a child.

On April 24, he auditioned for several officers hoping to convince the army that he should be allowed to serve as an "entertainment specialist." He played his songs, told some stories, and was summarily rejected.

With the rigors of basic training staring him in the face—and neither he nor Marjorie was convinced he could make it through boot camp alive—he made a last-minute attempt to ship out again. But regulations had been tightened at the N.M.U. hiring hall: before he could get his papers, he would have to go over to Naval Intelligence and confront a crisp, young lieutenant, who apparently spotted Woody's name on a certain list and asked, "Mr. Guthrie, how long have you been a member of the Communist Party?"

Woody said he wasn't a member of the Communist Party.

"I've never met one yet that would admit it," said the crisp, young lieutenant.

In a later account of the confrontation, Woody said he explained to the man that while he had played frequently for the Communists, he'd also played frequently for CBS radio and was willing to play for just about anyone who'd pay him. But, he added, he wasn't ashamed of playing for Communists or of being

dentified with them. "If you call me a Communist, I am very
>roud because it takes a wise and hard-working person to be a
Communist. The Communists may change their policies very fast,
>ut this old world changes faster than that. If you say the Com-
nunists make mistakes, show me one of the mistakes and I will
how you ten made by your Republicans and Democrats. You
:an't make me feel ashamed of the Communists."

Nor could the lieutenant give Woody papers enabling him to
hip out.

And so, there was no choice but to submit himself to the army.
n a moment of darkest irony, Woody Guthrie was inducted on
May 7, 1945—the day Germany surrendered to the Allies and
hundreds of thousands of Americans danced in the streets. He
vas sent to Fort Dix in New Jersey.

He decided, from the very start, to make the best of it. If he had
:o be a soldier, he was going to work at it and concentrate on it
and become a good one. "I marched better than all the other men
n our company," he wrote to Marjorie, optimistically, after his
first day at Dix. "The healthy look and planning is the thing I
ike about the Army. . . ."

But no matter his intentions, Woody Guthrie and the army
seemed to exist on different planes of reality. Neither could quite
comprehend the other. The army, for example, was at a loss
when it came to finding a uniform that vaguely approached a
decent fit for him. Consequently, he always looked a droopy
ness. Even his dog tags didn't work: they had a defective clasp
and would fly off during calisthenics. His second day at Fort Dix,
he volunteered to help with some painting and, predictably
enough, smeared the one set of fatigues he'd been issued. He
vas still paint-spattered when, after several days of indoctrination
at Dix and several days on a train, he arrived at Sheppard Field,
a dusty Army Air Force base in northern Texas, for his basic
raining.

On the scorched drill field, with the asphalt turning to a sticky
gumbo beneath his feet (and preventing him from learning how
:o execute a crisp, precise "to the rear, march"), the drill instruc-
or always seemed to be looking his way when he had to itch or
pull "some kind of wormy web" off his face. Just to be safe, he
saluted everything in sight—which irked him, "almost like hav-
ng three teeth drilled by a buzzing machine"—and yet he man-

aged to be daydreaming when a general passed by one day . .
and then had to do some fast talking to keep from being disciplined. He was helpless on the obstacle course, giving his platoon
"one of the best laughs of their Army lives" as he fell into the
water hole and couldn't make it up the fence. He was excited
about learning how to shoot an M-1 rifle, but the first day of
target practice, "a rain come up and I got cold and got to shaking
all over and shot a pretty low score." He was stumped by his
pup tent.

There were some satisfactions, though. He was quite happy
with his test scores in typing (27 words per minute) and I.Q.
(112). He loved going to the informational movies that were
shown most afternoons, although he was horrified by the army's
infamous venereal disease epics. "You can go ahead and forget
any worries or ideas about me and other women," he wrote to
Marjorie. "I feel a fear of disease in me. . . . I always was a
coward about VD. I have seen several friends have VD in one
shape or another. . . . They told me on the ships how it ached,
stung, pained and plagued you, and the sight of its sores, swell-
ings and corruptions did throw a big fear in me." He wrote about
his fear frequently in the weeks that followed, terrified and intrigued by it, occasionally attempting to laugh it off, as when he
speculated that VD occurs because your "protective glands can't
operate properly when you stand on line outside a door with your
penis in one hand and a dollar in the other."

More than anything else, though, he was conscious—for the
first time in his life—of being old. He was thirty-two, an adult,
surrounded by children. His face was tan and wizened and weathered; theirs were soft, peach-fuzzed, and filled with the bug-eyed
wonder of their first real adventure away from home. His age
worked in his favor sometimes, as several of the drill instructors
considered his induction a bizarre and unfair fluke. One of them,
after asking Woody how he "got into this mess," congratulated
him: "I just wanted to tell you. You take it all in good spirit."

In June, he was visited by Mary and the children. Mary, still
living in El Paso, wasn't exactly eager to make the trip, but she
figured it was important for the kids to see their father again after
four years—even if he hadn't expressed much interest in seeing
them. Since their separation, Woody had sent letters and money
on occasion, and toys for the children one Christmas, and copies

of his record albums, but that was all . . . and Mary didn't mind that he'd kept his distance. She wanted to forget about Woody and those painful years, and wasn't even much interested in reading *Bound for Glory* when it was published. She skimmed the book, she later recalled, but didn't read it "page for page."

"I feel a little nervous," Woody wrote to Marjorie, anticipating the visit, "because she still feels toward me as sexual as ever." Actually, *he* was the one who started coming on as soon as Mary arrived, but was promptly deflected by the news that she'd fallen in love and was intending to remarry. They spent the next several days together, and took the children to visit Charley Guthrie in Oklahoma City. At one point, they stopped in a Woolworth's photo booth and Woody posed with each of his children. He made a considerable effort to look proud and soldierly, but succeeded only in seeming glum and uncomfortable.

Mary hadn't changed at all, he wrote to Marjorie. "She wanted to know if my views were as communistic as they once were and I told her a little more so. She asked me if I still paced the floor and pulled my hair and had restless fits. . . . One thing is now, forever and always settled: We could never pretend to dwell in the same house again." But then, he claimed, he had known from pretty near the start that they were incompatible, and had stayed with Mary only for "convenience." "I think I must have been trying to be so cruel and mean that she would bless the day I would leave and stay gone." And yet, he was unnerved now that it had turned out exactly as he had planned. Mary seemed quite happy to be rid of him, and though the news of her impending marriage lifted the "weight of conscience" that had been bothering him since their separation, there also was a twinge of disappointment that he could be replaced so easily.

In any case, the idea of formally getting married suddenly assumed a new importance in his letters to Marjorie. There was no point in waiting any longer, he maintained. They could make it legal as soon as he finished boot camp and her divorce was final. Basic training was winding down now. In mid-June, he reported: "I have been classified and qualified and mystified and bona fide for to be a teletype operator." He hoped he would be assigned to teletype school at a base closer to home, where she'd be able to visit him. They would have a military wedding of sorts, with Woody in uniform.

But as those plans progressed—and especially after Mary's

visit—he seemed to become less sure of himself. His letters, which had been light and airy, ironic and wonderfully descriptive in the first weeks of boot camp, grew more darkly personal. They alternated between giddy, explicit sexuality and utter depression. He worried that Marjorie was wavering again. He complained that her letters seemed stiff and formal and disturbingly infrequent. "I send you an average of two letters each day," he fretted. "I wonder where all my letters get lost. You never speak of getting them and you never comment on their contents." And: "Schedules and routines are the basis of life, but tell me more about your passion also. Tell me something super extry sensual. Don't be shy on the sex side, because that's where we found [Cathy] . . . Gosh momsy, if you could only know how warm and stiff my penis gets when I write you these words."

In early July, he was transferred to Scott Field, near Alton, Illinois, just across the river from St. Louis, to attend teletype school. His early impressions of the base were favorable. He liked the neat red brick barracks and the gleaming lines of B-29's over at the airfield. The whole place smacked of efficiency and order. Gradually, though, he slipped into the same dark mood that had plagued him through the last days of basic training and now, in the first frightening, unfamiliar moments in a new situation, the depression grew deeper still.

On July 9, the day after he arrived at Scott, he wrote her two very dreary letters in which he invented all sorts of reasons why she wouldn't come to visit, why they wouldn't be married, why she would finally come to her senses and ditch him: "I have considered myself from the point of looks, and they are the worst; from money, and there will never be any; from personality, and found none; from the ability to carry on a common sensible conversation and I can't even promise to do that. . . . You see a hundred things every hour to be glad about; I see everything I can to be sad about. . . . I can't promise you one solitary thing for certain except uncertainty, and you can't give yourself to any man who offers so little. These terrible, empty and hopeless storms have always been my real wife, and you should be the first to know it."

In the second letter, he even questioned the integrity of his political commitment: "I tried to pretend that . . . the social gains of the trade unions and the war workers made me glad, but my act was thin . . . because I only walked to my window and looked at the rot in the alley" instead of actually doing something about it. He lacerated himself until there was nothing left to attack, and then: "The real feeling I feel is that if we was to ever marry and you would go away, I would want to die. I am trying to look down and . . . see all the things that might take you away, and I do it so I can later say that I knew it all along."

The next day, though, he received a cheery and reassuring note from Marjorie, saying that she was, indeed, coming to visit as soon as possible. Embarrassed by his effusions of the past several days, he wrote back, "No, I am not as hopeless as those two hopeless letters." Just a bit worried about the future, he admitted.

But still, interspersed, a hint of uncertainty; the word "nervous," which always had carried a certain emotional charge in Woody's life, back to the days of his mother's "nervous" condition, began to insinuate itself into his letters. Sitting on his bunk that first Saturday night, listening to a swing band play in the distance for the young soldiers and their girls in the gymnasium, choosing to write to Marjorie rather than attend the dance himself, he imagined the bodies pressed together on the dance floor, the "sex tales" and fast talk whispered nervously into perfumed ears, the furtive worries about looking right and acting acceptably, the hopes and fears as the bodies leaned and swayed together. "Not all scientists will agree with me," he wrote, "but this sort of vulgar nervousness sets up a nervous limitation which paralyzes defense glands . . ."

And if that wasn't entirely clear, he set out to explain his theories more fully several days later: "Not to tell you of my desires, to pretend not to have them, or to switch them off to the side would only cause nervous damage and confusion to both of us." He added that he was hoping for a love letter as a thirty-third birthday present, and then began to get specific: "I feel my penis ease out of your womb and I ask you to take him in your mouth and lick him with your tongue. You may never know that the night you gave him the nice kissings and sucks was the night I felt closest and most completely together. . . . You may have a speck of a query in your mind about this new thing of sucking me, mama. I will say this. It has a big number of good points. It is a change and a variation. It is clean. It is healthy because it kicks the last of the bashful conventions out the door. I realize very well that your womb and vagina can not rouse themselves to the state of a come if you are tired and weary which you generally are. I cannot curse you for your work. Yet you can use your lips to give me as great a pleasure. And when you learn this one thing, you will never see your husband go out and get drunk nor stay with other girls." With that piece of nervous business off his chest, he felt "clear now of those wonders and worries. . . . I have no passion to dwell in any of the past and ignorant centuries when the love of and for the body was branded as bad. It is my best and most exact science." He also asked her if, when she came to visit, she could wear the "purpledy peasant skirt and blouse you wore up to Almanac House to give me your key?"

Marjorie arrived in St. Louis on July 20, wearing her peasant outfit, and stayed for ten days. Her divorce wasn't final yet, so they weren't able to be married, but they pretended it was a honeymoon anyway. Woody found a dinky room in a fleabag boardinghouse in Alton for her, and was quite solicitous throughout the week. One of their few fights occurred when he blew up because she would only take one salt tablet, instead of the two he thought were necessary for her to withstand the brutal heat. There also was a horrible moment when Marjorie, exploring Alton while Woody was in teletype class one day, came upon a public swimming pool with the sign: "No dogs or Jews allowed." Woody was so angry that he promised to contact the Communist Party in St. Louis and have them do something about it. For the most part, though, the week passed smoothly.

He continued to write letters to her even while she was there. Their correspondence had become a personal journal of sorts for him, his most satisfying means of expressing himself, and so it only seemed natural for him to continue. After meeting her at the train the first night and establishing her in her room—Marjorie was too tired from the trip for anything more than a kiss good night—Woody returned to the barracks and, disgusted with himself, wrote: "Here you are, after 10 weeks gone, and I've wrote you 10 hundred letters telling you what all kinds of speeches, confessions, weepings and love songs I'm going to tell you about, and here you are in front of my eyes, and not one word comes out." He continued the letter most nights while she was there, cataloguing all their various adventures: "We had a session of lovemaking which I caused to be too hasty, then after supper we had some more honeymooning which was a tiny bit closer to a success. But our walks and swims tired us out and we went to sleep hugging."

After Marjorie left, on July 30, he fell into another depression. There was nothing to look forward to now, except teletype class, which he hated and was determined to find a way out of. "I never felt so useless. I feel bored and mean and disgusted," he wrote to her. He tried selling himself to the army again as an entertainer, but "they all look at my red background and get afraid to transfer me. . . . I took ten typing drills today and only two were correct."

His next gambit was to claim that his deformed elbow rendered him incompetent as a teletypist. He wrote to his commanding officer: "I say it is a waste of public money, time and energy to try to make me a teletypist. First, because of my crooked elbow, which I broke at the age of six, second because of my age and third, because every arrow in my life points to the fact that I am an entertainment specialist." The commanding officer responded with a harsh lecture on the importance of discipline in the army, and Woody decided on a new strategy: passive resistance. The next week he received a 26 on a typing test for which the passing grade was 70, but all *that* accomplished was to get him washed back a week in the course, and another tongue lashing from his commanding officer, who said: "They sent you here for me to make you into a teletype officer and, by Jehovah, I'm going to make you into a teletype officer."

Then, another shock. Sitting in the PX one afternoon, with the jukebox blaring, he heard one of his own songs, "Oklahoma Hills," come on, sung by his cousin Jack Guthrie, "word for word, just like I sung it for two years in Los Angeles." Investigating further, he discovered that Jack Guthrie was credited with having written the words and music.

After some initial outrage Woody's reaction was surprisingly reasonable: "Jack is not a vicious or mean guy, just vastly adventurous and romantically inconsiderate. . . . I don't want to make him too sore at me. I'll write Capitol Records and see what they allow. Fact of the matter is, if he becomes hugely successful, he may come in my direction for material and ideas, and it may be that I can convince him to become a singer of progressive songs." His anger was tempered further by the news that Moe Asch was about to release another album of his songs, called

Struggle, including some of his heavier political material, like "1913 Massacre" and his song about the Ludlow strike.

But there was still the sobering reality of teletype class to contend with, and Woody settled upon a final strategy: he would work hard, complete the course as quickly as possible, and graduate so that he could go home for a two-week furlough. He played little games to make the exercises more interesting. "I sang songs to the four-beat exercises. Come home mom-my. Come home dad-dy. Come home Cath-y, and then I imagined that every group of letters was another person joining the Communist party."

On the evening of August 9, he was standing in the hall, smoking a cigarette during a break in his three-hour teletype class, when he heard a great commotion. Men were piling out of the classrooms. He saw his teacher leading the charge down the hall, screaming: "The Japs, men! The Japs gave up! The atom bomb! I just heard it on the radio. They surrendered. It's all over!"

After the formal surrender on August 14, all classes were canceled and the men were given two-day passes into St. Louis, which led Woody to observe: "Peace hit St. Louis harder than the war ever did." He brought his guitar into town and tried to make some money playing in the bars, but most of the patrons seemed more interested in hearing the wistful, poignant wartime songs on the jukeboxes. Eventually, he reconciled himself to a bottle of sweet rum down by the Mississippi River docks and fell asleep there, awakening the next morning with his first hangover of the postwar era.

After that, Scott Field slowly settled back into a tense approximation of normality as the men waited to find out when they would be sent home. Teletype classes resumed as if nothing had happened. Calisthenics and marching drills continued too. Woody tried to keep himself busy by doing some creative work. He wrote a short story about his experiences hoboing through Santa Fe, and sent it off to *Pacific* magazine; he also wrote several war ballads celebrating individual feats of heroism. One was the story of three Russian sisters, two of whom committed suicide rather than sleep with the Nazis; the third became a prostitute, pumping the Germans for information, which she slipped to the partisans—it was a story that intrigued Woody, and which he'd use again later on. He'd also, from time to time, be swept away by waves of loneliness and passion, pouring out long, ardent sexual epics to Marjorie, and continuing his campaign to have her respond in kind: "You really ought to write your lover some letters as hot as he writes you. He worries and wonders why you keep refusing." Her response was an oblique request to tone it down, to write more about his past or the things he was reading and doing.

Gradually, as August slipped into September, he began to suspect—as did some of the other older men—that the end of the war hadn't made any difference in his status as far as the army was concerned. Rationally, he figured, there couldn't be much use for a reluctant thirty-three-year-old teletypist now that the war was over. But his experiences with the army had been somewhat less than rational from the start. Could they actually be thinking of sending him overseas to serve in the occupation forces in Europe or Japan? Was it possible that he'd have to serve out his full two-year hitch? His teletype classes continued apace, and he worked hard at them, for fear of further extending the ordeal. "The war," he wrote, "is more of a grind now that it's over than it was before."

He began to receive reports of old friends and enemies in the music world resuming their lives and careers. Pete Seeger married Toshi Otah, a young woman he'd met at a square dance. Alan Lomax wrote that the record companies and networks seemed as thickheaded as ever, perhaps more so. But there were, apparently, *some* opportunities: Burl Ives was riding the gravy train, with radio shows and acting jobs and *Time* magazine stories about him. And Sophie Maslow was cranking up *Folksay*, and wanted to know if Woody would be discharged in time for a fall tour . . . or would she have to find someone else to do it?

Finally, he couldn't stand it any more and skipped out. He took a train to New York in early September, and Marjorie promptly shipped him right back to Scott Field. Returning, he entertained visions of firing squads or the brig. Officially, he was AWOL. He feared a court-martial. But the army, such a magnificent and tightly disciplined machine in war, had become a clomping, arthritic, and elephantine bureaucracy almost overnight. It seemed utterly mystified by the logistics of peace, handcuffed by the enormity of its own dissolution. Protests were rising among G.I.'s around the world who wanted to go home. Congress was deluged by thousands of "Bring the Boys Home" telegrams each day. Given the general mayhem, Woody Guthrie was merely a buck private who'd stretched a two-day pass out for several days. He was confined to base for a week.

In late September, he graduated from teletype school . . . and nothing happened. There was no furlough home, no permanent assignment overseas or to another base, no discharge. He did have to transfer to a different barracks because he was now a teletype school graduate but, aside from that, the army seemed to have no plans for him whatever. He considered the possibility that they'd forgotten him entirely, and tried desperately to make his presence felt by filling the post's suggestion box with ideas and advice, mostly concerning a folk music festival he wanted to stage. For a time, he was assigned duty as a barracks guard and wrote to Marjorie: "A barracks guard is a long word for janitor."

Then, a bit of good luck. He was offered the choice of being a clerk-typist or sign painter until he received a permanent assignment. He chose sign painting, of course, and worked at it with much the same ardor as he'd devoted to setting tables in the merchant marine . . . and with some of the same flourishes. In addition to his quota of "Keep off the Grass" signs and trash barrels to label, he found a vacant outdoor bulletin board and began painting the news of the day on it each morning in brilliant color. "I painted my news board all up with red and brown frost colors and made all the men shiver and shake," he wrote to Marjorie one day in early October. Soon crowds would gather as he worked, more curious about Woody's embellishments than the actual headlines: "Death Toll Mounting in Okinawa Storm" or "I. G. FARBEN MONOPOLY CONFISCATED BY ALLIES" or "CHUNGKING COMMUNISTS TAKE RAILWAY." Sometimes there would be reminders like "FIRE PREVENTION EVERY WEEK," accompanied by an appropriate cartoon, and occasional weather reports like "FROST TONIGHT, GOOD DUCK HUNTING," which was followed the next day by a cartoon of duck hunters going berserk with their shotguns and the headline "SERIOUS DUCK SHORTAGE LOOMS," which brought a complaint from his commanding officer about too many jokes and capital letters on the news board. "I'd like to have a job for Hearst writing all those big red headlines," he confided to Marjorie.

Woody's news board made him something of a celebrity in camp and he quickly found ways to take advantage of his status, showing up at the PX each night and entertaining the boys with his music and cartoons. "I sat around the PX last night and drew portraits in pencil (free). The boys bought me two or three beers, to keep me in an adventurous mood. One fellow even lent me a dollar. I nearly dropped my pencil.''

When not writing letters or painting signs, he practiced his guitar, hoping to get in shape for his postwar career. He was, he wrote, developing a new style that borrowed from Leadbelly, the Carters, Roy Acuff, and a little from Josh White. It sounded something like the dust bowl songs, ''only more like the tone and sound of a deep banjo. In fact, my guitar strings are tuned banjo style, or what is called 'open G'—you strike all of the strings open and get a G chord. It is lonesomer for some pieces, and the dance tunes are easier to play.''

He was filled with hopes and plans for the future. He wanted to reorganize the Almanac Singers, adding Sophie Maslow's dancers to the troupe and Will Geer as master of ceremonies. He also dreamed of staging programs together with Marjorie and was thrilled when she wrote that the Philadelphia Art Alliance had asked them to do a ''joint'' concert. ''Well,'' he responded, ''the secret of dancing is in the joints and all my past singing has been in joints, so who could do a joint appearance any better?''

But despite his various diversions, he was suffering. ''I never remember being in any earthly predicament that my imagination could not find ways to enjoy, but I have exhausted every pretense and lost the knack of making this Army life ring with a shallow sound of satisfaction,'' he wrote in late October, with still no word about furlough, reassignment, or discharge. ''To try to even lie to you or myself as to the love of painting signs . . . is a cheap lie and you probably guessed it already. It seems like a hundred pound sack of frogs and snakes are tied to each of my arms, my mouth is full of rabbit hair and my brain is caught in a net it can't get out of.''

He couldn't be sure if it was the army or his own boredom, but there was an odd, drifty sensation, an inability to concentrate or keep track of what he was doing. ''Confused states of mind, a kind of lonesomeness, a nervousness stays with me no matter how I set myself to reading, painting or playing my guitar. Without trying to make it sound too serious, it never does get quite straight in my head.''

In his letter writing, too, Woody appeared to have little control over where his mind was taking him. Sometimes he seemed to lose track of himself, to become discursive and confused . . . but correspondence remained his only solace. On November 3, he sent Marjorie six separate letters. Two days later, a routine account of his activities evolved into a detailed and joyous description of his masturbatory history. "Childish or not, habit or not, it has always been very strong in me. . . ."

He described his first twinges of sexuality, sitting in high school in Okemah, staring at a girl in class or the teacher, and then: "You feel your penis get real hard and hot against your leg, between your leg and your clothing, a tight, nice fit. . . . You move your knee in a little rocking back and forth way and the clothing of the girl you take off in your visioning. If you are real expert, you can make this process go on for twenty or thirty minutes.

"As I got older, I got a little more arty and found out that the hand was the most natural thing to use." He began masturbating regularly—several times a week—during his high school year, in cool, dark, and private afternoon places, feeling a bit guilty, but always looking forward "to more of the pleasure, instead of back on it as a mistake."

He stopped after he met Mary, at least until he started spending so much time on the road, and then stopped again with Marjorie, until she went to Wilmington and "then when I rode boats (This was a very good season for it. Sea rough. Emotions high. Death close. Very imaginative), and then when I came back from the ships I remember having several sessions in our house—sessions during which I commenced to realize that maybe I was too passionately developed for you. . . . I could see that in spite of your good trying, the business of sex for sex's sake wasn't felt very strongly in you. To me it was the center of everything. I wanted it to be intellectual and beautiful, even scientific, but there was and still is a wildness that I would like to feel, a self-forgetfulness, a more daring and thrilling, surprising something. I felt like that you somehow couldn't feel this way, this wilder way, and so when you would leave the house and be gone all day to your classes, the feeling to just come would come over me so strong that, well, I welcomed my hand to give me the pleasure and feeling of relief."

Having made that rather embarrassing revelation, he recouped by saying that it was the vision of Marjorie that fueled all his recent masturbatory fantasies, "in my bunk—in the shower—at the writing desk," and he closed by maintaining that while "there are some that would try to make me feel guilty or ashamed," he refused to countenance them. He would not be made to feel guilty about his own body, his own sexuality. "I am not and never will be ashamed of any times I have done this."

The following day, November 6, he received his two-week furlough and orders to report to an air base near Las Vegas, Nevada, when it was over.

Woody and Marjorie finally were married when he arrived home. The wedding took place at City Hall in New York, and he was in uniform. The witnesses were Sophie Maslow and another Martha Graham dancer, Sascha Leibig. Cathy Ann Guthrie remained at home in Coney Island, although Woody later would claim that she had served as flower girl. The ceremony itself was perfunctory and the subsequent honeymoon a bit rushed, as Woody was nervous about arriving promptly at his new base.

But there was nothing for him to do in Las Vegas, not even a signpainting job. It was generally assumed by his commanding officers that Private Guthrie would be mustered out soon, most likely before Christmas, so there really was no point in assigning him a job.

Lacking anything better to do, he wrote letters. His correspondence, which had been extraordinary in its emotional complexity and detail since the very first, felicitous letters about boot camp, became a dark, convoluted, and frightening maze in which he spent the month of December 1945, lost at times, looking for a way out, the strings of words becoming endless and confused, retracing his paths and retracing them again, a terrifying journey that often spun well out of control. His letters lengthened to forty and fifty pages, choked with hundreds of words per page in a small, tight, relentless, and neat script . . . and he mailed several letters each day, one running on into the next, each stopping only because of the dim, belated realization that it had grown too thick to fit inside an envelope. Merely as a physical feat, his output some days was staggering.

His physical surroundings, the other men, the daily routine all fell away now, and he seemed to exist alone in that December desert just outside Las Vegas, examining his past down to details like the contents of his father's bureau the day he visited the old man for the first time in that fleabag rooming house in Little Juarez in Pampa. He wrote about his mother's fits and his father's ability to cry. Every idea, every image was distended, then re-

cycled and stretched again. Even his salutations at the top of each
letter became encyclopedic: "My Dear, darling, legal, sinful,
angel queen, married, hatched and hog-tied wife." One day he
decided to make a list of the albums he wanted to record for Moe
Asch, and the list kept growing and growing until it topped out
at seventy albums, including *War Heroes of World War Two,
Prostitutes and Gamblers, Outlaws and Inlaws, Me, You, Cars I
Owned, Reno Jail* (each man a song), *Holidays Around the World,
Paid in Full.*

But more than anything else, the letters were marked by their
insistent, naked, intense, and often lyrical sexuality. He began
where he'd left off, describing masturbation: "I laid there for
about an hour [on my bunk] and saw all kinds of pictures of my
dear, sweet, pretty, good, smart angel darling wife, and after my
tummy got soaked in some sort of a hot juice I held my balls and
my penis in my hands." Gradually, as he wandered deeper into
his darkness, the idealized vision of Marjorie fell away too and
he became obsessed with her unwillingness to perform oral sex.
"I do find that when you shiver and shudder and refuse to share
my most selfless feelings (sex desires with all the trimmings), I
get to where my mind is all confused and rattled, I don't know
what to say or what to do and get to where I feel all day long
like my bodily presence means no more to you than a barber, a
beautician, a masseur or some kind of brother. I hate and revolt
against this."

In the midst of this harangue, which continued on and off for
several weeks, Woody made another startling revelation: he was
writing love letters to other women. Specifically, he was writing
to a young woman in New Jersey named Annette Berger, who,
apparently, had written him a fan letter . . . and also to another,
unnamed, woman. On December 7, he taunted Marjorie: "You
may and then again you may not know that today I come to you
after dripping my words across sheets of paper for two other
women." He added that in his letter to Annette, "I turned myself
completely free and did write hotter than the welding torch."

As the month progressed, his vicarious fling with Annette became more and more bizarre. She seemed to be responding
warmly to his advances. He wrote to her about Marjorie. She
then wrote to Marjorie about Woody. He then proposed to Marjorie that he relieve some of Annette's obvious sexual frustrations:
"I feel I could make ardent love to any two women and still have

time to study books and write songs. This feeling has been inside me ever since we have been wedded. . . . I told Annette that if she needed bodily love to help her through her season, I was not the type of man to turn my back.''

At times, in the midst of this strange journey, he would begin an apology that invariably turned into either a defense of his avalanche of words or another wallow in self-pity. "A man like me is half-coward . . . afraid your love for him would dry up if he did not cover your doorstep with noisy pages." He was afraid, he said, that some strong man would come along and make her realize that "there's a dead horse in your field."

Occasionally, he seemed to jerk himself into a fitful awareness of what he was doing and how odd it was. "What are these letters that I set around this camp and blow up into barrage balloons? Maybe these words will someday be used against me. Maybe I'm not entitled to use sheets of paper and a pen and a wife for my hired psychoanalyst. I like the thought that someday these words may be read by eyes outside the family. . . . I guess I'm reveling and wallowing in it too much. . . . I know my mind feels airier after a long session of pen slinging."

And later: "You may accuse me of falling from my noble place as a communist thinker by entering into such a forum, with sex spoken of as the workers speak and talk it along our streets of the nation. You may call their phrases vulgar and untrained, but to me their forms of speech are much more clear, more powerful, with more courage and poetry than all your schools in which our leaders smile to see us learn empty grammar. . . . A man's most basic character, most basic wants, hopes and needs come out of him in words that are poems and explosions."

These sometimes grand attempts to rationalize his Las Vegas siege were the beginnings of his journey back from wherever it was that he'd been, the first acknowledgments of a world outside. There were frequent detours and relapses still, but toward the end, as Christmas approached, he seemed intent on returning to what he considered to be his normal self. "I feel good tonight," he wrote to Marjorie on December 19, "because I have set out to get rid of all this lonesome junk I have been carrying about. . . . Truth is, I really went as screwy as I can go, and the pains seem to be all gone."

The next day, though, there was a final bizarre convulsion. He was writing an amiable enough letter to Marjorie about a movie he'd just seen when, suddenly, his prose seemed to spin totally out of control: "Just dizzy. Woozy. Blubberdy. And scrubberdy and rustlety, tastlety, I was saying. Fantiffy, fantiffy, fantoy, fantoy. Poodle de doodle de dum dum. Doodle doodle dum. Cockle a doodle daylight, my old hen lays eggs for the railroad men. . . . This is the soberest drunk I ever got on," and then it passed as abruptly as it had come on.

The next day he was discharged.

CHAPTER 9

Stackabones

In 1946, Coney Island was best known for its gaudy neon entanglement of roller coasters, fun houses, and merry-go-rounds, an area along the boardwalk that always seemed faded and peeling despite its flashy colors; it was laced with greasy hot dog and knish stands, and ramshackle ski-ball parlors wallpapered with kewpie dolls; the streets were littered with cotton candy shreds and hot dog wrappers that swirled and eddied in the sea breeze. But beyond the clangor, and largely unnoticed, there was a modest Jewish neighborhood—mostly garment workers, waiters, mom and pop storekeepers, poor people, drained and ravaged after fifteen years of war and economic crisis, living in shabby row houses on an earlobe-shaped peninsula jutting out into a filthy sea. New York's garbage washed ashore at Coney Island beach; the water usually was thick with condoms, bobbing along like so many jellyfish.

On summer weekends, hundreds of thousands of people would stream out from the subway terminus and swarm the beach, filling the air with a lather of sweat and salt and suntan oil. A constant, low-level din would rise from the waterfront, punctuated by giggles and shrieks, and shimmer back toward the rowhouse blocks where clusters of elderly Jews sat in the shadows of their porches, glumly watching as the rest of New York paraded before them in terry cloth and sunglasses. Occasionally the natives would emerge from the shadows to go shopping or take a walk, descending the front steps with arms shielding their eyes against the glary sun, looking as if they'd just come out from a bunker after a long siege.

In winter, the beach achieved a certain dull grandeur: pale sand and steel-blue water under an imposing mother-of-pearl sky, the boardwalk empty enough so that each step sounded a satisfying *clonk*, the coarse spray from the breakers, carried by the sea breeze, glossing the neighborhood with a constant mist. On dim, blustery March days the utter drabness of it all could be overwhelming; the residents and row houses, both, battered and submissive.

By contrast, Woody and Marjorie's apartment seemed a luminous island of creativity. The three tiny rooms were stuffed with books, records, Woody's cartoons and art, musical instruments, people playing musical instruments, and, as often as not, a fair number of neighborhood kids hanging out or in semi-permanent residence.

It was located on the first floor rear of 3520 Mermaid Avenue, down a dark hallway. The front door opened into the living room, dominated by a convertible sofa (where Woody and Marjorie slept) and an upright piano, which faced each other from opposite walls—the room was so small that when the bed was opened at night, it jammed up against the piano. There also was a wall-length bookcase extending into Woody's triangular desk at one end of the room, a few casual lamps and tables, a comfortable chair, and one window. There was a Mexican tapestry on the wall above the sofa and several touches that made it quite clear that this was Woody Guthrie's house: a jar full of guitar picks on the piano, violins and mandolins and guitars strewn about and tucked into corners, Woody and Cathy's drawings pasted haphazardly on walls and doors, small sculptures of Woody's invention—Sophie Maslow remembers a little "plant" made of popsicle sticks, buttons, shells, and other wisps of this and that, that Woody had "potted" and placed on the windowsill.

Two doorways interrupted the piano wall, at front and rear, one leading to the little kitchen and the other to Cathy's room, which was generally considered to be the highlight of the house, especially by other children. Its walls were covered with huge, gorgeous flowers that Woody had painted; a paper screen shielding the radiator had splendid cartoons of children cavorting about.

A wooden gate was fixed across the doorway, so the entire room could serve as a playpen at times. At other times—as when Cisco and Bina were visiting—a cot was unfolded and it became the guest room. There were two windows, which made Cathy's the lightest room in the house, and Marjorie built a small staircase down from one of the windows to the tiny square of ground that served as a backyard—a parody of a backyard, really—where Woody stored the various scraps of wood, metal, seashells, and assorted garbage that he transformed into pieces of sculpture, each called a "Hoodis" (since that was what Cathy called them), which he would build for the edification and pleasure of the local kids in much the same manner as he'd constructed the wind machine for the men of the *William B. Travis*.

There was, particularly in those early days, a certain magic about their home. Anyone who knew the Guthries realized they had serious problems—Woody's drinking and amatory adventures, Marjorie's bossiness, a persistent series of professional disappointments—but there also was a deep, unshakable bond between them, a shared purpose, a sense of destiny. It was an intimacy that flowed from the tacit assumption that their marriage was going to be different from most, a high-stakes gamble that would produce spectacular results . . . of one sort or another. They seemed to glow with the intensity of their struggle. Alan Lomax noticed it one morning when he came to visit and found Woody and Marjorie still entwined on their living room sofa bed, two tiny, gorgeous people on a bed the size of a Kleenex; they were so small the bed seemed king-sized, and the apartment a mansion. "They were absolutely adorable together, like two beautiful birds nestled there," he remembered. "I'd never seen such pretty love in all my life. They were like two little elves in love, and I felt like a big bear and very protective."

For the neighborhood kids, the mere fact that an Okie guitar player and a glamorous modern dancer had chosen to settle in that community of tailors and meatcutters was exciting enough . . . but then, to find that these people were not only exotic but also open and curious and caring—Woody, willing to sit and play his guitar for hours with any of the teenage novices who were beginning to make pilgrimages out to Mermaid Avenue from all over the city; and Marjorie, more than happy to listen to and commiserate with anyone at length about his or her personal problems. Their house became a magnet for troubled kids. There was a succession of adolescents spending nights, weeks, months, and—in a few cases—years on the cot in Cathy's room.

Rosalind Richman, who lived around the corner and probably logged more nights on the cot than any other neighborhood kid, remembered what it was like:

I met the Guthries through my sister, Shirley. We were very poor in our family and unhappy, always fighting . . . and these people were buoyant, open, optimistic. Maybe it was because I was just eighteen and impressionable, maybe it was in relation to the drabness in all our lives, but they both—Woody and Marjorie—seemed so *special* to me.

With me, the stronger bond was with Marjorie, because I really needed the mother support. . . . But I really loved that man too. There was a sweetness to him, despite the exterior roughness. Woody was always very *present* with you. He never said much, I don't think he ever *asked* me about anything . . . and I never told him about how miserable I was in my home. I didn't have to, though; he just knew. . . .

Woody and Marjorie just seemed to fit together. Not because they were alike, or similar. Actually, they were very different: Marjorie, with her city refinement and dancing and theater and aesthetic tastes so different than his— and yet, they fit. They even began to look the same after a while. . . . But the big thing was—at least to me—that in my house there never was a lot of laughter and in that house, somehow, there always was. And music. And Cathy . . . now, there again, maybe it was the drabness of my life, but that little girl was completely unique—a joyous bubble, a miraculous child. . . .

Indeed, Cathy seemed the physical manifestation of all that was good about Woody and Marjorie together. It was remarkable how nearly she approached the creative ideal they'd been fantasizing about, how close she came to the spirit of Railroad Pete. She began to speak at an early age and, once started, never seemed to stop. She was alert, brighteyed, and curly-haired . . . though not quite beautiful; the sort of child who'd make up little rhymes and sing them to herself while hopping about, playing with her dolls, drawing pictures . . . and keeping a sharp eye on everything else going on inside the house.

Actually, Woody and Marjorie never spent all that much time taking care of her. He was off at the war and she still kept a dancer's schedule, so Cathy was left with a series of day nurses (paid for by Marjorie). But they were devoted parents nonetheless, and determined to keep as complete a record as possible of her life and doings. They maintained a precise diary those first few years, with entries almost every day, sometimes from both parents. Woody was, predictably enough, the more ardent diarist. On April 28, 1943, he wrote of his two-month-old daughter: "Woke up—singing and laughing and talking. Ate breakfast—laughed—gooed—kicked feet in bath—flipped and flopped and splashed in the water. Diaper: raised feet over head. Sang tenor . . ."

On April 29: "Sucked fingers . . . gurgled . . . cooed . . . Dictated outline of a policy plan to oust John L. Lewis from the CIO. Sent telegram to Phil Murray stating she was behind him in move to oust Lewis. Bowel movement. Changed diaper."

When Woody went off to sea, the diary became Marjorie's responsibility. She tended to be more prosaic, lapsing at times into extended accounts of things like Cathy's chewing ability, but always with an intensity that was, at once, loony and winning: "Today is my birthday [October 6, 1943] and I must say it started out badly but ended just fine! We had another bad breathing night! I finally stuffed cotton in my ears! It helped a little! You slept, but not well because your nose is all clogged up. . . . The next Big News is that we received a lovely letter from Woody! It just says hello, but so nicely! That was perfect timing too!" And although Marjorie never missed the really important events like first steps or words, the pressure of dance classes and three hours of commuting into and out of Manhattan each day inevitably prevented her from doing the diary justice, and so it fell to Woody to catch up when he came home from his various jaunts, at which times he would attempt to list every new skill Cathy had mastered and everything else that had happened to her while he'd been gone.

Woody seemed to become even more attached to Cathy as she grew older and began to speak. He called her by a variety of nicknames—Stackabones, Cathy Bones, Stackaroony, Cathy Rooney, and just plain Stacky. He would, from time to time and just for the fun of it, try to list Cathy's entire vocabulary. At other times, he would simply sit and listen to her, fascinated, writing down whole conversations, fifteen-minute chunks of language. As on the night of November 19, 1944, when he filled page after page with a verbatim account of her bedtime ritual, the various ways—after being tucked in her crib—that she tried to regain her mother's attention: "Make more uh-uh [go to bathroom] . . . Make chewing gum . . . Nite nite nite nite . . . Kissie . . . Hurt nosie, hurt nosie . . . Want wow wow . . . Go see Bubby [grandmother] . . . More uh-uh . . . Want to kiss daddy cheek . . . more daddy cheek . . . Nite nite . . . More uh-uh . . . Chain chain chain chain . . . Mommy mommy mommy mommy mommy mommy mommy . . .''

Sometimes, when left alone with Cathy and her playmates, Woody would imagine himself the principal of the "How Joo Doo Nursery School" and write elaborate reports for the parents. On one occasion, he described Cathy and her upstairs friend, Dinny, making an important discovery:

DINNY: Chair aw wet.
CATHY: Cheah aw wet, yeah.
D: How did ya make it?
C: (Silent)
D: You didn't make it like me. How did ya?
C: (Puzzled but says nothing)
D: (Examines very close her female parts)

From there, the report evolved into a riotous account of Dinny chasing Cathy around the house, trying to seduce her, while Cathy—demurely unaware of his lascivious intent—managed, just barely, to evade his grasp. The two eventually came to rest in the bathroom, where, transfixed by all the pretty bottles in the medicine cabinet, they were overheard making "yum, yum, yum, yum . . .'' noises.

In all of this, Woody often appeared to be more a conspirator than a parent. And in his heart, he was. His innocence, the childlike quality of wonder that all his friends since Matt Jennings had noticed immediately and loved, was more than just a pose—he actually seemed able to shed thirty years of experience and see the world as Cathy did; to really understand the danger and exhilaration of making new discoveries, the stark terror of being small in an outsized world, the all-encompassing joy of being

cuddled and loved . . . and, most of all, the bouncy, open rhyminess of being a kid. It was somehow inevitable, once he returned from the army and began spending more time with her,
that he and Cathy would become collaborators in fact as well as
spirit—they had so much in common, creatively. He began writing down the little rhymes that she casually tossed off each day,
and using them as the basis for songs:

> *Take me riding in the car, car*
> *Take me riding in the car, car*
> *Take you riding in the car, car*
> *Take you riding in the car.*

They were utterly artless songs; some didn't even have tunes,
but were merely chants. They were truly *children's* songs,
though—written as children might write them, without much of
the condescension inherent in songs for children composed by
adults. They were so simple, in fact, that many adults didn't
understand them; a number of Woody's friends throught they
were boring and trite (although they *were* grateful when he'd
spend hours serenading their children), and were disappointed
that the great political activist was wasting so much time writing
things like:

> *I put my dolly's dress on*
> *I put my dolly's pants on*
> *I put my dolly's hat on*
> *And she looks hike this . . .*

CHORUS:

> *O, well, she looks like this-o*
> *O, well, she looks like this-o*
> *Tra la la la la la lo*
> *And she looks like this.*

Or:

> *Why can't a bird eat an elephant?*
> *Why, oh why, oh why?*

Because an elephant's got a pretty hard skin,
Goodbye, goodbye, goodbye.

Luckily, Moe Asch understood. Woody used his studio several times during 1946 and 1947 to record batches of children's songs. Usually it was a deadly serious operation—far more serious than the loose sessions with Cisco and the others—with Marjorie taking an active role, making suggestions and changes. It also was relatively successful—the children's albums sold better than Woody's more "serious" works, sometimes as many as a thousand copies, and became a staple in progressive nurseries across the country. Each was packaged with a little book of lyrics. One had a lovely series of photographs of Marjorie and Cathy on the beach at Coney Island; another was festooned with Woody's drawings of kids at play. In the booklet for *Work Songs to Grow On*, Woody explained his purposes:

> Now I don't want to see you use my songs to divide nor split your family all apart. I mean, don't just buy these records and take them home so your kids can play around with them while you go off and do something else. I want to see you join right in, do what your kids do. Let your kids teach you how to play and act these songs out. . . .
>
> Please, please, please don't read nor sing my songs like no lesson book, like no text for today. But, let them be a little key to sort of unlock and let down all your old bars.
>
> Watch the kids. Do like they do. Act like they act. Yell like they yell. Dance the way you see them dance. Sing like they sing. Work and rest the way the kids do.
>
> You'll be healthier. You'll feel wealthier. You'll talk wiser. You'll go higher, do better and live longer here amongst us, if you'll just only jump in here and swim around in these songs and do like the kids do.
>
> I don't want the kids to be grownup. I want to see the grown folks be kids.

Although Moe Asch appreciated the quality of the children's songs, his real hopes for Woody lay in other areas. He was especially impressed by the man's ability to make the radical past come alive in songs like "1913 Massacre," and was determined to keep him moving in that direction. When Woody returned from the army, Asch offered him several hundred dollars to write a series of ballads about an event that still was a painful memory to many American leftists (including Asch himself) twenty years after the fact—the Sacco and Vanzetti case.

Woody took the job gladly, and ruminated—uncharacteristically—at length about how he might convey the anguish of the two Italian immigrants, wrongfully convicted of murder and robbery, awaiting death in the electric chair. He called the assignment "the most important dozen songs I've ever worked on," and began filling a notebook with ideas in March of 1946, trying to imagine how the two must have felt arriving in America: "I can just see you walking into our big Eastern cities for your first time. I guess you walked along a good bit faster than I did, this is because I always did walk awful slow and look around a lot . . ." He saw them passing through a chamber of horrors in the streets that were supposed to be paved with gold, and their anger rising as they saw: "Faces against walls, an eye gone, an ear missing, no teeth, open boils, sores of the syph and you heard there was no cure. There was no cure known, and the words whirled and spun around in your head. No cure for the people. No cure for the streets."

But despite Woody's ability to identify with their alienation and also, perhaps, their martyrdom, the songs wouldn't come . . . at least, no really memorable songs came. The old country tunes, which had served so well for the Dust Bowl Ballads and the Columbia River songs and all the others, seemed unnatural and trite when applied to the agony of Sacco and Vanzetti; the results were superficial and forced. Woody recorded some of his attempts for Asch in 1946, but never was quite satisfied with them. After traveling to Boston and Plymouth in November of that year, hoping that a firsthand look at the various sites of the case might help, he implied failure in a letter to Asch: "I feel like the trip to Boston was just a little bit hurried and hasty. I did not get to go to all the spots plainly mentioned in the pamphlets and books. . . . So I say, let's forget about the Sacco and Vanzetti album for the time being. It will be lots better when I can get a car and my own way of traveling from one scene to the other one. I'm drunk as hell today, been that way for several days. . . . I refuse to write these songs while I'm drunk and it looks like I'll be drunk for a long time."

Years later, Asch released an inferior collection of the songs Woody recorded before he gave up on the project, with the inscription: "Commissioned by Moses Asch—1945. Composed and sung by Woody Guthrie—1946-47."

The inability to finish the Sacco and Vanzetti songs to his own satisfaction reflected a deeper problem that was beginning to affect much of Woody's "serious" songwriting. His work was becoming rather ponderous and self-righteous; he seemed to have lost his sense of humor (except for the children's songs). He had stopped writing anthems and was concentrating on ballads, which tended to continue on for verse after verse—verses that often were beautiful and moving, but usually too literary and complex to be sung to any but the most devoted listeners. One of his more impressive works of the period was "The Ballad of Isaac Woodward," about a black veteran who was blinded by police in the South after trying to use a "white" bathroom in a bus stop. The incident had caused a wave of outrage, and an all-star rally in support of Woodward was held at Lewisohn Stadium in New York, on August 16, 1946. Cab Calloway, Orson Welles, Milton Berle, Billie Holiday, and many others performed for a crowd of 31,000. "Cab Calloway and about 15 or 20 big bands were ahead of me on the program," he later wrote. "And for two whole hours I didn't hear nine words of fighting protest. Isaac was the last one on the program, and I sung right after he made his talk." But Woody's performance was a disaster. The ballad was so long that he couldn't remember all the words, so he had to write them down and set them on a music stand . . . and the wind kept blowing them off. He'd lost nearly all his audience long before he reached the final verse:

> It's now you've heard my story, there's one thing I can't see
> How you can treat a human being as you have treated me.
> I thought I fought in the islands to get rid of their kind,
> But I can see the fight's not over, now that I am blind.

He was still as prolific as ever, perhaps *too* prolific. He wrote songs the way other people worked crossword puzzles, at the end of his morning newspaper ritual. Marjorie remembered him flipping through the paper each day (he preferred the tabloid *Daily News*), coming across stories that interested him and clipping them out. He'd write song titles, inspired by the clips, on as many as a half dozen blank sheets of paper—then lie back on the couch, thinking. Then he'd pick up his guitar and strum a few bars, then type out a verse on the typewriter, then back to the couch, then up again . . . until he'd composed a song to fit each title.

The results usually weren't very inspired, though. The "newspaper" songs he wrote during this time—partly a result of Moe Asch's prodding, partly a playing out of his old Almanac House theories about ballads—were a confirmation of another of his old Almanac House theories: you can only write what you see. What he "saw" and cared about most intensely during that period was his daughter Cathy, and the songs he wrote for her breathed with the life and humor of his very best work.

More than that, they were an island of innocence and calm in a world that seemed to be growing increasingly hostile toward him.

A few days after Woody was discharged from the army, a meeting of folk singers was held in the basement of Pete Seeger's house on Macdougal Street in Greenwich Village. Most of the old Almanac gang was there, gathered to discuss the possibility of building a new musical organization for the postwar era. Since many of them were married and had families now, it was obvious that an Almanac House-style commune no longer was appropriate; Seeger suggested a loose-knit union of songwriters to stage occasional hootenannies, provide a library of protest songs for unions and other progressive groups, and maybe even send people out to perform at meetings and on picket lines. The organization would be so ecumenical as to include, in addition to the old regulars, some less radical sorts like Oscar Brand, Tom Glazer, and Josh White; and even non-folk performers—jazz singers and composers of pop tunes—would be welcome as long as their hearts were in the right place.

And so People's Songs was born. A slate of officers and a board of directors (including Woody Guthrie) were elected; a small office was leased from a left-wing theater company on Forty-second Street, and a monthly bulletin mimeographed. The first bulletin opened with a ringing manifesto: "The people are on the march and must have songs to sing. Now, in 1946, the truth must reassert itself in many singing voices. . . ."

There was a good deal of enthusiasm at the start, much of it provided by the first members of a new generation of folk singers—city kids who'd been raised on the music and its accompanying mythology in left-wing homes and, especially, in camps like Unity, Beacon, and Wo-Chi-Ca (an acronym for Workers' Children's Camp). At the heart of the new generation—bureaucratically, if not creatively—was a young man named Irwin Silber. He was a counselor at Camp Wo-Chi-Ca, a student at Brooklyn College, and founder of the American Folksay Group, which consisted of teen-age folk singers and square dancers (Irwin's specialty was left-wing square dance calls). When People's Songs opened, Silber and friends began hanging around the offices, happily stuffing envelopes, sweeping floors, and lapsing into awed silence when one of the Old Lions like Leadbelly or Guthrie ambled in. Silber was *so* devoted that, within a year, he was handed the job of executive secretary and was running the place.

For the old-timers, the feeling was something on the order of a class reunion. At one of the first board of directors meetings, Pete Seeger and Lee Hays entertained themselves by passing a sheet of paper back and forth, gleefully collaborating on the lyrics for "If I Had a Hammer . . ."

The old Almanac hope that the C.I.O. would become the official home of the folk song revival seemed to have returned, stronger than ever. It looked as if 1946 was going to be the biggest, angriest year for organized labor since 1941, with the unions trying to win major pay raises for their members after four years of wartime wage and price controls. Already, in January, the meatcutters, steel workers, and auto workers had gone out on strike. When the electrical workers joined them, Seeger, Guthrie, and Hays—the Almanac Singers reunited, minus Lampell—hopped a plane to Pittsburgh and played for a massive, cheering rally of Westinghouse strikers and their supporters downtown. Thousands of People's Songs bulletins were dumped from rooftops and used as song sheets. Flying home, an exhilarated Woody wrote: "We sang two songs made up this day for the situation here at Westinghouse. The crowd roared like the ocean in a rock canyon. Good to see and feel . . ." and he began filling a notebook with union song ideas:

Tune of "Will the Circle Be Unbroken"—will the union stay unbroken.

Needed: a sassy tune for a scab song.

Need of pointing out in song that you got to rise above simple porkchop unionism.

Song: Pride of an aircraft worker as he sees a plane zooming overhead. Chorus: "If Douglas died tomorrow, we'd still be making planes . . ."

But the ideas never were followed through; the promise of the Pittsburgh trip proved illusory. The labor movement had changed. It no longer needed hard-nosed radicals (or their musical accompanists) to lead organizing drives. Most of those battles had been won, the basic industries organized, and, once the postwar strike wave abated, the unions were well established as American institutions. Already, several of the more canny leaders like Joe Curran of the National Maritime Union were moving to dislodge Communists from positions of authority—often the very same Communists who'd helped bring them to power in the first place. It was a retrenchment that probably would have happened in any case—accountants, not militants, were needed to run pension plans and the other accouterments of modern trade unions—but political developments outside the labor movement tended to hurry the process along.

The grand Anglo-American-Soviet alliance blew apart during those first months of 1946. On February 9, Stalin delivered a speech to a Soviet party congress in which he stated that the United States and its capitalist allies represented a graver threat to the Soviet Union than Nazi Germany ever had. He predicted that war against the capitalists was inevitable, probably sometime in the 1950's . . . when America would be mired in another great depression.

A month later, Churchill responded with his famous "Iron Curtain" speech, and the cold war had begun.

These events did not exactly take the American Communist leadership by surprise. The party had begun shifting to a more militant posture a year earlier: after a clear signal from Moscow (via the French Communist Party), Earl Browder was dumped in the spring of 1945, along with his moderate policies. He was replaced by the old war-horse William Z. Foster, who wouldn't have been caught dead offering his hand in friendship to J. P. Morgan, as Browder had done during the war.

Woody did his best to keep up with the complicated political developments. He was still in basic training at Sheppard Field when the first rumors about Browder began to spread, and he wrote to Moe Asch: "Is there a new line? If so, what is? I heard some sort of a rumor that Browder cast the lone vote on some sort of argument or decision. What was it about? What were the details? Be sure you send me a copy of the *Sunday Worker* once in a while. I want to keep posted even if I do get roasted."

A month later, when Browder's fall was public knowledge, he wrote to Marjorie: "The change will be a good one. Browder has done well but he is too old and needs a rest, as his health is bad." He also favored Foster's decision to re-establish the Communist Party: "If there is no party, the outsiders get the wrong idea . . . that it had to close its doors like a failed fruit stand, or we are going mysteriously underground." Not only was he going to stand with the party ("Lord knows, I owe them . . . the only guidance and recognition and pay that I've ever tasted"), but he also was predictably angry at the people beginning to criticize Stalin: "The whole world cannot trick Joseph Stalin because he is too scientific for them."

But if it appeared that Woody had made his decision with his eyes open, it's doubtful that he—or any of the legion of sympathizers existing at the party's periphery—realized how drastic the implications of the hardening line were. Certainly, the naïfs who organized People's Songs were surprised by the increasingly cold shoulder they were getting from the labor movement. At the C.I.O.'s annual convention in November of 1946, a resolution was passed stating: "We resent and reject the efforts of the Communist Party or other political parties and their adherents to interfere in the C.I.O. This convention serves notice that we will not tolerate such interference." The irony was that the Communists had lobbied *for* that particular resolution, the alternative being outright expulsion from the C.I.O. It was a true measure of their desperation that they viewed its passage as a victory; it would be their last victory for quite some time.

In a way, the prospect of a witch hunt was more palatable to radicals—it confirmed the beginnings of the final crisis of capitalism—than the deeper, less obvious problem leftists were facing: the very real possibility that the times had passed them by. After the grand, stirring battles of the past fifteen years, the Great Depression and the struggle against fascism, they were confronting a new and truly implacable foe—prosperity. Much of their potential constituency, the American working class, no longer could be considered downtrodden proletarians, but were incipient consumers. Woody Guthrie's Okies still held their high-paying jobs in the California defense plants (thanks, in large part, to the Communist menace); and now they were busy lining up for new cars and refrigerators, and beginning to nose around the burgeoning tract house developments in Orange County. In fact, if American workers were worried about anything—aside from the long waits for consumer goods—it was that the Russians would come over, take away all their hard-won possessions, and establish slave-labor camps.

Even in the area of culture, where political radicals had been the innovators during the Popular Front days of the 1930's, the Left seemed to be slipping . . . if not wholly irrelevant. Communists were about the only people, aside from staunch conservatives (like the former populist movie directors Frank Capra and John Ford), who still were celebrating small-town America. The Common Man had given way to the existential hero, riddled with anxiety. Abstract expressionist art, the sweet anarchy of Charlie Parker's sax, and psychological thrillers were all the rage in intellectual circles. The Communists, meanwhile, weren't even sure they *believed* in psychology. After strenuous internal debate, Freud was discarded on the grounds that economics, not sex, was at the root of anxiety.

For a time, as the Left circled its wagons and grew more defiant, it was possible to believe the movement actually was growing stronger. People's Songs boomed during its first year, quickly gaining a thousand subscribers to its bulletin . . . and then leveling off. Attendance at the hootenannies rose from 80 at the first one, held in Pete Seeger's basement, to 112, to 300 at the Newspaper Guild hall, to the 1,000 that *Time* magazine reported attending a hoot at Irving Hall in April 1946. Twenty folk singers performed, *Time* said, and "the smallest and the loudest was Woody Guthrie. . . . The lyrics were black and white (and sometimes red) versions of current events. The result was not always good singing or good logic."

Several months later, *The New York Times* sent a reviewer over to investigate a hootenanny at Town Hall: "People's Songs, it seems, is more concerned with controversies than music. Within the first 15 minutes of song, two leading political figures were brought up for ridicule and scorn. . . .

"In an entertainment of this sort, the required essence is contagion. If one is infected, no doubt the evening becomes great fun. To his sincere chagrin, this reviewer found himself immune."

The *Times's* immunity, and all the other "political" criticism, only served to confirm the radicals in their belief that folk music was the true *people's* idiom; indeed, Charles Seeger's old political analysis of the music seemed to have penetrated the Left entirely now, and folk singers became part of the ceremonial trappings for any self-respecting Communist meeting. There developed, central to this phenomenon, the bizarre notion that since the music was inherently egalitarian, *anyone* should be able to perform it. Pete Seeger, for one, often appeared to feel cheated when the audience didn't sing along with him; and it was true, a thousand people singing "This Land Is Your Land" in four-part harmony, Pete directing them with one arm and plunking his banjo with the other, could be an inspiring sight. But there also was the tendency to allow anyone with the right politics and the ability to suss out a G chord to take the stage at a hootenanny and play his or her latest composition, which inevitably was titled something like "Listen, Mr. Bilbo." Alan Lomax, among others, was dismayed to hear the music he loved diluted by amateurs and led a faction that lobbied for virtuosity at People's Songs board of directors meetings, but to little effect.

There was, meanwhile, something of a boom market for folk singers—every I.W.O. lodge seemed to want one for its next meeting—and so People's Songs launched a booking agency, People's Artists, that handled people like Seeger, Guthrie, Josh White, and a host of lesser lights. At the same time, the more mellow and accessible folk performers were beginning to crack the nightclub circuit. Café Society, which was owned in part by the Communist Party, and the Village Vanguard both featured occasional folk singers—including Pete Seeger, who rapidly was becoming the best known of the lot.

Woody Guthrie had never been a very mellow performer, and was becoming even less so. His enthusiasm for the sing-along business was only occasional . . . and he had no patience at all with the incompetents who'd begun cluttering up the stage. He was losing his temper with audiences more frequently now—it had become almost a trademark—taunting and deliberately offending them when he sensed they were bored with his endless ballad verses. "Going on after Woody Guthrie was like attending your own wake," Oscar Brand remembers. "He would test the audience. If he felt they weren't attentive enough, he'd start playing the wrong chords . . . or just not change chords at all. I have heard him sing the same verse of 'Gypsy Davy' three, four times in a row. Sometimes, I figured, it was because he had simply forgotten the next verse, but often he was just mad at the audience. He'd go right up to the front of the stage and sing an incredibly bawdy verse, and stare this wild stare, and make everyone very tense and uncomfortable. Sometimes he came close to being booted off stage; a couple of times, I think he was."

In between songs, Woody often indulged in long, discursive stories which seemed to unravel endlessly without much point. Occasionally, though, he'd turn this to his advantage. One night he seemed locked into a helpless, meandering tale about a group of neighborhood ladies who'd picketed the local market to protest high meat prices, and the butcher who sympathized with them, and the fruit-and-vegetable man who was a loudmouth and a reactionary and was hated by everyone in Coney Island, and who "came running out sailing his arms in the air and yelling at the pickets. And a couple of pickets just told him, 'Aw, go drop dead,' and he dropped dead."

And then, before the audience could recover, he was off into his next song.

Such moments were rare, though. He still conveyed the same sense of having stumbled accidentally onstage that he'd used so brilliantly in the past to set up his humor, but now the punch lines often were muffled or missing entirely, and all that remained was the aimless confusion. The fact was that he really *did* stumble onstage at times. Some of his friends were quite concerned about Woody's incessant boozing, and Marjorie agreed that it was becoming a serious problem. But she also was aware that he was under a good deal of self-imposed pressure, struggling through a frustrating period of creative indecision. He seemed unable to concentrate on anything. He wasn't sure, at any given moment, if he wanted to be writing or performing, or both . . . or either; and he didn't do *anything* very well as a result. He'd often come home from People's Artists gigs upset because the audience hadn't taken him seriously enough. "They thought they'd bought themselves an *entertainer*," he'd tell Marjorie, who would try to comfort him by suggesting that he didn't *have*

to go out performing all the time. The bookings certainly didn't
bring in all that much money, and he might just as well stay
home and concentrate on his writing, if that was what he truly
wanted. On several such occasions, he announced huffily to People's Artists that he was no longer accepting bookings. But the
writing inevitably proved lonely and difficult—*Bound for Glory*
was turning out to be a tough act to follow—and he'd start missing the hoots and the audiences. So he'd go out performing again,
and then forget the words to "Tom Joad" or hear people whispering in the third row, get angry at the crowd, get drunk, feel
lost and frightened and unappreciated, and rush back to the relative safety of his typewriter.

The steadily declining political situation didn't help much,
either. For one thing, he was able to perform less and less frequently for his favorite audiences—union crowds. He couldn't
even play for his beloved National Maritime Union anymore. But
more than that, there was the claustrophobic sense of declining
possibilities, the bitter realization that his work was, in all like-
lihood, doomed to the periphery of the culture . . . unless he sold
out and went commercial like Burl Ives or Josh White, who, he
wrote to Moe Asch, were carrying on "strange love affairs" with
the bosses. "I have decided long ago that my songs and ballads
would not get the hugs and kisses of the capitalist 'experts' simply because I believe that the real folk history of the country finds
its center and hub in the fight of the union members against the
hired gun thugs of the owners. . . . It's not just a question of
you as an artist, selling out and becoming harmless to the owning
side. No, you are never actually bought or bribed till they have
decided that they can use you in one way or another to rob, to
deceive, to blind, to confuse, to misrepresent, or just to harass,
worry, bedevil and becloud the path of the militant worker on his
long, hard fight from slavery to freedom."

Woody was beginning to lose control of the anger that he'd
always been able to harness as the fuel for his best songs; the
rage that he'd once controlled like a stiletto was becoming a
bludgeon. He'd always been something of an anarchist, balking
at the merest conventions of language. He'd never say, "I only
have one or two cigarettes," but always "one or three." Now,
though, the rebellion deepened and spread to some bizarre areas.
His driving, which never had been very steady, became a campaign to flout every known traffic law and terrorize his friends.

He'd run red lights, go down one-way streets the wrong way, and make sudden, lurching U-turns across the traffic islands on the Belt Parkway. He burned his way through the series of second- and third-hand touring cars he owned during those years, all of which were named Totsy, after Cathy's stroller.

He seemed intent on shaking people up at every opportunity, offending them, forcing them to react, get angry, wake up. There always was the expectation, when Woody was in a group of people, that he would do something outrageous. One night at Pete Seeger's house, a covey of folk singers had gathered to play for the new Polish delegate to the United Nations, a prim and dowdy woman bureaucrat in the Stalinist mold. Toward the end of the evening, they were singing "Black-eyed Susan," an improvising song, and all the performers were coming up with stately verses about peace and brotherhood and amity between nations. When it came Woody's turn, he bellowed:

> *Backed her up against the wall,*
> *Here I come, balls and all*
> *Hey, pretty little black-eyed Susie . . .*

The telling of outrageous Woody Guthrie stories became a favorite pastime in left-wing circles, and several of the best were told by John Henry Faulk, the radio personality from Texas who later gained a certain notoriety when he sued CBS for blacklisting him. Faulk was an occasional drinking buddy of Woody's, and they often performed together at fund-raising parties in much the same way as Woody and Will Geer did.

One night, Faulk and Woody and Elizabeth Lomax went to a party for the Spanish Relief Fund, hosted by a prominent society woman in her posh town house on the upper East Side. It was a grand, spacious place, with a huge fireplace and a half dozen butlers in full battle dress, and the woman—who flitted about in a toreador costume studded with diamonds, and puffed on an exquisite onyx-and-gold cigarette holder—had gathered some very wealthy sympathizers together there.

From the start, it was obvious that Woody was going to be in rare form that night. He swooped down on the hors d'oeuvres and gathered clumps of them in each hand, stuffing them into his mouth and chomping noisily, licking his lips and washing each mouthful down with prodigious gulps of liquor. In order to divert

Woody from the hors d'oeuvres before he demolished the lot of
them, Faulk decided to introduce him to the hostess. As it happened, Woody was affecting a little plastic cigarette holder at the
time, which he'd use occasionally to puff his Camels or Herbert
Tareytons. As soon as he spotted the hostess's onyx-and-gold
model, he pulled his plastic one from his pocket and, in a series
of elaborate, Chaplinesque gestures, put her cigarette into his
holder, his cigarette into her holder, his holder into her mouth
and hers into his, and walked off, grinning, the holder clamped
in the side of his mouth, Roosevelt style. After a while, the
woman approached Faulk and said, "It was a charming joke, but
that cigarette holder really is dear to me and I'd hate to lose it."

Faulk grabbed Woody and told him to give it back.

"Cain't."

"Why the hell not?"

"Lost it."

"Well, what . . . how could you possibly . . . ?"

"I went outside, and then I came back and I didn't have it."

"Come on, Woody. Don't pull that shit on me. Cough it up."

The hostess had spotted them arguing, and heard the end of
the conversation. She summoned a butler. "Eric, go get a flash-
light and go out with Mr. Guthrie and look for my cigarette
holder."

So they went outside and Woody said, "I lost it under a car,
in the gutter," and the butler got down on his hands and knees,
flashing under each of the cars with Woody giving him directions. "Jesus Christ," Faulk said. "You know damn well that
the only way that damn cigarette holder is under those damn cars
is if you *threw* it there." But Woody insisted the butler finish the
search. Eventually they gave up and went inside, and Faulk was
offering to buy the woman a replacement when he saw Woody
lurch over to the silver collection plate, piled with contributions
from the guests, and pour all the money down his shirt. The party
stopped cold, everyone staring. Woody was grinning and patting
his shirt. "Somebody shoot at me," he said. "You cain't hit me
now!"

Faulk rushed over and grabbed him. "Woody, you little son
of a bitch, you're making a shambles of this whole thing. That
money doesn't belong to these people, it's for a cause. It's for
some poor, half-starved Spanish kids sitting in refugee camps in
France. So give it back, for chrissake. Now."

Woody pulled out his shirttail and the money fluttered to the carpet, where several butlers fell upon it immediately and put it back on the tray. Then Woody ambled over to the hostess, took her cigarette holder from his pocket, took one of her cigarettes, put it in her holder, and gently placed the holder in her mouth.

"You little bastard," Faulk said. "You had it all the time."

"Just didn't want to embarrass that man by making it seem like *he* couldn't find it and I could."

Of course, not all fund-raising parties were so disastrous. Woody's performances at People's Artists bookings improved markedly when he was accompanied by any of a number of young women folk singers like Hally Wood (who was, for the moment, Johnny Faulk's wife), Jolly Smolens, or Jackie Gibson. He'd be reminded then of the old days with Lefty Lou in Los Angeles, and slip happily into the comfortable old harmonies. On the way home in Totsy, there would be an obligatory lunge at his singing partner . . . which could be deflected easily enough, although more than a few women were flattered to be stalked by the legendary Guthrie, and acquiesced. His extramarital doings tended to be flings rather than full-blown affairs, and usually were not very memorable to either party. "It was mostly just cuddling," recalled Hally Wood, who brought Woody home one night after her marriage to Faulk was over. "It was something I'd been wondering about for years, and I was sorry it didn't work out better." Jackie Gibson, who slept with Woody several times during a five-year period, also remembered him as a distinctly unspectacular lover.

He continued, even after his discharge from the army, to conduct several dalliances by mail—the most persistent correspondent being young Annette Berger. He seemed to have no real desire to *act* on the sentiments he poured forth in his letters to the girl; at least, he made no serious effort to meet her . . . until he and Marjorie had a tiff one day and he rounded up Cisco for an impromptu scouting expedition to Orange, New Jersey, where Annette lived. As they approached the Berger family store, Woody grew nervous and asked Cisco to go in first for an evaluation. Cisco went in, came out, said, "Nope," and they promptly drove home.

Marjorie tolerated these escapades, but just barely. It wasn't so much that she was jealous: Woody's sexuality was so innocent and playful, and anything but furtive, that it was hard to be threatened by it—but it *was* embarrassing. The Annette Berger affair was soon, via Cisco, the talk of New York. Nor did Woody make much effort to be discreet when he was on the prowl at the various social gatherings he attended without Marjorie. His nights on the town added to the constant tension in the marriage. There always seemed to be pressure of some sort weighing on them: not enough living space, not enough money (he collected unemployment for a time), Marjorie dancing most days and exhausted when she came home at night, the creative frustrations he was facing, the fact that her father still wouldn't acknowledge the marriage, the politics of the times . . .

They would fight. Actually, Marjorie fought and Woody sulked. He never raised his voice, just huffed about conspicuously until she noticed that he was angry about something and tried to pry it out of him. She'd lose her temper then because he was so stubborn and uncommunicative, and start yelling . . . and he'd storm out. After a few nights on the couch at Seeger's or Faulk's (or anyone else's), there would be a spectacular reconciliation and they would be ecstatic together again for several weeks.

It was an exhausting way to live, though, and by September of 1946, when they decided to share a house in the Pocono Mountains near Stroudsburg, Pennsylvania, with the Lomaxes and Faulks, they were looking for a way to break out of their tiring pattern. In fact, Woody and Marjorie considered the vacation a trial run for a permanent demi-separation. They would spend weekends together in Stroudsburg, then Marjorie would return to Coney Island with Cathy during the week, while Woody remained alone in the country, with enough peace and quiet to do his work without all the diversions and interruptions that proved so bothersome in the city.

After a wonderful first weekend in Stroudsburg, with everyone skinny-dipping together in a local stream and Woody spending hours trying out his new children's songs on the Lomax and Faulk kids, Marjorie returned to New York and wrote him a long letter in which she announced her determination to make their marriage work, and hoped the new arrangement would ease it along. She admitted the Annette Berger business and all their other problems had been difficult, but they had only "served to heighten my understanding of people. . . . So while you are still a bit of a problem child to me, you are also my lover and teacher and inspiration." She compared him to Martha Graham: "I have always felt that knowing her and you both so well has been the greatest lesson of my life. It is exciting and shocking to realize how organized as artists you both are . . . and how, in all the rest of living, there isn't the slightest sign of organization and always more complications than there should be. . . . I see myself as a perfect balance for you. I want most of all to make you not just happy, but to feel full of energy and vitality, and to feel good at least. . . ."

Woody responded with a notebook-length sex letter, interspersed with more lyrics to children's songs. "We've got to give our love in this middle season that same smack of forbidden fruit which gave us our good hot start," he wrote. "We must not go around grieving for the conventions we are breaking nor the restrictions we are destroying. . . . The vision of you naked down in Scramblo Creek is so plain in me that my little (or big) farmer is all hot and hard wanting you to touch him, lick him, and to kiss him, to make him all nice and slick with your spit and to open your little legs and let him come in. . . . What has mama nature put there in you that is the world's best drugstore for me? Why is the spit in your mouth my best medicine? And why does my belly tickle and my balls tingle and my pecker stay so hot and so stiff at the very thought of you? . . . Let's run off somewhere behind the barn . . . and come about three or four good times apiece next time you come down here. . . . Let's have a few festivals of seed planting . . . I've got several gallons of fresh milk backed up inside me."

In point of fact, their first week's separation worked rather *too* well: their second weekend in the country was so idyllic and passionate that they could barely stand the parting that Sunday. "I don't know if I really want to live this way very long," Marjorie wrote him from Coney Island the next day. "I feel a new, strange love. Maybe it was the vacation . . . or perhaps our new sex life is at the bottom of it all." Which was just about all Woody needed to send him rushing down from the Poconos, ready and willing to try life together in Coney Island once more.

They would make it work this time, they vowed. He would concentrate on his writing. There would be no more bookings, no more diversions. Marjorie suggested that he write a letter to the *Daily Worker* announcing his new policy and explaining that his retreat wasn't caused by any desire to run from the big fights, but an attempt to face them in his own creative way. They decided to spend a few dollars per month on a vacant room around the corner from their apartment, to serve as an office for Woody. They fixed it up with a desk and chair, his typewriter, books, and papers. He was going to take another, final stab at writing his merchant marine novel, with no interruptions.

Except, of course, for really important things like Jimmy Longhi's political campaign. He was running for Congress in 1946, endorsed by an unlikely combination of the Republican and American Labor parties—the same parlay that had won a seat for progressive Vito Marcantonio in Manhattan—but Jimmy was considered a heavy underdog against the Democratic machine in a district that included Brooklyn's tough waterfront section. Woody and Cisco traveled the docks, performing from the back of a flatbed truck; during their breaks, a loudspeaker played a Longhi campaign song contributed by Frank Sinatra. Despite the high-powered entertainment, Jimmy lost a surprisingly close contest.

And then there was the Frederick Douglass Club, the Communist Party's Coney Island headquarters, which operated a storefront several blocks down from the Guthrie apartment on Mermaid Avenue, and always needed volunteers for one thing or another. Woody's most famous contribution was a paint job—brilliant red—but he also delivered a memorable talk one evening: "Trade Unions—What They Mean to You and Your Family."

The real distractions, of course, were all in Woody's head. He just couldn't seem to find the right creative groove for any sort of sustained work. He would sit at the typewriter and, as always, words would pour out—but rarely did they have much to do with *Ship Story*, which was the working title for his book. He wrote letters to the *Daily Worker* and People's Songs, blurbs promoting Moe Asch's latest albums, short articles, and great gobs of free verse that included striking passages, but overall were hackneyed, Popular Front-style valentines to "the people":

I ALMOST BELIEVE THAT I HAVE SEEN AS MANY FACES AND PLACES AS ANY OF US.

    FORTY SIX OF THESE FORTY EIGHT, MEXICO, CANADA, TOWNS, CITIES, FARMS AND VILLAGES, AFRICA, SICILY,

FREIGHT TRAINS AND SHIP CONVOYS, AND THE BRITISH
ISLES.

   AND I WALKED AND RODE LOW ENOUGH AND SLOW
ENOUGH TO SEE THE PEOPLE AND EVEN TO HEAR THEM
TALK

   AND EVEN TO STOP AND TALK TO THEM AND TO LIVE
AND SING AND WORK AND EAT WITH THEM

   AND THIS WAS BEFORE I HEARD ABOUT THE PEOPLE AS A
WORD

   I HAD NOT HEARD ANY WORD I COULD SPEAK AND BRING
ALL OF YOU BACK IN MY MIND AGAIN

   BUT EVERYTIME I MET AND TALKED AND SUNG WITH A
NEW STRANGER I DID THINK BACK OVER MOST OF THE OTH-
ERS AND MAYBE ALL OF THEM

   I JUST DID NOT KNOW I WAS THINKING ABOUT ALL OF
YOU

   BUT THIS HARD AND EASY TRAVELING DOES GIVE ME THE
RIGHT TO GUESS AT WHAT THE PEOPLE ARE

   A RIGHT TO SAY ALL OF YOU

   A RIGHT TO HEAR AND TO SEE AND TO SING ALL OF
YOU . . .

The sad part was that he *did* have an uncanny fix on the spirit
and cadences of the country; as Clifton Fadiman had said of
Bound for Glory, America seemed to spill from his guitar and
typewriter . . . but less frequently now, and certainly not when
he struggled for the big picture in the bloated images of his free
verse. He was at his best describing individual people and specific events; capturing the rhythms of their speech and the sub-
tleties of their perception. He seemed able to do that so easily at
times that it was, perhaps, difficult for him to believe it was
important or real.

Although Woody paid lip service to the ideal of simplicity, he
was burdened by the constant pressure to produce greatness: "I
feel now like I have felt before, that these words are such a force,
such a pressure, such a bomb inside me, that if I fail to get them
out and written down here . . . they will expand and actually
explode and destroy me like wax paper." The reason for all the
urgency, he explained, was the developing political crisis, a situation as explosive as the words in his head. In short: "The
workers are anxious for my words."

If so, they were about the only ones. Nobody else seemed very interested anymore. Joy Doerflinger was dead after a long, tragic siege in the hospital. Even Marjorie was too busy with her dancing and child-rearing and commuting to shepherd him through *Ship Story* as she had with *Bound for Glory*. He was all alone in his ratty little office, and lonely, and gradually moved all his equipment, piece by piece, back to Mermaid Avenue, where at least there was coffee, and Cathy, and all the other welcome interruptions of his life.

The few times he sat down and actually tried to write his novel, the results were rather strange. He had been working on it intermittently for more than three years now; his original concept had changed several times and the various incarnations lay atop each other like alluvial strata. The first few chapters, those he'd started writing even before he put out to sea, were a fairly straightforward account of his courtship with Marjorie—confused at times (he couldn't decide whether to use real names or pseudonyms), and sometimes overdone, but often quite moving. The next several chapters were precisely detailed but disjointed accounts of life at sea. There were some fine moments, authentic swatches of shipboard talk culled from Woody's notebooks, but without any real purpose or direction. Each of the last few chapters had a very definite direction, though. Apparently they were the ones that Woody had been working on since the war, and they invariably ended with a wildly improbable sex scene involving Pat Lukas (Woody's alter ego) and a different, exotic woman—in one case, a Baltimore society matron in the back seat of her Packard; then, in Sicily, with a peasant girl in a hayloft.

Eventually he deposited the entire mess, unfinished, on Bill Doerflinger's desk at Dutton in the spring of 1947 and, in due course, received a letter from Doerflinger saying that it might be best to forget about *Ship Story* and try something else. Woody was somewhat relieved, oddly enough. He had felt an obligation to Dutton after signing the contract for *I Want to Be Right* in the spring of 1943, and now Doerflinger had told him it wouldn't really be necessary to live up to that deal. "Of course," the editor added, "we'd be interested in seeing anything else you'd want to write . . ."

Woody wasn't sure what else he *could* write. He really wanted to go back again and explain more about his past, his childhood in Oklahoma and Texas—but he was afraid that *Bound for Glory* had pretty much covered that territory, at least in the eyes of anyone who'd be in a position to *publish* his work.

Still, he couldn't seem to stop writing about it. He puttered for a time with a concert script called "High Balladry," which included all sorts of exquisite details about his childhood unreported in *Bound for Glory*, interspersed with appropriate songs. He never quite finished the script, but years later it would be used as the basis for a series of concerts celebrating his work. He also wrote an autobiographical sketch for a book of his lyrics that Moe Asch intended to publish, called *American Folk Song*, which was a charming though essentially repetitive account of his life . . . and the most extensive piece of his writing actually to see print in the postwar years.

The only other subject he seemed able—and thrilled—to write about with any success was his daughter Cathy. He wrote several wonderful sketches about playing with her, walking her to nursery school past the gauntlet of Coney Island shopkeepers, and other accounts of her daily life, which were published in *Two to Six* magazine in 1946 and 1947.

She seemed an unending source of wonder; his stories about her were as simple and beautiful as his children's songs. One of the best was called "Child Sitting," in which he described the rigors of taking care of Cathy on a day when she was home sick from school:

Sam, the newspaper man, ran in with his arms full of coloring books, a jar of sticky paste, a big red balloon, another box of crayons, all sent from the candy store by Marjorie on her way to work. Sam ran back out again to sell his papers and magazines and Cathy was waving, "'Bye, Sem." She held up the jar of paste first and told me, "Deddy here, opinnit."

"Play with your other things," I told her . . .

"But, Deddy, I wanta just paste."

"Color."

"Paste."

"Cut."

"Paste, Deddy. Silly. Don't ya know what paste is?"

"Draw me a nice big, big, big picture."

"I'll paste ya one."

"Dolls."

"My dolls asked me to paste 'em a s'prize."

"Draw with a pencil."

"But, Deddy, ya cain't paste nuthin' with a pencil."

Cathy proceeds with the paste, of course, while Woody tries to work on his merchant marine novel. Eventually she asks him to come and unstick her hand—it's stuck on the telephone—and he discovers:

> The whole box of kleenex tissues were pulled out and pasted on top of one another, like diapers folded flat in a laundry. The color books had paste between their pages. She had cut out chains, pumpkins, baskets, fruit of every kind, masks with eyes, noses, mouths, that looked like people you know. She had smeared her cheeks with paste like Mommy does her cold cream, and painted her finger-nails with it, the way her grandma had showed her. Every-thing on the bed was stuck to everything else. I picked up the pasted basket to carry away into Cathy's room and the rest of the mess on the bed all followed me. There was no more paste in the jar . . .

Even though they were in no financial condition to build a family—Marjorie was borrowing money regularly from her parents to make ends meet—the Guthries decided they wanted more children. In December of 1946, Marjorie announced that she was pregnant again and Woody revived all his old fantasies about Railroad Pete.

One day when he was pulling Cathy over to the beach in her wagon and Margorie, just pregnant, was trailing behind, watching them, she had a vision of a picture in a book she'd read as a little girl: a young boy with no shoes and his pants rolled up just as Woody looked now—carrying firewood in his arms. Oddly, she even remembered the boy's name: Arlo. She ran to Woody and told him about her vision, and he said, "Fine, that's what we'll call him."

"No, really," she said. "We don't have to. It's just that you reminded me of the drawing."

"No, really," he said. "I'd like to."

* * *

Woody began the new year, 1947, in chipper fashion. He stapled together one of his little newspapers, called "The Reckless Observer," and sent it to friends and relatives. It announced Marjorie's pregnancy, the birth of Daniel Seeger, and the death of Joy Doerflinger. There was a letter from Gwen Guthrie in El Paso, about her new bike, and a brief item: "Ugliest Guthrie Brother Located—George, working at Douglas aircraft, visited New York recently in his new car."

He'd begun work on another novel, called *House of Earth*, which represented a new creative direction: he was writing about things he'd remembered from his childhood but, for the first time, not about himself. The main characters were a high plains farmer named Arthur Hamlin and his wife, Ella Mae, probably based on Guthrie cousins; and in just a few pages, he managed to capture the windy emptiness and sweep of the Texas panhandle: Arthur, a dreamer, wants to replace his rotting old wooden farmhouse with one made of adobe brick. He has a government pamphlet telling him how to build his dream house. Ella Mae, the more practical member of the family, thinks it's a crazy idea . . . and Arthur follows her about while she's doing the chores, trying to convince her. He finally lures her into an incredibly long, detailed love scene ("He touched the tip of his tongue to each of her teeth, one at a time and felt the vacant gums in two places where teeth were out . . ."), which takes place in the barn, with Arthur reading occasionally from the government pamphlet, proselytizing his wife passionately.

Woody showed the first chapter to Alan Lomax, who thought it was astonishing. "There was a moment in my life," he'd later recall, "when I considered dropping everything I was doing, and just helping Woody to get published. It was, quite simply, the best material I'd ever seen written about that section of the country." It also was all that he'd ever see of *House of Earth*. After fiddling with a second chapter, Woody gave up on it.

Cathy Ann Guthrie celebrated her fourth birthday on February 6, in a new pink birthday dress. Woody had, by now, taken to saving almost everything she produced. Her drawings were labeled and dated, her rhymes catalogued, bits and snatches of conversation preserved . . .

MAMMA: What makes your cheeks so red?
CATHY: My applesauce, my milk, my rouge and the wind.

Cathy's birthday was on Thursday. Woody spent most of Saturday at his typewriter, writing free verse and watching a fine, gentle snowfall. Most of his poems that day were the usual love letters to "the people," although he also wrote one called "My Wild Woman," which expressed some frustration with Marjorie's (apparent) renewed sexual conservatism, and then evolved into a lovely erotic tribute to her. Late that evening, he performed at a Town Hall hootenanny honoring Sonny Terry, and was quite pleased that Marjorie—for a change—decided to accompany him.

The concert evidently was one of Woody's better performances, and he sat down at the typewriter first thing Sunday morning to describe it . . . but he didn't get very far. He had to leave in late morning to go to Elizabeth, New Jersey, for what he considered to be a real treat—an appearace before a union audience, the electrical workers at Phelps-Dodge, who were celebrating the end of an eight-month strike, and mourning the death of Mario Russo, a union leader who'd been murdered while on picket duty.

Marjorie took Cathy for a walk to visit her parents in Sea Gate. They returned in early afternoon, had lunch, and then played together quietly in the living room for a time. Cathy sat on the couch, proudly wearing her new pink birthday dress, listening to the radio. In midafternoon, Marjorie had a sudden, disturbing thought: she wondered if she was getting enough vitamin C for the new baby. She decided to make a quick run over to the fruit stand across the street, and buy some oranges. She told Cathy to answer the phone if it rang.

She was gone no more than five minutes.

When she returned, smoke was pouring from 3520 Mermaid Avenue. She could not see, at first, what was happening for all the smoke . . . but it was her apartment. Arthur Young, the boy from upstairs, was there and he had a blanket. Then she saw, it was Cathy in the blanket and Cathy was gone. She was still alive, but she was just gone. The dress was gone.

A doctor was summoned, the ambulance was there, and she was inside it with Cathy, who was semi-conscious and whimpering, still in the blanket—and Marjorie did not have any idea what had caused the fire, or how it could have happened so quickly and do what it had done. She looked down at Cathy, whose face was the only part of her body that hadn't been utterly seared and even her face was beginning to blister, and she thought: Please, God, let her die. Don't make her suffer. Don't let her live like this. . . .

They went to Coney Island Hospital and Cathy was sent to the emergency room. Marjorie could hear, from just outside the doors, Cathy crying in there. The doctors came out and told her that it was very serious indeed, and all they could do now was wait. She began making phone calls. She called her brother Mutt in Brooklyn, whose wife, Clare, had been an English ambulance driver and presumably could deal with such a horrible situation. She wanted only calm people around her now. She called Sophie Maslow, and then realized that Sophie was pregnant and probably would be very upset by the news—she was thinking *very* clearly now—and so she asked Sophie to put Max on. And she told him, and they came to the hospital.

The doctors were giving Cathy intravenous feeding through her foot, and needed someone to hold the foot. Marjorie came in and held it for a while, then the others took turns. Then the doctors said they needed blood, and so she called Ross's candy store next to her house and asked for volunteers; several of the neighborhood kids responded immediately. Cathy cried through much of the afternoon, but along toward evening she seemed to feel a bit better and began singing her little rhymes in the emergency room.

Woody left the Phelps-Dodge workers in late afternoon and decided to stop in at Moe Asch's studio on his way home—Moe usually was there on Sunday—and see if any copies of his latest album of children's songs, *Work Songs to Grow On*, were available yet. The albums weren't ready, but the little books of lyrics were and he took a half dozen home to show Marjorie and Cathy. He arrived home in early evening, smelled the smoke in the hallway, and found a note on the door: "Go to Coney Island Hospital immediately."

Later he would write that Cathy was "laughing and singing in her bandages" when he arrived. He went directly to the emergency room, held her foot for a time, then came out and was very quiet. He and Marjorie spent the night there, on a bench in the hall; she sat upright and Woody stretched out, with his head in her lap. Cathy died in the morning.

They went home to survey the wreckage, and there wasn't very much. Just the couch, the radio, the end table that the radio had been sitting on, a bit of the wall was singed—it looked like a bolt of lightning had struck, but the firemen suspected it was a spark from the cheap wiring in the radio, an electrical fire. Marjorie and Clare began to clean up. That afternoon, close friends arrived—Cisco and Bina, Jimmy Longhi. At one point, Marjorie's parents came by, Isidore Greenblatt setting foot inside their house for the very first time. Marjorie began to cry and said to her father: "I don't want you here when my children are dead. I want you here when they're alive."

Aside from that, they were very quiet. Woody was dazed; the life had gone out of his eyes. Toward evening, Cisco and Jimmy took him for a walk along the beach. The three sailors, who'd been through so much together, were close enough to know that there was nothing that possibly could be said now. And then, suddenly, Woody was flopped down on his back in the sand, his arms and legs flailing furiously and a wounded animal yowl building in his throat, increasing in force and intensity until it pierced the noise of the breakers and seemed to hover like a cloud along the beach.

And then it stopped.

He stood up, shook the sand out, and began to walk home. Shortly afterward, he wrote in his notebook: "And the things you fear shall truly come upon you . . ."

"This is to test the typewriter after it came thru the bath of Cathy's fire. This piece about Blind Sonny was rolled up in my typewriter when I left the house here to sing down in Elizabeth, New Jersey.

"I am going ahead now and finish up this letter on this same piece of scorched and smoked paper just to show myself that such a thing as a no good wartime radio wire shorting out and burning little Miss Stackabones to death has not stopped me nor slowed down my thinking, but has made my old bones jump up wider awake to fight against this kind of a greed that sells such dangerous wirings."

There was no funeral. Woody and Marjorie tried to continue their lives as normally as possible. Several days after Cathy's death, they even performed a children's program together at the Barbizon Plaza Hotel in Manhattan, singing and dancing the very songs that must have been most painful to them. A number of friends attended—Will and Herta Geer, Sophie Maslow, several folk singers—amazed that the show was taking place at all.

But despite the attempts to present a brave front, their suffering was transparent. Marjorie was beside herself with guilt for having left Cathy alone in the house; quite a few people quietly blamed her for the death. Woody seemed blasted away, vacant and draggy, in a state of shock. Several weeks after the fire, he learned that Oscar Brand—never a close friend—recently had burned his hand. "He was like a mother hen, entirely solicitous," Brand recalled. "He told me all about the fires in his family, his mother, his sister, and how you always had to be very careful. He seemed to really believe that everyone he loved was doomed to go up in smoke. It was not at all like the normal, gruff Woody. He insisted on carrying my guitar case that day, to protect my hand."

He spent the month of February locked in the apartment, writing exhaustive responses to every last person who'd sent a condolence note, even those he didn't know. He typed his responses on long, legal-sized paper, single-spaced, kept carbon copies of each one, and signed them all: Woody, Marjorie, Cathy, and Pete. Each was different—to Mother Bloor, the aging Communist leader, he wrote what a wonderful revolutionary Cathy would have been; to her classmates, how devoted she was; to his sister Mary Jo, how happy and creative she'd been. He wrote dozens of letters, and each one continued on for thousands of words, and each was different.

By March, the condolence letters had stopped coming and his responses all were written. He wrote a poem to Arthur Young, the boy upstairs, thanking him for trying to save Cathy. He wrote three songs about the Centralia, Illinois, mine disaster that killed 111 people. People's Songs published the three in a special edition of its bulletin, but they really weren't very memorable. He seemed generally at a loss. . . .

In the days just after Cathy's death, he'd received a telegram from the Bonneville Power Authority: "BPA interested in your singing Columbia River songs at National Rural Electric Cooperative convention at Spokane, April 21 thru April 23. Good chance your songs to come into their own out here where they were meant to be sung. Might arrange other appearances. Are you interested? How much besides expenses?"

He was in no shape to consider the offer very seriously at first, but the more he thought about it, the more attractive it seemed. Marjorie agreed that the trip might be just what he needed—he hadn't been out West in years. He could visit his family in Oklahoma and Texas on the way out, and then swing through Califonia on the way back, performing at the various People's Songs outposts there.

Just before he left, though, there was another shock. Jackie Gibson was pregnant, the result of an unsuccessful attempt to fend off a drunken Woody on Pete Seeger's couch one midwinter night. She wanted money for an abortion. Cisco, discussing the matter with Woody and Marjorie one evening, volunteered to say that he'd slept with Jackie too and thus take the weight off Woody's shoulders. Woody said little at the time, but then—without Marjorie's knowledge—he wrote a scandalous letter to Jackie, which alternated between frenzied erotica and a plea *not* to have the abortion. He said he didn't want another of his children to die, but didn't offer any plans or alternatives. Jackie was understandably outraged, and went ahead and paid for the abortion herself, vowing never to speak to the man again.

He took the train to Chicago, then south to Pampa, where not only Uncle Jeff and Allene still were living, but also Woody's older brother Roy and his wife, Ann. Jeff was working as a night watchman, and Allene was a clerk at the carbon-black factory west of town. Roy was working in the oil business. It was good to see them all again, but depressing too. He wrote to Marjorie that they couldn't pronounce the word "fascist," and called the black section of Pampa "niggertown." Jeff, of course, badgered Woody about cranking up their old vaudeville act, maybe even taking it to New York. But Woody wasn't buying: "If I hooked up with them again, I'd let myself and my ideas get pushed out the rear window. . . . I remember now why I started walking out and down that Pampa road in 1936. . . ."

From Texas, he hopped a Greyhound bus through Colorado, Utah, Wyoming, and Idaho to Spokane. He seemed happy, revisiting the sights of his old hobo days. He remembered the spot in Raton Pass where a truck driver had thrown some cinnamon rolls out the window to him in 1935, then a dry-goods salesman had picked him up and given him a ride all the way to Denver, letting *him* drive the car for the last hour: "I never felt any better, richer, nor any bigger in my whole life . . ." He loved the idea of traveling the West again: "I'd like to form a gypsy family folksong dancing band and come up through here on a busking trip. Between saloons and union places we ought to make enough money to keep on our traveling shoes."

Arriving in Spokane, he was surprised and excited to find telegrams from a dozen different Left organizations, from Seattle to Los Angeles, inviting him to perform. *People's World*, his old newspaper, was offering to pay him real money—twenty-five dollars per week—to revive his column. "This is an awful nice hotel . . . just a little too fascisti to satisfy my higher ideals. But Spokane ain't that way at heart," he wrote to Marjorie. "I like the Pacific Northwest more every time I see it. The folks out here got a good shot of the old free and easy pioneer spirit in them. They still ride the tough grass and dig in the hills."

He spent May Day in San Francisco and May 2 in Oakland, where he "marched and sung for the telefone girls, but the police broke us up." He sent Marjorie fourteen postcards that day, and two more on May 3.

But Marjorie had fallen into a deep funk, alone in the house, and there was nothing he could do to cheer her up. "While I was shopping in a store I heard a kid scream and I could hardly hold back the tears that swelled in my throat," she wrote to him. "It seemed like I had heard our Stacky crying and calling for me and then I relived again what I seem unable to ever get out of my eyes and ears and heart. . . . And I always see things like Stacky half asleep running to the toilet or I can hear her making sounds in her little bed. Oh daddy, will we ever be able to enjoy kids again?"

She tried to keep herself busy, cleaning and recleaning the house. She fancied herself Woody's secretary, and did valuable work for him, arranging his California schedule. She even pulled his old army letters from a trunk and arranged them chronologically in a loose-leaf binder. She went to the movies often, to get her mind off things, but one night: "Just as I was walking out and putting on my coat, I saw a little curly head standing at the candy counter . . . for a second I almost thought I saw Stack . . ."

It's probable that Woody hadn't yet received her sad letters or was unaware of her suffering, because at the end of a generally innocuous letter from San Francisco, he wrote viciously: "I still feel full of various doubts about us, but not so full as most of these other people I meet and talk to each day. I love you in a way that is purely primitive with none of the intellectual trimmings you need so badly. But I have never been able to feel that you could love me in these same ways. I met one girl up in Spokane who"

Incredibly, the letter ended there.

Marjorie couldn't believe he could be so sadistic. She was crushed: "The letter just stopped there and that was all! If I told you I laughed, it would be a lie. If I told you I cried, you'd be upset. So what shall I tell you? . . . How can I write that I love you when you tell me I don't know what it's all about? . . . I'm lonely and blue and very much in love with my husband and want to know that he loves me too. . . ."

Arriving at Earl Robinson's house in Los Angeles—Earl had taken to writing movie scores—Woody found a pile of sad letters from Marjorie waiting for him, and was immediately contrite:

> I started out on this six weeks trip sort of half way expecting it to be a bum deal for you and for me and for everybody else. In your present pregnant condition I guess it does seem dreary and bad for me to be out here knocking around so sporty and so free. I almost wish in some ways I'd never come out at this time but had flew right back home from Spokane.
>
> I wish I'd come on back home and worked on our songs and stuff together and then took this damnable western tour after Pete was big enough to come with us (and Repeate) (and Stacky).
>
> You know me good enough to know that I cant write no female woman very much of a lovers letter. I always get all bogged down in the nakedest and lowest forms of just wild and crazy sexual night horses and day dreams. I will tell you once more again that I think I'm fairly certain that I'm wedded and latched onto the pertiest and the smartest little mommy dudios in all of them big waxed studios. . . .
>
> Don't be afeard so much that my love juices are dripping down onto pages of letters to any other girl, nor into words spoke into any other lady's ears. This hasn't took place and it's not going to happen. So just keep your goidle and your pants on, Turtle, and save every little drop of your boxing, wrestling, debating, arguing, clawing, biting, kissing, screwing, fucking, laying and hip swaying for me.
>
> I love you so much I can't see nor think straight. . . .

Hollywood was rather jittery that spring. Investigators were snooping around. A congressional committee—the House Un-

American Activities Committee (HUAC)—was planning to hold hearings on the Communist influence in the movie business that October, and the town was buzzing with it. The official reaction in Hollywood Left circles was jaunty assurance: HUAC had held hearings before (Woody, in fact, was named as a Communist in 1941, in testimony which had him seducing the troops at Fort Dix in New Jersey at a time when he actually was in California), and not many people had taken the committee seriously. It was a right-wing road show—noisy, but unable to inflict any real damage. Nonetheless, with the change in the political atmosphere, there was no sense in taking any chances and the "progressives" were reining in and behaving cautiously.

Despite the hint of paranoia in the air, there was plenty to keep Woody busy in Los Angeles. There were all sorts of appearances, including a folk-song party at the home of Eddie Albert, the actor, who later sent a warm note thanking him for the music. There also was business to be transacted at Capitol Records, where Woody opened negotiations for his rightful share of "Oklahoma Hills." Eventually, he would be given a writing credit (along with Jack Guthrie) and a share of the royalties. He tried to find his cousin in Los Angeles, hoping that they might do some singing together, but Jack was a fairly big country music star now, and out on tour when Woody arrived in town. He did, however, find Lefty Lou . . . still married and living happily as a housewife in the San Fernando Valley. They spent an uncomfortable hour together. Maxine thought he seemed troubled and weird, and also that he'd picked up a touch of a New York accent.

He *was* troubled, of course. Cathy's death was still shaking loose skeletons, opening musty closets of pain and fear in his mind. The trip West had compounded his preoccupation with the past. He seemed, at times, lost in it. One night, sitting with Irving Lerner, the movie director, Woody told the story of the trip that he, his brother, his father, and Uncle Jeff had taken to the Chisos Mountains in search of Jerry P. Guthrie's silver mine, and Lerner had said that it sounded like it might make a good screenplay, a possibility that Woody began to consider seriously.

The combined weight of memory and the political tension in Los Angeles was a familiar and frightening sensation. As always, Woody reacted defiantly to the political threat. As usual, he wasted his defiance on people he loved. After a visit with his

Aunt Laura and cousin Amalee in Sonora, he wrote a letter that
started off sweetly, as a thank-you note, and evolved into a dia-
tribe: "The big rich landlords, gambling lords, rulers and owners
are cussing the Communists loud and long these days. The Communists always have been the hardest fighters for the trade unions,
good wages, short hours, nursery schools, cleaner workshops and
the equal rights of every person of every color. Communists have
the only answer to the whole mess. That is, we all ought to own
and run every mine, factory, timber track, just as we own our
post office and our post office is run so good because it is owned
and bossed by the whole country. So you can call me a Communist from here on. I've been working with them since 1936 in
this same way."

His anger couldn't exorcise the fear, though. He felt haunted.
"Your old man is in hard shape," he wrote to Marjorie in mid-
May. "I don't know what has hit me. I've never felt this low
before. . . . What the hell good is a career? I mean, if we can't
do it together or to stay home and have kids together."

And again: "Every day seems like it's no go. I don't feel like
doing very much of anything. All scrabbled up."

He had bookings arranged through the middle of June, but
decided to drop them. He was tired of the road and scared, and
wanted to go home.

CHAPTER 10

What Am I Gonna Do When My Shock Time Comes?

He worked with unaccustomed discipline now. He sat each day at the little desk in the Coney Island living room, and the words poured out. His time of confusion had passed; he knew what his priorities were, even which bookings to accept and reject. He cut way down on his drinking. He stayed at home more often. This was, quite clearly, the work he should have been doing all along. When Joy Doerflinger separated the "Silver Mine" chapter from *Bound for Glory*, she'd said it was worth a book in itself, but Woody figured she was simply trying to ease the pain of excision, and he hadn't given the idea much thought. But Cathy's death, and the obsession with the past that followed, had brought her suggestion to mind once more. And Irving Lerner's reaction to the story—that it might make a good movie— erased any lingering doubts Woody may have had.

His first working title for the manuscript was *Study Butte*, after the tiny mining village nearest the site of Jerry P. Guthrie's lost claim, but he later changed it to *Foolish Gold* and then—much later—to *Seeds of Man*. He began with the Guthrie family's attempt to regroup after a disaster—his mother's illness and his father's mysterious fire. The similarities between Clara's death and Cathy's, between his father's business failure and his own disappointments, between his mother's debilitation and his own . . . *nervousness*, obviously were very much on his mind. Surely, the connections were far too tenuous to draw any real conclusions, but the very act of raising the questions, of bringing some of them out into the open, held certain satisfactions. Finally, he could tell his father off. In the remarkable scene that dominated Chapter 2, a scene he would rewrite time and again, he exorcised some of the pain and confusion that had been festering since childhood. He did it gently, though, and with a good deal of insight. Charley Guthrie was made to seem more pathetic than blustery . . . and Woody himself, more blustery than understanding: "I seen this stuff that was gonna wham into our family a long time before it really happened. I seen what papa's badge and gun jobs, and his land trading were doing every day to Mama . . . Big Pistols . . . Big fistfights . . . Shootings, swappings, tradings, cheating of the worst and lowest kind.

". . . It's been stuff like this, by the day, by the hour, by the ten or fifteen years that wrecked the family. Mama cried with her head down a hundred spells a day, while all of us had our eye on the money—the dough, the long green, the coin, the deeds to that land, the title to that property . . ."

The story billowed as he wrote. Woody, Jeff, and Charley Guthrie remained the central characters in the search for the lost silver, but Roy Guthrie was subtracted from the traveling party and replaced by a fictitious cousin, Eddie Moore, whose experiences in World War I had rendered him impotent and slow-witted. Not surprisingly, Woody conjured up a dark, sexy girlfriend named Helen Cliffman for himself in Pampa and another, equally sexy Mexican girlfriend in Terlingua, near the Chisos Mountains. But his most felicitous invention was an old shaman named Rio— part Indian, part Mexican, and a full-blooded Marxist—who uses his mystical powers to restore Eddie's wits and urges in Terlingua, and also lectures Charley on social injustice.

Although Woody's work habits had become more disciplined, his writing remained unpolished and raw. He still had little sense of structure, only a vague notion of how to build dramatic tension or sustain a story. He seemed to get lost in his scenes and thrash about; he felt the need to have each of his characters describe what he or she was feeling at all times. His descriptive passages were, at once, glorious and dizzying: "This was a sandyland country, this Pecos country, here all around us. Sandy desert bushes. Sandy cactus of every kind, slim and long, fat and thick, wide and low, high and skinny, curly, twisty, knotty, stickery, thorny, daggery-knifed, razor sharp; hot darts, burning needles, fuzzy needles, cutting edges, stinging leaves and blistering stems. I saw a whole world of sword and dagger weed and limb—a new world to my eyes. The feel and breath of the air was all different, new, high, clear, clean and light. None of the smokes and carbons, none of the charcoal smells of the oil fields. None of the sooty oil-field fires, none of the blackening slush pond blazes, none of those big sheet-iron petroleum refineries, none of those big smokey carbon-black plants.''

Although many of the characters' speeches evolved similarly into soaring, melodic soliloquys, the cumulative weight of all the words was, ultimately, numbing. And there was a new stylistic twist that made wading through Woody's dense prose even more difficult: he had decided to try to replicate, as closely as possible, the *sound* of the southwestern and Mexican dialects his characters were speaking, in much the same way that his children's songs were an attempt to re-create the sound of children playing with words.

As a result, his Texans tended to lapse into unintelligible grunts and wheezes, their speeches a forest of apostrophes (''I wisht Charlie 'n' Woodrow wouldn't of been s'damn quick t' tell 'im we'd ride 'em down t' th' Perseedeo turnoff,'' Eddie says at one point). His Mexicans were even worse, blatant and often embarrassing caricatures. Rio, for example: ''I gon' ask Addie for me, Rio, to please throw down hisa chew 'backa, his dirty snoffa, speet run down chin. I say he love de cegarette bot not every cegarette he see, joosta only thesa kind wheech Woody smoke, wheech Woody moosta roll for Addie. I come to Addie een his dreams; he t'ink when I tal heem tonight on the truck what he eeza to do . . .''

No doubt *Study Butte* would need quite a bit of editing before it could be published, but that didn't matter. The purposeful clatter of Woody's typewriter had brought new optimism to the apartment on Mermaid Avenue. The place was beginning to fill with children again: Gwen Guthrie, age eleven, came from El Paso to spend the summer. She was soon joined by Arlo Davy Guthrie, who was born without much fuss on July 10, 1947 . . . and Woody and Marjorie were determined not to stop there. They dreamed of a family troupe—the Singing Guthries—and Arlo was followed by another son, Joady Ben (after Tom Joad), in December of 1948, and then a daughter, Nora Lee, little more than a year later, in January of 1950.

There was more good news, too, in the months after Arlo's birth. Capitol Records sent Woody a check for the incredible sum of $1,155.56, his share of the "Oklahoma Hills" royalties. It was "the biggest chunk of free enterprise I've got so far," he wrote, and he used a good part of it to buy Totsy II, a two-door Ford, from the "mad Russian on Surf Avenue." He also learned that a country and western group called Maddox Brothers and Rose were going to record his old ballad "The Philadelphia Lawyer" (which they subsequently did, to very little effect).

He was feeling optimistic again. In the free verse that he continued to churn out even while banging away at *Study Butte*, he compared himself—favorably—to his literary heroes. Whitman, Carl Sandburg, Robert Burns, and Pushkin, among others, were summoned and dispatched. He celebrated himself with a fervor that once had been reserved only for "the people":

> *The world has already built me a legend . . .*
> *This more than anything else*
> *Is what makes me a poet in the folking field*

He sought to confirm his lofty status by compiling a list of the praise people had showered on him over the years, including the famous quotes from Steinbeck, Fadiman, and all the others. He called it "Things They Said About Woody Guthrie All Along."

He still accepted bookings from People's Artists, but only important ones. In November of 1947, he traveled to Chicago for the first People's Songs national convention. A month later, he was paid a hundred dollars to sing for striking tobacco workers in North Carolina. He quickly ran into trouble there, though, when he wrote a picket line song that included the verse:

> *All colors of hands gonna work together*
> *All colors of eyes gonna laugh and shine*
> *All colors of feet gonna dance together*
> *When I bring my CIO to Caroline, Caroline*

The problem was, of course, that the union was segregated and the organizers insisted that he cut the verse. "I [said] that if the line got the blue pencil, me and my guitar hit the road for home," he reported in the *Daily Worker*. But the union held firm, and the white workers boycotted the meeting where he was to have played. "It cut me to my bones to have to play and sing for those negroes with no other colors mixing in."

For the most part, though, *Study Butte* kept Woody out of action. He even resigned from People's Songs for a time, arguing that the book was keeping him so busy that he couldn't possibly contribute very much to the organization. Which was just as well, because People's Songs and much of the American Left were moving inexorably toward a major disaster in 1948, fueled by the Communist Party's decision to throw its weight behind the third-party candidacy of Henry Wallace for President.

The alliance between People's Songs and Henry Wallace was an inspired mating of innocents. It produced a great many enthusiastic rallies and a staggering amount of bad music. The pages of the People's Songs bulletin soon were filled with campaign songs. Irwin Silber contributed some Wallace square dance calls ("Promenade, promenade, every gal is a Wallace babe"), and even Alan Lomax was moved to descend from his lofty plateau of virtuosity and compose (with E. Y. "Yip" Harburg) a truly dreadful number called "I've Got a Ballot," to the tune of "I've Got Sixpence." But the uncontested star of the show was Pete Seeger, who sang at the Progressive Party's July convention in Philadelphia, and again at the massive Wallace rally in Yankee Stadium later that summer, and then during a courageous tour of the South with the candidate himself (both Wallace and Seeger were pelted with tomatoes and eggs) in September.

Woody remained at the periphery, composing several inconsequential Wallace songs and appearing with Cisco on the stump occasionally. Later, he would write a letter to People's Songs criticizing the generally sappy level of work during the campaign: "How a man with such a long road of sensible travels behind him, Alan Lomax, could expect such a shallow jingly and insincere number as 'I've Got a Ballot' to touch the heartstrings and conscience of the hard-hit masses, is a problem beyond me. I never did hear a living human being call his vote a 'magic little ballot.' People I have seen call their vote a number of things, none of which are nearly as cutiepie, as highly polite, as flippant, as sissy nor effeminate as this song. . . ."

Woody said that he'd complained during the campaign about the type of songs being sung, but "being a slow talker by nature,

I was cut down by such able lips as Lomax . . . and others, and others, who seemed so surely and certainly, so proudfully, to have it all figured out,'' and while Woody could be accused of indulging in a cheap post-mortem, it *was* certainly true that the People's Songs brigades had lost all sense of perspective in the heat of the campaign.

They believed they were making history. Lomax often described it as "the first singing campaign since Lincoln's." And Irwin Silber, on the very eve of the election, was predicting that Wallace would pull a respectable five to ten million votes, which surely would be enough to establish the new party permanently. The truth was, though, that about the only people left on the Progressive Party bandwagon were the members of the band. The public had come to perceive Henry Wallace as an ill-disguised front for the Communist Party, whose support he refused to disclaim. His final total was a meager one million votes, fewer even than the Dixiecrat segregationist candidate, Strom Thurmond, and no threat at all to the victorious Harry Truman.

Although there were those who remained optimistic in defeat— Alan Lomax wrote a song called "Keep A-Growin'," which included the memorable lyric: "When Wallace is elected in '52, We'll have a fair and happy land"—the effect of the campaign on People's Songs was terminal. After several months of ruminating on the role of folk music after the deluge, the organization collapsed in a heap in February of 1949.

Nor was People's Songs the only casualty of the Wallace debacle. The C.I.O. moved quickly to expel all remaining Communists, even whole unions (like the United Electrical Workers). Entertainers with left-wing reputations began finding it more difficult to get work as an insidious blacklist slipped into Hollywood, and later into New York's radio, television, and recording industries. The scourge spread through the government (where workers were investigated and forced to sign "loyalty" oaths), and then through academia. Anyone who'd ever joined a committee against racism, anyone who'd supported the "wrong" side in the Spanish Civil War, anyone who could be called a "premature antifascist," anyone who seemed suspiciously idealistic, one-worldy, permissive, well read, or immune to the lures of materialism, was suspect. The great fear caused many people with a blemish in their past—a petition signed, a brief fling with the Young Communist League (because they had good parties)—

to consider changing their names, moving to a new town, leaving the country. Some who'd never felt the faintest blush of altruism themselves were trapped because a brother or an uncle had. Very few escaped the panic; one way or another, no one was untouched.

But, as was often the case in difficult times, the hard-core Communists managed to negotiate the passage better than most. They still believed what they believed, and were proud of it. There always was a suitable Marxist interpretation for every new development, even Armageddon. As they had thirty years earlier, during the Palmer Raids, the leaders laid romantic plans for going underground. At the same time, they purified the ranks in a series of paranoid kangaroo courts (in which members usually were hauled up on charges of "white chauvinism" or some such thing, and tried by their erstwhile peers, a significant number of whom were—by this time—covert F.B.I. informants). Despite the subsequent history of witch hunts and hysteria, the naming of names and ruining of lives that seemed to convince the rest of America that there was indeed a Communist menace amok in the land, the party itself was no longer an even vaguely credible political force. It was more a rubble of former idealists, still arrogant and bitterly hoarding their own special truth, able to marshal small crowds to rally in support of the Rosenbergs and other martyrs, but burnt-out cases nonetheless . . . too old to deny the struggles and dreams of a lifetime, perpetrators and victims of a huge tragedy that very few others could understand.

By September of 1949, when a proletarian mob routed a Paul Robeson concert in Peekskill, New York, the Left was in utter disarray. The spectacle of beery blue-collar types attacking their would-be saviors, many of whom had been bused to the concert from New York City by various left-wing organizations, was a fitting symbol for the end of an era.

Woody's fortunes mirrored the times. Within weeks after the Peekskill riots, he and Marjorie delivered an 842-page version of *Seeds of Man* to an editor Alan Lomax had recommended at the publishing house of Duell, Sloane and Pearce. The editor mulled over the manuscript, and finally told Marjorie—Woody was waiting downstairs in the car, too nervous to be present for the final judgment—that it was the work of a great talent, but too huge and unwieldy, demanding too much work . . . and certainly far too sexy to be published in the United States. "Perhaps in England someday," she recalled him saying, and relayed the message to Woody in the car, who refused to make any further effort to sell the book.

The failure of *Seeds of Man* was a turning point. Already, in the year before it was submitted, Woody's creative energy had begun to dissipate. He seemed to dawdle his way through much of 1949, spending his days down on the beach with the kids, working only sporadically on his nearly completed manuscript. He still dabbled in poetry, and had developed a new habit of sending angry letters to public officials. He warned Attorney General Tom Clark that fear caused cancer and "if you are full of fears about socialism, sir, then you are surely spreading your killing fears through your own self." He wrote to President Truman in favor of disarmament: "Your face will look a whole lot blanker if the little atoms blow our world away—all of your pals and kinfolks along with the rest of us. I'm not ready to blow just yet. Your pal, Woody Guthrie."

The post-war rush of science and technology had left him at a loss. And yet, he was fascinated by the abstractions of modern science (if not the realities). Albert Einstein was a particular hero and, according to several accounts, Woody went down to Princeton University and visited the man one day. It was in response to Einstein's theories about the bending of light and the shape of the universe that Woody composed a song that seemed to fit the spirit of the times quite precisely:

> If I cain't go east nor west
> If I cain't go north nor south
> I can still go in and out
> I can still go round and round
>   And around and around and around . . .

He was writing as many songs as ever, but few of any consequence. His children's songs continued to be charming (but less consistently so) and his other songs remained perfunctory, with the notable exception of "Plane Wreck at Los Gatos (Deportees)," which he composed after reading, early in 1948, that a plane deporting migrant farm workers back to Mexico had crashed. It was the last great song he would write, a memorial to the nameless migrants "all scattered like dry leaves" in Los

Gatos Canyon, where the plane crashed, and with the memorable chorus:

> Goodbye to my Juan, goodbye Rosalita
> Adios mis amigos, Jesus y Maria.
> You won't have a name when you ride the big airplane.
> All they will call you will be . . . deportees.

The song, as he wrote it, was virtually without music—Woody chanted the words—and wasn't performed publicly until a decade later when a schoolteacher named Martin Hoffman added a beautiful melody and Pete Seeger began singing it in concerts.

Briefly, in 1949, Woody had a job (via Alan Lomax) writing and singing songs about venereal disease for a radio program sponsored by the U.S. government. He produced at least nine such songs, a few of them clever and moving, but most just plain outrageous:

> I tossed her two dimes and six pennies
> I stumbled up and down her slick trail
> Three weeks from then
> I had a fireball on my rail . . .

He seemed, in many instances—and especially in the seventeen songs he machine-gunned out after the Peekskill riots—to be simply filling in the blanks, using the same old songs and concepts over and over, plugging in new facts to fit old situations. There was a tired, resigned quality to much of his work. Even his poetry was becoming introspective and depressed. One day he scrawled across a huge sheet of wrapping paper:

> Yes, he's gone a little daffy trying to sweat out an honest
>   dollar
> But my man
> Could have been an artist
>   to say some good—
> But not no more
> Nope not no more
> Not anymore

The little apartment on Mermaid Avenue had become down-right claustrophobic with two babies in the back room. The level of tension was higher than ever before. Woody was drinking more heavily again, and behaving very strangely at times. One afternoon he lost his temper and came charging at Marjorie with a kitchen knife. She screamed, "Woody!" which shocked him back to his senses, after which he apologized profusely . . . but the incident stayed in her mind.

He wasn't as close to the children as he'd once been, either; no child seemed able to replace the memory of Cathy Ann. He changed their diapers, and took them to the beach and to Nathan's for hot dogs and sodas, and sang for them as always, but he wasn't quite as patient or loving as before, and often was unnerved by their constant chatter and bawling. His dealings with Arlo were espe-cially volatile. Arriving within months after Cathy's death and after years of Railroad Pete mythologizing, Arlo probably would have had a difficult time in any case. But the problem was compounded by the fact that he just wasn't a very pleasant baby, always croupy and colicky, whiney and uncomfortable. Woody tried hard, with sand castles and "Hoodises" and the little songs he would write; he gave Arlo the nickname "Dybbuk" or "Dyb" after he and Marjorie went to see the Yiddish play *The Dybbuk*, but his feelings always seemed somewhat mixed. Within a month after Arlo's birth, he wrote: "Today I slammed my door with hate and the wind blew back acrost little Arlo . . . and you cried all morning till I opened that same old door with love."

One afternoon, probably in the summer of 1949, John Henry Faulk came out to Coney Island to discuss a radio program Alan Lomax was trying to arrange for the two of them at CBS. Woody had custody of Arlo for the day, and suggested they all go out for a walk along the beach. As they walked along, Arlo started wailing for some reason and wouldn't stop. Woody scolded him once, twice, told him, "Shut up!" and Arlo cried all the more. Finally, as an incredulous Faulk looked on, Woody took a hand-ful of sand and jammed it in Arlo's mouth. "Goddammit, Woody, you crazy son of a bitch, cut that out!" Faulk screamed, and Woody, stung and embarrassed, tried his best to comfort his son.

Marjorie never found out about that incident, but she realized that the situation in the cramped apartment was growing desper-ate—and would become still worse in a few months when their third child was born. In November of 1949, she wrote to the

Guggenheim Foundation, pleading (unsuccessfully) for a fellowship for Woody: "Can you picture a man writing in the corner of a tiny room which is our living room, bedroom, entrance to all visitors, with children crying and laughing around his feet, with baby sitters asking questions of him every few minutes, with the phone ringing and I necessarily answering as briefly as possible and that is hardly brief because I conduct much of my administrative work on the phone?

"No one could ever call Woody a shirker if they could see the amount of work he does in a day . . . For his sake, I want him to feel that he contributes to the home. It is so important because it is these desperate feelings that grip him and make him miserable with himself, and sometimes us too. And then he runs away from us who love him and want him to be happy and becomes a hermit in the midst of a living world."

Despite the passionate tone of the letter, some friends thought Marjorie was growing colder and more distant. She was filled, as always, with motherly love and good cheer, but sometimes it seemed that her militant concern about other people's problems was merely a smoke screen, a way of keeping them from prying into *her* rather confused life . . . just as she'd once used her interest in "the issues" to fend off boys in the back seats of cars in Philadelphia. There was a certain theatricality to everything she did—a tendency to rationalize, to prettify, to put the best face on an increasingly awful situation. She tended to shrug off Woody's erratic behavior, knowing that it was quite impossible to deal with him rationally about things like his drinking and gadding about.

And so it was that when Woody was indicted for writing obscene letters to a young woman in California, and brought to trial in federal court, Marjorie's reaction was more resignation than shock.

After discovering the joys of erotica during the war—and finding that some women didn't at all mind receiving the fruits of his passion—Woody had continued his correspondence from Mermaid Avenue, mailing off letters to various prospects from right under Marjorie's nose, receiving few replies . . . but no real objections either. He was especially attracted to the other dancers in Martha Graham's group; he filled notebooks with fantasies about each of them and implied, at one point, that he'd dispatched several "half-hot" letters to the beautiful Pearl Lang, who had refused to answer.

It was a disturbing but not very threatening pastime—and was recognized as such by Marjorie and the other women who knew him and made allowances because he was Woody Guthrie, and considered rather odd to begin with. His fantasies remained essentially unchanged, very much like the letters he'd been sending Marjorie through the years, although he occasionally drifted off into more perverse areas. Reminiscing about his childhood adventures in a notebook addressed to Marjorie in 1947, he wrote: "I done things with bunches of kids that even you might think a little too far over on the side of animal heating: We played all sorts of lover's games out around the barn with the breeding stud and jack and mare. We played hotel and sweetheart games with the fat brood sow, the young colty, the baby calfs, the growing lambs, the goats, and had love affairs with the chickens." He defended these, though, saying that city kids no doubt had the same urges but a different set of opportunities.

Still, as innocuous as it seemed to Marjorie and the others who knew him, Woody's letter writing was bound to get him into trouble sooner or later. And it did in February of 1948. After receiving a letter from Lefty Lou's younger sister, Mary Ruth, telling of the untimely death of his cousin Jack Guthrie, Woody responded with great sympathy . . . and no small amount of passion. This letter, of February 18, 1948, was followed by two more—one of them apparently included unexplained newspaper clippings of grisly murders—which frightened and outraged Mary Ruth. She promptly brought them to the U.S. Attorney in Los Angeles, who said that Woody Guthrie should be prosecuted for sending obscene materials through the mails, and warned Mary Ruth that the man seemed dangerous and demented, and she would do well to contact the authorities if he ever crossed her path again. She decided to press charges.

Woody was outraged. He didn't believe that such a thing could happen. Immediately, he wrote a summary of the case in his defense, addressed to "The Honorable Court of My Feelings and to the Honorable Judge of My Conscience":

I stand here accused of being guilty of a so-called crime of writing a bundle of insulting love letters to a certain young lady here in this room.

If these letters had been letters of hate, I would feel guilty of every crime in the pages of our law books. These letters are not hate letters, they are all and every word of them love letters.

And if you can find a single drop, one little ounce of hurtful hate in all of these yellow pages of my letters to this girl, I'll be glad to let you chain me up and lock me away in the dirtiest jail in the world.

He went on to say that he'd only been trying to comfort the woman. "You've already heard that she was once in love with my cousin, Jack Guthrie, and how he died in the veterans hospital with tuberculosis. I thought in every way that I could offer her a pardnership with me."

His conscience was clear. In fact, he inferred that his legal troubles were of a piece with the HUAC hearings, the blacklist, and the other attempts to limit free expression. He saw himself as yet another victim of right-wing fanaticism and, to a great extent, Marjorie agreed and blamed the judiciary for treating the whole thing so seriously.

The legal proceedings dragged on for almost two years. Woody hired his pal Jimmy Longhi to be his lawyer and entered a defiant plea of not guilty at first, but later changed it to guilty with the understanding that Judge Harold Kennedy—who wasn't at all sympathetic to Longhi's arguments that his client was a creative man, perhaps a bit eccentric, but a genius nonetheless and engaged in the promulgation of art—would go easy on him. The trouble was, though, that Woody had no intention of going easy on the judge. He noted: "My judge can't even say the word, sex, without thinking the word, maniac. I'd ought to be up on the judging bench looking down at him . . ." And when the time came in late November of 1949, with Marjorie eight months pregnant, and the judge asked Woody if he regretted having sent the letters, he said he didn't regret anything. It was his right as an American to say or write anything he pleased. In fact, he was proud of what he'd done, if it really *was* obscenity, because "obscene" meant "of the low and common people," and that was what he wanted to be.

The judge sentenced him to 180 days in jail.

Woody told several friends that jail was what he'd been wanting all along. It would be a nice respite, he said, a quiet place where he could do some writing. Marjorie recalls: "I wanted to say to the judge, 'You can't do this. He'll just go in there and meet all sorts of interesting characters and have a fine old time. I'm the one who's going to suffer. I need him to take care of the kids.' But Jimmy didn't think that would help, so I didn't say it."

Actually, Woody did seem to have a pretty good time at the West Street jail. Christmas was approaching, and he decided to organize a gala pageant for the inmates. Meanwhile, Longhi was pulling every string he could find, trying to get the sentence rescinded . . . and, with a bit of luck and some friends in the right places, he succeeded in springing Guthrie after just a few weeks in stir. But when they released Woody on December 22, he was outraged. He wanted to stay in, at least until Christmas, and put on his pageant.

"Well, he had a point," Marjorie agreed. "The least they could have done was let him come back and do the Christmas show for those poor guys."

Although he tried not to show it, Pete Seeger was shaken by the failure of the Wallace campaign and the subsequent death of People's Songs. He'd invested a great deal of time, energy, and faith in both. And now all he had left was a handful of invitations to perform for the few remaining "progressive" groups that hadn't disappeared in the conservative tide. Aside from those, there just wasn't very much work to be had—not even for the man who'd become the most popular figure in folk music. One day Fred Hellerian, a veteran of Irwin Silber's youth group and Camp Wo-Chi-Ca, stopped in at the Seeger house and found Pete sprawled, very uncharacteristically, across a couch, despondent. "I guess," Pete said, "I ought to think about getting a job in a factory."

Hellerman was part of a sextet that gathered at Seeger's house to harmonize informally on Wednesday afternoons. The others were Lee Hays, Jackie Gibson, and her two roommates, Greta Brodie and Ronnie Gilbert. But Jackie soon went to work raising defense funds for the eleven Communist leaders on trial for conspiring against the U.S. government, and Greta Brodie drifted off, which left a quartet of Seeger, Hays, Hellerman, and Gilbert. They were an interesting combination: Hellerman's baritone fit snugly between Hays's bass and Seeger's tenor, and Gilbert had an impressive voice that seemed capable of almost anything. They began arranging some of the old folk standards to fit their talents, and started singing together publicly. They performed on Oscar Brand's weekly folk music program on WNYC as the No-Name Quartet, but soon decided to call themselves the Weavers, after a militant play by the German leftist Gerhart Hauptmann.

"It was still pretty informal," Hellerman recalls. "In fact, we almost broke up. Ronnie was supposed to go to California for some reason, and I was thinking of doing graduate work at the University of Chicago. But we really wanted to stay together, just for the pure pleasure of the singing, so Pete started thinking about how we could make some money. He said he'd sung down at the Village Vanguard before, and maybe we could get a job there."

The Weavers opened at the Vanguard in late 1949, at about the same time as Woody Guthrie was beginning his hitch at the West Street jail. Max Gordon, the owner of the club, had his doubts about the viability of a folk quartet, but he loved Seeger and figured that anything Pete was involved with couldn't be all bad. He needn't have worried, though: the Weavers soon were packing the Vanguard with enthusiastic fans, including a small circle of music business executives who were impressed by the group's sound and curious about its commercial possibilities. One of those most impressed was an aggressive young man named Howie Richmond, a former publicist just starting to establish himself as a music publisher.

Richmond's specialty was novelty songs, which happened to be very big at the time. Nonsense lyrics like "Mairzy Doats" and the Woody Woodpecker theme song had been doing quite well on the Hit Parade. Richmond recently had made a bundle on a modified novelty number called "Music Music Music" and was in the market for more. The first time he heard the Weavers, he sensed a gold mine—they were a classic novelty act, with at least a half dozen sure hits, like the Israeli folk song "Tzena Tzena Tzena," which, in a way, was reminiscent of "Music Music Music."

Nor was Richmond the only one impressed by the Weavers. Representatives from Decca Records and Columbia (whose man, Mitch Miller, would later become famous as the sing-along king of the late 1950's) were beginning to make inquiries; every night at the Vanguard seemed to bring a new offer. Pete Seeger remembered all the false starts and commercial fiascos the Almanac

Singers suffered, and decided not to fool around this time. He contacted a friend from the Wallace campaign, Harold Leventhal, and asked him to manage the group. Leventhal, a soft-spoken, cigar-smoking man, had dual qualifications for the job: he'd had experience in the music business as a song plugger for Irving Berlin, and he was a Communist, which meant he could be trusted. Leventhal, in turn, recruited a high school friend from the South Bronx, Pete Kameron, to share the responsibilities.

The first order of business was a recording contract. Mitch Miller of Columbia wanted to sign the group and, for a time, it looked like he'd get them. But then at the last minute Dave Kapp, the garrulous president of Decca, waded in with a better offer. Kapp had reservations about the group, though. Folk music had never sold, and he wasn't certain this bunch would do any better—he'd signed them mostly because Columbia had seemed so interested—and so he decided to present them to the public rather cautiously, wrapped in a gossamer cloak of violins and chorus provided by Gordon Jenkins, who, in addition to being Decca's house arranger and orchestra leader, had loved the Weavers from the moment he heard them at the Village Vanguard. Their first record was "Tzena Tzena Tzena" with a version of Leadbelly's lovely "Irene" on the flip side; on both sides, the label read: "by Gordon Jenkins and the Weavers."

"Tzena" did nicely enough as a novelty song, but the real surprise was "Irene," which became a huge success, the most popular song of 1950. By the spring of that year, the Weavers were the hottest thing in the record business: "Irene" was followed by a string of hits—"On Top of Old Smokey," "Wimoweh," "Kisses Sweeter Than Wine," and the song that Woody Guthrie had written in 1935 to commemorate a dust storm, "So Long, It's Been Good to Know You."

Meanwhile, Howie Richmond and his associate, Al Brackman, had made an important discovery. They'd found they could copyright and make money from traditional songs—songs that everyone had assumed were public property, like "On Top of Old Smokey"—if there was a "substantial change" in the music or lyrics. And, in fact, the Weavers were making substantial changes all over the place—smoothing out the rough edges, cutting and rewriting verses, emphasizing the choruses ("We need songs with good choruses," Howie Richmond told them). Not only were traditional folk songs changed, but also those composed by known

authors. Leadbelly's "Irene" was shortened and bowdlerized—
even the name was changed to "Goodnight Irene"—to fit the
public taste.

Folk music had reached the masses finally, but not quite in the
way Alan Lomax had hoped a decade earlier. It had come in
through the back door, as the idiot—'novelty"—stepchild of pop
music. It was greasy smooth and harmonious, very different from
the surging, anguished cry Lomax had fallen in love with in the
prison camps of the South.

To some purists, and also to political types like Irwin Silber,
the Weavers had sold out. The spectacle of Pete Seeger singing
in a tuxedo was disturbing enough; but the idea that he would be
a party to the dilution of the music he loved—for *commercial*
purposes—was mind-boggling. The Weavers even stopped coming around to the hoots that Irwin Silber still promoted, a last
vestige of the People's Songs days, as the group adopted a quiet
policy of avoiding the more obvious Left functions in the (vain)
hope that it might sneak past the blacklist. Seeger, who felt tremendously uncomfortable with that policy (and with other aspects
of commercial success: he wore red socks with his tuxedo), often
would sneak out and perform at radical fund-raising parties on
his own. For the most part, though, he was a willing participant
in activities he would have gagged on just a few years earlier.

Although the purists had a point, the Weavers were convinced
they were reacting in the most sensible way to a difficult political
situation. Harold Leventhal remembers telling Silber that the
group couldn't come to a hootenanny one night because they
were supposed to appear on a television show. Silber protested
that television was decadent and Leventhal responded: "Irwin,
take a drive up to Harlem and see how many antennas they got
there already." And it was true that even though the Weavers
were presenting only a pale copy of what the music could be,
they were breaking important new ground. What's more, for many
people—the veterans of the struggles of the 1930's and 1940's—
the Weavers were a reminder that the spirit of those times lived
on—undercover for now—but lived on nonetheless.

Woody certainly had no moral problem with adapting "So
Long" for commercial use when the time came. Ten years earlier, he had turned the song into a jingle for pipe tobacco . . .
and now it became a perky love song, with little of the humor or
bite—and none of the dust—of the original. He did most of the

revising himself, sitting on the floor of Gordon Jenkins's suite in a midtown hotel, writing down the words on a huge roll of wrapping paper. He also attended the recording session, where, he later bragged to his sister Mary Jo, the song was sung by a twenty-voice chorus and played by a thirty-piece orchestra. "They shipped 125,000 [copies of the record] in the first ten days it was released, and printed up already an unheard of 25,000 copies of sheet music to prime the markets," he wrote. "We get pretty close to a penny per record sold, three cents on every sheet of music peddled, six cents (I think) every time a radio station plays the record."

He also received a $10,000 advance, which arrived at just the right time. A few months earlier, in October of 1950, Marjorie had reached the end of her patience at Mermaid Avenue—the place simply was too small for three children—and decided that she was going to have to find a larger apartment, no matter the cost. She found one easily enough in the nearby Beach Haven garden apartment complex. Their new address was 59 Murdoch Court, a nondescript three-story building across from the Coney Island Hospital.

For the first time in their marriage, Woody and Marjorie actually had their own bedroom. Not only that, there was a glorified closet in which Woody could do his writing, a bedroom for the kids, a living room, a modern kitchen, and a terrace. The rent, however, was $120 per month—as opposed to $35 at Mermaid Avenue—and Marjorie had no idea how they would ever afford it. Luckily, the advance for "So Long" arrived within a month after they made the move. It was more than enough, of course, to take care of the rent; it also enabled them to repay their debts, buy a new car—Totsy III—and there even was $2,400 left over for Marjorie to invest in a long-held dream: the Marjorie Mazia School of Dance, which opened a year later in Sheepshead Bay, just a few blocks from their new apartment.

The impact of the Weavers rippled out through the folk music community. Even before "So Long" was recorded, Woody was benefiting from the group's success. Howie Richmond, always on the lookout for new material, heard about Woody's vast repertoire from Seeger and the others. He offered to publish and promote Woody's songs, paying him twenty dollars per week as an advance against royalties on an open-ended basis . . . which was something of a windfall at the time. The agreement was negotiated by Harold Leventhal's associate, Pete Kameron, who was serving as Woody's business manager while also being employed by the Richmond Organization—an interesting juxtaposition that didn't bother Woody very much. All he knew was that Kameron and Richmond had enough confidence in his future to pay him good money, with no guarantee that his songs would ever make them a penny, and no one had ever done that before.

What's more, Howie Richmond had given him a splendid new toy: a tape recorder, with the instructions that Woody was to sing everything he knew into the machine. He strung a rope across the bedroom and dangled the microphone from it—he hated to sing sitting down—and began making tapes. He recorded more than fifty hours' worth of songs in all, announcing the name of each and occasionally adding a note like: "I made this one up in the year of 19 and 41 when I was working for the folks at the Bonneville Power Authority." He sang without much expression or feeling, in a voice that had become dry and husky over time, with little of its former power.

His lyrics had power enough, though. Richmond developed the habit of listening to the tapes at home in the evening, with his girlfriend, and he was struck by the incredible diversity of all that Woody had seen and done. There were not, perhaps, as many Hit Parade-type songs as he had hoped, but there was something more. The songs made Howie feel patriotic. One he'd never heard before—"This Land Is Your Land"—could easily be the national anthem, he thought. And there were others, like "Pastures of Plenty," that existed on a level somewhere beyond pop music. He decided that the best strategy was to get those songs as wide a hearing as possible, even if it entailed some financial sacrifice; to *give* them to the schools if necessary, get them in the textbooks . . and they might become American standards that would be sung forever. It was a classy, low-key, long-term strategy, with the advantage of being both high-minded and astute. The sale of sheet music choral arrangements for "This Land," for example, might be enormous someday.

But not very soon. When Woody came round to the Richmond offices, as he often did in his increasingly aimless ramblings about the city, there rarely was much in the way of news for him. He didn't seem to mind, though. Just the idea that they knew him here, and were working for him, was enough. He'd spend hours with Pete Kameron, talking about things he'd read in the paper—long, looping discourses that often didn't have much of a point. A favorite topic now was Korea—he was siding with the North Koreans and Chinese Communists, of course (and even appeared at one of Irwin Silber's hoots with an outrageous song celebrating the death of an American general). Kameron was a man who enjoyed conversation, no matter how fractured it sometimes seemed—as opposed to Moe Asch, who'd grown tired of watching one of his favorite performers fall apart—and Woody began to hang out at the Richmond offices more frequently. He was tolerated with a mixture of amusement and chagrin. Once he showed up in the middle of the night, and simply decided to wait in the hall until morning. Unfortunately, though, the police found him sleeping there and he was arrested for loitering. The next day Howie Richmond was summoned to the precinct station and was ready to berate the cops for pinching a distinguished composer when he spotted Woody chatting blithely with the arresting officers, not at all disturbed by his night in jail. Richmond, and most other people, assumed that his brains had been scrambled by alcohol.

It was not a difficult assumption to make. He showed all the classic signs of alcoholism. There was a boozy, light-headed quality to him; his walk had become a lurch, and his speech often was decidedly slurred. What's more, he looked like a bum. Photographs taken of Woody in Washington Square Park in 1952 show him with a full beard and long, curly hair, looking very much like a biblical prophet . . . or a vision from a future time, the late 1960's, and a state of mind not yet even vaguely imagined.

One night he materialized at the posh Blue Angel nightclub, where the Weavers were playing, and couldn't get in because he was smelly and bedraggled and the headwaiter refused to believe he was a friend of the performers. Eventually he found Harold Leventhal, who dressed him up in a borrowed jacket with a table napkin for a cravat, and eased him in through the kitchen. It may have been that night, or perhaps another like it, that he stumbled into the back seat of Pete Seeger's car and fell asleep. Not noticing his passenger, Seeger drove all the way up the Hudson River to his new home in the little town of Beacon, New York, and was not entirely pleased when Woody hopped out at the end of the ride, an uninvited house guest. Pete didn't like seeing Woody very much anymore. "He's a pain in the neck when you're with him," Seeger would tell friends, then add guiltily: "But I kind of miss him when he's gone."

Marjorie found she was frightened by him. It was ironic: finally they were living in a nice apartment and had some money, and finally the commercial people were interested in Woody's work . . . but success hadn't helped at all. He was, in fact, worse than ever. He was without purpose, drifting, unable to concentrate on anything. He'd pretty much stopped writing and performing. He flunked an audition at Decca Records. He would forget which songs he'd sung into the tape machine for Richmond, and repeat the same ones over and over. He signed up for courses at Brooklyn College, paid for by the government under the G.I. bill, but dropped out after a month. He'd disappear for days at a time, then barge into the house—often at some ridiculous hour, often drunk—and flop out on the couch, oblivious, with a glazed, ugly look on his face, and Marjorie would be frightened then that he was going to lose his temper and do something awful. She wasn't sure *what* he was capable of doing anymore. One day she watched as the baby, Nora, started toward Woody—who was out on the couch as usual—and then stopped, as if she were scared of him; and Marjorie knew that even the baby sensed that there were times when Woody was potentially dangerous. There were other times, of course, when he seemed his normal self, but even those were beginning to take on an extravagant and frightening quality. One day he piled everyone into the car and went to Manhattan, where he bought four-year-old Arlo an eighty-dollar guitar, and one for the little girl next door as well, since she happened to be along for the ride.

Marjorie, fearing for her children, was beginning to think seriously about divorce. She decided to encourage his travels. She practically pushed him out the door each time he mentioned the possibility of visiting some long-lost friend or relative. Starting in 1949, he began to bounce around the country almost as persistently as he had in the mid-1930's. Each spring, it seemed, he would make a pilgrimage to the west coast, popping in on embarrassed friends and relatives along the way.

Usually he traveled alone, and by bus, but gradually, as the years passed, the trips became more chaotic. He'd drink away his bus fare and have to resort to his former, more desperate means of transportation. He hitched rides and hopped trains, both considerably more difficult for a man approaching the age of forty (and wavering noticeably at the edge of the road) than they'd been for a lithe teen-ager during the Depression. Nor was he able to charm his way to many bowls of chili anymore—the waitresses in the diners were young girls and he was a middle-aged drifter, bearded and shaggy, a bothersome, frightening old man.

In the spring of 1950, he made a particularly disastrous crossing to California and had to place an emergency call to his brother George to come and retrieve him near Barstow. George found him sitting dazed outside a truck stop—apparently they wouldn't let him inside—and unable to walk. His legs had cramped up, he said, coming across the desert. His clothes were in tatters and it had been a long time since he'd shaved or bathed. There were no explanations, though, not even after George spent several days nursing him back to health. There *never* seemed to be explanations—to anyone—anymore. Woody hadn't ever been much of a talker, and he was becoming less of one now.

An odd thing was happening, too, with his writing. It was beginning to bulge and warp crazily, like images in a fun-house mirror. In some ways, it seemed a natural progression—or, perhaps, disintegration—from his army letters to his children's songs to *Study Butte* to the madder, free style he was slipping into: the increased rhyminess, the prolixity, the confusing attempts to replicate obscure dialects. And still, beneath all the embellishments, there was a strange, dizzy power to it.

By 1951, when he initiated another of his erotic correspondences, his language had become swirling and vertiginous, a joyous spew of words that strained against all conventions and was, at once, brilliant and quite mad. The object of his affections this time was Jolly Smolens, a former secretary at People's Songs and occasional singing partner of his, and the excuse for writing was a scheme he had to start a new singing group, a looser (and racially integrated) alternative to the "Weavery people." Quickly, though, the letters turned to more basic matters:

Since you come here and swum here the other night I've been seeing what you might spiritually and soulfully describe as little shafty, shifty drafty drifty beams and rays and legs of lights and shapely shadows of old hopes too olden gone for any earthling to have to even to try to tell or to describe to any other worldster.

It's been a little more than one year ago now since my ownself and MGM have really and truly enjoyed what you might roughly describe as zexxzzuoll intrakourzen; and so, I guess, you just made my old crazy cup to run and to spill over all nineteen of its sides and edges. . . .

Jolly Honey Girl, you know, us boys surely must be bilt a good bit different from you galz. You know, honey girl, I've walked and paced and tramped and tromped up and down this here room here and have shottoff andspewedoff and squirtedoff twenty or fifty million seeds of man out from the headend of my penis you know, just like a cottonwoody tree, just sorta thinking of how warm and how juicey and how nice and good and how hot and how fine your vagina's lips are going to feel sucking around the shape and form of my maley organ, until, and until, my own balls (testicles) and coddy sack, honey, meet and greet and rub up real tightagainst your own womb lips and openings and your little hole of sweetness . . .

The references to "seeds of man" had begun to proliferate in his poems and letters (and as the last title for his Chisos Mountains odyssey). He obviously was quite concerned about his virility, which seemed to be fading . . . along with much of the rest of his personality. His life had become a series of long silences, interrupted by occasional antic outpourings of words on paper.

The rhyming games and linguistic anarchy extended even to his address (Beach Haven became "Bitch Heaven" in "New Jerk Titty") and to his own name, which he garbled and distended and mocked. He signed himself "WWWW Gee Gee Gee Gee" and "WW Geehawker" and "Goody Wuthrie" and "Woodridge Duthridge" and, quite frequently, "Woodvine Twiner" as well as many others. His handwriting, which once had been tight and precise, began to spill out of line and past margins. In fact, he now had two distinct handwritings—his normal script and an austere, terrifying print that he used mostly when drunk or angry. Often, he wrote with different-colored pens and pencils—sometimes each word was a different color, sometimes each *letter*— and his scrawl took on the tense, garish look of a kidnap note. He left his mark everywhere—in marginal notes on his typewritten letters, in comments scribbled across the pages of the books he read. In October of 1950, when Moe Asch re-released *Dust Bowl Ballads*, Woody wrote all over his copy of the booklet of lyrics and pictures that Asch issued to accompany the album. Every picture required a comment: "I sung in many a tent like this—WG" and "and I sung and talked with a few 100 like this—WG."

He had acquired, it seemed, the habits of a chronic graffiti artist . . . only worse, because it was his own life and work he was defacing, his own self that he seemed alienated from. He left his name everywhere; it was affixed dutifully on every page of every letter he wrote, as if he were trying to convince himself that he really was still there.

In February of 1951, Woody suffered an acutely ruptured appendix and nearly died. The problem was, he later wrote to Jolly Smolens, that the doctor had mistaken his abdominal pains for a stomach virus that was making the rounds in Coney Island. Woody drank a bottle of milk of magnesia and ate several bars of Ex-Lax to ease the cramps, then passed out and was taken to Coney Island Hospital. "Normally, this is not a serious operation," Marjorie wrote to his friends, asking them to come visit. "But leave it to Woody to be the exception to the rule. He was truly lucky to survive."

He remained in the hospital for several weeks after, receiving visitors and entertaining the other patients. He made up songs about his medications, the nurses, and the injections they gave him. Al Brackman, Howie Richmond's associate, brought him several cartons of cigarettes one day, which Woody promptly tore open and distributed to the other smokers on the ward. He seemed, his visitors reported, a bit loopy from all the medication, but happier than he'd been in some time.

One of his visitors was a kid Woody had never seen before. He was about twenty years old, dressed like a cowboy and carrying a guitar. He said his name was Buck Elliot and that he'd been an admirer of Woody's for many years. He asked if he might play something for him on the guitar. Woody winced, and said the guy in the next bed had just gotten off the operating table. Then he said, "Go over to the window. . . . See my kids down there?" Buck saw the kids. "Why don't you go out and visit with them?"

But Buck Elliot wasn't to be disposed of so easily. When

Woody was released from the hospital, Buck started hanging around the house. Then he moved *into* the house, another in the series of wayward kids who'd established residence with the Guthries over the years. Buck's real name, it turned out, was Elliot Adnopoz. He was from Brooklyn, a doctor's son. He'd fallen in love with cowboys and rodeos as a child but, unlike most children, had never let go. He wore a cowboy hat, and tried to talk like he thought a cowboy would, and played the guitar because that's what cowboys did. He'd first heard Woody Guthrie on Oscar Brand's radio program, and then saw him perform at one of Irwin Silber's hootenannies, and decided to incorporate into his routine the image of the dusty little stranger who ambles into town, writes a ballad about social injustice, then hops a train into the sunset. Which distinguished him not at all from the dozens of other kids who'd knocked on Woody's door over the years, enraptured by his legend. What did distinguish Buck Elliot—who soon changed his name to Ramblin' Jack Elliot for no apparent reason—was his persistence, and his musical talent, and the fact that he was an uncanny mimic. He could imitate Woody perfectly. It was downright eerie, and Woody would shake his head and giggle: "He sounds more like me than I do."

Intrigued, Woody took the kid under his wing. He brought him to parties, took him for walks along the beach ("I've had more salt water go in and out of my asshole than you've ever *seen*," he'd tell the kid when recounting his merchant marine adventures), played the guitar with him for hours, taught him everything he knew and several things he didn't. Afternoons, they would drive along the Belt Parkway in Totsy III, Woody with his chin jutted out, a quart of Ballantine ale between his legs, thumbs hooked onto the very bottom of the steering wheel, keeping up a constant patter: "Greyhound bus drivers say this is the most comfortable way to drive. . . . They learn it in bus drivers school. . . . Nine jillion Greyhound bus drivers drive exactly like this here. . . . Helps the reflexes. . . . You can reach down and stash the booze real quick if the cops come. . . ."

He was nonplussed by the kid. He was flattered, but also frightened. Ramblin' Jack was such a good mimic that he was beginning to ape the elements of Woody's disintegration: the lurching walk, the slurred speech that seemed to burst forth after considerable effort, the little shakes and uncertainties, the distance, the fogginess. . . . Woody could look at Jack and see himself fading. He drank to stop thinking about it, and the drinking made him worse—and Jack, a mirror, reflected that too. He'd get angry at Jack, make fun of him, humiliate him, tell him to get lost, but the kid was very persistent.

In September of 1951, Marjorie sent Woody and Jack out to paper Coney Island with announcements of the opening of the Marjorie Mazia School of Dance. Woody wrote proudly of the school—and its 150 pupils—to his sister Mary Jo, but had other, less charitable feelings about it too. Marjorie was so wrapped up in the place that she seemed to have little time for him anymore. He suspected she was having affairs with other men—the school was just a smoke screen—and became wildly jealous. There were several drunken episodes, one of which apparently took place in the school itself, in front of her students. She kicked him out of the house, but he begged his way back in again. She threatened him with divorce. She was afraid for her children, she told friends. She wanted him out of her life . . . but he always seemed able to arouse her sympathy, and she relented a dozen different times. Their divorce scenes were becoming a set routine, part of the dizzy horror of his life.

After one such episode, in November of 1951, he decided to go to Florida—the only state he'd never seen. He wanted to visit Stetson Kennedy, an old friend who was living picturesquely in an abandoned bus at the edge of Beluthahatchee Swamp, just south of Jacksonville. Kennedy was a quietly outrageous character, a writer and activist best known for infiltrating the Ku Klux Klan in the 1930's and exposing its secret rituals in a book called *I Rode With the Ku Klux Klan*. In 1950 Kennedy had decided to run for the U.S. Senate as a write-in integrationist candidate. The campaign garnered him several hundred votes and the renewed enmity of the Ku Klux Klan, which threatened periodically to burn him out.

By the time Woody arrived at the Jacksonville bus station a year later, the Kennedys had settled into a life of laconic vigilance at the swamp. They still lived in the abandoned bus, which was equipped with a lean-to kitchen, a privy located behind a palmetto clump, and a cache of small arms and ammunition to fend off the Klan . . . if it ever came to that. They spent their days lolling about, watching the alligators cruise through the cypress and water lilies, and making sporadic attempts to build a dam and create a lake that, Stetson was positive, would turn the property into an attractive residential area (which it did, twenty years later).

Woody was asleep on the pavement, his head propped on his guitar, and wearing five shirts—he often served as his own suitcase on the road—when Stetson came to retrieve him at the bus station. He was given an outdoor hammock with zip-up mosquito netting to sleep in, and slipped easily into the swamp life. His arrival coincided with the appearance of a thousand gallons of apple juice at Beluthahatchee—a payment in kind to Stetson's neighbor, a lawyer named Gerald Hart, from a backwoods client— which they allowed to sit in the sun and ferment until it was potent, and then they began selling the stuff to the locals in gallon jugs. They also consumed a fair amount of it themselves, and used the emptied jugs as targets for the daily rifle drills that Woody organized in anticipation of the KKK. He had found an old Swiss army rifle, and developed the technique of balancing it against a log and shooting it off like a mortar. Woody was so adamant about the Klan threat that one night Kennedy and his friend Hart staged a mock (and decidedly drunken) Klan attack, firing a volley over Woody's hammock which sent him spinning out and careening through the barbecue coals.

But while he appeared to be enjoying himself and forgetting his domestic troubles, Woody was quietly sending a series of desperate letters to Marjorie. On November 14, he wrote: "I've never been this miserable in my life before. . . . I never felt this lonesome and doneful before. . . . [If you knew] just how blue and empty I'm feeling, you'd tell your heart to open up your shut doors and let this crazy boy in just another time."

He tried several different strategies in the next few days, flattering her, writing love letters, promising to go back to work again, describing in detail an idea for a new book about a man who gets knocked down a flight of stairs in a whorehouse and wakes up in the mental ward of a hospital, promising to pick up *Seeds of Man* once more and shorten it so it could be sold commercially, and, finally, confronting her defiantly:

No matter how far this divorce between us has gone.
No matter how many good points it has for you and me
  to love freely.
I will never sign my signature of agreement to it.
I'll stop it every possible way I can.

> *For the sake of our kids and for the sake of all of us as a*
> *   family, I'll never, ever, to my dying day agree*
> *To this crazy divorce idea.*

After pleading for mercy by mail for about a week, he returned to New York to see if his letters had won him a reprieve. They hadn't. Marjorie was standing fast this time. Apparently, he arrived on her doorstep in rough shape and she wouldn't even let him into the house, so they spent a tense afternoon driving around Coney Island in the car, talking it out. Afterwards, he returned to the city and, still unwilling to give up, started writing to her again:

> *To the exact extent*
> *That I let myself drift away from your love*
> *Eternal, endless*
> *And awful and terrible calamity will hit me in every way.*

It was an ugly winter. He wandered about, sleeping on friends' couches, touching Moe Asch, Pete Kameron, and the other regulars on his hit list for money. He would disappear for weeks at a time. No one was ever sure whether he was in town or out, nor were many people curious. When a young academic, interested in Woody's music, asked Marjorie where he could be located, she said bitterly, "I don't know. He went out to mail a letter three months ago, and I haven't seen him since." The word spread around town that Woody was on the skids, and friends winced when they saw him coming. Soon he ran out of couches and moved into a series of fleabag hotels, some of them rancid places on the Bowery.

Occasionally, he would try to pull himself together and visit the children. After spending a day in March watching them frolic in the snow, he wrote a lovely little piece describing them at play and concluding: "I know I never will be able to figure out why it is that this old crazy private landlord profity system makes it so hard for me and my family to stick together. . . ."

In April, he turned up in Okemah. He wanted to spend a few days with his old friend Colonel Martin, who now was a bartender, but Colonel's wife was horrified by the stench and sight of him, and wouldn't let him in the house. He took a room at the

Broadway Hotel instead, and roamed the old, familiar streets of the sad and ghostly town, remembering the days when it was vital and optimistic, noticing the changes—the old Fort Smith and Western depot torn down, the desolation along Broadway, the general torpor. He walked over to the schoolhouse hill, and around back to where his gang house had been. Of course, it was gone too. He sat evenings in the hotel writing long, desperate letters to Marjorie, attributing all his recent failings to alcohol and tobacco, and promising to kick both habits. "I wish you'd grab my next bottle out of my hand and break it over my head. . . . Some of the best folks I know waste and wreck their whole lives fighting this crazy habit. . . . To kick me out the door like you do (when I need help most of all) does not help. . . . Let's don't kick anybody out our door anymore. The use of alcohol and tobacco are both a dizzy kind of sickness and they make me weak enough without your pushing me out." And there was one particular kind of weakness he seemed most concerned about: "I feel terribly afraid of everything connected with the act of sex . . . the sudden loss of this sexual ability, my fear of not being sexually attractive all add up to a very strong, nervous, fearful feeling that amounts to hate. . . . I knocked all my sexual attraction out of myself simply simply out through the necks of all those sickly bottles. . . . That bottle is my disease, and just about my only disease." He signed one of the letters: "Your man once, Woody," and another simply: "Me lost."

He had paid a month in advance at the Broadway Hotel (fifteen dollars), but stayed only a few days. He was back in New York again by early May and, in a poignant twist that was calculated to have an effect on Marjorie, had moved into the very same little rooming house on Fourteenth Street where they'd first made love a decade before, almost to the very day. There, he started rewriting *Seeds of Man* again, in longhand, on the backs of his original pages, with a seventeen-year-old Marjorie as a character—his girlfriend, replacing Helen Cliffman. He hoped his efforts at productive labor would win her back. He promised, once more, to quit drinking. He wrote her a cutie-pie letter, which began: "Dear Pritty Sweety Lovely Dovely Sugartit Marjorie," and held out the promise of "a new kiss I got in from the factory," and also the resumption of all-night "skadges" (leg massages) as in the old days. He signed it: "Yore other boy."

As a matter of fact, Marjorie *had* gone and gotten herself another boy: Tony Marra, her auto mechanic. It was, admittedly, a liaison born out of desperation. She was terribly lonely, especially after the last few harrowing years; and she also hoped the specter of a big, tough Italian boyfriend would fend off Woody, and convince him it was over. But when she found out where he was and what sort of mood he was in, her heart softened and she suggested they go out on a "date," where, she thought, she would explain the new situation and offer the possibility of getting together every so often.

The date was a disaster. Woody couldn't tolerate the thought of another man. The next day, in his severe print-style handwriting, he wrote:

> Thanks once more for clearing up all the airs and atmospheres between us. I feel lots freer now in a very good way to go out and locate myself a womban. I'm so very sorry I cant go along with your ideas about birth control. I'm not dictating to you any such ball and chainery as to ask you not to have any more babies for your next husband. You wouldn't even think of asking or taking my advise on any such personal sexual matters and I kindly believe I'll be highly unable to zip my zippering of creation as you so modernly suggest. Life owes me one more wife and three more kids and you might as well prepare yourself to hear the news. . . .
>
> I know how you're smiling that smile of perfection of yours. I know I can hear you psychoanalyzing every word I write and every breath so far I've breathed. I took sick of your analyzing and your double analyzing a good long time ago. I hate your nagging. I hate your bossyness. I hate your weak attempts to be my lord and my master. I hate to hear you preach to me about what all is wrong with me when if I only wished to fall so low I could lecture and preach to you three times as many things twice as wrong and truer and deeper wrong than all your lectures to me have been.
>
> You're not my soul nor my conscience nor any kind of a goddess that I've got to live and breathe and do and act just soso to please. I'll spend the rest of my life trying my level best to displease you in every earthly way I know how. . . .

The letter went on for several more pages, and became still more vituperative. He accused her of having an affair with Uncle Sid, the family dentist, and a lesbian relationship with one of the baby-sitters. He repeated the line "No more Marjorie" over and over, and his handwriting fell apart at the end, except for the last few words: "I hate everything about you."

It was an alarming letter—he never did mention Tony—and so, in its way, was the apology that followed the next day:

> I don't claim to lie to myself nor to you nor to our three fine kids and tell you that your present affair with Tony doesn't hurt me, because it does. . . . [But] none of your Tony Boys can ever miss you, crave you, need you, and want you not half as much as I do. . . . I don't even think I could come to an erection or a sexual ejaculation or an orgasmic climax with any other woman, and I highly doubt if you could come to such a healthy and normal conclusion with any other Tony as you've learned to come to with me. Please come back to me Marjorie. Be my helping hand again. Please don't let me die again. Woody once again.

Two days later, on the evening of May 15, Marjorie came home from a night on the town with Tony and found Woody there instead of the baby-sitter. He had cut the telephone wire and was holding the scissors in his hand. She could tell, in that first instant before either of them did or said anything, that he was beyond reason; his eyes were glazed and crazy, his lips tight, and then he came after her with the scissors.

She ran down the hall to the bedroom, thinking: It takes two people to have a fight, and I'm not going to do it. I'm just going to go limp. She flopped on the bed. Then he was on top of her, and she didn't know where the scissors were, but he was pummeling her with his fists and, she noticed, he seemed to be frothing at the mouth. The odd thing was that neither of them was making any noise. She wasn't screaming, and he wasn't saying anything at all. And another odd thing she noticed: he hadn't been drinking. He was sober, and yet crazier than she'd ever seen him drunk.

Then he stopped hitting her, got off the bed, and slumped into a chair, heaving, his eyes still mad and glary and staring at her.

"Woody," she said as calmly as she could, "I have to go to the bathroom."

He rose partway from the chair, and seemed ready to follow her. She moved with a rush to the bathroom, and slammed the door. She figured he'd followed her and was waiting outside. It was possible that he still had the scissors. She tried to collect her thoughts. If she could make it to the terrace, out through the children's room, she could go to the neighbors' and call the police. He wouldn't hurt the children. They were sleeping—was it possible that they'd slept through the whole thing?—and she had to believe he wouldn't hurt them, and she knew she had to get out of the bathroom. She started, then stopped. Was the terrace door locked? She wasn't sure.

She dashed again, and then she was pounding on the neighbors' windows, and then calling the police, who came quickly. She went out to the hall and followed the cops in, a few steps behind, and she heard one of them say to Woody, quite calmly, "Want a cigarette?"

"Yup."

He was on the bed now. The cop was sitting in the chair. "You know," the officer said. "I know who you are. I know your songs."

They started to talk quietly, and Marjorie slipped in and listened. After a while, she said, "Woody, you're sick . . . and you weren't drinking, and you shouldn't be that way. I don't know what it is and you don't know what it is, but you're sick."

She called Earl Robinson (who'd moved back to Brooklyn after being blacklisted in Hollywood and was giving guitar lessons at Marjorie's school) and asked him to come over to help. Then she sat down on the bed with Woody, and comforted him until morning.

That day, May 16, Earl Robinson drove them to Kings County Hospital, and Woody checked himself in. He remained there for three weeks in a detoxification program for alcoholics. Although no diagnosis was made, hospital records noted a "bluntness of affect" (meaning that Woody didn't talk or express himself very much) and "sensitivity in the sexual sphere with regard to the last time he slept with his wife." He was released on June 5, and returned to the little room on Fourteenth Street and began writing letters to Marjorie again. He seemed determined to convince her that alcohol was his only problem: "All my running and my running and my blind cowardly running hasn't been because of any fault of yours nor any fault of my own. I loved you every time I walked out from you. . . . It was the dope in me, the alcohol in me that forced me to behave so wildly. It turned me into a senseless raving idiot.''

Her refusal to sleep with him—his violent attack had become, apparently, no more than that in his mind—was the "biggest pain I've so far felt," and he intended to work hard to regain her love. In that respect, he thanked Tony for "doing such a fine job keeping me sober. . . . If he does my job better than I can do it, he's the best man, anyhow, and he deserves all of the pleasures that you and the kids can give him.''

In addition to his letters now, there were constant phone calls and visits. Marjorie recorded each new episode in her day book:

June 5—"Woody out [of the hospital]. Long walk and talk. Jack [Elliot] here.''

June 7—"Beach all day. Woody is upset, calls. Goodbye!''

June 8—"Woody calls and we talk. And we talk tonight too . . .''

June 10—"Woody here, upset.''

June 11—"Drunk again. Cisco.''

June 12—"Woody here. Drive Woody's things to New York.''

June 13—"Woody's here. Tries a last time. Drunk and ready to die.''

On June 14, Woody called her and said he was going to go up on the roof and jump off the building and kill himself if she didn't ditch Tony and let him back in again. He sounded confused and drowsy, and she couldn't quite figure out where he was, but gambled that it was Fourteenth Street and called the cops—it took several phone calls before she found the right precinct—and then had Tony drive her in.

They arrived to find the police there with Woody, who was stretched out on the bed in his dingy cubicle, apparently drunk and obviously bewildered. An ambulance came and he was taken off, to Bellevue Hospital this time. He later wrote to Seeger that he spent a week on the "padded cell floor" and then three weeks on a normal ward where the doctors decided to "whack off my hernia.''

At Bellevue, Woody's mental problems were diagnosed as "schizophrenia," but the doctors seemed rather puzzled by his case. One of them told Marjorie, "Mrs. Guthrie, your husband is a very sick man, and we don't know what to do with him."

So they let him out on July 15, the day after his fortieth birthday, and he showed up at Beach Haven that afternoon—much to Marjorie's surprise—drunk and disorderly. The events of that evening aren't entirely clear, but Woody apparently attacked one of the children—possibly Arlo—because he refused to go to bed. The next day, having meekly checked back into the drunk tank at Kings County Hospital, he wrote: "Alcohol made me thrash my kids with my fists because they played around my house too loud when (I figured) they should have been asleep. I took my fists to my own wife in one of my senseless, alcoholic fits of jealousy."

Whatever really did happen that night, it plagued Woody for months after. He apologized continually to the children in the notebooks he kept during his various hospital stays:

> I'll never lose my temper again in that old alcohol stuff that drove me to hit you that night (like I did) because you wouldn't go to sleep on your bed, remember? I remember it now so plain that it hurts me now even worse than it hurts you. That's the worst mistake I ever made in my born days. I say to you be nicer to your kids than I was to mine. I take it all back. I regret it to my last day. I regret it. I do regret it. Forgive me for it. Please forgive me for it. Forget it ever did happen. Let me forget that I got so angry that night and hit you so hard. We'll both forget it, won't we? We'll both pretend it never did happen, won't we? Yes we will. Yes, we will.

And:

> Arlo you must have known yesterday in that back seat of Totsy car that you were saving my lost life when you told me that I was a better daddy than that other one. I had 10,000 deadly doubts that riz up and flew when you told me that. No doctor will ever be able to do me as much good as you did yesterday in Totsy's back seat.

Despite his terrible guilts and fears, Woody recovered his spirits at Kings County rather quickly. Once again, he was absolutely

positive that he would conquer his drinking problem and resume
his life as before. He even began writing songs:

> Pacing this ward in Bellevue
> Pacin' Kings County too
> I'm gonna pace on outta my psycho ward
> Gonna pace back, baby, to you.

Which was precisely what Marjorie was concerned about. She
was emotionally exhausted by now, frustrated and angry and
wondering what *really* was the matter with Woody. One thing
was clear: she couldn't have him bouncing in and out of mental
hospitals, and terrorizing her family between padded cells.

She began making phone calls, hoping to find someone who'd
understand Woody's problem and be able to do something about
it. One of the few reasonable suggestions came from Dr. Joseph
Vortis, who was Earl Robinson's brother-in-law. He suggested
that there was a new insulin shock therapy program at Brooklyn
State Hospital that might prove effective in Woody's case. She
made inquiries there, and then visited Woody in Kings County
and explained the situation to him, and he agreed to transfer
voluntarily to Brooklyn State for sixty days of treatment and evaluation. He was moved there on July 22, 1952, and subjected to
an intense series of physical and psychological examinations.
Hospital records include a vivid description of Woody's condition
at that time:

> He was noted as a thin, scrawny looking white male look-
> ing somewhat older than his 40 odd years, because of his
> lined face and weather-beaten features. On the ward he is
> co-operative with ward personnel and mixes and talks with
> other patients. At interview he is quite co-operative but
> appears withdrawn and emotionally inaccessible. He is ex-
> tremely fidgety and does not seem to be able to sit still for
> a moment. He is constantly jumping up from his chair and
> walking around the room or lighting a cigarette. Patient's
> movements are jerky and athetoid in nature, which makes
> him appear loose-jointed. Many of these movements are
> random and purposeless. His speech too is hesitant with
> many jerky pauses. He exhibits inconstant facial grimaces,
> the most frequent of which is a sniff. His face, despite all

the random movements, remains expressionless with only an occasional smile brightening his features. The patient is at all times coherent and relevant, he tends to be somewhat rambling in his productions and when talking becomes preoccupied so that it is difficult to interrupt him. He is quite productive and spontaneous but speaks in a jerky ebb and flow fashion with many hesitancies and pauses. He exhibits no language deviations and reaction time is normal. His affect is markedly dulled. He can talk about what must be to him highly emotionally charged material, without showing any visible signs of emotional disturbance. This marked blunting plus the patient's athetoid movements form a striking contrast. In speaking of his past, he admits to have periods of marked depression, from which he would try to escape with alcohol. Patient exhibits no psychotic trends. He has no ideas of grandiosity, persecution or reference. During the interview, he spoke at great length about his early childhood days in Okla., of the songs he learned from his mother, his father's drinking and the horror of watching his mother during her spells. There appeared to be feelings of ambivalence toward the father. Patient then roughly traced his life through his first marriage and a brief try at respectable conformity in Texas, his years of wandering the west and mid-west as a minstrel and interpreter for the migratory workers, who were devastated by the dust storms and the great depression. His story is essentially the same as that given by his wife [in the admitting statement]. It is since he was discharged from the Army in 1945 that he feels he has hit the skids. He stresses the marked sense of failure that he tried to drown with alcohol, the patient goodness of his wife as contrasted with his own fits of drunken jealousy and impulsive wandering. He is well oriented in all spheres; recent and remote memory good; retention and recall good; counting and calculation adequate; school and general knowledge good; abstractions excellent; insight partial; judgment good. Physical examination on admission essentially negative.

The examiner—a Dr. Marlowe—concluded that "this is one of those cases which stubbornly defies classification. In it, it has elements of schizophrenia, psychopathy and a psychoneurotic anxiety state, not to mention the mental and personality changes occurring in Huntington's chorea, at this patient's age. As such, examiner chooses to defer diagnosis until such time as further observation has made the picture clearer.''

The tentative, almost offhand inclusion of Huntington's chorea—Woody, no doubt, had mentioned it when recounting the family history—was the first official suggestion that Woody might, indeed, be suffering from the same disease that killed his mother. But the young examiner obviously was confused about the nature of the illness, since he didn't realize that the ''psychoneurotic anxiety state'' and all those other conditions he was describing were *symptoms* of Huntington's chorea. But then, he'd probably never seen a case of it before. It was so rare that it existed, for most doctors, merely as another oddity in their medical school texts. They learned only that it was a hereditary, degenerative disease of the central nervous system which featured random, purposeless movements (thus it was called chorea—as in ''choreography''), as well as mental imbalance, and that nobody knew very much about what caused it. It was, at best, a midterm exam question, and certainly not the sort of thing a young doctor expected to encounter in real life.

But it was enough to rouse the interest of Dr. Marlowe's superiors at Brooklyn State Hospital. On August 20, just before Woody was scheduled to begin the insulin shock therapy, a conference was held to review his case. It was decided that a final diagnosis not be made until a neurologist was consulted, and that the insulin treatments be postponed pending the neurologist's findings.

Woody was told about none of this. All he knew was that groups of doctors were inspecting him periodically, and that they asked about his mother on several occasions. It was odd, he thought, that they were so curious about his mother, since he was absolutely convinced that his problem was alcoholism, pure and simple, and it was his *father* who'd been the drunk in the family.

In a letter he never mailed, he told his sister Mary Jo not to worry about him. ''You're just associating me with mama, thinking surely since she broke down and died like she did over those long, slow years that I am bound and destined to break the same as she did. All the good doctors I talk to tell me there is no

connection between Huntington's Korea which mama had, and
my own trouble whatever my own will be named and labeled."

Having made a brave stab at convincing himself of that, he
turned his attention to the insulin shock treatments he was about
to receive. "I was scared witless when I first moved over here,"
he wrote to Seeger, "and heard everybody moan and groan in
their comas and shocks, but [then] I saw how they laff their heads
off telling one another what they screamed about." Usually,
though, he wasn't so sanguine. He saw the grim hospital ward
as a prison, where "every step leads me to another barred window and another locked door." The only reason he was willing
to tolerate such agony, he wrote, was the prospect that Marjorie
might love him again.

As always, he was deeply affected by the human suffering
around him. He saw the men on his ward as victims of the capitalist system. He studied and described them with love and respect: the kid who talked to himself and wrote all day on a pad
of paper with no lead in his pencil; the guy who stood in the
bathroom all day wiping himself with toilet paper ("Who was it
that made this man feel so dirty?" he wondered); the combat-
fatigued veteran who paraded around singing, "I'm a schizo-
freeny . . ."; the man in the bed next to him who peed defiantly
on the floor each night. He played chess with a kid who'd discuss
his every move with an imaginary partner, and he also played
with another veteran who would dream each night that he was
back in some godforsaken jungle, and scream hysterically and
tear his bedclothes and sheets to shreds. "Most patients are of
such a sensitive type," he wrote, "that they seem in many ways
to run a step or two ahead of most average people. They have an
odd, curious way of knowing at one glance almost all there is to
know about anybody."

When the other patients glanced at Woody, they saw—no
doubt—just another loony. He was the guy who sat at the table
all day writing the letter that he never sent. He wrote hundreds
upon hundreds of pages in the months that he spent in Brooklyn
State Hospital in 1952. Some of it was as powerful as anything
he'd ever written, all of it was directed to Marjorie, some via
Tony, most of it pleading for another chance, reviewing the events
of the past months and years, apologizing for his behavior, worrying about Tony taking over his "rightful" place, and describing his physical condition in precise detail: "Here's my funny

old feeling over me again. That lost feeling . . . out of control, jumpy, jerky, the least little thing knocks my ego down below zero mark. Everything cuts into me and hurts me several times more than it should. . . . No bodily pains; just like my arms and legs and hands and feet and my whole body belong to someone else, not to me. . . .''

He tried to write songs, much as he always had, penciling in a title at the top of a page . . . but usually the words didn't come and all that was left was a series of titles: "Why Did It Hit Me?" "I Wanta Go Home," "Drunkard's World," "A Little Faith," "Social Drinker," "My World Is Hell," and so on. Occasionally he would squeeze out a short verse:

> *What am I gonna do*
> *What am I gonna do*
> *What am I gonna do*
> *When my shock time comes?*

On September 3, he was examined by the consulting neurologist—a Dr. Perkins, according to hospital records—who immediately saw that this was a fairly classic case of Huntington's chorea. A diagnosis was entered in capital letters: "PSYCHOSIS ASSOCIATED WITH ORGANIC CHANGES IN THE NERVOUS SYSTEM WITH HUNTINGTON'S CHOREA."

For some reason, though, they still didn't tell Woody. The day after the diagnosis was made, he wrote: "I asked the head lady nurse in our office today, Thursday, September 4, 1952, if and when I'd start my insulin treatments and she told me the name of a certain world famous doctor studying my case which doctor, she says, says there's a big big question now whether to even give me these insulin treatments. . . .''

The uncertainty frightened him. He turned to his writing even more intensely than before, keeping a detailed diary, which began with a thirty-seven-page entry on September 6, ostensibly addressed to Marjorie and Tony, going on about the usual things, but also: "I don't think anybody will find any tracks of insanity or hereditary disease in me, except for my mother's death by Huntington's Chorea which I've read in a heavy book or two is not pass-onable."

On September 8, he admitted that he was anxious to meet his new doctor, to find out what kinds of treatment he needed. "Remind myself again this morning that I'm still the world's best ballad maker, and nobody can ever take that away from me." He decided that divorce from Marjorie was inevitable, and he might as well start looking for another wife on September 22, when his sixty days would be up and he could check himself out.

On September 9, he didn't feel very well. "Just try to hide my dizziness so no one else will see me or notice it. . . . Paper and pencil is my only little dose of relief for me . . . carving my psychopathetic thoughts." He told the doctor he was still suffering from alcoholic dizzy spells, and was asked how long it had been since he'd had a drink. "Forty-five days," he replied, and the doctor said, "That's a long time to stay dizzy," and asked him to walk a straight line. The doctor didn't venture any opinion as to why he might still be dizzy, though, and Woody decided it had to be the alcohol, or maybe: "My dizzy spell . . . is when I get hungry."

On September 10, he reflected on the possibility of painting signs again for a living, and wrote a poem about Tony, who "reflects a manliness I've always wanted to."

On September 11, he got his "heart tapped on by some world famous specialist. . . . Old sinky feeling just hit me again . . . can't be from hunger, we just finished our midday meal. . . . Dizzy spell hung on bad while I racked and stacked the dishes." Afterwards, he went out and lolled in the sun, reading the Alcoholics Anonymous pamphlets an attendant had given him, and decided it was a sure cure for his troubles. "I feel all soaked and full of alcohol (like an old cobwebby bottle left after a wild party)."

On September 12, he decided he wasn't going to perform anymore. All he'd ever gotten from it was "my wife and my kids took from me, and a new daddy already going through his movements." But then he realized that "this crazy line of thinking is just another big pile of my wasteful self-pity." He felt another dizzy spell coming on, and went to the bathroom and looked at his face in the stainless-steel mirrors, looked at it closely and saw hints of his mother. "Face seems to twist out of shape. Can't control it. Arms dangle all around. Can't control them. Wrists feel weak and my hands wave around in odd ways. I can't stop. . . . Awful afraid of people seeing me break down. Try to stall it off and act different. . . . All these docs keep asking me about how my mother died of Huntington's Chorea. They never tell me if it's pass-onable or not. So I never know. I believe every doctor ought to speak plainer so us patients can begin to try to guess partly what's wrong with us. . . . If it's not alcohol which has me, I wonder what it's going to be. . . ."

On September 14, he was up—as usual—at the crack of dawn, sleepier than usual because a raver on the ward had gone into a tirade that night about the dirty Communists and filthy Jews. He began to think about Alcoholics Anonymous and decided it might not be the answer after all, since it didn't deal with the problems of capitalism. Then the doctors came in and asked about his mother again. "Got me worried a bit. Wondering. Could it be that I'm taking an early stage of the same disease? Sure love to read some books on it so I'll sort of know what to expect. . . . It sure does put a new light on the subject, don't it? Maybe chorea is my paycheck for beating you all like I did." He began to think about dying: "Cathy Ann showed me the proper fashion to go. She taught me the tricks. Don't worry. Don't bother your head about me. Don't. Don't. . . . This don't split us. It don't part us. It brings us all closer together."

On September 15, he told a pal in the bathroom about how his mother died with that "old three-way disease of chorea," which, he said, consisted of "St. Vitus dance, epilepsy and mild insanity." But he was "not of the opinion that chorea can be passed on to any child. I was born before mama took her chorea anyhow."

On September 16, he made sure to remind himself again to check out all the books he could find about the "mental disease, chorea. It had me bad worried a few days but I remember (over again) that I've read . . . that chorea's not transmittable from parent to child. Good." He became defiant then, ranting about the "Hoover gang" at the F.B.I., and speculating that Tony might be a G-man sent to spy on him. He felt compelled, later, to list all the things he was good at. He was the best chess player in his ward, and the hardest worker at his kitchen job. "I'm a good writer. I know more about these patients here than any of you doctors and nurses know. I can take any idea or current event of today or back yonder in history and make it rhyme and make it zing all around this world of yours. I can play my guitar and my mandolin and my fiddle better and faster and louder than I ever could in my drunken days, and I can still sing by heart and without looking at any kind of printed page several thousand of the best balladsongs you've ever heard. . . ." He began to wonder about all the writing he'd been doing lately and decided it was like "going into a self-protective trance. I can't always remember, when I come out of it, how it was in that trance."

On September 17, he grew concerned because Marjorie—who'd been visiting regularly (as had Jack Elliot, but practically none of his other alleged friends)—hadn't arrived with the new clothes he'd asked for. He then slipped into a long, pitiful reverie about beating the children on the night before he checked into Kings County two months earlier.

On September 18, there was a new patient on the ward, a priest: "The church commits life's worst criminal sin when it pumps our bodies full of ideas about love and then denies us love's greatest outlet."

On September 20: "My dizzy head hits worse than ever now. Funny how I wake up so clear and already so danged woozy all over. Sorta stumbled through my kitchen job worse than ever. . . . Forget little things. Keep seeing my end in sight. Keep telling you all not to feel guilty about my condition. I wonder if it could be chorea? If it is, I wonder if there's any kind of cure for it? . . . I guess I'd best not try to discharge myself out of here any too fastly after all. I'd ought not to be at large feeling like I feel now."

Apparently, on that day or the next, the doctors told Woody that he was suffering from Huntington's chorea. It is impossible to know exactly what they told him, how candid or calculating they may have been. It seems likely, though, from subsequent events, that he reacted much as he had twenty-five years earlier when the doctors told him about his mother. He simply refused to accept the ugliness and finality of what they were saying. If the doctors were indeed frank, it was a message far too horrible to contemplate rationally in any case: his brain was dying. He was slowly losing control of his mind and body, and had been for some time. He would continue to slowly lose control of his mind and body until there was nothing left to him but a quivering, vegetable sack of skin and bones, his brain depleted and rotting inside a cavernous skull.

He didn't want to hear that he was sentenced to spend the next fifteen years trapped within an increasingly senseless, writhing body. He didn't want to hear any details. He just wanted to get out of there, to leave that place, to go.

In the charming letter he wrote requesting that he be discharged, he stubbornly insisted that he was "an alcoholic going through some of the curious feelings of alcoholic withdrawal, but no pain serious enough to hinder me from working in all capacities to help my wife to provide, and to take care of our three small children." At the same time, though, he acknowledged, "I am already tracking down all the library books, pamphlets, articles, essays, speeches, lectures on that peculiar mixture of mental diseases called by the name of Huntington's Chorea. I want to do some writing of my own on that disease, chorea."

He concluded: "My paper page ends here but not any of my good memories toward you all," and signed it: "Woodrow Wilson Guthrie."

On September 22, they let him out and he ran.

CHAPTER 11

Jesus My Doctor

The problem was where to go.

It was the autumn of 1952, and the New York folk scene had shattered. Alan Lomax was in England, having fled a bad marriage and the blacklisters. Earl Robinson, unable to find any other work, had latched on as a music teacher in a left-wing private school. Leadbelly was dead. John Henry Faulk was being hounded off the radio because he'd performed at fund-raising parties with people like Woody Guthrie. Sonny Terry and Brownie McGhee had retreated to the relative safety and obscurity of Harlem. Moe Asch still recorded folk music, but was more cautious now about "topical" material. Several members of the old gang, most notably Burl Ives, had cooperated with the House Un-American Activities Committee. "The future of Burl Ives should be interesting," the ever-militant Irwin Silber wrote in *Sing Out!*, his slapdash successor to the People's Songs bulletin. "We've never seen anybody sing while crawling on their belly before."

After leaving the hospital, Woody turned first to Marjorie . . . but quickly found that she wasn't going to take him back, not even after his (hospital-imposed) months on the wagon and the diagnosis of his disease. The doctors said that his erratic behavior probably had been caused by Huntington's chorea, but they couldn't tell her much more than that—except that it was serious, hereditary, degenerative, and incurable. There was, therefore, no guarantee that Woody wouldn't go berserk again, and she wasn't about to submit her family to any further experiments. When he came to visit her after his release, she took him for a walk along the boardwalk and told him how she felt.

Woody was bitterly disappointed that the reconciliation he'd been dreaming about through the long months at "Brooklyn State Hopey House" had turned out to be a mirage, but he accepted Marjorie's decision. He figured the safest course of action was to leave town. "I'm less and less jealous every day, but I don't believe it's good policy for me to range around too close to Murdock's Courtin Place for now," he wrote. "It's just been these past couple of days that I've been able to admit or face up to the fact that somewhere in this world there is even a man by the name of Tony. . . ."

Lacking anything better to do, he drifted up the Hudson River valley to Pete Seeger's house—but Pete was off in Los Angeles with the other Weavers, making a last stand before they, too, would be closed out by the blacklist. Woody spent several days with Toshi Seeger and the children, and wrote Pete a selectively truthful account of his hospital stay:

> They analyzed me as being partly in the first pains of alcoholic withdrawal period, plus a certain percentage of the mental disease my mother had, Huntington's Chorea. They're not plumb sure about my dizzy spells I feel now twice every day. . . . All us alky boys go through some odd sorts and flavors of craving.
>
> There are lots of kinds of chorea and nobody is plumb sure about what kind I'll most likely have, if any. They say it aint deadly nor fatal so my days in yonder hospital weren't quite wasted if they got me off my bottle or helped me get strong enough to bypass Whiskeytown. Chorea keeps me just as dizzy and a good bit cheaper.
>
> Doctors all told Marjorie to get a divorce from me for the safety of the kids, which is the hardest part of my troubles at this time. She's willing to talk later about a rematch between us if my chorea stays mild enough for a few seasons.

Pete realized the situation probably was more serious than Woody made it out to be, and wrote a moving reply: "We are all with you and want to be able to help pull you through these hard times. . . . You once wrote a song called 'Dust Can't Kill Me.' As long as you keep that attitude uppermost in your head, why I guess we'll be a long way toward winning."

But Woody never received the letter. He'd already left for Los Angeles, which seemed the only logical place to be. The Weavers were there. Cisco Houston had a regular radio show on KFAC. Will Geer had bought some property and was determined to wait out the blacklist in the relative seclusion of Topanga Canyon, just north of Los Angeles, and Butch and Bess Hawes were in hibernation nearby. It sounded rather hospitable and Woody hit the road in early October, sending Marjorie barbed postcards along the way. One showed a man and woman in bed, separated by four children, and the words: "They said that nothing would ever come between us." Another had a fat couple in divorce court: "I don't know what's come between us." On the back of the latter, Woody wrote: "All fooling aside, I feel lots better about being no more a burden on yous . . ."

And, in fact, he did seem to make a remarkable recovery after settling in Topanga. The canyon was a wild, craggy pathway through the coastal mountains, snaking from the San Fernando Valley to the Pacific Ocean. It was a newly settled area, favored by blacklist victims and Hollywood bohemians looking to get away from it all. Land was so cheap that even Woody Guthrie could afford to buy a sizable, if somewhat godforsaken, piece of property—the only means of access was a long climb up a steep hill—several months after he arrived.

At first, though, he lived in Will Geer's remarkable compound, which included a huge garden and a public theater, and was a halfway house of sorts for lost souls and refugees from the political storms of the period. Geer and company would perform Shakespeare and agitprop for free each Sunday in a rustic amphitheater on the property, and make a little money on the side by selling hot dogs. As blustery and full of himself as ever, Geer simply refused to let the blacklist get him down and dragged all his friends along, munching hot dogs and reciting *Coriolanus* quite splendidly. Another popular favorite that season was *Alice in Plunderland*, in which Woody played the Mad Hatter.

He was given a small cabin, adjacent to Will and Herta's house, to live in. He did his own cooking—invariably canned chili—in a barbecue pit out front, and felt so much at ease that he routinely wandered about in the nude, a state of grace that tended to bother Herta Geer (but not nearly as much as the erotic letters he began sending her children). For the most part, though, Woody and the Geers left each other—happily—to their own devices.

He was greeted throughout the canyon as a visiting celebrity, the Old Lion of folk music. There was a round of hootenannies featuring Pete Seeger (and, occasionally, other Weavers), Butch and Bess Hawes, the Geers, a black woman named Odetta, who had a positively earth-shattering voice, and assorted young folk singers . . . but Woody was the centerpiece, the main attraction, and, sometimes, the beneficiary—seventy dollars was raised at one such party for his continued maintenance. The various tics and shakes, the slurred speech and other "symptoms" the doctors had noticed at Brooklyn State Hospital all were so subtle—they had insinuated themselves gradually over the course of many years—that most of his old friends didn't notice much of a change in him. To them, the odd little mannerisms, the way he walked and talked *were* Woody. It was true that at times he seemed less certain than in the past, but often he was as clear and sharp as ever. Pete Seeger remembers sitting in a room full of singers, improvising verses to "Acres of Clams" one evening, and Woody putting everyone to shame with a clever account of a visit from the F.B.I., which culminated:

> He asked, "Will you carry a gun for your country?"
> I answered the F.B.I. "Yay!"
> "I will point a gun for my country,
> But I won't guarantee you which way!"

His confidence had returned. He wrote to Marjorie that he was fighting off the disease: "It will all wear off, little by little, day by day; I feel my dissssy spppells a bit around here but not as dizzzzery as I felt them [in the hospital]." He was writing songs once more, a slew of songs about the war in Korea, a place which obviously had special meaning for him: "Korea and me . . . you gotta agree . . . both gotta get free . . ." He also addressed his condition more directly:

> This world it's hit me in my face
> It's hit me over my head

> *It's beat me black and blue and green*
> *But still, though, I ain't dead.*

To prove it, he decided to buy the plot of Topanga land, and start looking for "wife #3." He bought eight acres from Bob DeWitt, a local real estate dealer, for a down payment of $250 (which was forwarded by Pete Kameron). He called it Pretty Polly Canyon, after the old folk tune, and dreamed of establishing a town called Woody Burgh on its scraggly heights: "I'll build up my Dancing Tree Ranch here along my Pretty Polly Canyon spot into one burgh and one city towne where it'll always be against the good law for any citizen to ask you even one question about your whole case history, where you've come from and where you're heading towards."

As for wife number three, he wrote to Marjorie that he hoped she would be "dark skind, Spanish or Negro, Oriental, Asiatic or whichever." His first choice, however, was Ruth Waldman, a young medical student who'd visited him frequently on the ward at Brooklyn State. He offered himself to her by mail, but was gently rebuffed. She said that she was going to medical school in Switzerland, and wouldn't be back for five years. Woody claimed not to be disappointed, though. In a subsequent letter to Marjorie, he allowed that it probably was best to move slowly toward wife number three, because "I don't want my next womban, whoever she may be, to kick me out of bed for calling her Marjorie in my dreams."

Such lines had their effect on Marjorie, who would make occasional teary phone calls to Herta Geer, asking about poor Woody. "We are really never ever apart—just because of the children," she wrote to him. "I'm always happy when I remember you are their dads!" Her dancing school was prospering now, and she was able to buy a little house of her own in Howard Beach, an eerily vacant corner of Brooklyn at the edge of Jamaica Bay. In the process of moving, she unearthed old scrapbooks and notebooks, remnants of Cathy and their life together. "I still can't imagine moving without you," she wrote, adding hastily that Tony was giving "wonderful help." But still, she closed: "Let's always be the world's best lovers in even this seemingly impossible world. . . . Always, your best gal . . ."

Marjorie's wistful vacillations tended to make Woody very angry. "You don't love me anymore," he wrote. "You pity me."

Invariably, a sad letter from Marjorie would bring a vicious response from Woody and then—as always—an effusive apology: "I take back all my bad crazy words that I tried to write on Herta's brokedown corona portable. . . . I stay dizzier these days only when this cloudy cloud of useless hate tries to hover and to hang and to blow in cold between us." He wasn't drinking, he assured her, and recently had found a great deal of satisfaction working with clay on the potter's wheel in Bob DeWitt's barn. "I can be much more myself in my clay working than any kind of art medium. Hours pass and I don't know where they go."

In late November, though, he stopped writing. After three weeks without a word from him, Marjorie wrote on December 18: "No mail is something I don't quite understand . . . unless you are so busy with work or so sick that you can't write . . . and yet I feel it is not either. . . . I feel you are angry and hurt and wishing you could forget these past ten years." But he shouldn't forget, she continued, because of their children. Arlo, especially, seemed "a little version of you." She begged him to keep in touch: "How shall I tell you how much I think about you and worry about you. The night after we moved into the new house, I cried all night."

But there was no response. Finally, in late January of 1953, she called Herta, who went into a tizzy: "Oh, Marjorie! It's so awful! Woody's run off . . . with a woman! He's run off with Anneke Marshall, and she's so young and I thought she and David were so happy . . ."

He met Anneke in the pottery shed. He'd seen her at several of the hootenannies, an attractive girl who asked him to sing "Green Corn" one night, but there hadn't been any real contact between them. She was, apparently, happily married—*just* married—to a rigorously handsome man, an aspiring writer and actor named David Marshall, who worked at putting down tile floors in the San Fernando Valley while waiting for the lightning to strike. Anneke didn't know very much about folk music—in truth, she thought it was pretty simple-minded—and wasn't aware of Woody's legend or status. All she knew was that he didn't seem to care very much when he performed . . . and she didn't like that, being the sort of woman who cared passionately about virtually everything.

And so she was rather surprised by the warm, pleasant sensation she felt when she walked into the pottery shed that day and saw Woody at the wheel. He smiled at her, but didn't say anything. They worked quietly, side by side, for about an hour and then he asked if she'd like to go for a walk. She agreed, and they went off to visit his property.

Anneke had been born in eastern Pennsylvania, and her maiden name was Van Kirk. She came from a sophisticated, academic family, and was an art student before she met Marshall. She was about Woody's height, with light brown hair and sharp Scandinavian features. But she was distinctive more because of her manner than her appearance. She was smart and quick and enthusiastic, with a tendency to take charge of any situation—she was, in that sense, quite similar to Marjorie. She was only twenty years old and looked her age, but seemed much older. She was headstrong, rebellious (but not very "political"), and something of a bohemian, given to wearing long peasant skirts and going about with no shoes on. She talked about books and art and movies that first afternoon—they both loved Charlie Chaplin, who'd recently been forced to leave the country because of his left-wing politics—and they spent several peaceful hours together, basking in the sun on Woody's hillside. She found herself utterly charmed by the man.

They met each afternoon in the pottery shed after that, and spent Christmas Eve together, being driven through the canyon on the back of a truck filled with children, singing carols. Soon after, she invited Woody to come live with her and David in the small house they'd just purchased (with help from her family). She was, by now, quite in love with him. And while some of it was, no doubt, a product of his need to be mothered and her desire to take care of the poor guy, there also was a fairly strong physical attraction. He seemed, to her, a perfect little creation. He had a mature, weathered, intelligent face beneath the wild mop of hair. But the big surprise was that his body was perfectly shaped and muscled, with smooth skin like a young boy. The only imperfection was an awful hernia that squished when he made love . . . which wasn't very frequently, although she found him to be a gentle and sensitive lover when roused.

For his part, Woody was bemused by all the attention. Just a few months earlier he'd almost given himself up for dead in a mental ward, and now a beautiful young woman was in love with him. Surprisingly, there were no sexual fantasies or other ruminations about Anneke in his notebooks. No mention of her at all, in fact, except for an attempted song:

> *Anneke, Anneka*
> *What does it mean?*
> *What could it mean?*
> *Anyhow, anyway Anneke girl*
> *The pertiest name*
> *That my memory has seen.*

He spent nearly a month with the Marshalls before making his move. Finally, he told her, "I'm going to be leaving you now. I'm going back to Polly Canyon to live." When she asked him why, he said that two men couldn't live in the same house loving the same woman. She helped pack his things, and then drove him to Pretty Polly, where he apparently was intending to establish residence in a pup tent. She couldn't bear the thought of him up there all alone and, that night, told her husband that she was in love with Woody and wanted to be with him. David asked her to wait several days, and think it over before making a final decision. She did, and two days later took off for New York City with Woody.

There they hooked up with Jack Elliot, who was now the proud owner of a Model A Ford (and could drive about imagining that he actually was a dust bowl refugee) . . . and, with the back seat piled with boxes of Woody's *Seeds of Man* manuscript, the three of them took off for Stetson Kennedy's Florida retreat. Anneke, thrilled to be on an adventure after her brief attempt at domesticity, scrawled across the back window: "Move Old A Crate."

Beluthahatchee was deserted. The Kennedys had left for an indefinite stay in Europe, leaving the place unattended. The Klan, ever vigilant, had ransacked the bus for evidence of Communism and miscegenation after Stetson's departure and destroyed all the furniture. Woody and Anneke didn't mind, though; it was their first home together, and they were quite happy there—Woody working on *Seeds of Man*, Anneke sketching and writing, Jack Elliot hanging about awkwardly.

Woody worked on the book almost every day, and made some interesting revisions. He eliminated the confrontation with his father in Chapter 2, since he now knew the answers to most of the questions he'd been asking about the past. It hadn't simply been Charley's "badge and gun jobs" and land trading that sent his mother reeling. It had been Huntington's chorea, passed down from Nora's father, George Sherman, the man who'd drowned mysteriously in Little Deep Fork. But Woody didn't want to be reminded of all that now. He was reborn, the disease was fading—it wasn't inexorable, there was no family curse. So he cut the scene and worked around it.

At the top of the first page of this new draft, he wrote a reminder: "Make my own dialect more straighter as per my dad. Cut down on so many repititions," but he seemed entirely unable to follow his own advice. The speeches and descriptions became bloated and gross, overrunning his intentions, spilling out of control. The idea of *gold*, for example, sent him hurtling off interminably: "Cellar diggers gold, well drillers, toothy fillers, salty rivers, redblood Indians, rootabaggers, back benders, heavy lifters, highway drifters, bums, hoboes, lobo wolfers, cradle robbers, gravey diggers . . ."

His language had loosened another notch in the general direction of madness. In March, he sent a whirling, tumultuous letter to Marjorie and the kids, which began:

> It wasnt just because any of you are so smart or so good looking as you think you are, nor it wasnt just on account of how loud I can hear these bullyfrogs singing about you off down here in Beluthahatchee Lake, nor how I see that sexymoss yonder dancing to all my ballads my frogs keep singing about—it wasnt any of them things thats making me whale away tonight here and write to you; I want to have some reasonable excuse at least to tell you partways anyhow about Little Anny in this letter; and she lots more than me is in back of my writing it to you; it was your nice big perty perty picture you painted for us, Missy Puffy Duffy [Puffy was his name for Nora], for us to hang up down here in our cowboy indian house; and yours, too, Old Man Joadsy Boatsun, your goofy goofy funny picture showing me and Annyhow all of you nice big bubbles bubble up in our water hole down here in Beluthahatchee Lakey Pond where we sneak away (dern neart) every day with some kind of a store boughten bar of stinkery dam soap and we stand there and we scrub and we rub and we screeble and we scrabble and we damn neart rub one anothers

hair, hide and skin plumb off just trying to keep a teensybit cleaner than all of our alligator friends, and our crockidile friends, and our snakey friends, and all of our birdy and animal friends that get to be so many down in this hotwater country that you just cant quite count all of them in ten hundred life-terms . . .

And it went on like that for thousands upon thousands of words.

Rather than worry—or, at least, wonder—about Woody's skidding style, Anneke began to imitate it, uncannily, in much the same way as Jack Elliot had appropriated everything else about him (Woody, made even dizzier by the sense that he was living in a hall of mirrors, soon banished Elliot from the swamp). In a letter to Marjorie that March, Anneke strutted her newfound style:

> Received your missal this aft. and Arlo Larlow BeeLow Barlow's finest and we were mighty glad you wrote, sending the third masterpiece to complete the trio. Pity you can't sit your fanny down and take, rob, steal, beg or borrow the time to write a minor epistle, expressing in the finest high flown language, what the kids are doing at that exact moment, whether the sun is shining his brightest and happiest or whether the dreariest of rains is sobbing and moaning around the house on Sheepshead Bay.

Marjorie was alarmed and perplexed by all this, surprised that an intelligent young woman would take up with a man who was, quite obviously, disintegrating. She decided that Anneke was along for a brief ride at best, blinded by the glamour of hanging out with a Great Folk Hero; she also was more than a little jealous. Not knowing how else to handle the situation, Marjorie once again performed a spectacular feat of incorporation, welcoming Anneke officially into the Guthrie family . . . and even venturing some homely advice: "Don't feel bad because you're only 21, remind Woody of his youth."

Anneke, outraged and not at all willing to allow Marjorie to draw up a new family plan with everyone's role neatly defined, including her own, lashed back:

> You know how I feel about keeping the "tribe" together; I told you that I would always try my best to give

Woody's kids my love. . . . But, Marjory, despite all your fond hopes, I know that we, you and I, can never be as close as you would wish. . . . You, to me, symbolize a series of wonderful, happy days in the younger years of a person I love very dearly; but something went wrong, something backfired . . . something got all fouled up. It doesn't matter what the cause or reason, it happened. . . . For me, there is no joy in the thought that we are all one . . . because we are not. You are you . . . I am I, so I think that I would be happier . . . far far happier if we remained in our separate corners of the earth.

Now it was Marjorie's turn to be outraged. In a letter dated "April 1 . . . the day of fools," she insisted, *"Nothing went wrong. And I swear to you nothing backfired."* If it wasn't for the kids, she wrote, Woody still would be living with her. But the doctors had said the "strains and pressures" of family life would be too much for him and so, regretfully, they were apart. Remarkably, Marjorie never really spelled out the reasons why the doctors didn't want Woody to stay with the family. She never mentioned Huntington's chorea. She did, however, lay down several broad and rather nasty hints: "This is one case in a million. . . . Perhaps Woody doesn't speak too much now but later he will begin to unravel his story. Don't let it frighten you or cause you sorrow."

It is not entirely clear how much Anneke *did* know about the disease at this point. The party line was that Woody had been sick, but was feeling much better now—a recovery attributable, in large part, to Anneke's presence. On at least one occasion, though, in a note apologizing to her for one of his temper tantrums, Woody hinted that his troubles might be more serious than he'd allowed: "It [his temper] could be the sprigs and sprouts of real or imaginary sicknesses; it could be many more things; but, I am not at all certain that any of them will ever get one drop better; they most likely will get terribly and terribly and more terribly worse, so don't say I didn't tell you . . ."

But even if their conversations were more specific, even if Woody had said the magic words and told her he was suffering from Huntington's chorea, it's apparent that Anneke had no idea of what that meant. Because, that spring, she decided that she wanted to have a baby with Woody . . . and was quite happy to learn, in June, that she was indeed pregnant.

The prospect of a baby imposed some reality on their idyll, at least for Anneke. A baby couldn't be raised in an abandoned bus at the edge of a swamp. Arrangements would have to be made. They'd been scraping along on the monthly royalty checks from Pete Kameron, which weren't nearly enough, and Anneke had been forced, on occasion, to pick rutabagas at a local farm to raise money for groceries. Woody wasn't doing much to help the situation—in part, because he was increasingly oblivious and logy, but also because he was convinced that prosperity was just around the corner. He was going to make a concert tour of Europe as "America's Greatest Balladeer" and, oddly enough, for a time that spring it seemed that such a trip might actually be arranged.

For nearly a year, Woody had been corresponding with Ken Lindsay, the manager of the International Bookstore in London, who was a Guthrie fan and claimed there were thousands like him all over the Continent. At first, all Lindsay wanted was to sell Woody's records in his store and, perhaps, to distribute Asch records in Europe. The idea of a tour simply was a thought in passing, but it ballooned . . . especially in Woody's mind. Lindsay's eventual proposal certainly wasn't overwhelming: "This friend, Alex Korner and his wife, will give you accommodation in their house for as long as you'd like to stay. They suggest that you come over in January of next year. We shall arrange publicity and concerts. . . ."

But then Stetson Kennedy began writing from Europe, encouraging Woody to come over, and Alan Lomax waded in with an idea that sounded like the real thing. The BBC was "interested in doing a biography of you and it would be all the better if you were here to be the principal actor. . . . I think you will have a great time here. People will like you very much and it is fairly cheap and extremely pleasant. . . ."

By the time Lomax's letter arrived, though, there was no longer any real possibility of a European tour.

On the morning of June 10, Woody went out to prepare breakfast in the barbecue pit next to the bus. He readied the coffee pot and stacked wood for the fire. Then he took the can of white gasoline that he used as a starter, and began to pour. . . . There was a flash and an explosion, and suddenly the fire was shooting back toward Woody—a live ember from the night before had touched it off, apparently—and he jerked back, spilling the gasoline on his arm, and the fire raced up it, past his elbow. He staggered back screaming, falling to the ground and rolling about. Anneke raced into the bus and came out with some oleo, which she spread on the wound—it was his right arm—but the skin slid off as she rubbed the oleo on, and she gasped. Woody was pale and terrified and whimpering. Anneke then ran to the farmer down the road, the man who'd hired her to pick rutabagas, and he agreed to drive them—at five miles per hour, it seemed—into Jacksonville, where they refused to treat Woody at the public clinic because Beluthahatchee was in the wrong county. They told Anneke to go to St. Augustine. Too stunned to argue, she took Woody to a nearby private hospital, St. Vincent's, where they treated him—but rather reluctantly, as the admission notes suggest:

> Pt. threw gasoline on an open fire, blazed and burned his arm. Pt. says he plays stringed instruments, receives $100 per month royalties on songs he has written. The patient is a peculiar—He wears shaggy hair and beard which he says is to keep mosquitos away.
>
> Wife Anneke Louise wife—22 says mar. about a yr. ago in New York—Pt. has six chil by two other wives—Now says they are not married but Pt. is not divorced—says divorce is pending in Juarez, Mex.
>
> This couple are drifters—came down here several months ago. Pt. is supposed to be a musician—folk music—has quite a history.

The doctors dressed the wound and gave Woody painkillers, and then he and Anneke were left to walk from the hospital to the Jacksonville bus station, where they caught a bus back to Beluthahatchee.

That evening, Anneke broke down and asked Marjorie for help. She called first, then—still shocked by what she'd seen that day and needing to exorcise it—wrote Marjorie a letter, describing the fire in great detail: "You probably know what it's like to see someone catch on fire, blaze . . . crawl about in agony . . . I never did see anyone hurt in this way before."

Marjorie told Anneke that Woody was covered by Blue Cross, then wrote a letter offering to come down and help. To Woody, she added, "Hold on, honey, and remember the Guthries can take an awful lot. . . . I suppose you are wondering again about fire . . . . Let's stop it right here. . . . It was an accident, and so were all the other fires."

The next days were awful. At first, Anneke thought Woody's arm might be infected. It was turning colors and she called the hospital, but they assured her that was just part of the healing process. Then the arm began to stink, and there was no question in her mind *that* wasn't part of the healing process. She went through the Yellow Pages, trying to find a doctor who'd treat Woody; most wouldn't come out to the swamp, but one finally did—an old navy doctor—and saved the arm and, most probably, Woody's life. Afterwards, Anneke wrote to Marjorie: "Did you ever smell an infected area? Ewww! It's grim. Sour sweet. It makes me sick. You know, this climate is rotten for healing."

It was summer now, and the swamp was a steam bath. Woody was in agony, and Anneke at a loss. She decided the best thing would be to go back to Topanga, and asked her family for bus fare. In July, they left Beluthahatchee and returned to California, stopping in Mexico along the way so that Woody could get a quickie divorce, arranged by Jimmy Longhi with Marjorie's reluctant approval. She felt that if Anneke was going to have a baby, it might as well be legal. Jimmy wrote to Woody in Florida, asking for a "protective document which will protect the kids financially in the event that you strike it rich some day," and then gave him the name of a lawyer in Juárez. The divorce wouldn't cost him anything; it was all being handled from New York. "It'll only take an hour," Jimmy assured him, "and then you can be on your way."

Woody and Anneke returned to Topanga to find that their sudden departure six months earlier had set off a wild and improbable chain of events. David Marshall had received a great deal of sympathy after Anneke dumped him, especially from the Geers—Will even landed him a small movie role—and most especially from Herta Geer, who fell in love with him. Herta was now pregnant by David, Will was off in New York licking his wounds, and Topanga was scandalized. It was generally agreed that Woody was to blame for setting the events in motion, and the reception wasn't very warm when he and Anneke returned this time.

They moved into her old house, and Woody, whose arm was scarred and immobile, did his best to continue with *Seeds of Man*,

dictating it to Anneke, who made small improvements and cor-
rections along the way, like changing "womban" to "woman"
each time. She also handled his correspondence, dashing off
clever, but rather huffy letters to Woody's various relatives in an
attempt to establish herself firmly in their minds as the new Mrs.
Guthrie. It was an effort grounded in jealousy as much as pride:
Anneke still was irked that Marjorie, quite obviously, considered
herself the *real* Mrs. Guthrie despite everything. Most of the
letters landed harmlessly, but one touched off a bitter exchange
with another old, huffy letter writer—Woody's father. Charley
Guthrie, stunned by yet another fire in the family and concerned
about Woody's state of mind, became parental and solicitous in
response to Anneke's report of recent events. He sought to soothe
Woody, but also offered some advice: this new book he was
writing might be more successful than *Bound for Glory* if it was
a bit less vulgar. Anneke jumped to Woody's defense then, re-
plying that *Seeds of Man* was a work of art and that artistic
integrity was the most important thing, and that she'd be curious
about Charley's definition of "success" in any case.

"I only meant to persuade him to keep his verbiage within the
bounds of common decency," he responded, adding that books
with vulgar language usually were "relegated to the limbo of
filthy tripe and unreadable trash." Then the man who'd once
been the most dashing figure in Okemah, Oklahoma, closed with
a definition of "success" in response to Anneke's query:

"My definition of a successful person: One who is least like
me. Love, Papa."

In September, Anneke took a job with the phone company in
Santa Monica and Woody was left alone in the house all day.
For a time, he tried typing out *Seeds of Man* with his left hand,
but gradually gave up on that . . . and just about everything else.
The fire and subsequent agony had taken the starch out of his
attempts to pretend he was recovering from Huntington's chorea;
the Jacksonville affair seemed the final confirmation that there
was no escaping the family curse. Fire would always be waiting
for him, as it had for his mother.

Although he might have regained the use of his hand with
exercise and therapy, he chose to just let it hang there. Indeed,
he seemed to flash it about, displaying it to other people, *foisting*
it upon them, often unbandaged and disgusting, an announcement
and constant reminder that there could no longer be any illusions.

He was terribly lonely in the house without Anneke. He was beginning to miss New York, and his family. He wrote charming letters to the children in Howard Beach, and they responded in kind.

From Arlo: "Woody I love you so much. I can't stop it. I love you for sending me all those pictures and notes for me to look at . . ."

From Joady: "Do you feel good? When are you going to get better? When are you going to get better, a little better, and come back to your hospital?"

Anneke, of course, noticed his deepening despair. He'd almost stopped talking, making his wishes known only through shrugs, grimaces, and an occasional mumbled phrase. It had been so long since they'd actually sat down and had a conversation that she was beginning to wonder if they'd *ever* really talked. He'd also stopped bathing and shaving, his hair was matted and smelly, and not even their marriage ceremony, performed at the Los Angeles Hall of Justice in December, with Anneke quite pregnant and just able to squeeze into her good tweed skirt, could lift him from the doldrums. After that, Woody began leaving scattered hints about returning to New York and resuming his career—Anneke never could figure just how he was able to get his message across without talking, but he did—and she agreed that a change of scene might be good for him. He had friends in New York, and contacts.

They left in January of 1954, with Anneke eight months pregnant. She did all the driving—Woody was too foggy to do much of anything—in a 1937 Hudson Terraplane, which seemed precarious from the start and quickly broke down in the Nevada desert, requiring a new ninety-dollar radiator. Exhausted, they stopped in Denver, where Jeff and Allene Guthrie were now living.

"My son, Robbie Gid, answered the door and screamed," Uncle Jeff later recalled. "He said there was a man at the door covered with hair, and I went to get my pistol. The man at the door said, 'It's me, Woody. Don't you know me?' I knew his voice. I gave him a haircut and he got in the bath tub and he came out looking like Woody. . . . Anneke was the slouchiest thing I'd ever seen. She had an old dress on she must have been wearing for 10 years, right down to her ankles. She was an old country, backwoodsy gal. They were traveling with some money.

He'd bought this Gibson mandolin and decided to give it to me—it was a $160 mandolin. I had a *bois d'arc* fiddle and he said he'd give me anything for it, so he gave me $50 and the mandolin. It was the one he'd always called my 'squawlin panther' fiddle. . . . He wasn't shaking or anything then, just acting unconcerned-like. I didn't know, but I figured he had the same disease that all them Shermans had. . . .''

They arrived in New York in the dead of winter, with no idea of where to go or what to do. They visited Tiny Robinson, Leadbelly's niece, who was happy to put them up for several days until they found a dreadful apartment on the Lower East Side—near Leadbelly's old place—a shadowy fifth-floor walk-up on East Fifth Street. It consisted of one small room and an alcove, and was so cold that Woody kept the gas stove running full blast, all the time.

The move to New York hadn't done very much to lift his spirits; in fact, he seemed worse than before. They owned a junky portable record player and he would sit all day listening to his old albums over and over and over again. He didn't read the newspapers anymore, but occasionally would flip through one of Anneke's books—her prized possessions, mostly classics—and scrawl comments across them: "This is against the people," or "This one here is mighty fine," defacing the books, ruining them. Anneke was bored by the incessant record playing and angered by the destruction of her books, but he seemed so lost and pathetic and sad that she didn't have the heart to come down on him. She'd try to coax him toward the bath, away from the record player, away from the quart bottles of ale that were proliferating again, but she didn't want to upset him. She was afraid that he'd run away, and she knew he'd never be able to make it alone, and she wasn't ready to let go of him.

Sometimes he'd walk down the five flights (Anneke would always remember the sound of his unsteady steps on the stairs, and hoping he'd make it without falling) and visit his old associates in the city. Sometimes he would bring her along, proudly—his new wife. He brought her to Howie Richmond's office, and Howie was shocked by the sight of a disheveled Woody and an equally messy "16-year-old girl who was very pregnant and who Woody introduced as his wife, as if it were a perfectly normal situation." There were rumors out in town that Woody's brain had been eaten away by syphilis, and Howie was beginning to believe them.

One of the few people who showed them any kindness was Bob Harris, who owned Stinson Records and the Union Square Music Shop with his father, Herbert Harris, and had distributed many of Woody's albums for Moe Asch. In fact, the Harrises *still* were releasing new Woody Guthrie albums—much to Asch's dismay—culled from the marathon recording sessions that Woody and Cisco had done for Moe ten years earlier. The initial agreement between Asch and Harris (Asch would record and Harris distribute) had been vague enough so that no one was sure who had the right to decide what would be released and what wouldn't. As a result, both Asch and Harris were selling Guthrie records (still not very many of them, but there *did* seem to be a small cult starting out there)—Asch on his Folkways label, Harris on Stinson. It was a complex and ridiculous business that seemed destined to wind up in court (but never was resolved) . . . and so it's conceivable that Bob Harris was making his pilgrimages to Woody and Anneke's dingy apartment with gifts of new albums and, occasionally, money just to stay on Woody's good side. As it happened, Woody didn't even appear to be *aware* of the dispute and probably wouldn't have cared much if he had been, as long as the records were being released and were available. And all Anneke knew was that someone, for whatever reason, was being kind.

Marjorie probably would have been more than happy to take care of all of them—Woody, Anneke, *and* the baby—but Anneke never would have allowed that. Woody decided, perhaps with her prodding, that he didn't want to see Marjorie or the kids either and he wrote a frightening, almost hallucinatory letter to that effect, which he sent to Marjorie via Harris's music store:

> I don't firmly think that my presence around there can make matters a bit better than they are when I stay gone. . . . I couldn't walk into that accursed house out there which Tony bought for you. And face that mother of yours that told me so many times how it was just an act of god that he took away Cathy to punish ye and me for ever falling in love in the first place (for which I can't condemn or curse out every member of the Jewish faith on account of her own personal hatred towards me).

You'll grow lots healthier
If you just quit expecting me
To visit your sweet cemetery.
Not in fifty lifetimes.
Leave me be.
Leave me alone.

Anneke went into labor on the morning of February 22, 1954. She calmly gathered her things and boarded a bus to Bellevue Hospital, with only a copy of *Moby Dick* to keep her company. Woody was in such awful shape that she didn't even think to wake him. Later that day she gave birth to a baby girl, who was named, according to her husband's wishes, Lorina Lynn Guthrie.

But Woody himself was nowhere to be found. Days passed, and he didn't come to visit. Finally Marjorie, who'd been keeping close tabs on the situation despite everyone's desire that she stay away, went up to the apartment and found him there, surrounded by empty liquor bottles, woozy and delirious. "Woody," she said.

"Uh."

"Woody, you're a father again. Anneke had a little girl."

"Uh."

"Woody, you're sick. You should go to the hospital."

He was in no condition to agree or disagree with that assessment, though, and Marjorie felt that it probably wasn't her place to call the ambulance and have him moved. So she left him there, passing word of his indisposition to Anneke through Jack Elliot's father, Dr. Adnopoz.

Woody never did visit Anneke in the hospital, and she was very worried about him. She asked Tiny Robinson to help her and Lorina home, dreading the scene that would, no doubt, be waiting for her there and not wanting to face it alone. But the apartment was clean when she opened the door, and covered—every wall was covered—with happy little cartoons that Woody had drawn, welcoming Lorina Lynn. He looked well, too; somehow, he'd located a last bit of dignity and pulled himself together again. It seemed a miracle.

Lorina's birth inspired Woody, briefly. There was another short, sad burst of activity. Will Geer had established an East Coast version of his Topanga playhouse—he called it Folksay Theater—in a midtown loft, and Woody began writing playlets for him. Most were dramatizations of folk songs, the sort of thing he and Will had been doing together since the migrant camps, but distended and bizarre now. For example, the ballad of the three Russian sisters that Woody had written during World War II was transformed into the raucous tale of a Russian prostitute who castrated her German clients and dropped their members through a hole in the floor. Will Geer thought it was very funny, but a bit much. And he didn't know *what* to make of Woody's language, which was beginning to look like some archaic form of English, with many words ending in "e" and "y," the vowels and consonants routinely doubled and tripled. One play that he wrote, *Skybally*, had Anneke, Jack Elliot, and himself as the main characters and included a chilling re-creation of his fire in Florida, filled with dizzy embellishments:

WOODY (HANGS FIDDLE ON SAME TWIGGYLIMB) HEY WAIT ABOUT A MINUTE HERE FRIENDS AND LET ME DASHLE AND SPLASHLE SOME OF MY JUG HERE OF WHITE GASOLENE DOWN ON OUR DERNDAMN FIRE I AINTA GUESSIN SHE'SA GONNTA TAKE OFF AT ALL AS DAMP AND AS WET AND AS SOGGRY AS IT LOOKS.

JACK (STRIKES MATCH AND DROPS INTO COOKPIT) I DONT THINK SHES TAKIN AHOLD ONE DAM LITTLE DERN BIT IS IT IN HERE ANNY? I CAINT SEE ME NARY A BLAZEE OF NARYA KIND HERE CAN YOU?

ANNY (BLINDED BY SMOKEY SMOKE) UHHHHM. HUHM? ME? SEE WHICH? ME? NO? MATCH? I CANT EVEN SEE HOW TO STAND UP.

WOODY (CARRIES GALLON TIN CAN PROM FENDER OF JAL-LOPY) OUTTA MY DAMND WAY YOU BLATTY YOU BATTY BLIND BIRDS YOU BOTH OF YOU'RE SISSYS IN TH' FIRST DE-GREE DONT EVEN KNOW HOWTA MAKE A WOODFIRE BURN SISSYS ((POURS SOME GAS INTO SMALLER TIN CAN ON COOKTABLE) HERE STAND IT BACK GITIT OUTTA MY WAY OUT OUT OUTTY PLEASEY PLEASY PLEASY I'LL JUST DUMP MY LITTLE TINNY CAN RIGHT OFF DOWN HERE RIGHT ON TOPPA Y'R SMOKERY OLD FIREBOX AND YA'LL SEE'ER JUM-PAT UP AND DANCE JUST AS PERTY AS YAD PLEASE AND JUST BLAZE AROUND AND JUST BURN AROUND AS PERTY AS YA'D ASK.

ANNY ((GRABS AT CAN)) No NONO DONT THROW THAT

WHILE THAT LITTLE SPARK IS DOWN IN THERE DONT DON-
TYA DONTYA

JACK ((STUMBLES BLIND)) I'M JUST SA DAMND BLIND BY
OUR DANGD SMOKE HERE THAT I CANT SEE ME ONE DAMND
THING.

ANNY ((SEES FIREBLAZE JUMP UP TO FILL BARBECUE PIT
& TO ROAR ON UP TO BLAZE IN TINCAN IN WOODY'S HAND))
THRROW IT OHHH FOR GOD SAKE MANN THROW IT THROW
IT THROW IT

WOODY ((WALKS A STEP OR TWO TO GET CLEAR OF JACK
AND ANNEKE TO TOSS HIS HOT BURNING CAN OF GAS OFF
DOWN TOWARDS LAKE AND SLOSHES GASOLINE UP AND
DOWN HIS ARM IN TRYING TO TOSS HIS CAN AWAY & AS
JACK RUBS AND STAGGERS BLINDED AROUND IN WEEDS WE
SEE ANNY GRAB A POUND OF OLEO UP IN HER HANDS AND
RUN DOWN PATH TO WHERE WOODY ROLLS ON DAMPISH
GRASSY GROUND TO TRY TO PUT BLAZEY FIRE OUT THAT
CRAWLS UP AND DOWN HIS ARM FROM HIS SHOULDER ON
DOWN TO HIS FINGERS))((TO ANNY)) OOOOHHHHMH OH?
OHHH YESSS YES YESSS F'R GOD SAKES RUB IT RUB IT
RUBBBBB ME . . .

Woody's plays were considered far too weird to be used, but
then everyone associated with Folksay Theater was a bit crazy in
the spring of 1954 and he seemed not much worse, by and large,
than anyone else. Geer himself, sleeping on an army mattress at
Marion Tanner's house in Greenwich Village—she was the model
for *Auntie Mame*—was unhinged and rickety after the dissolution of
his marriage. And then there was Art Smith, a blacklisted actor
who was an integral part of the company. He'd fall into wild rages
and prowl the streets looking to kill Elia Kazan, the famous director, who—he believed—had fingered him to the HUAC investigators. Even the location of Folksay Theater was notably unstable,
moving from loft to cellar to hole-in-the-wall club, always one step
ahead of the fire marshals. The quality of performance varied from
week to week too, depending upon who was available—usually,
though, the talent pool was larger than the potential audience. Harold Leventhal, unemployed now that the Weavers were blacklisted,
stood by the door and accepted contributions from the loyal dozens
who'd inevitably manage to find out where Folksay was being performed each week and who kept it alive.

Woody showed up most of the time and often insisted on playing, even though his right hand and arm were almost useless. Will Geer didn't have the heart to tell his old friend that he was making a fool of himself; and neither did Anneke, who would bring the baby along and wince as Woody struggled bravely; and neither did Jack Elliot, just back in town, who played halting duets with Woody, often slowing down so as not to embarrass him; and neither did Moe Asch, who recorded Woody and Jack Elliot playing together—Woody's last, painful sessions—even though he was disgusted by what had become of America's finest ballad writer; and neither did Bob Harris, who lent Woody a wire recorder that he lugged up to Harlem for sessions with Sonny Terry and Brownie McGhee that were as sad as his other attempted performances; and neither did Sonny Terry, who, through his blindness, could sense that Woody was drifting away . . . diminishing . . . lost. No one had the heart to tell him that his performing days were over. And then, as he gradually slipped back into a mindless stupor and stopped *trying* to do anything, no one had to tell him.

Anneke took a secretarial job with Bellevue Hospital that spring and, reluctantly, left Lorina in Woody's care each day. She'd return home to find the baby wet, undiapered, and bawling wildly in a soaking crib; and Woody passed out on the bed. Sometimes, when they were down to a last few dollars, he would demand that they play chess to decide whether the money would be spent on food or booze—and, being an excellent chess player, he usually won. Anneke didn't know how much more of this she could handle; she felt paralyzed, unable to confront him, unable to say, "You crazy bastard, what do you *mean* you want to spend our last few bucks on booze?"

An explosion was inevitable, and it came one evening when Bob Harris was visiting. Anneke had just finished washing Lorina's diapers—an exhausting job, especially after a long day at work—and had them stacked neatly by the bed. Woody, drinking ale and talking to Harris, lurched and spilled some ale on the floor. Without thinking, he grabbed several diapers from the pile and began mopping it up. "Use a rag!" Anneke screamed, yanking the diapers out of his hand. Embarrassed, he shoved her and she slapped him across the face, and then they were down on the floor, rolling around, and she was choking him and banging his head against the floor. He was so weak she might have strangled him if she hadn't come to her senses, suddenly realizing that it was Woody—poor, pitiful Woody—she was trying to murder. She was shocked by her anger and so, apparently, was he.

Several days later, he left.

He and Jack Elliot raised about eleven dollars playing in Washington Square Park, then joined two young folk-singing friends of Jack's and drove across country, straight through to San Diego in three days. Woody and Jack left the others there, and went over to the train yards, looking to hop a freight to Los Angeles. The railroad bulls stopped them though, and demanded identification. "I didn't have anything in my wallet," Jack Elliot remembered. "Woody had lots of ID. He had his seamen's union card and a document testifying that he was a legitimate, bona fide author and several other things, and he began bawling me out in front of the cops, 'You always gotta have your ID, kid. You gotta have your *i-den-ti-fi-ca-tion* on ya at all times,' and the cops really dug that, I guess, because they let us go our way unmolested. Woody always had a way with cops."

They went to Topanga and stayed with Butch and Bess Hawes. Bess noticed immediately that Woody had deteriorated. He seemed weird and distant. "He'd kind of phase out on you all the time," she recalled. "I remember going home once and he was sitting out in the backyard, stark naked, and I had three children and seven bags of groceries that I nearly dropped, and I said, 'Hello, Woody,' and he just didn't say anything. I got very nervous about having him there alone with the kids and all. We really didn't know what was the matter with him—he looked kind of wasted. I thought Jack Elliot was pretty strange too, although he always was quiet and self-effacing. But he was such an incredible mimic of Woody that I'd hear him say something in another room, and think it was Woody. It was all pretty eerie. We finally talked it over and decided we should tell them to leave."

Woody went up to Pretty Polly Canyon. He told Jack to go buy some food. "I bought a quart of Olympia ale and some hot dogs," Jack recalled. "And when I got back up to his mountain, Woody was gone. Next time I heard from him, he sent me a postcard from the jail in Olympia, Washington. Same place as the ale."

Hitching and hopping freights, lurching along highways and through railroad yards, this was to be Woody's very last trip across America. It was the summer of 1954. Eisenhower was President and the nation was at peace. The great Red Scare seemed to be running out of steam (in spirit, if not in fact), as Senator Joseph McCarthy recently had made a fool of himself on national television attempting to prove that the army was riddled with Communists. Woody rode the empty boxcars—there weren't many hoboes anymore—watching it all pass by, the long rows of fruit trees in the great valleys, the fields of wheat and corn shimmering hypnotically, the superhighways filled with speeding diesel trucks, the new shopping centers and supermarkets stuffed with unimaginable abundance, the television antennas sprouting in areas that hadn't even had electricity the last time he'd passed through.

He went north first, along the Pacific coast, sending Anneke a postcard from Santa Barbara: "I'm heading up to Frisco to hire out as a seaman in Harry Bridges' hiring hall to dump me off yonder in Asia most any old spot or place. Love still, Weedy Seedy Guthrie."

Apparently the N.M.U. wouldn't have him, though, and he continued on up the coast, getting busted in Olympia and sending Jack Elliot the postcard. It wasn't the only jail he'd visit that summer. He didn't make much of an effort to conceal himself from the police—sleeping on sidewalks, in alleys, flopped out in boxcars—and was picked up almost every night for vagrancy or drunk and disorderly, and usually let out the next morning. But the nights in jail weren't nearly so bad as the visits with old friends and relatives, who didn't want to see him. Uncle Jeff was disgusted when Woody passed through Denver this time, "looking like Jesus" once again. Uncle Claude Guthrie, who ran a machine shop in Tulsa with his half brother Gid, wouldn't even come out from the back room to *talk* to Woody, much less put him up.

In El Paso, he visited Matt Jennings and Mary and his children, who he assumed had been adopted by Mary's new husband (Woody had signed adoption papers in 1947, but wasn't aware that they'd never been filed). He arrived at Matt's house just before sunrise one day, wearing a blue shirt, black pants, battered shoes, and "no other article of clothing on his body," Matt remembered. He was carrying a copy of *Microbe Hunters* by Paul de Kruif, which he'd bought in a bus station. Matt fixed breakfast and tried to get him to go to sleep on the couch, but Woody was more interested in talking about *Microbe Hunters* and playing Matt's fiddle records on the hi-fi. He seemed drunk and was waving a pint of whiskey about conspicuously, but Matt noticed that he never drank from it. The bottle was full.

Later he went to visit Mary, who wasn't quite so happy to see him as Matt had been, and fell asleep on her couch . . . and urinated on it. He was terribly embarrassed and told her that he was helpless, and wanted to stay there since no one else would take care of him. Mary began to cry, and their daughter Sue—a poised, sharp high school girl now—took over. "Daddy," she said, "I've missed you very much and I love you, but Mom has made a good life for us here and it hurts her to have you stay, and so maybe you'd better just go."

Woody put his arm around Sue and said, "What time does the next bus leave?"

Several weeks later, on August 29, 1954, the Columbus, Ohio, *Citizen* reported the following:

CITY PRISON HOUSES DISTINGUISHED AUTHOR AND COMPOSER—AND HOBO
By Eugene Grove

"Saturday's child," the proverb says, "has far to go."

And Woodrow Wilson Guthrie, citizen of New York City and the world at large, surely must be a Saturday child. He has gone far in search of the Big Rock Candy Mountain.

The journey of Woody Guthrie, successful author, successful musician and successful hobo, however, was temporarily detoured—for the 12th time in six weeks—by an enforced stay in jail. This time, it was the Columbus City Prison.

"I don't mind," Guthrie said, gazing abstractedly out a window. "Give me a chance to get a shower and couple of meals. And they give me a suspended sentence too.

"Some of the jails I been in they get tough, but most places are like this—if you're just passing through, the judge understands and suspends the sentence." Woody was arrested for trespassing on railroad property, held overnight for court and released.

"I was sleeping in a flat car," he said.

"On a Pennsy express I caught in East St. Louis . . ." his voice trailed off in a chuckle. "They call it their 'fast' express.

"It's hard to tell what you can do. Some places they throw you on a train to get you out of town and other places, like here, they drag you off a freight and stick you in jail."

Woody paused, lit a cigarette with an awkward, stiff-handed motion. "Burned my hand in Florida last year," he explained. "They told me I'd never use it again.

"Before the officer hauled me off, the brakeman slipped me a dollar. Something like that always happens just when you get to starving.

"I can safely say that Americans will let you get awful hungry but they never quite let you starve."

Woody went on to talk about his wartime experiences and *Bound for Glory*, and bragged about several songs he'd written, most notably "So Long" and "Oklahoma Hills." Then:

"But mostly I just like to bum around. Every spot has its good points and I like to see them all.

"I went out to Los Angeles on this trip to see about a lot I bought out there. I hadn't kept up on the payments and I went to see the real estate man. Then I beat it up to Vancouver to a hospital. I got a heart condition and I heard they could fix it, but they couldn't. . . .

"Time to go. Where'd I put my book? Oh, there it is." He picked up the only possession he had with him, a book entitled "Yogi Philosophy and Oriental Occultism," by Yogi Ramacharaha. "I'd say I'm a religious man," he said. "But I ain't got no favorites. I sorta like them all."

Several days later, he was back in New York and living with Anneke again on East Fifth Street. He talked about resuming his career and visited all his old contacts, but he couldn't fool himself or anyone else any longer. He felt stumbly and deranged, confused and out of control. He visited Pete Kameron, who had five hundred dollars in royalties from *Songs to Grow On* waiting for him, but Woody seemed incapable of figuring out what to do

with the money. Kameron suggested that he put half in the bank
and send the other half to Marjorie, which he did.

Three days later, on September 16, 1954, he checked himself
back into Brooklyn State Hospital.

"Marjorie Guthrie called me up this morning," Anneke wrote to
him. "She was sniffing and weeping . . . she said you had gone
into the hospital but didn't tell me anything I didn't know would
happen. I had a grim feeling this morning that I wouldn't see you
again tonight. This poor old bed is going to feel mighty empty
with you gone. And you are gone. The pack of half-opened cigarettes still lies on the table and I came in through the window
because I didn't have the key. I hated to come home to nothing,
like I have these past few months. But if you are doing OK by
yourself, I don't mind too much. I dread Sunday. I'll feel very
embarrassed . . . all [of us] trooping up to see you in your little
hospital."

The hospital records noted, with some wonderment: "*Both* wife
two and three visiting patient and appear friendly . . . wife 3
somewhat unusual in manner, but very realistic." As for Woody:
"Disease affecting his playing, easily upset, periods of self-de-
structiveness, dizzy spells . . . socializes very little on ward . . .
preoccupied with burned hand, receiving physiotherapy for hand
. . . may not as yet require extensive hospitalization."

After several weeks of evaluation, it was decided that Woody
could leave the hospital and spend weekends with Anneke, who
was determined to play her role in the unfolding tragedy with
aplomb. She would stand by her husband, even though it was
clear that there was nothing left for Woody but a gradual, frustrating diminution. She wrote to his sister Mary Jo: "I love him
like I love the free wind and the wild grass, like the sweet heady
smell that comes before the thunder storm. . . . I love him like
I love every good and beautiful thing here on my earth, and I
will always see that he is as happy as it is in my power to make
him."

She found a small apartment in Coney Island for their weekends together, just around the corner from 3520 Mermaid Avenue. It wasn't the most convenient place for her to live, especially
with the long commute to Manhattan for work each day, but she
hoped Woody would feel more comfortable in familiar surroundings.

She had been forced to make some quick decisions about the care and feeding of their baby after Woody ran off in June. Through a friend, she'd found an elderly couple in Queens who were willing to keep Lorina for several weeks while she tried to make long-term arrangements; but the "several weeks" stretched into months, and the elderly couple became de facto foster parents, with Anneke taking the baby on occasional weekends . . . but, more often, visiting her in their home. Now, though, in her effort to make a weekend home for Woody, she decided to start taking the baby more frequently. She would ride the subway to Queens after work on Friday and pick up Lorina, then another subway to Brooklyn to pick up Woody at the hospital, then a third subway to Coney Island with both of them in tow. She worked hard at this for several months, but found that none of it made much difference: Woody seemed just barely there, and the baby—more attached now to the foster parents than to her—wasn't very happy either. By March of 1955, the hospital records noted: "Continues to visit wife—wife says tends to become depressed, reads continuously . . . hopeless . . ."

He was reading now in much the same way as his mother had gone to the double features at the Jewel Theater in Okemah. It was a way of shutting out the world, of not having to deal with anyone or think about how he appeared to others ("looks at floor and tries to control involuntary movements," a diagnostic report noted). It's not clear that he had the presence of mind to comprehend all that he was reading—especially the more weighty volumes like Bertrand Russell's *The Analysis of Matter*, which he proudly carried about the hospital. He certainly wasn't lucid enough, except on rare occasions, to do the sort of nonstop writing that had kept him busy in the past, and reading seemed the next-best thing.

As it happened, the book that gave him the most comfort was the Bible. "I don't much believe," he wrote, "that our key secret of life will be found on these printed pages of paper," but "I see my words of soulful healing lots plainer in my bibledy book. . . . God is my best doctor, Jesus is my tippytop best teacher on every work."

Even in his most ardent moments as a Communist, Woody had never quite lost faith in Jesus, the raggedy socialist outlaw (not unlike himself) who loved the poor and drove the bankers from the temple. But the Jesus he turned to now was a different, more fundamental Christ—the Savior, pure and simple. He threw himself on the mercy of Preacher McKenzie's total-immersion Christ, the ultimate healer. Facing the most horrible reality that a man can face, Woody decided that heaven was his only out—and loving Jesus the only means of transportation. When he was able to steady his mind and hand long enough for a letter to Anneke, or to Marjorie and the kids, it would be awash with religiosity of the most primitive sort: "I hear my words from Jesus run my crazified wards around my Brooklyn Stater place here a good deal more than I can hear the words of any of my other biggy doctors."

He wrote a song called "Jesus My Doctor," in a scraggly handwriting that wandered up and down the page:

> *Christ youre still my best doctor*
> *Jesus youre still my best doctor*
> *Christ youre still my best doctor*
> *You can cure what ails me*

Then, after two similar verses:

> *Jesus Jesus Jesus Jesus*
> *Jesus Jesus Jesus Jesus*
> *Jesus Jesus O My Jesus*
> *You cured all thats worried me.*

Woody was so sure that Christ would save his soul that he was now able—for the first time—to face up to the disease that was wasting his body. In December of 1954, he finally admitted to his father: "I've got the 1st early signs and symptoms of a dizzy disease called Huntington's Chorea, same disease that Mama had which lets me stay dizzy in my head everyday without paying my barman one penny."

And he wrote a poem which began:

> *Huntington's Chorea*
> *Means there's no help known*
> *In the science of medicine*
> *For me . . .*

And closed with the hope that "maybe Jesus can think up a cure of some kind."

His cloudy mind, his scarred and shaky hands, prevented him from doing very much writing in the hospital—and the writing he did was increasingly illegible—but Anneke had a typewriter in Coney Island, which was easier to use, and there, on weekends, he tended to forget Jesus and fall into wild fits of retyping old songs—"Shenandoah," "The Streets of Laredo," "Rosewood Casket"—on yellow legal pads, always ending with the line "End of Shenandoah [or whatever], but not of me." A verse of "Cumberland Mountain Farms," which his mother had taught him, came out looking like this:

> *ITSA Hundert'N twenty some mile t' Shittyyynooger*
> *ITSA BOUT THAT SAME DISSTANCE T'' PURCELL*
> *ITSA TRILLIONE JILLIONE MILES T' CYVVYLIIZZA-*
> *TIUNE*
> *HERE I'MA STANDIN IN THESE LOWEREST PARTSA*
> *HELLLLL*

At the bottom of the page, he signed it:

> *I ME WOODY GUTHRIE TWENTYE NINE ELEVEN*
> *WESTY THIRTYSIX*
> *POORE DAMND BROOKLYNE TWENTY FOURE,*
> *NEWDY YERK*
> *MAY GONE SA DAMNLY QUICKLY SOONE*
> *NINETEENE HUNDRITDTHE & DOUBLEDY FIVE*

Occasionally, but far less frequently than before, he would have bursts of his old delusional enthusiasm, firing off letters to Asch and Harris, proposing new albums or books or plays or singing groups. Anneke indulged him in these fantasies for the most part; but then, gradually, she stopped.

The months were passing very, very slowly for her. His condition worsened, but so imperceptibly that he almost always seemed the same. She drifted back into the world, and away from him. She moved from Coney Island to a more convenient apartment in Brooklyn. She acknowledged the obvious and allowed the elderly couple in Queens to adopt Lorina. She fell in love with another man, and told Woody she was intending to file for divorce. He understood the situation, she thought, although he still sent her long, unreadable letters from the hospital, written on paper towels stuffed haphazardly into envelopes, her address smeared and crazy—she wondered how the letters ever reached her.

By the summer of 1956, it was all over. She wrote him a last letter, en route to Mexico for her divorce: "I'll just say that you left me a long time ago, and that you are clinging to the thought that I am still there . . . where I was two years ago. But I'm not. . . . It is my ambition, when I get back from Mexico and when Lorina is all taken care of, to go to either Korea, with some group, or Alaska. This from Anneke Van Kirk. Love . . . always."

With Anneke out of the picture, Marjorie moved back in. She resumed the role she'd always played most comfortably, unabashedly treating Woody as a child—*her* child. She was remarried now, but not to Tony Marra, who'd proven a bit too racy and undependable for the long haul. Her husband was Al Addeo, a carpenter and jack-of-all-trades whose deceased wife, Florence, often had taken care of the Guthrie children. Al was not a brilliant man, and Marjorie's friends wondered what she saw in him. But he was loyal and kind, and malleable. More than anything else, Marjorie needed someone to do a man's chores about the house and dance studio; she also was looking for someone who wouldn't be jealous of her resumed role as Woody's official "wife" and keeper of the flame.

Early in 1956, a meeting was held at Earl Robinson's house in Brooklyn to discuss what to do about Woody's financial affairs now that he was no longer capable of handling them himself. It was attended by the people who considered themselves Woody's closest friends: Robinson, Pete Seeger, Lee Hays, Marjorie, Harold Leventhal, and several others. Leventhal, the business expert, suggested that a trust fund be established to organize and promote Woody's songs and writings, collect his royalties, and disburse them to his children. This sounded easy enough, and everyone agreed that it should be done. But Woody's affairs were in a ridiculously tangled state. There was the Asch vs. Harris situation, neither of whom kept the most elaborate sales records, and there was the rather vague contract that Pete Kameron (now departed for California) had entered into with Howie Richmond, and there was the question of who owned the rights to all the old Almanac Songs, as well as several hundred others that Woody had written or helped write on the backs of paper bags, napkins, and menus over the past twenty years. It would be years before Leventhal could say that the Guthrie estate was in reasonable order—and, even then, there were some questions (like the exact record sales) that never would be resolved.

In any case, the Guthrie Children's Trust Fund was launched, with Leventhal, Pete Seeger, and Lou Gordon as trustees. Gordon was a union official and not a very close friend of Woody's, but everyone figured that any self-respecting "progressive" committee should have a representative from the ranks of labor.

Unfortunately, though, there was a major flaw in the Guthrie Children's Trust Fund. The "children" as defined in the incorporation papers were *Marjorie's* children. Arlo, Joady, and Nora were the only ones who could legally receive money. And while that would later appear to be a deliberate disinheritance, it was more an innocent oversight: no one seemed to remember that Woody *had* other children. Mary hadn't been heard from in years, and Anneke's child had been adopted by people who'd made it clear they wanted no part of Woody Guthrie or his estate. In any case, the division of spoils seemed a rather moot point, since Woody was averaging only about $1,000 per year in royalties. In fact, there was some concern that there wouldn't be enough in the fund to cover the children's college educations. As a result, it was suggested that a benefit concert be staged to raise some money.

The concert, held on March 17, 1956, at Pythian Hall in New York, proved memorable. Millard Lampell prepared a script that interlaced Woody's songs and autobiographical writings, and managed to convey—for the very first time—the awesome diversity of his work. But more than that, the concert was a reunion of sorts—of the Almanac Singers, and the People's Songs gang and the rest of the left-wing folk music community. For the first time in years they were all out in the open and celebrating one of their heroes. More than a thousand people filled the hall that night and the program closed with the entire cast singing "This Land Is Your Land."

As the last verse ended, the spotlight swung suddenly to the balcony and settled on a spidery little man with salt-and-pepper hair who struggled to his feet and saluted the audience with a clenched fist—a perfect gesture, quite in keeping with the defiant spirit of the evening. Pete Seeger, tears streaming, began the first verse of "This Land" again, and now the entire audience was up and cheering the man in the balcony, and singing his song.

Years later, Seeger and others would look back on the evening as an important moment in the rebirth of the folk music revival. It was more than that, though: it was the beginning of Woody Guthrie's canonization.

Perhaps it was the sudden adulation, perhaps simply a desire not to be stuffed and mounted so soon, but Woody became rather rambunctious in the months after the concert. He found that he could check himself out of the hospital without much fuss, and began turning up unexpectedly around town. Sometimes he would find his way to the various haunts in Greenwich Village where young folk singers were beginning to congregate, and allow himself to be fussed over. He'd often visit Lee Hays, who lived upstairs from Earl Robinson and had a typewriter; or Harold Leventhal, the man now in charge of the money; or Marion Tanner, who always had a houseful of strange people. He wasn't in the best shape—drooling at times, unable to control his bowels, and very, very uncertain, especially when trying to light cigarettes. One day he accidentally set fire to Harold Leventhal's couch. Another time, Leventhal received a phone call: Woody was going berserk at Marion Tanner's house. By the time Leventhal arrived, though, he'd calmed down and Harold took him out and bought him some new clothes, then put him in a taxi back to the hospital.

But Woody wanted out of the hospital. He told the doctors he was certain that with his newfound fame he could earn a living out in the world. The doctors were doubtful. His "ability to function," they noted, was "highly questionable." Still, since he'd admitted himself voluntarily, there was no way they could hold him and, on May 23, 1956, he checked himself out.

He staggered several miles across Brooklyn to Lee Hays's apartment, arriving there with a gallon of wine late in the evening. He announced that he was starving, and Lee asked Earl Robinson's son, Perry, who was having a jam session with several young musician friends downstairs, to make Woody Guthrie some food. The kids worshipfully came upstairs with their guitars and a plate of ham and eggs, which Woody pushed and prodded about clumsily until half was eaten and the other half on the floor, and then he asked for more. The kids wanted Woody to sit in with them, but he could barely handle the guitar; he felt more at home at the typewriter, where he camped out for the rest of the night, filling page after page with erotic songs and poems:

> *Gotta havey perty girly alla my timey*
> *Gotta havey perty girly alla my timey*
> *I feely miserable alla mye time*
> *If I cainta grabby perty girly alla my time.*

Hays didn't want to go to sleep for fear that Guthrie, chain smoking, would set fire to the place, but eventually Lee passed out and awakened the next morning to find erotic poems and songs *pasted* all over his walls. He put Woody in a cab, and sent him over to Harold Leventhal's apartment.

But Woody never arrived there. Instead, he hopped a bus heading west, his destination uncertain. He made it as far as New Jersey, where he was arrested for vagrancy because he didn't have money for the fare. He told the policeman that he was sick, not drunk, and needed to go to a hospital. The officer called Leventhal, who confirmed the story, and Woody was taken to Greystone Park—a massive state institution as bleak as its name—in Morris Plains, New Jersey, where he would remain for the next five years.

He called it "Gravestone," and panicked when he learned that he was stuck there. Because his admission hadn't exactly been voluntary, he couldn't check himself out as he had in Brooklyn. He wrote anguished letters to Marjorie, who didn't answer—she was off in the mountains with the children, teaching dance at a summer camp. He couldn't understand why she wouldn't write to him, why no one seemed to care anymore:

> Six biggy loney somey hard months here since I seed any or alla you o god please justa donty ya ever let me suffer this lonesome without you way this long no more . . . and I do really die from my loneysomeness here when you guys in my gang there just never do ever writey me no letters here nor drop over ta see me. . . . So how now would you feel if you are me if you was me 6 months in here and notta dam dam dam dam vizitor off no dam kind. Whatty kind of dam nurse what kind offa dam secretary do you

tryta call yourself here Marjy anyhows what dam dam
kind—If I've ever doney one meany baddy thing for alla
you guys ta be offa onna biggy strikey against me I am
hereby apologizin and Ill be gladdy to granta you all all
your demands you ever ever demanden off me.

Lovey Me.
       Writey me.
              Savey me.
                     Lordey God, Woody.

He did receive one visit that summer, from Harold Leventhal
and Fred Hellerman, who were amazed by how happy he seemed.
He liked Greystone better than Brooklyn, he said. The awful
buildings were surrounded by vast lawns, and trees and flowers.
There also was the site of George Washington's revolutionary
army encampment nearby, which he enjoyed wandering through.
He said to Hellerman, "This is the best damn place to be these
days. It's the only place in the country where I can get up on a
stool and start screaming, 'I'm a Communist. I'm a Communist,'
and no one can do a goddamn thing about it. If *you* do that,
they'll arrest you."

In all, Woody seemed disturbingly sane . . . especially when
compared to the comic-opera psychiatrist who, in a thick Viennese accent, reviewed the case with Leventhal and Hellerman. "Guthrie, Guthrie," he said, rummaging his desk for
the file. "Ah, Guthrie! A very sick man. Very sick. Delusional! He says he has written more than a thousand songs!
And a novel too. And he says he has made records for the
Library of Congress . . ."

"He has," Leventhal said.

In the fall, when she returned from the mountains, Marjorie began visiting Woody every few weeks with the kids. They would
pile into Al Addeo's car on Sundays, and sit with Woody under
a big tree—he called it his magic tree—on the grounds. Sometimes they'd take him out for lunch at a diner, the children nervous and shy and watching as Woody tried to direct the food
toward his mouth, struggling, spilling, and Marjorie chattering
all the while: "Oh, Woody, you're just having a tough old time
of it today, aren't you?" Rather than ignore his troubles, she was

forcing the kids to confront Woody's illness and accept it. And while that was admirable, there was a strained, nervous undercurrent to their times together, the kids embarrassed and Woody—who was so proud that he wouldn't allow anyone to light his cigarettes for him—never acknowledging that there was anything out of the usual about his behavior. And no one, *no one*, ever talking about the most obvious and frightening aspect of it all: the children could get it too. The disease had been passed from George Sherman, who fell off his horse and drowned, to his daughter Nora, to her son Woody, to . . . Each of his children had a fifty-fifty chance of getting it.

In the first months after she'd found out that Woody had Huntington's chorea, Marjorie questioned several doctors about the disease. She asked Jack Elliot's father, Dr. Adnopoz, and her family pediatrician and the doctors she met at parties and in the course of her work—but none of them knew very much, except that it was very rare. The most helpful, if one can call it that, was a doctor from Pittsburgh, a friend of her parents, who said, "Do you want to know what your husband is going to look like?" and began flailing his arms and head about wildly.

In truth she really didn't *want* to know all that much. She realized from the start that her children were at risk, but there would be no way of knowing whether they had it until they reached middle age, and she wasn't about to spend the next thirty-five years worrying. She wanted their lives to be as normal as possible, but she knew—especially after they began visiting Woody regularly—that they were going to start asking questions someday and she had no idea what she would tell them.

It was Joady who asked. They were riding home from Greystone one Sunday and he asked, "Could I get sick like Woody?"

"Yes," she spluttered, gasping. "But don't worry about it now. If it happens, it won't happen for a long, long time. Anyway, lots of families have problems like this and they get by, so we will too."

And, for many years after, that was the extent of family discussion on the subject. If the children were frightened—and, no doubt, they were—they kept their fears to themselves.

Between visits, Woody wrote letters to Marjorie that were—because of his deteriorating handwriting—virtually illegible. Only with a good deal of effort could she pick out some of the words.

September 14: "Rabbi Slonsky [another patient] makes me read to him my good gideon's bibel here every day. . . . Teach our kids to read to pray to God to believe to know Jesus and you'll never see any of them turn out to be delinquents. Pray together and stay together."

September 17: "Today I did helpy to tie down our wildest loudyest most constant complainer to God His Very Own Self— Bobby Rosenstein. . . ."

October 2: "You can use alla me and alla my moneys there Marjorie just any old way you please. . . . I know that God'll pay you more moneys for 'This Land' than He did for 'So Long.' " (Later, in an undated letter, Woody modified this intention somewhat: "I'm asking you Marjyreena to write me up some kind of a legal notice a legal letter of some sort givin alla my moneys over to my first church of Christ Scientist Boston Mass over and above any sum stated by you to help care for you and our four world shakers.")

October 4: "Eisenhower can't be my big chiefy bossyman till he makes alla my United States alla my races all equal. . . . . I vote for my communist candidates anyhow that'll be the only ones ta ever even partways tryta give birth ta my racey equality."

October 14: "Please Marjy I really do need your good helps lots more now Marjy than I ever did . . . don't desert me, don't you ever quit me, I die dead if you do. . . . Sex and all aint possible by me not no more sex is just not possible with me anymore. I'm just like another one of alla your little babies cryin after you o my sweety little Marjorie weepin after you."

In November of 1956, his oldest daughter, Gwen, gave birth to a daughter and Woody was a grandfather.

In December of 1956, his father died in an Oklahoma City hotel room at the age of seventy-seven. In one of the very last letters he was able to write, Woody comforted his sister Mary Jo:

Marjoree wrote to me that you wrote to her on the day after our dear father Charley Edward Guthrie passed on to his greaty goody everloving and heavenly and holy saintly reward as in the promises of my savior my deary sweety Jesus M. Christo and so I say lets not be worrie eyedy weery eyedy nor tearyful eyedy nor now sorrowdy hearted down here on our lowlow earthful worldly planet to see

him passy on up to the everlovin fingers of our good good
lorde and our saver there Jesus my only goody earthyful
boy to Jesus my only true hearted earthly man But I say to
all of you I say to you all let's be gladdy let's be just be
thankful let's all be really happy day for just once in our
earthly lives here to see our father go to his new earth and
on into his new builty heavenly by gods very own hands
and all of us struggle our bests to live such a godlyful kind
of earthy life here we will each and all and everyone one
of us here enter on in into gods great eternal glory at the
day of our deathy. Amen Amen.

Harold Leventhal continued to visit, often bringing Lee Hays,
Fred Hellerman, and other old friends with him, as well as cigarettes, candy (Woody seemed to have acquired an insatiable appetite
for sweets), books, and records. Leventhal was depressed and
frightened by the hospital. He feared for Woody's safety, often
slipping a few dollars to the attendants in the hope that they'd take
special care of him. Woody never complained, though. He seemed
determinedly cheery when visitors came, entertaining them with
gossip about the other patients ("Ya see that guy over there? He
eats books. Said *Bound for Glory* was one of the best he ever tasted
. . ."), and refusing to accept pity or condescension.

Soon after he arrived at Greystone, he asked Leventhal to bring
him a guitar, and Harold did—but Woody returned it on the next
visit, saying matter-of-factly that he couldn't do much with it anymore, and the other patients probably would bust it up before long.
Then he asked for a typewriter, which Leventhal brought—but that
was returned, too, before very long. In one of his last letters, December 12, 1956, he acknowledged to Marjorie: "I just guess I
have to really face my fact in my earthly case here all off my goody
pooky writing days are just all out and all over anyways."

On December 14, there was another typewritten letter in which
he described a new patient on the ward who ate cigarette butts
off the floor and never said anything. He invited the kids to
"comey visit me in my magicy tree againe . . ." and wrote on
the envelope: "God You See, Me I Donte."

It was his last letter.

The following July, Marjorie wrote to Mary Jo that Woody had
"stopped writing anything this winter. . . . He will never be able

to live away from constant care. He is obviously ill . . . his balance is pretty poor. In fact I requested that he get permission to go outdoors more often and the doctor said he was hesitant because he does not hold his head erect and could easily get in the way of automobiles.'' She added that Woody had suffered through a difficult winter, but was feeling much better now after another hernia operation. She hoped that he might even start writing again. ''Now that he is feeling so much better I think a few good words from you would be welcome and if he is inspired he can still try to write even though it's hard with his arm.''

Mary Jo wrote to Woody, and so did his children, and so did lots of other people, but, after forty-five years of spilling his every thought and dream and feeling and intention on paper, he could no longer control his body sufficiently to respond.

A year or so later, Alan Lomax returned from England and decided to visit the man who'd been his greatest discovery. He found Woody gray and gaunt, but still defiant. They walked around the hospital grounds—Woody uncertain, but refusing any help—and came to Washington's encampment, where Woody attempted a halting little joke: ''Ya see that, Alan? George Washington shit there.'' They returned then to the ward, where a crowd seemed to be awaiting Woody's arrival. ''Everyone seems to like me around here,'' he said. ''Don't know why.'' Then he went inside alone, disappearing beneath a sea of arms and hands patting, welcoming him home.

Lomax would always remember the moment. ''He told me goodbye with the iron calm of a totally possessed human being going to his death place. He did it without a quiver, with the pride of someone who knew what he was about—steel hard, tough, unbreakable. You'd think that with all the disease and his enormous insatiable sexuality, the heavy drinking and smoking and fornicating and running and chasing and playing and doing everything, he might have lost himself. But through that whole thing he was like an arrow in flight: Never a waver. He was aimed someplace; he was aimed back there to that ward. It was his destiny, those people. I felt chills of awe in his presence that afternoon.''

CHAPTER 12

Dust Can't Kill Me

In the late 1950's, Lee Hays—who loved casting himself as an elder statesman and master storyteller—began to notice that young people would listen politely, as always, to his stories about the Weavers and the Almanac Singers and political struggles gone by, but what they *really* wanted to hear about was his friendship with Woody Guthrie. He'd tell them his dozen or so Guthrie stories, suitably embellished, but that wouldn't be enough. They'd want to know more. What did he look like? Did he actually ride the freights? Was *Bound for Glory* true? How did he die?

One summer, when Hays had latched on as the entertainment coordinator at a resort in the Adirondacks, a young waiter kept pestering him and Lee, irritated, finally demanded, "Why are you so damned interested in Woody Guthrie? The man's been out of commission for years. Why is he so important to you?"

The waiter, obviously a thoughtful sort, replied, "Most kids reach a point where they really want their freedom. You hate school, your parents—anything that stands in the way. All you can think about is getting *out*. You want to hitch a ride, hop a freight, go wherever you want. Woody, I guess, represents that kind of freedom for me."

On Sunday afternoons, Hays would go down to Washington Square Park in Greenwich Village and watch the young folk singers—they were becoming a horde now—whanging away at their guitars, singing, "Goin' down the road feelin' bad . . ." with all the grit their adenoids could muster. Many of them affected—uncannily—a certified Guthrie slouch, ratty old clothes, facial stubble, and aroma. Hays would wander through the crowd, asking them, "Who was Woody Guthrie?"

"He was a rich rancher's son who ran away."

"He sailed a boat to Alaska."

"He killed a man."

"He died of syphilis."

"He's out there somewhere, riding the boxcars."

Lee Hays never would hear a better explanation of the phenomenon than the one offered by the young waiter at the mountain resort, but he still was perplexed by it. He thought of all the talented people he'd known in his life—some of them every bit as charismatic and colorful as Woody Guthrie—and how easily most had been forgotten. Pete Seeger was the finest musician he'd ever known, far superior to Guthrie . . . but it was Woody, not Pete, who was becoming part of the national mythology, slowly but surely. The mechanics of this bizarre consecration seemed maddeningly obscure. Hays couldn't figure how all these kids even *knew* about Woody—*Bound for Glory* was out of print, his records had never sold . . . and yet, it was the Guthrie spirit, as much as anything else, that was fueling the wild resurgence of folk music sweeping the country.

It began in 1958, with the Kingston Trio—three young college types with short hair and no rough edges—singing the old folk ballad "Tom Dooley," which became the most popular song of the year. They followed it with a succession of dry-cleaned, button-down folk song hits, including a version of the old Bess Lomax/Almanac Singers favorite, "The Train That Never Returned." Soon other well-scrubbed and antiseptic folk trios and quartets were popping up all over the place—the Limeliters, the Brothers Four, the Tarriers, and, now that the political heat was off, the Weavers again (minus Pete Seeger)—and most of the groups included a handful of Woody Guthrie songs in their repertoires. The Kingston Trio, for example, sang "Hard Ain't It Hard" on their first album and, in the next few years, would record "This Land," "Pastures of Plenty," "Hard Traveling," and "Deportees," among others.

The appearance of folk music on the pop charts was nothing new, of course. The Weavers had been there in the early 1950's, and Harry Belafonte's calypso (considered folk music of a sort) after that. But there were some important differences now. For one thing, folk music wasn't coming in the back door, as a novelty item, this time. It was being encouraged by the music establishment as a safe, congenial replacement for rock and roll, which had been crippled by military inductions (Elvis) and plane crashes (Buddy Holly et al.), and sullied by payola scandals, various libidinous difficulties (Chuck Berry's statutory rape conviction, Jerry Lee Lewis's marriage to his thirteen-year-old cousin), and the fact that rock and roll was enabling black performers to reach white audiences on a large scale for the very first time—a rather abstract form of racial mixing, but considered improper in many parts of the country nonetheless. The specter of financial impropriety, wholesale lasciviousness, and integration was enough to start talk of government intervention of some sort . . . and there was a growing sense in the music business that it might be best to cool it for a while. In that context, three white boys singing "Michael, Row the Boat Ashore" seemed decidedly less dangerous than, say, Fats Domino lecherously memorializing the "thrill" he found on "Blueberry Hill." And while the record company executives—whose concern about social responsibility and the appearance of propriety was strong, but not quite on a level with their interest in profits—never made much of an effort to purge sex or soul from their catalogues, they *did* succeed in transforming folk music into a commodity.

But there were other, less squalid reasons for what soon became known as the "folk boom." There was the rebirth of political activism after the frightened McCarthy years, especially in the civil rights movement in the South, which was a *singing* movement from the very start. The Highlander Folk School in Tennessee, still thriving twenty years after Pete Seeger and Woody Guthrie had visited on their way to Oklahoma in 1940, was training civil rights activists like Dr. Martin Luther King and teaching them songs like "We Shall Overcome," which was a reworking of a Baptist hymn ("I'll Be All Right") that first had been used by black tobacco workers in the 1940's.

The college campuses were stirring, too. The practical, G.I. bill generation of the late 1940's and early 1950's had cleared out, replaced by a more affluent, more adventurous and intellectually curious (and, perhaps, less enterprising) group of students—kids who, by and large, didn't remember the Great

Depression and were beginning to wonder about the frantic, un-questioning materialism of their parents. A timid, rather self-centered nonconformity became acceptable again. The nihilistic Beat poets and writers enjoyed a vogue; and while there were a few, faint glimmerings of a renewed idealism, more young peo-ple seemed to be using the Bomb as an excuse for philosophizing and end-of-the-world hedonism than working to ban it.

Pete Seeger was working to ban it. With few other bookings available because of the blacklist, he traveled from campus to campus in the 1950's, always encouraging the kids to get in-volved politically and musically, showing them how easy it was to pick up a guitar or banjo and start making music for them-selves. He'd also tell them about his old friend Woody Guthrie, an angry little man from Oklahoma who rode the boxcars during the Depression, who fought against the big shots, and who was the best songwriter he'd ever met, and then he'd sing a few of Woody's songs.

His audiences usually were familiar with folk music, even be-fore the Kingston Trio came along. The college students of the 1950's had grown up singing traditional songs like "Shenan-doah" and "The Erie Canal" in their school music programs—largely as a result of Alan Lomax's promotional efforts over the years (and, because of Howie Richmond's shrewdness, many of them already knew "This Land" and "Pastures of Plenty," too). But now, Seeger—using Woody as a prime example—showed them how the music was more than just history, how it could be used to express anger, to protest against social conditions. "Make your own music," he'd tell them. "Write your own songs about the things you care about." It didn't happen all at once, and it wasn't just Seeger's influence, but the seeds were planted and soon guitars seemed to be sprouting on campuses everywhere.

By 1959, when a young man named Robert Zimmerman enrolled at the University of Minnesota, knowledge of Woody Guthrie's music was commonplace among the folk singers and hangers-on in Dinkytown, the bohemian section of Minneapolis. Zimmerman had dreamed of becoming a rock-and-roll star, but now—like many oth-ers his age—he shifted his interest to folk music. It seemed freer, more artsy and collegiate, and, in a way, more rebellious than rock. He played the harmonica and guitar occasionally in local coffee-houses, calling himself Bob Dylan—no one knew why he chose that particular name, though it sounded vaguely literary. He would sit in friends' apartments and listen to records, old 78's of Woody Guthrie and Cisco Houston singing together, and of Woody alone singing his *Dust Bowl Ballads* in that rough, lonesome, distant voice. One day a friend asked if he'd ever read Guthrie's autobiography, *Bound for Glory*. Dylan hadn't, and he scoured the campus for a copy—the library, the bookstores, everywhere—before finding a faculty member who happened to have one. He read the book in a day, and carried it around for weeks afterward, pulling friends aside and forcing them to listen to passages: "Hey, you gotta hear this! Woody's riding on a freight train with these two kids and it starts to rain . . .

Much as Jack Elliot had before him, Dylan decided to remake himself in Woody's image. He learned all the songs, and held his guitar the way Woody did in the pictures, and dressed as he thought Woody might (and loved the fact that his hair was curly like Woody's), and invented a rambling past. According to Anthony Scaduto's biography of Dylan, friends began to tease him about the fixation. At one party, for example, they told him, "Hey, Bobby, Woody's here! He's outside and he wants to see you." And he ran out into the snow, knowing full well that Woody wasn't going to be there, but wanting it to be true so badly that he had to go out anyway, shouting, *"Woody, where are you?"*

One of Dylan's earliest songs—and his first really good one—was called "Song to Woody," the melody cribbed from "1913 Massacre":

> *I'm out here a thousand miles from my home*
> *Walkin' a road of the men who've gone down.*
> *I'm seein' your new world of people and things,*
> *Your paupers and peasants and princes and kings.*

> *Hey. hey Woody Guthrie I wrote you a song*
> *'Bout a funny ol' world that's a-comin' along.*
> *Seems sick an' it's hungry, it's tired an' it's torn.*
> *It looks like it's a-dyin' an' it's hardly been born.*

> *Hey, Woody Guthrie but I know that you know*
> *All the things that I'm a-sayin' an' many times more.*
> *I'm a-singin' you the song, but I a-can't sing enough.*

'Cause there's not many men that done the things
*   that you've done.*

Here's to Cisco an' Sonny an' Leadbelly too,
An' to all the good people that traveled with you.
Here's to the hearts and the hands of the men
That come with the dust and are gone with the wind.

I'm a-leavin' tomorrow. but I could leave today,
Somewhere down the road someday.
The very last thing that I'd want to do
Is to say I've been hittin' some hard travelin' too.

By late 1960, Dylan had learned that Woody was confined to a hospital in New Jersey. He phoned the place several times, but they said Mr. Guthrie couldn't come to the phone. Patients *were* permitted to receive visitors, though, and Dylan took off to see him. He arrived in January of 1961, and sent a postcard back to friends in Minneapolis: "I know Woody. I know Woody . . . I know him and met him and saw him and sang to him. I know Woody—Goddamn."

In 1959, a New Jersey electrician named Bob Gleason and his wife, Sidsel, heard a radio broadcast of the script that Millard Lampell had written for the 1956 Woody Guthrie benefit concert. At the end of the program, listeners were encouraged to write Woody at Greystone Park—he loved getting mail. Bob Gleason was a Guthrie fan from way back (he even remembered the "Woody Sez" column in the *Daily Worker*) and Sid, who came from Montana, had actually met Woody out West in the 1930's. Since they lived near the hospital, the Gleasons decided to see if there was something more they could do for Woody than just writing.

As it happened, there was. After several visits to Greystone, they started bringing him to their home on weekends, and the word quickly spread through the New York folk community that Woody was receiving visitors on Sundays in East Orange, an easy bus ride from the city. Soon the Gleasons' apartment was jammed with folk singers, anxious to play for their hero. They literally would sit at his feet and sing his songs—he only liked to hear *his* songs—as Woody leaned back in a chair, beaming and occasionally dispensing praise or advice: "Don't play the guitar s'damn loud. I can't hear the words," or "That's good. That's *damn* good."

His physical condition had deteriorated markedly since he'd entered Greystone. The little twitches and shakes had become gross, unpredictable lurches of his arms and legs and torso. Despite heavy medication, he was in constant motion. The worst of it seemed to be his right arm, which would fly up and strike his forehead with such force that sometimes, when they hadn't clipped his nails at the hospital, he'd gash himself with his thumb and blood would pour down his face. As a result, Sid Gleason began to clip his nails and, indeed, take responsibility for much of the rest of his personal hygiene. She also found that she could hook Woody's right hand into one of his belt loops when the spasms came so that he wouldn't hurt himself. He still was able to walk, but he looked like he was walking across a trampoline. His speech was a slurred, guttural rumble and difficult to understand if you weren't used to it. He never spoke much, in any case, and occasionally seemed to slip into a sort of trance, and no one could reach him.

Usually, though, his mind was crystal clear. He would entertain the Gleasons with tall tales about his past:

"I've made twenty-six record albums and had a bastard child for each one of them."

"Only place I ever was kicked out of was a whorehouse in Butte, Montana, and that was because I was makin' so much money with my guitar the girls couldn't do any business."

"I picked Greystone because it was the prettiest damn booby hatch I came across. When it was time and I knew I was gonna have to stay *someplace*, I went around scouting out hospitals and Greystone looked pretty good, so I fixed it so that I'd get arrested and sent there."

"I used to be able to visit Franklin Roosevelt any time I wanted. And Einstein too. I was the only person they let interrupt Einstein when he was working."

When they picked Woody up at the hospital each Sunday morning, he'd open and close the car windows several times—he hated the fact that the hospital windows were barred and locked—and then ask Bob Gleason, "Got a smoke?" Usually, he'd emerge from the ward with fan letters stuffed in his pockets, sleeves, socks, and coat, sticking out at all angles, causing him to look something like a scarecrow. After a bath and change of clothes (and more rebellious window opening), he and Sid would sit down with the letters and she'd ask him what he wanted to say in response to each.

"Tell them, tell them," he'd say.

"Tell them what, Woody?"

"Ask Pete," he'd say if he didn't have an immediate response and then, flustered: "Tell them, tell them . . ."

About noon, the guests would start to arrive. Marjorie and the kids, who found it far easier to get to East Orange than Greystone, came most weekends—and soon the Guthrie Children's Trust Fund was reimbursing the Gleasons for food, stamps, and other expenses. Pete Seeger often would be there, and Harold Leventhal, and occasionally Alan Lomax would rumble in. The real energy on Sunday afternoons came from the younger folkies, though—the kids who worshipped Woody and wanted him to hear them play: Ernie Marrs, Ralph Rinzler, John Cohen, Lionel Kilburg, Peter LaFarge, and Mel Lyman (who later would become a communal messiah of sorts and require his followers to listen to Woody's music) among others. Arlo Guthrie was now old enough to join the rest, and though he played the guitar a little too loudly for Woody's taste, he did write a song about a math test—to the tune of "So Long"—that showed promise.

The Gleasons' home became a youth hostel for wandering folk singers. Bob Dylan lived with them for several weeks after he came to town, listening to the tapes Bob Gleason had compiled of the Sunday-afternoon sessions, and of Woody's old record collection—vintage recordings of the Carter Family, Jimmie Rodgers, and the others. Over the course of several months, a real rapport seemed to develop between Woody and Dylan, with Woody often asking the Gleasons if "the boy" was going to be there on Sunday. "That boy's got a voice," he told them. "Maybe he won't make it with his writing, but he can sing it. He can really sing it." And when it came time for Dylan to make his New York debut at Gerde's Folk City, Sid Gleason gave him one of Woody's suits to wear for the occasion. It was an investiture whose symbolism was lost on no one.

The Sunday afternoons were so much fun, and the course of Woody's disease so gradual, that it often was possible to forget the utter tragedy of the situation, and just enjoy the good times. But then some old friend of Woody's would arrive in town—Jack Elliot, Cisco Houston, his sister Mary Jo—and be so shaken by his appearance that all the Gleason regulars would be forced to remember that the man was indeed dying. Jack Elliot returned from a self-imposed five-year exile in Europe and spent an afternoon hiding his face under a pushed-down cowboy hat and crying as he played all of Woody's old favorites, listening with horror as Woody, so happy and excited that Jack was back, tried to sing along on "Goin' Down the Road," but couldn't really make it: "Anna ainna gonna be treed thizzawayy . . ."

The folk boom and the promise of finally being able to make a living with his guitar was what brought Jack Elliot back home, and it also was what brought Cisco Houston back to New York at Harold Leventhal's behest. Cisco, who'd been selling encyclopedias out West, finally had a shot at the nightclub career he'd always wanted. Leventhal was even able to book him on a tour of India for the U.S. State Department. He was idolized by the crowd at the Gleasons', not only because he was acknowledged to be Woody's closest friend, but because he was a genuinely sweet man, and a very brave one. Shortly after he arrived in New York, Cisco learned that he was going to die from stomach cancer. He kept performing until the very end, when they almost had to carry him on and off the stage at Gerde's. And he always maintained that he wasn't nearly as courageous as his good friend Woody. In reminiscences he taped with Lee Hays near the end, he said, "I don't consider my case nearly as bad as some. When I go out to see Woody, and I see this broken man going in and out, back and forth from the hospital room, trembling and shaking, and just at the end of all the—well, of all the good things in life, just sort of breathing and walking around, enjoying this in a very limited way—the way he faces all this is with tremendous courage. . . .

"You know my situation, which could be a matter of weeks, or months before the wheel runs off. Nobody likes to run out of time. But it's not nearly as great a tragedy as Hiroshima, or the millions of people blown to hell in a war that could be avoided. Those are the real tragedies in life. What's happening to me and Woody are just mistakes of nature, things that eventually someday will be overcome."

On an afternoon in February of 1961, Woody's friends gathered to play some music for him at One Sheridan Square, the Greenwich Village nightclub that formerly had been Café Society. Lee Hays remembered Cisco walking in, riddled with cancer, and seeing Woody there, shaking so badly that he barely could hold on to his seat. "Cisco went over to him," Hays remembered, "and kissed Woody on the forehead and Woody, who always was a macho sort and never much for physical contact, seemed to lift his head up in order to be kissed. It was a stunning moment."

Cisco died on April 29, 1961.

The party for Woody at One Sheridan Square was one of many held during those years. His friends seemed to seize on any excuse to rent a hall, round up the old-timers once more, and pay homage. There was a hootenanny bar mitzvah for Arlo, and a hootenanny publication party for the paperback version of *Bound for Glory*; Oscar Brand, Hally Wood, Lionel Kilburg, and others also held parties in his honor. In addition, the Gleasons often would bring Woody to the city for concerts and, especially, to see the battalions of angry young bucks singing in Washington Square on Sundays. It must have seemed remarkable to Woody— all these kids from places like Queens and Great Neck, playing the fiddle and banjo like they came from the Blue Ridge Mountains, singing in that high nasal style like his mother . . . and some of them really doing it quite well. Often someone would spot Woody and a crowd would gather around him, the young bucks suddenly drained of anger and full of awe, gaping, competing for a spot close by, hoping to get a chance to play their latest for the rickety old man.

"Is that *really* Woody Guthrie?"

"God, he looks awful!"

"Whatsa matter with him?"

"They say he's in the last stages of syphilis."

One Sunday, Woody nearly went berserk when he overheard a kid say that he was dying of syphilis. Slurred and blathering, he grabbed the kid and tried to explain that it wasn't syphilis, it was Huntington's chorea. *Huntington's chorea* that came from his mother, and not from sleeping with whores or living out on the road. There was nothing, *nothing* he could have done about it. Nothing.

He still was agitated when the Gleasons loaded him back into the car that afternoon, and he decided that it probably was time to start talking to the reporters who'd been asking for interviews. He hadn't ever wanted to talk about the disease—and, in truth, he never actually *did* say very much when interviewed—but he'd rather have people know that he was suffering from Huntington's chorea than think it was syphilis.

And so he spoke with Robert Shelton of *The New York Times*, who wrote: "A giant, in the form of a wispy little guitar picker, has been among us." There were other newspaper articles: the New York *Post, The Village Voice,* England's *Melody Maker. Time* magazine designated Woody as one of the founding fathers of folk music. *Sing Out!,* fat now with advertising from the record companies, kept track of his physical condition, his various comings and goings around town, and, from time to time, would reprint one of his more obscure songs. *Mainstream,* the one Communist magazine that managed to survive the Cold War, had an entire Woody Guthrie issue.

The spate of articles coincided with the second wave of the folk boom: the appearance, in the early 1960's, of a school of bitter young political singers—people like Dylan, Tom Paxton, and Phil Ochs—all of whom were very much, and rather self-consciously, in the Guthrie tradition. They wrote songs about rampaging materialism and race hate, and published them in *Broadside,* a mimeographed sheet started by Gordon Friesen and Sis Cunningham, the old Almanac Singers, to provide a forum for political music. Bob Dylan contributed "Talking John Birch Society Blues" to the first issue, and his new songs appeared frequently in the magazine thereafter.

Just as the Almanac Singers had gone out to the picket lines, the new generation of protest singers went South to serenade the civil rights workers. Dylan, Paxton, Ochs, Joan Baez, and others joined the marches and demonstrations. Pete Seeger was there too—a respected elder now, a symbol of continuity, still rigidly principled and unbowed; he was personally invited by Dr. Martin Luther King to march with him from Selma to Montgomery, Alabama. More than anyone else—more than Alan Lomax, who had spent his life promoting a folk song revival and yet, now that there was one, resented the idea of affluent young kids trying to sound rural—Seeger derived great personal satisfaction from the flowering of new talent. He was thrilled by the brilliant, piercing songs that suddenly were all about. Every kid with a guitar in Greenwich Village seemed to have an original ballad about social injustice. At the Monday-night hootenannies at Gerde's Folk City, they would troop up to the microphone one after the next, dour and pained and terminally earnest . . . and, occasionally, eloquent and sensitive and funny. Overnight, folk music seemed to have become the primary means of expression for an entire generation.

Dylan was, of course, the best of the lot. Though he was initially regarded as merely another Woody Guthrie imitator, and then as Woody's heir apparent (and later as a traitor because he didn't live up to the Old Guard's political expectations), Dylan was very much his own man from the start. He never really had any political goals—just a personal vision. His songs were far more artful and complex than Woody's, filled with oblique references and exotic imagery. His vision was darker, less optimistic, and, ultimately, less concerned with the problems of the world than the sour emptiness of life. His early songs did seem firmly rooted in the left-wing folk tradition, though: ballads like "The Lonesome Death of Hattie Carroll" and anthems like "Blowin' in the Wind" and "A Hard Rain's Gonna Fall" sent old-timers like Seeger and Irwin Silber into fits of rapture. The quality of Dylan's rage was such that it began to create an audience for political music beyond the traditional confines of academia, bohemia, and the Left. Slick, pop folk groups—especially Peter, Paul and Mary—were beginning to record dandified versions of protest songs. Even Pete Seeger's "Where Have All the Flowers Gone?" and "If I Had a Hammer" were sneaking onto the pop charts. The folk boom was making everyone rich.

By 1963, *Time* magazine could put Joan Baez on its cover and say: "Anything called a hootenanny ought to be shot on sight, but the whole country is having one." The ultimate hootenanny took place that summer, when 37,000 people and an approximately equal number of musical instruments gathered for three days at the Newport (R.I.) Folk Festival. It was an impressive display of the music's diversity and appeal, with room onstage for everyone from aging Mississippi Delta blues players to Peter, Paul and Mary. But it was the young protest singers—Sis Cunningham called them "Woody's Children" in the festival program notes—who dominated the show. According to Paul Nelson, editor of *The Little Sandy Review*, they also seemed to dominate the audience: "Neophyte non-conformists, the young men were courteous, polite, affected in a sort of pseudo-Western manner, all dressed in blue or tan jeans, all trying hard to look, walk, talk, act in a way both highly humane and eminently road-weary.

The hair was erratic, the clothes as rumpled as parents would allow; the accent was drugstore cowboy, that non-regional dialect of the Shangri-La West that Bob Dylan and Jack Elliot hail from, that mythical nowhere where all men talk like Woody Guthrie and are recorded by Moses Asch.''

The commercial sharks moved in after that. The big record companies, seeing how well Dylan and Baez were selling, suddenly were open to any new kid with a guitar, a sneer, and a vibrato. Would-be talent scouts seemed to lurk about the edges of Washington Square Park on Sundays and Gerde's on Monday nights. Two-bit entrepreneurs entered the market with hootenanny gewgaws. A *Hootenanny* magazine darkened the newsstands briefly. And the ABC television network scheduled a weekly program called "Hootenanny," which became infamous in the folk music community when it blacklisted Pete Seeger. Many top performers boycotted the show as a result, although Seeger—typically—encouraged them to appear on it anyway and use it as a political platform.

But it wasn't the sharks so much as the singers themselves who brought about the commercial dilution and eventual collapse of the folk boom. Bob Dylan wasn't a folklorist like Alan Lomax, dedicated to preserving and promoting a beloved tradition . . . nor was he a singing political organizer like Seeger, who saw the music as a homemade "people's" alternative to Tin Pan Alley. He didn't disdain popular music—Elvis Presley had been his first hero. He'd chosen folk music because it seemed to offer more creative freedom than the formula pap of rock and roll. But all the old formulas had been washed away with the arrival of the Beatles and the surge of English creativity. Dylan was excited and intrigued when he heard the Animals sing "House of the Rising Sun"—a song he had recorded—as a rock tune, with electric guitars. He began to experiment quietly with rock musicians, and debated whether to make the great leap. He'd never made any deep commitment to folk purity or simplicity; in truth, he couldn't understand why the old-timers were so adamant about the music. And he was getting tired of their constant sniping as he explored his art and deepened his themes and moved away from didactic politics and—worst of all in their eyes, it seemed—became *popular*.

The internal politics of folk music began to reflect, in a strange, distorted way, the vast changes taking place out in the country.

The kids were challenging the old, conservative (in this case, fossilized left-wing) traditions. After a bloated and generally unsatisfactory 1964 festival, the 1965 version of Newport was shaping up as a war—between the young and the old, the electric and the acoustic, the personal and the political. Alan Lomax, who presided over the death of the folk song revival as he'd presided over its birth, started things off on precisely the wrong note. After a typically rhapsodic series of introductions of old, acoustic Delta blues players, he gave a rather snotty welcome to the Paul Butterfield Blues Band, a young, electrified outfit from Chicago—something to the effect that the old-timers didn't need any machines or gimmicks to make their music, but here are some young guys who do. . . . Albert Grossman, who was Dylan's manager (and soon to be Butterfield's), approached Lomax angrily after that, and then—incredibly—the two of them were at each other, wrestling on the ground and throwing ineffective punches, actually having a *fight* over it.

An obscure blues band from Chicago playing with electricity was one thing, but when Dylan materialized on the last night of the festival with an electric guitar and a four-piece rock band, there was chaos. Half the audience seemed to be dancing and cheering, the other half booing. Backstage, there was a heated debate among the old-timers as to whether to pull the plug. Seeger was threatening to get an ax and cut the power cables. After all the lonely years of five-dollar bookings at I.W.O. halls, of being blacklisted and red-baited but keeping the music (and the political dream that went along with it) alive despite it all, Pete saw his life's work being snatched right out from under his nose, the music incorporated into the popular mainstream by the very kid he'd hoped would carry on the tradition that Woody had personified. He didn't go ahead and chop the power cables that night, but Dylan retreated from the stage after two raucous numbers . . . and then returned with his acoustic guitar, sang "It's All Over Now, Baby Blue," and left.

And it was all over. Sooner or later, nearly all the popular folk singers would follow Dylan into electricity. Even Seeger eventually would record an album with electronic instruments backing him. Folk music would keep a small, purist following, but the folk "style" would become a major influence on the creative explosion in popular music that took place in the late 1960's, eventually settling in as one of rock's many hyphenated subdivisions, a rather syrupy cul-de-sac known as folk-rock.

Meanwhile, Woody Guthrie had become a cultural institution strong enough to weather the vagaries of folk boom or bust. By the mid-1960's, he (or, rather, his estate) was averaging $50,000 per year in royalties. Asch, Stinson, and even RCA—which included his *Dust Bowl Ballads* in its "Legendary Performers" series—released new versions of his old recordings. In 1964, an elegant three-record set of his Library of Congress interview with Alan Lomax was released by Electra. In 1965, a collection of his poetry and short prose, titled *Born to Win*, was published; in later years, a heavily edited version of *Seeds of Man* and a collection of the "Woody Sez" columns would see print posthumously.

But most of the royalties came from other people's versions of Woody's songs. "This Land Is Your Land" often was mentioned as a possible replacement for "The Star-Spangled Banner" as the national anthem. It was used as an advertising jingle by United Airlines and the Ford Motor Company, and was the theme song for George McGovern's 1972 presidential campaign. In 1975, untold millions of children across the country sang it simultaneously one morning to open the first annual Music in Our Schools Day. It also was recorded by the Wayfarers, Glen Yarborough, the Kingston Trio, the Brothers Four, the Limeliters, the New Christy Minstrels, Peter, Paul and Mary, Trini Lopez, Harry Belafonte, Jay and the Americans, Glen Campbell, Bing Crosby, the Staple Singers, Tex Ritter, Connie Francis, Country Joe McDonald, Paul Anka, Jim Croce, the Mike Curb Congregation, and the Mormon Tabernacle Choir—few of whom could have realized that they were singing a song originally intended as a Marxist response to "God Bless America."

Indeed, there was a growing fear among Woody's old associates, especially the hard-liners like Irwin Silber, Gordon Friesen, and Sis Cunningham, that Woody's legacy was being expurgated, that his native radicalism was being toned down for public consumption, that his anger and bitter humor were being replaced by a happy-go-lucky vapidity, the mindless optimism inherent in his book titles. When the U.S. Department of the Interior cited Woody for his songs about the Pacific Northwest, and the Bonneville Power Authority named a substation after him in 1966, Sil-

ber raged: "They're taking a revolutionary, and turning him into
a conservationist."

Marjorie Guthrie, who tended to emphasize Woody's optimism
at the expense of all else, was considered the primary culprit by
Silber and the hard-liners. But there were others equally to blame.
There was a persistently dim-witted band of academic folklorists
who, in an impressive marshaling of footnotes and citations
theorized that Woody was merely a pure and simple country boy
seduced by the big-city radicals. There also were, most insidious
of all, the various marketing experts working to promote him a
the godfather of folk music (with Marjorie's tacit acquiescence
of course). The cover of the paperback version of *Born to Win*
seemed the ultimate product of their vulgar efforts. It proclaimed
"Nitty-Gritty Songs and Snatches from the Boss Father/Hero of
Bob Dylan, Joan Baez, Donovan, The Lovin' Spoonful, The Mamas and The Papas and Everyone Else in the Mainstream of Pop
Music Today."

But the debate over Woody Guthrie's public image wasn't
nearly as bitter as several other, more intimate controversies surrounding Marjorie's stewardship and personality in the early
1960's. Her aggressive cheeriness was beginning to seem a bit
more aggressive than cheerful at times, and while she might profess that *she* wasn't going to sit around worrying about her children's fate, the constant tension—and it was, largely, a quiet
tension, since the kids rarely mentioned the disease or their feelings about it—clearly was taking its toll.

A bitter controversy erupted over the trust fund revenues in
1960, when Bill Guthrie—Woody's oldest son—arrived in New
York after a stint in the Navy and asked for money to go to
college. Marjorie's response was not very charitable. She wondered aloud why Bill had chosen that particular moment to appear
on the scene, after nearly twenty years of no contact with his
father. Even though Woody already was something of a legend,
he still wasn't earning very much money at that point—the royalties for 1960 totaled only about $6,000. The trust fund wasn't
in any position to pay for *her own* children's educations, much
less Bill's, and so the trustees (acting on Marjorie's wishes, apparently) told Bill there was nothing they could do about helping
him with college. Shaken by the sight of his near-helpless father
in the hospital and angered by the rejection from the trustees, Bill

returned home to California and died soon after when his car collided with a railroad train.

Though there was never any evidence that Bill had committed suicide, Harold Leventhal felt deeply guilty about the whole affair, and several years later when the trust fund was a bit more flush, he worked out a scheme whereby Woody's two oldest daughters, Gwen and Sue, were *hired* by the fund and received a regular stipend.

Furthermore, Marjorie was involved in a messy dispute with Bob and Sid Gleason over Woody's transfer back to Brooklyn State Hospital in 1961. The Gleasons had developed a very close, protective, almost familial relationship with Woody during the two years they'd cared for him, and felt that Marjorie was "taking him away" because she was jealous. And while it's possible that Marjorie did resent their attempts to usurp what she considered her rightful place, the truth was that she'd been trying to get Woody out of Greystone almost from the very start, and well before he'd met the Gleasons. Beginning in 1958, she conducted a running battle with the Veterans Administration over whether Woody was eligible to be admitted to a V.A. hospital. The case dragged on until April of 1961, when the V.A. informed Woody: "Your nervous condition is not service-connected for the purpose of hospital care or outpatient treatment." With all other possibilities seemingly foreclosed, Marjorie moved him back to Brooklyn.

The Gleasons were so offended that they never visited him in the hospital again, nor did Marjorie ever invite them to visit Woody at her home in Howard Beach, where he now spent Sunday afternoons. It was a petty, stupid rift that served none of them very well—and certainly not Woody, who must have wondered where the Gleasons had gone.

In July of 1962, on the occasion of Woody's fiftieth birthday, Marjorie wrote to Mary Jo:

> Woody is failing all the time, and his visits on Sundays are growing shorter. After a few hours he really can't take the noise and gets overly excited. I suppose the greatest change is that he finds it difficult to speak and has begun to say less and less. And when he does say something, and I don't understand him and ask him to repeat he gets exasper-

ated. . . . According to the nature of his illness, he should be showing signs of mental deterioration. And since they [the doctors] can't understand him, they keep asking me about his condition. And all that I can say is that he's as alert as he's ever been. When he speaks it's usually a funny comment. . . .

Perhaps his concentration is failing a bit. Nowadays when we get mail, I usually don't read the whole thing . . . I usually read it myself and tell him the essence of the news, or read just parts of letters. He doesn't even open his mail . . . just too hard to manage, although he does remarkably well with his cigarettes.

Just a few weeks ago he had another hernia operation. He is unable to go home for a month, so we visited him there. And just 24 hours after the operation he walked off his bed and down the hall to the bathroom . . . and he has been walking ever since! Of course, his walk is poor . . . practically staggers, but determined he is . . . and many is the time I catch him when he almost falls.

In January of 1964, *Sing Out!* reported that Woody had "deteriorated in the past year" and visitors were being discouraged. His condition *was* worse, but the real problem was an onslaught of scruffy kids with guitars—the stories of Dylan paying homage had become legend and every nascent protest singer seemed to think that a pilgrimage to Brooklyn State was a necessary way-station on the road to success. One afternoon, Marjorie came in and found a kid in a pea jacket squatting in front of Woody, who was sitting in his wheelchair, and just staring at him. Marjorie took the boy aside and said, "He's not an animal in the zoo. He has *feelings*. How do you think he feels about you staring at him like that?"

She still encouraged visits from Woody's friends, but most weren't very anxious to come. Will Geer flatly stated that he just couldn't bear to see Woody like that. Matt Jennings came up once from El Paso, saw Woody writhing uncontrollably on the bed while a young girl sang "Reuben James" a bit too sweetly, and was terribly upset. Jimmy Longhi came a few times, and was struck by how it only seemed to get worse—there was never the slightest remission. Pete Seeger came more than most, and once brought Sonny Terry and Brownie McGhee with him. Sonny could *feel* Woody shaking in the bed. "He couldn't say anything, but I could tell he liked it when I started doing 'Lost John' with all my whoops and everything. He always did love that."

Seeger also sent Woody letters from all over, often addressing him as "my friend and teacher," telling him how popular folk music was becoming. In 1964, he wrote from Moscow: "Woody, every day I live I realize more my debt to you as a poet and musician. I mean I'm trying to be one, and what I half-learned from you have been the most valuable lessons of my life."

The young folk singers, the ones who hadn't known him when he was well, and therefore couldn't imagine the horror of his deterioration, were more persistent visitors than Woody's old friends. Even Arlo Guthrie had only the vaguest pre-hospital recollections of his father; like the others, he'd mostly learned Woody's style from recordings. One Sunday afternoon early on, when Woody could still speak fairly well, he took Arlo out to the backyard at Howard Beach and had him memorize the old, radical verses that he'd written for "This Land" in 1940, and which no one was singing now that the song had become a patriotic anthem. He was afraid that if Arlo didn't learn them, they'd be forgotten . . . and Arlo always made sure after that to add the verse about the sign that said "Private Property" ("But on the other side, it didn't say nothin' . . . That side was made for you and me . . .") when he was with a group of people singing "This Land."

In general, Woody's Sunday-afternoon visits were difficult for the children. Howard Beach was a very conservative working-class neighborhood, and the Guthries were considered dangerously artsy and bizarre well before Marjorie's former husband began to show up, shaking and spluttering, often insisting on taking *all* his clothes off in the backyard and sometimes flying into noisy temper tantrums, ruining Sunday afternoons for the neighbors. "I guess the parents told the kids to kind of stay away from us," Arlo remembered, "which only made us more interesting to the kids. We weren't very popular in that neighborhood . . . but after a while, we began to realize that it wasn't *Woody's* fault and it wasn't ours—it was just that some people were narrow-minded and dumb. In a way, Woody taught us that what other people thought didn't make any difference."

Nora, who had always dreaded visiting him at the hospital, also was embarrassed at first; but one afternoon toward the end—

when she was about fourteen years old, and starting her career in modern dance (and gaining the poise and assurance that many good dancers seem to have)—she happened upon Woody, who was quietly trembling on the living-room couch, and she realized that this odd little man was her *father*, even though she never remembered him being anywhere but in a hospital and anything but frightening, and she might not have another chance to spend time with him. So she sat down near him—and he noticed her, and looked at her, and it was the one quiet moment they ever shared together.

Gradually, as Woody continued to deteriorate, the Sunday-afternoon visits became briefer and more difficult. On the way back to the hospital in the evening, they'd invariably stop at a local hot dog stand, where Woody would eat a half dozen frank-furters (but not the rolls) and drink four root beers, to the amazement and alarm of the rest of the family. His appetite, especially for sweets, had grown beyond all reason, and yet he continued to lose weight. His body, in constant motion, burned up more energy than he could ever hope to produce. He grew frail, his bones brittle and his system vulnerable to disease. His senses dulled—often he'd burn himself with a cigarette and not notice it; his clothes were studded with burn marks. One day an arm flew up and his elbow shattered against a tile wall, which precipitated a major crisis since he wasn't able to heal very well and the arm became infected. He was forced to spend months in bed, being fed intravenously . . . and he never really was strong enough to walk after that.

By 1965, he had stopped speaking entirely and could only communicate by pointing a wildly flailing arm at ''yes'' and ''no'' cards that Marjorie had made for him. Then, after a while, he could no longer even do *that*. All he had left were his eyes, which he blinked in recognition when Marjorie entered the room and, sometimes, when she asked him a question or told him something. The real horror, Marjorie was convinced, was that Woody could still understand what she was saying. He could still think and know. There was an active mind trapped inside the tumultuous decrepitude of his body.

She still had no idea what the disease really was. She watched it destroy Woody, and she didn't know how or why it was happening . . . and part of her still didn't *want* to know, but there also was a growing anger and frustration, a desire to do something about it. Then, in 1966, she received a phone call from Dr. John Whittier, who was studying Huntington's chorea patients at Creedmoor State Hospital in Queens, and was interested in Woody's case. He admitted there wasn't much he could do for Woody at this late stage, just make him a bit more comfortable on a smaller ward at Creedmoor . . . but he said he'd be willing to answer any questions Marjorie had about the disease. She immediately arranged an appointment, and Whittier told her all he knew—which still wasn't very much, but more than she could ever possibly have imagined.

It began with a modest country doctor named George Sumner Huntington. He was born in 1850, in the village of East Hampton, Long Island, where both his father and grandfather had been doctors before him. After graduating from medical school, Dr. Huntington decided to set out on his own and moved—at a friend's behest—to Pomeroy, Ohio. But he was haunted by his memories of the rare hereditary disease that his father and grandfather had noted among some of their patients. He remembered riding with his father on his rounds one day. They were on the Amagansett road when they suddenly came upon "two women, both tall, thin, almost cadaverous, both bowing, twisting, grimacing. I stared in wonderment, almost in fear. What could it mean? My father paused to speak with them, and then we passed on. . . ."

He also remembered "two married men, whose wives are living, and who are constantly making love to some young lady, not seeming to be aware that there is any impropriety in it. They are suffering from chorea to such an extent that they can hardly walk, and would be thought by a stranger to be intoxicated. They are men of about 50 years of age, but never let an opportunity to flirt with a girl go past unimproved. The effect is ridiculous in the extreme."

Huntington decided to write a paper about the phenomenon, using his own observations as well as notes from his father and grandfather. The result, delivered to the not very august Meigs and Mason Academy of Medicine at Middleport, Ohio, was a startlingly accurate description of a very subtle disorder. He called it "hereditary chorea," adding that there didn't seem to be any real name for it, not even among its victims, who normally didn't talk about it. When pressed, they would call it "*that* disorder."

In addition to the flailing movements—which were common to

other diseases—Huntington observed that hereditary chorea could only be passed from parent to child, that it manifested itself in middle age, and that there was a marked tendency toward insanity. The observations of three generations of Huntingtons enabled him to give a fairly precise description of the disease's hereditary characteristics: "When either or both parents have shown manifestations of the disease . . . one or more of the offspring almost invariably suffer from [it], if they live to adult age. But if by any chance these children go through life without it, the thread is broken and the grandchildren and great-grandchildren of the original shakers may rest assured that they are free from the disease."

Huntington's description was not the first, only the most precise—and especially remarkable in his ability to predict the genetic theories of Gregor Mendel, which wouldn't be rediscovered by science for another thirty years. Earlier, in 1841, Dr. Charles Oscar Waters of New York had written to a friend describing a "singular convulsive affection" that was "markedly hereditary, and is most common among the lower classes." Unfortunately, his account was marred by several other, less than scientific observations: "It may not be amiss to state that the last person who came under my observation and who had the reputation of being an honest man, informed me that, in his own case, this involuntary action of the muscles ceased under the influence of all instrumental music, except that of the common Jew's harp."

Huntington's paper received wide circulation, but the amount of solid information about the disease remained minimal until well into the twentieth century. Brains of Huntington's chorea victims were autopsied, and found to be vastly diminished—"sort of like rotten melons" was the way Dr. Whittier would describe them. But no one had any idea what caused the brain cells to die, or whether there was any particular type of cell that was affected.

One area of research that proved quite interesting—though only indirectly rewarding—was the genetic tracing of Huntington's disease families. In 1916, Drs. C. P. Davenport and Elizabeth Muncie traced 962 choreics from the New England area back to four family groups who came to Salem and Boston in the seventeenth century. In 1932, Dr. P. R. Vessie did further research into one of those families: three men from the village of Bures in England, who came to America on John Winthrop's boat in 1630. Vessie found that several of the women descendants of this family were hanged during the famous Salem witch trials, and another was forced to endure a water trial at Fairfield, Connecticut, in 1693. Both hereditary studies found that affected families often had a tendency toward large numbers of children, criminal behavior (especially sex crimes), depression, and suicide.

Gradually, scientists began to gain a better sense of the areas of the brain most affected by the disease. They found severe damage in several crucial midbrain areas, especially those known as the caudate nucleus and the putamen, which are believed to have a great deal of influence on movement and balance. But there also was cell loss throughout the rest of the brain, and particularly in the frontal lobe of the cortex—an area generally associated with a person's sense of self and social awareness. The brain, of course, was far too sophisticated an organ for researchers ever to pin down which areas caused which personality disruptions in hereditary chorea patients. In fact, it was difficult to say which disruptions were indeed caused by the disease; no doubt, alcoholism and the long years of confinement in mental hospitals accelerated Woody's degeneration, but it was impossible to say where the disease left off and Woody began.

There was no way of knowing, for example, whether he would have written erotic letters if not for the disease. Choreics seemed to suffer a loss of control over a wide range of emotions and desires—sexuality, anger, depression, elation, giddiness—but the severity varied from case to case. Dr. Whittier explained to Marjorie that the illness (which he pointedly called Huntington's *disease*, as opposed to chorea, because there obviously was more to it than just choreiform movements) tailored itself to each individual, exaggerating personal characteristics that already were there, and unmasking others that had been hidden. Thus, it was fairly safe to say that the disease had some effect on Woody's rhyminess and prolixity, especially the frenzied nature of his later writings. And while it would be absurd to suggest that Huntington's disease *made* Woody Guthrie a brilliant songwriter, Dr. Whittier (and, later, Marjorie Guthrie herself) would wonder aloud if the disease hadn't worked like a drug on Woody, as a creative spur (in much the same way that some artists use alcohol and other drugs), enhancing his natural rhyminess, forcing the brain to continually rewire itself as cells died, forcing new, wonderful, and unexpected synaptic pathways to open (which also led to some unexpected and not so wonderful behavior), forcing the brain to become—in effect—more creative to survive; and then, after a point, exhausted and starving for energy, the synapses and ganglia short-circuiting . . . preventing him from *concentrating* on anything, making him fidgety, antsy, causing him to lose perspective and, eventually, his creative sense of himself.

Of course, that was only a theory—less than a theory, the wildest of speculation. It was impossible to say *anything* with any certainty except that brain cells died, and personality changes took place. Woody Guthrie and Huntington's disease were bound together inextricably; there was no way to separate them, no way to guess when and where and how the disease began to affect his judgment; and no way to figure what he might have done (or who he might have been) without it.

By the late 1970's, more progress had been made toward understanding the disease—and the brain itself—but both remained essentially mysterious. It was known, by then, that the brain was as much a chemical as an electrical instrument—minute chemical variances triggered the electronic interactions of the cells—and that Huntington's disease severely reduced the levels of several vital brain chemicals. But it wasn't known if the reduced chemical levels caused the cells to die, or if the dying cells caused the reduced chemical levels, or both. Nor was it known *when* cells began to die—whether the process started at birth, or in middle age when the first symptoms began to appear. There still was no way of detecting the disease in advance, no way of curing it, and no way—aside from heavy doses of tranquilizers to modify the flailing a bit—of treating it.

And it continued its grisly march through the Guthrie family.

Gwen Guthrie began to behave erratically in 1964, after visiting her father for the first time in many years. She left her husband and three children and wandered about the country; she seemed to lose track of where she was at times—staying with relatives for weeks on end, not knowing when or how to leave. She had three illegitimate children who were eventually placed in foster homes. She told her mother, "I can't do the things I'm supposed to, and I don't know why." In 1965, a doctor at the UCLA Medical Center told her that she had Huntington's disease. When she died of it in 1976, she weighed only sixty-seven pounds and was shaking so violently that two attendants had been needed to feed her—one to hold her down and another to put the food in her mouth.

Sue Guthrie's marriage also had fallen apart and she was having difficulty performing the simplest chores—like diapering a baby or doing the shopping. She was diagnosed as having the disease in 1974.

Anneke's daughter, Lorina Lynn, turned out to be an intelligent and headstrong girl who much resembled her Aunt Clara . . . and, like Clara, she died tragically and young, in an auto accident in California, at the age of nineteen.

Meanwhile, after meeting with Dr. Whittier in 1966, Marjorie Guthrie had decided she was going to press the fight against Huntington's disease, even if there was nothing she could do to prevent it from striking her own children (who, as 1980 began, were still free of it . . . but waiting). In 1967, she formed the Committee to Combat Huntington's Disease in order to raise money for research, and to provide counseling and support for HD families. Eventually, she closed the Marjorie Mazia School of Dance, and devoted her life to CCHD.

One of the last things Woody Guthrie did before he died was to listen to a recording of his son Arlo singing a long, convoluted talking blues about how he'd been arrested for littering in Stockbridge, Massachusetts, and how he'd parlayed that "criminal record" into a means of dodging the draft and avoiding the war in Vietnam. The song—which would bring Arlo more fame and commercial success by the age of nineteen than Woody had achieved in his entire life—was stitched together by a wry little chorus, a jingle that Arlo had written as a radio commercial for a friend's restaurant:

> You can get anything you want at Alice's Restaurant
> You can get anything you want . . . at Alice's Restaurant
> Walk right in, it's around the back
> Just a half a mile from the railroad track
> You can get anything you want at Alice's Restaurant.

And as Woody listened to Arlo describing how he went to the draft board in New York and was "injected, inspected, detected, infected, neglected and selected," perhaps he heard an echo of his own timing and inflection . . . *that stew was so thin that even some of these here pollli-TISH-uns could see through it . . . or* maybe he was thinking back even farther than that, to Charley Edward Guthrie—his father—at the top of his game, entertaining the courthouse crowd down at Parson's drugstore in Okemah each morning with tall tales and patter, spinning out alliterations and exaggerations, twists and turns and pregnant pauses . . . *We-ell, you know how it is with Almighty-High Gene Debs and that Squeal of Treason crowd . . .*

Or maybe Woody wasn't thinking anything at all, maybe so many cells had died in his brain that he *couldn't* think very much anymore; maybe the smile that Harold Leventhal saw flickering as Woody listened to the record was just an atavistic twinge, an involuntary response—to a voice that was soothing and familiar, a voice that sounded like home.

He died several weeks later on October 3, 1967. There wasn't very much left of him at the end. He weighed less than one hundred pounds. His skin was waxy and translucent, his bones sticking up through it. He was so weak that he didn't even have the energy to shake very much anymore; his movements were constant, but almost gentle now—like a soft breeze riffling the surface of a lake.

Marjorie came to the hospital the night before he died, saw his eyes blink slightly in recognition, and knew that it was the last time she'd ever see him. A priest was there, and offered to say something. Marjorie told him they weren't Catholics, but that Woody had always believed in the validity of all religions and so it might be nice if he said a prayer. The priest read the 23rd Psalm. Then Marjorie got up on her tiptoes, arching over the steel bars at the side of Woody's bed, and kissed him goodbye.

Early the next morning, the hospital called and told her that Woody's ordeal was finally over.

Marjorie called Harold Leventhal and asked him to make all the arrangements. She didn't want a funeral, a burial, or any other kind of service. She just wanted him cremated. Harold found an old left-wing funeral parlor in Brooklyn and saw to the cremation. Then he called Pete Seeger, who was on tour in Japan, and told him the news. Then he began to call some of Woody's other close friends and relatives, as well as the Associated Press and United Press International. Within an hour, the wire services were carrying news of his death and it was all over the radio—

along with musical tributes on many stations, "This Land" and "So Long" and "Oklahoma Hills." That evening, all three television networks announced Woody Guthrie's death on their nightly news shows. That evening, too, Bob Dylan, recuperating from a near-fatal motorcycle crash, called Harold Leventhal and offered to be part of any memorial service or concert that was being planned. A memorial concert *was* held at Carnegie Hall several months later to benefit the Committee to Combat Huntington's Disease, and Dylan made his first public appearance since his accident—along with Arlo Guthrie, Pete Seeger, and a score of Woody's other friends—singing an appropriately angry and very satisfying hard rock version of "I Ain't Got No Home in This World Anymore."

Within a week after Woody Guthrie died, Marjorie received a drab olive canister from the crematorium—his ashes. It looked like an institution-size can of beans. Much to the dismay of the children, she decided that they should all go out to Coney Island together and spread Woody's ashes to the winds there, over by the jetty that separated Coney Island from Sea Gate—Woody's favorite spot on the beach.

Arlo and Nora didn't want to go. They were opposed to any sort of ceremony, no matter how informal. But Joady said, "Well, look, we've got to do *something* with the ashes."

And so they went.

There were, however, several logistical problems to be solved before Woody's ashes could be spread to the winds . . . like figuring out how to open the can. After some discussion, Marjorie located a beer-can opener and pried several holes in the top, but for some reason—none of them could quite understand why—the ashes just wouldn't pour out when they reached the jetty and were standing there at the end of it, on the rocks, with the sun shining and the wind blowing dramatically.

"It's not coming," Arlo said, waving the can about. "What should I do?"

No one had any ideas, and so he just heaved the can out into the ocean, where it bobbed insistently and, for a moment, seemed to be heading back toward the jetty rocks—was the tide coming in?—before it finally submitted, and went under. Marjorie and the kids stood there not knowing what to do next, staring now at the empty ocean, at the spot where the can had gone down, the wind whipping in their faces.

"Well," Marjorie said, trying to imagine what Woody might suggest under the circumstances. "Why don't we go to Nathan's and have a hot dog?"

<u>God Blessed America</u>
This Land ~~was made for you~~ for you & me

778
W

This land is your land, this land is my land
From ~~the~~ California to the ~~Staten~~ Island,
From the Redwood Forest, to the Gulf stream waters,
<u>God blessed america for me.</u>

As I went walking that ribbon of highway
And saw above me that endless Skyway,
And saw below me the golden valley, I said:
~~God blessed america for me.~~

I roamed and rambled, and followed my footsteps
To the sparkling sands of her diamond deserts,
And all around me, a voice was sounding:
God <u>blessed</u> america for me.

Was a big high wall ^there that tried to stop me
A sign was painted said: Private Property,
But on the back side it didn't say nothing —
God blessed ~~america~~ for me.

When the sun come shining, then I was strolling
In wheat fields waving, and dust clouds rolling;
The voice was chanting as the fog was lifting:
God blessed america for me.

One bright sunny morning in the shadow of the steeple
By the Relief office I saw my people —
As they stood hungry, I stood there wondering if
God blessed america for me.

                    * all you can write is
                      what you see.

original copy
of this song

                              Woody G——
                              N.Y., N.Y., N.Y.
                              Feb. 23, 1940
                              43rd St & 6th Ave,
                              Hanover House

NOTES

Since I am not an academic and didn't intend to write a "scholarly" biography, I haven't felt the need for exhaustive footnoting and documentation. The notes that follow are merely an organized way of thanking the many people who cooperated with me, and acknowledging certain books and manuscripts that proved valuable along the way. As noted in the Preface, much of the material was culled from Woody Guthrie's private papers—although I have tried, where possible, to corroborate Woody's version of the events of his life with interviews and research.

CHAPTER 1. Life's Other Side

Dr. Guy Logsdon, chief librarian at the University of Tulsa, was invaluable in the preparation of this chapter. Not only did he give me access to microfilm copies of the Okemah newspapers from 1902 to 1929, but freely shared his own research into Woody's early life—collected over a twenty-year period—and many hours of wise counsel. He also directed me to several obscure scholarly papers and books, such as *The Longest Way Home* by William E. Bittle and Gilbert Geis (Wayne State University press), which is a well-researched history of the black separatist movement in Okfuskee County. Other valuable books were: *Grass Roots Socialism* by James Green (Louisiana State University Press); *Eugene Debs* by Ray Ginger (Collier); *Democratic Promise: The Populist Moment in America* by Laurence Goodwyn (Oxford University Press); *The Autobiography of Will Rogers* (Avon) and *Will Rogers* by Richard M. Ketchum (Touchstone); *Once in the Saddle* by Lawrence Ivan Seidman (Mentor), several standard histories of Oklahoma, including the W.P.A. Writers Project *Guide;* plus *Kumrids* by Charley Edward Guthrie and, of course, *Bound for Glory*.

Woody's sister Mary Jo and her patient husband, Hulette Edgmon, were extremely helpful—giving me the names of distant Guthrie cousins, guiding me through Okemah, feeding me, and talking my ear off. Mary Jo led me to Woody's ancient uncles, Jeff and Claude, who gave detailed descriptions of Woody's parents and grandparents. Claude, who was well over ninety years old, remembered his father, Jerry P. Guthrie, very clearly, and he was there the day Nora Guthrie was taken to the mental hospital. Jeff Guthrie knew more about Woody than did Claude, and was a major source of information for Chapters 2, 3, 4, 10, and 11. Other helpful members of the family included: Woody's brother George Guthrie, his sister-in-law Ann Guthrie and her daughter Mary Ann, and cousin Amalee Creason, who also helped with Chapters 2, 3, 4, and 9.

In addition, Mary Jo introduced me to Wayne Lovelady, who, in turn, led me to many longtime Okemah residents: Bill Stanford, the town barber, who was there when Clara died, Albert Hill, Clifford Hooper, Hugh Stanley, W. George, Hubert Weaver, Walter Byam, and Mrs. V. K. Chowning.

Other sources included: Blanche (Giles) Konkal, Grace (Giles) Newbern, Mr. and Mrs. Glenn Dill, Ora Tanner, Floyd "Red" Moore, and his sister Gladys Gordon, who was there the day Woody went to visit his mother at the hospital in Norman.

CHAPTER 2. Wheat Fields Waving ...

Sylvia Ann Grider, of Texas A and M University's English Department, provided much the same sort of assistance with this chapter as Guy Logsdon did with the first. A native of Pampa, she had interviewed many of the people who'd known Woody and were no longer alive, such as Eulys McKenzie, and was happy to share her research with me. She also taught me something of the history of the town, and corrected my spelling of Cudahy bacon.

But the bulk of the information in this chapter (and the next several) came from extensive interviews with Mary (Guthrie) Boyle and her brother, Matt Jennings. Both were very gracious, suffering through long interviews and many late-night phone calls. Most of the family members mentioned earlier— especially Uncle Jeff—were helpful here, as well as Woody's cousin Geneva Adkins, who served as my guide in town. Others interviewed included: Rufe Jordan, Nat Lunsford, Pauline Lee, Lillian Snow, Violet Pipes, Roy Buzbee, Ted Gikas, and Cluster Baker. Thom Marshall, then editor of the Pampa *Times*, provided valuable assistance and good company throughout.

The brief history of country music relies a good deal on Bill C. Malone's *Country Music, USA* (University of Texas Press), as well as conversations with Martha Hume, Chet Flippo, Matt Jennings, and Bob Orman of the Country Music Hall of Fame; also many happy hours of listening to records by the Carter Family, Jimmie Rodgers, and others. Guy Logsdon introduced me to the glories of Bob Wills and the Texas Playboys, and also provided much of the data about the dust bowl that appears near the end of the chapter.

Pete Seeger told me where Woody had gotten the tune for "So Long" and many of his other songs, often singing the original lyrics over the phone; consulting with Pete about the musical background of Woody's songs was one of the more pleasant aspects of my research.

CHAPTER 3. Here Come Woody and Lefty Lou

Not only did Maxine "Lefty Lou" Crissman remember nearly every song she and Woody sang together, every conversation they had, and every joke he told, but she also saved many of the letters they received during their days on KFVD, as well as the songbooks they sent out to listeners and Woody's unforgettable "Santa Monica Examine 'Er."

Most of the information about Woody's hobo days early in the chapter comes from family sources, as well as Floyd Moore and James "Curly the Kid" Isenberg, and *Hard Travelin': The Hobo and His History* by Kenneth Allsop (New American Library).

There are lots of books about the Wobblies, but John Greenway's *American Folk Songs of Protest* (University of Pennsylvania Press) and *The Case of Joe Hill* by Philip Foner (New World) have specific information about the I.W.W.'s musical heritage.

Carey McWilliams was a valuable source of information about California in the 1930's, especially the small-town nature of Los Angeles . . . and the corrupt politics described in Chapter 4. We had several telephone conversations, and I found his books *Southern California: An Island on the Land* and *Factories in the Fields* (Peregrine, Smith) to be excellent. Also helpful was *Upton Sinclair* by Leon Harris (Crowell). Malone's *Country Music, USA* includes sections about Gene Autry, the rise of the singing cowboy, and the Mexican "X" stations, but most of the color came from Maxine Crissman.

CHAPTER 4.   I Ain't a Communist . . .

Many books have been written about the Communist Party U.S.A.—virtually all of them flawed by ideological ax-grinding of one sort or another. My most valuable source of information was the *People's Daily World* itself (and, in later chapters, the *Daily Worker*). *The American Communist Party* by Irving Howe and Louis Coser (Da Capo) is vituperative and militantly anti-Stalinist, but covers the basic facts. Other books included: *A Long View from the Left* by Al Richmond (Delta); *The Autobiography of an American Communist* by Peggy Dennis (Lawrence Hill/Creative Press); *Politics Past* by Dwight Macdonald (Viking Compass); *Part of Our Time* by Murray Kempton (Delta); *American Hunger* by Richard Wright (Harper & Row); *We Are Many* by Ella Reeve Bloor (International); *The Romance of American Communism* by Vivian Gornick (Basic); *A Fine Old Conflict* by Jessica Mitford (Knopf); *The Radical Soap Opera* by David Zane Mairowitz (Avon). Also the following books about the general political and social mood of the 1930's: *USA* by John Dos Passos (Signet); *To the Finland Station* by Edmund Wilson (Vintage); *The Glory and the Dream* by William Manchester (Little, Brown); *Brother Can You Spare a Dime* by Milton Meltzer (Mentor); and *Let Us Now Praise Famous Men* by James Agee and Walker Evans (Ballantine).

The information about the American labor movement, which begins in this chapter and continues throughout the book, comes from Ed Sadlowski, Jerry Wurf, and other labor leaders of the 1970's, as well as the following books: *John L. Lewis* by Saul Alinsky (Vintage); *Toil and Trouble* by Thomas R. Brooks (Delta); *Strike* by Jeremy Brecher (Straight Arrow); and *Labor's Giant Step* by Art Pries (Pathfinder).

John Steinbeck's famous novels *The Grapes of Wrath* and *In Dubious Bat-*

tle are both excellent descriptions of the Okies in the valley, as is Carey McWilliams' aforementioned *Factories in the Fields*. Other sources included: *Long Road to Delano* by Sam Kushner (New World) and *A Western Journal* by Thomas Wolfe (University of Pittsburgh Press).

Interviews for this chapter included: UCAPAWA organizers Luke Hinman and Dorothy Healy (who later became a member of the Communist Party's Central Committee); Ed Robbin, the late Will Geer, Herta Geer, Burl Ives, and Al Richmond.

CHAPTER 5. American Spirit

The information about New York City that appears at the beginning of this chapter was taken from several almanacs, guidebooks, and histories available at the New York City Historical Society. The information, later in the chapter, about New York as a "red" city comes from many, many interviews with former Communists, as well as the following books: *Pete* by Simon Gerson (New World), which is about Pete Caccione—a CP member of the New York City Council in the 1940's; *Humboldt's Gift* by Saul Bellow (Avon); and Helen Lawrenson's *Stranger at the Party* (Popular Library) and *Whistling Girl* (Doubleday).

The history of the Lomax family and the early days of the folk revival comes from interviews with Alan Lomax, Bess (Lomax) Hawes, Pete Seeger, Earl Robinson, and the late Nicholas Ray. Other sources included: John Lomax's *Cowboy Songs, Negro Songs as Sung by Lead Belly*, and *The Adventures of a Ballad Hunter* (Macmillan); *Folk Songs of North America* by Alan Lomax (Doubleday); *The Incompleat Folksinger* by Pete Seeger (Fireside); and *Hard-Hitting Songs for Hard Hit People* by Alan Lomax, Pete Seeger, and Woody Guthrie (Oak), from which John Steinbeck's famous quote about Woody was taken. About the only book that has been written about the Left's love affair with folk music is *Great Day Coming* by Serge Denisov (University of Illinois Press), which is grievously flawed by its cold war sensibility. Oscar Brand's *The Ballad Mongers* (Minerva) is a tepid history of the folk song revival, and only marginally useful.

I'd like to thank Joseph Hickerson of the Library of Congress Folk Music Archives for making those facilities available to me, including the taped reminiscences of Alan Lomax and Charles Seeger, and such precious items as tapes of the "Back Where I Come From" and "Columbia School of the Air" radio programs. Woody Guthrie's Library of Congress interview with Alan Lomax is available on Electra records. The *Dust Bowl Ballads* are available on both RCA and Folkways.

The discussion of the impact of the Popular Front on culture was drawn from varied sources, including conversations with many of the people already mentioned, as well as Leo Humitz, Ann Banks, and Angus Cameron. Also the following books: Richard H. Pells's *Radical Visions and American Dreams* (Harper Torchbook); *Writers on the Left* by Daniel Aaron (Oxford); *The Dream and the Deal* by Jerre Mangione (Equinox); *Martha Graham* by Don McDonagh (Popular Library); *Documentary Expression and Thirties America* by William Stott (Oxford); *Lay My Burden Down* by B. A. Botkin (Chicago); Lionel Trilling's novel *The Middle of the Journey* (Avon); the play *Tobacco Road* by Jack Kirkland (Samuel French), which was based on Erskine Caldwell's novel; and *The Solitary Singer* by Gay Wilson Allen (Grove), which is a biography of Walt Whitman.

The research departments at both NBC and CBS helped to reconstruct Woody's network radio career, as did Norman Corwin, Davidson Taylor, and Henrietta Yurchenko. John Hammond's *On Record* (Ridge Press/Summit Books) is a good history of the music business during this period.

CHAPTER 6.   Talking Union

Most of this chapter came from the Almanac Singers themselves: Pete Seeger, Millard Lampell, Lee Hays, Bess (Lomax) Hawes, Arthur Stern, Gordon Friesen, and Sis Cuningham. Also Camilla Horne, Jean Karsavina, Earl Robinson, and Studs Terkel. The *Daily Worker* kept track of the Almanacs on its entertainment page, and I also consulted the appropriate editions of the *World-Telegram* and *Post* for their accounts of the "This Is War" fiasco. Unfortunately, most of the Almanac Singers' records are no longer available—except for *Talking Union* on Folkways.

Gunther Von Fritsch, Stephen Kahn, and Sam Moment helped explain Woody's month on the Columbia River, as did a research paper by Harry Menig of Oklahoma State University.

CHAPTER 7.   Like a Wild Wolf . . .

Obviously, most of the information in this chapter (and the remainder of the book) came from Woody and Marjorie Guthrie's private papers. Woody's "Little Rat" story was found in his unpublished novel *Ship Story*, and later confirmed by Marjorie.

Other sources included: Sophie Maslow, Max Blatt, William Doerflinger, Earl Robinson, Sonny Terry, Brownie McGhee, the various Almanac Singers; also *The Portable Rabelais* (Penguin) and *Mother* by Maxim Gorky (Progress).

CHAPTER 8.   Poems and Explosions

Jimmy Longhi and I spent an afternoon together at his home in London and he was kind enough to let me look at his unpublished account of the merchant marine adventures, titled *Woody, Cisco and Me*, but I also depended on Woody's letters, notebooks, and the more plausible sections of *Ship Story*, as well as Cisco's account of the wind machine, as recorded by Lee Hays.

Jim Kweskin has begun work on a comprehensive Woody Guthrie discography, which includes the exact dates of many of the early Asch sessions (but is decidedly incomplete, due to Moe's haphazard bookkeeping). Much of the music that Woody, Cisco, and the others produced during those sessions is still available on Folkways and Stinson records. *The Martins and the Coys* is not generally available, but Alan Lomax has a copy of the set released by English Decca and played it for me.

Other sources included: Moe Asch, Jackie (Gibson) Alper, Bina (Rosenbaum) Bernard, and *V Was for Victory* by John Morton Blum (Harcourt Brace Jovanovich).

CHAPTER 9. Stackabones

The primary sources for the sad story of Cathy Ann's death were Sophie Maslow, Jimmy Longhi, the Geers, and Marjorie herself. Other sources for this chapter included: Rosalind (Richman) Riversong, Oscar Brand, Tom Glazer, Irwin Silber, Fred Hellerman, John Henry Faulk, Hally Wood Faulk, Charles Weiner, Jackie Alper, Ronnie Gilbert, Jolly (Smolens) Robinson, Vera Lerner, Pete Seeger, Lee Hays, and Amalee Creason.

Also *American Folk Song* by Woody Guthrie (Oak); *The Best Years: 1945-1950* by Joseph C. Goulden (Atheneum); *American Communism in Crisis* by Joseph Starobin (University of California Press); and the bulletin of People's Songs. The complete version of "Child Sitting" can be found in the collection of Woody's writings, *Born to Win* (Collier).

CHAPTER 10. What Am I Gonna Do . . .

The story of Woody's indictment for writing obscene letters comes from records provided by the U.S. Attorney's office in Brooklyn, plus interviews with Maxine Crissman, Jimmy Longhi, and Marjorie. Others interviewed for this chapter included: Harold Leventhal, Pete Kameron, Jack Elliot, Eric Barnouw, Jolly (Smolens) Robinson, Stetson Kennedy, and the various Weavers. Howie Richmond, Al Brackman, and Jay Mark of the Richmond Organization all were helpful, and were kind enough to let me listen to the tapes that Woody made for Richmond in the early 1950's.

The background on the Wallace campaign comes from Joseph C. Goulden's aforementioned *The Best Years* and also his compilation of H. L. Mencken's 1948 campaign coverage, *Mencken's Last Campaign* (New Republic); also *Gideon's Army* by Curtis McDougal (Marzani and Munsell); *The Crucial Decade* by Eric F. Goldman (Vintage); *Scoundrel Time* by Lillian Hellman (Bantam); *Senator Joe McCarthy* by Richard H. Rovere (Harper Colophon). Clancy Sigal's novel *Going Away* (Popular Library) gives a good sense of the shattering effect that the demise of the Communist dream had on the party's sympathizers.

Woody's medical records were obtained, after much struggle, from the New York State Department of Mental Health, with the stipulation that a qualified psychiatrist review them first. Dr. Joseph Wortis, the man who suggested that Woody be sent to Brooklyn State in the first place, agreed to spend an afternoon with me at the hospital, reviewing the records.

CHAPTER 11. Jesus My Doctor

Obviously, Anneke Van Kirk was the primary source for this chapter. It was the first time she'd allowed herself to be interviewed about a very painful period in her life, and I appreciate her cooperation. Other interviews included: the Geers, Bess (Lomax) Hawes, Mrs. Alfred Koeth, and various members of the family, especially Sue Guthrie.

Harold Leventhal explained the tangled state of Woody's business affairs and opened the books of the Guthrie Children's Trust Fund so that I could see the exact figures for myself. The 1956 concert was remembered in great detail by Pete Seeger, Bina (Rosenbaum) Bernard, Earl Robinson, and Rosalind (Richman) Riversong.

CHAPTER 12. Dust Can't Kill Me

Bob and Sid Gleason were very helpful here, answering all my questions, allowing me to listen to their tapes of the Sunday sessions, and showing me their photographs. Also Lee Hays, Pete Seeger, Matt Jennings, Jimmy Longhi, and the others who visited Woody in the hospital, and Dave Marsh, Martin Burman, and Albert Grossman (who refused to deny that he and Alan Lomax had had a fistfight). Also the following books: *Dylan* by Anthony Scaduto (Signet); *Baby Let Me Follow You Down* by Eric Von Schmidt and Jim Rooney (Anchor); *Minstrels of the Dawn* by Jerome Rodnitzky (Nelson Hall); *Death of a Rebel* by Marc Eliot (Anchor); and *Mystery Train* by Greil Marcus (Dutton).

The research into Huntington's disease was perhaps the most difficult work of the book. Dr. Nancy Wexler, who was executive director of the Commission for the Control of Huntington's Disease, reviewed those portions of the manuscript that were related to the disease, and invited me to attend a weekend seminar for the scientists involved in basic HD research. Others interviewed included Dr. Milton Wexler, Dr. Judith Walters, Dr. Ntinos Myrianthopoulos, Dr. John Whittier, and Dr. Thomas Chase—most of whom also gave me treatises and research studies they had written about the disease. Marjorie Guthrie provided much of my initial information, including a copy of Dr. Huntington's original monograph. In order to understand what all of these people were talking about, I first had to acquaint myself with the workings of the brain, which I did by reading the following: *The Mind of Man* by Nigel Calder (Viking Compass); *The Conscious Brain* by Steven Rose (Knopf); *The Brain Changers* by Maya Pines (Signet); and *The Dragons of Eden* by Carl Sagan (Ballantine).

Finally, the Guthrie children graciously shared their memories of Woody's last years with me, even down to the difficulties they had in spreading his ashes to the sea.

ACKNOWLEDGMENTS

There are several people at *Rolling Stone* who deserve credit for starting me off on this road: Dave Marsh, who came up with the idea of a story about Arlo; Jann Wenner, who assigned it; Chet Flippo, who loaned me the records; and Harriet Fier, who edited it.

After suggesting that I write the book, Harold Leventhal provided constant support—and not simply the office space, occasional Xeroxing, and telephone use that he offered so graciously. From the start, he understood exactly what I was trying to do, and his tactful advice was quite helpful, as were his assistants Irene Allong and Sarah Posnick.

Irma Bauman, who is Marjorie Guthrie's close friend and assistant, should also be acknowledged, as well as the work of the Woody Guthrie Foundation, which is dedicated to keeping Woody's name and work alive. It is located at 250 West 57th Street, New York, N.Y. 10019.

And, of course, I'd like to thank Bob Gottlieb and Martha Kaplan of Knopf.

INDEX

ABOUT THE AUTHOR

Joe Klein is a contributing editor of *New York* magazine. The winner of several journalism awards, he is the author of PAY-BACK. He lives in Brooklyn, New York.